M01 40005 23804

P9-DCJ-512

DATE DUE

MAR 3 1 1982		
MAR 3 1 1982		
AUG 1 1986		
DEC 13 1991		
JUL 28 1994		
OCT 2 5 1999		
MAY 0 5 2003		
OCT 1 6 2007		

DEMCO 38-297

RENNER LEARNING RESOURCE CENTER
ELGIN COMMUNITY COLLEGE
ELGIN, ILLINOIS 60120

UNITED STATES FOOD LAWS, REGULATIONS, AND STANDARDS

UNITED STATES FOOD LAWS, REGULATIONS, AND STANDARDS

Y. H. HUI

Humboldt State University

A WILEY-INTERSCIENCE PUBLICATION

JOHN WILEY & SONS

New York • Chichester • Brisbane • Toronto

RENNER LEARNING RESOURCES CENTER
ELGIN COMMUNITY COLLEGE
ELGIN, ILLINOIS

344.73
H 899 u

Copyright © 1979 by John Wiley & Sons, Inc.

All rights reserved. Published simultaneously in Canada.

Reproduction or translation of any part of this work
beyond that permitted by Sections 107 or 108 of the
1976 United States Copyright Act without the permission
of the copyright owner is unlawful. Requests for
permission or further information should be addressed to
the Permissions Department, John Wiley & Sons, Inc.

Library of Congress Cataloging in Publication Data

Hui, Yiu H
   United States food laws, regulations, and standards.

   "A Wiley-Interscience publication."
   Includes index
   1. Food law and legislation—United States. I. Title.

KF3875.H8   344′.7′042   78-26668
ISBN 0-471-03182-8

Printed in the United Stated of America

10 9 8 7 6 5 4 3 2

053885   ITNBD ZBDRUOZBR BMIHRBBI IBMHBD
            IBBLLOD YTIMUMMOD MIDLB

PREFACE

In the absence of a modern reference source, it is difficult for an interested person to obtain basic information on and to understand the system of federal food regulations in the United States, its complexity, and its comprehensiveness. For example, one might ask: What are the types of legislation that exist with regard to food standards and inspections? What legislations regulate the standards for drinking water and alcoholic beverages, the use of food additives in food, or the safety of food preparation equipment? Other questions might be different in form, such as: Which federal agencies are involved in the enforcement of such legislations? How are they organized, what types of work do they perform, and what are their specific statutory responsibilities? Further, what is the relationship of two federal agencies that may have jurisdictional conflict? What kind of cooperation exists between a federal agency and a state authority in regard to food regulations? Other interests might revolve around the legal requirements for television claims of the nutritive values of food products, the ingredients or nutritional composition of pet foods, the occurrence of "unavoidable" food contaminants, and the marketing of powdered forms of alcoholic beverages. All these questions and more might be raised.

There is no recent publication that discusses United States food laws and regulatory agencies in a coordinated and systematic manner, especially regarding the queries mentioned above. The pertinent information does not exist in a cohesive form but is scattered in various federal publications, making it difficult to assemble and study the materials. Hopefully, this book helps to fill the existing vacuum. Its chief purpose is to provide a basic understanding of the major food regulatory agencies in the United States and of the regulations they promulgate concerning food inspections, standards, specifications, and related matters.

This book is divided into 7 chapters, each describing a federal agency that has at least some degree of statutory responsibilities in enforcing food laws, especially in regard to food standards, definitions, and inspections. Food is defined by the Congress to include food and drink for human and animal consumption.

Each chapter contains part or all of the following information: 1) a brief description of the organizational structure of the agency, with a simplified chart attached to the appendix; 2) the agency's role in food inspection and the establishment of food grades and standards; 3) relevant statutory responsibilities assigned to the agency; 4) a list of lay and professional publications issued by the agency and related to food inspections and standards; 5) a discussion of some of the food regulations promulgated by the agency; 6) a list of food standards established by the agency, with some specific examples attached to the appendix; 7) the relationship to other governmental agencies in the performance of specific statutory responsibilities; 8) foreseeable changes in the organization of the agency, the food inspection regulations and standards promulgated by the agency, and the inclusion of new statutes; 9) directions for obtaining the original sources of material discussed in the book and in other related publications; 10) methods of enforcement; and 11) miscellaneous information such as important Supreme Court decisions, controversial microbiological quality standards, problems of corporate responsibility, major jurisdictional conflicts, standardization of food package sizes, and other related materials.

Each chapter is provided with an appendix that may include such information as examples of definitions, standards, specifications, and grades for selected food items, subpart and section titles of some relevant parts contained in the *Code of Federal Regulations*, and organization charts of the federal agencies discussed in the book.

There is a number of legal terms and documents that are used and referred to frequently in this book. Most individuals and organizations that are involved in this specialized area of food laws are familiar with them already. However, they are briefly explained here so that the information serves as a reminder for some and as background material for others. Specifically, the meanings of *Statutes at Large*, *Public Law, United States Code, Federal Register*, and the *Code of Federal Regulations* are presented in the following paragraphs.

Laws enacted by the Congress are published in the final and permanent form in the *Statutes at Large*. This publication is issued in volumes, each of which contains those laws passed during a calendar year, although some old issues may contain varying periods of legislation. The *Statutes at Large* divides all the legal papers into groups such as proclamations, treaties and executive agreements, concurrent resolutions, private acts and resolutions, and public acts and resolutions. All the materials belonging to one group are assembled in a continuous series for the entire period covered by the volume. When a specific statute is cited, an abbreviation is used. For example, the citation "84 Stat. 1620 et seq." means Volume 84 of the *Statutes at Large*, starting from page 1620 and continuing with the following pages. These pages are concerned with the Egg Products Inspection Act. The abbreviation "Sec. 3, 84 Stat. 1620" means Section 3 of page 1620 in Volume 84 of the *Statutes at Large;* Section 3 is the Declaration of Policy for the Act.

It is difficult to define the difference between *Public Law* and Private Law. "Legislation classed generally as public may be listed as that in which the interest of the government is paramount, particular, or outweighs the other considerations of the act; that in which by the nature and scope of the act, the interest of the public as a whole is affected." This was stated in 1950 by the General Services Administration, which was and still is partially responsible for the editing and compiling of the *Statutes at Large.* In general, most food laws, especially those relating to food standards and inspections, are public laws. For example, PL 91-597 was enacted on December 20, 1970. This means that Public Law number 597 was enacted during the 91st Congress of the United States on the date shown. The act was entitled Egg Products Inspection Act.

At the time of current writing, the *United States Code* is in its 9th edition. It contains a consolidation and codification of all the general and permanent laws of the United States that were in force on January 1977. By statutory authority this edition may be cited "U.S.C. 1976 ed."

The authority for preparing and publishing this publication was issued under Section 202(c) of Title 1 of the Code. Previous editions were published in 1926, 1934, 1940, 1946, 1952, 1958, 1964, and 1970. Because many of the general and permanent laws required to be incorporated in this Code are redundant, obsolete, and inconsistent, the Judiciary Committee of the House of Representatives is currently revising and enacting the Code into law, title by title. As the project proceeds, bills have been passed to revise, codify, and enact into law various titles of the Code. When this work is completed all the titles of the Code will be legal evidence of the general and permanent law of the United States, and recourse to the numerous volumes of the *Statutes at Large* for this purpose will be unnecessary.

Each year a supplement to the latest edition is published, and this supplement contains the general and permanent laws of the United States enacted during the sessions of Congress of that particular year.

The *United States Code* is divided into titles that are expected to number 50. The citation "21 U.S.C. 1031 to 1056" refers to Title 21 of the *United States Code*, Sections 1031 to 1056. Title 21 is related to food and drugs, whereas Sections 1031 to 1056 are concerned with the Egg Products Inspection Act.

The *Federal Register* is published daily, Monday through Friday, and there is no publication on Saturdays, Sundays, or on official federal holidays. It is published by the Office of the Federal Register, National Archives and Records Service, and the General Services Administration, under the Federal Register Act (49 Stat. 500, as amended, and 44 U.S.C. Chapter 15) and the regulations of the Administrative Committee of the Federal Register (Title 1 of the Code of Federal Regulations, Chapter 1). Distribution is made only by the Superintendent of Documents, U.S. Government Printing Office.

The *Federal Register* provides a uniform system for making available to the public regulations and legal notices issued by the federal agencies. These include Presidential proclamations and Executive orders and federal agency documents having general applicability and legal effect, documents required to be published by the Act of Congress, and other federal agency documents of public interest. There are no restrictions on the republication of material appearing in the *Federal Register*.

Again, abbreviation is used in the citation of information appearing in the *Federal Register*. The citation "36 FR 9814" (sometimes a date may accompany the citation, such as May 28, 1971) refers to Volume 36 of the *Federal Register*, page 9814, and such a page number was published on May 28, 1971. The regulations for enforcing the Egg Products Inspection Act as promulgated by the Food Safety and Quality Service of the United States Department of Agriculture began on that page.

The *Code of Federal Regulations* is a codification of the general and permanent rules published in the *Federal Register* by the Executive departments and agencies of the Federal government. The Code is divided into 50 titles, each of which is subdivided into chapters that usually carry the name of the issuing agency. Each title represents broad areas subject to federal regulation, and each chapter is further sectioned into parts that cover specific regulatory areas.

The Code is revised annually, and the dates of issue for the new revisions are as follows: January 1, Title 1-16; April 1, Title 17-27; July 1, Title 28-41; and October 1, Title 42-50. The cover of each volume should be consulted for the revision date. The contents of the *Federal Register* are required to be judicially noticed (44 U.S.C. 1507), and the *Code of Federal Regulations* is prima facie evi-evidence of the text of the original documents (44 U.S.C. 1510).

Individual issues of the *Federal Register* keep the Code up to date. To determine the latest version of any given rule, these two publications must be used together. Further, the cumulative "List of CFR Sections Affected" (issued monthly) and the "Cumulative List of Parts Affected" (appearing daily in the *Federal Register*) together may assist a user to ascertain if there have been any amendments since the revision date of the specific Code volume.

Each volume of the *Code of Federal Regulations* contains amendments published in the *Federal Register* since the last revision of that volume. Note that effective dates and publication dates in the *Federal Register* are usually not the same and that care must be exercised in determining the actual effective date. In instances where the effective date is beyond the cut-off date for the Code a note is inserted to reflect the future effective date.

The subject index to the Code, which is revised annually and supplemented periodically, is contained in a separate volume entitled *General Index*. This volume also contains a table of *Code of Federal Regulations* titles, chapters, and parts, and alphabetical list of subtitles and chapters, and lists of current and superseded volumes.

Again, reference to materials in the Code is usually given in abbreviation. For example, the citation "7 CFR 2859" means Part 2859 of Title 7 of the *Code of Federal Regulations*. Title 7 is "Agriculture," and Part 2859 is entitled "Inspection of eggs and egg products." Sometimes the citation may indicate a section, such as Section 2859.900 (or, 7 CFR 2859.900), which has a section title of "Requirements for importation of egg products or restricted eggs into the United States."

This is a reference book and, as such, can be used by a large audience. It is expected, however, that the materials will be of special interest to the following individuals and organizations.

1. College or university students and instructors in the following fields: food science, food chemistry, dietetics, nutrition, public health, and law.
2. Federal and state regulatory officers at the administrative, technical, and field levels, who are assigned the responsibility of establishing and enforcing standards and regulations relating to food, drinking water, agriculture, and health.
3. Physicians and scientists engaged in public health disciplines.
4. Ranking corporate officers in the food industry with supervisory roles in production, quality control, advertising, sanitation, regulatory affairs, and related responsibilities.
5. Government and private attorneys who have *recently* engaged in the practice of this specialty--food law. It is noted that a lawyer experienced with and specializing in food laws is usually very familiar with one particular aspect of this book. However, it is hoped that this book serves as a good reference source for information about agencies and statutes that he is not working with and may be interested in.
6. Libraries of major universities, especially those with government document centers and law schools.

This book is not a comprehensive treatment of the total system of federal food regulations in the United States. Basic limitations on the size of a book of this nature confine the discussion to only a selected number of federal agencies and statutes. The selection is based on their direct bearing on and relative importance to food standards, inspections, and related regulatory aspects as they exist in this country. The omission of any material should be judged in this light. Two such examples of omission are the Occupational Safety and Health Administration (Department of Labor) and the Bureau of Customs (Department of the Treasury). The first has authority over the setting of safety regulations in food processing plants that have as their aim the protection of the workers. The second issues many special regulations governing the importation and exportation of food and drink for human consumption.

Federal statutes require all federal agencies to use federal specifications and standards for the procurement of subsistence items. Thus, for example, the General Services Administration, the Department of Defense, and the Veterans Administration all issue their own food product specifications and standard documents. This book does not deal with this type of information because of the lack of space and the scheduled massive federal government reorganization in procurement practices, including the issuance of food specifications and standards. However, interested parties may obtain the necessary information from the following documents, which are available at the time of current writing. (1) Publications issued by the Department of Defense: *Consolidated Stock List, FSC Group 89 subsistence, Federal Supply Classification Listing of the Department of Defense Specifications and Standardization Documents*; and *Microbiological Requirements and Methodology for Food in Military and Federal Specifications*. (2) *Index of Federal Specifications and Standards* issued by the General Services Administration. (3) *Federal Hospital Subsistence Guide* issued by the Veterans Administration.

There are certain kinds of information that this book either does not deal with or is concerned with only to a limited extent. For example, statutes concerning food stamps, food prices, and other monetary or economic aspects are not discussed. In addition, apart from a limited number of special situations, in general the book is not concerned with the legal analyses of specific court cases.

This book contains a fair amount of legal and technical information, most of which is paraphrased from original documents, and the interpretation is entirely the author's. Every reasonable effort has been made to assure accurate interpretation and paraphrasing. Because of the voluminous amount of materials involved, the author does not assume any liability for errors or omissions. Persons using this source should always consult the original document referenced to obtain further details and should use their own interpretations when necessary. Furthermore, the legal information contained herein cannot and should not be used as prima facie evidence in a court of law. The book is not meant to teach the practice of law, and, if legal advice is needed, the professional service of an attorney-at-law should be obtained.

Since one of the book's objectives is to make the information available to scientists, among others, some of the discussion and examples given are related to mathematical, chemical, physical, and/or biochemical data. The use of scientific and technical terms assumes certain basic background in these fields, but, for the most part, this use has been kept to a reasonable minimum.

The *United States Government Manual* provides a limited account of practically every federal agency in the country. It is published annually by the Office of the Federal Register, the National Archives and Records Service, and the General Services Administration, and it may be obtained from the Superintendent of Documents. A small amount of information appearing in this book is obtained from this publication, in which case it is cited as the *Government Manual*.

Because practically all the resource materials discussed are government publications, it is useful to attend to the question of the length of time it takes to obtain such materials from a government source. When requesting information it is fair to allow at least one month for a government reply. The answer may be faster if a request is sent to a specific individual in a federal agency soliciting specific and standard information. On the other hand, the purchase of any material from the Government Printing Office may take longer. Addresses of government agencies discussed are given in Appendix 8. Those of private organizations are given in the text.

A book of this nature always suffers one inherent disadvantage--change. All federal laws, regulations, documents, and agencies undergo change constantly. Though it is not possible to avoid this obvious handicap, an attempt is made to minimize its impact. The information is presented in such a manner that only extensive and major changes will affect the content of this book. It is expected that no changes can influence its most important objective: "...to provide a basic understanding of the major food regulatory agencies in the United States and of the regulations they promulgate concerning food inspections, standards, specifications, and related matters." But it would be useful to remember that to obtain any of the reference sources discussed, one should always request the latest issue or edition.

In order to keep abreast of new developments in food laws, food regulations, and agency changes, one should read the *Federal Register* and the *Food Chemical News* (published weekly by Food Chemical News, Inc., 420 Colorado Building, 1341 G Street, N.W., Washington, D.C. 20005). The first publication is a well-known government document and is available in most major university government document centers and in law school libraries. It is too expensive for a personal subscription, though most food industries and law firms engaged in this specialty are subscribers. The *Food Chemical News* is a private publication, has been in existence since 1959, and is also too expensive for a personal subscription. Interested individuals, law firms, food industries, and university libraries subscribe to this publication.

Unless otherwise specified, the *Code of Federal Regulations* discussed in this book is the 1977 edition.

In the presentation of materials, the author is neutral, adheres to facts, and avoids personal opinions. Any controversial legal or scientific issue mentioned is accompanied by pro and con discussion.

Y. H. Hui

Arcata, California
January 1979

ACKNOWLEDGMENTS

I would like to express my most sincere appreciation to the many individuals who have contributed to the completion of this book. In the past few years, a number of government officials in responsible positions have provided me with invaluable information. Although there is not enough space to name them individually here, I wish to extend my thanks to them for their generosity and assistance. Obviously, the entire editorial and production staff of Wiley-Interscience played an important role in the publication process. I am especially indebted to Drs. S. F. Kudzin and M. M. Conway, the editors, Ms. F. Tindall, the editorial supervisor, and Mr. P. Malchow, the production supervisor. I acknowledge special thanks and recognition to Mr. E. Schimps, Head, Documents Section, Humboldt State University Library, who from 1971 has never failed to be concerned, helpful and informative in all facets of my year-to-year research. He is one of the individuals without whose aid the project could not have been finished. I am deeply grateful also to Dr. D. Blucher of Humboldt State University who conscientiously and painstakingly proofread and criticized the original manuscript. The contribution of Mrs. M. Farr, Professor Emeritus of Humboldt State University, is too enormous to put into words. She has continuously provided inspirational, emotional and moral support over the many years of my research and writing, never ceasing to express her total confidence in my potential and ability during my periods of agony of self-doubt.

Moreover, she has assisted me financially and spent countless hours proofreading the typeset materials. She is a true friend, the kind of person one meets once in a lifetime. Ms. M. Rodgers, a professional typist/graphic designer associated with Humboldt State University, typeset the entire book on an IBM Selectric composer. The excellent quality and professionalism of her work is self-evident. Her highly commendable skill can only be paralleled by the fortitude with which she has tolerated my sometimes excessive and unreasonable work-demand. She has my heartfelt thanks and appreciation.

CONTENTS

CHAPTER 1

DEPARTMENT
OF AGRICULTURE

INTRODUCTION

In 1862 Abraham Lincoln signed the congressional act that created the United States Department of Agriculture (USDA). This department is now one of the cabinet level federal agencies that exist within the executive branch of government. The secretary of Agriculture heads the department. With the exception of management, administrative, and legal offices, all agencies within the USDA related to the substance of agricultural business are grouped under six different offices of function. A simplified chart of the USDA's organization appears in Appendix 1-1. The offices of special interest to this book are: Food and Consumer Services, Marketing Services, and International Affairs and Commodities Programs. Each of these offices is headed by an assistant secretary of Agriculture. Another important unit that should be mentioned is the Office of Communication. This office has compiled a list that gives sources of information within the USDA Office of Communication and the various agencies of the department. The organizational listing of the USDA is described in a telephone directory that is published by the agency and revised regularly. A general description of the responsibilities, activities, and organizational structure of the USDA is provided in the Government Manual and various consumer pamphlets that it issues.

The USDA administers a number of federal statutes, many of which are described in the publication "Compilation of statutes, relating to the Agricultural Marketing Service and closely related activities" (see Table 1-1). Some of these are presented in this chapter.

One major legislation administered by the USDA is the Agricultural Marketing Act of 1946 (7 U.S.C. 1621-1627, 60 Stat. 1087 as amended). The act authorizes the USDA to perform many functions, the most relevant of which are:

1. Authorization of grading, inspection, and certification of all agricultural products. Such services are permissive or voluntary.
2. Making certifications prima facie evidence in court.
3. Prohibition of misrepresentation with respect to such services.

The USDA issues a number of lay publications that are of interest; these are listed in Table 1-1. For example, pamphlet FSQS-6 lists all lay publications that are available, many of which are discussed in this chapter. Because of frequent government reorganization, the publication code numbers and issuing offices may vary though the titles and contents usually remain the same or nearly the same.

Two publications listed in Table 1-1 relate to food standards and grades. "Food quality--What you can do about the USDA grades" describes the meaning of grade standards, whereas "How to use USDA grades in buying food" provides examples of food grade standards. Although these publications are written for the

TABLE 1-1.   United States Department of Agriculture General Publications on
Food Standards and Relevant Statutes

Publication Number (date)	Title of Publication
FSQS-6 (December 1977)	Information available from USDA's Food Safety and Quality Service
AMS-562 (1975)	Food quality--What you can do about the USDA grades
HG-196 (1977)	How to use USDA grades in buying food
Agricultural Handbook No. 341 (February 1977)	USDA standards for food and farm products
AMS-548 (1977)	Federal food standards
Agricultural Handbook No. 492 (September 1975)	Compilation of statutes related to the Agricultural Marketing Service and closely related activities

consumer, they serve as a useful introduction to the topic. A brief discussion of their contents follows.

In a retail store, beef packages may carry labels such as "USDA prime" or "USDA choice"; these are grades for beef. Grades for many food products have been established by the USDA, which sets up a standard that defines the requirements for a particular grade. "Grades are often said to be the language of commerce--and standards are the dictionary that gives definition and meaning to that language." When one separates a basket of apples into homogeneous groups in appearance and quality, one grades the apples. A grade is thus also a level of quality. Obviously, the criteria for grade standards vary from product to product. Also, with reference to most food products, new grade standards may be added and old ones revised or amended. The USDA now has grade standards for dairy products, fruits and vegetables, eggs, poultry, and meat. Some examples are given in the following.

The label "U.S. Grade AA butter" means it is best quality and has a delicate sweet flavor, whereas "Grade A butter" is almost as good and usually sells for a lower price.

When one buys eggs, the grade and size must be considered. Grades for eggs are: U.S. Grade AA (or Fresh Fancy Quality), U.S. Grade A, and U.S. Grade B. Grades AA and A eggs are best for frying and poaching because they do not spread very much in the pan and the yolk is firm and not easily broken. Grade B eggs are just as good to eat, but the white is thinner and the yolk may be flatter than in AA and A eggs. As far as the size of eggs is concerned, a dozen "small" eggs must weigh at least 18 ounces, "medium" 21 ounces, and "large" 24 ounces.

Beef grades are as follows: U.S. prime, U.S. choice, U.S. good, U.S. standard, and U.S. commercial. Prime beef is the best, most expensive, tender, juicy, and flavorful; choice beef, such as high quality steaks and roasts, is quite tender and juicy, with good flavor; good beef is not as juicy and flavorful but fairly tender; and commercial beef is not very tender, requiring long and slow cooking with moist heat such as pot roasting or braising, although if cooked properly, it has a good rich flavor.

The publication "USDA standards for food and farm products" (Table 1-1), lists practically all the agricultural and food products for which the USDA has established standards of quality. Because consumer confusion has frequently arisen over the meanings of the grade standards and food identities issued by the various federal agencies, the USDA distributes the bulletin "Federal food standards" (Table 1-1) for clarification. Since different chapters in this book provide elaborated explanations and references for food grades, standards, identities, and specifications established by federal agencies, no further details are presented on this topic at this stage.

As indicated in Appendix 1-1, the Assistant Secretary for Food and Consumer Services within the USDA supervises a number of services, two of which are the Food Safety and Quality Service and the Food and Nutrition Service. They are discussed in the text that follows.

FOOD SAFETY AND QUALITY SERVICE

The title of this office is self-explanatory; its major responsibility is to assure the quality and safety of those food products that the U.S. Congress has placed under the jurisdiction of the USDA. This responsibility is shared by a number of divisions and programs and those that are of concern to this book include: Fruit and Vegetable Quality Division, Meat Quality Division, Poultry and Dairy Quality Division, and Meat and Poultry Inspection Program. Each of these is discussed in the sections that follow.

Fruit and Vegetable Quality Division

This division is headed by a director who supervises, among others, the Fresh Products Branch and the Processed Products Branch. These branches standardize, grade, and inspect fruits and vegetables. These services are voluntary, the users pay the fees, and the Agricultural Marketing Act of 1946 provides the basic statutory authority.

The regulations promulgated for fresh products are located in 7 CFR 51, titled "Fresh fruits, vegetables and other products (inspection, certification, and standards)." The authority for the provisions of this part was issued under Sections 203, 205, 60 Stat. 1087 as amended, 1090 as amended, and 7 U.S.C. 1622, 1624. This part provides information on the basic regulation for voluntary grading and inspection services and the standards and specifications for fresh fruits and vegetables.

The basic regulation is composed of the following: administrative procedure, definitions of common terms, inspection service, appeal inspection, licensing of inspectors, schedule of fees and charges at destination markets and shipping point areas, requirements for plants operating under continuous inspection on a contract basis, and miscellaneous such as denial of inspection service, approved identification, and others. This complicated regulation is partially simplified in a lay publication, "Official grade standards and inspection for fresh fruits and vegetables" (see Table 1-2). It is summarized briefly as follows, although details should be obtained from 7 CFR 51.

Official inspection services are offered on a fee for service basis. In terminal markets and at shipping points, the inspector examines a commodity and issues a certificate that identifies its condition or quality and indicates its compliance with federal specifications or grades or those designed by the seller or buyer. These certificates are legally acceptable as prima facie evidence in all federal and most state courts.

The division has cooperative agreements with various state agencies to render federal/state inspection services. Under these agreements, thousands of federally licensed officials perform inspection work at points of origin. The division establishes basic inspection policies and procedures and furnishes overall direction.

One example is continuous inspection service, which is made available to packers at shipping points and in terminal markets. The service was originally designed to aid packers who pack in consumer size containers, but at present it may be used by packers who pack in containers of any size. During the full time packing conducted at the packing plant, one or more inspectors are assigned to observe plant conditions and preparation and packing of the product. He makes frequent quality checks on the commodity from the packing lines and examines samples of the packed products to determine whether they comply with the U.S. grade or specifications for which the commodity is being packed. The fee charged

TABLE 1-2.   Selected Publications Distributed by Fruit and Vegetable Quality
             Division

Publication Number (date)	Title of Publication
AMS-520 (December 1963)	Official grade standards and inspection for fresh fruits and vegetables
Marketing Bulletin No. 56 (January 1975)	Inspection and grading service for processed fruits and vegetables
File Code 162-A-1, 2, 3, 4 5, etc. (1977)	Inspection of processed fruits and vegetables under quality assurance program
Unnumbered, undated	Visual aids approved for use in ascertaining grades of processed fruits and vegetables
AMS-569 (1976)	Facts about: Grade names for fresh fruits and vegetables
AMS-570 (1976)	Facts about: Study drafts on U.S. grade standards for fruits and vegetables

for any type of service follows a prearranged schedule. Both the U.S. grade standards and the inspection services are permissive and their use voluntary.

Apart from written standards and grades for fresh fruits and vegetables, there
are visual aids. A company is authorized and licensed by the USDA to manufacture and sell visual aids to the public. Such aids include color charts illustrating the
different color classifications defined in the standards for grades of fresh tomatoes,
the minimum shades of color for the different varieties of apples, and color photographs for Florida citrus showing limits for defects. More information may be obtained from the Fruit and Vegetable Quality Division.

According to 7 CFR 51, the USDA has established U.S. standards for the
following: basic trading grades, grades of products for processing, and grades of
nuts and special products; consumer standards for certain products; and specifica-

tions for damaged products. All these grade standards and their legal citation are described in the publication "USDA standards for food and farm products" (see Table 1-1). However, they have been adapted from 7 CFR 51 (1977) and are listed alphabetically as follows. The section number for each standard is given in parentheses.

United States Standards Basic Trading Grades

Anise, sweet (2900)

Apples (300)

Apricots (2925)

Artichokes, globe (3785)

Asparagus, fresh (3720)

Avocados, Florida (3050)

Beans, lima (3805)

Beans, snap (3830)

Beet greens (2860)

Beets (375)

Blueberries (3475)

Broccoli, bunched
Italian sprouting (3555)

Brussels sprouts (2250)

Cabbage (450)

Canteloupes (475)

Carrots, bunched (2455)

Carrots, topped (2360)

Carrots with short
trimmed tops (2485)

Cauliflower (540)

Celery (560)

Cherries, sweet (2646)

Collard or broccoli
greens (520)

Corn, green (835)

Cucumbers (2220)

Cucumbers, greenhouse (3855)

Dandelion greens (2585)

Dewberries and blackberries
(4270)

Eggplant (2190)

Endive, escarole, or
chicory (3535)

Garlic (3880)

Grapes, American (Eastern
type) bunch (3610)

Grapes, juice (European
or Vinifera type)
(4290)

Grapes, table (European
or Vinifera type)
(880)

Grapefruit (California
and Arizona) (925)

United States Standards Basic Trading Grades (continued)

Grapefruit (Florida)
(750)

Grapefruit (Texas and
states other than
Florida, Arizona, and
California) (620)

Honey dew and honey
ball type melons
(3740)

Horseradish roots
(3900)

Kale (3930)

Lemons (2795)

Lettuce (2510)

Lettuce, greenhouse
leaf (3455)

Limes, Persian
(Tahiti) (1000)

Mushrooms (3385)

Mustard greens and
turnip greens (1030)

Nectarines (3145)

Okra (3945)

Onions, Bermuda-Granex-
Grano type (3195)

Onions, common green
(1055)

Onions, Creole (3955)

Onions (other than
Bermuda-Granex-Grano and
Creole types) (2830)

Onion sets (3980)

Oranges (California and
Arizona) (1085)

Oranges (Texas and states
other than Florida, California,
and Arizona)
(680)

Oranges and Tangelos,
Florida (1140)

Parsley (4000)

Parsnips (4010)

Peaches (1210)

Pears, summer and fall
(1260)

Pears, winter (1300)

Peas, fresh (1375)

Peas, Southern (2670)

Pepper, sweet (3270)

Pineapples (1485)

Plums and prunes
(1520)

Potatoes (1540)

Potatoes, seed (3000)

Radishes (2395)

Raspberries (4320)

Rhubarb (field-grown) (3665)

Romaine (3295)

Shallots, bunched (1630)

United States Standards Basic Trading Grades (continued)

Spinach leaves, fresh
   (1730)

Spinach plants (2880)

Squash, fall and winter
   (4030)

Squash, summer (4050)

Strawberries (3115)

Sweet potatoes (1600)

Tangerines (1770)

Tangerines, Florida (1810)

Tomatoes, fresh (1855)

Tomatoes, greenhouse (3345)

Turnips or rutabagas (2610)

Watermelons (1970)

United States Standards for Grades of Products for Processing

Apples (340)

Asparagus, green (4075)

Beans, fresh shelled
   lima (355)

Beans, snap (3240)

Beets (40)

Berries (860)

Blueberries (2025)

Broccoli (425)

Cabbage (4120)

Carrots (4140)

Cauliflower (3220)

Cherries, red sour, for
   manufacture (4340)

Cherries, sweet, for
   canning or freezing
   (4360)

Cherries, sweet, for
   export for sulfur
   brining (4380)

Corn, sweet (3365)

Cranberries, fresh
   (3030)

Cucumber, for pickling
   (4170)

Currants (1950)

Grapes, American (Eastern
   type) bunch for processing
   and freezing (4400)

Grapes, mechanically
   harvested American
   (Eastern type) for
   processing and freezing
   (2150)

United States Standards for Grades of Products for Processing (continued)

Mushrooms (3435)

Okra (3635)

Onions (4190)

Peaches, fresh freestone,
  for canning, freezing,
  or pulping (3695)

Pears, for canning (1345)

Peas, fresh shelled, for
  canning or freezing
  (4210)

Peas, southern (3585)

Peppers, sweet (1465)

Potatoes (3410)

Raspberries (1710)

Spinach (2695)

Strawberries, growers'
  stock for manufacture
  (4415)

Strawberries, washed and
  sorted for freezing
  (4435)

Sweet potatoes for canning
  or freezing (1660)

Sweet potatoes for dicing
  or pulping (1685)

Tomatoes, green (1930)

Tomatoes, Italian type,
  for canning (2976)

United States Standards for Grades of Nuts and Special Products

Almonds, in the shell
  (2075)

Almonds, shelled (2105)

Asparagus, Plumosus
  (4455)

Brazil nuts, in the shell (3500)

Christmas trees (3085)

Filberts, in the shell
  (1995)

Mixed nuts, in the shell
  (3520)

Peanuts, cleaned Virginia
  type in the shell (1235)

Peanuts, shelled Runner
  type (2710)

Peanuts, shelled Spanish
  type (2730)

Peanuts, shelled Virginia
  type (2750)

Pecans, in the shell
  (1400)

Pecans, shelled (1430)

Peonies in the bud, cut
  (4475)

United States Standards for Grades of Nuts and Special Products (continued)

Tomato plants (4505)

Walnuts (Juglands Regia),
  shelled English (2275)

Walnuts, in the shell
  (2945)

United States Consumer Standards

Beet greens (3170)

Broccoli, Italian sprouting
  (400)

Brussels sprouts (2050)

Carrots (495)

Celery stalks (595)

Corn, husked on the cob (810)

Cranberries, fresh (2775)

Kale, fresh (975)

Parsnips, fresh (2310)

Potatoes (1575)

Spinach leaves, fresh (1750)

Tomatoes, fresh (1900)

Turnips, fresh (2425)

Miscellaneous Standard

United States specifications for the classification of damaged or repaired packages
of fresh fruits and vegetables (6000)

For illustration, Appendix 1-2 reproduces the U.S. standards for grades of
strawberries, 7 CFR 51.3115, and Appendix 1-3 reproduces the official identification
marks for grading and inspection of fresh products by the USDA, 7 CFR
51.49.

The regulations promulgated by the USDA for the voluntary grading an inspection of processed products are located in 7 CFR 52, "Processed fruits and
vegetables, processed products thereof, and certain other processed food products." This part provides three types of information: basic regulation, standards

for inspection by variables and determination of fill weights, and standards for grades of processed fruits and vegetables. The authority for the provisions of this part was issued under sections 202 to 208, 60 Stat. 1087, as amended and 7 U.S.C. 1621 to 1627.

The basic regulation provides information similar to that given for 7 CFR 51, such as administrative procedure, inspection service, appeal inspection, and fees and charges. The pamphlet "Inspection and grading service for processed fruits and vegetables" (see Table 1-2) has paraphrased some of the legal information for the general public. These voluntary services are described as follows.

There are four basic inspection services available: continuous inspection, pack certification, lot inspection, and unofficial sample inspection. Under the continuous inspection service, the inspector stays in the plant at all times. He makes continuous in-process checks of preparation, processing, and packing operations and certifies the grade (or quality) and condition of the finished products. Under the pack certification program, the inspector may examine and certify the entire pack of products under a cooperative quality assurance program in qualified plants, or he may inspect and certify only designated portions of production. He is not necessarily present at all operating shifts. Under lot inspection, the inspector checks specific lots for quality and condition of the food products and container. The lot can be of any size and located in places other than a processing plant. Under the unofficial sample inspection, a party submits samples to the nearest USDA office for inspection.

Before the division will begin in-plant inspection services, a plant survey is required. Such a survey is also required if a processor wishes to use a U.S. grade designation on the label of products inspected on a lot basis. Only products processed in approved plants may use the grade labeling. In addition to the initial plant survey, surveys must be repeated at least annually if official inspection or grade labeling is to be continued. The plant survey is based on the Food and Drug Administration's (FDA) good manufacturing practices sanitation guidelines, which are discussed in Chapter 6. After the inspector has approved the plant sanitation, facilities, equipment, and operation, in-plant inspection services may begin.

In addition to providing quality, quantiy, and condition certification, the division also assists volume buyers in translating their needs into exact purchase specifications, which may be USDA standards or the buyer's own requirements. The supplier, whether selected or awarded by bids, may be required to have the deliveries certified by the division as to specifications compliance.

On August 6, 1975 (40 FR 33043 to 33046) and October 20, 1975 (40 FR 48933 to 48935) the division announced a new quality assurance program to be incorporated into the regulations for the inspection of processed products. It has issued a set of internal documents for the program (see Table 1-2), which is briefly described as follows.

The policy of this program is to assist processing plants in the development and implementation of complete or partial quality control programs. It is expected that these programs will facilitate consistent production of safe, wholesome, and uniformly high quality processed products. The division will rely on the inspection results of other approved quality control programs such as those of the FDA. This will reduce the division's inspection effort.

United States Department of Agriculture inspector(s) are assigned to a processing facility on a year-round, in-plant contract after the plant has met plant survey requirements of the division's regulations (see 7 CFR 52.81). The inspections verify that the processors' quality control program complies with that of the division. A user of this service assigns quality levels to all lots produced and records and evaluates all other procedures used within a particular plant. The processor is permitted to use all USDA in-plant inspection procedures, sampling plans, instructions, acceptance and rejection criteria, forms, and reports. Designated grade marks and the officially sampled stamp may also be used. At present, the documents for this quality assurance program are divided into six parts (Table 1-2). The first part provides general information on the following: statement of policy and intent of the program, introduction to the program, definitions applicable to the program, guidelines for development of a quality control program, summary of responsibilities, USDA published documents or procedures available for use under the program, implementation of the program, program verification groups, quality assurance verification sampling, group verification procedures, and action by contractor on quality assurance verification. The other five parts are related to the quality assurance program in the following aspects: Part 2, verification report form; Part 3, method of implementation; Part 4, procedure for determining significant deviations; Part 5, fill weight verification guide--pears; and Part 6, product grouping and verification rates. For further details, consult the original documents. Also, refer to Chapter 6 for general information on quality assurance programs conducted by the FDA.

To interpret the various factors that determine quality in the U.S. grade standards for processed fruits and vegetables, the division has developed a number of visual aids, color guides, and standards. These aids guarantee the uniformity of the interpretation. The division has also made these aids available to members of the food industry. To maintain quality control, these aids are of particular service to manufacturers during their processing operations.

The types of visual aids available include the following: special plastic and glass color comparators; photographic color slides and prints; black and white photographs and drawings; and wax models depicting color, shape, and types of defects. A number of commercial firms have been granted licenses by the USDA to manufacture and sell such visual aids. An interested person should obtain the publication "Visual aids approved for use in ascertaining grades of processed fruits and vegetables" (Table 1-2), which lists the types of aids available and the locations of the manufacturers.

Apart from the publications indicated in Table 1-2, the division has prepared numerous inspection instructions and procedures manuals or handbooks for certain specific processed fruits or vegetables. They are comprehensive, detailed, and priced. A list of available publications with their cost may be obtained from the division.

The second type of information contained in 7 CFR 52 is related to U.S. standards for inspection by variables and for determination of fill weights. The purpose of the standards for inspection by variables is to:

1. Designate and define symbols and terminology associated with statistical quality control;
2. Prescribe a procedure for collecting and recording data that are adaptable for use in statistical quality control; and
3. Provide a statistical procedure for determining compliance of a variable, which may be any measurable product characteristic, with a specified requirement.

These standards are supplemented by the standards for determination of fill weights that adapt the former to the determination of fill of container, based on fill weights, for canned fruits and vegetables and related products. Further information on the use of statistical procedures is presented at the end of this chapter.

According to 7 CFR 52, U.S. standards for grades have been established for the following food products. The section number is included in parentheses.

United States Standards for Grades of Processed Fruits and Vegetables

---

Apples, canned (2161)	Applesauce, canned (331)
Apples, dried (2481)	Apricots, canned (2641)
Apples, dehydrated (low moisture) (2341)	Apricots, dehydrated (low moisture) (3871)
Apples, frozen (361)	Apricots, dried (5761)
Apple butter, canned (2801)	Apricots, frozen (5521)
Apple juice, canned (301)	Apricots, solid-pack, canned (6241)
Apple juice, concentrated, frozen (6321)	Asparagus, canned (2541)

Asparagus, frozen (381)

Beans, canned baked (6461)

Beans, dried canned (411)

Beans, green and wax, frozen (2321)

Beans, lima canned (471)

Beans, lima frozen (501)

Beans, speckled butter (lima) frozen (5241)

Beets, canned (521)

Berries, frozen (5881)

Blackberries and similar berries, canned (551)

Blueberries, canned (581)

Blueberries, frozen (611)

Broccoli, frozen (631)

Brussels sprouts, frozen (651)

Carrots, canned (671)

Carrots, frozen (701)

Cauliflower, frozen (721)

Cherries, red tart pitted, canned (771)

Cherries, red tart pitted, frozen (801)

Cherries, sweet canned (821)

Cherries, sweet frozen (3161)

Chili sauce, canned (2191)

Corn, cream style, canned (851)

Corn on the cob, frozen (931)

Corn, whole kernel, canned (881)

Corn, whole kernel, frozen (911)

Cranberry sauce, canned (951)

Cranberries, frozen (6281)

Dates (1001)

Figs, dried (1021)

Figs, kadota, canned (2821)

Fruit cocktail, canned (1051)

Fruit jelly (1081)

Fruit preserves (or jams) (1111)

Fruits for salad, canned (3831)

Grape juice, canned (1341)

Grape juice, concentrate, sweetened, frozen (2451)

Grapefruit, canned (1141)

Grapefruit, frozen (1171)

Grapefruit and orange for salad, canned (1251)

Grapefruit juice (6121)

Grapefruit juice, concentrated, frozen (1221)

Grapefruit juice, dehydrated (3021)

Grapefruit juice and orange juice, canned (1281)

Grapefruit juice and orange juice, concentrated, blended, frozen (1311)

Grapefruit juice for manufacturing, concentrated (3481)

Grapes, canned (4021)

15   (continued)

Hominy, canned (3281)

Leafy greens, canned (6081)

Leafy greens (other than spinach), frozen (1371)

Lemon juice, canned (5481)

Lemon juice, concentrated for manufacturing (3951)

Lemonade, concentrate, frozen (1421)

Limeade, concentrate, frozen (2521)

Melon balls (6361)

Mushrooms, canned (1481)

Okra, canned (3331)

Okra, frozen (1511)

Okra and tomatoes, tomatoes and okra, canned (3421)

Olives, green (5441)

Olives, ripe, canned (3751)

Onion rings, breaded, frozen (4061)

Onions, canned (3041)

Orange juice, canned (1551)

Orange juice, dehydrated (2981)

Orange juice, concentrated, canned (2251)

Orange juice, concentrated for manufacturing (2221)

Orange juice, pasteurized (5641)

Orange juice from concentrate (5681)

Orange marmalade (1451)

Peaches, dehydrated (low moisture) (3911)

Peaches, dried (5801)

Peaches, frozen (3551)

Peaches, clingstone, canned (2561)

Peaches, freestone, canned (2601)

Pears, canned (1611)

Pears, dried (5841)

Peas, canned (2281)

Peas, frozen (3511)

Peas and carrots, canned (6201)

Peas and carrots, frozen (2501)

Peas, field and blackeye, canned (1641)

Peas, field and blackeye, frozen ((1661)

Peppers, sweet, frozen (3001)

Pickles (1681)

Pimentos, canned (2681)

Pineapple, canned (1711)

Pineapple, frozen (1741)

Pineapple juice, canned (1761)

Plums, canned (1781)

Plums, frozen (2911)

Porks and beans, canned (6441)

Potatoes, french fried, frozen (2391)

Potatoes, hash brown (6401)

16   (continued)

Potatoes, white, canned (1811)

Prunes, dehydrated (low moisture) (3231)

Prunes, dried, canned (5601)

Prunes, dried (3181)

Pumpkin (squash), canned (2741)

Raisins, processed (1841)

Raspberries, canned (3311)

Raspberries, frozen (1871)

Sauerkraut, canned (2951)

Spinach, canned (1901)

Spinach, frozen (1921)

Squash (cooked), frozen (1941)

Squash (summer type), canned (3581)

Squash (summer type), frozen (1961)

Strawberries, frozen (1981)

Succotash, canned (6001)

Succotash, frozen (2011)

Sweet potatoes, canned (2041)

Sweet potatoes, frozen (5001)

Tangerine juice, canned (2071)

Tangerine juice, concentrated for manufacturing, canned (2931)

Tomatoes, canned (5161)

Tomato catsup (2101)

Tomato juice, canned (3621)

Tomato juice, concentrated (5201)

Tomato paste, canned (5041)

Tomato puree (tomato pulp), canned (5081)

Tomato sauce, canned (2371)

Turnip greens with turnips, frozen (3731)

Vegetables, mixed, frozen (2131)

United States Standards for Grades of Honey and Sugar Products

Honey, comb (2861)

Honey, extracted (1391)

Maple sirup for processing (5921)

Maple sirup, table (5961)

Molasses, sugarcane (3651)

Refiners' sirup (6041)

Sugarcane sirup (3101)

United States Standards for Grades of Miscellaneous and Processed Products

---

Cherries, sulfured (741)   Potatoes, white, peeled (2421)

Olive oil (1531)   Sauerkraut, bulk (3451)

Peanut butter (3061)

Appendix 1-4 reproduces U.S. standards for grades of grapefruit juice and orange juice (or orange juice and grapefruit juice). Appendix 1-5 reproduces official identification for grades, inspections, and quality controls for processed fruits and vegetables. According to Table 1-2, the pamphlet AMS-569 defines grades and grade standards and explains uniform grade term policy adopted in 1976. Also, the publication AMS-570 summarizes the steps in developing grade standards for fresh and processed fruits and vegetables and explains how to participate in the process.

The Agricultural Marketing Service of the USDA has signed a number of official agreements with the FDA in regard to grading and inspection of food products. These agreements apply to various divisions under the Food Safety and Quality Service. For example, on April 19, 1977 (42 FR 20350 and 20351) an official Memorandum of Understanding was announced between the two agencies concerning the grading and inspection of food products. This agreement does not apply to egg products and grains including rice, dry beans, peas or lentils. Because this agreement is of general applicability, its contents are briefly described as follows.

According to the agreement, the USDA, that is, its various divisions or offices, will:

1. Provide the FDA with a list of food plants under the voluntary inspection and grading programs of USDA with all the relevant details of the contracts; the USDA will immediately notify the FDA of any insanitary conditions that may result in the services being withdrawn, terminated, and so on.
2. Institute appropriate USDA regulatory action if any plant deficiencies cited by the FDA are substantiated and not corrected.
3. Will not inspect or grade products seized or considered for actions by the FDA. Will reinspect previously USDA-cleared products.
4. Will not assign grades or permit the use of USDA official identification marks on any products considered adulterated or for action by the FDA.
5. Inform the USDA of any products rejected for inspection and grading by USDA. Recondition, segregation, and disposal of such products may be necessary.
6. Furnish information on any products considered for action by the FDA.

7. Report on the inspection certificate any pertinent codes or other marks that will serve to identify the specific goods that are inspected or graded.
8. Provide the FDA with detailed information when a USDA inspector or employee is subpoenaed as a witness.

According to the agreement, the FDA will:

1. Recognize that the voluntary grading and inspection provided by the USDA will aid the FDA enforcement programs. Such services will not diminish FDA authority but will minimize its inspections in USDA-inspected plants. A USDA inspector will only familiarize plant management with FDA requirements and compliance procedures and will not act as an FDA inspector.
2. Team inspect with a USDA inspector when both are present at the same time and discuss and cooperate with each other.
3. Request from USDA relevant information on food products considered for action by the FDA. Take into consideration USDA inspection certificates and other available data.
4. Immediately notify the USDA of any objectionable conditions discovered by the FDA in USDA-supervised plants and other food plants.
5. Mark seized products so that they will be recognized by USDA inspectors.
6. Ascertain that products acceptable to one agency will not be rejected by the other.
7. Review, when requested, labels and other official marks for products inspected by the USDA for compliance with FDA misbranding prohibitions.

The Fruit and Vegetable Quality Division also has, as mentioned briefly earlier, cooperative agreement with the food and agricultural departments of the individual states. Each agreement carries its own file code number. The legal authority for the agreement is issued under the Agricultural Marketing Act of 1946 (7 U.S.C. 1621 et seq.) and the applicable laws of the individual state. There are many specific provisions in each agreement, and in the following samples of the contents are described. Details on individual agreements may be obtained from the division.
According to the agreement, the USDA (i.e., the division) will:

1. Train and supervise inspectors in the interpretation and application of grades, methods of performing inspections, and preparation of certificates.
2. Oversee the examination and licensing of inspectors.
3. Issue licenses; furnish standard notes, forms, and certificates; and arrange methods of payments for services performed.

According to the agreement, the state agency will:

1. Employ only federally licensed inspectors.
2. Obtain concurrence from the division in the selection, assignment, and work load of each employee.
3. Establish reasonable and adequate fees and collect them for services performed. Fees are usually comparable to those established at the federal level.
4. Develop a system of accounting, fund appropriations, collection, handling, and safekeeping of fees and salaries and for other monetary management.

It is mutually understood and agreed that:

1. Shipping point inspection certificates issued under the agreement will be joint federal/state certificates.
2.· Inspection work will be conducted in accordance with federal rules and regulations, although special arrangements may be made.
3. Mutual approval is needed for the assignment of personnel for certain inspection work.

Meat Quality Division

This division is headed by a director who supervises, among others, the Meat Grading Branch and the Standardization Branch. This division provides voluntary grading and certification services. The regulations promulgated to govern such services are stated in 7 CFR 53, "Livestock, meats, prepared meats, and meat products (grading, certification and standards)." This part was issued under the authority of Section 203, 60 Stat. 1087, as amended; Section 205, 60 Stat. 1090, as amended; 7 U.S.C. 1622, 1624; and 10 FR 74, as amended.

The regulations are divided into two aspects: basic regulations and established standards for different livestock carcasses and their products. A brief discussion of the basic regulations is presented as follows.

When the division approves an application for grading service, it will provide determination, certification, and other identification of the grade, class, or other quality of livestock or products in accordance with federal standards. There are standards for livestock or meat of cattle, sheep, or swine in carcass form or for wholesale cuts of such meat, other than pork wholesale cuts. The services are available for items shipped or received in *interstate* commerce. For intrastate trade, one may also obtain such service with proper permission from the division.

The services are also made available to state and local agencies under authorized cooperative agreements. However, the most important point is that the division will provide services for livestock and products *only* if they have been derived from animals slaughtered in federally inspected establishments or operated under officially recognized state meat inspection authorities.

The division will furnish services for imported meat only if it is marked so that the name of the country of origin appears on most of the major retail cuts. The marking of meat of foreign origin must comply with very stringent regulations before the owner or his representative is permitted to utilize the grading services of the division. Details of the requirements may be obtained from 7 CFR 53. It is the responsibility of the applicant to notify the meat grader performing the service whenever imported meat is offered for grading.

For clarity, some terms of common usage in the grading of meat and meat products are defined as follows. Within the same kind of species, the livestock or product may be subdivided according to differences in physical characteristics. This is "class." A "grade" refers to the subdivision of livestock or product according to conformation, finish, and quality in livestock and meat. All these are preference factors. "To grade" means to define the quality such as grade or class according to a standard. "Quality" expresses the relative degree of excellence, which is actually a combination of the inherent properties of the livestock or product. "Yield grade" indicates how much trimmed, boneless, major retail cuts can be obtained from the carcass or wholesale cuts--rounds or legs, loins, ribs or racks, and chucks or shoulders. "Quality grade" explains two factors: palatability (how lean?), and the conformation of the carcass (primal cut?).

Two kinds of grading services are specifically indicated in the regulations: Meat Acceptance Service and the Carcass Data Service. The division issues a small publication, "USDA's acceptance service for meat and meat products" (Table 1-3). Some of the information is presented as follows.

Large volume meat buyers such as the military, prisons, hospitals, restaurants, schools, hotels, steamship lines, and airlines depend heavily on the "acceptance service." Generally, the buyer specifies what he wants, awards the contract by bid, and mandates that the products be certified by federal graders. The fee for the service is usually paid by the supplier who, in turn, adds the cost to the price that the buyer pays. The cost usually adds up to about a fraction of a cent per pound. For a small price, the buyer is guaranteed the quality of the meat.

The Meat Acceptance Service of the division is based on USDA-approved Institutional Meat Purchase Specifications, commonly called IMPS. These specifications are the end products of extensive testing and development conducted by the division in conjunction with various segments of the meat industry. At present there are specifications available for a number of meat products. They have been prepared to make their use as easy as possible; each item is numbered and may be referred to simply by number. Also, each item listed in these specifications is described in careful detail. When a purchasing agent orders any item--for instance, Item 1301 (cubed steaks, special)--there is no doubt on the part of the supplier or the federal meat grader as to exactly what is wanted. The Veterans Administration

TABLE 1-3. Selected Publications Distributed by Meat Quality Division

Publication Number (date)	Title cf Publication
Marketing Bulletin NO. 47 (July 1974)	USDA's acceptance service for meat and meat products
AMS-545 (April 1975)	Carcass data service
C&MS-8 (August 1968)	USDA's beef carcass evaluation service
Technical Bulletin No. 1232 (1961)	Beef characteristics as related to carcass grade, carcass weight, and degree of aging
MB-45 (1968)	USDA Yield Grades for Beef
MB-49 (1970)	USDA Grades for Pork Carcasses
MB-51 (1970)	USDA Grades for Slaughter Swine and Feeder Pigs
MB-52 (1970)	USDA Yield Grades for Lamb

has incorporated such specifications directly into their master subsistence procurement reference source, that is, the Federal Hospital Subsistence Guide which is not discussed in this book (for an explanation, see the preface).

To start with, the purchasing agent obtains from the Government Printing Office copies of the Institutional Meat Purchase Specifications General Requirements and the various specifications concerning the meat and meat products he wishes to purchase (see the list of specifications that follows). Most suppliers already have copies of these publications. Next, he lists the items he wants and indicates the grade, weight range, state of refrigeration, and other variables. After a contract has been awarded by bids, a copy of the purchase document is sent to the nearest USDA meat grading supervisor, who will be asked by the supplier to examine the product on delivery. The meat grader is responsible for accepting the product and certifying that it is in compliance with specifications. The federal grader stamps each acceptable meat item or the sealed carton in which it is contained with a shield-shaped stamp bearing the words "USDA Accepted as Specified" or similar official statement. This method assures the purchaser of a wholesome product (only meat that has passed inspection for wholesomeness will be examined for "acceptance") of the grade, trim, weight, and other options requested. This system also encourages competitive bidding and usually results in overall lower costs, permits long-range planning, and eliminates controversies between the buyer and seller over compliance of product.

All currently available IMPSs are listed as follows:

1. Institutional Meat Purchase Specifications--General Requirements, effective August 1971.
2. Institutional Meat Purchase Specifications for Fresh Beef--Series 100, effective January 1975.
3. Institutional Meat Purchase Specifications for Fresh Lamb and Mutton--Series 200, effective January 1975.
4. Institutional Meat Purchase Specifications for Fresh Veal and Calf--Series 300, effective July 1975.
5. Institutional Meat Purchase Specifications for Fresh Pork--Series 400, effective January 1975.
6. Institutional Meat Purchase Specifications for Cured, Cured and Smoked, and Fully Cooked Pork Products--Series 500, effective June 1971.
7. Institutional Meat Purchase Specifications for Cured, Dried, and Smoked Beef Products--Series 600, effective January 1970.
8. Institutional Meat Purchase Specifications for Edible By-products--Series 700, effective January 1971.
9. Institutional Meat Purchase Specifications for Sausage Products--Series 800, effective July 1976.
10. Institutional Meat Purchase Specifications for Portion-cut Meat Products--Series 1000, effective March 1970.

Among these specifications, the IMPSs--General Requirements is a very useful reference booklet. It describes in great detail the conditions that must be fulfilled if one wants to derive maximal benefits from the specifications. The contents of this publication include the following: inspection, ordering data, certification of products for delivery (chilled or frozen), disposition of certificates, cost, time limitation, state of refrigeration, packaging and packing, closure, sealing, marking, examination for condition of containers, condition of product at time of delivery, special notice, waivers and amendments to specifications requirements, and institution inspection. If interested, one may obtain any of the specifications and study the details since space limitation prohibits an inclusion of an example of an IMPS in the appendix.

The publication "Carcass data service" (Table 1-3) explains the second grading service provided by the Meat Quality Division. This service is carried out with the joint effort of the cattle and beef industry, the Meat Quality Division, and state agencies. It provides cattle feeders and producers with carcass data that determine the quality and yield grade factors of the carcasses and their by-products. This is especially important to persons who *may not own* the carcass, but who were financially interested in the live animal at some point during its development. The service works this way.

Producers and feeders purchase specially designed eartags used for official identification from an authorized source. Each animal whose carcass data is needed will be assigned one of the bright orange, shield-shaped, and serially numbered eartags [see 7 CFR 53.19(f)]. In the slaughter house, the federal meat inspector removes the tag from the ear, attaches it to the carcass, and then informs the official meat grader. After the usual chilling process, the tagged carcass will be evaluated by the grader with respect to quality and yield grade factors. The information will be recorded on a special form that is then sent to a Carcass Data Center in the headquarters of the Meat Quality Division. The center processes the data and returns them to the cooperator--cattle producer and feeder organizations, state departments of agriculture, and so on--from which the tags were initially purchased. The cooperator then forwards the data to the producer or feeder who originally purchased the eartag. A fee is charged for each data form processed and returned. Some of the important value-determining carcass characteristics include conformation, maturity, marbling, quality grade, packer's warm carcass weight, adjusted fat thickness, ribeye area, kidney pelvic and heart fat, yield grade, and evaluation data.

A third grading service not described in 7 CFR 53 is explained in the publication "USDA's beef carcass evaluation service." This program attempts to certify detailed carcass information from specific slaughter cattle. The service is used extensively by breed associations, beef cattle producers, agricultural experimental stations, and others. The carcass evaluation service is based on positive identification of the live animal and its carcass. It is suitable, therefore, for use in sire evaluation and other performance-testing programs.

A special form called the "Beef Carcass Evaluation Report" is used by the meat graders who provide any or all of the information listed. Other information or characteristics of the carcass can also be obtained if they are requested. For a nominal fee, an estimate of ribeye area and yield grade may also be made if such information is needed. When less detailed information is requested, such as only carcass grade and weight, it may be furnished on a regular grading certificate.

If the service is desired, the producer should notify the nearest division's Meat Grading Branch and provide the following information: location of the federally inspected slaughter house, the number of animals involved, the factors desired to be evaluated, data and time of slaughter, and who is to be billed for the service.

In spite of the many similarities between the Beef Carcass Data Service and the Beef Carcass Evaluation Service, they differ in one important aspect. The latter service requires that the official meat grader be informed in advance of the date and location of slaughter. As a result, this particular service becomes useful only to producers, feeders, or other interested persons who own the cattle just prior to slaughter. On the other hand, the Beef Carcass Data Service serves mainly feeders or producers who do not own the animals at the time of slaughter. This service requires no specific action on the part of participants other than the purchase and installation of the specially designed eartags. As a result the Data Service is more readily available to a larger segment of the livestock and meat industry since it is easier to use.

The Meat Quality Division has also issued a number of publications such as MB-45, MB-49, MB-51, MB-52, and Technical Bulletin No. 1231 (Table 1-3) that describe grades or yield grades for beef, pork carcass, lamb, and others. A list of slaughter livestock, their carcasses and products for which this division has established standards, and grades and specifications are presented in the list that follows. They have been adapted from 7 CFR 53 (1977), and the section numbers are given in parentheses.

Carcass beef (7 CFR 53.100 to 53.105), Standards for grades of quality and yield of steer, bullock, bull, cow, and heifer.
Veal and calf carcass (7 CFR 53.107 to 53.112), Standards for grades of veal and calf carcass.
Lamb, yearling mutton, and mutton carcasses (7 CFR 53.114 to 53.119), Standards for grades of quality and yield.
Vealers and slaughter calves (7 CFR 53.120 to 53.124), Standards for grades.
Slaughter lambs, yearlings, and sheep (7 CFR 53.130 to 53.135), Standards for grades of quality and yield.
Pork carcasses (7 CFR 53.140 and 53.145), Standards for grades of barrow, gilt, and sow.
Swine (7 CFR 53.150 to 53.159), Standards for grades of slaughter barrows, gilts, sows, and feeder pigs.
Cattle (7 CFR 53.201 to 53.209), Standards for grades of quality and yield of steer, bullock, bull, cow, and heifer.

Appendix 1-6 reproduces the standards, grades, and specifications for veal and calf carcasses (7 CFR 53.107 to 53.112), and Appendix 1-7 reproduces 7 CFR

RENNER LEARNING RESOURCES CENTER
ELGIN COMMUNITY COLLEGE
ELGIN, ILLINOIS

53.16 and 53.19, the official certificates, and identifcation marks for grades, standards, and acceptance.

The grading of meat is a very complicated and technical process, and the division has developed various sophisticated literature, visual aids, tools, and other paraphernalia to facilitate the process. Some of these are occasional publications called "Instruction." Table 1-4 gives three examples. They are usually issued to supervisors and meat graders. For example, G 14 explains the operation of the car-

TABLE 1-4. Selected Publications Distributed by Meat Quality Division

Publication Number (date)	Title of Publication
LS Instruction 918 (MG)-2 Rev. 6, G 16 (March 3, 1971)	Examination, Acceptance and Certification Service
LS Instruction 918 (MG)-1 G 14 (September 21, 1973)	Evaluation and Certification of Carcass Data, Grades, and Weight
LS Instruction 918 (MG)-1 Rev. 6, G 15 (November 7, 1975)	Grading Methods and Procedures

cass data program and the certification of carcass weight and grades; G 15 describes how to class quality, grades, and roller brand; and G 16 explains the various services offered other than meat grading and the procedures to be followed in performing these services. One may obtain from the division a list of available publications and informational tools such as posters and films.

Because of the importance of meat and meat products, most states have their own meat grading and/or certification programs. However, some states need assistance. At present, the division has cooperative meat grading agreements with a few states such as Nevada, Hawaii, North Carolina, and Virginia. Each agreement carries its own file code number. The authority for the provisions in these agreements was issued under 7 U.S.C. 1621 et seq. and the applicable laws of the states. Sample contents of an agreement are as follows.

The federal agency will train, supervise, and license state meat graders to apply and interpret official grade standards, grading methods and procedures. To obtain a license, the employee must pass an examination given by the federal agency. The latter will establish fee schedules.

On the other hand, the state agency will use only federal certificates, grades, standards, and identifications. It will employ only federally licensed individuals and pay for the service of any borrowed federal grader.

It is mutually agreed that both agencies will approve state grader assignments, and the federal agency must approve the agreement signed between the state agency and an applicant for service. For more details, consult the original document.

The relationship between the Meat Quality Division and the FDA is focused on the latter's approval of the ingredients used in the manufacturing of the ink used to apply official grade identification to meat carcasses and cuts.

Poultry and Dairy Quality Division

This division is headed by a director who supervises both voluntary and mandatory grading and inspection services. The discussion that follows is divided into two parts: poultry programs and dairy programs.

Poultry Programs

The division provides both voluntary and mandatory services and derives its authority from two federal statutes. The Agricultural Marketing Act (7 U.S.C. 1621 et seq.) authorizes the division to perform voluntary inspection and grading services for poultry, eggs, and rabbits. The fee for these services is paid by the user. The Egg Products Inspection Act (PL 91-597 , December 29, 1970, 21 U.S.C. 1031 to 1056, 84 Stat. 1620 to 1635) authorizes the mandatory inspection of egg products and surveillance for shell eggs. The U.S. Government assumes the cost of these programs. Because of the various services available, it is difficult to sort out the basic differences among them. Table 1-5 lists the federal regulations promulgated by the division for each service and the basic differentiating characteristics.

The Egg Products Inspection Act contains the following features:

1. Mandatory inspection of egg products, which include whole eggs, whites, yolks, and various blends in liquid, frozen, and dried form.
2. Thorough and continous inspection of the product processing plants and the entire operation from the selection of a shell egg for breaking to the final products. A final check is applied to the product after pasteurization, cooling, and packaging.
3. Mandatory application to eggs and egg products in interstate, foreign, and intrastate commerce.

TABLE 1-5. Inspection and Grading Regulations for Poultry Products as Promulgated in Title 7 of Code of Federal Regulations (1977)

Part[a]	Part Title and Statutory Authority under which Each Part Was Issued	Statutory Requirement (cost)	Grade Standards Established	Inspection
55	Voluntary inspection of egg products and grading. Authority: Sections 202 to 208, 60 Stat. 1087 to 1091; 7 U.S.C. 1621 to 1627.	Voluntary (fee for service)	No[b]	Yes
56	Grading of shell eggs and United States standards, grades and weight classes for shell eggs. Authority: Section 205, 60 Stat. 1090, as amended; 7 U.S.C. 1624.	Voluntary (fee for service)	Yes	No
59	Inspection of eggs and egg products. Authority: 84 Stat. 1620 et seq., 21 U.S.C. 1031 to 1056.	Mandatory (no fee)	No[b]	Yes
70	Voluntary grading of poultry products and rabbit products and United States classes, standards, and grades with respect thereto. Authority: 60 Stat. 1087; 7 U.S.C. 1621 et seq.	Voluntary (fee for service)	Yes	No

[a] At time of current writing, the parts are being recodified as a result of government reorganization. Thus, 7 CFR 55, 56, 59, and 70 will eventually become 7 CFR 2855, 2856, 2859, and 2870, respectively. Note that the difference is the two extra prefix-digits, "28."

[b] The USDA uses the grade standards established by the FDA (see Chapter 6).

28

4. Regulation of the distribution of certain qualities of shell eggs in commerce. Use of nationwide standards, grades, and weight classes for eggs in commerce. "Restricted" shell eggs are defined to include dirties, checks (eggs with cracked shells but not leaking), incubator rejectors, inedibles, leakers, and eggs unsuitable for human consumption; in addition, they are regulated with reference to their selective disposal and distribution. For example, the act provides authority to destroy all restricted eggs except checks and dirty eggs that may be shipped to officially inspected plants to be properly segregated and processed.
5. Prohibition of individual states from requiring state origin labeling of shell eggs except for noncontiguous areas (Hawaii, Alaska, Puerto Rico, and the Virgin Islands) of the United States. Individual states may require the name, address, and license number of the person processing and packaging eggs.
6. Mandatory application to those that break only a few cases of eggs each week, as well as to highly mechanized operations producing many thousand pounds of egg products a day. Registration is required of all individuals who handle (grade and pack) shell eggs for retail stores, households, restaurants, institutions, or food manufacturers; producer/packers with more than 3000 hens, who pack eggs that ultimately reach the consumers; and all hatcheries.
7. Cooperation between the federal government and state agencies to enforce various provisions of the act, with the latter to be reimbursed for services performed.
8. Equal treatment of imported egg and egg products and domestic products.
9. Provision of requirements for exemptions, record keepings, detentions, and penalties for violations.

The regulations for implementing the Egg Products Inspection Act, promulgated in 7 CFR 59, provide information on the following:

1. Administrative procedures and definitions for terms used.
2. Scope of inspection and relation to other authorities.
3. Eggs and egg products not intended for human consumption and exemptions from requirements.
4. Performance, application, inauguration, and denial of service.
5. Records and related requirements for eggs and egg product handlers and related industries.
6. Administrative detention and appeal of an inspection or decision.
7. Certification, identification, and marking of products.
8. Inspection, reinspection, condemnation, and retention.
9. Entry of materials into official egg product plant.
10. Sanitary, processing, and facility requirements and laboratory work.
11. Exempted egg product plants and registration of shell egg handlers.

12. Inspection and disposition of restricted eggs.
13. Identification of restricted eggs or egg product not intended for human consumption.
14. Imports.

Table 1-6 provides a few of the publications that have translated some of the legal language of the act and the implementing regulations in 7 CFR 59 into layman's terms. Selected aspects of 7 CFR 59 are briefly described in the following paragraphs.

TABLE 1-6. Selected Publications Distributed by Poultry and Dairy Quality Division

Publication Number (date)	Title of Publication
AMS-560 (November 1974)	Handled with care, Egg Products Inspection Act
PA-866 (June 1973)	USDA egg products inspection--A safeguard for quantity buyers
PS-238 (April 1971)	The egg and the law
PS-253 (May 1972)	The egg and the law--Part two
Marketing Bulletin No. 46 (August 1975)	USDA's acceptance service for poultry and eggs
Agriculture Handbook No. 75 (August 1975)	Egg grading manual
Agriculture Handbook No. 31 (March 1977)	Poultry grading manual

The legal definitions for certain eggs and egg products are as follows. An "egg" is defined as the shell egg of a domestic turkey, chicken, goose, duck, or guinea. When an egg is an incubator reject, it has been removed from incubation during the hatching process because of infertility or nonhatchability. An inedible egg may be described as yellow rot, black rot, white rot, or mixed rot. It may be a sour egg or an egg with stuck yolk, green white, blood ring, or embryo chick. It may also be a moldy or musty egg. An egg with break or crack in the shell and shell membrane and content exposed or exuded is a leaker.

An egg product includes any frozen, dried, or liquid eggs with or without added ingredients, except when the egg part exists in a relatively small proportion. Some nonegg products as defined by law are: egg substitutes, imitation egg products, freeze-dried products, eggnog mixes, milk and egg dip, cake mixes, French toast, and sandwiches containing eggs or egg products. Certain eggs are exempt from federal inspection, for example, eggs for sale by a producer with less than 3000 hens for egg production or directly to a household consumer for use by the buyer and his family and nonpaying guests.

The regulation provides detailed information on sanitary, processing, and facility requirements. According to the plant requirements, the plant should be free from objectionable odors, dust, and smoke-laden air. Rooms should be kept free from refuse, rubbish, waste materials, odors, insects, rodents, and from any conditions that may constitute a source of odors or engender insects and rodents. There should be an efficient drainage and plumbing system for the plant and premises. Drains and gutters should be properly installed with approved traps and vents. The water supply (both hot and cold) should be ample, clean, and potable, with adequate pressure and facilities for its distribution throughout the plant or portion thereof utilized for egg processing and handling operations and protected against contamination and pollution.

All equipment and utensils used should be of appropriate design, material, and construction. These conditions permit the examination, segregation, and processing of eggs and egg products to be efficient, sanitary, and satisfactory. They allow easy access to all parts for thorough cleaning and sanitizing. Whenever practicable, all equipment should be made of metal or other impervious material that will not affect the product by chemical action or physical contact.

Any operation involving processing, storing, and handling of shell eggs, ingredients, and egg products should be sanitary and conducted as rapidly as practicable. Pasteurization, heat treatment, stabilization, and other processes should follow approved requirements. All operations should prevent any deterioration of the egg products. All loss and inedible eggs or egg products are placed in a container clearly labeled "inedible" and containing a sufficient amount of approved denaturant or decharacterant, such as FD&C brown, blue, black, or green colors; meat and fish by-products; grain and milling by-products; or any other approved substance that will accomplish the purposes. Shell eggs should be crushed and the substance should be dispersed through the product in amounts sufficient to give the product a distinctive appearance or odor.

If interested, one should consult 7 CFR 59 for further details. Appendix 1-8 reproduces the inspection and identification marks for eggs and egg products.

As can be seen in Table 1-5, the regulations for the voluntary inspection and grading of egg products are stated in 7 CFR 55. This program is used for any service required but not covered by the mandatory service. For example, the regulations provide for the following kinds of services:

1. Inspection of the processing of products containing eggs in official plants.
2. Sampling and laboratory analysis of products.
3. Quantity and condition inspection of products.
4. Laboratory analysis of samples (with or without added ingredients) of products submitted to the laboratory by the applicant.

An operator may apply for service on a fee basis or a resident inspection basis. For example, in a resident inspection service, the inspector is authorized to:

1. Make such observations and inspections as he deems necessary to enable him to certify that products have been prepared, processed, stored, and otherwise handled in conformity with prescribed regulations.
2. Supervise the marking of packages containing products eligible for official identification.
3. Retain, under his supervision, labels with official identification, marking devices, samples, certificates, seals, and reports of inspectors.
4. Deface or remove any official identification from any package containing products if they have not been processed in accordance with prescribed regulations or are not fit for human consumption.
5. Issue a certificate on request on any product processed in the official plant.
6. Use retention tags or other devices and methods for the identification and control of products not in compliance with the regulations or held for further examination. The same applies to any equipment, utensils, rooms, or compartments found to be unclean or otherwise in violation of the regulations. None of the products or other items may be released for use until it has been made acceptable. Such identification will only be removed by an inspector or grader.

For further details on the inspection and gradings of egg products, one should consult 7 CFR 55.

The regulations also present the official U.S. standards for palatability scores for dried whole eggs. It describes in detail the preparation of samples for palatability test (7 CFR 55.800) and palatability scores for dried whole eggs (7 CFR 55.820).

As indicated in Table 1-5, the Poultry and Dairy Quality Division also administers the regulations promulgated in 7 CFR 56, "Grading of shell eggs and United States standards, grades and weight classes for shell eggs."

The egg grading program is voluntary. If an egg packing plant wants its eggs to carry the U.S. grade shield such as Grade AA, A, or B, it may employ the program. The official grade shield certifies that the eggs have been graded for quality and size under federal/state supervision.

Table 1-6 includes the publication "Egg Grading Manual," which explains in detail how shell egg standards are set and how they are graded according to quality, standard, and wholesomeness. If interested, one should consult this publication or 7 CFR 56. In the following, some aspects of the regulation are discussed.

The grading service for shell eggs requires an official grader to determine the class, quality, quantity, or condition of a large lot of eggs by examining specific and representative samples and to issue an official grading certificate. Sometimes the grading service involves continuous supervision, in an official plant, of the handling or packaging of any product. The grading service is based on the U.S. standards, grades, and weight classes for shell eggs. Also, with proper authorization, grading service may be rendered with respect to products bought and sold on the basis of institutional contract specifications or those of the applicant.

All grading services are subject to supervision at all times by the applicable state supervisor, circuit supervisor, area supervisor, and national supervisor. Such service will be rendered where facilities and conditions are satisfactory, and where the requisite graders and samplers are available. Whenever the supervisor of a grader has evidence that the latter has incorrectly graded a product, he should make the necessary alterations prior to shipment of the product from the place of initial grading.

Any person who is a federal or state employee or the employee of a local jurisdiction or a cooperating agency possessing proper qualifications may be licensed by the division as a grader if he so applies.

An application for any noncontinous grading service on a fee basis may be made in any office of grading or with any grader or sampler at the nearest location where the service is desired. Such application may be made orally (in person or by telephone), in writing, or by telegraph.

An application for continuous grading service on a resident basis or continuous grading service on a nonresident basis must be made in writing on forms approved by the division. Such forms may be obtained at the national, area, or state grading office.

According to the "Egg Grading Manual" and the regulation in 7 CFR 56, in order for cartoned eggs to be grade labeled, several requirements must be met. They are listed as follows:

1.   The eggs must be graded by and identified under the supervision of a licensed

grader. The eggs may be graded by an authorized company employee but then must be check graded by the supervising grader.

2. Eggs to be packed in consumer packages and marked U.S. Grade AA or A must be packed from eggs of current production.
3. Eggs to be packed in consumer packages and identified as U.S. Grade AA, "Fresh Fancy," or U.S. Grade A under the quality control program must be packed from eggs produced during a specified testing period.
4. Establishments that pack eggs with official marks in consumer packages must meet the facility and operating requirements set forth in the USDA regulations.

Under the federal/state grading program provision is made for the grade identification of the packaged product, whether packed in a 30-dozen case or a 1-dozen carton. Usually the grade mark is applied to 30-dozen cases by means of a rubber stamp. The stamp also specifies the date of grading. In many instances when eggs are packed for delivery on purchase contracts to institutions, a paper tape must be placed across the top of the case and the grade mark or acceptance mark stamped partially on the tape and partially on the case to effectively seal the case. There are other specific provisions in regard to the mechanics of grade labeling.

According to 7 CFR 56, the following U.S. standards, grades, and weight classes for shell eggs have been established, with the relevant section numbers in parentheses:

1. United States standards for quality of individual shell eggs (200 to 212).
2. United States grades and weight classes for shell eggs (216).
3. United States consumer grades and weight classes for shell eggs (216 to 218).
4. United States procurement grades and weight classes for shell eggs (221 to 223).
5. United States wholesale grades and weight classes for shell eggs (226 to 228).
6. United States nest-run grade and weight classes for shell eggs (230 to 234).

Appendix 1-9 reproduces the U.S. consumer grades and weight classes for shell eggs. Appendix 1-10 reproduces the official identification marks for the products.

The voluntary grading of poultry and rabbit products is described in 7 CFR 70 (see Table 1-5). In this part U.S. classes, standards, and grades for these products are also established. Some aspects of the grading regulations are discussed in the following.

The grading service provided by the division includes:

1. Determination of the class, quality, quantity, or condition of any product by

examining each unit or representative unit drawn by a grader.

2. Issuance of a grading certificate with respect to the examination.
3. Identification of the graded product.
4. Determination that, with reference to an official plant, the product has been processed, handled, and packaged in accordance with regulations.
5. Any regrading or appeal grading of a previously graded product.

"Poultry" means any kind of domesticated bird, including, but not limited to, chickens, turkeys, ducks, geese, pigeons, and guineas. A rabbit means any domesticated rabbit, whether dead or live.

"Ready-to-cook poultry" means any dressed poultry from which the protruding pinfeathers, vestigial feathers (hair or down as the case may be), head, shanks, crop, oil gland, trachea, esophagus, entrails, reproductive organs, and lungs have been removed; and with or without the giblets; and that is ready to cook without need of further processing. It also includes any cut-up or disjointed portion of such poultry or any edible part. A "ready-to-cook rabbit" means any rabbit that has been slaughtered for human consumption, from which the head, blood, skin, feet, and inedible viscera have been removed and that is ready to cook without need of further processing.

According to the regulations in 7 CFR 70, the following kinds of service are provided by the division:

1. Grading of ready-to-cook poultry and rabbits in an official plant or at other locations with adequate facilities.
2. Grading of specified poultry food products in official plants.
3. Any one or more of the different services applicable to an official plant may by rendered in the establishment.

The grading service is based on the U.S. classes, standards, and grades as contained in the regulation. However, it is available for products bought and sold on the basis of institutional contract specifications or those of the applicant. Such approved specifications form the basis of grading.

All products to be graded must have been inspected and passed by the Meat and Poultry Inspection Program (MPIP; see later discussion). Squabs and domesticated game birds (including, but not limited to, quail, pheasants, and wild species of ducks and geese raised in captivity) may also be graded if they have been inspected and passed by the same program.

In general, the grading regulations in 7 CFR 70 contain the following broad topics: general provisions, basis of service, performance of service, application for grading service, denial of service, identifying and marking products, reports, fees and charges, grading, grading certificates, appeal of a grading or decision, and sanitary requirements, facilities, and operating procedures.

According to 7 CFR 70, the U.S. classes, standards, and grades established for poultry and rabbit products are as follows, with the section numbers in parentheses:

1. United States classes of ready-to-cook poultry (200 to 206).
2. United States standards for quality of ready-to-cook poultry and specified poultry food products (210).
3. United States standards for quality of ready-to-cook poultry (220 to 222).
4. United States standards for quality of specified poultry food products (230 to 231).
5. United States grades for ready-to-cook poultry and specified poultry food products (240).
6. United States consumer grades for ready-to-cook poultry and specified poultry food products (250 to 252).
7. United States ready-to-cook grade of poultry for further processing (260).
8. United States procurement grades for ready-to-cook poultry (270 to 271).
9. United States classes of ready-to-cook rabbits (300 to 302).
10. United States standards for quality of ready-to-cook rabbits (310 to 322).
11. United States consumer grades for ready-to-cook rabbits (330 to 332).

Appendix 1-11 reproduces the U.S. standards for quality of ready-to-cook poultry, and the official identification for grades of poultry and rabbit products is presented in Appendix 1-12.

To help federal personnel and the industry to understand and perform grading of poultry products, the division has issued a publication called "Poultry Grading Manual" (see Table 1-6). This government document is very useful for the poultry industries and regulatory agencies and especially in the teaching area. The general contents of this publication are as follows:

1. Introduction: standards and grades and general use of standards and grades.
2. Grading and inspection programs: inspection services, grading services, and official identification marks for ready-to-cook poultry.
3. Grading ready-to-cook poultry and poultry food products: determining condition, determining quality, examining birds and parts, standards of quality for ready-to-cook poultry, poultry parts, poultry food products, and grades.
4. Classes of poultry: chickens, turkeys, ducks, geese, guineas, and pigeons.
5. Grading live poultry: determining class, determining condition, quality factors for individual birds, combining quality factors, suggested standards of quality, and bird examination.
6. Planning a grading school: location and time of the school, equipment and

facilities, and suggested programs.

Two selected aspects of the materials in this publication are described as follows.

Ready-to-cook poultry is graded for condition in processing plants following evisceration. Decomposition (slimy or slippery condition of the skin, or putrid or sour odor) renders it (or them) ineligible for grading. In addition, birds showing certain conditions cannot be graded. Such birds must be sent back for further processing if grading is done at the processing plant. When grading is performed elsewhere, the number of birds found with these conditions would be recorded, and the lot would be classified as "No Grade." These conditions are:

1. Protruding pinfeathers.
2. Bruises requiring trimming.
3. Lungs or sex organs incompletely removed.
4. Parts of the trachea present.
5. Vestigial feathers.
6. Feathers.
7. Extraneous material of any type inside or outside of the carcass (e.g., fecal material, blood).

The quality of ready-to-cook poultry is determined by, among others, the extent of frozen defects. Discoloration and drying out of the skin of poultry carcasses during storage is commonly called "freezer burn." This defect detracts from the appearance and sales value of the carcass and, in the case of either moderate or severe freezer burn, lowers the quality of it. Other freezing defects of significance are darkening of the carcass due to slow freeze or defrosting, and, in the case of consumer-packaged poultry or parts, seepage of moisture from the product, resulting in clear, pinkish, or reddish layers of ice. The standards of "A" quality for ready-to-cook poultry require that the bird be practically free from defects that result from handling or occur during freezing or storage. The following defects are permitted if they, alone or in combination, detract only very slightly from the appearance of the carcass, part, or specified poultry food product:

1. Slight darkening over the back and drumsticks, provided that the frozen bird or part has a generally bright appearance;
2. Occasional pockmarks due to drying of the inner layer of skin (derma); however, none may exceed the area of a circle 1/8 inch in diameter for poultry weighing 6 pounds or less, and 1/4 inch in diameter for poultry weighing over 6 pounds;
3. Occasional small areas showing a thin layer of clear or pinkish colored ice.

Further details may be obtained from the original document.

The Egg Products Inspection Act is being administered simultaneously by the USDA and the FDA. Thus to delineate each agency's responsibility, a Memorandum of Understanding was announced on February 4, 1972 (37 FR 2686 to 2687). The specific jurisdiction and duties of the FDA are discussed in Chapter 6 of this book. Those of the USDA (i.e., of the division) are as follows.

The division will have exclusive jurisdiction in official egg product plants and exempted egg product plants; in checking egg products, packers, and other firms engaged in marketing eggs, including hatcheries, to determine the disposition of restricted eggs (check, dirty, incubator reject, inedible, leaker, or loss); and over imported egg products.

According to the agreement, the USDA (i.e., the division) will:

1. Notify the FDA whenever shell eggs or egg products are shipped illegally in commerce to receivers for which the FDA has exclusive jurisdiction.
2. Determine whether retail stores comply with the law in their purchases and sales of shell eggs.
3. Check imported shell eggs for proper labeling and disposition of restricted eggs and notify the FDA before releasing any lot for domestic commerce.
4. Notify the FDA when applications are made to import shell eggs into the United States.

This division also has a cooperative agreement with each of the 50 states. There are two types of agreement, one for a State Trust Fund and the other a Federal Trust Fund. For the former, fees for services are collected and held in trust by the state and applications for service are between the state and the individual firms. Under the latter, contracts for services are between the USDA and the individual firms, and the fees are collected and held in trust by the U.S. Government.

The agreements are used for all programs, both voluntary and mandatory, and for all products. The legal authority that provides for the signing of the agreement is found in the Agricultural Marketing Act of 1946 (7 U.S.C. 1621 et seq.) and the applicable laws of the state. Each agreement has its own file code number; the substance of a sample agreement is as follows:

1. To provide nationwide cooperative grading service for:
    a. Voluntary grading of egg products, shell eggs, poultry, and rabbits,
    b. Mandatory inspection of egg products, and
    c. Regulatory surveillance inspection of shell egg handlers and their applicable records.
2. To advise producers and processors with reference to improved methods and practices of handling, processing, standardizing, grading, packaging, and marketing of poultry, eggs, egg products, and rabbits.

The division will train, supervise, and license individuals to grade and inspect products and issue certificates; perform plant surveys; and approve facilities, labeling and packaging, chemicals, and other associated paraphernalia. The state agency will use only official standards, regulations, and certificates; perform both voluntary and mandatory inspection services; and assist the federal agency in informing and educating all interested parties about grade standards and the inspection process.

It is mutually agreed that all services will be performed on a cooperative basis. Fees for all services, including grading, sampling, weighing, and inspection, will be based on the regular schedule currently employed at the federal level. Mutual approval is needed for including any additional and/or supplemental arrangements in the agreement.

Dairy Programs

The programs cover both voluntary and mandatory services relating to dairy products. The authority to carry out the service is provided by some provisions of the Agricultural Marketing Act of 1946 and the Process or Renovated Butter Provisions of the Internal Revenue Code of 1954. The former authorizes voluntary and the latter mandatory services.

Details of regulations for the voluntary services are described in 7 CFR 58, "Grading and inspection, general specifications for approved plants and standards for grades of dairy products." There are three types of information:

1. Regulations governing the inspection and grading services of manufactured or processed dairy products.
2. General specifications for dairy plants approved for USDA inspection and grading service.
3. United States standards for grades of various dairy products.

The publications "Dairy inspection and grading services" and "Dairy products inspection service--aid for quantity buyers" (Table 1-7) provide a general understanding for the general public about the regulations. A brief discussion is provided in the following paragraphs, but details should be obtained from 7 CFR 58.

The division offers four major programs: plant surveys, inspection and grading, laboratory service, and the resident grading and quality control service. An interested party must make a request and be qualified for any voluntary services; fees are based on a scale. To carry out its inspection and grading services, the division depends heavily on the grade standards they have established for various dairy products.

The plant survey is the basic program. A plant must meet the requirements of the "General Specifications for Approved Dairy Plants" according to 7 CFR 58. This will qualify the plant for other services such as grading, inspection, sampling, testing, and certification of various dairy products. Every 3 months the division revises the publication "Dairy Plants Surveyed and Approved for USDA Grading Service" (see Table 1-7). It lists all those dairy plants in the United States that have been subjected to facility study and sanitation investigation. These plants have passed the test and are qualified to apply for other services. Additional plants are added to the list periodically.

TABLE 1-7. Selected Publications Distributed by Poultry and Dairy Quality Division

Publication Number (date)	Title of Publication
MB-48 (November 1974)	Dairy inspection and grading services
AMS-366 (1960)	Dairy products inspection service--aid for quantity buyers
Revised every 3 months	Dairy plants surveyed and approved for USDA grading service
Farmer's Bulletin No. 2259 (May 1975)	Judging and scoring milk and cheese
Agricultural Handbook No. 51 (January 1977)	Federal and state standards for the composition of milk products (and certain non-milk fat products)
Unnumbered (August 1976)	General instructions for performing farm inspections according to the USDA recommended requirements for milk for manufacturing purposes and its production and processing for adoption by state regulatory agencies
Unnumbered (August 1976)	Guidelines for the control of abnormal milk and screening tests for its detection

The inspection and grading of dairy products is the oldest program offered by the division. It is used extensively by dairy manufacturers, buyers, wholesalers, processors, restaurant owners, and others. This service makes extensive use of the division's grade standards. The division also extends their acceptance service of grading and inspection to volume dairy product buyers such as schools, restaurants, steamship and airline companies, Veterans Administration, Department of Defense, and state and local government agencies (e.g., hospitals, nursing homes, and prisons). This acceptance service is similar to that for fruits and vegetables, livestock, or poultry products. The division examines and certifies that a supplier's delivery has complied with contract specifications. Official stamps, certificates, and so on are also required.

The laboratory service monitors the class, quality, conditions, and keeping properties of all dairy products. Specialists in the laboratory establishment make chemical and bacteriological determinations of the products. A number of such laboratories are maintained in different parts of the country. They also perform tests on dairy and nondairy products for industry and other federal agencies on a fee-for-service basis. The dairy technicians have the training and equipment to check almost any kind of food product.

The resident grading and quality control service aims at serving the approved dairy plants. It provides quality checks on incoming raw material, in-processing controls, and sanitation. Grading and certification of the finished product are provided by an inspector stationed at the plant on a full-time basis. The program thus combines plant survey, inspection, grading, and laboratory services. To obtain the service, the plant must be approved and possess an approved laboratory.

The regulation in 7 CFR 58 provides detailed specifications for each plant that manufactures, processes, and packages any of the following categories of dairy products: nonfat dry milk, instant nonfat dry milk, dry whole milk, and dry buttermilk; butter and related products; cheese; cottage cheese; frozen desserts; pasteurized process cheese and related products; and whey, whey products, and lactose.

According to 7 CFR 58, the USDA has established the following U.S. standards for grades of the indicated product(s), with the section numbers in parentheses:

1. Bulk American cheese for manufacturing (2455 to 2460).
2. Monterey (Monterey Jack) cheese (2465 to 2471).
3. Colby cheese (2475 to 2481).
4. Cheddar cheese (2501 to 2506).
5. Nonfat dry milk (spray process) (2525 to 2541).
6. Nonfat dry milk (roller process) (2550 to 2562).
7. Swiss cheese, Emmentaler cheese (2570 to 2574).
8. Dry whey (2601 to 2606).
9. Butter (2621 to 2635).
10. Dry buttermilk (2651 to 2657).

11.   Dry whole milk (2701 to 2708).
12.   Edible dry casein (acid) (2800 to 2808).

The USDA also has established the following: U.S. scorched particle standards for dry milks (2670 to 2678), U.S. sediment standards for milk and milk products (2726 to 2731), and U.S. standards for instant nonfat dry milk (2750 to 2759). Appendix 1-13 reproduces the U.S. standards for grades of Colby cheese, and the official identification for graded and inspected products appears in Appendix 1-14.

As indicated in Table 1-7, the division issues the publication "Federal and State standards for the composition of milk products (and certain non-milk-fat products)." This document, Handbook No. 51, is very important and useful in teaching, enforcement, and legal purposes. Some details are presented in the following.

Handbook No. 51 is one of long standing and continued importance over a wide area of interest. When the division is developing U.S. standards and specifications for dairy products, it receives related information from state regulatory authorities. The combined materials are incorporated into this publication, which is published periodically to update current development. This publication serves as a ready reference to identify and compare the standards for composition of dairy products. Many interested parties utilize this publication. These include the dairy industry, libraries, law firms, academics, state regulatory authorities, and other federal agencies. At present, standards of dairy products among different states are quite uniform, and this has been attributed to the frequent and extensive utilization and distribution of Handbook No. 51.

The information contained in Handbook No. 51 has been derived from correspondence, laws, rules, and regulations furnished by federal, District of Columbia, state, and commonwealth officials who are in charge of enforcing the laws and regulations pertaining to milk and milk products.

Change in legislation will necessarily change the standards contained in the publication. The division has compiled the information but is not responsible for the establishment or enforcement of dairy legislature.

The commonwealth, District of Columbia, and state standards are applicable to products produced and marketed within their respective jurisdictions, whereas the federal standards promulgated by the FDA apply to products entering into interstate commerce. Products with no standard listed may lawfully be shipped in interstate commerce and will be regulated under the supervision of the Federal Food, Drug and Cosmetic Act which is administered by the FDA and is discussed in Chapter 6.

Table 1-7 indicates that the division issues other publications which deal with the scoring of milk and cheese, instructions for farm inspections, and guidelines for the control of abnormal milk. They are very useful reference materials and should be consulted if interested since space limitation prohibits a discussion of their contents here.

Apart from the voluntary programs reviewed in the preceding paragraphs, the division also carries out a mandatory inspection of the manufacture of processed or renovated butter. The Process or Renovated Butter Provision of the Internal Revenue Code of 1954 forms the basis for the service. The regulations for this act are described in 7 CFR 171, "Sanitary inspection of process or renovated butter." The authority for the provisions of this part was issued under Section 4817, 68A Stat. 573; 26 U.S.C. 4817, 4826, 7235(c).

Process or renovated butter is defined as "butter which has been subjected to any process by which it is melted, clarified, or refined and made to resemble butter." Butter is defined as that food product made exclusively from milk or cream, or both, with or without common salt, although the legal definition is much more complicated.

The regulations provide requirements for the processing plants, equipment and facilities, processing and sanitary practices, inspection of the raw materials and finished product, labeling, record keeping, and so on. The act authorizes the Secretary of Agriculture (i.e., the division) to withdraw inspection from any factory where there is failure to comply with the regulations, condemn and seize raw materials and process or renovated butter deemed unhealthful or unwholesome, and investigate violations.

The raw materials consisted mainly of butter produced on farms having one or two cows. It was common practice for farmers to deliver the butter to their grocery store, where it was sold for cash or traded for other foods. The local stores sold the butter to the butter processor. This type of farm butter making and trading no longer exists, and the last butter processing and renovating plant closed in 1967. Since that time no new operations of this type have been started. In case such a plant is established, the division is prepared to supply the inspection service discussed earlier.

When it carries out its grading and inspection services, the division cooperates with the FDA according to the general agreement signed between the two agencies (42 FR 20350 and 20351), which has been discussed previously. The USDA (i.e., the division) has another Memorandum of Understanding with the FDA on "*Salmonella* in non-fat dry milk products" (40 FR 8846 and 8847, March 3, 1975).

A number of cooperative agreements have been signed between the division and various state agencies such as departments of agriculture, food, or even public health. Such agreements serve two objectives: (1) provide federal/state inspection and grading services and (2) advise producers and others on all aspects of manufacturing and marketing of dairy products.

There is a master agreement that provides for federal/state inspection and grading service for dairy products (butter, cheese, dry milk, etc.). Individual states become signatories to the agreement. States enter the agreement on a voluntary basis. There is little or no need for the services in states where there is no production or manufacturing of dairy products. The legal authority that provides for the signing of the agreement is found in the Agricultural Marketing Act of 1946 (7 U.S.C. 1621 et seq.) and the applicable laws of the individual state. The substance of a sample agreement is as follows. According to the agreement, the division will:

1. Assume responsibility for the administrative and technical supervision of inspection, grading, sampling, weighing, and laboratory services.
2. Issue federal licenses to all federal and state employed and qualified graders, inspectors, and samplers.
3. Collect and handle all fees and charges for services furnished under the agreement.

According to the agreement, the state agency will:

1. Inform and educate all interested parties regarding improved methods and practices of producing, handling, processing, standardization, inspection, grading, packaging, and marketing of dairy products.
2. Adopt all federal official standards and grades.
3. Assign personnel to assist the federal agency in performing inspection and grading services.

It is mutually agreed that all procedures and regulations relating to grades and services will be those of the federal agency. Fees will be paid on a prescheduled scale. Certificates will be either federal/state or straight federal. If interested, one should contact the division to obtain more information on the cooperative agreements between the federal government and a state authority.

Meat and Poultry Inspection Program

The Meat Poultry Inspection Program (MPIP) inspects the slaughtering of certain domestic livestock and poultry and the processing of meat and poultry products. It has jurisdiction from the time that livestock and poultry are received at the slaughtering establishments until the finished products are distributed in commerce to consumers or for other purposes. This prevents the sale and distribution of adulterated or misbranded meat and poultry products, and it applies to all products in interstate or foreign commerce. The program reviews foreign inspection systems and packing plants that export meat and poultry to this country and reinspects imported products at ports of entry.

This program derives its authority from four major federal statutes: the Federal Meat Inspection Act (34 Stat. 1260, 79 Stat. 903, as amended, 81 Stat. 584, 84 Stat. 91, 438, 21 U.S.C. 71 et seq., 601 et seq., 33 U.S.C. 466 to 466K), the Poultry Products Inspection Act (82 Stat. 791 et seq. and 21 U.S.C. 451 et seq)., the Agricultural Marketing Act (7 U.S.C. 1621 to 1627), and the Humane Slaughter Act (7 U.S.C. 1901 to 1906).

The major requirements of the Federal Meat Inspection Act are as follows:

1. Antemortem inspection cf cattle, sheep, swine, goats, and horses slaughtered for human consumption.
2. Postmortem inspection of the carcasses of the same animals and their prepared parts for distribution.
3. Inspection of prepared meat food products.
4. Prohibition of the distribution of adulterated or misbranded carcasses, their parts, and meat and meat food products.
5. Regulation of the marking, packaging,and labeling of the meat and meat food products.
6. Meat processing plants must conform to uniform sanitation and inspection requirements.
7. Inspection and certification of all meat food products for export.
8. Regulation of the importation of animal carcasses, their parts, and meat and meat food products that are for human consumption.
9. Identification of all equine products for human food.
10. Identification and denaturation of all cattle, sheep, swine, goats, or equine products not intended for human consumption.
11. Exemption of custom slaughtered animals and products and certain operations in the unorganized territories from the requirements or placement under exclusionary provisions. Custom slaughterers are permitted to engage in the business of buying and selling without losing their exemption as custom slaughterers.
12. Regulation of the storage and handling of carcasses, their parts, and meat and meat food products by specified classes of individuals engaged in such business for commerce or import.
13. Meat processors and operators in related business must keep records, be registered and fulfill other requirements.
14. Distribution in commerce of "4D" (dead, dying, disabled, or diseased) animals and their carcasses are regulated.
15. Financial, technical, and scientific assistance are provided by the federal government to state agencies to improve intrastate meat inspection service.
16. The federal government has immediate authority to cover intrastate meat processing plants producing products that are hazardous to health if the state

does not act to remove the hazard.

17. If a state meat inspection program is equal to or better than the federal one, it is a "nondesignated" state. "Designated" states are those that do not maintain an inspection program at least equivalent to that of the federal government; federal inspection will be extended to the intrastate meat operations in these states.

18. The effectiveness of a state program must be constantly assessed and federal support be available when necessary.

19. Under certain circumstances, the federal meat inspection service may be denied to an applicant, and violative articles may be detained and seized.

20. The federal government is authorized to use seizure, condemnation, and injunction for any violation of the act.

21. The federal government is authorized to request reports, issue administrative subpoenas, and take certain other enforcement actions.

Most major provisions in the Poultry Products Inspection Act are quite similar to those in the Federal Meat Inspection Act, although they apply to all poultry and poultry products instead.

To enforce the two acts, the MPIP conducts numerous activities; some most important ones are indicated as follows:

1. Each product is inspected a number of times--before slaughter, after slaughter, and during processing, packaging, and labeling.

2. All domestic and imported products are monitored for drug, pesticide, and industrial chemical residues, including suspicious animals, flocks, and herds. The FDA and the Environmental Protection Agency (EPA) are alerted for illegal residues.

3. The use of all chemical additives in the production of meat and poultry products is regulated. Some uses of such chemicals include improving flavor, color, and shelf life of a product, and some requirements for their uses are:
   a. Approved by the FDA.
   b. Limited to specified amounts.
   c. Meeting a specific, justifiable need in the product.
   d. Not promoting deception as to product freshness, quality, weight, or size. For example, dye or color is not permitted in fresh meat since its red color can make raw meat appear leaner and fresher than it is.
   e. The label carries required statement about the chemicals.

4. All labels must be informative and accurate and must comply with all prescribed regulations.

5. Standard, composition, and identity have been developed for many meat and poultry products. For example, "beef with gravy" product must contain 50%

beef (cooked basis), whereas the minimum meat content for "gravy with beef" is 35% (cooked basis).

6. The MPIP has an epidemiology unit that traces causes of food-borne hazards involving meat and poultry. It works with local, state, and other federal agencies to identify any hazardous products.
7. The inspection laws, regulations, procedures, administration, and operations of a foreign country's overall program must meet domestic requirements before they are approved. Each foreign plant must be certified by its government for export to the United States. The plant is inspected by its government officials or U.S. experts. Labels of foreign products are checked for accuracy, and samples are routinely examined by MPIP officials.

Appendix 1-15 presents the organizational structure of the MPIP, which is composed of two main offices of functions: Scientific and Technical Services and Field Operations.

Two major responsibilities of the Scientific Services Staff with reference to meat and poultry and their products and ingredients are as follows:

1. The analysis, detection, evaluation of, and/or establishment of tolerances for residues of pesticides and related substances, food and color additives, industrial chemicals, drugs for therapy, growth, feed efficiency of animals, and toxic trace elements.
2. The identification, detection, evaluation and control of:
   a. Microorganisms with reference to growth, spoilage, toxin, and pathogen.
   b. Antibiotic residues.
   c. Phytoxins and mycotoxins.

One major responsibility of the Technical Services Staff is to develop, revise, and issue regulations, procedures, and instructions for or relating to:

1. Inspection or exemption from inspection of meat, poultry, and related products.
2. Establishment of product standards and approval of methods of preparation and ingredients used in the formulas for meat, poultry, and related products.
3. Marking, labeling, and packaging of the products.
4. Approval of plants, facilities, equipment, and environmental considerations for inspection and inspector safety.

Some major activities of the Field Operations are as follows:

1. Participates in the planning, organizing, directing, controlling, and coordina-

ting MPIP cooperative activities with states and other government agencies directed toward protecting the consuming public from product adulteration or misbranding.

2. Administers activities relating to the import and export of meat, poultry and their products, including inspection and certification to assure their compliance with U.S. federal requirements.
3. Coordinates all relevant activities to assure compliance by meat, poultry, and allied industries with federal laws and regulations.
4. Supervises all regional operations.

The MPIP has promulgated a voluminous amount of regulations relating to the inspection and certification of meat and poultry food products. They are stated in Chapter III of Title 9 of the Code of Federal Regulations. The title of each part is described in Table 1-8, together with the issuing statutory authority. To assist the MPIP personnel and industrial members to interpret and utilize the regulations, the headquarters in Washington, D.C. has issued very comprehensive inspection manuals, such as the Meat Poultry Inspection Manual.

One can obtain a general idea of the regulations contained in each part by studying its title in Table 1-8. It is not possible to discuss all of them in detail here. In the following, with the exception of a few parts, a brief discussion is presented for each part indicated in Table 1-8.

Definition (9 CFR 301). A number of common terms used in the regulations for meat inspection are defined. For example, a meat product is adulterated if it contains any poisonous or deleterious substance that may render it injurious to human health.

Application for Inspection and Other Requirements (9 CFR 302). The regulation explains what kind of establishements require inspection. Special provisions are applied to the District of Columbia and to designated states, territories, and/or designated plants endangering public health. For example, inspection is required for any establishment in which livestock are slaughtered for transportation or sale in commerce. All livestock and products entering an official establishment and their prepared products are required to be inspected, handled, stored, prepared, packaged, marked, and labeled in accordance with regulation.

Exemptions (9 CFR 303). The requirements and regulations do not apply to a number of situations. For example, one exemption is the slaughtering by an individual of livestock of his own raising. He prepares and transports in commerce the carcasses, parts, and meat and meat food products exclusively for use by himself, his family, nonpaying guests, and employees.

TABLE 1-8. Part Titles of Chapter III of Title 9 of Code of Federal Regulations
(1977)

Part	Part Title and Statutory Authority under which The Part Was Issued [a]

Subchapter A Mandatory Meat Inspection

301 Definitions
302 Application of inspection and other requirements
303 Exemptions
304 Applications for inspection; grant or refusal of inspection
305 Official numbers; inauguration of inspection; withdrawal of inspection reports of violation
306 Assignment and authorities of program employees
307 Facilities for inspection
308 Sanitation
309 Antemortem inspection
310 Postmortem inspection
311 Disposal of diseased or otherwise adultereated carcasses and parts
312 Official marks, devices, and certificates
314 Handling and disposal of condemned or other inedible products at official establishments
315 Rendering or other disposal of carcasses and parts passed for cooking
316 Marking products and their containers
317 Labeling, marking devices, and containers
318 Entry into official establishments; reinspection and preparation of products
319 Definitions and standards of identity or composition
320 Records, registration, and reports
321 Cooperation with states and territories
322 Exports
325 Transportation
327 Imported products
329 Detention; seizure and condemnation; criminal offenses
331 Special provisions for designated States and Territories; and for designation of establishments which endanger public health and for such designated establishments
     Authority: Sections 21, 301, 81 Stat. 584, 588, 592, 593, 595.
335 Rules of practice governing proceeding under the Federal Meat Inspection Act
     Authority: Section 21, 34 Stat. 1264, as amended (21 U.S.C. 621);37 FR 28464, 28477.

Subchapter B Voluntary Inspection and Certification Service

350 Special services related to meat and other products
     Authority: 34 Stat. 1260 to 1265, as amended; 41 Stat. 241, Section 306; 46 Stat. 689, Sections 203, 205; 60 Stat. 1087, as amended; 7 U.S.C. 2201; 19 U.S.C. 1306; 21 U.S.C. 71 to 91, 96; 7 U.S.C. 1622, 1624, unless otherwise noted
351 Certification of technical animal fats for export
     Authority: Sections 203, 205; 60 Stat. 1087 and 1090, as amended, 7 U.S.C. 1622, 1624

(continued)

50 Department of Agriculture

TABLE 1-8 (continued)

Part	Part Title and Statutory Authority under which The Part Was Issued

354 Voluntary inspection of rabbits and edible products thereof
Authority: Sections 203, 205, 60 Stat. 1087, 1090; 7 U.S.C. 1622, 1624; 37 FR 28464, 28477

355 Certified products for dogs, cats, and other carnivora; inspection, certification, and identification as to class, quality, quantity, and condition
Authority: Sections 203, 205, 60 Stat. 1087, 1090; 7 U.S.C. 1622, 1624

362 Voluntary poultry inspection regulations
Authority: Sections 203, 205, 60 Stat. 1087, 1090; 7 U.S.C. 1622, 1624; 37 FR 28464, 28477

Subchapter C Mandatory Poultry Products Inspection

381 Poultry products inspection regulations
Authority: Section 14 of the Poultry Products Inspection Act, as amended by the Wholesome Poultry Products Act (21 U.S.C. 451 et seq.); the Talmadge-Aiken Act of September 28, 1962 (7 U.S.C. 450); and subsection 21(b) of the Federal Water Pollution Control Act, as amended by PL 91-224 and by other laws [33 U.S.C. 1171(b)]

Subchapter D Humane Slaughter of Livestock

390 Designation of methods
Authority: Section 4, 72 Stat. 863; 7 U.S.C. 1904

391 Identification of carcasses of certain humanely slaughtered livestock
Authority: Section 4, 72 Stat. 863; 7 U.S.C. 1904

---

[a] With the exception of parts 331 and 335, all other parts were issued under the authority of 34 Stat. 1260, 79 Stat. 903, as amended; 81 Stat. 584, 84 Stat. 91, 438; 21 U.S.C. 71 et seq., 601 et seq., 33 U.S.C. 466 to 466k.

Application for Inspection; Grant or Refusal of Inspection (9 CFR 304). Before an inspection is granted, each person conducting operations at an establishment is required to submit an application. It should provide complete drawings of all facilities with detailed specifications such as water supply, plumbing, drainage, refrigeration, equipment, lighting, floor plans, and other pertinent data. The operator is notified as to whether the application is granted or refused, and reasons for refusal are included.

Official Numbers; Inauguration of Inspection, Withdrawal of Inspection; Reports of Violation (9 CFR 305). An official number is assigned to each establishment granted inspection and is used to identify all inspected and passed products prepared there. Each official establishment is required to be separate and distinct from an official establishment, except for a poultry products processing establishment operated under federal or state inspection. Sanitation and adequate facilities are required before the inauguration of the establishment. The U.S. Government may withdraw inspection from an official establishment where the sanitary conditions are such that its products are rendered adulterated, or for failure of the operator to destroy condemned products as required.

Assignment and Authorities of Program Employees (9 CFR 306). A supervisor is assigned to each inspection program, and all MPIP employees should have access at all times, day or night, whether the establishment is in operation or not, to every part of the premise. The officer uses a numbered badge as the official identification for entering an establishment.

Facilities for Inspection (9 CFR 307). Office space, including necessary furnishings, light, heat, and janitor service, should be provided by the official establishments, rent free, for the exclusive use for official purposes of the inspector and other MPIP employees. All other facilities and conditions necessary for the efficient conduct of inspection and maintenance of sanitary conditions should be provided.

Sanitation (9 CFR 308). There are numerous requirements governing the sanitation problems in an establishment and the products manufactured there. Some examples are as follows. There should be abundant light, of good quality and well distributed, and sufficient ventilation for all rooms and compartments to insure sanitary condition. The drainage and plumbing system should be efficient, and all drains and gutters should be properly installed with approved traps and vents. The water supply should be ample, clean, and potable, with adequate facilities for its distribution in the plant and protection against contamination and pollution.

Antemortem Inspection (9 CFR 309). Unless otherwise approved, all livestock offered for slaughter in an official establishment should be examined and inspected on the day of and before slaughter. All livestock showing, on antemortem inspection, symptoms of anaplasmosis, listeriosis, ketosis, leptospirosis, pseudorabies, parturient paresis, scrapie, rabies, grass tetany, tetanus, transport tetany, purpura hemorrhagica, strangles, azoturia, infectious equine encephalomyelitis, toxic encephalomyelitis (forage poisoning), dourine, acute influenza, generalized osteoporosis, glanders (fancy), acute inflammatory lameness, or extensive fistula will be identified as "U.S. Condemned" and disposed of in accordance with regulations.

Postmortem Inspection (9 CFR 310). A careful postmortem examination and inspection should be made of the carcasses and their parts of all livestock slaughtered
at an official establishment. Unless otherwise approved, it should be made at the
time of slaughter. The head, tail, tongue, thymus gland, and all viscera and blood of
such animal to be used in the preparation of meat food or medical products should
be handled in such a manner as to identify them with the rest of the carcass and as
being derived from the same animal, until the postmortem examination of the carcass and its parts has been completed. Such handling will include the retention of
the eartags, backtags, implants, and other identifying devices affixed to the animal.
Each carcass, including all detached organs and other parts, in which any lesion or
other condition is found that might render the meat or any part unfit for food
purposes, should be retained for a second and subsequent inspection. The identity
of such retained products should be kept until the final inspection has been completed. Retained carcass or parts should not be washed or trimmed without the
supervisor's authorization.

Disposal of Diseased or Otherwise Adulterated Carcasses and Parts (9 CFR 311).
Each carcass or its part should be disposed of in accordance to the disease or condition with which it is identified. For example, carcasses too emaciated to produce wholesome meat or that show a serious infiltration of muscle tissues or a
serous or mucoid degeneration of the fatty tissues should be condemned. Yellow
fat conditions caused by nutritional factors, characteristic of certain breeds of livestock or sometimes seen in sheep, should not be confused with icterus. If otherwise
normal, such carcasses should be approved and passed for human food. An individual organ or other part of a carcass affected with a neoplasm should be condemned.
If there is evidence of metastasis or that the general condition of the animal has
been adversely affected by the size, position, or nature of the neoplasm, the entire
carcass should be condemned.

Official Marks, Devices, and Certificates (9 CFR 312). The types of official marks,
devices, and certificates are as follows:

1. Marks and devices to identify inspected and passed products of cattle, sheep,
    swine, goats, or equine.
2. Antemortem inspection marks and devices.
3. Seals for transportation of products.
4. Marks and devices in connection with postmortem inspection and identifica-
    tion of adulterated products and insanitary equipment and facilities.
5. Import inspection marks and devices.
6. Export inspection marks, devices, and certificates.
7. Detention marks and devices.

Appendix 1-16 reproduces some of these official marks, devices, and certificates.

Handling and Disposal of Condemned or other Inedible Products at Official Establishments (9 CFR 314). Carcasses and their parts and products condemned at official establishments having facilities for tanking should follow a certain procedure in the disposal. Those with no tanking facilities must perform the disposal according to another procedure. Tanks, fertilizer driers, and other equipment used in the preparation of inedible products should be properly equipped with condensers and other appliances that suppress any unpleasant odors. Livers condemned on account of fluke infestation may be shipped from an official establishment only for purposes other than human food and only if they are first freely slashed and then identified, and handled as provided by the regulations.

Rendering or Other Disposal of Carcasses and Parts Passed for Cooking (9 CFR 315). Carcasses and parts passed for cooking may be rendered into lard, pork fat, or tallow in accordance with specific regulations, or they may be used for the preparation of meat food products, provided they are heated to at least 170° F for at least 30 minutes either prior to use in or during the preparation of the finished product.

Marking Products and Their Containers (9 CFR 316). Authorization is required to make devices bearing official marks and for putting them on a product. The use and removal of such marks must be supervised by a MPIP employee. The operator of each official establishment is required to furnish such ink and burning brands and any other device for marking products with official marks. Ink used must assure legibility and permanence of the markings, and the color must provide acceptable contrast with the color of the product to which it is applied. No product is permitted to be removed from the official establishment unless it has been marked in accordance with the regulations. Outside containers of inedible grease, tallow, other animal fat, or a mixture are required to be marked conspicuously with the word "inedible" prior to removal from the point of filling.

Labeling, Marking Devices, and Containers (9 CFR 317). The labeling and packaging of meat food products is of great importance in relation to consumer acceptance and deception. The following provides the general contents of the information covered under this part:

1. Requirement for labeling and its supervision by a program employee.
2. Definition for a label and the required features.
3. Approval of abbreviations of markings of inspection required; preparation of

marking devices bearing inspection legend prohibited unless prior approval obtained; exception to the requirements.

4. All labels must have approval.
5. Modifications of approved labels permitted by inspector in charge.
6. Approved labels to be used only on products to which they are applicable.
7. Deviations such as printing labels in foreign language permissible for products for foreign commerce.
8. General and specific prohibitions and requirements for labels, containers, and related practices.
9. Equine products specifically labeled.
10. Reuse of official inspection marks or containers bearing such marks and labels prohibited unless authorized.
11. Labeling, filling of containers, and handling of labeled products must comply with regulations.
12. Requirements for the relabeling of products.
13. Requirements for the storage and distribution of labels and containers bearing official marks.
14. Reporting of obsolete labels.
15. Requirements for the labeling and containers of custom prepared products.
16. Interpretations and statement of labeling policy for cured products.
17. Jar closures requirements.

Some examples of labeling of meat food products are described as follows. When cereal, vegetable starch, starchy vegetable flour, soy flour, soy protein concentrate, isolated soy protein, dried milk, nonfat dry milk, or calcium reduced dried skim milk is added to sausage as approved, special labeling is required. Immediately next to the product name, the label should show the name of each such added ingredient (e.g., "Cereal Added," "With Cereal," "Potato Flour Added," "Cereal and Potato Flour Added"), as the case may be.

When products such as loaves are browned by dipping in hot edible oil or by a flame, the product name on the label should be accompanied by the words "Browned in Hot Cottonseed Oil," "Browned by a Flame," or similar descriptions.

The term "spring lamb" or "genuine spring lamb" is applicable only to carcasses of new-crop lambs slaughtered during the period beginning in March and terminating not beyond the close of the week containing the first Monday in October.

The word "fresh" should not be used on labels to designate a product that contains any sodium nitrate, sodium nitrite, potassium nitrate, or potassium nitrite, or salt used for preservation.

Terms such as "farm" or "country" should not be used on labels in connection with products unless such products are actually prepared on the farm or in the country. If the preparation is only similar to that used on the farm or in the country, these terms may be used if they are qualified by the word "style" in the same size and style of lettering. Also, the term "farm" may be used as part of a brand designation when qualified by the word "brand" in the same size and style of lettering and followed by a statement identifying the locality in which the product is prepared. Sausage containing cereal should not be labeled "farm style" or "country style," and lard not rendered in an open kettle should not be designated as "farm style" or "country style."

Packages for sliced bacon should have a transparent opening designed for viewing the cut surface of a representative slice. For example, for single-packed sliced bacon, the transparent window should be designed to reveal at least 70% of the length (the longest dimension) of the representative slice and to have a minimum width of 1½ inches. It should be located not more than 5/8 inch and 3/4 inch from the top (or bottom) edge of a 1-pound or smaller package and one larger than 1 pound, respectively.

Entry into Official Establishments; Reinspection and Preparation of Products (9 CFR 318). Apart from certain exemptions, no product is permitted entry into an official establishment unless it has been previously prepared in an official establishment, inspected, passed, and is identified by an official inspection legend. When any article for use as an ingredient in the preparation of meat food products enters and while staying in an official establishment, it is required to bear a label showing the name and the amount or percentage of its contents. Carcasses of game animals and personal (i.e., not for commercial purposes) livestock may be brought into an official establishment for preparation, packaging, and storing in accordance with specific regulations. All ingredients and other articles used in the preparation of any product should be clean, sound, healthful, and wholesome. Accurate information must be furnished to the inspectors regarding all procedures involved in product preparation, including product composition and any changes in such procedures essential for inspection control of the product.

Records, Registration, and Reports (9 CFR 320). Every person, firm, or corporation that engages in the business of slaughtering any animals or preparing, freezing, packaging, or labeling any carcasses or their parts for use as human or animal food is required to keep records that will fully and accurately disclose all transactions involved. Some such records include the following:

1. Bills of sale, invoices, bills of lading, and receiving and shipping papers. They provide the required information for any transaction in which any livestock, carcass or its part, meat, or meat food products is purchased, sold, shipped, received, transported, or otherwise handled by the person.
2. Shipper's certificates and permits are required to be kept by consignees of in-

edible products shipped under official seals.

All persons engaged in the business must be registered with the MPIP. Each operator should furnish all relevant and accurate information needed by MPIP employees for making their daily reports of the amount of products prepared or handled under their supervision within the establishment and other required reports, such as sanitation.

Exports (9 CFR 322). The regulation provides details on the following: manner of affixing stamps and marking products for export; export stamps and certificates and instructions concerning issuance; transferring products for export; prohibited clearance of vessels and transportation without certificates or specific exemptions; and prohibition of the exportation of uninspected and uncertified tallow, stearin, oleo oil, and so on.

Transportation (9 CFR 325). No person is permitted to sell or transport in commerce any product suitable for human consumption unless the product and its container bear the official inspection legend as required or exempted. No carrier is permitted to transport any carcass, its parts, or meat or meat food products unless and until a certificate is made and furnished to such carrier in one of the forms prescribed. This does not apply to any product offered for importation into the United States if it is conveyed to an authorized place of inspection in railroad cars or other means of transport. Packages, sealed with special official import meat seals of the USDA or with customs or consular seals, are treated similarly. The U.S. parcel post is deemed a carrier, and the regulations apply, whenever applicable, to transportation by parcel post. The operator of a ferry is deemed a carrier, and the regulations apply to transportation by ferry of any products loaded on a truck or other vehicle.

Imported Products (9 CFR 327). The provisions of the regulation apply to products derived from cattle, sheep, swine, goats, horses, mules, and other equine, if suitable for human consumption. Conditions for importation of products must comply with the provisions listed as follows:

1. Eligibility of foreign countries for importation of products into the Unted States.
2. Applicable regulations that products must comply with before importation is permitted.
3. Requirement of foreign certificates for imported products.
4. Information required in the application by the importer for inspection of products for importation.

5. Requirements relating to movement prior to inspection, sealing, handling, bonding, and assistance for products for importation.
6. Maintenance in sanitary condition for the equipment and means of conveyance used in handling import products.
7. Conditions for using burlap wrapping for foreign meat.
8. Conditions relating to samples, inspection of consignments, refusal of entry, and marking.
9. Receipts to importers for import product samples.
10. Sampling and inspection of foreign canned or packaged products bearing trade labels.
11. Notification of customs regarding inspection findings of foreign products offered for importation and handling of articles refused entry.
12. Marking of products and labeling of their immediate containers for importation.
13. Marking, labeling, and application of official inspection legend to the outside containers of foreign products.
14. Requirements for small importations for importer's own consumption.
15. Acceptances of "U.S. inspected" and "passed" and similarly marked products exported to and returned from foreign countries.
16. The handling, transportation, and entry into an official establishment for products after importation.
17. Special exemption for specimens for laboratory examination and similar purposes.
18. Importation of foreign inedible fats is governed by denaturation and special marking of containers.
19. Special inspection procedures for chilled fresh or frozen boneless manufacturing meat.
20. Official import meat inspection marks and seals.

Detention; Seizure and Condemnation; Criminal Offenses (9 CFR 329). The regulations provide details on the following:

1. Subjection of any article or livestock suspected of violating the law to an administrative detention for a period of 20 days. An official "U.S. Detained Tag" is affixed to the article or livestock.
2. Proper procedure for the notification of detention to the owner of the article or livestock detained or his agent or person having custody.
3. Proper procedure for notification of governmental authorities having jurisdiction over article or livestock detained.
4. Proper procedure for the movement of article or livestock detained and removal of official marks.

5. Subjection of any violative articles or livestock to judicial seizure and condemnation either under the Federal Meat Inspection Act or other applicable federal statutes.
6. Authority of the MPIP to conduct criminal proceedings against various offenses.

Rules of Practice Governing Proceedings under the Federal Meat Inspection Act (9 CFR 335). The regulations provide details on the following:

1. Rules applicable to refusal or withdrawal of inspection service under Section 401 of the Federal Meat Inspection Act (21 U.S.C. 671).
2. Rules applicable to withdrawal of inspection service for failure of an establishment to destroy any condemned carcass or part thereof or any condemned meat or meat food product.
3. Rules applicable to refusal or withdrawal of inspection service for failure of an establishment to maintain sanitary conditions.
4. Rules applicable to suspension of assignment of inspectors for forcible assault or threaten thereof, intimidation of, or interference with any inspection service employee.

According to 9 CFR 319, the following lists the general categories and specific types of food products for which definitions and standards have been established by the MPIP. The section numbers are given in parentheses.

Raw meat products

Miscellaneous beef products (15)	Miscellaneous pork products (29)

Cooked meats

Barbecued meats (80)	Roast beef parboiled and steam roasted (81)

Cured meats, unsmoked and smoked

Corned beef (100)	Cured beef tongue (103)
Corned beef brisket (101)	Cured pork products, unsmoked or smoked (104)
Corned beef round and other corned beef cuts (102)	Chopped ham (105)

Sausage generally: fresh sausage

Sausage (140)	Breakfast sausage (143)
Fresh pork sausage (141)	Whole hog sausage (144)
Fresh beef sausage (142)	Italian sausage products (145)

Uncooked, smoked sausage

Smoked pork sausage (160)

Cooked sausage

Frankfurters, frank, furter, hotdog, wiener, vienna, bologna, garlic bologna, knockwurst, and similar products (180)	Cheesefurters and similar products (181)
	Liver sausage and braunschweiger (182)

Luncheon meat, loaves, and jellied products

Luncheon meat (260)	Meat loaf (261)

Meat specialties, puddings, and nonspecific loaves

Scrapple (280)	Bockwurst (281)

Canned, frozen, or dehydrated meat food products

Chili con carne (300)	Tamales (305)
Chili con carne with beans (301)	Spaghetti with meatballs and sauce, spaghetti with meat and sauce, and similar products (306)
Hash (320)	
Corned-beef hash (303)	Spaghetti sauce with meat (307)
Meat stews (304)	Tripe with milk (308)

(continued)

Canned, frozen, or dehydrated meat food products (continued)

Beans with frankfurters in sauce, sauerkraut with wieners and juice, and similar products (309)

Lima beans with ham in sauce, beans with ham in sauce, beans with bacon in sauce, and similar products (310)

Chow mein vegetables with meat and chop suey vegetables with meat (311)

Pork with barbecue sauce and beef with barbecue sauce (312)

Beef with gravy and gravy with beef (313)

Meat food entree products, pies, and turnovers

Meat pies (500)

Meat snacks, hors d'oeuvres, pizza, and specialty items

Pizza (600)

Fats, oils, and shortenings

Oleomargarine or margarine (700)

Mixed fat shortening (701)

Lard, leaf lard (702)

Rendered animal fat or mixture thereof (703)

Meat soups, soup mixes, broths, stocks, and extracts

Meat extract (720)

Fluid extract (721)

Meat salads and meat spreads

Deviled ham, deviled tongue, and similar products (760)

Potted meat food product and deviled meat food product (761)

Ham spread, tongue spread, and similar products (762)

Miscellaneous

Breaded Products (880)   Liver meat food products (881)

Appendix 1-17 reproduces the standards of identity for some raw and cooked meat products. To educate the consumers in general, the MPIP issues a pamphlet, "Standards for meat and poultry products--a consumer reference list." This pamphlet lists practically all items of products for which the MPIP has established standards, with required percentage of meat and poultry indicated. The following illustrates some examples:

Beans in Sauce with Meat. At least 20% cooked or cooked and smoked meat.

Chop Suey (American style) with Macaroni and Meat. At least 25% fresh uncooked meat.

Dumplings and Meat in Sauce. At least 18% fresh uncooked meat.

Ham Salad. At least 35% ham (cooked basis).

Pork Sausage. Not more than 50% fat; may contain no by-products or extenders.

Vegetable and Meat Casserole. At least 25% fresh uncooked meat.

Space limitation prohibits the presentation of more examples. However, this list is probably the only publication available that provides such comprehensive listing of the standards with easy reference to the percentage of meat contents. It is a very useful tool for teaching purposes especially in nutrition and food science.

One of the most important aspects of the Federal Meat Inspection Act is its provisions governing the relationship between the MPIP and state authorities. According to Table 1-8, 9 CFR 321, "Cooperation with states and territories" and 9 CFR 331, "Special provisions for designated States and Territories; and for designation of establishments which endanger public health and for designated establishments," are the regulations promulgated to administer the specific provisions of the act. A discussion on such regulations is presented below.

The MPIP administrator is authorized to cooperate with any state (including Puerto Rico) or any organized territory in developing and administering the latter's meat inspection program. This is to ensure that the individual state will impose and enforce requirements at least equal to those under the federal programs with respect to official establishments and products prepared there for human consumption within its jurisdiction. Any interstate or foreign commerce will be under federal supervision. Such cooperation is authorized if the jurisdiction has enacted a law imposing mandatory ante- and postmortem inspection, reinspection, and sanitation requirements at least equal to the federal requirements with respect to all or certain classes of persons engaged in slaughtering livestock or otherwise preparing products solely for distribution within such jurisdiction. The same cooperation is extended to record keeping, registration of specified classes of operators, disposal of dead, dying, disabled, or diseased livestock, and handling of products not suitable for human consumption.

Any federal cooperation includes advisory, technical and laboratory assistance, training, and financial aid. Such contributions may not exceed 50% of the estimated total cost of the state or territorial program. According to this state/federal program, the MPIP is authorized to utilize employees and facilities of any state in carrying out federal functions. Thus there are some states in the country that have their own meat inspection programs that receive assistance from the MPIP. Those states that are unwilling or unable to conduct their own inspections that would be equivalent to those of the federal government have requested the MPIP to assume inspection responsibility. Such states are labeled as "designated" states. At present, the following states are under the MPIP: California, Colorado, Connecticut, Guam, Kentucky, Massachusetts, Minnesota, Missouri, Montana, Nebraska, Nevada, New Jersey, New York, North Dakota, Oregon, Pennsylvania, Puerto Rico, Tennessee, Virgin Islands of the United States, and Washington.

Also, the MPIP has established criteria and procedures for "designating" establishments with operations within the jurisdiction of a state that would clearly endanger the public health, the disposition of products, and the application of regulations. Such an establishment will be placed under federal inspection. For example, the endangering of public health applies if any meat or meat food product prepared at the establishment is adulterated in any of the following respects:

1. It bears or contains a pesticide chemical, food additive, or color additive that is legally unsafe or was intentionally subjected to radiation in an illegal manner.
2. It contains added poisonous substance that may be harmful to health.
3. It consists of any filthy, putrid, or decomposed substance; was prepared from meat or other ingredients exhibiting spoilage characteristics; was prepared from a carcass affected with a disease transmissible to humans and its condemnation would be required; or is a ready-to-eat pork product that has not been treated to destroy trichinae.
4. It has been prepared under insanitary conditions.
5. It is the product of an animal that died other than by slaughter.

6.   Its container is composed of harmful substances.

When an MPIP inspector identifies such an establishment, he will informally advise the operator of the deficiencies detected and report his findings to his superior or the regional director. After a careful study of the report, the regional director may, if the facts so warrant, issue a written notification to the appropriate state officials for effective action under state or local law to prevent any hazard to public health. If effective action is not taken, a written notification is issued to the operator of the establishment, specifying the deficiencies involved and allowing 10 days to present his views or make the necessary corrections and notifying him that failure to correct such deficiencies may result in designation of the establishment and its operator. Any nonaction on the part of the operator will result in its designation as completely under federal control. Such establishment will no longer be permitted to prepare meat food products unless the operator proceeds with the regular procedure of obtaining official inspections and complying with all other federal requirements.

Apart from formal regulations, the MPIP has issued two types of internal documents to implement the state/federal cooperative programs. One document is the cooperative agreement signed between the MPIP and the state authority. Basically, each agreement contains three types of information. It states the duties of the federal agency, most of which have been described previously, and it delineates the responsibilities, some of which are as follows:

1.   It recruits, selects, and employs state personnel to perform the relevant duties, to be paid in accordance with state salary system.
2.   It assigns and supervises such personnel in their inspection work and other services according to state law and agreement provisions.
3.   It keeps a complete accounting of the total cost of developing and operating the state inspection program and provides the MPIP a copy of the data.
4.   It arranges an annual official public auditing of the accounts.

Other terms of the agreement include the following:

1.   Periodic reviews of state programs, including subordinate municipal or county inspection programs, are conducted by federal and state officials.
2.   The MPIP conducts in-plant surveys at each establishment granted inspection under this agreement whenever necessary to assure that operations and facilities and the conduct of inspections at the establishment are in accord with provisions under the state law at least equal to the provisions of the Federal Meat Inspection Act and supplementary instructions of the federal agency.

The second internal document issued by the MPIP is MPI Directive 910.1, "Review of certified State meat and poultry inspection programs," or any similar recently published document. This directive sets forth the MPIP's procedures for determining the status of state inspection programs. The general contents of this document are as follows: purpose, responsibility, requirements, operations endangering public health, review-exempt plants, requirements to be used when reviewing plants, instruction for completing establishment review and evaluation report, and guidelines for selection of intrastate plants. Selected aspects are discussed in the following paragraphs.

With reference to the information on requirements, there are seven basic requirements that must be adequate in all federal plants, and state plants must also meet them if they are to be judged on an equal basis. Federal inspections are required to indicate and certify their findings with respect to these requirements. The seven requirements are:

1. Ante- and postmortem inspection.
2. Reinspection (processing).
3. Sanitation.
4. Potable water.
5. Sewage and waste disposal control.
6. Pest control.
7. Condemned and inedible material control.

With reference to "operations endangering public health," the document provides additional details. Corrective action must be taken immediately for any of the deficiencies identified. Some additional undesirable operations are:

1. Use of nonpotable water in edible product departments of the establishment.
2. Improper sanitation that results in: (a) bacterial growth and development in or on product, (b) foreign matter entering product, or (c) failure to control vermin and insects.
3. Use of unsound meat/poultry in processing food products.

The publication provides very detailed guidelines for selection of intrastate plants for review. For example, the number of intrastate plants to be reviewed per quarter must be determined on a specific basis, as is the method of determining the category and percentage of unacceptable items. A very complicated statistical procedure is to be used for a plant selection, as is the procedure for determining the "mix" of slaughter, slaughter/combination, processing, and exempt plants.

Regulations governing mandatory poultry products inspection are stated in 9 CFR 381. The overall contents of this part are fairly similar to those provisions described in 9 CFR 301 to 331 but are applicable to poultry products instead. Examples of some topics include: definitions, exemptions, application for inspection, sanitation, operating procedures, ante- and postmortem inspection, handling and disposal of condemned or other inedible products at official establishments, labeling and containers, entry of articles into official establishments, and imported poultry products. The cooperative relationship between federal and state authorities for poultry inspection programs is also similar to that for meat. In the following, three selected aspects of the regulations are discussed.

Certain Requirements Governing Operating Procedures

All operations and procedures involving the processing, and other handling or storing of any poultry product should be clean and result in sanitary processing, proper inspection, and the production of unadulterated poultry and poultry products. Any room, compartment, or other place in an official establishment where any poultry product is processed should not house or handle any "adulterating" materials.

When thawing frozen ready-to-cook poultry in water, absorption of moisture should be avoided. Some approved thawing methods are as follows.

1. Use continuous running tap water below 70° F. Complete thawing is necessary to permit thorough examination before any further processing.
2. Placing frozen ready-to-cook poultry into cooking kettles without prior thawing is permitted only when a representative sample of the entire lot has been thawed and found to be sound and unadulterated. Thawing may be accomplished in cookers where the water is heated to enable the cooking process to begin immediately following completion of thawing. Any thawing technique should not result in a weight larger than the frozen weight. When whole carcasses or parts are thawed for repackaging as parts, it is not acceptable to re-cool the parts in slush ice. However, they may be held in tanks of crushed ice with the drains open, pending further processing or packaging.
3. The poultry may be thawed in recirculated water at less than 50°F for an optimal period.

Cut-up poultry should be processed from chilled carcasses, and the parts should not be rechilled in ice, water, or both. They may be held temporarily in crushed ice pending further processing and packaging. The ice must be in containers continuously drained.

Remove from the premise as often as possible any offal resulting from evisceration of the poultry. Poultry products should be packaged in containers that are clean and with no potential adulterants and can withstand normal distribution without breaking or changing shape. Barrels or other containers used for packaging poultry products should be lined with paper or other material that remains intact when moistened.

When certain poultry products are in an official establishment or being transported between establishments, they should be placed under protective coverings. The latter should be capable of excluding any foreign substances such as dust and dirt and should take into consideration the means of transporting the products.

Temperatures and procedures necessary to chill and freeze ready-to-cook poultry are very important. They must insure prompt removal of animal heat, preserve the condition and wholesomeness of the poultry, and assure that the products are not adulterated. A description of the chilling and freezing procedures used at the official establishment is required to be filed with the inspector in charge. Some selected aspects are presented as follows.

All poultry that is slaughtered and eviscerated should be chilled immediately after processing so that the internal temperature is reduced to $40^{\circ}F$ or less unless such product is to be frozen or cooked immediately at the establishment. Eviscerated poultry to be shipped from the establishment in packaged form should be maintained at $40^{\circ}F$ or less, except that during further processing and packaging operations, the internal temperature may rise to a maximum of $55^{\circ}F$. However, immediately after packaging, the poultry is placed under refrigeration at a temperature that will promptly lower the internal temperature of the product to $40^{\circ}F$ or less, or the poultry is placed in a freezer. Poultry to be held at the plant in packaged form in excess of 24 hours should be held in a room at a temperature of $36^{\circ}F$ or less.

Poultry carcasses and their major parts should be chilled to $40^{\circ}F$ or lower within the times specified as follows.

Weight of Carcass	Time (hours)
Under 4 pounds	4
4 to 8 pounds	6
Over 8 pounds	8

Only ice produced from potable water may be used for ice and water chilling. The ice should be handled and stored in a sanitary manner. If of block type, the ice should be washed by spraying all surfaces with clean water before crushing. The temperature of the chilling media in the warmest part of any poultry chilling system should not exceed $65^{\circ}F$ or any specified temperature in the regulations.

To facilitate continuous processing operations, poultry carcasses and major parts may be held overnight in chilling tanks. The latter should contain water-saturated ice, refrigerated water, or other approved cooling media that will maintain all poultry in the tanks at a temperature of 40°F or lower. The same temperature is required if other practices such as reicing, recirculation of the chilling medium, holding product in refrigerated rooms, or use of increased amounts of ice are used to chill the tanks.

Giblets should be chilled to 40°F or lower within 2 hours from the time they are removed from the inedible viscera. Any of the acceptable methods of chilling the poultry carcass may be followed in cooling giblets.

Labeling and Packaging of Poultry Products

Examples of provisions governing the labeling and packaging of poultry products are presented in this section.

The label should show the name of the product. If the product has a standard of identity, use the prescribed name. If not, use either the common or usual name of the food or a truthful descriptive designation.

For fresh or frozen raw whole carcasses of poultry product, the name should be either of the following forms. The name of the "kind" (e.g., chicken, turkey, or duck) is preceded by the qualifying term "young," "mature," or "old" or the appropriate class (e.g., hen or rooster) name. The name of the kind may be used in addition to the class name, but the absence of the qualifying age or class is not acceptable as the name of the product. However, the name "chicken" may be used without such qualification with reference to a ready-to-cook pack of fresh or frozen cut-up young chickens, or a half of a young chicken, and the same applies to the name "duckling." The class name may be appropriately modified by changing the word form, such as using the term "roasting chicken" rather than "roaster."

Poultry products containing light and dark chicken or turkey meat in quantities other than the natural proportions must have a qualifying statement indicating the types of meat actually used. When the product contains less than 10% cooked deboned poultry meat or the character of the light and dark meat is indistinguishable, the qualifying statement will not be required, unless the product bears a labeling referring to the light or dark meat content. The required statement must be in type at least one-half the size and of equal boldness as the name of the product; for example, "Boned Turkey (Dark Meat)". The chart on page 68 prescribes the relationship between the required statement and the content of light and/or dark meat used.

The term "chicken meat," unless modified by an appropriate adjective, is construed to mean deboned white and dark meat, whereas the term "chicken" may include other edible parts such as skin and fat not in excess of their natural proportions, in addition to the chicken meat. If the term "chicken meat" is listed

Label Terminology	Light Meat %	Dark Meat %
Natural proportions	50 to 60	50 to 35
Light or white meat	100	0
Dark meat	0	100
Light and dark meat	51 to 65	49 to 35
Dark and light meat	35 to 49	65 to 51
Mostly white meat	66 or more	34 or less
Mostly dark meat	34 or less	66 or more

and the product also contains skin, giblets, or fat, it is necessary to list each such ingredient.

Boneless poultry products should be labeled in a manner that accurately describes their actual form and composition. It should specify the form of the product (e.g., emulsified, finely chopped) and the kind name of the poultry. If the product does not consist of natural proportions of skin and fat, as they occur in whole carcass, the label should also include terminology that describes the actual composition. If the product is cooked, it should be so labeled. Natural proportions of skin, as found on a whole chicken or turkey carcass, is considered as follows: chicken (20% raw, 25% cooked) and turkey (15% raw, 25% cooked).

When the labels bear a chemical analysis, such products must be analyzed on a lot basis by an impartial laboratory to determine products compliance with data shown. Such laboratory results should be made available to the inspector in charge. Any protein percentage shown should be a minimum and any fat, carbohydrate, or caloric content should be a maximum.

Some false or misleading labeling or containers are as follows:

1. Official grade designations such as the letters A, B, and C may be used only if the articles have been graded by a licensed federal or federal/state grader and found to qualify for the indicated grade.
2. Terms having geographical significance with reference to a particular locality may be used only when the product was in that locality.
3. The terms "All," "Pure," "100%,"and similar descriptions should not be used on labels for products to identify the content unless the product is prepared solely from a single ingredient.

4. The calendar date should express the month and day for all products. The year is also required for products hermetically sealed in metal or glass containers, dried or frozen products, or any other products for which a year identification will avoid misunderstanding or misleading consequences because of their special distribution and marketing practices. Each calendar date must be qualified (e.g., "packing" date, "sell by" date, or "use before" date), with or without a further qualifying and approved phrase (e.g., "For Maximum Freshness" or "For Best Quality") and other acceptable ones.

Packaged products that require special handling to maintain their wholesome condition should prominently display on the label the statement "Keep Refrigerated," "Keep Frozen," "Keep Refrigerated or Frozen," "Perishable--Keep Under Refrigeration," or other approved similar statements.

The immediate containers for products that are frozen during distribution and intended for thawing prior to or during display for sale should bear the statement "Shipped/Stored and Handled Frozen for Your Protection, Keep Refrigerated or Freeze."

Standards for Poultry Products

The MPIP has established specifications, definitions, standards of identity, or composition for a number of poultry products. This is necessary to cover the principal constituents and specific name of any such product in order to prevent sale of the product under false or misleading labeling and/or to protect public health. See page 70 for a description of the kinds and classes of poultry and the applicable cuts of raw poultry as established by the MPIP.

Some examples of the kinds, classes, and cuts of poultry are as follows. A broiler or fryer is a young chicken (usually under 13 weeks of age) of either sex that is tender--meated with soft, pliable, smooth-textured skin and flexible breastbone cartilage. A young turkey is a turkey (usually under 8 months of age) that is tender-meated with soft, pliable, smooth-textured skin, and breastbone cartilage that is somewhat less flexible than in a fryer/roaster turkey. Sex designation is optional.

"Backs" include the pelvic bones and all the vertebrae posterior to the shoulder joint. The meat will not be peeled from the pelvic bones. The vertebral ribs and/or scapula may be removed or included without affecting the appropriateness of the name. Skin should be substantially intact. "Quarters" consist of the entire eviscerated poultry carcass, which has been cut into four equal parts but excludes the neck.

According to 9 CFR 381 and the publication "Standards for meat and poultry products--a consumer reference list," the following poultry products have standards of identity established by the MPIP:

Kinds of Poultry

1. Chickens
2. Turkeys
3. Ducks
4. Geese
5. Guineas

Classes of Chicken

1. Rock Cornish game hen or Cornish game hen
2. Rock Cornish fryer, roaster, or hen
3. Broiler or fryer
4. Roaster or roasting chicken
5. Capon
6. Hen, fowl, baking, or stewing
7. Cock or rooster

Classes of Turkeys

1. Fryer/roaster turkey
2. Young turkey
3. Yearling turkey
4. Mature turkey or old turkey (hen or tom)

Classes of Ducks

1. Broiler duckling or fryer duckling
2. Roaster duckling
3. Mature duck or old duck

Classes of Geese

1. ˙Young goose
2. Mature goose or old goose

Classes of Guineas

1. Young guinea
2. Mature guinea or old guinea

Applicable Cuts of Raw Poultry

1.	Breasts	12.	Quarters
2.	Breasts with ribs	13.	Breast quarter
3.	Wishbones (pulley bones)	14.	Breast quarter without wing
4.	Drumsticks	15.	Leg quarter
5.	Thighs	16.	Thigh with back portion
6.	(Kind) legs	17.	Legs with pelvic bone
7.	Wings	18.	Wing drummette
8.	Backs	19.	Wing portion
9.	Stripped backs	20.	Cut-up poultry
10.	Necks	21.	Giblets
11.	Halves		

Baby food

  High poultry dinner
  Poultry with broth
    (strained or chopped)

Beans and rice with poultry

Breaded poultry

Cabbage stuffed with poultry

Canned boned poultry

  Boned (kind), solid pack
  Boned (kind)
  Boned (kind), with broth
  Boned (kind), with specified
    percentage of broth

Cannelloni with poultry

Chicken cordon bleu

Creamed poultry

Eggplant parmigiana with poultry

Egg roll with poultry

Entree

  Poultry or poultry food product and
    one vegetable
  Poultry or poultry food product with
    gravy or sauce and one vegetable

Poultry a la Kiev

Poultry a la King

(continued)

Poultry almondine

Poultry barbecue (or minced
  poultry barbecue)

Poultry blintz filling

Poultry Brunswick stew

Poultry burgers

Poultry cacciatore

Poultry casserole

Poultry chili

Poultry chili with beans

Poultry chop suey

  Chop suey with poultry

Poultry chow mein, without noodles

Poultry croquettes

Poultry croquettes with
  macaroni and cheese

Poultry dinners (a frozen product)

Poultry empanadillo

Poultry fricassee

Poultry fricassee of wings

Poultry hash

Poultry lasagna

Poultry livers with rice and gravy

Poultry paella

Poultry pies

Poultry ravioli

Poultry roll

  Poultry roll with natural juices
  Poultry roll with broth
  Poultry roll with gelatin

Poultry salad

Poultry scallopini

Poultry soup

  Ready-to-eat
  Condensed

Poultry stew

Poultry stroganoff

Poultry tamales

Poultry tetrazzini

Poultry wellington

Poultry with gravy

  Gravy with poultry

Poultry with gravy and dressing

Poultry with noodles or dumplings

  Noodles or dumplings with poultry

Poultry with noodles au gratin

Poultry with vegetables

Stuffed cabbage with poultry

Sauce with poultry or poultry sauce

The following are some examples showing the standards of poultry products and the minimum percentage of poultry ingredients required. The complete list is found in the publication "Standards for meat and poultry products--a consumer reference list," published by MPIP.

Chicken Cordon Bleu. At least 60% boneless chicken breast (raw basis), 5% ham and either Swiss, Gruyere, or Mozzarella cheese. If breaded, no more than 30% breading.

Poultry Chili with Beans. At least 17% poultry meat (cooked deboned basis).

Poultry Empanadillo. At least 25% poultry meat including skin and fat (raw basis).

Poultry Stew. At least 12% poultry meat (cooked deboned basis).

Stuffed Cabbage with Poultry. At least 8% poultry meat (cooked deboned basis).

Apart from the two acts discussed earlier (Federal Meat Inspection Act and Poultry Products Inspection Act), the MPIP also administers certain provisions of the Agricultural Marketing Act. They provide *voluntary* inspection and certification services for a number of other products related to meat and poultry. The regulations are promulgated in 9 CFR 350, 351, 354, 355, and 362 (see Table 1-8).

According to 9 CFR 350, "Special services relating to meat and other products," the following services are available:

1.   Identification Service. A meat or other product that is federally inspected and passed domestically or on importation is officially marked for identification. Such product(s) may be divided into smaller or combined into larger units and still maintains its "legal" identity if the handling has been supervised by MPIP personnel and the resulting products marked and identified officially.

2.   Certification Service. At the request of a purchaser, supplier, exporter, or others, inspectors may make certification regarding livestock products intended for human consumption (including casing) to be exported, as meeting conditions or standards that are not or are in addition to those ordinarily imposed by federal or state regulations and laws.

3.   Food Inspection Service. An inspection and certification service for wholesomeness relating to the manufacturing of a food article may be furnished on application. Applicable regulations of MPIP apply to the preparation, labeling, and certification of the food article prepared under such service.

4. Reindeer Inspection Service. The service inspects and certifies the wholesomeness relating to the slaughter of reindeer. All applicable regulations of the MPIP apply to such slaughter and the preparation, labeling, and certification of the reindeer meat and products prepared under such service.

The fee for each of the above services is paid by the user.

According to 7 CFR 351, "Certification of technical animal fats for export," certification in a prescribed form is available for specific lots of technical animal fat for export. The fat should be rendered from materials derived from carcasses or their parts that had been inspected and passed and that came from animals slaughtered under supervision. After an examination of the product and the information obtained from various sources including the exporter, an MPIP employee makes a certification of such fat for export and a prescheduled fee is paid by the user for the service.

The regulations indicate that the processes to be supervised and examinations to be conducted should be as follows:

1. All processes used in the preparation of certified technical animal fats at any official plant is subject to supervision by an inspection. The preparation is required to follow the prescribed regulation.
2. Supervision maintained to determine a plant's compliance with regulations ranges from full time coverage of the entire plant to one or more reviews per month.
3. Coverage is at least once a month if the plant consistently handles only raw materials acceptable for the preparation, and maintenance of this procedure is certified in writing by the plant operator.
4. Coverage is at least once a week if the plant consistently handles some acceptable and some unacceptable raw materials for the preparations; uses separate equipment for processing and separate rooms, compartments, and equipment for receiving and storing the respective types of raw materials and technical animal fats; and if the plant operator certifies in writing that he is maintaining this complete physical separation procedure.
5. Coverage will be full time during the receiving of raw materials and their preparation into certified technical animal fat, if the plant handles some acceptable and some unacceptable raw materials for the preparation and uses the same rooms, compartments, and equipment, with only time separation between receiving, processing, and storing the respective types of raw materials and technical fats.

According to 7 CFR 354, "Voluntary inspection of rabbits and edible products thereof," the basis of service is as follows. Any inspection service will be for condition and wholesomeness of the rabbits and their products, and only rabbits processed in official plants according to regulations may be inspected. Any eviscerated rabbit in an official plant with inspection service will be so inspected, and no dressed rabbits or uninspected products are permitted entry into such a plant. All services are subject to supervision at all times by a responsible supervisor and rendered where facilities and conditions are satisfactory and the requisite inspectors are available.

The inspection procedure is as follows. Unless exempted, products to be further processed will be prepared and handled in an official plant under the supervision of an inspector. An official antemortem inspection of rabbits is made on the day of slaughter. Dying or dead rabbits on the premises are disposed of according to regulations. Rabbits with any disease or condition that would cause condemnation of their carcasses on postmortem inspection are condemned. Such rabbits are neither dressed nor conveyed into any department of the plant where rabbit products are prepared or held. They will be disposed of accordingly. During antemortem inspection those rabbits that do not plainly show, but are suspected of being afflicted with, any disease or condition that may cause condemnation in whole or in part on postmortem inspection are segregated from other rabbits and held for separate slaughter, evisceration, and postmortem inspection, for which the inspector will be notified. Correlation of ante- and postmortem findings is performed. When live rabbits, affected by a contagious disease transmissible to man, are brought into an official establishment, they are segregated. Their handling and slaughtering are dealt with separately and differently.

With reference to the postmortem inspection service, the following regulations apply. No viscera or its part are removed from any rabbits to be processed under supervision in any official plant, except at the time of evisceration and inspection. Each such carcass will be opened to expose the organs and the body cavity for proper examination by the inspector and are prepared immediately afterward as ready-to-cook rabbit. Each carcass and its parts is held for further examination if it has any lesion or disease or other condition rendering it unfit for human consumption and a final decision cannot be made on first examination. The identity of each such carcass and its part is maintained until a final examination has been completed. If it is found to be unsound, unwholesome, or otherwise unfit for human consumption, it will be condemned and treated to prevent its use for human consumption and to preclude dissemination of disease through consumption by animals. If it is found to be sound, wholesome and fit for human food, it will be so certified.

According to 7 CFR 355, "Certified products for dogs, cats, and other carnivora; inspection, certification, and identification as to class, quality, quantity, and condition," the following selected information is presented. On application, an inspection may be granted at a plant where animal food products are to be prepared. The application must conform to, and the plant meet with, certain requirements. The owner or operator of an applicable or approved plant must apply to the MPIP for inspection, certification, and identification of their products. One very important aspect contained in the regulation is the "composition of certified products," which is briefly described as follows.

The composition of certified animal food products is indicated in Table 1-9, which should be referred to in conjunction with the following details:

Canned Certified Maintenance Food for Dogs, Cats, and Other Carnivora

1. The food should contain a level of minerals and vitamins generally recognized to be essential to the nutritional value of the food.
2. Vegetables and grains and their derivatives used as ingredients should be of good quality, free from discoloration, mold, smut, and insect infestation, and otherwise fit for animal consumption.
3. Inedible material such as tankage, dried blood, and bone meal should not be used as ingredients.
4. Semimoist products should have a soft granular consistency and be shelf stable.

Certified Animal Protein Supplement.

They may contain not more than 3% wheat flour or other processing aid acceptable to the MPIP, which should be of good quality, free from insect infestation, and otherwise fit for animal consumption.

Certified Pet Food Supplement.

They may contain various cereals, flours, vegetables, flavorings, seasonings, and other processing aids acceptable to the MPIP, which should be of good quality, free from discoloration, mold, smut, and insect infestation and otherwise fit for animal consumption.

Canned Certified Variety Pet Food

1. They should contain a variety of vegetables and may contain other ingredients that are favorable to adequate nutrition.
2. Vegetables and grains and their derivatives used as ingredients of the product should be of good quality, free from discoloration, mold, smut, and insect infestation, and otherwise fit for animal consumption.

All certified products for dogs, cats, and other carnivora should use only ingredients that are normal to the animals, favorable to adequate nutrition, and classed by MPIP as conforming with requirements in the preparation of the product.

According to 7 CFR 362, "Voluntary poultry inspection regulations," the content is concerned with the voluntary inspection services provided for poultry products not covered by the mandatory regulation of the Poultry Products Inspec-

TABLE 1-9. Composition of Certified Animal Food Products. Adapted from 9 CFR 355.29

Food	Meat, Poultry, Horse Meat, Mule Meat, or their approved by-products or combinations (%)[a]	Protein(%)	Fat (%)	Moisture(%)	Sufficient Amount of Freshly Ground Bone or Other Acceptable Agent to Insure Decharacterization of Product for Human food purposes
Canned certified maintenance food	30 or more	10 or more	not specified	27 or less (for semi-moist product)	not required
Certified animal protein supplement	95 or more	15 or more	3 or more	not specified	required
Certified pet food supplement	50 or more	11 or more	3 or more	74 or less	required
Canned certified variety pet food	25 or more	8 or more	2 or more	75 or less	not required

[a] Use uncooked weight; per cent obtained by relating this weight to the total weight of product. Some, but not all, of the ingredients may be replaced in all except certified pet food supplement by whale meat, fish, and animal food poultry by-products.

77

tion Act. The poultry covered by these regulations include any migratory water fowl and other non-domesticated game bird or squab, whether live or dead. For example, pheasants and quail. The following types of service may be furnished when a proper application is submitted and approved.

1. Inspection Service. At the request of any person intending to export any such slaughtered poultry or their products for human food, the inspectors may make certification regarding their exportation status and indicating their compliance with conditions or standards that are not or in addition to those ordinarily imposed by the mandatory regulations.

All services must be paid by the applicant according to a prescheduled formula. The MPIP may deny or withdraw any service for specified reasons such as the operator's fraudulent or deceptive practices.

Another important federal statute administered jointly by the MPIP and other offices within the USDA is the Humane Slaughter Act of 1958 (7 U.S.C. 1901 to 1906). This act establishes the use of humane method of slaughter as a policy of the United States and requires that packers who wish to sell meat and meat products to agencies of the federal government must use USDA-approved methods of slaughtering. Section 2 of the act (7 U.S.C. 1902) contains the following provision:

> No method of slaughtering or handling in connection with slaughtering shall be deemed to comply with the public policy of the United States unless it is humane. Either of the following two methods of slaughtering and handling are hereby found to be humane:
> (a) in the case of cattle, calves, horses, mules, sheep, swine, and other livestock, all animals are rendered insensible to pain by a single blow or gunshot or an electrical, chemical or other means that is rapid and effective, before being shackled, hoisted, thrown, cast, or cut; or
> (b) by slaughtering in accordance with the ritual requirements of the Jewish faith or any other religious faith that prescribes a method of slaughter whereby the animal suffers loss of consciousness by anemia of the brain caused by the simultaneous and instantaneous severance of the carotid arteries with a sharp instrument.

The USDA has promulgated regulations in 9 CFR 390 and 391 to implement the act. According to 9 CFR 390, "Designation of methods," the federal government provides instruction on the slaughtering of animals with chemical (carbon dioxide), mechanical (captive bolt or gunshot), and electrical (stunning with electric current) means. According to 9 CFR 391, "Identification of carcasses of certain humanely slaughtered livestock," the federal government has issued a certain statement of policy. With respect to the statement, the USDA will, based on current information, periodically publish in the Federal Register, as a notice, a table listing the names of the official establishments operating under the Federal Meat Inspection Act that use humane methods of slaughter and incidental handling, the official establishment numbers, and the species of livestock being slaughtered in such establishment using such methods. The most recent notice was announced on February 8, 1977 (42 FR 8114 to 8137). According to this notice, the establishment number is branded on each carcass of livestock inspected and passed at that establishment. The table of listing should not be understood to indicate that all species of livestock slaughtered at a listed establishment are slaughtered and handled by humane methods unless all such species are listed for that establishment in the table. Nor should the table be understood to indicate that the affiliates of any listed establishments use only humane methods.

Table 1-10 lists a number of useful publications issued by the MPIP for use by its personnel and the meat and related industries. A brief description is provided for each publication.

TABLE 1-10. Selected Publications Distributed by USDA Meat Poultry Inspection Program

Publication Number (date)	Title of Publication
MPI-2 (May 1977)	Accepted meat and poultry equipment
MPI-6 (September 1977)	Manual for compliance officers
MPI-8 (March 1977)	List of chemical compounds authorized for use under USDA meat, poultry, rabbit, and egg products inspection programs
Agricultural Handbook No. 191 (June 1975)	U.S. inspected meatpacking plants/A guide to construction, equipment, layout
Unnumbered (semiannual)	Meat and poultry inspection directory

The "U.S. inspection meat packing plants/a guide to construction, equipment, layout" provides interpretation and judgment for the federal meat inspection regulations with reference to sanitation and facilities. Its table of contents is as follows:

1. Description of plans and specifications that must accompany application for inspection.
2. Location of establishments.
3. Water supply plant drainage and sewage disposal system.
4. Plant construction, lighting, ventilation, and refrigeration.
5. Equipment.
6. Design and construction of equipment.
7. Equipment installation.
8. Hand-washing facilities, sterilizers, drinking fountains, and connections for cleanup hoses.
9. Facilities for processing edible products.
10. Design, equipment, and operation of slaughtering departments and related areas.
11. Required slaughtering facilities for cattle, sheep, goats, calves, hogs, and horses.
12. Welfare facilities for plant employees.
13. Inspector's office.

The publication "Accepted meat and poultry equipment" provides information on the following: equipment acceptance program, plants coming under inspection, equipment other than that commercially available, transfer of equipment between plants, bakery equipment, procedure for obtaining equipment acceptance, chemical clearance, listing of accepted equipment, equipment standards, and accepted commercially available equipment.

The MPIP reviews plant equipment, including materials used in its construction and provisions for its sanitary maintenance in proposed use. Basically, the concern is sanitary design, construction, installation, and maintenance. Equipment acceptable in sanitary design and construction may not be accepted unless its operation and output meet certain requirements. Such approval is needed to assure that the right equipment is used at the beginning instead of correcting any problems that result later. This is a constructive and preventive approach with advantages for the processor, equipment merchant, consumer, and inspection service.

The evaluation and approval apply to used as well as new equipment. Any equipment already installed, capable of producing acceptable products, and kept clean do not need approval. It must, however, be acceptable to the inspector in charge at the point of use, who may also exempt other equipment, including simple hand tools, equipment used for preparing packaging materials, equipment for handling or transporting packaged goods, equipment used in inedible departments, central cleaning systems, utensil and equipment cleaning machinery, and many others.

The publication "Manual for compliance officers" is to provide the procedures for obtaining compliance with the two federal statutes (the Federal Meat Inspection Act and the Poultry Products Inspection Act) and the respective regulations. It also outlines the evidence needed to establish a violation and the manner in which it must be obtained, maintained, prepared, and submitted. The contents of the manual are: responsibilities and performance; compliance programs; definitions; detecting and documenting violations; exemptions; detentions, seizures, and condemnations; disposition of violations; activity reports; and conclusion. All employees in the MPIP are responsible for being alert to, and reporting, alleged violations and other irregularities under the provisions of the two acts, and related laws and regulations. This includes, but is not limited to, violations and irregularities alleged or otherwise occurring within or by establishments under federal inspection or elsewhere in the production, processing, and distribution of meat and poultry products. The procedure for reporting alleged violations or irregularities is prescribed.

The publication "List of chemical compounds" provides meat and poultry inspectors with a list of nonfood compounds authorized for use in federal and state inspected plants. It also lists nonfood compounds authorized by the Poultry and Dairy Quality Division for use on shell eggs. The National Marine Fisheries Service of the Department of Commerce (see Chapter 2) considers the list of substances as acceptable for use in plants under its inspection program. A nonfood compound is defined as any agent proposed for use in a federally inspected plant but not intended as an ingredient of a meat, poultry, rabbit, or egg product.

The publication "Meat and Poultry Inspection Directory" is a very comprehensive publication describing the names, addresses, titles, official numbers, and other pertinent data of government personnel, meat and poultry industries, establishments, and other relevant agencies such as state and local authorities that participate in the MPIP. The table of contents of this publication are as follows:

1. Key program personnel.
2. United States Department of Agriculture MPIP offices.
3. Officers-in-charge of compliance staff area offices.
4. Meat and Poultry Inspection Compliance offices.
5. State program officials.
6. Official state codes and abbreviations by region.
7. Scientific services laboratories.
8. Certified laboratories.
9. Meat establishments under USDA inspection by number.
10. Poultry establishments under USDA inspection by number.
11. Equine and other species establishments under USDA inspection.
12. United States Department of Agriculture-approved establishments for food inspection service.

13. United States Department of Agriculture-approved cold storage warehouses and establishments for identification service.
14. United States Department of Agriculture-certified export establishments.
15. United States Department of Agriculture-approved import establishments.
16. United States Department of Agriculture-certified animal food plants.
17. Inedible fat shippers.
18. Establishments under USDA inspection by state and city.
19. Establishments under USDA inspection cross-referenced by name and number.
20. Foreign meat and poultry establishments.

This publication is used extensively by large volume meat and poultry buyers to ascertain whether the products have been produced in an official establishment under federal or state inspection.

The MPIP has a very close working relationship with the FDA in a number of areas. The most important ones are as follows:

1. The MPIP issues certain requirements governing the use of chemical substances in any of the meat and poultry products. It makes sure that none of the permitted uses is contrary to any relevant regulation promulgated by the FDA. The two agencies cooperate in their regulatory controls over the use of food additives, coloring, spices, and other related chemical and biological substances in meat and poultry products.
2. The MPIP will not normally exercise any regulatory authority over food products that contain less than 3% meat and/or less than 2% poultry as ingredient(s). Such products are under the jurisdiction of the FDA.
3. According to an announcement made on June 2, 1975 (40 FR 25079), the two agencies cooperate in the recall (by FDA) and disposition of Class I and II recalled products for human consumption. Such meat and poultry products have been processed under MPIP inspection and supervision. The FDA is recalling certain ingredient(s) under its jurisdiction that have been used to prepare those products. The agreement delineates each agency's specific responsibilities. Chapter 6 of this book describes the duties of the FDA and provides more details on the arrangement. According to the agreement, the MPIP will:
   a. Evaluate processing procedures in consultation with the FDA to determine the need for the secondary recall of USDA meat and poultry inspected products.
   b. Initiate a secondary recall of meat and poultry products, when necessary, and monitor and determine the effectiveness of the recall.
   c. Issue news releases after consultation with the affected firms and the FDA.
   d. Inform the FDA of the identity and amounts of USDA inspected meat and

poultry products containing ingredients under FDA recall.
  e. Advise the FDA of the method of disposition to be used, such as destruction of the products.
4. The MPIP cooperates with the FDA in the regulatory programs involving drug, pesticide, and industrial chemical residues in animal feeds and in meat and poultry (40 FR 16228 and 16229, April 10, 1975). Meat and poultry may become contaminated with illegal residues of these substances from several sources, including the presence of these residues in animal feeds at actionable levels. Chapter 6 describes the duties of the FDA and provides more details on the arrangement. According to the official agreement, the MPIP will:
  a. Provide the FDA with a list of establishments under MPIP supervision, including any subsequent changes.
  b. Promptly provide the FDA with all available information on the findings of illegal drug, pesticide, or industrial chemical residues in edible tissue samples of meat or poultry.
  c. Report to the FDA any MPIP investigation results initiated by information from the FDA.
  d. Support a FDA regulatory action under the Federal Food, Drug and Cosmetic Act involving drug residues in meat and poultry by providing reports, documents, samples, and MPIP personnel for testimony.
  e. Provide the FDA with details on MPIP testing and sampling programs for residues in meat and poultry, such as number and location of samples tested, residues analyzed, methodology used, and results obtained.
  f. Advise the FDA whenever the MPIP seeks an action of tolerance from the Environmental Protection Agency for a pesticide residue in meat or poultry so that FDA may assess the need for similar action level or tolerance in animal feed.

According to an announcement on August 3, 1977 (42 FR 39330 to 39337), the MPIP has solicited views on certain recommended changes in meat and poultry mandatory inspection under the two federal statutes. A consulting firm has been hired to find possible ways to lower the cost of inspection and remove any unnecessary regulatory burden placed on industry while assuring no loss of consumer protection in regard to meat and poultry products. The firm has finished its study and prepared a detailed report, which is summarized in the announcement. This notice is asking all interested parties to submit comments with reference to the changes in the inspection procedure recommended by this report. If interested, one should study this notice together with the report since the available information will give a very good background for the MPIP and at the same time delineate some of the major changes that may occur if public approval is secured.

FOOD AND NUTRITION SERVICE

According to Appendix 1-1, the Assistant Secretary for Food and Consumer Services also supervises the Food and Nutrition Service. This service coordinates the work of a number of divisions and staffs. Those that concern the present chapter include the Child Nutrition Division, Special Supplemental Food Division, and the Nutrition and Technical Services Staff. Their work is discussed below in the following paragraphs.

Statutes Administered

The service administers a number of federal statutes, most of which are effective for a certain period and then have to be extended by the U.S. Congress and the Executive Branch of the U.S. Government. However, in view of certain unique provisions, they are included for discussion in this chapter. Two such statutes are: the National School Lunch Act of June 4, 1946, as amended (60 Stat. 230 et seq.; 42 U.S.C. 1751 et seq.) and the Child Nutrition Act of 1966, as amended (80 Stat. 885 et seq.; 42 U.S.C. 1779 et seq.). Because of very complicated legislative history, no attempt has been made to make the citations all inclusive.

Under these two statutes, child nutrition programs have been developed under federal auspices to "safeguard the health and well-being of the Nation's children and to encourage the domestic consumption of nutritious agricultural commodities and other foods." Federal cash and donated food assistance are provided to the nonprofit public and private schools and child care institutions through various programs. Because of their unstable legal status, most of the regulations promulgated to implement the acts are not discussed here. For reference purposes, the regulations are located in 35 FR 753, 32 FR 12587, 40 FR 30923, 35 FR 6255, 40 FR 60057, 39 FR 3549, 35 FR 14065, and 39 FR 44729. The following discussion focuses on two major aspects, meal components and new foods.

Meal Components

According to the two statutes, to participate in the child nutrition programs, schools and child care institutions must agree to the following:

1. Operate the food service on a nonprofit basis for all children without regard to race, color, or national origin.
2. Provide free or reduced-price meals to children unable to pay the full price. These must not be identified or discriminated against in any way.

3. Serve meals that meet the minimum nutritional requirements established by the Secretary of Agriculture.

Condition (3) makes it one of the few peace-time situations where the federal government issues and *enforces* guidelines that define the nutritional need of the people and, in this case, children. Thus, for example, before 1977 the service established the minimum food components for the following categories of meals.

Type A School Lunch

1. One-half pint of milk as a beverage.
2. Two ounces (edible portion as served) of lean meat, poultry, or fish; or 2 ounces of cheese; or one egg; or ½ cup of cooked dry beans or peas; or 4 tablespoons of peanut butter; or an equivalent quantity of any combination of these foods.
3. Three-fourths cup serving of two or more vegetables or fruits or both. Full-strength vegetable or fruit juice may be counted to meet not more than ¼ cup of this requirement.
4. One slice of whole-grain or enriched bread; or one serving of corn bread, biscuits, rolls, muffins, or similar, made of whole-grain or enriched meal or flour.
5. One teaspoon of butter or fortified margarine.

Breakfast

1. One-half pint of fluid whole milk as a beverage or on cereal or for both.
2. One-half cup of fruit or full-strength fruit or vegetable juice.
3. One slice of whole-grain or enriched bread; or an equivalent serving of corn bread, biscuits, rolls, muffins, or similar, made of whole-grain or enriched meal or flour; or ¾ cup or 1 ounce (whichever is less, volume or weight) of whole-grain cereal or enriched or fortified cereal; or an equivalent quantity of any combination of these foods.

Supplemental Food

1. One serving of milk or full-strength fruit or vegetable juice; or an equivalent quantity of fruit or vegetable.
2. One serving of whole-grain or enriched bread or cereal; or an equivalent serving of corn bread, biscuits, rolls, muffins, crackers, or cookies made of whole-grain or enriched meal or flour.

The federal program permits exceptions under various circumstances. Table 1-11 illustrates the amount of food to be served to children of different age groups required to fulfill the meal component requirements.

New Foods

Table 1-11 contains the statement "lean meat (edible portion as served) or an equivalent quantity of alternate." When the word "alternate" was introduced, it also started a new era of "meal replacement" in an institutional setting, that is, the child nutrition programs. The service embarked on one of the few peace-time and nonmilitary situations of replacing traditional food components with new and nutritious items that make use of abundant agricultural commodities.

Table 1-12 lists those publications that are currently available and provide detailed information on these new food items. According to the publication "Using new foods to improve USDA child nutrition programs" (item 1 in Table 1-11), "new foods"are "food ingredients or food components that have been put together in a new form or a new composition, usually as an answer to a specific need or problem. They may also be familiar foods redesigned to meet new needs." This publication provides simple answers to questions such as:

1.   What are "new foods"?
2.   How does the USDA decide which new foods to approve?
3.   Why do many new foods seem to emphasize protein?
4.   What are the new foods being considered for the child feeding programs?

At present, the service has developed five major types of new foods.

Textured Vegetable Protein

The Food and Nutrition Service issued the following instructions in FNS Notice 219 (item 2 in Table 1-12).

"Textured vegetable protein products meeting the following requirements may be used as an alternate to meet part of the minimum requirement of two ounces of cooked meat specified for the Type A School Lunch." It may also be used to meet any meat and meat alternate requirements of the food patterns served under the USDA child nutrition programs. The requirements for the textured vegetable protein products are as follows. "The vegetable protein product shall be prepared and served in combination with ground or diced meat in the form of meat patties, meat loaves, meat sauces, meat stews, or in similar foods made with poultry or fish. Ratio of hydrated vegetable protein product, moisture content 60 to 65 per

TABLE 1-11. Specific Amount of Foods Served to Children of Different Age[a] Groups for Fulfillment of Minimum Meal-component Requirements in USDA Child nutrition Programs

Breakfast

Age (years)	Cup of Milk	Cup of Juice or Fruit	Slice of Bread or Equivalent	OR	Cup of Cereal or Equivalent Quantity of Bread and Cereal
1 to 3	1/2	1/4	1/2		1/4
3 to 6	3/4	1/2	1/2		1/3
6 to 12	1	1/2	1		Equivalent quantity of both bread and cereal

Lunch or Supper

Age (years)	Cup of Milk	Lean Meat (edible portion as served) or Equivalent Quantity of Alternate	Cup of Vegetables or Fruits or Both Consisting of Two or More Kinds	Slice of Bread or Equivalent
1 to 3	1/2	1 oz	1/4	1/2
3 to 6	3/4	1 1/2 oz	1/2	1/2
6 to 12	1	2 oz	3/4	1

Supplemental Food

Age (years)	Cup of Milk or Juice or Equivalent Quantity of Fruit or Vegetable	Slice of Bread or Equivalent
1 to 3	1/2	1/2
3 to 6	1/2	1/2
6 to 12	1	1

[a] For meal patterns of infants 0 to 4 months, 4 to 8 months, and 8 to 12 months, consult 40 FR 60057 (December 31, 1975).

TABLE 1-12. Selected Publications and Regulations Issued by Food and Nutrition Service on Various New Foods Used in the Child Nutrition Programs

Item	Publications and regulations
1	"Using new foods to improve USDA child nutrition programs," revised, 1972.
2	"Textured vegetable protein products (B-1) to be used in combination with meat for use in lunches and suppers served under child feeding programs," February 22, 1971, FNS Notice 219.
3	"Information on using textured vegetable protein in child feeding programs," November 1971.
4	"Acceptable textured vegetable protein products," April 1976.
5	"7 CFR 210 Appendix A: Alternate foods for meals, cheese alternate products," 39 FR 31514 (August 29, 1974).
6	"Listing of acceptable cheese alternate products," first revision, February 23, 1976.
7	"Information on using protein fortified, enriched macaroni-type products in child nutrition programs," September 1972.
8	"List of processors and private label distributors of protein fortified, enriched macaroni-type products," December 7, 1972.
9	"7 CFR 210 Appendix A: Alternate foods for meals, enriched macaroni products with fortified protein," 39 FR 11248 (March 27, 1974).
10	"7 CFR 220 Appendix A: Alternate foods for meals formulated grain-fruit products," 39 FR 11249 (March 27, 1974).
11	"Listing of acceptable formulated grain-fruit products," January 21, 1976.
12	"Guidelines for the formulation of CN pizzas (Type 1 and Type 2) for use in the Food and Nutrition Service, Child Nutrition Programs," July 1973.
13	"List of companies producing pizza products according to guidelines for the formulation of CN pizzas (Type 1) for use in the food and nutrition service," September 1976.
14	"Philadelphia cup-can school lunch program" June 1971, FNS Notice 271.
15	"Guidelines for items to be credited as bread equivalents," April 1974, FNS (CN) Instruction 783-9.

cent, to uncooked meat, poultry, or fish in the combination shall not exceed 30 parts per 70 parts, respectively, on basis of weight."

Thus items 2 to 4 in Table 1-12 provide detailed information about the textured vegetable protein. They provide the following important data:

1. Background materials.
2. Forms of textured vegetable protein products.
3. Requirements for using the products in school lunch recipes.
4. Procedures for calculating the amount of raw meat, the products, and water to use.
5. Recipes using the products.
6. Ingredients, chemical composition, and biological value of the products.
7. Listing of processors and private label distributors of those products acceptable for use in the child-nutrition program.

Basic information on textured vegetable protein may be obtained from any current textbooks and/or technical and scientific reviews on the topic. Such materials are not discussed here. As an illustration, the ingredients required by the service for making the products include: food grade oilseed or cereal flours or derived protein concentrate or isolates, alone or in combination with one or more of the following optional ingredients: edible fats or oils, carbohydrates, binders, stabilizers, natural or artificial flavors, colors, amino acids, vitamins, and minerals.

Cheese Alternate Products

According to items 5 and 6 in Table 1-12, the service has issued the following instructions.

"Schools may utilize cheese alternate products...as a food component meeting the meal requirements.... Cheese alternate products shall be prepared and served in combination with natural or processed cheese.... The quantity, by weight, of cheese alternate product in the combination shall not exceed that of the natural or processed cheese." All cheese alternate products used must meet specific requirements.

Items 5 and 6 in Table 1-12 provide the following information:

1. The terms and conditions that govern the use of cheese alternate products as a food component meeting the meal requirements of child nutrition programs.
2. The ingredients, physical and functional properties, meltability, texture and consistency, slicing and grinding character of the products.
3. Nutritional specifications.
4. Biological value of protein in the products.
5. List of manufacturers of cheese alternate products acceptable for use in the child nutrition programs.

Some requirements governing the use of ingredients in manufacturing the products are as follows. All ingredients should be of food grade products. Protein should derive from animal sources and lipid, from plant or animal sources. Lipids should contain less than 50% saturated fatty acids. Both protein and lipid should combine with water, fats or oils, salts, carbohydrates, vitamins, and minerals in a proportion necessary to meet compositional specifications. All ingredients must comply with regulations and laws of the USDA and FDA.

Some physical characteristics of the products should be: 15 g of product in shredded form on a slice of bread must melt to a smooth consistency and lose shred identity in a maximum of 3 minutes when placed in a conventional oven pre-heated and set at 500°F.

Protein Fortified, Enriched Macaroni-type Products

The service has issued the following instructions, "One ounce of dry enriched macaroni products with fortified protein may be used to meet not more than one-half of the meat or meat alternate requirements when served in combination with one or more ounces of cooked meat, poultry, fish, or cheese. The size of servings of the cooked combination may be adjusted for various age groups."

Items 7 to 9 in Table 1-12 provide detailed information on the products, including:

1. Background materials and nutritional value of the products.
2. Yield information, that is, how much of the product can replace 1 ounce of cooked meat.
3. Types of products available and recipes for using the products.
4. Requirements for using the products in child nutrition programs.
5. Listing of processors and private label distributors of the products.
6. The products must comply with the FDA standard of identity and label statement of ingredients.

According to the FDA standard of identity, the product is manufactured by drying formed units of dough made with one or more of the milled wheat ingredients designated and other ingredients to allow the finished product to meet the protein requirements. Edible protein sources, including food grade flours or meals made from nonwheat cereals or from oilseeds, may be used. Vitamins and minerals are added to bring the product into conformity with requirements. Safe and suitable ingredients may be added. The proportion of the milled wheat ingredient is larger than the proportion of any other ingredient used. Each such finished food, when tested by official methods, should meet a number of specifications. For example, the protein content is 20% or more by weight (on a 13% moisture basis). The protein quality is not less than 95% that of casein as determined on the cooked food by a prescribed method. The total solids content is 87% or more by weight. Each food product contains 5 mg of thiamin, 2.2 mg of riboflavin, 34 mg of niacin or niacinamide, and 15.5 mg of iron.

Formulated Grain-fruit Products

The service has issued the following instructions, "Formulated grain-fruit products may be used as an alternate to meet the bread/cereal and the fruit/juice requirements in the breakfast pattern specified...."

Items 10 and 11 in Table 1-12 provide some basic information on the products. There are two types: grain type and grain-fruit type. A grain type product is required to have grain as its primary ingredient, whereas a grain-fruit type has fruit as its primary ingredient. Each type must have at least 25% of their weight derived from grain, and all ingredients must comply with requirements under the USDA and FDA. The product must also comply with prescribed nutritional specifications. Item 11 in Table 1-12 lists the manufacturers of acceptable formulated grain-fruit products.

Child Nutrition Pizzas

The service has issued guidelines for use "in developing pizza products that will meet the meat/meat alternate, bread, and butter or fortified margarine requirements and part of the vegetable/fruit requirement of meals served under" the child nutrition programs. Items 12 and 13 in Table 1-12 provide the following information on this special product:

1. Types of pizzas.
2. Forms, weights, food components, and examples of the products.
3. Ingredients, yield, and labeling of the products.
4. Product evaluation and acceptance.
5. List of companies producing pizza products according to guidelines for the formulation of child nutrition pizzas for use in the child nutrition programs.

Some product specifications are as follows. There are two types of child nutrition pizzas--Types 1 and 2. Type 1 contributes three components of the meal components, and Type 2 contributes four.

1. Type 1 meets the meat/meat alternate, bread, and butter, or fortified margarine requirements.
2. Type 2 meets the meat/meat alternate, bread, and butter, or fortified margarine requirements, and at least 1/4 cup of the vegetable/fruit requirement.

The pizzas must be frozen or unfrozen, cooked or uncooked, weigh at least 4 ounces "as served" for Type 1 and 5½ ounces for Type 2. The requirements for the food components are as follows:

1. Meat/meat alternate:
    a. Cheese only. At least 2 ounces of cheese per serving.
    b. Cheese and meat/meat alternates. At least ½ ounce of cheese with either cooked meat, poultry, or fish or meat, poultry, or fish combined with textured vegetable protein products to be equivalent to 2 ounces of cooked meat as prescribed.
2. Bread. The crust must weigh at least 1 ounce "as served."
3. Butter or fortified margarine. At least 1 teaspoon (0.17 ounce) per serving.
4. Vegetable/fruit (applies to Type 2 only). At least ¼ cup per serving. Quantities over this amount are allowed, but crediting is limited to ¼ cup.

Miscellaneous New Foods

One new item served to school children is the "Philadelphia cup-can school lunch program" (see item 14 in Table 1-12). The lunches, as served, consist of an individual can of combination food (stews, beans and franks, spaghetti and meatballs, etc.) and the necessary supplements to meet all the requirements of the Type A lunch. The cans are heated in inexpensive ovens, and the heated food is eaten by the children directly from the cans with the supplements. The overall simplicity of the program and the fact that this program can be utilized for at-the-desk feeding, makes it adaptable to schools with no facilities and/or no cafeterias.

Item 15 in Table 1-12 contains guidelines to determine what a bread equivalent is. The basic meal component requirements include, among others, one slice of whole-grain or enriched bread, or a serving of corn bread, biscuits, rolls, muffins, or similar, made of whole-grain or enriched meal or flour. The requirement, as stated, has been interpreted quite literally over the years, and, consequently, has somewhat restricted the use of otherwise appropriate and acceptable bread alternates and given rise to much confusion as to the kinds and types of creditable bread items. The guidelines list those items that can replace bread or serve partially as equivalents: one bagel weighs 40 grams, one serving of French or Vienna bread weighs 24 g, one salt stick weighs 25 g, and one serving of stuffing bread weighs 80 g. Some types of products do not qualify as bread equivalents and, consequently, may not be credited toward meeting the bread requirement in meals served under the child nutrition programs. They include sweet-type foods (cakes, cookies, pies, etc.), snack type foods such as hard, thin pretzels, corn chips, and other extruded and/or shaped items made from grain. Cereal products such as rice, bulgur, and pastas are not credited toward meeting the bread requirement since they are needed to round out the meals for both satiety and nutrients.

Since many sections of the two acts (National School Lunch Act and Child Nutrition Act) are periodically amended, extended, and revised by the U.S. congress, the regulations promulgated by the USDA to implement the acts are also subjected to frequent revision. Consequently, much of the information discussed under the Food and Nutrition Service will undergo corresponding changes. However, it is emphasized that the material presented above serves only as an illustration and not an updated reference source of the requirements established by the federal government (via the Food and Nutrition Service) to regulate the quantity and quality of foods served to infants and children under congress-mandated food and nutrition programs. The Code of Federal Regulations and the Federal Register should be consulted for the latest references.

FEDERAL GRAIN INSPECTION SERVICE

Statutes Administered

According to Appendix 1-1, the Assistant Secretary for Marketing Services supervises, among others, the Federal Grain Inspection Service. This service administers the voluntary and mandatory requirements of the U.S. Grain Standards Act of October 21, 1976 (90 Stat. 2867 et seq.; 7 U.S.C. 71 et seq.) and the voluntary requirements of the Agricultural Marketing Act of 1946 (7 U.S.C. 1621 to 1627).

The basic objectives of the Grain Standards Act are to ensure that grain may be marketed in an orderly and timely manner and that trading in grain may be facilitated. Some major provisions of this act are as follows:

1. Provides for a national official inspection system for grain.
2. Establishes official U.S. standards of quality, quantity, and condition for corn, wheat, rye, oats, barley, flaxseed, grain sorghum, soybeans, mixed grain, and other grains if the circumstances warrant. Such standards may be revoked if necessary, and the act requires uniform application of such standards by inspection personnel.
3. Provides for mandatory inspection, weighing, and certification for grains to be exported outside of the United States. All grains to be transferred out of or into an export elevator at an an export port location are required to be officially weighed. All grains must have official or other approved standards. Official inspection and weighing may be waived under certain circumstances.
4. Provides for the mandatory *certification* of the grade and weight of a lot of grain that has been officially inspected and weighed while being transferred into or out of a grain elevator, warehouse, or other storage or handling facility.

5. Establishes standards for accurate weighing and weight certification procedures and controls, including safeguards over equipment calibration and maintenance for grain shipped in interstate or foreign commerce.

6. Permits the effective date to be one calendar year after a standard has been officially promulgated by the service.

7. Makes it illegal for a person to engage in trade of a grain with an official standard in either interstate or foreign commerce while describing such grain as being of any grade other than the one officially assigned. No person is permitted to describe a grain by any false or misleading grade designation.

8. Authorizes permissive or voluntary inspection of any grain engaged in domestic commerce in accordance with established standards or other approved criteria. An interested party must apply for such service.

9. Makes official certificates for inspection prima facie evidence in a court of law.

10. Authorizes the designation of any individual or state or local government agency as an official agency for the conduct of all or specified functions involved in certain types of official inspection at approved locations. The person or agency to be designated must comply with a number of prerequisite requirements before such designation.

11. Permits inspection by official samples, submitted samples, or otherwise in commerce within the United States and Canada.

12. Permits the use of modern mechanical and electronic grain-sampling equipment.

13. Authorizes agreements with the Canadian government with respect to the official inspection and weighing in Canadian ports of United States export grain transshipped through Canadian ports.

14. Authorizes the charging and collection of reasonable inspection fees to cover the estimated cost incident to the performance of official inspection by the service's personnel.

15. Requires the operator of a grain handling facility to comply with a number of prerequisite requirements before official weighing is rendered by the service.

16. Requires the testing of all equipment used in the sampling, grading, inspection, and weighing of grain located at all grain elevators, warehouses, or other storage or handling facilities at which official inspection or weighing services are provided by the service.

17. Provides for licensing of grain inspectors for 3-year, renewable periods.

18. Authorizes the refusal, renewal, suspension, or revocation of licenses.

19. Authorizes the refusal of inspection and weighing services and the institution of civil penalties.

20. Requires the keeping of and access to records for all transactions involving

grain, such as inspection, weighing, purchases, sales, transportation, storage, weighing, handling, treating, cleaning, drying, blending, and other activities.

21. Institutes criminal penalty against any individual who commits any offense specifically prohibited by the act. The person will be guilty of a misdemeanor and, if convicted, will be subject to imprisonment for not more than 12 months, or a fine of not more than $10,000 or both. For each subsequent offense, the person will be guilty of a felony and, if convicted, will be subject to imprisonment for a maximum of 5 years or a fine of $20,000 maximum or both. An example of a prohibited act is knowingly and falsely counterfeiting an official certificate.

22. Requires the registration of all persons engaged in the business of buying, handling, weighing, or transporting grain for sale in foreign commerce. There are many exemptions to this requirement. For example, no registration is needed for any producer of grain who only incidentally or occasionally sells or transports grain that he has purchased.

23. Prohibits any state or other political subdivision to "require the inspection or description in accordance with any standards of kind, class, quality, condition, or other characteristics of grain as a condition of shipment, or sale, of such grain in interstate or foreign commerce, or require any license for, or impose any other restrictions upon, the performance of any official inspection or weighing function...by official inspection personnel."

Regulations Promulgated

The regulations, standards, and gradings of this act are described in detail in 7 CFR 26. The authority for the provisions in this part was issued under Section 8, 39 Stat. 485; Section 16, 82 Stat. 768; 7 U.S.C. 84, 87e; 27 FR 16210, as amended; and 33 FR 10750.

The regulations in this part provide the details with reference to a national inspection system for grain. The purpose of this system is to promote the uniform and accurate application of the official grain standards and to provide such inspection services as may be required by the act or desired by the grain industry.

According to the regulations and the act, "official inspection" is interpreted to include the following:

1. Performed by official inspection personnel.
2. May be original inspection, reinspection, or appeal inspection.
3. Determination and certification of either:
   a. The kind, class, quality, or condition of grain in accordance with established standards or

b. The condition of vessels and other carriers or receptacles for the transportation of grain insofar as it may affect the quality or condition of such grains;

c. Upon request of any interested party applying for inspection, the quantity of sacks of grain or other facts related to grain under other approved criteria.

4. The technique of determination includes sampling, inspecting, examining, testing, grading, and other methods.

"Official weighing" is interpreted to include the following:

1. Performed by official inspection personnel.
2. Determination and certification of the quantity of a lot of grain under established standards and based on the following:
   a. Actual performance of weighing or its physical supervision, including the physical inspection and testing for accuracy of the weights and scales and the physical inspection of the premises at which the weighing is performed;
   b. Monitoring of the discharge of grain into the elevator or conveyance.

The regulations specifically emphasize that certain kinds of inspection services are not authorized and cannot be performed. For example, any agricultural commodity or processed grain product not covered by the official grain standards cannot be inspected. Also, a grain cannot be inspected on the basis of an unofficial standard.

There are at least 10 types of official inspection services. Some examples include: official sample (lot inspection), type sample (lot inspection), warehouseman's sample (lot inspection), submitted sample inspection, quality information inspection, checkweighing, sampling, stowage examination, and other miscellaneous services. An explanation for some of these services follows.

Under the official sampling, lot inspection, the official inspector samples an identified lot of grain, inspects the grain in the sample, and issues an official certificate about the examination.

Under the warehouseman's sample, lot inspection, a licensed employee of a grain elevator or warehouse samples an identified lot of grain and submits the sample and a report to an official inspection agency. The official inspector then inspects the grain in the sample, grades the sample, files a report, and issues a certificate.

Under the quality information inspection, the inspector makes frequent and periodic examinations of grain being loaded aboard or discharged from a ship, for official grade or factors. He files a report and issues a certificate about the result.

One of the major tasks is to obtain an official sample of grain. With some exceptions such as exporting grain, official samples of grain may be obtained by licensed employees of official inspection agencies, authorized employees of the service, licensed employees of grain elevators or warehouses, and other individuals who are licensed to sample grain under a contract with the service.

Some details of the method and order of inspection service are described as follows. First, all sampling, testing, grading, and related inspection services are required to be performed by official inspection personnel or other designated agents. Second, such inspection will be based on a list of items that must be considered in the order described: careful inspection of grain, prescribed tests and examinations, review of previous inspection if any, and other pertinent and necessary information. Third, the sampling must be proportional or random and determinations must be based on a careful and accurate examination, testing, or analysis. The source of the sample must be clearly detailed. There are other details such as record of documents, order of service, and conflict of interest. They are all carefully described in the regulations.

Another very important aspect of the inspection service is the recognition and licensing of official inspection agencies. Some procedural requirements are listed as follows:

1. Before any agency or person may operate an official inspection agency to perform official inspection services, including the issuance of certificates, they must make an application or be designated by the service.
2. Notice of the application will be published in the Federal Register, and interested parties will be given opportunity to submit comments in writing.
3. On the basis of the comments received and other information available to the service, a decision to approve or deny the application will be made.
4. The applicant must fulfill certain requirements for designation as an official inspection agency. In addition to many specific data, other requirements include: trade need, citizenship status, conflict of interest, and the proper staffing with duly qualified official inspection personnel. Most important of all, the applicant must possess the proper equipment and facilities.
5. Some of the duties of the official inspection agencies include: proper staffing, rendering specific services, securing license for each staff member, providing such licensed personnel with training and supplies, supervising the staff, establishing fees and charges, reporting inspection volumes and other details, and notification to government officials regarding service and other changes.

Any interested party should both consult 7 CFR 26 and request information from the service with reference to the regulations governing mandatory inspection, grading, weighing, and certification of grain to be exported; and mandatory grades for grains to be transported in interstate commerce.

As the process of grain inspection is very complicated, the service has issued a large "Grain Inspection Manual (see Table 1-13). The purpose of this manual is to provide a guide to the proper sampling, inspection, grading, and certification of the various grains under the provisions of the U.S. Grain Standards Act, as amended. It is prepared in the form of a manual for ready reference and for use by official inspection personnel, agricultural commodity graders and others engaged in the inspection and marketing of grain.

TABLE 1-13. Selected Publications Distributed by Federal Grain Inspection Service

Publication Number (date)	Title of Publication
Instruction No. 918 (GR)[a]	Grain inspection manual, covering the sampling, inspection, grading, and certification of grain under the United States Grain Standards Act as amended
HB-3 (January 1971)	Inspection handbook for dry beans
HB(918)-1 (1974)	Inspection handbook for the sampling, inspection, and certification of dry peas, split peas, and lentils
HB(918)-2 (March 1975)	Inspection handbook miscellaneous processed commodities
HB(918)-4 (December 1975)	Sanitation inspection handbook for beans, peas, lentils, and processed commodities
Unnumbered[b]	Notices and instructions

[a] The manual is constantly being revised. Replacement sheets and inserts are added to update the materials.

[b] Publication irregular. Request to be put on mailing lists; also refer to the text.

According to 7 CFR 26, the service has established U.S. standards for the following grains (section number in parenthese): barley (201), corn (351), flaxseed (501), grain sorghum (551), mixed grain (451), oats (251), rye (401), soybeans (601), and triticale (651).

As mentioned earlier, the service also administers certain provisions of the

Agricultural Marketing Act. The regulations are promulgated in 7 CFR 68, "Regulations and standards for inspection and certification of certain agricultural commodities and products thereof." The authority for the provisions in Part 68 was issued under Sections 203, 205, 60 Stat. 1087, 1090, as amended, and 7 U.S.C. 1622, 1624.

The regulations are related to the voluntary inspection and certification of a number of agricultural commodities that do not fall under the U.S. Grain Standards Act. Part 68 provides information on inspection and appeal inspection, general provision, authorized inspections, licensed inspectors and samplers, fees and charges for certain federal inspection services, and miscellaneous information. For example, under the section inspection, the regulations provide details on kind and availability of service; regulations not applicable for certain purposes; who may inspect commodities; who may obtain service; how to make application; form of application; when application may be withdrawn; accessibility of commodities; lot inspection; sample inspection; issuance, form, and disposition of inspection certificates; and issuance of corrected certificate.

According to the regulations, the inspection of agricultural commodities is based on standards promulgated by the service or approved specifications prescribed by other federal agencies, trade associations, or an individual applicant. The service will provide voluntarily requested services for commodities shipped or received in interstate commerce or at important central markets and other places designated if it is so desired. To facilitate such services, the service has established U.S. standards for the following agricultural commodities (section number in parentheses): beans (191), rough rice (201), brown rice for processing (251), milled rice (301), whole dry peas (401), split peas (501), and lentils (601).

Table 1-13 lists a number of publications that are very useful for various parties in this field. For example, the inspection handbooks for dry peas, split peas, lentils, dry beans, and miscellaneous processed commodities are all specifically designed by the service to serve as guides to the proper sampling, inspection, grading, checkweighing, checkloading, and certification of the agricultural products. They serve as ready reference for use by inspection officials, grain industrial personnel, large volume grain product buyers, and others. The sanitation handbook noted in Table 1-13 is designed specifically for an inspector. It outlines in detail the procedure for checking the sanitation of processing plants that handle those agricultural products.

Agreements with Other Government Agencies

Apart from standards and grades, the wholesomeness and cleanliness of the grain must also be assured. This is normally done by the FDA. On May 29, 1974, the

FDA and the Agricultural Marketing Service of the USDA announced (39 FR 18695 and 18696) that an official Memorandum of Understanding had been signed between the two agencies in relation to the inspection and grading of grain, rice, and pulses. This agreement is applicable to the Federal Grain Inspection Service. The delineated responsibilities are as follows. Specifically, the service will, among other duties,

1. Notify the FDA immediately of any plants where inspection services have been or will be suspended because of sanitation or other criteria violation.
2. Notify the FDA of any plants that have failed to correct objectionable defects discovered by the FDA.
3. Provide in the standards for grain, rice, and pulses the permissible levels of deleterious substances, assuring that they do not exceed allowances set by the FDA.

The FDA will specifically, among other duties:

1. Team inspect with any service inspectors if they are present in a plant.
2. Immediately notify the appropriate service field office concerning the details of serious, objectionable sanitation conditions, or handling practices.
3. Provide the service with details on any products against which seizure action is being contemplated or has been initiated.

It is mutually agreed that both the FDA and USDA will cooperate jointly and with the grain, rice, and pulse industries in the improvement of sanitation and food handling practices in the processing plants. Both agencies will mutually exchange data and cooperate in the development of the sampling plans, methodology, and guidelines for determining natural and unavoidable defects common to grain, rice, and pulses. The original document should be consulted for further details.

The service also has cooperative agreements with various state agencies. These agreements apply to certain provisions of the Agricultural Marketing Act and they are signed under the joint authority of 7 U.S.C. 1621 et seq. and the applicable statutes of the state. Each agreement carries a specific file code number and copies may be obtained from the service. The information contained in each agreement varies; some typical arrangements are as follows.

The state agency has full responsibility for providing inspection services on commodities covered by the agreement. These include staffing, assignments, facilities, and some basic instructional materials. The state agency should adopt all grain and commodity standards established by the service. It will train inspectors to interpret grades and perform inspections and will establish fees and charges to be assessed for services rendered, which must be consistent with those of the federal agency for comparable services.

The service will have full responsibility for grading accuracy, interpretation of specifications and standards, establishment of appropriate inspection techniques and methods, and the development of inspection instructions, handbooks, training aids, and guidelines. The service will provide supplemental training in the inspection services and supervise official inspection personnel to guarantee proper methods and criteria. It will give examinations and issue licenses to successful individuals. Inspectors so licensed will be permitted to issue official inspection certificates.

It is also mutually agreed that changes and exceptions in fundings must be approved by both parties. Both state and federal employees must have a similar merit system, and only federal personnel will be authorized to supervise and/or conduct appeal inspections and issue appeal certificate. Again, interested parties should consult the original document(s) for further details.

FOREIGN AGRICULTURAL SERVICE

According to Appendix 1-1, the Assistant Secretary for International Affairs and Commodity Program supervises, among others, the Foreign Agricultural Service. Within the Foreign Agricultural Service, according to Appendix 1-18, one special function of the Administrator's office is Correspondence Control, which, among others, encompasses communication dealing with International Organization Affairs. At present, the Executive Director of the International Organization Affairs is also the chief coordinator of all activities relating to the participation of the United States in the international body, the Codex Alimentarius Commission. Because of frequent Government reorganization and title changes, the Foreign Agricultural Service within the USDA is considered as providing the general leadership in this particular coordinating responsibility.

Codex Alimentarius Commission

The term "Codex Alimentarius" is approximately translated as food standards. The Codex Alimentarius Commission is an international body established in 1963 by the Food and Agricultural Organization (FAO) of the United Nations and the World Health Organization (WHO). Information about the Commission may be obtained from the latest Procedural Manual, which is published jointly by FAO/WHO. The following describes the work of the commission; the material has been adapted from the manual.

The primary objectives of the commission regarding food products are the protection of consumer health and facilitation of world trade. These are achieved by the establishment of uniform international food standards, which are collectively known as the Codex Alimentarius. The latter is also the title of an FAO/WHO publication for such standards. These standards also include recommendations in terms of guidelines, codes of practice, and other advisory provisions that aim at promoting the purposes of the standards.

The Codex Alimentarius includes standards for all the principal foods for distribution to the consumer. The foods may be raw, semiprocessed, or processed. Materials for further processing into foods are included to the extent necessary to achieve the purpose of the Codex Alimentarius as defined. The standards take into consideration the composition, minimum quality, food hygiene, adulterants, food additives, industrial contaminants, food colors, residues of pesticide and related substances, packaging, labeling and presentation, methodology in sampling and analysis, and other related factors.

Full and associate member nations of the WHO and FAO may request permission to join the commission. This commission has a number of subsidiary bodies or committees, some of which are concerned with administration, others with broad food topics; the majority are assigned specific commodity work. The diagram shown in Figure 1-1 is adapted from the Procedural Manual and illustrates the administrative profile and the different committees within the Codex Alimentarius Commission. It is important to remember that each member of this commission is a country.

For further details on the organization and working details of the commission, refer to the Procedural Manual. As of April 9, 1976, there were 114 member countries in the commission, with 31 from Africa, 26 from Asia, 29 from Europe, 22 from Latin America, 4 from Southwest Pacific, and 2 from North America. The last two countries are Canada and the United States.

The procedure for the establishment of an international food standard is as follows:

Procedural Sequence 1. The commission intends to establish an international *Codex standard* for a particular commodity or product and will designate one subsidiary or other body to begin the process.

Procedural Sequence 2. The selected subsidiary body or committee prepares a preliminary *proposed draft* standard. The preparation incorporates all appropriate and available data that have been developed by any international organization, usually in the food trade. The chairman of the committee submits this draft to the commission's secretariat.

Procedural Sequence 3. The secretariat sends the proposed draft to the associate and full member countries of FAO and WHO and to the international association(s) affected, soliciting their comments.

Procedural Sequence 4. After the comments have been received, they are sent to the initiating subsidiary body, which may, after deliberation, amend the proposed draft.

Procedural Sequence 5. The secretariat then submits the proposed draft to the commission, intending to adopt it as a *draft standard*. The commission may refer the proposed draft to a special body or committee before adopting it as a draft standard or may request this body to accomplish sequences 6, 7, and 8.

Procedural Sequence 6. The draft standard is rerouted by the secretariat back to the international association(s) and all associate and full member countries of the FAO and WHO.

Procedural Sequence 7. After further comments have been received, they may be sent to the initiating subsidiary body, which may, after deliberation, amend the draft standard.

Procedural Sequence 8. The secretariat submits the draft standard to the commission with a view to adopt it as a *recommended standard*.

Procedural Sequence 9. The recommended standard is forwarded to all full and associate member countries of WHO and FAO and to the international organization(s) affected. All countries will inform the secretariat regarding the acceptance of the recommended standard in accordance with the commission's acceptance procedure, which is discussed in the following paragraph. Countries belonging to the FAO/WHO but not to the Commission are usually provided an opportunity to accept the recommended standard.

Procedural Sequence 10. If the acceptance response from the various member countries is agreeable to the commission, the recommended standard is published in the Codex Alimentarius as a worldwide *Codex standard*.

A member country of the commission may accept the recommended standard in one of three ways: full acceptance, target acceptance, or acceptance with specified deviations. When full acceptance is forwarded, the country will permit the product to be distributed freely within its territorial limit under the identity as prescribed in the standard as long as the product complies with all requirements and conditions. The identity includes the name and the description of the product. When a target acceptance is expressed, the country states that it will accept the product standard within a specified period, usually a number of years. In the mean-

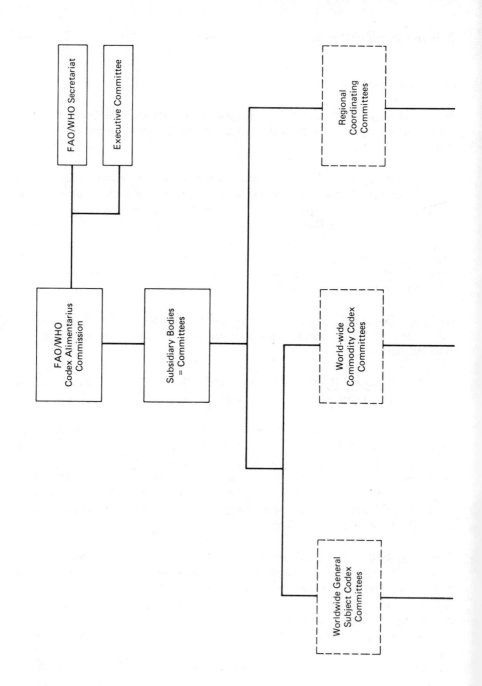

FAO/WHO Secretariat

Executive Committee

FAO/WHO Codex Alimentarius Commission

Subsidiary Bodies = Committees

Regional Coordinating Committees

World-wide Commodity Codex Committees

Worldwide General Subject Codex Committees

104

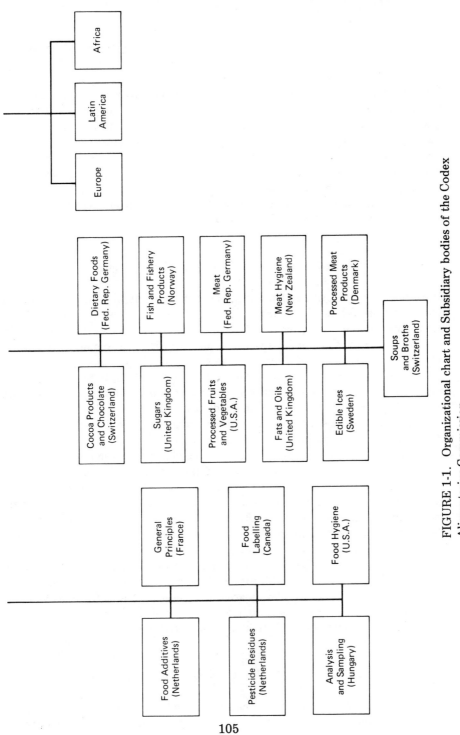

FIGURE 1-1. Organizational chart and Subsidiary bodies of the Codex Alimentarius Commission

105

time, the country will not handicap the distribution of any such product that conforms to all conditions of the standard. When a country accepts the standard with specified deviations, it means that, apart from specifically detailed deviations, it will fully accept the product standard. The assumption is made that if such a product complies with the general standard and the deviations, it is permitted to be freely distributed in the country. One should refer to the Procedural Manual for other variations of the acceptance procedure.

The commission now meets periodically, usually annually, and the report of the meeting is published by the FAO/WHO.

The Commission and Role of the United States

Through the coordinating activity of the Foreign Agricultural Service in the USDA and with financial assistance from the Department of State, the United States participates as a full member in the commission. In comparison with U.S. food standards (also see Chapter 6), a Codex standard for a given commodity is essentially a combined standard of identity and minimum standard of quality.

The United States has a vital interest in such standards, both as an exporter and importer. It participates actively in the standard establishment process and seeks, wherever possible, to have standards that reflect acceptable marketing and manufacturing practices and good food law regulations, especially with reference to the conditions and requirements in the United States.

Much of the work of the commission is conducted through its committees or subsidiary bodies, each chaired by one of the participating member countries. According to Figure 1-1, the United States chairs two committees, one on food hygiene and the other on processed fruits and vegetables. It has other U.S. Government representatives and industry advisors as members in the other committees of the commission. This helps to gain experience and at the same time assures that U.S. interest is maintained. The Foreign Agricultural Service has designated two main coordinators of U.S. representation, one from the USDA and the other from the FDA. They work closely with various domestic groups of representatives from various government food regulatory agencies, especially the USDA and the FDA. Table 1-14 lists the representatives from the United States participating in the development of Codex standards for the different commodities.

STATISTICS, STANDARDIZATION, GRADING, AND SAMPLING

Statistics plays a major role in enforcing food standards, inspections, gradings, and related regulatory activities. It is not possible to manufacture a large number of

TABLE 1-14. Specific U.S. Federal Government Agency Representative and Corresponding Commodity Codex Committee

Committee	Purpose	U.S. Agency Sending Representative
Joint FAO/WHO Committee of Government Experts on code of principles concerning milk and milk products	To establish international standards of composition and standard methods of sampling and analysis for milk and milk products	USDA
Codex committee on food additives	To recommend international tolerances for individual food additives in specific food items	FDA
Codex committee on pesticide residues	To recommend international tolerances for pesticide residues in specific food products	USDA
Codex committee on food hygiene	To develop basic principles for food plant sanitation and for handling food in international trade	FDA
Codex committee on food labeling	To draft provisions on labeling applicable to all foods	FDA
Codex committee on general principles	To define purpose and scope of Codex Alimentarius	USDA
Codex committee on methods of analysis and sampling	To determine best method of analysis and sampling for products for which Codex standards are in preparation	FDA
Codex committee on cocoa products and chocolate	To recommend international standards for cocoa products and chocolate	FDA

(continued)

TABLE 1-14 (continued)

Committee	Purpose	U.S. Agency Sending Representative
Codex committee on sugars	To recommend international standards for all types of carbohydrate sweetening	USDA
Codex committee on fats and oils	To recommend international standards for fats and and oils of animal, vegetable, and marine origin, including margarine and olive oil	FDA
Codex committee on fish and fishery products	To recommend international standards for fresh, frozen, or otherwise processed fish	NMFS[a]
Codex committee on foods for special dietary uses	To develop general guidelines, principles, and standards for selected dietetic foods	FDA
Codex committee on processed fruits and vegetables	To recommend international standards for all types of processed fruits and vegetables	USDA
Codex committee on honey	To recommend international standards for types of honey	USDA
Codex committee on meat hygiene	To develop international codes of practice for meat hygiene	USDA
Codex committee on processed meat products	To develop international standards for processed meat products, including consumer packaged meat	USDA
Codex committee on fresh meats	To develop international standards and/or codes of practice for classification and grading of carcasses and cuts of beef, lamb, mutton, pork, and veal	USDA

Codex committee on edible ices	To elaborate worldwide standards as appropriate for all types of edible ices, including mixes and powders used for their manufacture	FDA
Codex committee on soups and broths	To elaborate worldwide standards for soups, broths, bouillons, and consomme	USDA
Joint Economic Commission of Europe/Codex Alimentarius group of experts on standardization of fruit juices	To recommend international standards for fruit juices	FDA
Joint Economic Commission of Europe/Codex Alimentarius group of experts on standardization of quick frozen foods	To recommend international standards for quick frozen foods but not including meat, poultry, fish, and fruit juices	USDA

[a] NMFS = National Marine Fisheries Service (see Chapter 2).

109

products that are completely free from defects. One practice is to divide them into groups of equal level of quality. Another method is to permit the marketing of a lot of products with a certain legally authorized percentage of defective ones. Assume there are 1000 cans of salmon or peaches to be inspected and/or graded. Some cans may have indentations or leaks. Some peaches may have rot, and some salmon may be in broken pieces rather than in firm chunks. Some central questions that must be answered before this particular lot of canned goods is permitted to be marketed include the following:

1. How many "distorted" cans will this lot be permitted to have in order to be legally acceptable?
2. How many cans have to be opened for checking to assure that the remaining ones will be a reasonable reflection of the conditions of those already opened?
3. What kind of defects are the salmon or peaches permitted to have and to what extent?
4. How will one quantitate the defects?
5. How much time is alloted for the examination of 1000 cans of the products?
6. How frequently must such types of products be checked?
7. How many inspectors and/or graders are available for examining 1000 cans of the products?
8. How objective is the decision in regard to product quality such as color, texture, and other organoleptic characteristics?

Providing answers for these questions and making the right decision regarding the acceptability of the lot of products is very important. Any inaccurate or biased procedure/decision will be fairly costly to either the consumer or the manufacturer. In addition, public confidence in the government's seal of approval, identification, grades, and other official markings may be affected. Most important of all, as prima facie evidence in a court of law, government certification, inspection, grading, and sampling can be challenged by the attorney defending or suing for his client(s). Thus the scientific techniques used and conclusions drawn by the food regulatory agency in its inspection and grading services may be subjected to approval or rebuttal by experts in the field in a court trial. Statistical analysis is so vital that practically every regulatory agency for food products, both federal and state, has a specially trained group of statisticians.

Some of the basic duties of a statistician in this specialty are to: (1) assist in the development of standards and grades, (2) define the quality of a product, (3) devise a procedure for sampling, (4) evaluate the quality of a product, and (5) analyze the data mathematically.

Recently, statisticians in the USDA have developed the method of attribute grading, which is briefly explained as follows. Depending on the product, the grader decides on the number of samples to be checked. He examines the products and identifies any factor that deviates from a fixed value (e.g., dark green or light green instead of golden yellow for a ripe peach). Such a deviation is labeled as a defect. The grader passes through the products in the samples and counts the defects. He ascertains the grade to be assigned to that lot from which the samples were obtained by its correlation with the number of defects so identified in a special table. Also, the defects are categorized into three levels of undesirability: minor, major, or critical defect. A critical defect is one that seriously affects the usability of the product for its intended purpose. A major defect is one that materially affects the usability of the product for its intended purpose. A minor defect is one that materially affects the appearance of the product but is not likely to affect the usability for its intended purpose. An insignificant defect is a flaw in the product that does not materially affect appearance or the usability for its intended purpose. The appropriate chart specifies the frequency of each category of defect permitted in a limited number of samples to be assigned a certain grade, although insignificant defects are not recorded.

The USDA has issued different types of official statistical information to serve the purpose of performing inspection, grading, evaluation and certification in a most scientific and acceptable manner. They are listed as follows:

1. 7 CFR 42, Standards for condition of food containers.
2. 7 CFR 43, Standards for sampling plans.
3. Each grade standard and/or standard of identity for any particular commodity issued by the USDA may also carry certain information such as defects and other quality factors and means of sampling, grading, inspection, and other evaluation techniques. Inspection manuals issued for reference use by USDA personnel usually carry detailed instruction on using statistical measures.

Some general ideas about the role of a statistician in this regulatory activity is explained by R. P. Bartlett, Jr., in the following articles:

1. "A statistician looks at standardization," January 1970, Agricultural Marketing.
2. "A statistician looks at grading by attributes," February 1970, Agricultural Marketing.
3. "A statistician looks at sampling plans," June 1970, Agricultural Marketing.

The following discussion has been adapted from 7 CFR 42. The regulation in this part outlines the procedure to be used to establish the condition of containers in lots of packaged foods. It is used to determine the acceptability of a lot based on specified acceptable quality levels and defects or any approved alternate plan. In addition, any other sampling plan in the special tables provided with a larger first sample size than that indicated by the lot size range may be specified if approved. The regulation or approved alternate plan is applied when the USDA is requested to certify the condition of filled primary containers or shipping cases or both and, unless specified, the USDA normally examines both. The regulation is not applicable to inspection lots of less than 50 shipping cases or 300 primary containers. When the primary container is the shipping case, the number 50 applies.

There are some very common terms used in statistical procedures for food grading and inspection:

Acceptable Quality Level (AQL).   The AQL is expressed in terms of defects per 100 units. Lots having a quality level equal to a specified AQL are accepted approximately 95% of the time when using the sampling plans prescribed for the AQL.

Acceptance Number.   The number in a sampling plan that indicates the maximum number of defects permitted in a sample for considering a lot as meeting a specific requirement.

Rejection Number.   The number in a sampling plan that indicates the minimum number of defects in a sample that will cause a lot to fail a specific requirement.

Defects Classifications.   They are the critical, major, minor, and insignificant defects as explained previously, except the classifications apply to containers.

Operating Characteristic Curve.   A curve that gives the probability of acceptance as a function of a specific lot quality level. It shows the discriminatory power of a sampling plan, that is, how the probability of accepting a lot varies with the quality of the containers offered for inspection.

Another aspect of the regulation is related to the lot acceptance criteria, which are stated as follows:

1.   The acceptability of the lot is determined by relating the number and class of defects enumerated on the worksheet to the acceptance and rejection numbers shown in various tables for the respective sample size and AQL.
2.   Consult the AQLs for the respective class of defects as provided.
3.   Refer to the appropriate sample size and AQL and compare the number of defects found in the sample with the acceptance and rejection numbers in the sampling plan.
4.   Accept the lot after examining the single sample or first sample of a double sampling plan when the numbers of critical, major, and the combination of

critical, major, and minor defects do not exceed the applicable acceptance number for the corresponding defects. Reject the lot when the number of critical, major, and/or combination of the three defects equals to or exceeds the applicable rejection number for the corresponding defects.

Thus 7 CFR 42 provides tables for the following:

1. Sampling plans for normal condition of container inspection.
2. Sampling plans for tightened condition of container inspection.
3. Sampling plans for reduced condition of container inspection.
4. Defects of containers: metal containers, glass containers, rigid and semirigid containers (excluding metal and glass), and flexible containers.
5. Defects of label, marking, or code.

The following discussion has been adapted from 7 CFR 43, "Standards for sampling plans." According to the regulations, certain definitions are as follows. The term "attributes" refers to the measurement of a given factor, noting and recording the presence or absence of some characteristic (attribute) in each of the units in the group under consideration. The "limited quality" is expressed in terms of percent defective or defects per 100 units. Lots inspected under the prescribed standards that have a 10% probability of acceptance are referred to as a lot having a quality level equal to limiting quality. "Consumer's risk" is defined as the risk a consumer takes that a lot will be accepted by a sampling plan even though the lot does not conform to requirements. In the standards prescribed, the risk is nominally set at 10%. "Consumer protection" is defined as the ability of a sampling plan to reject unacceptable supplies. This is measured as the complement of the probability of acceptance for the limited quality lots; and the consumer protection is 90% in these standards.

The regulation provides selected single and double sampling plans for inspection by attributes. They are to serve as a source of plans for developing sound specifications, standards, or sampling and inspection procedures. In the "master table," a sampling plan is selected by first determining the sample size or sizes and AQL to be used. Then the applicable acceptance and rejection numbers are located at the intersection of the sample size(s) row and AQL column. These numbers, together with the sample size or sizes, constitute a sampling plan. Thus 7 CFR 43 provides a number of tables, including: (1) master table of single and double sampling plans and (2) numerous operating characteristics curves.

As mentioned in the preface of this book, periodic government reorganizations will result in changes in those regulations promulgated by the agency or agencies affected. As of June 27, 1977, a recodification with some slight title changes was made in some parts of Title 7 of the Code of Federal Regulations, which is presented in Table 1-15. However, it is emphasized that all the information presented above for Chapter 1 remains essentially the same notwithstanding the changes.

TABLE 1-15. Parts Recodified in Title 7 of the Code of Federal Regulations.
Adapted from 42 FR 42514 (June 27, 1977).

Old Part	Changed to New Part[a]
42	2842
43	2843
51	2851
52	2852
55	2855
56	2856
58	2858
59	2859
70	2870
171	2871

[a] Note the additional prefix "28."

APPENDIX 1-1. Simplified organization chart for the USDA.

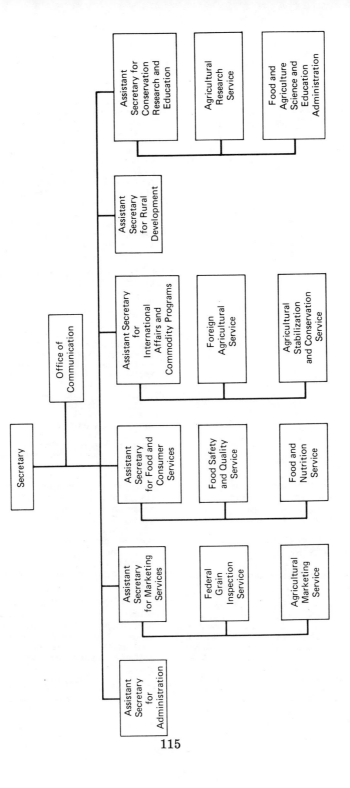

115

APPENDIX 1-2. United States standards for strawberries, reproduced from 7 CFR 51.3115 to 51.3124 (1977).

Subpart—United States Standards for Grades of Strawberries

Source: §§ 51.3115 to 51.3124 appear at 30 F.R. 6711, May 18, 1965, unless otherwise noted.

GRADES

§ 51.3115   U.S. No. 1.

"U.S. No. 1" consists of strawberries of one variety or similar varietal characteristics with the cap (calyx) attached, which are firm, not overripe or. undeveloped, and which are free from mold or decay and free from damage caused by dirt, moisture, foreign matter, disease, insects, or mechanical or other means. Each strawberry has not less than three-fourths of its surface showing a pink or red color.

(a) *Size.* Unless otherwise specified, the minimum diameter of each strawberry is not less than three-fourths inch.

(b) *Tolerances.* In order to allow for variations incident to proper grading and handling the following tolerances, by volume, are provided as specified:

(1) *For defects.* Not more than 10 percent for strawberries in any lot which fail to meet the requirements of this grade, but not more than one-half of this tolerance, or 5 percent, shall be allowed for defects causing serious damage, including therein not more than two-fifths of this latter amount, or 2 percent, for strawberries affected by decay.

(2) *For off-size.* Not more than 5 percent for strawberries in any lot which are below the specified minimum size.

§ 51.3116   U.S. Combination.

"U.S. Combination" consists of a combination of U.S. No. 1 and U.S. No. 2 strawberries, except for size: *Provided,* That at least 80 percent, by volume, of the strawberries meet the requirements of U.S. No. 1 grade.

(a) *Size.* Unless otherwise specified, the minimum diameter of each strawberry is not less than three-fourths inch.

(b) *Tolerances.* In order to allow for variations incident to proper grading and handling the following tolerances, by volume, are provided as specified:

(1) *For defects.* Not more than 10 percent for strawberries in any lot which are seriously damaged, including therein not more than one-fifth of this tolerance, or 2 percent, for strawberries affected by decay. No part of any tolerance shall be allowed to reduce for the lot as a whole, the percentage of U.S. No. 1 strawberries required in the combination, and individual containers (cups or baskets) may have not less than 65 percent U.S. No. 1 strawberries: *Provided,* That the entire lot averages within the required percentage.

(2) *For off-size.* Not more than 5 percent of the strawberries in any lot may be below the specified minimum size.

§ 51.3117   U.S. No. 2.

"U.S. No. 2" consists of strawberries which are free from decay and free from serious damage caused by dirt, disease, insects, mechanical or other means. Each strawberry has not less than one-half of its surface showing a pink or red color.

(a) *Size.* Unless otherwise specified, the minimum diameter of each strawberry is not less than five-eighths inch.

(b) *Tolerances.* In order to allow for variations incident to proper grading and handling the following tolerances, by volume, are provided as specified:

(1) *For defects.* Not more than 10 percent for strawberries in any lot which are seriously damaged, including therein not more than three-tenths of this tolerance, or 3 percent, for strawberries affected by decay.

(2) *For off-size.* Not more than 5 percent for strawberries in any lot which are below the specified minimum size.

UNCLASSIFIED

§ 51.3118   Unclassified.

"Unclassified" consists of strawberries which have not been classified in accordance with any of the foregoing grades. The term "unclassified" is not a grade within the meaning of these standards but is provided as a designation to show that no grade has been applied to the lot.

APPLICATION OF TOLERANCES

§ 51.3119   Application of tolerances.

(a) The contents of individual packages (cups or baskets) in the lot, based on sample inspection, are subject to the following limitations:

(1) For a tolerance of 10 percent or more, individual packages (cups or baskets) in any lot shall have not more than one and one-half times the tolerance specified, except that when the package contains 25 specimens or less, individual packages shall have not more than double the tolerance specified: *Provided,* That the averages for the entire lot are within the tolerance specified for the grade.

(2) For a tolerance of less than 10 percent, individual packages (cups or baskets) in any lot shall have not more than double the tolerance specified, except that at least one defective and one off-size specimen may be permitted in any package: *Provided,* That the averages for the entire lot are within the tolerances specified for the grade.

DEFINITIONS

§ 51.3120   Overripe.

"Overripe" means dead ripe, becoming soft, a condition unfit for shipment and necessitating immediate consumption.

§ 51.3121   Undeveloped.

"Undeveloped" means that the berry has not attained a normal shape and development due to frost injury, lack of pollination, insect injury, or other causes. "Button" berries are the most common type of this condition.

§ 51.3122   Damage.

"Damage" means any defect or any combination of defects, which materially detracts from the appearance, or the edible or shipping quality of the strawberries.

§ 51.3123   Serious damage.

"Serious damage" means any specific defect described in this section; or an equally objectionable variation of any one of these defects, any other defect, or any combination of defects, which seriously detracts from the appearance, or the edible or shipping quality of the strawberries. The following specific defects shall be considered as serious damage:

(a) Soft berries;

(b) Badly deformed berries;

(c) Badly bruised berries;

(d) Decayed or leaky berries;

(e) Berries badly caked with dirt; and,

(f) Berries with less than one-half of surface showing pink or red color.

§ 51.3124   Diameter.

"Diameter" means the greatest dimension measured at right angles to a straight line running from the stem to the apex.

APPENDIX 1-3. Approved identifications for the grading, inspection, and so on of fresh fruits and vegetables, reproduced from 7 CFR 51.49 (1977).

Shields with plain background.

FIGURE 2.

(b) *Inspection legends.* The approved continuous inspection legends may be used on containers, labels or otherwise indicated on the package when: (1) The product has been packed under continuous inspection provided by the Inspection Service, (2) the plant in which the product is packed is maintained under good commercial sanitary practices, and (3) the product meets the requirements of such quality, grade, or specification as may be approved by the Administrator. The continuous inspection legends approved for use shall be similar in form and design to the examples in figures 3 and 4.

(c) *Combined grade and inspection legends.* The grade marks set forth in paragraph (a) of this section and illustrated by figures 1 and 2 of this section

§ 51.49 Approved identifications.

(a) *Grade marks.* The approved shield mark with the appropriate U.S. grade designation may be used on containers, labels or otherwise indicated on the package when: (1) The product has been packed under continuous inspection as provided by the Inspection Service, (2) the plant in which the product is packed is maintained under good commercial sanitary practices, and (3) the product has been certified by an inspector as meeting the requirements of U.S. Grade A, U.S. Grade No. 1, or a higher U.S. grade as shown within the shield. The shields with approved grade designation for use shall be similar in form and design to the examples in figures 1 and 2 of this section.

← BLUE
← WHITE
← RED

Shield using red, white and blue background.

FIGURE 1.

PACKED UNDER CONTINUOUS INSPECTION OF THE U. S. DEPT. OF AGRICULTURE

FIGURE 3.

PACKED BY

- -

- -

UNDER CONTINUOUS
FEDERAL-STATE
INSPECTION

FIGURE 4.

and the inspection legends set forth in
paragraph (b) of this section and illustrated by figures 3 and 4 of paragraph
(b) of this section may be combined into
a consolidated grade and inspection
legend for use on products which meet
the requirements of both of these paragraphs. See figure 5.

PACKED BY

- -

- -

UNDER CONTINUOUS
FEDERAL-STATE
INSPECTION

FIGURE 5.

(d) *Packer identification.* The packer's
name and address or assigned code number or other mark identifying the packer
as may be approved by the Administrator, shall appear on any container bearing grade marks or inspection legends
approved under paragraph (a), (b), or

(c) of this section, as illustrated by the
example in figure 6.

PACKER NO. 01

PACKED UNDER CONTINUOUS
FEDERAL - STATE INSPECTION

FIGURE 6.

(e) *Other identification marks.* Products may be inspected on a lot inspection
basis as provided in this part and identified by an official inspection mark similar in form and design to figure 7 of this

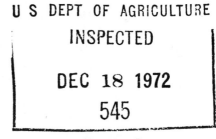

FIGURE 7

paragraph. The use of this mark or other
comparable identification marks may be
required by the Administrator whenever
he determines that such identification is
necessary in order to maintain the identity of lots which have been inspected
and certified.

[38 FR 7448, Mar. 22, 1973]

APPENDIX 1-4.   United States standards for grades of grapefruit juice and orange
juice (or orange juice and grape fruit juice), reproduced from
7 CFR 52.1281 to 1293 (1977).

Subpart—U.S. Standards for Grades of Grapefruit Juice and Orange Juice (or Orange Juice and Grapefruit Juice) [1]

SOURCE: §§ 52.1281 to 52.1293 appear at 37 FR 21155, Oct. 6, 1972, unless otherwise noted.

PRODUCT DESCRIPTION, TYPES, STYLES, AND GRADES

§ 52.1281   Product description.

(a) Grapefruit Juice and Orange Juice (or Orange Juice and Grapefruit Juice), hereinafter referred to as Grapefruit Juice and Orange Juice, is prepared from a combination of unfermented juices obtained from mature fresh grapefruit (Citrus paradisi) and mature sweet oranges (Citrus sinensis). The juice of oranges from the mandarin group (Citrus reticulata), however, may be added in such quantities that not more than 10 percent, by volume, of the orange juice ingredient consists of juice from citrus reticulata. It is recommended that the minor juice ingredient (either orange or grapefruit) provide not less than 25 percent, by weight, of the total soluble fruit solids present in the finished product.

(b) The fruit is prepared and the juice extracted and processed in a manner to assure a clean and wholesome product.

(c) Soluble solids, insoluble solids, Brix-acid ratios, and flavor may be adjusted by suitable manufacturing procedures.

---

[1] Compliance with the provisions of these standards shall not excuse failure to comply with the provisions of the Federal Food, Drug, and Cosmetic Act or with applicable State laws and regulations.

APPENDIX 1-4. (continued).

(d) The product is processed by appropriate physical means to assure its preservation through normal marketing channels. Such means include, but are not limited to:

(1) *Canning.* Processing with heat so as to assure the preservation of the juice in hermetically sealed containers.

(2) *Refrigerating.* Reducing the temperature of the product so as to extend its market life. The juice may or may not have been subjected to heat prior to refrigerating. It may or may not be packed in hermetically sealed containers.

§ 52.1232 Types.

The product may be identified as one of the following types:

(a) *Single strength type.* Composed of single strength grapefruit juice and orange juice, with or without added grapefruit juice concentrate and/or orange juice concentrate.

(b) *Reconstituted type.* Composed of grapefruit juice concentrate and orange juice concentrate and water, with or without added single strength grapefruit juice and/or single strength orange juice.

§ 52.1283 Styles.

(a) Unsweetened.
(b) Sweetened.

§ 52.1284 Grades.

(a) U.S. Grade A (or U.S. Fancy) is the quality of grapefruit juice and orange juice that:

(1) Shows no coagulation;
(2) Has a good color;
(3) Is practically free from defects;
(4) Has a good flavor; and
(5) Scores not less than 90 points when scored in accordance with the scoring system outlined in this subpart.

(b) U.S. Grade B (or U.S. Choice) is the quality of grapefruit juice and orange juice that:

(1) May show only a slight coagulation;
(2) Has a reasonably good color;
(3) Is reasonably free from defects;
(4) Has a reasonably good flavor; and
(5) Scores not less than 80 points when scored in accordance with the scoring system outlined in this subpart.

(c) Substandard is the quality of grapefruit juice and orange juice that fails to meet the requirements of U.S. Grade B.

FILL OF CONTAINER

§ 52.1285 Recommended fill of container.

The recommended fill of container is not incorporated in the grades of the finished product since fill of container, as such, is not a factor of quality for the purposes of these grades. It is recommended that the container be as full of grapefruit juice and orange juice as practicable and that the product occupy not less than 90 percent of the volume capacity of the container.

FACTORS OF QUALITY

§ 52.1286 Ascertaining the grade.

(a) *General.* Consideration is given to the degree of coagulation, the ratings for the factors which are scored, and the limiting rules which may apply.

(b) *Factors which are scored.* The relative importance of each factor which is scored is expressed numerically on the scale of 100. The maximum number of points that may be given such factors are:

Factors	Points
Color	20
Defects	40
Flavor	40
Total score	100

§ 52.1287 Ascertaining the rating for the factors which are scored.

The essential variations, within each factor which is scored, are so described that the value may be ascertained for each factor and expressed numerically. The numerical range within each factor which is scored is inclusive (for example, "18 to 20 points" means 18, 19, or 20 points).

§ 52.1288 Color.

(a) *(A) classification.* Grapefruit juice and orange juice that has a good color may be given a score of 18 to 20 points. "Good color" means that the juice mixture has a yellow-orange color that is bright and typical of the freshly extracted juice of oranges and either white fleshed grapefruit or red or pink fleshed grapefruit, and is free from browning due to scorching, oxidation, caramelization, or other causes.

(b) *(B) classification.* Grapefruit juice and orange juice that has a reasonably good color may be given a score of 16 or 17 points. Juice that falls into this classification shall not be graded above

Continued

APPENDIX 1-4. (continued).

U.S. Grade B, regardless of the total score for the product (this is a limiting rule). "Reasonably good color" means that the juice has a fairly typical color that may range from light yellow to light amber, may be dull or show evidence of slight browning, but is not off color.

(c) *(SStd) classification.* Grapefruit juice and orange juice that fails the color requirements of U.S. Grade B may be given a score of 0 to 15 points and shall not be graded above Substandard, regardless of the total score for the product (this is a limiting rule).

§ 52.1289 Defects.

(a) *General.* The factor of defects concerns the degree of freedom from small seeds and seed portions; from discolored specks, harmless extraneous material, and other similar defects; from juice sacs and particles of membrane, core, and peel in excess of that normally present in grapefruit juice and orange juice; and from free and suspended pulp.

(b) *(A) classification.* (1) Grapefruit juice and orange juice that is practically free from defects may be given a score of 36 to 40 points.

(2) "Practically free from defects" means that the juice may not contain more than 12 percent free and suspended pulp as determined by the method outlined in this subpart, and that any other defects present may no more than slightly detract from the appearance or drinking quality of the juice.

(c) *(B) classification.* (1) Grapefruit juice and orange juice that is reasonably free from defects may be given a score of 32 to 35 points. Such product shall not be graded above U.S. Grade B, regardless of the total score for the product (this is a limiting rule).

(2) "Reasonably free from defects" means that the juice may not contain more than 18 percent free and suspended pulp as determined by the method outlined in this subpart, and that any other defects present may no more than materially detract from the appearance or drinking quality of the juice.

(d) *(SStd) classification.* Grapefruit juice and orange juice that fails to meet the requirements of U.S. Grade B may be given a score of 0 to 31 points and shall not be graded above Substandard, regardless of the total score for the product (this is a limiting rule).

§ 52.1290 Flavor.

(a) *(A) classification.* (1) Grapefruit juice and orange juice that has a good flavor may be given a score of 36 to 40 points.

(2) "Good flavor" means the following with respect to the method of preservation used:

(i) *Refrigerated juice* or juice not subjected to high temperatures prior to refrigerating: "Good flavor" means a flavor that is fine, distinct, and substantially typical of freshly extracted grapefruit juice and orange juice which is free from off flavors and off odors of any kind;

(ii) *Canned juice* or juice that has been subjected to high temperatures: "Good flavor" means a fine, distinct grapefruit juice and orange juice flavor which is free from off flavors and off odors of any kind; and

(iii) The flavor of all juices may be affected only slightly by the process, the packaging, or storage conditions and the juice complies with the analytical limits listed in Table I.

TABLE 1—ANALYTICAL REQUIREMENTS—U.S. GRADE A

Type style	Single strength		Reconstituted	
	Unsweetened	Sweetened	Unsweetened	Sweetened
Brix (Degrees) Minimum	10.0°	11.5°	11.0°	12.5°
Brix-Acid Ratio—				
If Brix is less than 11.5°:				
Minimum	9.5:1		9.5:1	
Maximum	18.0:1		18.0:1	
If Brix is 11.5° or more:				
Minimum	8.5:1	10.5:1	9.5:1	10.5:1
Maximum	18.0:1	18.0:1	18.0:1	18.0:1
Oil—Maximum percent by volume	0.035	0.035	0.005	0.035

(b) *(B) classification.* (1) Grapefruit juice and orange juice that has a reasonably good flavor may be given a score of 32 to 35 points. Grapefruit juice and orange juice of this flavor shall not be graded above U.S. Grade B, regardless of the total score for the product (this is a limiting rule).

(2) "Reasonably good flavor" means a flavor less desirable than "good flavor" because of excess bitterness, terpenic, processing, storage, or container flavors but is not seriously objectionable and is free from off flavors and off odors of any kind. Such juice complies with the analytical limits listed in Table II.

TABLE II

ANALYTICAL REQUIREMENTS—U.S. GRADE B

Type Style	Single strength		Reconstituted	
	Unsweetened	Sweetened	Unsweetened	Sweetened
Brix (Degrees) Minimum	9.5°	11.5°	11.0°	12.5°
Brix-Acid Ratio:				
Minimum	8.0:1	10.5:1	9.0:1	10.5:1
Maximum	None	None	None	None
Oil—Maximum percent by volume	0.055	0.055	0.055	0.055

(c) (SStd) classification. Grapefruit juice and orange juice that fails the requirements of the U.S. Grade B classification may be given a score of 0 to 31 points and shall not be graded above Substandard, regardless of the total score for the product (this is a limiting rule).

EXPLANATIONS AND METHODS OF ANALYSIS

§ 52.1291 Definitions of terms and methods of analysis.

(a) Brix. "Brix" means the degrees Brix of the juice when tested with a Brix hydrometer calibrated at 20° C. (68° F.) and to which any applicable temperature correction has been made. The degrees Brix may be determined by any other method which gives equivalent results.

(b) Acid. "Acid" means the grams of total acidity, calculated as anhydrous citric acid, per 100 grams of juice. Total acidity is determined by titration with standard sodium hydroxide solution, using phenolphthalein as indicator.

(c) Brix-Acid ratio. "Brix-Acid ratio" is the ratio of the degrees Brix of the grapefruit juice and orange juice to the grams of anhydrous citric acid per 100 grams of the juice.

(d) Free and suspended pulp. "Free and suspended pulp" means the percentage of pulp determined by the following method: Graduated centrifuge tubes with a capacity of 50 ml. are filled with juice and placed in a suitable centrifuge. The speed is adjusted, according to diameter, as indicated in Table No. III, and the juice is centrifuged for exactly 10 minutes. As used in this subparagraph, "diameter" means the overall distance between the bottoms of opposing centrifuge tubes in operating position. After centrifuging, the milliliter reading at the top of the layer of pulp

in the tube is multiplied by 2 to give the percentage of pulp.

TABLE III

Diameter (inches)	Approximate revolutions per minute
10	1,609
10½	1,570
11	1,534
11½	1,500
12	1,468
12½	1,438
13	1,410
13½	1,384
14	1,359
14½	1,336
15	1,313
15½	1,292
16	1,271
16½	1,252
17	1,234
17½	1,216
18	1,199
18½	1,182
19	1,167
19½	1,152
20	1,137

(e) Recoverable oil. "Recoverable oil" means the percent of oil by volume, determined by the Bromate titration method as described in the current issue of the Official Methods of Analysis of the Association of Analytical Chemists.[3]

LOT COMPLIANCE

§ 52.1292 Ascertaining the grade of a lot.

The grade of a lot of grapefruit juice and orange juice covered by these standards is determined by the procedures set forth in the Regulations Governing Inspection and Certification of Processed Fruits and Vegetables, Processed Prod-

[3] Copies may be obtained from this Association at Box 540, Benjamin Franklin Station, Washington, D.C. 20044.

Continued

APPENDIX 1-4. (continued).

ucts Thereof, and Certain Other Processed Food Products (§§ 52.1 through 52.87).

SCORE SHEET

§ 52.1293 Score sheet.

Size and kind of container_____ ---
Container mark ⎱ Cans_____ ---
       or   ⎰
Identification ⎰ Cases_____ ---
Label (including ingredient statement, if any)____ ---
Liquid measure (fluid ounces)_____ ---
Vacuum (inches)_____ ---
Style_____ ---
Brix (degrees)_____ ---
Acid (grams/100 gms: calculated as anhydrous citric ---
  acid)_____
Brix-acid ratio (:1)_____ ---
Pulp (free and suspended) (%)_____ ---
Recoverable oil (% by Volume)_____ ---
Degree of coagulation (None), (Slight), or (Serious)__ ---

Scoring factors		Score points		
Color_____	20	(A)	18–20	
		(B)[1]	16–17	
		(SStd)[1]	0–15	
Defects_____	40	(A)	36–40	
		(B)[1]	32–35	
		(SStd)[1]	0–31	
Flavor_____	40	(A)	36–40	
		(B)[1]	32–35	
		(SStd)[1]	0–31	
Total score_____	100	_____		---
Grade_____				---

[1] Indicates limiting rule.

APPENDIX 1-5. Approved identifications for the grading, inspection, and so on of processed fruits and vegetables and related products, reproduced from 7 CFR 52.53 (1977).

FIGURE 1.

MISCELLANEOUS

§ 52.53   Approved identification.

(a) *General.* Use of the approved identification marks described and illustrated in figures 1 through 10 of this section is restricted to processed products that:

(1) Are clean, safe, and wholesome;

(2) Have been produced in an approved plant;

(3) Are truthfully and accurately labeled;

(4) Meet the quality requirements for U.S. Grade C or better;

(5) Meet applicable fill weight and/or drained weight, condition of container criteria, Brix or other characteristics of a commodity related to market value; and

(6) Have been certified, or have been inspected and are eligible for certification, by an inspector; and, in addition, meet the specific requirements stated in paragraphs (b), (c), and (d) of this section.

(b) *Inspection (Continuous) grade and inspection marks.* The official marks approved for use by plants operating under USDA continuous inspection service contracts shall be similar in form and design to the examples in figure 1 through 10 of this section: *Provided,* That the official marks illustrated by figures 8 and 9 are limited to products packed by plants operating under an approved Quality Assurance type of inspection contract: *And provided further,* That the inspection marks illustrated in figures 1 through 4 may only be used on products packed by plants operating under USDA continuous inspection.

FIGURE 2.

Statement enclosed within a shield.

FIGURE 3.

PACKED UNDER
CONTINUOUS
INSPECTION
OF THE
U. S. DEPT. OF
AGRICULTURE

Statement without the use of the shield.

FIGURE 4.

(c) *In-plant inspection (other than
continuous) grade and inspection marks.*
The official marks approved for use by
plants operating under USDA inspection
service contracts (other than continuous) requiring a resident inspector shall
be limited to those similar in form and
design to the examples in figures 5
through 10 of this section; *Provided,*
That the official marks illustrated by figures 8 and 9 are limited to products
packed by plants operating under an approved Quality Assurance type of an inspection contract.

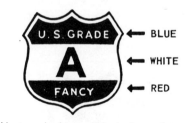

Shield using red, white, and blue background
or other colors appropriate for label.

FIGURE 5.

Shield with plain
background.

FIGURE 6.

Shield with plain
background.

FIGURE 7.

APPENDIX 1-5. (continued).

FIGURE 8

PACKED UNDER

QUALITY ASSURANCE

PROGRAM

of the

U.S. DEPT. OF AGRICULTURE

Statement without the use of the shield.

FIGURE 9

(d) *Approved plant-lot inspection grade marks.* Processed products that are produced in an approved plant and inspected and certified by an inspector on a lot basis may be labeled with an official grade mark, not in a shield design, such as is illustrated by marks (1) and (2) of figure 10. Failure to have all lots, bearing such official marks, inspected and certified shall be cause for the debarment of services and such other actions as provided for in the Agricultural Marketing Act of 1946.

(I) U. S. GRADE A

(2) U. S. CHOICE

Grade marks not in shield design.

FIGURE 10.

(e) *Sampling marks.* Processed products which have been packed under inspection as provided for in this section and products sampled for inspection on a lot basis as provided in this part may, at the option of the Department, be identified by an authorized representative of the Department by stamping the shipping cases and inspection certificate(s) covering such lot(s) with an officially drawn sampling mark similar in form and design to the example in figure 11 of this section.

128

Appendix 1-5

FIGURE 11.

(f) *Removal of labels bearing approved grade or inspection marks (figures 1 through 8)*. (1) At the time a lot of processed products, bearing approved grade or inspection marks (figures 1 through 8) is found to be mislabeled, the processor shall separate and retain such lot for relabeling. Removal and replacement of labels shall be done, under the supervision of a USDA inspector within ten (10) consecutive calendar days or within such period of time as may be mutually agreed by the processor and USDA.

(2) The processor shall be held accountable to the Department for all mislabeled products until the products have been properly labeled.

(3) Clearance for the release of the relabeled product shall be obtained, by the processor, from the inspector.

(g) *Licensing and identification of certain official devices*. The Administrator may issue licenses permitting the manufacture, identification, and sale of any official device designated as a USDA color standard, defect guide or other similar aid under such terms and conditions as may be specified by the Administrator. Licenses shall be available to all persons meeting conditions prescribed by the Administrator, shall be nonexclusive, and shall be recoverable for cause. No person shall manufacture, identify, distribute or sell any such official device except at the direction of or under license from the Administrator. Such official devices may be marked, tagged or otherwise designated with the prefix "USDA" together with other identifying words or symbols, as prescribed by the license.

(h) *Prohibited uses of approved identification*. Except as specified in this section, no label or advertising material used upon, or in conjunction with a processed product, as defined by these Regulations, shall bear a brand name, trademark, product name, company name, or any other descriptive material that incorporates, resembles, simulates, or alludes to, any official U.S. Department of Agriculture certificate of quality or loading, grade mark, grade statement (except honey and maple syrup which may bear such grade mark or statement), continuous inspection mark, continuous inspection statement, sampling mark or sampling statement, or combinations of one or more thereof.

[38 FR 25169, Sept. 12, 1973, as amended at 40 FR 48934, Oct. 20, 1975]

APPENDIX 1-6. Standards, grades, and specifications for veal and calf carcasses, reproduced from 7 CFR 53.107 to 53.112 (1977).

VEAL AND CALF CARCASSES

SOURCE: §§ 53.107 to 53.112 appear at 36 F.R. 22279, Nov. 24, 1971, unless otherwise noted.

§ 53.107 Scope.

These standards for grades of veal and calf are applicable to the grading of carcasses, sides, hindsaddles, hindquarters, foresaddles, and forequarters, and to the following primal wholesale cuts—legs, loins, racks, and shoulders. However, throughout these standards wherever the words "carcass" or "carcasses" are used these are intended to also mean such parts of carcasses and primal wholesale cuts.

§ 53.108 Differentiation between veal, calf, and beef carcasses.

Differentiation between veal, calf, and beef carcasses is made primarily on the basis of the color of the lean, although such factors as texture of the lean; character of the fat; color, shape, size, and ossification of the bones and cartilages; and the general contour of the carcass are also given consideration. Typical veal carcasses have a grayish pink color of lean that is very smooth and velvety in texture and they also have a slightly soft, pliable character of fat and marrow, and very red rib bones. By contrast, typical calf carcasses have a grayish red color of lean, a flakier type of fat, and somewhat wider rib bones with less pronounced evidences of red color. Calf carcasses with maximum maturity for their class have lean flesh that is usually not more than moderately red in color, their rib bones usually have a small amount of red and only a slight tendency toward flatness, and such carcasses are not noticeably "spready" or barrelly" in contour. Such carcasses, when split, have cartilages on the ends of the chine bones that are entirely cartilaginous, there is cartilage in evidence on all vertebrae of the spinal column, and the sacral vertebrae show distinct separation. Carcasses with evidences of more advanced maturity than described in this paragraph are classified as beef. Carcasses not classified as beef but whose color of lean is not comparable with their other evidences of maturity shall be classed as veal or calf in accordance with the following:

(a) Carcasses whose indications of maturity other than color of lean are within the veal class but whose color of lean is darker than dark grayish pink shall be classed as calf.

(b) Carcasses whose evidences of maturity other than color of lean are within the range included in the calf class shall be classed as veal provided they have a correspondingly lighter color of lean within the darker one-half of the range of color included in the veal class. For example, a carcass whose evidences of maturity other than color of lean are midway within the range of the calf class shall be classed as veal if its color of lean is not darker than midway within the darker one-half of the range of color included in the veal class.

(c) Carcasses with color of lean within the lighter one-half of the veal class shall be classed as veal provided their other evidences of maturity do not exceed that associated with the juncture of the calf and beef classes.

§ 53.109 Classes of veal and calf carcasses.

Class determination is based on the apparent sex condition of the animal at time of slaughter. Hence, there are three classes of veal and calf carcasses—steers, heifers, and bulls. While recognition may sometimes be given to these different classes on the market, especially calf carcasses from bulls that are approaching beef in maturity, the characteristics of such carcasses are not sufficiently different from those of steers and heifers to warrant the development of separate standards for them. Therefore, the grade standards which follow are equally applicable to all classes of veal and calf carcasses.

§ 53.110   Application of standards.

(a) Veal and calf carcasses are graded on a composite evaluation of two general grade factors—conformation and quality. These factors are concerned with the proportions of lean, fat, and bone in the carcass and the quality of the lean.

(b) Conformation is the manner of formation of the carcass. The conformation descriptions included in each of the grade specifications refer to the thickness and fullness of the carcass and its various parts. Conformation is evaluated by averaging the conformation of the various parts of the carcass, considering not only the proportion that each part is of the carcass but also the general value of each part as compared with other parts. Superior conformation implies a high proportion of meat to bone and a high proportion of the weight of the carcass in the more valuable parts. It is reflected in carcasses which are thickly fleshed and full and thick in relation to their length and which have a plump, well-rounded appearance. Inferior conformation implies a low proportion of meat to bone and a low proportion of the weight of the carcass in the more valuable parts. It is reflected in carcasses which are very thinly fleshed, and very narrow in relation to their length, and which have a very angular, thin, sunken appearance.

(c) Quality of lean—in all veal carcasses, all unribbed calf carcasses, and in ribbed calf carcasses in which their degree of marbling is not a consideration—usually can be evaluated with a high degree of accuracy by giving equal consideration to the following factors, as available: (1) The amount of feathering (fat intermingled within the lean between the ribs) and (2) the quantity of fat streakings within and upon the inside flank muscles. (In making these evaluations, the amounts of feathering and flank fat streakings are considered

in relation to color (veal) and maturity (calf).) In addition, however, consideration also may be given to other factors if, in the opinion of the grader, this will result in a more accurate quality assessment. Examples of such other factors include firmness of the lean, the distribution of feathering, the amount of fat covering over the diaphragm or "skirt", and the amount and character of the external and kidney and pelvic fat. In making these evaluations, feathering and flank fat streakings are categorized in descending order of quantity as follows: extremely abundant, very abundant, abundant, moderately abundant, slightly abundant, moderate, modest, small, slight, traces, practically none, and none. Figure 1 depicts the quality grade equivalent of various degrees of feathering and flank fat streakings in relation to color of lean (veal) or maturity (calf). From this figure it can be seen, for example, that the degrees of feathering or fat streakings associated with minimum Choice quality for veal increase from minimum traces for carcasses having the lightest color of lean to maximum traces for carcasses with a dark grayish pink color of lean.

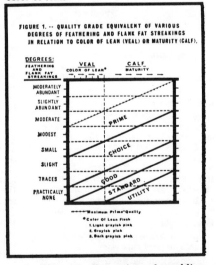

FIGURE 1. -- QUALITY GRADE EQUIVALENT OF VARIOUS DEGREES OF FEATHERING AND FLANK FAT STREAKINGS IN RELATION TO COLOR OF LEAN (VEAL) OR MATURITY (CALF).

(d) When grading cuts and marbling is not a requirement and when neither feathering nor flank fat streakings are available, quality is based on the firmness of the lean. The requirements relating to firmness of the lean are described

APPENDIX 1-6. (continued).

in the specifications for each grade and are based on the following degrees in descending order of firmness; extremely firm, very firm, firm, moderately firm, slightly firm, slightly soft, moderately soft, soft, very soft, and extremely soft. However, no credit is given to additional firmness of lean beyond "maximum slightly firm" in veal or beyond "maximum moderately firm" in calf.

(e) When grading ribbed calf carcasses or portions of such carcasses in which their degree of marbling is a consideration, the quality evaluation of the lean is based entirely on the characteristics of the lean as exposed in a cut surface. The official standards for grades of beef recognize nine different degrees of marbling. In descending order of amount these are as follows: abundant, moderately abundant, slightly abundant, moderate, modest, small, slight, traces, and practically devoid. Illustrations of the lower limits of eight of these nine degrees are available from the Department of Agriculture. These degrees of marbling and their illustrations also are used to describe and evaluate marbling in calf carcasses. Marbling requirements are included in each of the Prime, Choice, and Good grade specifications.

(f) To facilitate the application of the standards, no credit is given to degrees of feathering, flank fat streakings, or marbling beyond those associated with the quality grade equivalent of "Maximum Prime." "Maximum Prime" quality is represented by a development of each of these three factors which is two degrees greater than that specified as minimum for Prime.

(g) The quality indicating requirements referenced in the standards for each grade are based on their development in properly chilled carcasses and, when these relate to a cut surface of the lean, they are based on a cross section of the ribeye muscle between the 12th and 13th ribs. For legs and shoulders, these qualities shall be consistent with their normal development in relation to those specified for the ribeye muscle.

(h) The final grade of a carcass is based on a composite evaluation of its conformation and quality. Conformation and quality often are not developed to the same degree in a carcass and it is obvious that each grade will include various combinations of development of these two characteristics. Examples of how conformation and quality are com-

bined into the final quality grade are included in each of the grade descriptions. However, the principles governing the compensations of variations in development of quality and conformation are as follows: In each of the grades a superior development of quality is permitted to compensate, without limit, for a deficient development of conformation. In this instance the rate of compensation in all grades is on an equal basis—a given degree of superior quality compensates for the same degree of deficient conformation. The reverse type of compensation— a superior development of conformation for an inferior development of quality— is not permitted in the Prime and Choice grades. In all other grades this type of compensation is permitted but only to the extent of one-third of a grade of deficient quality. The rate of this type of compensation is also on an equal basis—a given degree of superior conformation compensates for the same degree of deficient quality.

(i) The colors of lean referenced in the standards reflect only the colors as present in normally developed veal and calf carcasses. They are not intended to apply to colors of lean associated with so-called "dark cutting" veal or calf. This condition does not have the same significance in grading as do the darker shades of pink and red associated with advancing maturity. The dark color of the lean associated with "dark cutting" veal or calf is present in varying degrees from that which is barely evident to so-called "black cutters" in which the lean is actually nearly black in color and usually has a "gummy" texture. Dependent upon the degree to which this characteristic is developed, the final grade of carcasses which otherwise would qualify for the Prime, Choice, or Good grades may be reduced as much as one full grade. In veal or calf otherwise eligible for the Standard grade, the final grade may be reduced as much as one-half grade. In the Utility grade this condition is not considered.

(j) Carcasses qualifying for any particular grade may vary with respect to their relative development of the various grade factors and there will be carcasses which qualify for a particular grade, some of the characteristics of which may be typical of another grade. Because it is impractical to describe the nearly limitless number of such recognizable combinations of characteristics, the standards for each grade describe only a veal or calf carcass which has a relatively similar development of conformation and quality and which also represents the lower limit of each grade.

§ 53.111   Specifications for official U.S. standards for grades of veal carcasses.

(a) *Prime.* (1) Veal carcasses with minimum Prime grade conformation tend to be moderately wide and thick in relation to their length. They are slightly thick-fleshed and have a slightly plump appearance. Legs are slightly thick and bulging. Loins and backs tend to be moderately full and plump. Shoulders and breasts tend to be moderately thick.

(2) Figure 1 in § 53.110 depicts the degree of feathering and flank fat streakings associated with minimum Prime quality for different colors of lean. The lean flesh is slightly firm, regardless of its color.

(3) A development of quality superior to that specified as minimum for the Prime grade may compensate, without limit, for a development of conformation inferior to that specified as minimum for Prime at an equal rate as indicated in the following example. A carcass which has midpoint Prime quality may have conformation equal to the midpoint of the Choice grade and remain eligible for Prime. However, regardless of the extent to which the conformation of a carcass exceeds the minimum of the Prime grade, a carcass must have minimum Prime quality to be eligible for Prime.

(b) *Choice.* (1) Veal carcasses with minimum Choice grade conformation tend to be slightly wide and thick in relation to their length. They tend to be slightly thin-fleshed and have little or no evidence of plumpness. Loins, backs, and legs are slightly thin and nearly flat. Shoulders and breasts tend to be slightly thin.

(2) Figure 1 in § 53.110 depicts the degree of feathering and flank fat streakings associated with minimum Choice quality for different colors of lean. The lean flesh is slightly soft regardless of its color.

(3) A development of quality superior to that specified as minimum for the Choice grade may compensate, without limit, for a development of conformation inferior to that specified as minimum for Choice at an equal rate as indicated in the following example: A carcass which

has midpoint Choice quality may have conformation equal to the midpoint of the Good grade and remain eligible for Choice. However, regardless of the extent to which the conformation of a carcass exceeds the minimum of the Choice grade, a carcass must have minimum Choice quality to be eligible for Choice.

(c) *Good.* (1) Veal carcasses with minimum Good grade conformation are rangy, angular, and narrow in relation to their length. They are thinly fleshed. Legs are thin and tapering and slightly concave. Loins and back are depressed. Shoulders and breasts are thin.

(2) Figure 1 in § 53.110 depicts the degree of feathering and flank fat streakings associated with minimum Good quality for different colors of lean. The lean flesh is moderately soft regardless of its color.

(3) A development of quality superior to that specified as minimum for the Good grade may compensate, without limit, for a development of conformation inferior to that specified as minimum for Good at an equal rate as indicated in the following example: A carcass which has midpoint Good grade quality may have conformation equivalent to the midpoint of the Standard grade and remain eligible for Good. Also, a carcass which has conformation at least one-third grade superior to that specified as minimum for the Good grade may qualify for Good with a development of quality equivalent to the lower limit of the upper third of the Standard grade. Compensation of superior conformation for inferior quality is limited to one-third grade of deficient quality.

(d) *Standard.* (1) Veal carcasses with minimum Standard grade conformation are very rangy and angular and very narrow in relation to their length. They are very thinly fleshed. Legs are very thin and moderately concave. Loins and backs are very depressed. Shoulders and breasts are very thin.

(2) Figure 1 in § 53.110 depicts the degree of feathering and flank fat streakings associated with minimum Standard quality for different colors of lean. The lean flesh is soft regardless of its color.

(3) A development of quality superior to that specified as minimum for the Standard grade may compensate, without limit, for a development of conformation inferior to that specified as minimum for Standard at an equal rate as indicated in the following example: A carcass which has midpoint Standard quality

APPENDIX 1-6. (continued).

may have conformation equal to the mid-point of the Utility grade and remain eligibility for Standard. Also, a carcass which has conformation at least one-third grade superior to that specified as minimum for the Standard grade may qualify for Standard with a development of quality equal to the minimum of the upper third of the Utility grade. Compensation of superior conformation for inferior quality is limited to one-third grade of deficient quality.

(e) *Utility.* The Utility grade includes those veal carcasses whose characteristics are inferior to those specified as minimum for the Standard grade.

§ 53.112 Specifications for official United States standards for grades of calf carcasses.

(a) *Prime.* (1) Calf carcasses with minimum Prime grade conformation tend to be moderately wide and thick in relation to their length. They are moderately thick-fleshed and have a moderately plump appearance. Legs tend to be moderately thick and bulging. Loins and backs tend to be moderately full and plump. Shoulders and breasts tend to be moderately thick.

(2) Figure 1 in § 53.110 depicts the degree of feathering and flank fat streakings associated with minimum Prime quality. The degree of marbling required for minimum Prime quality increases from minimum practically devoid for the very youngest carcasses classified as calf to a maximum moderate amount for carcasses with maturity at the juncture of the calf and beef classes. The lean flesh is moderately firm regardless of maturity.

(3) A development of quality superior to that specified as minimum for the Prime grade may compensate, without limit, for a development of conformation inferior to that specified as minimum for Prime at an equal rate as indicated in the following example: A carcass which has midpoint Prime quality may have conformation equal to the midpoint of the Choice grade and remain eligible for Prime. However, regardless of the extent to which the conformation of a carcass exceeds the minimum of the Prime grade, a carcass must have minimum Prime quality to be eligible for Prime.

(b) *Choice.* (1) Calf carcasses with minimum Choice grade conformation tend to be slightly wide and thick in relation to their length. They tend to be slightly thick-fleshed and have a slightly plump appearance. Legs are slightly thick but have little evidence of plumpness. Loins and backs are very slightly full and plump. Shoulders and breasts are slightly thick.

(2) Figure 1 in § 53.110 depicts the degree of feathering and flank fat streakings associated with minimum Choice quality. The degree of marbling required for minimum Choice quality increases from minimum practically devoid for carcasses at midpoint calf maturity to a maximum slight amount for carcasses with maturity at the juncture of the calf and beef classes. Marbling is not required for Choice quality in carcasses which are less than midpoint calf in maturity. The lean flesh is slightly firm regardless of maturity.

(3) A development of quality superior to that specified as minimum for the Choice grade may compensate, without limit, for a development of conformation inferior to that specified as minimum for Choice at an equal rate as indicated in the following example: A carcass which has midpoint Choice quality may have conformation equal to the midpoint of the Good grade and remain eligible for Choice. However, regardless of the extent to which the conformation of a carcass exceeds the minimum of the Choice grade, a carcass must have minimum Choice quality to be eligible for Choice.

(c) *Good.* (1) Calf carcasses with minimum Good grade conformation tend to be rangy, angular, and narrow in relation to their length. They tend to be thinly fleshed. Legs are thin and tapering and very slightly concave. Loins and backs are slightly shallow and depressed. Shoulders and breasts are thin.

(2) Figure 1 in § 53.110 depicts the degree of feathering and flank fat streakings associated with minimum Good quality. The minimum degree of marbling required for Good quality decreases from typical traces for carcasses with maturity at the juncture of the calf and beef classes to minimum practically devoid for carcasses midway in maturity within the more mature half of the range of maturity included in the calf class. In less mature carcasses, marbling is not required for Good quality. The lean flesh is moderately soft regardless of maturity.

(3) A development of quality superior to that specified as minimum for the Good grade may compensate, without limit, for a development of conformation inferior to that specified as minimum for Good at an equal rate as indicated in the following example: A carcass which has

APPENDIX 1-6. (continued).

midpoint Good grade quality may have conformation equivalent to the midpoint of the Standard grade and remain eligible for Good. Also, a carcass which has conformation at least one-third grade superior to that specified as minimum for the Good grade may quality for Good with a development of quality equivalent to the lower limit of the upper third of the Standard grade. Compensation of superior conformation for inferior quality is limited to one-third grade of deficient quality.

(d) *Standard.* (1) Calf carcasses with minimum Standard grade conformation are rangy, angular, and very narrow in relation to their length. They are very thinly fleshed. Legs are very shallow and depressed. Shoulders and breasts are very thin.

(2) Figure 1 in § 53.110 depicts the degree of feathering and flank fat streakings associated with minimum Standard quality. The lean flesh is soft regardless of maturity.

(3) A development of quality which is superior to that specified as minimum for the Standard grade may compensate, without limit, for a development of conformation inferior to that specified as minimum for Standard at an equal rate as indicated in the following example: A carcass which has midpoint Standard quality may have conformation equal to the midpoint of the Utility grade and remain eligible for Standard. Also, a carcass which has conformation at least one-third grade superior to that specified for the minimum of the Standard grade may qualify for Standard with a development of quality equal to the lower limit of the upper third of the Utility grade. Compensation of superior conformation for inferior quality is limited to one-third grade of deficient quality.

(e) *Utility.* The Utility grade includes those calf carcasses whose characteristics are inferior to those specified as minimum for the Standard grade.

APPENDIX 1-7. Official identifications for the grading and certification of livestock, meats, prepared meats, and meat products, reproduced from 7 CFR 53.18 and 53.19 (1977).

identification under the regulations for preliminary grade of carcasses and wholesale cuts.

Figure 1.

(b) A shield enclosing the letters "USDA" as shown below with the appropriate quality grade designation "Prime " "Choice," "Good," "Standard," "Commercial," "Utility," "Cutter," "Canner," or "Cull," as provided in the standards in Subpart B of this part and accompanied when necessary by the class designation "Bullock," "Veal," "Calf," "Yearling Mutton," or "Mutton," constitutes a form of official identification under the regulations to show the quality grade, and where necessary the class, under said standards, of steer, heifer, and cow beef, bullock beef, veal, calf, lamb, yearling mutton and mutton. The code identification letters of the grader performing the service will appear intermittently outside the shield.

Figure 2.

§ 53.18   Marking of products.

All products for which class and grade under the standards in Subpart B of this part, or compliance, is determined under the regulations, or the immediate and shipping containers thereof, shall be stamped, branded, or otherwise marked with an appropriate official identification: *Provided,* That except as otherwise directed by the Chief, such marking will not be required when an applicant only desires official certificates. The marking of products, or their containers, as required by this section shall be done by official graders or under their immediate supervision.

§ 53.19   Official identifications.

(a) A shield enclosing the letters "USDA" and code identification letters of the grader performing the service, as shown below, constitutes a form of official

(c) A shield enclosing the letters "USDA" and the words "Yield Grade," as shown below, with the appropriate yield grade designation "1," "2," "3," "4," or "5" as provided in the standards in Subpart B of this part constitutes a form of official identification under the regulations to show the yield grade under said standards. When yield graded, bull and bullock carcasses and eligible cuts from bull and bullock carcasses will be identified with the class designation "Bull" and "Bullock," respectively. The code identification letters of the grader performing the service will appear outside the shield.

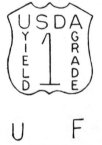

U   F

Figure 1.

(d) The letters "USDA" with the appropriate grade designation "1," "2," "3," "4," "Utility," or "Cull" enclosed in a shield as shown below, as provided in standards in Subpart B of this part, constitutes a form of official identification under the regulations to show the grade under said standards of barrow, gilt, and sow pork carcasses.

Figure 2.

(e) The following constitute forms of official identification under the regulations to show compliance of products:

Figure 1

Figure 2

Figure 3

Figure 4

Figure 5

APPENDIX 1-7. (continued).

The letters "AC," "XE," and "UF" shown in figures 1, 2, 3, and 4 are examples, respectively, of the code identification letters of the official grader performing the service.

(f) A shield-shaped eartag enclosing the letters "USDA," the words "Carcass Data Service," as shown below, and a serial number constitutes a form of official identification under the regulations for livestock and carcasses. Other information may appear on the backside of the eartag at the option of the purchasers.

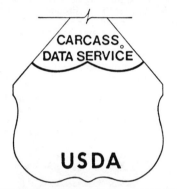

[34 FR 19338, Dec. 6, 1969 as amended at 38 FR 23317, Aug. 29, 1973]

§ 53.20 Custody of identification devices.

All identification devices used in marking products or the containers thereof under the regulations, including those indicating compliance with specifications approved by the Chief, shall be kept in the custody of the Branch, and accurate records shall be kept by the Branch of all such devices. Each office of grading shall keep a record of the devices assigned to it. Such devices shall be distributed only to persons authorized by the Department, who shall keep the devices in their possession or control at all times and maintain complete records of such devices.

[34 F.R. 19339, Dec. 6, 1969]

APPENDIX 1-8. Official identifications for the inspection of egg
and egg products, reproduced from
7 CFR 59.412, 59.414, and 59.415
(1977).

§ 59.412 Form of official identification symbol and inspection mark.

(a) The shield set forth in Figure 1 containing the letters "USDA" shall be the official identification symbol for purposes of this part and, when used, imitated, or simulated in any manner in connection with a product, shall be deemed to constitute a representation that the product has been officially inspected.

(b) The inspection mark which is to be used on containers of edible egg products shall be contained within the outline of a shield and with the wording and design set forth in Figure 2 of this section, except the plant number may be omitted from the official identification if applied elsewhere on the container.

FIGURE 1.

FIGURE 2

[36 FR 9814, May 28, 1971, as amended at 40 FR 20058, May 8, 1975]

§ 59.414   Products bearing the official inspection mark.

Egg products which are permitted to bear the inspection mark shall be processed in an official plant from edible shell eggs or other edible egg products and may contain other edible ingredients. The official mark shall be printed or lithographed and applied as a part of the principal display panel of the container but shall not be applied to a detachable cover.

§ 59.415   Use of other official identification.

Other official identification as shown in this section shall be printed or lithographed and applied as a part of the principal display panel, but shall not be applied to a detachable cover. The plant number may be omitted from the identification if applied elsewhere on the label or container. Such products shall meet all requirements for egg products which are permitted to bear the official inspection mark shown in § 59.412, except for pasteurization, heat treatment, or other such methods of treatment approved by the Administrator. Such products shall not be released into consuming channels until they have been subjected to pasteurization, heat treatment, or other approved methods of treatment.

(a) All nonpasteurized egg products, except as provided in paragraph (b) of this section, shipped from an official plant in packaged form shall be marked with the identification set forth in Figure 3 of this section. After pasteuriza-

EGG PRODUCTS

FOR FURTHER PROCESSING
IN AN OFFICIAL USDA PLANT

PLANT NO. 42

FIGURE 3.

tion or treatment, the product may bear the official inspection mark as shown in § 59.412.

(b) All nonpasteurized egg products, containing 10 percent or more added salt, shipped from an official plant in packaged form to an acidic dressing manufacturer shall be marked with the identification set forth in Figure 4 of this section.

UNPASTEURIZED
SALTED EGG PRODUCTS

FOR USE IN
ACIDIC DRESSINGS ONLY

PLANT NO. 42

FIGURE 4.

[36 F.R. 9814, May 28, 1971; 36 F.R. 10841, June 4, 1971]

APPENDIX 1-9. United States
consumer grades and weight classes
for shell eggs, reproduced from 7
CFR 56.216 to 56.218 (1977).

UNITED STATES CONSUMER GRADES AND
WEIGHT CLASSES FOR SHELL EGGS

§ 56.216   Grades.

(a) Fresh Fancy Quality shall consist
of eggs meeting the requirements as set
forth in § 56.42.

(b) *U.S. Grade AA.* (1) U.S. Consumer
Grade AA (at origin) shall consist of
eggs which are 85 percent AA quality.
The maximum tolerance of 15 percent
which may be below AA quality may consist of A or B quality in any combination, with not more than 5 percent C
quality or Checks in any combination
and not more than 0.30 percent Leakers
or Loss (due to meat or blood spots) in
any combination. No Dirties or Loss other
than as specified are permitted. This
grade is also applicable when the lot

consists of eggs meeting the requirements set forth in § 56.42.

(2) U.S. Consumer Grade AA (destination) shall consist of eggs which are
80 percent AA quality. The maximum
tolerance of 20 percent which may be
below AA quality may consist of A or B
quality in any combination with not more
than 5 percent C quality or Checks in
any combination and not more than 0.50
percent Leakers, Dirties, or Loss (due to
meat or blood spots) in any combination,
except that such Loss may not exceed
0.30 percent. Other types of Loss are not
permitted. This grade is also applicable
when the lot consists of eggs meeting
the requirements set forth in § 56.42.

(c) *U.S. Grade A.* (1) U.S. Consumer
Grade A (at origin) shall consist of eggs
which are 85 percent A quality or better.
Within the maximum tolerance of 15
percent which may be below A quality,
not more than 5 percent may be C quality or Checks in any combination, and
not more than 0.30 percent Leakers or
Loss (due to meat or blood spots) in any
combination. No Dirties or Loss other
than as specified are permitted. This
grade is also applicable when the lot
consists of eggs meeting the requirements set forth in § 56.43.

(2) U.S. Consumer Grade A (destination) shall consist of eggs which are 80
percent A quality or better. Within the
maximum tolerance of 20 percent which
may be below A quality, not more than 5
percent may be C quality or Checks in
any combination, and not more than 0.50
percent Leakers, Dirties, or Loss (due
to meat or blood spots) in any combination, except that such Loss may not exceed 0.30 percent. Other types of Loss are
not permitted. This grade is also applicable when the lot consists of eggs meeting the requirements set forth in § 56.43.

(d) *U.S. Grade B.* (1) U.S. Consumer
Grade B (at origin) shall consist of eggs
which are 85 percent B quality or better.
Within the maximum tolerance of 15 percent which may be below B quality, not
more than 10 percent may be Checks and
not more than 0.30 percent Leakers or
Loss (due to meat or blood spots) in any
combination. No Dirties or Loss other
than as specified are permitted.

(2) U.S. Consumer Grade B (destination) shall consist of eggs which are 80
percent B quality or better. Within the
maximum tolerance of 20 percent which
may be below B quality, not more than

10 percent may be Checks and not more than 0.50 percent Leakers, Dirties, or Loss (due to meat or blood spots) in any combination, except that such Loss may not exceed 0.30 percent. Other types of Loss are not permitted.

(e) Additional tolerances:

(1) In lots of two or more cases:

(i) For Grade AA—no individual case may exceed 10 percent less AA quality eggs than the minimum permitted for the lot average.

(ii) For Grade A—no individual case may exceed 10 percent less A quality eggs than the minimum permitted for the lot average

(iii) For Grade B—no individual case may exceed 10 percent less B quality eggs than the minimum permitted for the lot average.

(2) In lots of two or more cartons, no individual carton may contain less than eight eggs of the specified quality and no individual carton may contain less than 10 eggs of the specified quality and the next lower quality. The remaining two eggs may consist of a combination of qualities below the next lower quality (i.e., in lots of Grade A, not more than two eggs of the qualities in individual cartons within the sample may be C or Checks).

[32 F.R. 8233, June 8, 1967, as amended at 36 FR 9765, May 28, 1971; 38 FR 26798, Sept. 26, 1973]

§ 56.217 Summary of grades.

The summary of U.S. Consumer Grades for Shell Eggs follows as Table I and Table II of this section:

TABLE 1.—*Summary of U.S. Consumer Grades for Shell Eggs*

U.S. Consumer grade (origin)	Quality required [1]	Tolerance permitted [2]	
		Percent	Quality
Grade AA or Fresh Fancy Quality	85 percent AA	Up to 15	A or B.
		Not over 5	C or check.
Grade A	85 percent A or better	Up to 15	B.
		Not over 5	C or Check.
Grade B	85 percent B or better	Up to 15	C.
		Not over 10	Checks.

U.S. Consumer grade (destination)	Quality required [1]	Tolerance permitted [3]	
		Percent	Quality
Grade AA or Fresh Fancy Quality	80 percent AA	Up to 20	A or B.
		Not over 5	C or Check.
Grade A	80 percent A or better	Up to 20	B.
		Not over 5	C or Check.
Grade B	80 percent B or better	Up to 20	C.
		Not over 10	Checks.

[1] In lots of two or more cases or cartons, see Table II of this section for tolerances for an individual case or carton within a lot.

[2] For the U.S. Consumer grades (at origin), a tolerance of 0.30 percent Leakers or Loss (due to meat or blood spots) in any combination is permitted. No Dirties or other type Loss are permitted.

[3] For the U.S. Consumer grades (destination), a tolerance of 0.50 percent Leakers, Dirties, or Loss (due to meat or blood spots) in any combination is permitted, except that such Loss may not exceed 0.30 percent. Other types of Loss are not permitted.

TABLE II—TOLERANCE FOR INDIVIDUAL CASE OR CARTON WITHIN A LOT

U.S. Consumer grade	Case—minimum quality	Origin	Destination	Carton—minimum quality —number of eggs (origin and destination)
		Percent	Percent	
Grade AA or Fresh Fancy Quality	AA	75	70	8 eggs AA.
	A or B	15	20	2 eggs A or B.
	C or Check	10	10	2 eggs C or Check.
Grade A	A	75	70	8 eggs A.
	B	15	20	2 eggs B.
	C or Check	10	10	2 eggs C or Check.
Grade B	B	75	70	8 eggs B.
	C	5	10	2 eggs C.
	Check	20	20	2 eggs Check.

[28 FR 6347, June 20, 1963, as amended at 32 FR 8233, June 8, 1967; 37 FR 9458, May 11, 1972; 38 FR 26798, Sept. 26, 1973; 38 FR 27509, Oct. 4, 1973]

APPENDIX 1-9. (continued).

§ 56.218   Weight classes.

(a) The weight classes for U.S. Consumer Grades for Shell Eggs shall be as indicated in Table I of this section and shall apply to all consumer grades.

TABLE I—U.S. WEIGHT CLASSES FOR CONSUMER GRADES FOR SHELL EGGS

Size or weight class	Minimum net weight per dozen	Minimum net weight per 30 dozen	Minimum weight for individual eggs at rate per dozen
	Ounces	*Pounds*	*Ounces*
Jumbo	30	56	29
Extra large	27	50½	26
Large	24	45	23
Medium	21	39½	20
Small	18	34	17
Peewee	15	28	---------

(b) A lot average tolerance of 3.3 percent for individual eggs in the next lower weight class is permitted as long as no individual case within the lot exceeds 5 percent.

[20 F.R. 677, Feb. 1, 1955, as amended at 20 F.R. 10015, Dec. 29, 1955; 32 F.R. 8233, June 8, 1967]

APPENDIX 1-10. Official identifications for grades of shell eggs, reproduced from 7 CFR 56.35 to 56.38 (1977).

IDENTIFYING AND MARKING PRODUCTS

§ 56.35   Authority to use, and approval of official identification.

(a) *Authority to use official identification.* Authority to officially identify product graded pursuant to this part is granted only to applicants who make the services of a grader or supervisor of packaging available for use in accordance with this part. Packaging materials bearing official identification marks shall be approved pursuant to §§ 56.35 to 56.39, inclusive, and shall be used only for the purpose for which approved and prescribed by the Administrator. Any unauthorized use or disposition of approved labels or packaging materials which bears any official identification may result in cancellation of the approval and denial of the use of labels or packaging material bearing official identification or denial of the benefits of the Act pursuant to the provisions of § 56.31.

(b) *Approval of official identification.* No label, container, or packaging material which bears official identification may contain any statement that is false or misleading. No label, container, or packaging material bearing official identification may be printed or prepared for use until the printers' or other final proof has been approved by the Administrator in accordance with the regulations in this part, the Federal Food, Drug, and Cosmetic Act, the Fair Packaging and Labeling Act, and the regulations promulgated under these acts. The use of finished labels must be approved as prescribed by the Administrator. A grader may apply official identification stamps to shipping containers if they do not bear any statement that is false or misleading.

If the label is printed or otherwise applied directly to the container, the principal display panels of such container shall for this purpose be considered as the label. The label shall contain the name, address, and ZIP Code of the packer or distributor of the product, the name of the product, a statement of the net contents of the container, and the U.S. grademark.

(c) *Nutrition labeling.* Nutrition information may be included on the label of consumer packaged shell eggs, providing, such labeling complies with the provisions of Title 21, Chapter 1, Part 1, Regulations for the Enforcement of the Federal Food, Drug, and Cosmetic Act and the Fair Packaging and Labeling Act. Nutrition labeling is required when a nutritional claim or information is presented on the labeling of consumer packages. Labeling will not be approved by the Department without comments from the Food and Drug Administration regarding nutritional claims and test data. [40 FR 20055, May 8, 1975]

§ 56.36   Information required on, and form of grademark.

(a) *Information required on grademark.* (1) Except as otherwise authorized, each grademark provided for in this section shall conspicuously and legibly indicate the letters "USDA," and the U.S. grade of the product it identifies, such as "A Grade" (illustrated in Figure 2). The letters "USDA" shall be printed in a light color on and surrounded by a dark field, and the U.S. grade printed in a dark color on a light field.

(2) The size or weight class of the product such as "Large" and such terms as "Federal-State Graded" or words of similar import may be shown within the grademark, (illustrated in Figure 3). This information shall be printed in a dark color on a light field. However, such terms as "Federal-State Graded" need not be shown. The size or weight class of the product may be omitted from the grademark, provided, it appears prominently on the main panel of the carton.

(3) The plant number of the official plant preceded by the letter "P" may ap-

APPENDIX 1-10. (continued).

pear in the grademark. When not shown within the grademark, the plant identification must be shown elsewhere on the packaging material.

(b) *Form of official identification symbol and grademark.* (1) The shield set forth in Figure 1 containing the letters "USDA" shall be the official identification symbol for purposes of this part and when used, imitated, or simulated in any manner in connection with shell eggs, shall be deemed to constitute a representation that the product has been officially graded for the purpose of § 56.2.

FIGURE 1

(2) Except as otherwise authorized, the grademark permitted to be used to officially identify cartons of shell eggs which are graded pursuant to the regulations in this part shall be contained in a shield and in the form and design indicated in Figures 2, 3, and 6 of this section. The shield shall be of sufficient size so that the print and other information contained therein is distinctly legible and in approximately the same proportion and size as shown in Figures 2 and 3. The grademark shall be printed on the carton or on a tape used to seal the carton.

FIGURE 2

FIGURE 3

(3) Fresh Fancy Quality or AA grademark. Eggs which are packaged pursuant to § 56.42 and are to be grade marked shall be labeled with one of the following grademarks:

FIGURE 4

FIGURE 5

FIGURE 6

(4) Alternate Grade A mark: Eggs which are packaged pursuant to § 56.43 and are to be grade marked shall be

labeled with the grademark shown in Figures 2 and 3 of subparagraph (2) of this paragraph, or with the following grademark:

PRODUCED and MARKETED
under FEDERAL - STATE
QUALITY CONTROL PROGRAM

Figure 7

[28 FR 6343, June 20, 1963, as amended at 32 FR 8230, June 8, 1967; 40 FR 20055, May 8, 1975]

§ 56.37 Lot marking of officially identified product.

Each carton identified with the grade marks shown in Figures 2, 3, or 6 of § 56.36 shall be legibly lot numbered on either the carton or the tape used to seal the carton. The lot number shall be the consecutive day of the year on which the eggs were packed (e.g., 132), except other lot numbering systems may be used when submitted in writing and approved by the Administrator.

[35 F.R. 5664, Apr. 8, 1970]

§ 56.38 Rescindment of approved labels.

Once a year, or more often, if requested, each applicant shall submit to the Administrator a list, in triplicate, of approved labels which bear any official identification that have become obsolete, accompanied with a statement that such approvals are no longer desired. The approvals shall be identified by the date of approval, approval number, and the grade, weight class, and brand name of the product as applicable.

[40 FR 20056, May 8, 1975]

APPENDIX 1-11.   United States standards for quality of ready-to-cook poultry,
reproduced from 7 CFR 70.220 to 70.222 (1977).

STANDARDS FOR QUALITY OF READY-TO-
COOK POULTRY

§ 70.220   A Quality.

(a) *Conformation.* The carcass or part is free of deformities that detract from its appearance or that affect the normal distribution of flesh. Slight deformities, such as slightly curved or dented breastbones and slightly curved backs, may be present.

(b) *Fleshing.* The carcass has a well developed covering of flesh considering the kind, class, and part.

(1) The breast is moderately long and deep, and has sufficient flesh to give it a rounded appearance with the flesh carrying well up to the crest of the breastbone along its entire length.

(2) The leg is well fleshed and moderately thick and wide at the knee and hip joint area, and has a well-rounded, plump appearance with the flesh carrying well down toward the hock and upward to the hip joint area.

(3) The drumstick is well fleshed and moderately thick and wide at the knee joint, and has a well-rounded, plump appearance with the flesh carrying well down toward the hock.

(4) The thigh is well to moderately fleshed.

(5) The wing is well to moderately fleshed.

(c) *Fat covering.* The carcass or part, considering the kind, class, and part, has a well-developed layer of fat in the skin. The fat is well distributed so that there is a noticeable amount of fat in the skin in the areas between the heavy feather tracts.

(d) *Defeathering.* The carcass or part has a clean appearance, especially on the breast. The carcass or part is free of pinfeathers, diminutive feathers, and hair which are visible to the grader.

(e) *Exposed flesh.* Parts are free of exposed flesh, resulting from cuts, tears, and missing skin (other than slight trimming on the edge). The carcass is free of these defects on the breast and legs. Elsewhere, the carcass may have exposed flesh due to slight cuts, tears, and areas of missing skin, provided that the aggregate of the areas of flesh exposed does not exceed the area of a circle of the diameter as specified in the following table:

Carcass weight		Maximum aggregate area permitted	
Minimum	Maximum	Breast and legs	Elsewhere
None	1 lb, 8 oz	None	¾ in.
Over 1 lb, 8 oz	6 lb	do	1½ in.
Over 6 lb	16 lb	do	2 in.
Over 16 lb	None	do	3 in.

(f) *Disjointed and broken bones and missing parts.* Parts are free of broken bones. The carcass is free of broken bones and has not more than one disjointed bone. The wing tips may be removed at the joint, and in the case of ducks and geese, the parts of the wing beyond the second joint may be removed, if removed at the joint and both wings are so treated. The tail may be removed at the base. Cartilage separated from the breastbone is not considered as a disjointed or broken bone.

(g) *Discolorations of the skin and flesh.* The carcass or part is practically free of such defects. Discolorations due to bruising shall be free of clots (discernible clumps of red or dark cells). Evidence of incomplete bleeding, such as more than an occasional slightly reddened feather follicle, is not permitted.

Flesh bruises and discolorations of the skin, such as "blue back," are not permitted on the breast or legs of the carcass, or on these individual parts, and only lightly shaded discolorations are permitted elsewhere. The total areas affected by flesh bruises, skin bruises, and discolorations, such as "blue back," singly, or in any combination, shall not exceed one-half of the toal aggregate area of permitted discoloration. The aggregate area of all discolorations for a part shall not exceed that of a circle one-fourth inch in diameter for poultry weighing up to 6 pounds and one-half inch in diameter for poultry weighing over 6 pounds. The aggregate area of all discolorations for a carcass shall not exceed the area of a circle of the diameter as specified in the following table:

Carcass weight		Maximum aggregate area permitted	
Minimum	Maximum	Breast and legs	Elsewhere
None	1 lb, 8 oz	½ in	1 in.
Over 1 lb, 8 oz	6 lb	1 in	2 in.
Over 6 lb	16 lb	1½ in	2½ in.
Over 16 lb	None	2 in	3 in.

(h) *Freezing defects.* With respect to consumer packaged poultry, parts, or specified poultry food products, the carcass, part, or specified poultry food product is practically free from defects which result from handling or occur during freezing or storage. The following defects are permitted if they, alone or in combination, detract only very slightly from the appearance of the carcass, part, or specified poultry food product:

(1) Slight darkening over the back and drumsticks, provided the frozen bird or part has a generally bright appearance;

(2) Occasional pockmarks due to drying of the inner layer of skin (derma) (however, none may exceed the area of a circle one-eighth inch in diameter for poultry weighing 6 pounds or less and one-fourth inch in diameter for poultry weighing over 6 pounds);

(3) Occasional small areas showing a thin layer of clear or pinkish colored ice.

(i) *Backs.* A quality backs shall meet all applicable provisions of this section pertaining to parts, and shall include the meat contained on the ilium (oyster), pelvic meat and skin and vertebral ribs and scapula with meat and skin.

APPENDIX 1-11. (continued).

§ 70.221   B Quality.

(a) *Conformation.* The carcass or part may have moderate deformities, such as a dented, curved, or crooked breast, crooked back or misshapen legs or wings, which do not materially affect the distribution of flesh or the appearance of the carcass or part.

(b) *Fleshing.* The carcass has a moderate covering of flesh considering the kind, class, and part.

(1) The breast has a substantial covering of flesh with the flesh carrying up to the crest of the breastbone sufficiently to prevent a thin appearance.

(2) The leg is fairly thick and wide at the knee and hip joint area, and has sufficient flesh to prevent a thin appearance.

(3) The drumstick has a sufficient amount of flesh to prevent a thin appearance with the flesh carrying fairly well down toward the hock.

(4) The thigh has a sufficient amount of flesh to prevent a thin appearance.

(5) The wing has a sufficient amount of flesh to prevent a thin appearance.

(c) *Fat covering.* The carcass or part has sufficient fat in the skin to prevent a distinct appearance of the flesh through the skin, especially on the breast and legs.

(d) *Defeathering.* The carcass or part may have a few nonprotruding pinfeathers or vestigial feathers which are scattered sufficiently so as not to appear numerous. Not more than an occasional protruding pinfeather or diminutive feather shall be in evidence under a careful examination.

(e) *Exposed flesh.* Parts may have exposed flesh resulting from cuts, tears and missing skin, provided that not more than a moderate amount of the flesh normally covered by skin is exposed. The carcass may have exposed flesh resulting from cuts, tears, and missing skin, provided that the aggregate of the areas of flesh exposed does not exceed the area of a circle of the diameter as specified in the following table:

Carcass weight		Maximum aggregate area permitted	
Minimum	Maximum	Breast and legs	Elsewhere
None	1 lb., 8 oz	¾ in	1½ in.
Over 1 lb., 8 oz	6 lb	1½ in	3 in.
Over 6 lb	16 lb	2 in	4 in.
Over 16 lb	None	3 in	5 in.

Notwithstanding the foregoing, a carcass meeting the requirements of A quality for fleshing may be trimmed to remove skin and flesh defects, provided that no more than one-third of the flesh is exposed on any part, and the meat yield of any part is not appreciably affected.

(f) *Disjointed and broken bones and missing parts.* Parts may be disjointed, but are free of broken bones. The carcass may have two disjointed bones, or one disjointed bone and one nonprotruding broken bone. Parts of the wing beyond the second joint may be removed at a joint. The tail may be removed at the base. The back may be trimmed in an area not wider than the base of the tail and extending from the tail to the area halfway between the base of the tail and the hip joints.

(g) *Discolorations of the skin and flesh.* The carcass or part is free of serious defects. Discoloration due to bruising shall be free of clots (discernible clumps of red or dark cells). Evidence of incomplete bleeding shall be no more than very slight. Moderate areas of discoloration due to bruises in the skin or flesh and moderately shaded discoloration of the skin, such as "blue back" are permitted, but the total areas affected by such discolorations, singly or in any combination, may not exceed one-half of the total aggregate area of permitted discoloration. The aggregate area of all discolorations for a part shall not exceed the area of a circle having a diameter of one-half inch for poultry weighing up to 1 pound, 8 ounces; 1 inch for poultry weighing over 1 pound, 8 ounces, but not more than 6 pounds; and 1½ inches for poultry weighing over 6 pounds. The aggregate area of all discolorations for a carcass shall not exceed the area of a circle of the diameter as specified in the following table:

Carcass weight		Maximum aggregate area permitted	
Minimum	Maximum	Breast and legs	Elsewhere
None	1 lb., 8 oz	1 in	2 in.
Over 1 lb., 8 oz	6 lb	2 in	3 in.
Over 6 lb	16 lb	2½ in	4 in.
Over 16 lb	None	3 in	5 in.

(h) *Freezing defects.* With respect to consumer packaged poultry, parts, or specified poultry food products, the carcass, part or specified poultry food product may have moderate defects which result from handling or occur during freezing or storage. The skin and flesh shall have a sound appearance, but may lack brightness. The carcass or part may have a few pockmarks due to drying of the inner layer of skin (derma). However, no single area of overlapping pockmarks may exceed that of a circle one-half inch in diameter. Moderate areas showing layers of clear pinkish or reddish colored ice are permitted.

(i) *Backs.* B quality backs shall meet all applicable provisions of this section pertaining to parts, and shall include either the meat contained on the ilium (oyster) and meat and skin from the pelvic bones or the vertebral ribs and scapula with meat and skin.

§ 70.222   C quality.

(a) A part that does not meet the requirements for A or B quality may be of C quality if the flesh is substantially intact.

(b) A carcass that does not meet the requirements for A or B quality may be C quality. Both wings may be removed or neatly trimmed. Trimming of the breast and legs is permitted, but not to the extent that the normal meat yield is materially affected. The back may be trimmed in an area not wider than the base of the tail and extending from the tail to the area between the hip joints.

(c) C quality backs shall include the meat and skin from the pelvic bones, except that the meat contained in the ilium (oyster) may be removed. The vertebral ribs and scapula with meat and skin may also be removed, but the remaining portion must have the skin substantially intact.

[41 FR 23681, June 11, 1976; 41 FR 26565, June 28, 1976]

APPENDIX 1-12. Official identifications for grades of poultry and rabbit products, reproduced from 7 CFR 70.50 and 70.51 (1977).

this Part 70 and the applicable provisions of §§ 381.115 through 381.141 of 9 CFR Part 381. Poultry Products Inspection Regulations. Labeling requirements for ready-to-cook rabbits, except for the product name, shall be the same as for ready-to-cook poultry. For ready-to-cook rabbits the class name shall be shown on the label. The appropriate designation, "young," "mature," or "old," may be used as a prefix to the word rabbit" in lieu of the class name.

[41 FR 23681, June 11, 1976; 41 FR 24694, June 18, 1976]

§ 70.51   Marking graded products.

(a) *Information required on grademark*. Except as otherwise authorized by the Administrator, each grademark, which is to be used, shall include the letters "USDA" and the U.S. Grade of the product it identifies, such as "U.S. A Grade," and such information shall be printed in a light color on a dark field. In addition, a term, such as "Federal-State Graded," or "Government Graded," may be used adjacent to but not within the grademark.

(b) *Form of official identification symbol and grademark*. (1) The shield set forth in Figure 1, containing the letters "USDA" shall be the official identification symbol for purposes of this part, and when used, imitated, or simulated in any manner in connection with poultry or rabbits, shall be deemed prima facia to constitute a representation that the product has been officially graded for the purposes of § 70.2.

§ 70.50   Approval of official identification and wording on labels.

Any label or packaging material which bears any official grade identification shall be used only in such a manner as the Administrator may prescribe, and such labeling or packaging materials, including the wording used on such materials, shall be approved in accordance with and conform with the provisions of

FIGURE 1

(2) Except as otherwise authorized, the grademark permitted to be used to officially identify consumer graded

poultry and rabbit products, shall be of the form and design indicated in Figure 2 or 3 of this section. The shield shall be of sufficient size so that the print and other information contained therein is distinctly legible and in approximately the same proportion and size as shown in Figures 2 and 3.

FIGURE 2

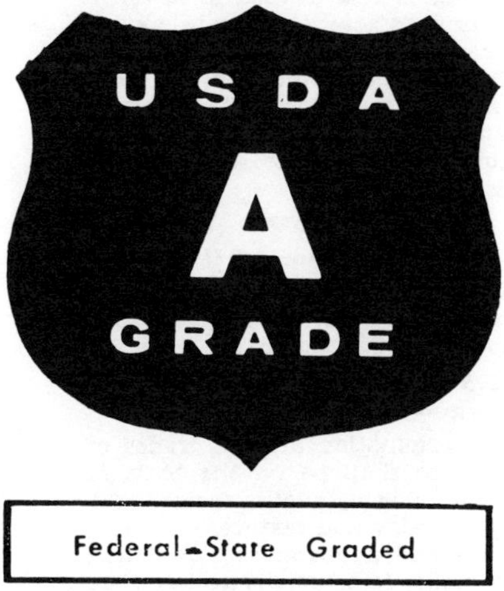

FIGURE 4

USDA
A
GRADE

FIGURE 3

(c) *Products that may be individually grade marked.* The grademarks set forth in Figures 2 and 3 may be applied individually to ready-to-cook poultry and rabbits and specified poultry food products for which consumer grades are provided in Subparts B and C of this chapter, or to the containers in which

such products are enclosed for the purpose of display and sale to household consumers, only when such products qualify for the particular grade indicated in accordance with the consumer grades.

(d) *Identification of U.S. Grade A— For Further Processing.* The grademark indicated in Figure 4, below, is restricted to turkeys meeting the requirements of § 70.260. The grademark may be applied only to master shipping containers and not to individual birds. The block containing the words "For Further Processing" in Figure 4 shall be located as indicated and shall be at least as wide and at least ¼ as high as the height of the grademark. The words "For Further Processing" shall be in the same boldness of type as the wording in the grademark.

Federal-State   Graded

FOR FURTHER PROCESSING

APPENDIX 1-13. United States standards for grades of Colby cheese, reproduced from 7 CFR 58.2475 to 58.2481 (1977).

Subpart J—U.S. Standards for Grades of Colby Cheese

SOURCE: The provisions of this Subpart J appear at 37 F.R. 25992, Dec. 7, 1972, unless otherwise noted.

DEFINITIONS

§ 58.2475 Colby cheese.

"Colby cheese" is cheese made by the Colby process or by any other procedure which produces a finished cheese having the same physical and chemical properties as the cheese produced by the Colby process. The physical attributes of Colby cheese are as follows: Uncolored to orange in color; a mild to mellow flavor similar to mild Cheddar cheese; softer bodied and more open textured than Cheddar. The cheese is made from cow's milk with or without the addition of coloring matter. It contains added common salt, contains not more than 40 percent of moisture, and in the water-free substance contains not less than 50 percent of milk fat, and conforms to the provisions of § 19.510 or § 19.512 as applicable, "Definitions and Standards of Identity for Cheese and Cheese products." Food and Drug Administration (21 CFR Part 19).

§ 58.2476 Types of surface protection.

The following are the types of surface protection for Colby cheese:

(a) *Bandaged and paraffin-dipped.* The cheese is bandaged and dipped in a refined paraffin, amorphous wax, microcrystalline wax, or any combination of such, or any other suitable substance. Such coating is a continuous, unbroken, and uniform film adhering tightly to the entire surface of the cheese.

(b) *Rindless.* The cheese is properly wrapped in a wrapper or covering, or by any other protective covering, which will not impart any color or objectionable odor or flavor to the cheese. The wrapper or covering is sealed with a sufficient overlap or satisfactory closure to prevent air leakage. The wrapper or covering is of sufficiently low permeability to water vapor and air so as to prevent the formation of rind and prevent the entrance of air during the curing and holding periods.

U.S. GRADES

§ 58.2477 Nomenclature of U.S. grades.

The nomenclature of U.S. grades is as follows: (a) U.S. Grade AA; (b) U.S. Grade A; (c) U.S. Grade B.

§ 58.2478 Basis for determination of U.S. grades.

The determination of U.S. grades of Colby cheese shall be on the basis of rating the following quality factors: (a) Flavor, (b) body and texture, (c) color, (d) finish and appearance. The rating of each quality factor shall be established on the basis of characteristics present in any vat of cheese. The cheese shall be graded no sooner than 10 days of age. The cheese shall be held at no lower than 35° F. during this period. The final

U.S. grade shall be established on the basis of the lowest rating of any one of the quality factors.

§ 58.2479 **Specifications for U.S. grades of Colby cheese.**

The general requirements for the U.S. grades of Colby cheese are as follows:

(a) *U.S. Grade AA.* U.S. Grade AA Colby cheese shall conform to the following requirements.

(1) *Flavor.* Is fine and highly pleasing, free from undesirable flavors and odors. May be lacking in flavor development or may possess a characteristic Colby cheese flavor. May possess a very slight acid or feed flavor, but shall be free from any undesirable flavors and odors. See Table I.

(2) *Body and texture.* A plug drawn from the cheese shall be firm. It shall have numerous small mechanical openings evenly distributed throughout the plug. It shall be relatively free from blind areas. It shall not possess sweet holes, yeast holes, or other gas holes. The texture may be definitely curdy or may be partially broken down if more than 3 weeks old. See Table II.

(3) *Color.* Shall have a uniform, bright attractive appearance. May be colored or uncolored but the color shall be uniform. See Table III.

(4) *Finish and appearance*—(i) *Bandaged and paraffin-dipped.* The rind shall be sound, firm and smooth providing a good protection to the cheese. The bandage shall be evenly placed on the end and over the entire surface of the cheese, free from unnecessary overlapping and wrinkles, and not burst or torn. The cheese surface shall be smooth, bright, and have a good coating of paraffin or wax that adheres firmly to the entire surface of the cheese. The cheese shall be free from mold under the bandage and paraffin. The cheese shall be free from high edges, huffing, and lopsidedness, but may possess soiled surface to a very slight degree. See Table IV.

(ii) *Rindless.* The wrapper or covering shall be practically smooth and properly sealed with adequate overlapping at the seams or sealed by any other satisfactory type of closure. The wrapper or covering shall be neat, and adequately and securely envelop the cheese but may be slightly wrinkled. Allowance should be made for wrinkles caused by crimping or sealing when vacuum packaging is used. The cheese shall be free from mold under the wrapper or covering and shall not be huffed or lopsided. See Table IV.

(b) *U.S. Grade A.* U.S. Grade A Colby cheese shall conform to the following requirements.

(1) *Flavor.* Is pleasing and free from undesirable flavors and odors. May be lacking in flavor development or may possess slight characteristic Colby cheese flavor. May possess a very slight bitter flavor, slight acid, or feed flavors but shall not possess undesirable flavors and odors. See Table I.

(2) *Body and texture.* A plug drawn from the cheese shall be reasonably firm. It shall have numerous mechanical openings but the openings shall not be large and connecting. It shall not possess more than two sweet holes per plug, and the plug shall be free from other gas holes. The body may be very slightly loosely knit and definitely curdy or partially broken down if more than 3 weeks old. See Table II.

(3) *Color.* Shall have a fairly uniform, bright attractive appearance. May be colored or uncolored but the color shall be uniform. Very slight waviness is permitted. See Table III.

(4) *Finish and appearance*—(i) *Bandaged and paraffin-dipped.* The rind shall be sound, firm, and smooth, providing a good protection to the cheese. The bandage may be slightly uneven, overlapped or wrinkled but not burst or torn. The surface shall be practically smooth, bright and have a good coating of paraffin or wax that adheres firmly to all surfaces of the cheese. The cheese shall be free from mold under the bandage. May possess the following characteristics to a very slight degree: Soiled surface and surface mold; and to a slight degree. Rough surface, irregular bandaging, lopsided and high edges. See Table IV.

(ii) *Rindless.* The wrapper or covering shall be practically smooth, properly sealed with adequate overlapping at the seams or sealed by any other satisfactory type of closure. The wrapper or covering shall be neat and shall adequately and securely envelop the cheese.

APPENDIX 1-13. (continued).

It may be slightly wrinkled but shall be of such character as to fully protect the surface of the cheese and not detract from its initial quality. The cheese shall be free from mold under the wrapper or covering and shall not be huffed but may be slightly lopsided. See Table IV.

(c) *U.S. Grade B.* U.S. Grade B Colby cheese shall conform to the following requirements.

(1) *Flavor.* Should possess a fairly pleasing characteristic Colby cheese flavor, but may possess very slight onion and the following flavors to a slight degree: Flat, bitter, fruity, utensil, whey-taint, yeasty, malty, old milk, weedy, barny and lipase; and the following to a definite degree: Acid and feed flavor. See Table I.

(2) *Body and texture.* A plug drawn from the cheese may be loosely knit and open and may have numerous sweet holes, scattered yeast holes and other scattered gas holes; and may possess various other body defects. Pinny gas holes, scattered yeast holes and other from the cheese may possess the following characteristics to a slight degree: Coarse, short, mealy, weak, pasty, crumbly, gassy, slitty, corky and loosely knit; the following to a definite degree: Curdy, and sweet holes. See Table II.

(3) *Color.* May possess the following characteristics to a slight degree: Wavy, mottled, salt spots, dull or faded. May be colored or uncolored, and color may be slightly unnatural. In addition, rindless Colby cheese may have a bleached surface to a slight degree. See Table III.

(4) *Finish and appearance*—(i) *Bandaged and paraffin-dipped.* The rind shall be reasonably sound, may be slightly weak, but free from soft spots, rind rot, cracks and openings of any kind. The bandage may be uneven and wrinkled but not burst or torn. The surface may be rough and unattractive but shall possess a fairly good coating of paraffin or wax. The paraffin may be scaly or blistered, with very slight mold under the bandage or paraffin but there shall be no indication that mold has entered the cheese. May possess the following characteristics to a slight degree: Soiled surface, surface mold, defective coating, checked rind, weak rind, and sour rind; and the following to a definite degree: Rough surface, irregular

bandaging, lopsided and high edges. See Table IV.

(ii) *Rindless.* The wrapper or covering shall be unbroken but may be definitely wrinkled. The wrapper or covering shall adequately and securely envelop the cheese. The following characteristics may be present to a very slight degree: Mold under the wrapper but not entering the cheese; to a slight degree: Soiled surface, surface mold, lopsided; and the following to a definite degree: Rough surface and wrinkled wrapper or cover. See Table IV.

TABLE I.—CLASSIFICATION OF FLAVOR

Identification of flavor characteristics	AA	A	B
Feed	VS	S	D
Acid	VS	S	D
Flat			S
Bitter		VS	S
Fruity			S
Utensil			S
Whey-Taint			S
Yeasty			S
Malty			S
Old Milk			S
Weedy			S
Onion			VS
Barny			S
Lipase			S

VS—Very Slight. S—Slight. D—Definite. P—Pronounced.

TABLE II—CLASSIFICATION OF BODY AND TEXTURE

Identification of body and texture characteristics	AA	A	B
Curdy	D	D	D
Coarse			S
Sweet holes		S	D
Short			S
Mealy			S
Weak			S
Pasty			S
Crumbly			S
Gassy			S
Slitty			S
Corky			S
Loosely knit		VS	S

VS—Very Slight. S—Slight. D—Definite. P—Pronounced.

TABLE III—CLASSIFICATION OF COLOR

Identification of color characteristics	AA	A	B
Wavy		VS	S
Unnatural			S
Mottled			S
Salt spots			S
Dull or faded			S
Bleached surface (rindless)			S

VS—Very Slight. S—Slight. D—Definite. P—Pronounced.

Table IV—Classification of Finish and Appearance

Identification of finish and appearance characteristics	AA	A	B
Soiled surface	VS	VS	S
Surface mold		VS	S
Mold under bandage and paraffin			VS
Mold under wrapper or covering (rindless)			VS
Rough surface		S	D
Irregular bandaging (uneven, wrinkled and overlapping)		S	D
Lopsided			S	D
Lopsided (rindless)		S	S
High edges		S	D
Defective coating (scaly, blistered, and checked)			S
Checked rind			S
Weak rind			S
Sour rind			S
Wrinkled wrapper or cover (rindless)	S	S	D

VS—Very Slight. S—Slight. D—Definite. P—Pronounced.

§ 58.2480   U.S. grade not assignable.

(a) Colby cheese which fails to meet the requirements for U.S. Grade B or higher shall not be given a U.S. grade.

(b) Colby cheese which does not comply with the provisions of the Federal Food, Drug, and Cosmetic Act shall not be assigned a U.S. grade.

(c) Colby cheese produced in a plant found on inspection to be using unsatisfactory manufacturing practices, equipment or facilities, or to be operating under unsanitary plant conditions shall not be assigned a U.S. grade.

EXPLANATION OF TERMS

§ 58.2481   Explanation of terms.

(a) *With respect to types of surface protection*—(1) *Paraffin.* Refined paraffin, amorphous wax, microcrystalline wax, or any combination of such or any other suitable substance.

(2) *Rindless.* Cheese which has not formed a rind due to the impervious type of wrapper, covering, or container, enclosing the cheese, or by any other means of handling.

(b) *With respect to flavor*—(1) *Very slight.* Detected only upon very critical examination.

(2) *Slight.* Detected only upon critical examination.

(3) *Definite.* Not intense but detectable.

(4) *Pronounced.* So intense as to be easily identified.

(5) *Lacking in flavor development.* No undesirable and very little, if any, Colby cheese flavor development.

(6) *Undesirable.* Those listed in excess of the intensity permitted or those not otherwise listed.

(7) *Feed.* Feed flavors (such as alfalfa, sweetclover, silage, or similar feed) in milk carried through into the cheese.

(8) *Acid.* Sharp and puckery to the taste, characteristic of lactic acid.

(9) *Flat.* Insipid, practically devoid of any characteristic Colby cheese flavor.

(10) *Bitter.* Distasteful, resembling taste of quinine.

(11) *Fruity.* A sweet fruitlike flavor resembling mature apples.

(12) *Utensil.* A flavor that is suggestive of improper or inadequate washing and sterilization of milking machines, utensils, or factory equipment.

(13) *Whey-taint.* A slightly acid flavor and odor characteristic of fermented whey caused by too slow or incomplete expulsion of whey from the curd.

(14) *Yeasty.* A flavor indicating yeasty fermentation.

(15) *Malty.* A distinctive, harsh flavor suggestive of malt.

(16) *Old milk.* Lacks freshness.

(17) *Weedy.* A flavor due to the use of milk which possesses a common weedy flavor.

(18) *Onion.* A flavor recognized by the peculiar taste and aroma suggestive of its name. Present in milk or cheese when the cows have eaten onions, garlic or leeks.

(19) *Barny.* A flavor characteristic of the odor of a poorly ventilated cow barn.

(20) *Lipase.* A flavor suggestive of rancidity or the odor of butyric acid, sometimes associated with a bitterness.

(c) *With respect to body and texture*—(1) *Very slight.* Detected only upon very critical examination and present only to a minute degree.

(2) *Slight.* Barely identifiable and present only to a small degree.

(3) *Definite.* Readily identifiable and present to a substantial degree.

(4) *Pronounced.* Markedly identifiable and present to a large degree.

(5) *Blind.* Lacking small mechanical openings characteristic of Colby cheese.

(6) *Firm.* Feels solid, not soft or weak.

(7) *Reasonably firm.* Somewhat less firm but not to the extent of being weak.

(8) *Curdy.* Firm when worked between the fingers, rubbery and not waxy.

(9) *Coarse.* Feels rough, dry, and sandy.

APPENDIX 1-13. (continued).

(10) *Mechanical openings.* Mechanical openings that are irregular in shape and are caused by variations in make procedure and not gas fermentation.

(11) *Sweet holes.* Spherical gas holes, glossy in appearance; usually about the size of BB shots.

(12) *Short.* No elasticity to the plug and when rubbed between the thumb and fingers it tends toward mealiness.

(13) *Mealy.* Short body, does not mold well and looks and feels like corn meal when rubbed between the thumb and fingers.

(14) *Weak.* Requires little pressure to crush, is soft but is not necessarily sticky like a pasty cheese.

(15) *Pasty.* Weak body and when the cheese is rubbed between the thumb and fingers it becomes sticky and smeary.

(16) *Crumbly.* Loosely knit and tends to fall apart when rubbed between the thumb and fingers.

(17) *Gassy.* Gas holes of various sizes and may be scattered.

(18) *Slitty.* Narrow elongated slits generally associated with a cheese that is gassy or yeasty. Sometimes referred to as "fish-eyes."

(19) *Corky.* Hard, tough, overfirm cheese which does not readily break down when rubbed between the thumb and fingers.

(20) *Pinny.* Numerous very small gas holes.

(21) *Broken down.* Changed from a curdy or rubbery condition to a waxy condition or further to a mealy or pasty condition.

(d) *With respect to color*—(1) *Very slight.* Detected only upon very critical examination and present only to a minute degree.

(2) *Slight.* Barely identifiable and present only to a small degree.

(3) *Definite.* Readily identifiable and present to a substantial degree.

(4) *Pronounced.* Markedly identifiable and present to a large degree.

(5) *Uncolored.* Absence of added coloring.

(6) *Wavy.* Unevenness of color which appears as layers or waves.

(7) *Unnatural.* Deep orange or reddish color.

(8) *Mottled.* Irregular shaped spots or blotches in which portions are light colored and others are of higher color. Also an unevenness of color due to combining the curd from two different vats, sometimes referred to as "mixed cured."

(9) *Salt spots.* Large light colored spots or areas.

(10) *Dull or faded.* A color condition lacking in lustre or translucency.

(11) *Bleached surface.* A faded color beginning at the surface and progressing inward.

(e) *With respect to finish and appearance*—(1) *Very slight.* Detected only upon very critical examination and present only to a minute degree.

(2) *Slight.* Barely identifiable and present to a small degree.

(3) *Definite.* Readily identifiable and present to a substantial degree.

(4) *Pronounced.* Marked identifiable and present to a large degree.

(5) *Wax or paraffin that adheres firmly to the surface of the cheese.* Thin or thick coating with no indication of cracking, breaking, or loosening.

(6) *Rind.* Hard coating caused by the dehydration of the surface of the cheese.

(7) *Firm sound rind.* Possessing a firmness and thickness (not easily dented or damaged) consistent with the size of the cheese and which is dry, smooth, and closely knit, sufficient to protect the interior quality from external defects; free from checks, cracks, breaks, or soft spots.

(8) *Burst or torn bandage.* A severance of the bandage usually occurring at the side seam, or the bandage is otherwise snagged or broken.

(9) *Wrapper or covering.* Transparent or opaque material (plastic film type or foil) next to the surface of the cheese, used as an enclosure or covering of the cheese.

(10) *Adequately and securely enveloped.* Wrapper or covering properly sealed, and entirely enclosing the cheese, with sufficient adherence to the surface to protect it from contamination and dehydration.

(11) *Smooth bright surface.* Clean, glossy surface.

(12) *Smooth surface.* Not rough or uneven.

(13) *Soiled surface.* Milkstone, rust spots, or other discoloration on the surface of the cheese.

(14) *Surface mold.* Mold on the paraffin or the exterior of the cheese.

(15) *Mold under bandage and paraffin.* Mold spots on areas that have formed under the paraffin or mold that has penetrated from the surface and continued to develop.

(16) *Mold under wrapper or covering.* Mold spots or areas that have formed under the wrapper or on the cheese.

(17) *Rough surface.* Lacks smoothness.

(18) *Bandage evenly placed.* Overlapping the edges evenly about one inch.

(19) *Irregular bandaging.* Bandage improperly placed in the hoop resulting in too much bandage on one end and insufficient on the other causing overlapping; wrinkled and loose fitting.

(20) *Lopsided.* One side of the cheese is higher than the other side.

(21) *High edge.* A rim or ridge on the follower side of the cheese, which is raised in varying degrees. In extreme cases it may bend over.

(22) *Defective coating.* Brittle coating of paraffin that breaks and peels off in the form of scales or flakes; flat or raised blisters or bubbles under the surface of the paraffin; check paraffin, including cracks, breaks or hairline checks in the paraffin or coating of the cheese.

(23) *Checked rind.* Numerous small cracks or breaks in the rind, sometimes following the outline of curd particles, sometimes referred to as "curd openings."

(24) *Huffed.* Swollen because of gas fermentation. The cheese becomes rounded or oval in shape instead of being flat.

(25) *Weak rind.* Thin and possessing little or no resistance to pressure.

(26) *Sour rind.* A fermented rind condition, usually confined to the faces of the cheese.

APPENDIX 1-14. Official identifications for grading, inspection, and so on of dairy products, reproduced from 7 CFR 58.49 to 58.51 (1977).

§ 58.50 Approval and form of official identification.

'(a) Any package label or packaging material which bears any official identification shall be used only in such manner as the Administrator may prescribe, and such official identification shall be of such form and contain such information as the Administrator may require. No label or packaging material bearing official identification shall be used unless finished copies or samples thereof have been approved by the Administrator.

(b) Inspection or grade mark permitted to be used to officially identify packages containing dairy products which are inspected or graded pursuant to this part shall be contained in a shield in the form and design indicated in Figures 1, 2, and 3 of this section or such other form, design, or wording as may be approved by the Administrator.

FIGURE 1

FIGURE 2

MARKING, BRANDING, AND IDENTIFYING PRODUCT

§ 58.49 Authority to use official identification.

Whenever the Administrator determines that the granting of authority to any person to package any product, inspected or graded pursuant to this part, and to use official identification, pursuant to §§ 58.49 through 58.57, will not be inconsistent with the Act and this part, he may authorize such use of official identification. Any application for such authority shall be submitted to the Administrator in such form as he may require.

FIGURE 3

The official identification illustrated in Figure 1 is designed for use on graded product packed under USDA inspection. Figure 2 is designed for graded product processed and packed under USDA inspection. Figure 3 is designed for inspected product (when U.S. standards for grades are not established) processed and packed under USDA quality control service. The official identification shall be printed on the package label, on the carton or on the wrapper and, preferably, on one of the main panels of the carton or wrapper. The shield identification shall be not less than ¾ inch by ¾ inch in size, and preferably 1 inch by 1 inch on 1-pound cartons or wrappers. Consideration will be given by the Administrator of a smaller shield on special packages where the size of the label does not permit use of the ¾ inch by ¾ inch shield.

(c) Official identification under this subpart shall be limited to U.S. Grade B or higher or to an equivalent standard of quality for U.S. name grades or numerical score grades when U.S. standards for grades of a product have not been established.

(d) A sketch, proof, or photocopy of each proposed label or packaging material bearing official identification shall be submitted to the Chief of the Inspection and Grading Branch, Dairy Division, Agricultural Marketing Service, U.S. Department of Agriculture, Washington, D.C. 20250, for review and tentative approval prior to acquisition of a supply of material.

(e) The firm packaging the product shall furnish to the Chief four copies of the printed labels and packaging materials bearing official identification for final approval prior to use.

[37 FR 22363, Oct. 19, 1972, as amended at 39 FR 987, Jan. 4, 1974]

§ 58.51   Information required on official identification.

Each official identification shall conspicuously indicate the U.S. grade of the product it identifies, if there be a grade, or such other appropriate terminology as may be approved by the Administrator. Also, it shall include the appropriate phrase: "Officially graded," "Officially Inspected," or "Federal-State graded." When required by the Administrator, the package label, carton, or wrapper bearing official identification for dairy products shall be stamped or perforated with the date packed and the certificate number or a code number to indicate lot and date packed. Such coding shall be made available to and approved by the Administrator.

APPENDIX 1-15. Simplified organizational chart for the Meat and Poultry Inspections Program

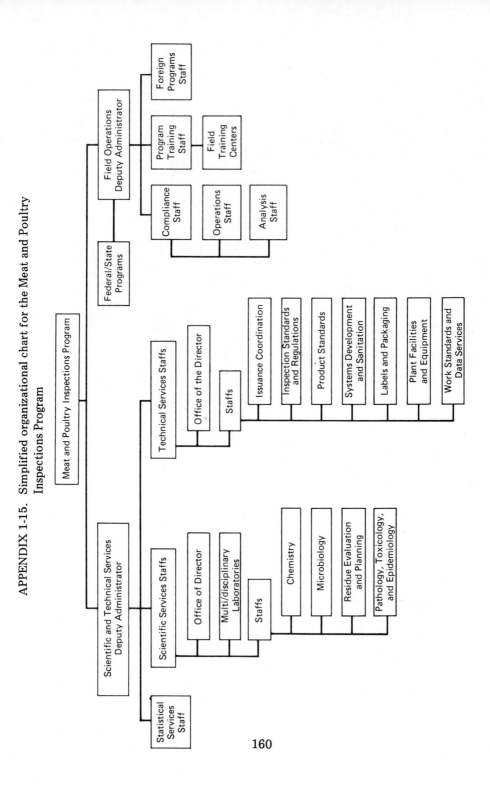

APPENDIX 1-16. Official marks, devices, and certificates used by the Meat Poultry Inspection Program, reproduced from 9 CFR 312 (1977).

PART 312—OFFICIAL MARKS, DEVICES AND CERTIFICATES

Sec.

AUTHORITY: The provisions of this Part 312 issued under 34 Stat. 1260, 79 Stat. 903, as amended, 81 Stat. 584, 84 Stat. 91, 438; 21 U.S.C. 71 et seq., 601 et seq., 33 U.S.C. 466—466k.

SOURCE: The provisions of this Part 312 appear at 35 F.R. 15573, Oct. 3, 1970, unless otherwise noted.

§ 312.1 General.

The marks, devices, and certificates prescribed or referenced in this part shall be official marks, devices, and certificates for purposes of the Act, and shall be used in accordance with the provisions of this part and the regulations cited therein.

§ 312.2 Official marks and devices to identify inspected and passed products of cattle, sheep, swine, or goats.

(a) The official inspection legend required by Part 316 of this subchapter to be applied to inspected and passed carcasses and parts of carcasses of cattle, sheep, swine and goats, meat food prod-

ucts in animal casings, and other products as approved by the Administrator, shall be in the appropriate form as hereinafter specified: [1]

For application to sheep carcasses, the loins and ribs of pork, beef tails, and the smaller varieties of sausage and meat food products in animal casings.

For application to calf and goat carcasses and on the larger varieties of sausage and meat food products in animal casings.

For application to beef and hog carcasses primal parts and cuts therefrom, beef livers, beef tongues, beef hearts, and smoked meats not in casings.

[1] The number "38" is given as an example only. The establishment number of the official establishment where the product is prepared shall be used in lieu thereof.

APPENDIX 1-16. (continued).

For application to burlap, muslin, cheesecloth, heavy paper, or other acceptable material that encloses carcasses or parts of carcasses.

(b) (1) The official inspection legend required by Part 317 of this subchapter to be shown on all labels for inspected and passed products of cattle, sheep, swine, and goats shall be in the following form[1] except that it need not be of the size illustrated, provided that it is a sufficent size and of such color as to be conspicuously displayed and readily legible and the same proportions of letter size and boldness are maintained as illustrated:

(2) This official mark shall be applied by mechanical means and shall not be applied by a hand stamp.

(3) The official inspection legend described in subparagraph (1) of this paragraph may also be used for purposes of Part 316 of this subchapter on shipping

containers, band labels, artificial casings, and other articles with the approval of the Administrator.

(c) Any brand, stamp, label, or other device approved by the Administrator and bearing any official mark prescribed in paragraph (a) or (b) of this section shall be an official device for purposes of the Act.

[35 F.R. 15573, Oct. 3, 1970; 36 F.R. 12002, June 24, 1971]

§ 312.3   Official marks and devices to identify inspected and passed equine products.

(a) The official inspection legend required by § 316.12 or § 317.2 of this subchapter to identify inspected and passed horse carcasses and parts of carcasses, or horse meat food products shall be in the appropriate form as hereinafter specified:[1]

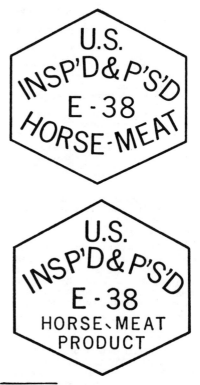

---

[1] See footnote 1 at end of section.

(b) The official inspection legend required by § 316.12 or § 317.2 of this subchapter to identify inspected and passed mule and other (nonhorse) equine carcasses and parts of carcasses, or equine meat food products shall be in whichever of the following form, is appropriate:[1]

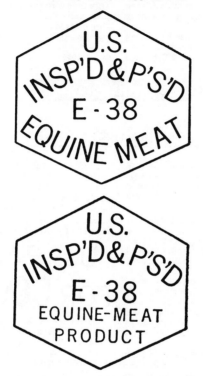

(c) Any brand, stamp, label, or other device approved by the Administrator and bearing any official mark prescribed in paragraph (a) or (b) of this section shall be an official device for purposes of the Act.

§ 312.4 Official ante-mortem inspection marks and devices.

The official marks and devices used in connection with ante-mortem inspection are those prescribed in § 309.18 of this subchapter.

§ 312.5 Official seals for transportation of products.

(a) The official mark for use in sealing railroad cars or other means of convey-

APPENDIX 1-16. (continued).

ance as prescribed in Part 325 of this subchapter shall be the inscription and a serial number as hereinafter shown [2] and any seal approved by the Administrator for applying such mark shall be an official device for purposes of the Act. This seal shall be attached to the means of conveyance only by a Program employee and he shall also affix thereto a "Warning Tag" (Form MP-408-3).

(b) The official mark for use in sealing railroad cars and other means of conveyance as prescribed in Part 327 of this

subchapter shall be the inscription and a serial number hereinafter shown below [3] and the import meat seal approved by the Administrator for applying such mark shall be an official device for purposes of the Act. Such device shall be attached to the means of conveyance only by a Program employee and he shall also affix thereto a "Warning Tag" (Form MP-408-3).

[35 F.R. 15573, Oct. 3, 1970; 36 F.R. 12004, June 24, 1971, as amended at 39 FR 36000, Oct. 7, 1974]

§ 312.6   Official marks and devices in connection with post-mortem inspection and identification of adulterated products and insanitary equipment and facilities.

(a) The official marks required by Parts 308 and 310 of this subchapter for use in post-mortem inspection and identification of adulterated products and insanitary equipment and facilities are:

(1) The tag (Form MP-427) which is used to retain carcasses and parts of carcasses in the slaughter department; it is black and white, and bears the legend "U.S. Retained." It is a three-section tag as used for hogs, sheep, goats, and calves and a five-section tag as used for cattle and equine.

(2) The "U.S. Retained" mark which is applied to products and articles as prescribed in Part 310 of this subchapter by means of a paper tag (Form MP-35) bearing the legend "U.S. Retained."

(3) The "U.S. Rejected" mark which is used to identify insanitary buildings, rooms, or equipment as prescribed in Part 308 of this subchapter and is applied by means of a paper tag (Form

MP-35 bearing the legend "U.S. Rejected."

(4) The "U.S. Passed for Cooking" mark is applied on products passed for cooking as prescribed in Part 310 of this subchapter by means of a brand and is in the following form:

U.S. PASSED
FOR COOKING

(5) The "U.S. Inspected and Condemned" mark shall be applied to products condemned as prescribed in Part 310 by means of a brand and is in the following form:

U.S. INSP'D AND
CONDEMNED

(b) The U.S. Retained and U.S. Rejected tags, and all other brands, stamps, labels, and other devices approved by the Administrator and bearing any official mark prescribed in paragraph (a) of this section, shall be official devices for purposes of the Act.

[35 FR 15573, Oct. 3, 1970, as amended at 38 FR 29214, Oct. 23, 1973; 39 FR 36000; Oct. 7, 1974]

[1] The number "38" is given as an example only. The establishment number of the official establishment where the product is prepared shall be used in lieu thereof.

[2] The number "2135202" is given as an example only. The serial number of the specific seal will be shown in lieu thereof.

[3] The term "F-351587" is given as an example only. The serial number of the specific seal will be shown in lieu thereof.

§ 312.7 Official import inspection marks and devices.

(a) When import inspections are performed in official import inspection establishments, the official inspection legend, required by Part 327 of this subchapter, to be applied to imported meat and meat food products shall be in the appropriate form[1] as hereinafter specified:

FOR APPLICATION TO CARCASSES, PRIMAL PARTS, AND CUTS, NOT IN CONTAINERS

FOR APPLICATION TO OUTSIDE CONTAINERS

(b) When import inspections are performed in official establishments, the official inspection legend, required by Part 327 of this subchapter, to be applied to imported meat and meat food products shall be the appropriate form as specified in § 312.2 of this Part.

---

[1] The number I-38 is given as an example only. The establishment number of the official import inspection establishment where the product is inspected shall be used in lieu thereof.

(c) When products are refused entry into the United States, the official mark, when required by Part 327 of this subchapter, to be applied to the products refused entry shall be in the following form:

(d) Devices for applying such marks will be furnished to Program inspectors by the Department.

[37 F.R. 21926, Oct. 17, 1972]

§ 312.8 Official export inspection marks, devices, and certificates.

(a) The official export meat inspection stamp required by Part 322 of this subchapter is a paper sticker bearing the following official mark, including the seal of the U.S. Department of Agriculture, with a serial number such as "D-5216200":

United States
Department of Agriculture
Animal and Plant Health Inspection Service
Meat and Poultry Products Inspection
U.S. Inspected and Passed

Such stamp is an official device for the purposes of the Act.

(b) The official export certificate required by Part 322 of this subchapter is a paper certificate form for signature by a Program employee bearing the legend:

United States
Department of Agriculture
Animal and Plant Health Inspection Service
Meat and Poultry Products Inspection

and the seal of the United States Department of Agriculture, with a certification that meat or meat food product described on the form is from animals that received ante-mortem and post-mortem inspection and were found sound and healthy and that it has been inspected and passed as provided by law and the regulations of the Department of Agriculture and is sound and wholesome. The certificate also bears a serial number such as "No. 184432."

APPENDIX 1-17. Definitions and standards of indentity for certain "raw meat products," "cooked meats" and "cured meats, unsmoked and smoked." They are reproduced from 9 CFR 319.15, 319.29, 319.80, 319.81, 319.100, 319.101, 319.102, and 319.103 (1977).

Subpart B—Raw Meat Products

§ 319.15 Miscellaneous beef products.

(a) *C h o p p e d   b e e f,   g r o u n d   b e e f.* "Chopped Beef" or "Ground Beef" shall consist of chopped fresh and/or frozen beef with or without seasoning and without the addition of beef fat as such, shall not contain more than 30 percent fat, and shall not contain added water, binders, or extenders. When beef cheek meat (trimmed beef cheeks) is used in the preparation of chopped or ground beef, the amount of such cheek meat shall be limited to 25 percent; and if in excess of natural proportions, its presence shall be declared on the label, in the ingredient statement required by § 317.2 of this subchapter, if any, and otherwise contiguous to the name of the product.

(b) *Hamburger.* "Hamburger" shall consist of chopped fresh and/or frozen beef with or without the addition of beef fat as such and/or seasoning, shall not contain more than 30 percent fat, and shall not contain added water, binders, or extenders. Beef cheek meat (trimmed beef cheeks) may be used in the preparation of hamburger only in accordance with the conditions prescribed in paragraph (a) of this section.

(c) *Beef patties.* "Beef Patties" shall consist of chopped fresh and/or frozen beef with or without the addition of beef fat as such and/or seasonings. Binders or extenders and/or partially defatted beef fatty tissue may be used without added water or with added water only in amounts such that the product's characteristics are essentially that of a meat pattie.

(d) *Fabricated steak.* Fabricated beef steaks, veal steaks, beef and veal steaks, or veal and beef steaks, and similar products, such as those labeled "Beef Steak, Chopped, Shaped, Frozen," "Minute Steak, Formed, Wafer Sliced, Frozen," "Veal Steaks, Beef Added, Chopped—Molded — Cubed — Frozen, Hydrolyzed Plant Protein, and Flavoring" shall be prepared by comminuting and forming the product from fresh and/or frozen meat, with or without added fat, of the species indicated on the label. Such products shall not contain more than 30 percent fat and shall not contain added water, binders or extenders. Beef cheek meat (trimmed beef cheeks) may be used in the preparation of fabricated beef steaks only in accordance with the conditions prescribed in paragraph (a) of this section.

(e) *Partially defatted beef fatty tissue.* "Partially Defatted Beef Fatty Tissue" is a beef byproduct derived from the low temperature rendering (not exceeding 120°F.) of fresh beef fatty tissue. Such product shall have a pinkish color and a fresh odor and appearance.

[35 FR 15597, Oct. 3, 1970 as amended at 38 FR 29215, Oct. 23, 1973]

§ 319.29 Miscellaneous pork products.

(a) *Partially defatted pork fatty tissue.* "Partially Defatted Pork Fatty Tissue" is a pork byproduct derived from the low temperature rendering (not exceeding 120° F.) of fresh pork fatty tissue, exclusive of skin. Such product shall have a pinkish color and a fresh odor and appearance.

Subpart C—Cooked Meats

§ 319.80 Barbecued meats.

Barbecued meats, such as product labeled "Beef Barbecue" or "Barbecued Pork," shall be cooked by the direct action of dry heat resulting from the burning of hard wood or the hot coals therefrom for a sufficient period to assume the usual characteristics of a barbecued article, which include the formation of a brown crust on the surface and the rendering of surface fat. The product may be basted with a sauce during the cooking process. The weight of barbecued meat shall not exceed 70 percent of the weight of the fresh uncooked meat.

§ 319.81   Roast beef parboiled and steam roasted.

"Roast Beef Parboiled and Steam Roasted" shall be prepared so that the weight of the finished product, excluding salt and flavoring material, shall not exceed 70 percent of the fresh beef weight. Beef cheek meat and beef head meat from which the overlying glandular and connective tissues have been removed, and beef heart meat, exclusive of the heart cap may be used individually or collectively to the extent of 5 percent of the meat ingredients in the preparation of canned product labeled "Roast Beef Parboiled and Steam Roasted." When beef cheek meat, beef head meat, or beef heart meat is used in the preparation of this product, its presence shall be reflected in the statement of ingredients required by Part 317 of this subchapter.

[35 FR 15597, Oct. 3, 1970, as amended at 38 FR 29215, Oct. 23, 1973]

Subpart D—Cured Meats, Unsmoked and Smoked

§ 319.100   Corned beef.

"Corned Beef" shall be prepared from beef briskets, navels, clods, middle ribs, rounds, rumps, or similar cuts using one or a combination of the curing ingredients specified in § 318.7(c) (1) and (4) of this subchapter. Canned product labeled "Corned Beef" shall be prepared so that the weight of the finished product, excluding cure, salt, and flavoring material, shall not exceed 70 percent of the fresh beef weight. Corned beef other than canned shall be cured in pieces weighing not less than 1 pound, and if cooked, its weight shall not exceed the weight of the fresh uncured beef. Beef cheek meat, beef head meat and beef heart meat may be used to the extent of 5 percent of the meat ingredient in preparation of this product when trimmed as specified in § 319.81. When beef cheek meat, beef head meat, or beef heart meat is used in preparation of this product, its presence shall be reflected in the statement of ingredients required by Part 317 of this subchapter. The application of curing solution to beef cuts, other than briskets, which are intended for bulk corned beef shall not result in an increase in the weight of the finished cured product of more than

10 percent over the weight of the fresh uncured meat.

[35 F.R. 15597, Oct. 3, 1970; 36 F.R. 11903, June 23, 1971, as amended at 38 FR 29215, Oct. 23, 1973]

§ 319.101   Corned beef brisket.

In preparing "Corned Beef Brisket," the application of curing solution to the beef brisket shall not result in an increase in the weight of the finished cured product of more than 20 percent over the weight of the fresh uncured brisket. If the product is cooked, the weight of the finished product shall not exceed the weight of the fresh uncured brisket.

§ 319.102   Corned beef round and other corned beef cuts.

In preparing "Corned Beef Round" and other corned beef cuts, except "Corned Beef Briskets," the curing solution shall be applied to pieces of beef weighing not less than one pound and such application shall not result in an increased weight of the cured beef product of more than 10 percent over the weight of the fresh uncured beef cut. If the product is cooked, the weight of the finished product shall not exceed the weight of the fresh uncured beef cut.

§ 319.103   Cured beef tongue.

In preparing "Cured Beef Tongue," the application of curing solution to the fresh beef tongue shall not result in an increase in the weight of the cured beef tongue of more than 10 percent over the weight of the fresh uncured beef tongue.

APPENDIX 1-18. Simplified organizational chart of the Office of the Foreign
Agricultural Service

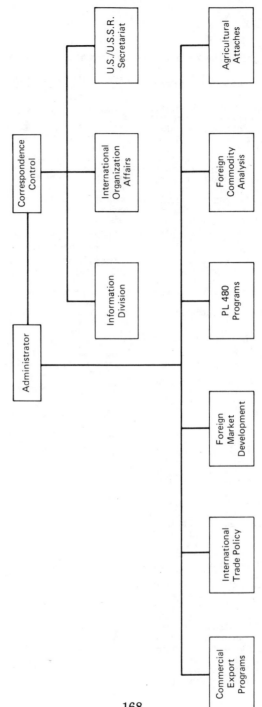

CHAPTER 2
DEPARTMENT
OF COMMERCE

INTRODUCTION

The U.S. Department of Commerce is another federal agency at the cabinet level within the executive branch of the U.S. Government. This department directs a huge number of other federal agencies, two of which play a very important part in food standards and inspections. One is the National Bureau of Standards (NBS) and the other, the National Oceanic and Atmospheric Administration. Refer to Appendix 2-1 for a simplified organizational structure of the Department of Commerce.

NATIONAL BUREAU OF STANDARDS

Introduction

The NBS was established by an act of the U.S. Congress (the Enabling Act or the Organic Act) of March 3, 1901 (31 Stat. 1449, as amended; 15 U.S.C. 271 to 286). The main purpose of the NBS is to: provide technical assistance in establishing commodity measurement and performance standards; develop federal product safety standards required by law; provide scientific and technological services for industry and government; establish a technical basis for equity in trade; and disseminate technical, scientific, and engineering information to the public and government agencies. Thus its overall goal is to strengthen and advance the nation's science and technology and to facilitate their effective application for public benefit.

Most of the official activities and regulations of the NBS are described in 15 CFR 10, 12, and 200 to 265. Those parts relevant to this book are discussed later. A booklet entitled "National Bureau of Standards at a glance" listed in Table 2-1, together with similar publications, provides some basic information about the agency; Appendix 2-2 presents its organizational structure. The technical programs of the NBS are conducted by four institutes, each headed by a director who is responsible for the development and direction of the institute's research and technical programs.

One of these four institutes is the Institute for Applied Technology. It is con-

TABLE 2-1. General Publications on and Published by the NBS

1. National Bureau of Standards at a glance; revised periodically.
2. Mission of Office of Weights and Measures; undated and unnumbered.

cerned with the application of technology to the solution of a number of identified societal problems. The areas in which the institute's major programs are concentrated include building technology, electronics, and fire research and safety. It is composed of three centers and two divisions. One of these two divisions is called the Standards Application and Analysis Division. The division facilitates domestic and international commerce by providing technical and administrative assistance to public and private organizations involved in the application and development of regulatory and voluntary standards. It also provides guidance to the engineering and product standards programs in the NBS. This division supervises a number of offices, three of which are of concern to this book. They include the Offices of Weights and Measures, Standards Development Services, and Metric Information.

Office of Weights and Measures

This office exists to provide leadership and technical resources that will assure the accuracy of the quantities and quantity representations in all commercial transactions in the United States, to supervise the standardization of weights and measures system in the country's commerce in order to provide protection equally to buyers and sellers, and to promote uniformity in such a system. Some of these roles produce regulations and activities that directly affect the consumers since they are concerned with the accuracy of scales in the supermarket, the commodity packages, the farm milk tank, the neighborhood gasoline pump and the taximeter, the truck scale, and the fuel/oil meter. Almost every weighing and measuring device used in the nation's commerce is affected; some are closely related to food. In Table 2-1, the brochure "Mission of the Office of Weights and Measures" is a good reference source for information about this agency.

The legal authority of this office is derived from certain provisions of two federal statutes: the Enable Act or Organic Act of 1901 (15 U.S.C. 272) and the Fair Packaging and Labeling Act of 1966 (15 U.S.C. 1454).

Specifically, this office has been assigned the following statutory authority:

1. "The provision of means and methods for making measurements consistent with those (*the national*) standards" [15 U.S.C. 272(a)].
2. "Cooperation with other governmental agencies and with private organizations in the establishment of standard practices, incorporated in codes and specifications" [15 U.S.C. 272(d)].
3. "Advisory service to Government agencies on...technical problems" [15 U.S.C. 272(e)].

The office conducts the following authorized activities:

1. "The study and improvement of instruments and methods of measurements" [15 U.S.C. 272(3)].
2. "Cooperation with the States in securing uniformity in weights and measures laws and methods of inspection" [15 U.S.C. 272(5)].
3. "Prosecution of such research in engineering...as may be necessary to obtain basic data pertinent to the functions specified herein" [15 U.S.C. 272(18)].
4. "The compilation and publication of general scientific data resulting from the performance of the functions specified herein...when such data are of importance to...manufacturing interests or to the general public and are not available elsewhere" [15 U.S.C. 272(19)].

With reference to the other statute, the office has the following responsibility: "the conduct of such studies, investigations, and standards development activities as are necessary to achieve the objectives of the Fair Packaging and Labeling Act" (31 FR 6746; 32 FR 3110). Further details on this aspect are presented later.

In fulfilling its mission, the office has engaged in a wide range of activities. The three areas that most concern this book are: the National Conference on Weights and Measures; standards, handbooks, and model laws and regulations; and packaging practices. They are discussed in the paragraphs that follow.

National Conference on Weights and Measures

This is the major mechanism through which the office works with federal, state, and local officials, representatives of industry, trade associations, and consumer groups, all of whom make up the conference. It meets annually, and the director of the Office of Weights and Measures is the executive secretariat for the conference. Table 2-2 lists the reference sources for information on the conference. The five main objectives of the conference are obtained from the publication "The National Conference on Weights and Measures--Its Organization and Procedure" and are reproduced as follows:

1. Provide a national forum for the discussion of all questions related to weights and measures administration as carried on by regulatory officers of the States, Commonwealths, Territories, and Possessions of the United States, their political subdivisions, and the District of Columbia.
2. Provide a mechanism to establish policy and coordinate activities within the Conference on matters of national and international significance.
3. Develop a consensus on model weights and measures laws and regulations, specifications, and tolerances for commercially-used weighing and measuring devices, and testing, enforcement, and administrative procedures.

4. Encourage and promote uniformity of requirements and methods among weights and measures jurisdictions.
5. Foster cooperation among weights and measures officers themselves and between them and all of the many manufacturing, industrial, business, and consumer interests affected by their official activities.

TABLE 2-2. Publications Issued by the NBS Concerning the National Conference on Weights and Measures

Publication Number and Date	Title of Publication
Unnumbered, Undated	The National Conference on Weights and Measures --Its organization and procedure
NBS Miscellaneous Publication 377	Index to the Reports of the National Conference on Weights and Measures (1905 to 1971)
Variable[a]	Report of the National Conference on Weights and Measures
Unnumbered (revised March 1976)[b]	Weights and Measures Directory, List of State, Commonwealth, District and Major Local Weights & Measures Offices of the United States

[a] Annual Publication beginning with 1971; each report has its own publication number.

[b] Always request the latest issue.

This sponsorship by a unit of the NBS is exercised under authority of that portion of the Organic Act under which the NBS is authorized to provide "cooperation with the States in securing uniformity in weights and measures laws and methods of inspection."

At present the annual attendance of this conference has exceeded 500, and practically all state administrative officials related to weights and measures participate. The conference develops many technical and general recommendations in the field of weights and measures administration, and its programs explore the entire area of this economically important segment of governmental regulatory service. Within the limitations of applicable federal authorization and policy, the NBS publishes and distributes reports of the proceedings of the meetings of the conference, reports of conference committees, and model laws, regulations, specifications, and tolerances adopted by the conference. Through the years, the NBS, via the Office of Weights and Measures, has exerted a strong leadership over the conference. Many of the technical publications are very useful and are discussed later on.

Federal food laws control the interstate commerce of edible items; city, county, and state regulatory officials are often required to promulgate their own standards and regulations as well as to enforce them. Every consumer often assumes that the weighing scale is accurate, and the package of meat, sugar, flour, or ice cream contains the amount it claims on the labels. This assumption is correct most of the time, although there is definitely a need for a city or county office that provides properly trained personnel to police any unfair dealings. Thus the conference assembles the decision-making officials and generates uniformity among the regulations issued by them concerning weights and measures. This conference provides no regulatory power, but it offers coordination and technical advice.

Table 2-2 also includes another useful publication, "List of State, Commonwealth, District and Major Local Weights and Measures Offices of the United States," from which one may obtain the name and location of the nearest weight and measure official.

Standards, Handbooks, Model Laws, and Regulations

All food items and their containers have measurement such as weight, height, volume, and other parameters. The standards for these units are established by the Office of Weights and Measures. Some relevant publications concerning weights, volumes, lengths, widths, and heights and other units of measurements are described in Table 2-3. Of special importance is the one-page leaflet titled "Household Weights and Measures." It provides information on the number of fluid ounces in one teaspoon, the approximate weight of one cup of flour, the number of pints in 1 quart, and so on. Table 2-3 also lists a number of publications on units and systems of weights and measures. These can be consulted for further details.

Among all the technical publications issued by the Office of Weights and Measures, Handbook No. 44 (see Table 2-4) has been adopted by the largest number of states. The specifications, tolerances, and other technical requirements for commercial weighing and measuring devices published in this government document comprise, in their latest form, all the current codes as adopted by the National Conference on Weights and Measures.

This publication is kept updated by the issuance of replacement sheets. Thus at any one time a well-kept copy in a document library should contain the most current information.

The main purpose of the technical requirements in Handbook 44 is to elimi-

TABLE 2-3. Selected Publications on Units and Systems of Weights and Measures
in the United States (All are issued by the NBS)

Publication Number and Date	Title of Publication
NBS Circular No. 593 (1958)	The Federal Basis for Weights and Measures
NBS Miscellaneous Publication No. 234 (November 1960)[a]	Household Weights and Measures
NBS Handbook No. 82 (1962)	Weights and Measures Administration
NBS Miscellaneous Publication No. 247 (1963)	Weights and Measures Standards of the United States, A brief history
NBS Miscellaneous Publication No. 286 (1967)	Units of Weight and Measure--Definitions and Tables of Equivalents
Unnumbered 1967[b]	Units of Measurement (Conversion Factors and Special Tables)
NBS Circular No. 1035 (January 1960, amended June 1975)	Units and Systems of Weights and Measures--Their Origin, Development, and Present Status

[a] Already out of print. Xerox copy of this two-page publication may be obtained.

[b] This article has actually been obtained from Publication No. 286.

nate from use all weights and measures and weighing and measuring devices that
fall into any of the following three categories:

1. The device is false.
2. The device is faulty. It is of such construction that it fails to repeat correct
    indications at all times or its adjustment is not reasonably permanent.
3. The device will facilitate the perpetuation of fraud.

Also, the requirements in Handbook 44 refrain from prejudicing any appara-

TABLE 2-4. Selected Handbooks Published by the NBS

NBS Handbook Number and Date	Title of Handbook
44 (1971)[a]	Specifications, Tolerances, and Other Technical Requirements for Commercial Weighing and Measuring Devices
67 (1958)[b]	Checking Prepackaged Commodities
94 (March 1965)	The Examination of Weighing Equipment
105-1 (1972)	Specifications and Tolerances for Field Standard Weights
112 (June 1973)	Examination Procedure Outlines for Commercial Weighing and Measuring Devices
NBS List of Publications, LP 56 (Revised April 1976) [c]	List of NBS Handbooks

[a] This is the fourth edition, and replacement sheets are constantly added to the 1971 copy. A new edition is expected.

[b] A draft of the revision was prepared in 1975. A new, revised edition is expected.

[c] Always request the latest issue.

tus that conforms as closely as practicable to the official standards. The conference recommends and encourages each participating state to promulgate and use such requirements in their regulatory control of commercial weighing and measuring apparatus. A similar recommendation is made with respect to local jurisdictions when their state authority does not promulgate any technical requirements such as specifications and tolerances.

The entire publication is divided into various codes, including a general code that applies to all other codes. Among the specific individual codes, four are of interest to this book: the codes for farm milk tanks, measure-containers, milk bottles, and berry baskets and boxes. Certain aspects of the code for measure-containers are as follows. According to the code for measure-containers, the containers include lids or closures if they are needed to enclose the commodity completely and are applicable to two types of situations.

One type includes those retail measure-containers used to determine, on the basis of liquid measure, the quantity of commodity from bulk supply. They are used only once and serve as the containers for the delivery of the commodity at time of retail sale. The second type includes prepackaged measure-containers intended for use only once to determine in advance of sale the quantity of a commodity on the basis of liquid measure. They serve as the containers for the delivery of the commodity, in either a wholesale or a retail market unit.

The code specifically excludes rigid containers used for cream, milk, or other dairy fluid products since containers for these products are covered by the code for milk bottles.

What are some examples that will fit these two applications? Retail measure-containers are now rarely encountered in present-day grocery store or supermarket merchandizing methods. For example, in the State of Oregon, food products including olive oil, cooking oil, vinegar and even molasses were at one time purchased at retail in containers covered by this section of the code. Such is no longer the case. In some states the only current examples of the use of this code for food products involve soft drinks. For example, fairly recently one could still purchase root beer to take home from A&W Drive-Ins measured from bulk into quart, half-gallon, and gallon single-service containers. Thus there are still instances where drive-in-type restaurants and refreshment stands sell soft drinks, apple cider, and other beverages in receptacles defined as retail measure-containers. In some states, retail measure-containers such as cardboard quart and pint containers may be used to fill, at the time of sale, potato salad, soups, puddings, and other foods in a delicatessen.

Prepackaged measure-containers include virtually all packages of ice cream, ice milk, sherbert, and mellorine sold in grocery stores. The "measuring" in these cases takes place at the plant level (during packaging filling), and not in the presence of the customer at the time of sale. Of course, because they are packaged, they would be subjected to other federal and state codes and laws. They have to be labeled in a manner that all of the requirements of the Fair Packaging and Labeling Act will be met, such as the identity of the commodity. the name and place of business of the manufacturer, packager, or distributor, and the net quantity placed on the principal display panel.

Some specifications for the retail measure-containers are: liquid pint (¼, ½, or 1), liquid quart (1), and gallon (½, 1, or multiple of 1). The "¼ liquid pint" may be replaced by "4 fluid ounces." The container must not be subdivided. Some specifications for prepackaged measure-containers are: liquid pint (½ or 1), liquid quart (1), and gallon (½, 1, 2½, 3½, or multiple of 1). Also, any capacity less than ½ liquid pint is permitted.

Each measure-container carries a specific capacity point that may be defined by "the top edge, a line near the top edge, or the horizontal cross-sectional place established by the bottom surface of the removal lid or cap when seated in the container."

One should be able to determine the capacity of a measure-container without distorting its normal assembled shape, which should be designed in some suitable geometrical form. The capacity point, if it is defined by a line, should be labeled by a statement in close proximity, identifying it as such. The capacity must also be defined by a clear statement in terms of prescribed units.

The use of a measure-container of rectangular cross section of a capacity of ½ gallon or over should be limited to the packaging, in advance of sale, of ice cream, sherbert, or other similar frozen desserts.

The code also defines the acceptance of tolerances, in excess and in deficiency, for measure-containers.

The importance of this code is recognized by the FDA, which, in its regulation for packaging and labeling (see Chapter 6), makes the following exceptions.

According to 21 CFR 1.24(a)(6), fruit sherbets, ice milk, French ice cream, ice cream, water ices, quiescently frozen confections (with or without dairy ingredients), special dietary frozen desserts, and other similar products, are permitted to express the net contents of 8-fluid ounces and 64-fluid ounces (or 2 quarts) in the form of ½ pint and ½ gallon, respectively, when the product(s) is(are) measured by and packaged in ½-liquid pint and ½-gallon measure-containers as defined in the code for measure-containers in Handbook No. 44.

Also, when the preceding products are measured by and packaged in 1-liquid pint, 1-liquid quart, and ½-liquid gallon measure-containers as defined in the handbook, they will be exempt from the "dual net-contents declaration requirement."

Also, the products, when measured by and packaged in ½-liquid pint, 1-liquid pint, 1-liquid quart, ½-gallon, and 1-gallon measure-containers as defined in Handbook No. 44, are exempt from the requirement that declaration of net contents be located within the bottom 30% of the principal display panel.

For information about the codes for farm milk tank, milk bottles, and berry baskets and boxes, consult Handbook 44. This handbook has been adopted by many state weights and measures officials, although such is not a mandatory requirement. This is an example of achieving uniformity in important food regulations in this country without a federal statute from the U.S. Congress. Some other important handbooks are described in Table 2-4. To determine which handbooks are available, refer to the document "List of NBS Handbooks" as indicated in that table.

As mentioned previously, the NBS, on recommendation from the National Conference on Weights and Measures, publishes model laws and regulations. Table 2-5 provides a list of such publications, some of which are related to food products. Such publications are models only and do not carry any regulatory power unless adopted by state authorities. One major publication is entitled "Model State Pack-

TABLE 2-5. Model Laws and Regulations Recommended by the National Confer-
            ence on Weights and Measures; published by the National Bureau of
            Standards

Publication Number and Date	Title of Publication
Unnumbered (1965)	Model State Weighmaster Law
Unnumbered (1975)	Model State Weights and Measures Law
Unnumbered (1975)	Model Weights and Measures Ordinance (for cities or counties)
Unnumbered (1966)	Model State Registration of Servicemen and Service Agencies Regulation
Unnumbered (1972)	Model Unit Pricing Regulation
Unnumbered (1973)	Model State Open Dating Regulation
Unnumbered (1975)	Model State Packaging and Labeling Regulation
Unnumbered (1975)	Model State Method of Sale of Commodities Regulation

aging and Labeling Regulation." It contains information on such topics as definitions for consumer package and label, declaration of identity and quantity, variations to be allowed for packages and net quantity, and numerous other requirements. Most of the information contained in this publication are being drafted into
the revision of Handbook No. 67, "Checking Prepackaged Commodities" (see
Table 2-4). This publication is being prepared with proper consideration for the
regulations issued by the FDA, Bureau of Alcohol, Tobacco and Firearms, USDA,
and the Federal Trade Commission in regard to food packaging and labeling. Similarly, Handbook No. 67 serves as a model only and does not have regulatory power.
Over the years, many states have adopted much of the model laws and regulations
in Handbook No. 67 into their regulatory programs. The State of California has
also adopted much of the information into its Business and Professions Code.

    With reference to Handbook 67, the Model State Packaging and Labeling

Regulation, and California laws and regulations, some very important and interesting court cases were settled in 1977.

On March 29, 1977, the U.S. Supreme Court ruled that states cannot enact food packaging laws different from those of the federal government. The court upheld decisions by lower courts that a California law used by a county official to ban the sale of Rath bacon and flour packaged by three companies is preempted by federal statutes.

Because of the importance and precedent-setting nature of this case, a brief discussion is presented as follows. Most of the pertinent legal references may be obtained from the final opinion of the Supreme Court (*Jones* v. *Rath Packing Co. et al*, No. 75-1053, March 29, 1977).

The discussion is divided into the following parts: (1) relevant regulation and law of California, (2) food companies involved and the federal statutes that govern their labeling and packaging practices, (3) relevant provisions of the federal statutes, (4) background history of the cases, and (5) the Supreme Court decision.

Relevant Regulation and Law of California. Section 12211 of the California Business and Professions Code states: "The average weight or measure of the packages or containers in a lot of any...commodity sampled shall not be less, at the time of sale...than the net weight or measure stated upon the package...."

In Title 4, California Administrative Code, Chapter 8, Subchapter 2, Article 5 details the regulation to implement section 12211 cited in the preceding paragraph. It sets forth statistical sampling procedures that an inspector uses to determine whether the average net weight of the contents of packages contained in lots is less than the net weight stated on the packages. Scientifically, such procedures provide allowances for unavoidable deviations of the net weights of the package contents due to variations in the manufacturing process. However, the statistical processes do not permit variations among the contents as a result of the distribution process. For example, during the course of any good distribution practice, there may be loss of weight resulting from moisture loss.

Food Companies Involved and Federal Statutes that Govern Their Labeling and Packaging Practices. The Rath Packing Company is a meat processor subject to federal regulation under the Wholesome Meat Act of 1967 (18 Stat. 584, as amended; 21 U.S.C. 601 et seq.). Among Rath's meat food products is bacon, which the company packages in containers for ultimate retail sale.

General Mills, Inc., the Pillsbury Company, and Seaboard Allied Milling Corporation all manufacture, package, and sell wheat flour. Wheat flour is a "food" under the Federal Food, Drug, and Cosmetic Act (52 Stat. 1040, as amended; 21 U.S.C. 301 et seq.) and a "consumer commodity" under the Fair Packaging and Labeling Act (80 Stat. 1296, as amended, 15 U.S.C. 1451 et seq.).

Relevant Provisions of Federal Statutes. The applicable federal legislation [15 U.S.C. 1453(a)(2); 21 U.S.C. 331(a), 343(e); 21 U.S.C. 601(n)(5), 610(b)] prohibits the distribution by the food industries of packaged bacon or flour unless the package bears a label containing an accurate statement of the net weight of the contents. Also, federal regulations require that the actual and labeled net weights be the same *at the time and place of packaging.* However, federal regulations make the following allowances [9 CFR 317.2(h)(2); 21 CFR 101.105(q)], "Reasonable variations caused by loss or gain of moisture during the course of good distribution practices or by unavoidable deviations in good manufacturing practice will be recognized. Variations from stated quantity of contents shall not be unreasonably large."

The Wholesome Meat Act (21 U.S.C. 678) contains the following preemptive clause, "Marking, labeling, packaging, or ingredient requirements in addition to, or different than, those made under this Act may not be imposed by any State or Territory or the District of Columbia with respect to articles prepared at any establishment under inspection in accordance with the requirements under...this Act...."

The Federal Food, Drug, and Cosmetic Act does not contain any relevant preemptive clause.

The Fair Packaging and Labeling Act contains the following preemptive clause (15 U.S.C. 1461), "It is hereby declared that it is the express intent of Congress to supersede any and all laws of the States...which are less stringent than or require information different from the requirements of...this Act or regulations promulgated...."

Background History of the Cases. Between April 1971 and March 1972 the Department of Weights and Measures in Los Angeles County ordered more than 100 lots of Rath bacon off sale after determining that the products were under weight according to California regulation. After some initial local court actions, the Rath Comapny filed suit at a U.S. district court on March 17, 1972. It requested declaratory and injunctive relief based on the allegation that certain state statutes were preempted by the Wholesome Meat Act.

From October to December of 1972 the Department of Weights and Measures in Riverside County, California, ordered off sale wheat flour manufactured by the three companies listed earlier (General Mills, Inc., Pillsbury Co., and Seaboard Allied Milling Corp.) because they were under weight according to California regulation. In July 1973 more bags of flour were ordered off sale. In the meantime (April 1973) the companies had brought suit in a U.S. district court requesting for declaratory and injunction relief against the county's actions. The county officials counterclaimed, alleging that some 30,618 bags of flour totaling 191,731 pounds had been ordered off sale and requested instead declarations antithetical to those requested by the companies as well as an injunction against their continuing violations of California law. In both bases the U.S. district court granted in part the relief as requested by the food industries. The court held that California Business and Professions Code Section 12211 and Title 4, California Administrative Code, Chapter 8, Subchapter 2, Article 5 are preempted by federal law and enjoined their enforcement. The cases were brought to the Federal Court of Appeals, which upheld the lower court decision. The State of California, on behalf of the county officials, requested the Supreme Court of the United States to review both cases. Thirty-three states and their attorney generals sided with the county officials of California in arguing that states should have the power to impose stricter standards in packaging in order to offer greater protection to consumers.

The Supreme Court Decision. The case was argued in front of the Supreme Court on December 6 and 7, 1976, and a decision was handed down on March 29, 1977. Seven justices, including the Chief Justice, agreed on the opinion, and two justices filed a separate opinion agreeing in part and dissenting in part with the majority's opinion, which is summarized as follows.

The provision in the Wholesome Meat Act preempts the law/regulation in California. The latter does not permit variations as a result of good distribution practice that may result in weight loss from moisture loss. Since it only permits allowance for reasonable manufacturing variations, it is "different than" the federal requirement. The latter permits both types of variations.

With reference to the Fair Packaging and Labeling Act, the California law/regulation is neither "less stringent than" nor "requires information different from" the federal statute. However, to permit the enforcement of the California standard would have been contrary to the purpose and objective of the U.S. Congress when it passed the federal statute. This is because the basic goal of the federal act is to facilitate value comparisons by consumers among similarly labeled/packaged products. Such comparison is not possible if two products do not contain the same quantity. When flour is packed in a manufacturing plant, it usually contains 14% to 15% of moisture, which is an indication that a similar quantity of flour solid will be in different bags of flour. Thus packages of flour that meet the federal labeling requirements and have the same stated quantity of contents can be expected to contain the same amount of flour solids even if variations from stated weight caused by loss of moisture are permitted. On the other hand, if a national milling firm packages its flour in accordance with a state regulation such as that of California, it will have to overpack. This is because of the lower humidity of such states. Other national millers that send their flour packages to states that conform to the federal regulation or have higher humidity would not have to overpack. Also, local millers that package and sell their flour within the same state do not have to overpack. Thus consumers in different parts of the country or state who attempt to compare the values of identically labeled packages of flour will not be comparing packages that contain identical amounts of flour solids and hence will be misled. This could frustrate the execution of the objective of the U.S. Congress, which is impermissible under the U.S. Constitution. Hence the state law must yield to the federal statute. The U.S. Supreme Court upheld the decision of the Federal Court of Appeals.

This discussion presents the legal aspects of this "test" case and also illustrates the role of the Office of Weights and Measures. Through the National Conference on Weights and Measures, the NBS published Handbook 67 and the Model State Packaging and Labeling regulation, both of which recommend the following:

> 12.1.1 Variations from Declared Net Quantity.--Variations from the declared net weight, measure, or count shall be permitted when caused by unavoidable deviations in weighing, measuring, or counting the contents of individual packages that occur in good packaging practice, but such variations shall not be permitted to such extent that the average of the quantities in the packages of a particular commodity, or a lot of the commodity that is kept, offered, or exposed for sale, or sold, is below the quantity stated, and no unreasonable shortage in any package shall be permitted.

This clause has been adopted by the State of California. The NBS has an influence on the weights and measures reguations in all states in this country.

Packaging Practices

The Office of Weights and Measures participates in the "voluntary regulation" of packaging commodities in two ways. Exercising part of its statutory authority inherent in the Organic Act of 1901, it assists in the development of model laws and regulations that aim at promoting uniformity in weights, measures, and quantities in which consumer commodities are packaged for retail sale and also provides cooperation and assistance to state and local officials to achieve such uniformity. Some of these packaging and labeling regulations have been discussed previously.

The Office of Weights and Measures contributes in another way by providing assistance and counsel to the packaging industry on means and methods for achieving the aims of the Fair Packaging and Labeling Act.

When Congress passed the Fair Packaging and Labeling Act in 1966 (PL 89-755, 80 Stat. 1296 et seq.) certain provisions were included to aim specifically at tackling the problem of too many package sizes and related undesirable side effects. The administration of these provisions was given to the Secretary of Commerce. At present the responsibility resides in the Office of Weights and Measures and Office of Standards Development Services within the NBS.

According to the provisions, the Secretary of Commerce *does not have the responsibility or the authority under the act to issue any regulations governing the packaging or labeling practices of private industry.* However, the secretary does have the responsibility and authority [see Sections 5(d), 5(e), 8, and 9(a)(1) of the act, 80 Stat. 1298] to:

1. Determine whether there is any undue proliferation of retail packaged consumer commodities with reference to weights, measures, and quantities.
2. Determine whether such proliferation impairs the consumer's ability to compare prices and values of the goods in the packages.
3. If such proliferation and impairment exist, request manufacturers, packers, and distributors of such commodity(commodities) to jointly develop a voluntary product standard for the commodity, with the participation of consumer representative.
4. Report to the U.S. Congress with a recommendation as to whether legislation providing regulatory authority should be enacted, when:
    a) after one year of the request for a voluntary product standard, no such standard is or will be published; or
    b) after such a standard has been published, its requirements are not observed.
5. Distribute to state officials and agencies all published standards and regulations resulting from the Fair Packaging and Labeling Act and transmitted to the Secretary of Commerce by federal agencies that have been given the responsibility to administer various sections of the same act.
6. Promote as much as possible uniformity in state and federal regulation of the labeling of consumer commodities.

The information contained in 15 CFR 12 implements the authority and responsibility indicated in the preceding list. The provisions of this part were issued under the authority of Sections 5(d), 5(e), 80 Stat. 1298, and 15 U.S.C. 1454. The regulation provides explanation for undue proliferation, procedure for the development of voluntary product standards, and report to the U.S. Congress.

The act does not furnish a detailed and definitive explanation for "undue proliferation." It does, however, point out that the condition of "undue proliferation" must be one that "impairs the reasonable ability of the consumers to make value comparisons" with respect to consumer commodities. Generally, therefore, the Office of Weights and Measures will determine "undue proliferation" on a case-by-case basis and, accordingly, is establishing by these procedures an orderly process for such determination.

In general, the industries concerned have sought ways in which they might reduce voluntarily the possible undue proliferation without being cited publicly. Industries are following two paths to accomplish this voluntary reduction. One way has been for the industry to informally develop their own program to reduce undue proliferation. The other is through participation in the formal voluntary product standards procedures of the NBS.

Each time an industry has developed a plan, it is submitted to the Office of Weights and Measures. If the plan is satisfactory, work under the Fair Packaging and Labeling Act on the problem of possible undue proliferation in that particular industry is discontinued. The evaluation may be reactivated if further information concerning undue proliferation is introduced or if there is failure to follow an accepted plan.

Many industries have introduced or are considering the introduction of packaged consumer commodities in metric sizes. The position of the Office of Weights and Measures is that round metric sizes such as 1 kg, 500 g, and 1 liter will not be construed to be either undue proliferation or noncompliance with the current package quantity standards. However, the industry is encouraged to take advantage of the process of metric conversion, to improve the rationalization of package sizes and to make further reduction of size variation.

Conversion to the metric system is underway. Many commodities are now or will be distributed in metric quantities for sale at retail. In order to assure the reasonable ability of consumers to make value comparison with respect to such commodities, rational metric quantity patterns will be developed with full participation by industry and consumer representatives. Coordination will be provided to assist each industry to develop a plan to convert to the metric system.

Rational metric quantity patterns will be needed to replace all current simplified quantity patterns that are either weight or volume units of the customary system. Additionally, industry plans will contain a timetable for phasing out customary system sizes.

At the time of present writing, a number of informal package quantity standards have been developed jointly by the industries and the government. This effort has resulted in some simplified quantity patterns of certain food packages. More details may be obtained from the Office of Weights and Measures. A number of formal voluntary product standards have also been established. One that relates to food is "paper ice bag sizes" (see Table 2-6). These formal standards are discussed later.

Office of Standards Development Services

The U.S. Department of Commerce has been assisting in the development of voluntary product standards ever since the 1920s. These standards are those developed according to departmental procedures that seek to establish nationally recognized requirements for particular products and to provide a basis for better understand-

TABLE 2-6. Some Relevant Voluntary Product Standards Obtained from "List of Voluntary Product Standards, Commercial Standards, and Simplified Practice Recommendations, NBS List of Publications No. 53, February, 1977"

Identification	Voluntary Product Standard Title
PS 14-69	Salt packages
PS 40-70	Package quantities of green olives
PS 41-70 (Errata, PS 41-71)	Package quantities of instant mashed potatoes
PS 44-71	Paper ice bag sizes
PS 48-71	Package quantities of cubed, sized, crushed, and block ice

ing between the buyers and the sellers of the products. These standards may include definitions, classes, sizes, dimensions, capacities, performance criteria, material specifications, marking requirements, installation, test procedures, and other similar information. Those standards most likely related to food are the quantities and sizes of food packages. At present the Office of Standards Development Services within the NBS assumes the major responsibility in the development of such standards.

The regulations contained in 15 CFR 10, titled "Procedures for the development of voluntary products standards," provide very pertinent and useful information regarding: advantages of the standards; roles of the Department of Commerce, producers, distributors, users, and consumers; initiating development of a new standard; development of a proposed standard; establishment of the standard review committee; development of a recommended standard; procedures for acceptance of recommended standard; procedure when a recommended standard is not supported by consensus; standing committee; publication of standard; review of published standard; revision or amendment of a standard; editorial changes, and withdrawal of a published standard. The provisions of 15 CFR 10 were issued under the authority of Section 2, 31 Stat. 1449, as amended, Section 1, 64 Stat. 371; 15 U.S.C. 272; Reorganization Plan No. 3 of 1946, Part VI.

Thus in 1966, when the Fair Packaging and Labeling Act requires the Secretary of Commerce to oversee the problem of undue proliferation of consumer commodities, the Office of Standards Development Services assumes the job of assisting in the development of package size standards, especially the formal ones. "Paper ice bag sizes" mentioned previously is an example of food package standard.

In general, at the present time of writing, a total of five voluntary products standards have been established by this office (see Table 2-6), all of which are related to food packages, although not all have resulted from the requirements of the Fair Packaging and Labeling Act. They have been developed in accordance with the general responsibility of the NBS in developing voluntary products standards as prescribed in 15 CFR 10.

The NBS has no regulatory power in the enforcement of such standards, but since they represent the will of the interested groups as a whole, their provisions soon become established as trade customs and become effective when the standards are referenced in sales contracts, procurement specifications, government regulations, and the like. The benefits that result from these standards will be in direct proportion to general recognition and actual use of the standards.

The voluntary product standard, PS 14-69, "Salt packages," is partly reproduced in Appendix 2-3.

Office of Metric Information

The relationship between food standards, definitions, and inspections and metric units is obvious. This office in the NBS is an appropriate place to seek information. However, other federal agencies also issue specific regulations regarding the use of metric units in a variety of foods and food-related accessories.

NATIONAL OCEANIC AND ATMOSPHERIC ADMINISTRATION (NATIONAL MARINE FISHERIES SERVICE)

Organization, General Activities, and Statutes Administered

The National Oceanic and Atmospheric Administration administers many programs and services; a major one is the National Marine Fisheries Service. This service is partly responsible for assuring the quality of seafoods consumed in this country. The mission, activities, organization, and details of this service are explained in its Annual Report to the U.S. Congress. The agency also publishes an organization directory that provides the names of the officials in charge of various divisions and offices. A detailed organizational chart of the service is attached to Appendix 2-4.

The service is divided into four main offices: Resource Research, Resource

Utilization, Resource Management, and International Fisheries. The Office of Resource Utilization is of interest to this book since it supervises, among other divisions, the Fishery Products Inspection and Safety Division. Refer to Appendix 2-4 for clarification. The office is headed by an associate director, whereas the division is headed by a national program manager, or an individual with similar title.

The major mission of the division is to guarantee the quality and safety of seafoods by a voluntary inspection service and to develop specifications and standards for sanitation, quality, grade, and identity for fishery products and processing establishments. Other roles include the development of inspection policies, education of consumer confidence in the program, management of inspection laboratory, and other activities. At the present time of writing, all services of the division are voluntary.

Two congressional acts provide the division with the necessary statutory authority. One is the Agricultural Marketing Act of 1946 (7 U.S.C. 1621 to 1627), the main objectives of which were discussed in Chapter 1 of this book, although fish and fishery products were not emphasized. This act is designed to handle the problems of marketing and usage of agricultural products that include fish and shellfish and their processed products. Among the numerous requirements of the act with respect to seafoods, the inspection and certification of the products in interstate commerce and the development of procurement standards and specifications rank high on the list.

The other major act is the Fish and Wildlife Act of 1956 [16 U.S.C. 742a-742k; 15 U.S.C. 713c-3(e); 15 U.S.C. 713c-3 Note; 23 FR 2304]. Among the numerous requirements of the act, the service is authorized to conduct continuing investigations and disseminate information concerning the production and flow to market of fishery products, the improvement of product and marketing practices, and the conduct of education and extension services relative to commercial and sport fisheries. Some of these responsibilities are directly or indirectly related to the inspection and grading of processed fishery products and to the establishment of grade standards for such products.

Voluntary Inspection Service

A brief summary of the voluntary inspection service for fishery products is given in the publication "Helping The Housewife Choose and Quality Control for Fishery Products" (see Table 2-7). The information is presented as follows.

The division started a new voluntary inspection program for fishery products in March 1974. At present four types of inspection service are established to assist the processor: In-plant product inspection, plant sanitation inspection, lot inspection, and consultative services.

TABLE 2-7. Selected Publications on Programs of Voluntary Inspection and
Grading of Fishery Products (All issued by National Marine
Fisheries Service Unless Otherwise Noted)

Publication Number & Date	Title of Publication
See footnote "a"	Helping The Housewife Choose
Unnumbered (May 1974)	Interim Sanitation Standard for Fishery Product Processing Establishments
See footnote "b"	APPROVED LIST Sanitarily Inspected Fish Establishments
Handbook No. 25[c]	NOAA Fishery Products Inspection Manual

[a] This article appears in NOAA (Quarterly Magazine) 5(1):59-61 (January 1975).

[b] A new copy is issued every 3 months.

[c] An ongoing project. A person must be on the mailing list to receive new pages as they are issued.

The most comprehensive service is in-plant product inspection, which combines all services available. A contract is set up and an inspector supervises the preparation, processing, and packaging operations in the plant. He examines the raw materials, the product during processing, and samples of the finished product. Plant sanitation is constantly being monitored by the inspector, who also advises the management in plant improvements and new product evaluations. Fees are charged according to a scale. Prime users of this service are producers and packers of fishery products. The inspector may spend 4 hours weekly to 8 hours a day in the plant, sometimes the whole year, depending on the plant size and the amount of service needed.

Plant sanitation inspection inspects the plant itself rather than the products processed. The inspector, with plant personnel, surveys the plant and identifies the strengths and weaknesses of the facility and the processing system. He then outlines correctional steps to upgrade sanitary practices and conditions. After the modifications have been made, the inspector will monitor the plant only once or twice weekly to ascertain that the hygienic conditions are kept. After all sanitary requirements are met, the inspector issues a certificate to indicate compliance of the plant facilities. A plant so certified is a Sanitarily Inspected Fish Establishment (SIFE). Fees are charged according to a scale.

Brokers and buyers of fishery products in the distribution chain are primary users of lot inspections. Warehouse, cold storage plants, processing plants, or terminal markets are locations where these inspections are conducted. In a lot inspection the inspector is concerned with the quality of the product and not involved with its processing or packaging. He examines samples and states whether the products comply with established standards in condition and quality. The buyer is assured of the fishery products because they have been federally and statistically sampled. Fees are charged according to a schedule.

When packers, processors, and brokers want to contract for specific services, including new product evaluations, label and product inspections, sanitation evaluation, and plant surveys, they may use the consultative services. These are normally a one-time service and usually do not require the lengthy presence of an inspector. Again, fees are charged according to a scale.

Some details of an inspection process are described below. An example of quality and grade is the proper flesh:breading ratio in a breaded fishery product. Grade A Shield and the official inspection mark require that the amount of flesh in the bread portions be standardized (e.g., in raw breaded portions, 75% flesh; in fish sticks, 72%; and in precooked breaded portions, 65%).

The inspector uses one of two methods to quantitate the amount of fish flesh in the portion or stick. One is the scrape method, where the inspector weighs samples of the finished breaded product, scrapes the batter and breading from the flesh, and weighs the flesh again. A precalculated mathematical formula provides him with the flesh:breading ratio. The other is the on-line method. Here, the inspector obtains a completed box of 15 portions from the production line and 15 portions from the front of the line where the items have been cut to the proper size but have not been otherwise processed. The inspector then weighs the portions and uses a mathematical formula to ascertain the percentage of flesh found in the completed portion. If the amount of flesh does not reach the required percentage, the inspector examines more samples to double check. Retesting is performed repeatedly while production corrections are being made. After the sample has been tested for proper weight and flesh:breading ratio, it is cooked, split, and checked for odor and taste, and it is determined whether bones or other foreign matter exist in the stick or portion. Each processing line is checked at least once an hour.

As for the inspection of frozen blocks of fishery products, periodic checks are made in the company laboratory. The frozen blocks are thawed, broken apart, and examined under strong light for bones and other foreign matter. The block is returned to the supplier or source if it proves to be substandard.

Although these inspection and grading services are not mandatory, they have certain distinct "legal" advantages. The certificate of quality of the products is recognized as evidence of fact in a court of law. A buyer is assured of the terms of his contract. The inspection service gives him a means of establishing the inventory loan value of his products, assists him in settling claims for damage to his product while it is being shipped, and gives him a basis for resolving disputes over product quality.

The official regulations promulgated by the agency to conduct such programs are referenced in the Code of Federal Regulations. Thus 50 CFR 260 describes the inspection and certification of fishery products. The authority for the provisions in Part 260 was issued under Section 6, 70 Stat. 1122; 16 U.S.C. 742e; Sections 203, 205, 60 Stat. 1087, 1090, as amended; and 7 U.S.C. 1622, 1624. Table 2-8 provides an outline of the information contained in 50 CFR 260. Some selected aspects are discussed in the following paragraphs.

TABLE 2-8. General Content of Subpart A (Inspection and Certification of Fishery Products) of 50 CFR 260

Subject Matter	Section Number
Definitions	260.6 to 260.7
Inspection service	260.12 to 260.30
Appeal inspection	260.36 to 260.14
Licensing of samplers and inspectors	260.47 to 260.51
Sampling	260.57 to 260.63
Fees and charges	260.69 to 260.81
Miscellaneous	260.86 to 260.93
Requirements for plants operating under federal inspection on a contract basis	260.96 to 260.104

According to the definition given, inspection service means sampling of products; determining their essential characteristics such as style, type, size, identity, class, quality, and condition; observing product preparation; checking sanitation of establishments; issuing certificates and reports, and other activities.

Some aspects of the process of inspection are as follows. An inspection service is required to be performed on the basis of appropriate U.S. standards for grades of processed fishery products; federal, military, or other government agency specification, contract specifications; or any written instruction approved by the supervising officer. Unless otherwise authorized, an inspection certificate may be issued only by an inspector and the certificate of loading must be issued and signed by an inspector or licensed sampler authorized to check the loading of a specific lot of processed products.

With reference to sampling, the inspector or licensed sampler should select samples, on request, from designated lots of processed products that are so placed as to permit thorough and proper sampling in accordance with regulations. Unless otherwise directed, the inspection personnel shall select samples from each lot in the exact number of sample units indicated for the lot size in the applicable single sampling plan or at the discretion of the inspector. Such single sample plans and acceptance levels are illustrated in 50 CFR 260.61(f).

In 50 CFR 260, Sections 260.86 to 260.93 (see Table 2-8) are grouped under the title of "miscellaneous." These sections describe approved identification and related information. Appendix 2-5 reproduces Section 50 CFR 260.86, which sets forth the official marks and legends for inspection, grades, officially sampled products, and acceptance per specifications.

The requirements for plants operating under federal inspection on a contract basis (see Table 2-8) include the following: application for a fishery products inspection service on a contract basis at official establishments, conditions for providing fishery products inspection service at official establishments, premises, buildings and structures, facilities, lavatory accommodations, equipment, personnel, and information on how operations and operating procedures shall be in accordance with an effective sanitation program. To illustrate what the materials cover, selected aspects are presented in the following paragraphs.

There are strict conditions relating to providing inspection service at an official establishment. The contracting party must agree to:

1. Use only wholesome raw material that has been handled or stored under sanitary conditions and is suitable for processings, to maintain the official establishment(s) designated on the contract in such sanitary condition, and to employ such methods of handling raw materials for processing as may be necessary to conform to the sanitary requirements prescribed or approved by the agency.
2. Adequately code each primary container and master case of products sold or otherwise distributed from a manufacturing, processing, packing, or repackaging activity, to enable positive lot identification and to facilitate, where necessary, the segregation of specific food lots that may have become contaminated or otherwise unfit for their intended use.
3. Not permit any labels on which reference is made to federal inspection to be used on any product that is not packed under fishery products inspection ser-

vice nor permit any labels on which reference is made to any U.S. grade to be used on any product that has not been officially certified as meeting the requirements of such grade, nor supply labels bearing reference to federal inspection to another establishment unless the products to which such labels are to be applied have been packed under federal inspection at an official establishment. Further details may be obtained from the original document.

The premises about an official establishment should be free from conditions that may result in the contamination of food, including the following:

1. Strong offensive odors.
2. Improperly stored equipment, litter, waste, refuse, and uncut weeds or grass within the immediate vicinity of the buildings or structures that may constitute an attractant, breeding place, or harborage for rodents, insects, and other pests.
3. Excessively dusty roads, yards, or parking lots that may constitute a source of contamination in areas where food is exposed.
4. Inadequately drained areas that may contribute contamination to food products through seepage or foot-borne filth or provide a breeding place for insects or microorganisms.

More published government documents on quality control system and sanitation standards for processing plants are described in the next section.

Quality Control Systems and Sanitation Standards for Processing Plants

According to 50 CFR 260.103(c), official "establishments operating under Federal inspection should have an effective quality control program as appropriate for the nature of the products and processing operations." In 1972 (37 FR 9328-9331, May 9, 1972; and 37 FR 16699, August 18, 1972) the National Marine Fisheries Service issued the following statement of policy and intent with reference to inspection, grading, and certification of fishery products.

To assist contracting parties in the orderly development of complete or partial quality control systems appropriate to their products and processing operations, the agency published guidelines for: (1) development of quality control systems --official establishments and (2) assessment and approval of quality control systems --official establishments.

Interested parties should consult these documents for more details since such information will assist the industrial personnel to improve the quality of their products and at the same time upgrade their fishery processing plants. In regard to any quality control system, the agency assumes the following positions:

1. Quality control plans will be developed in a simple, disciplined manner and will not be unnecessarily rigid. They will be assessed on their individual merits and demonstrated effectiveness, with the expectation that the plan has been developed using standard quality control principles and terms. During the on-site assessment of a quality control system, an appropriate establishment official will be invited to accompany the agency's survey team.
2. Official establishment reports pertinent to use by the agency are those recorded findings resulting from the performance of examinations and tests designated in the quality control scheme. Such information and results provide part of the basis for product certification.

The agency intends to rely on the results of approved quality control systems provided and operated by parties contracting for inspection services, so the amount of inspection effort required and performed by the agency may be systematically reduced in proportion to the amount of quality control effort provided by the contracting party.

It should be noted that the agency policy provides for partial as well as complete quality control systems, and since implementation of a quality control program is voluntary at official establishments, processors may proceed with developing and implementing a quality control program as their resources permit.

There are three other publications issued by the agency that deserve some attention (see Table 2-7). The publication "Interim Sanitation Standard for Fishery Product Processing Establishments" establishes the general sanitary requirements and is applicable to all types of plants supplying, processing, or storing fish. Compliance with this standard is mandatory if a plant wants to be officially approved by the agency (see later discussion). This standard shall be used to determine the processors' ability to produce wholesome and sanitary products. It shall not be used to determine the capability of an establishment to produce products that are in compliance with U.S. Grade Standards for fishery products. This publication should be used in conjunction with the regulations prescribed in 50 CFR 260.96 to 260.104 (see Table 2-8).

Every 3 months the division issues a revised copy of the publication "APPROVED LIST Sanitarily Inspected Fish Establishments" (Table 2-7). This reference document has been developed to determine which fishery products have been produced in processing establishments that have been sanitarily inspected, approved, and certified by the division as being capable of producing safe, wholesome products that are produced in accordance with the regulations promulgated.

To provide the user with a ready reference, the document is divided into three parts: Part 1, Establishments approved for sanitation; Part 2, Establishments approved for producing inspected fishery products; and Part 3, Establishments approved for producing animal feed products. The firms listed in this document have, at their own expense, voluntarily subscribed to the federal inspection services and have demonstrated their ability to meet rigid standards of sanitation and the capability to produce safe, wholesome fishery products.

It should be noted that the division does not infer that plants not appearing on this list fail to meet rigid hygienic standards; rather, the list is merely a compilation of those firms participating in the national fishery products inspection and safety program.

According to Table 2-7, the third publication is the "Fishery Products Inspection Manual." This document is not yet completed; it is an on-going project. It is divided into three parts, and Part I, "Inspection," contains: inspection service organization, contract negotiations, contract inspection, product evaluation, lot inspection, and many more details. Part II, titled "Grading," describes instructions for grading established standards for the various fishery products prescribed in 50 CFR 261 to 266. The content of Part III, titled "Certification," is not yet ready.

When it is completed, this document will probably be most useful both for government officials as well as industrial supervisory personnel. It contains references to most of the information needed by individuals and groups engaged in the fishery products business. If interested, one should request an incomplete copy of the manual and ask to be placed on the mailing list to receive future inserts.

Standards for Grades of Certain Fishery Products

The division also develops grade standards for fishery products. To date, more than 18 U.S. grade standards have been developed for frozen processed fishery products such as fish fillets and breaded shrimps. Such products, when produced and graded under the federal program, may carry the standard shield and inspection mark (see Appendix 2-5). However, as under the USDA grading programs, grade labeling is not required by federal law, even though products are officially inspected and graded. Also, standards for grades must be distinguished from those established by the FDA, which are standards of identity, minimum standards of quality, and standards of fill of container (see Chapter 6).

The following list describes those fishery products for which *United States Standards for Grades* have been established and whose citations appear in the Code of Federal Regulations. As an example, the U.S. Standards for Grades of Frozen Salmon Steaks in 50 CFR 262.200 to 262.249 are reproduced in Appendix 2-6.

Part 261	United States Standards for Grades of Whole or Dressed Fish
Subpart A	United States Standards for Grades of Whole or Dressed Fish (Sections 261.100 to 261.149)

Part 265	United States Standards for Grades of Crustacean Shellfish Products
Subpart A	United States Standards for Grades of Frozen Raw Headless Shrimp (Sections 265.100 to 265.149)
Subpart B	United States Standards for Grades of Frozen Raw Breaded Shrimp (Sections 265.150 to 265.199)
Part 266	United States Standards for Grades of Molluscan Shellfish Products
Subpart A	United States Standards for Grades of Frozen Raw Scallops (Sections 266.100 to 266.149)
Subpart B	United States Standards for Grades of Frozen Fried Scallops (Sections 266.150 to 266.199)

Importation and Exportation of Fishery Products

In addition to the programs discussed in the preceding section, the division also offers voluntary federal inspection services to exporters and importers of fishery products. The export inspection services are basically the same as the fee-for-service programs for domestic processors. An exporter can contract federal personnel to carry out lot inspection at any location before shipment. Both the buyer and/or exporter can set his own specifications or standards for the products that will be inspected and certified. The division can also furnish assistance with regard to the requirements of the country of destination. In sum, the service can provide an unbiased statement about the product, facilitate acceptance at foreign port, minimize delay at point of entry, eliminate most of the nontariff barriers to importation, and, finally, assist the export processors to upgrade the quality control in their plants.

On the other hand, the division assists importers who receive partially processed or prepared fishery items from abroad. More than 100 nations export fishery products to the United States. The Federal Food, Drug, and Cosmetic Act, as amended, requires that imported seafood products meet the basic requirements imposed on comparable items produced domestically for interstate commerce. These requirements include misbranding, labeling, adulteration, standards of identity, product definition, tolerances for pesticide residues, food additives, and good manufacturing practices. Refer to Chapter 6 for further details.

As a whole, the division provides four major types of assistance to importers:

1. Assists in contract and specification formulation, especially with reference to the Federal Food, Drug, and Cosmetic Act.

2. Certifies contract compliance of imported products.
3. Supplies technical assistance such as bacterial analysis and species identification.
4. Provides consultation on quality assurance plans, sanitation, facility, labeling, and other programs.

A useful reference source is: J. R. Brooker, "How to export fishery products to the United States." Food, Drug, Cosmetic Law Journal, May 1976.

Agreements with Other Federal Agencies

The National Marine Fisheries Service has signed agreements with two other federal agencies, namely, the USDA and the FDA.

On February 4, 1977 (42 FR 6872), it was announced that the service had signed a Memorandum of Understanding with the Fruits and Vegetables Division of the USDA in regard to the crossutilization of inspection personnel. The two agencies have agreed to carry out a mutual interest in providing inspection and certification to industry applicants on a fee-for-service basis in the most efficient and effective manner. They plan to maximize the use of trained food inspectors of the two agencies to crosslicense arrangements whereby requested inspection service for fishery products or processed fruits and vegetables can be accomplished.

Some responsibilities of the Fruits and Vegetables Division will be:

1. Provide inspectors for assignments in establishments operating under contract with the National Marine Fisheries Service in which the volume of pack inspected is predominantly fishery products.
2. Provide inspection service for fishery products processed in plants where the volume of pack is predominantly fruits, vegetables, or related products.
3. Provide the food industry with lot inspection service for fishery products and miscellaneous inspection and consultation services, including plant surveys and sanitation evaluations.

Some responsibilities of the National Marine Fisheries Service are as follows:

1. Evaluate some of the inspections performed by the other agency's inspectors.
2. Bear all travel and related expenses of the other agency's inspectors.
3. Provide inspection service for fruits and vegetables processed in plants where the volume of pack inspection is predominantly fishery products.

It is mutually agreed that:

1. The location and duration of assignments of either agency's inspectors will be pre-approved by both parties.
2. Where inspectors of one agency are crosslicensed to perform inspections for the other, the requesting agency shall be responsible for issuing appropriate license cards and other identification and shall also furnish training, supervision, and documents to carry out the assignment.
3. Additional specifications or guidelines may be issued according to needs and arrangement.

For further details, consult the original document.

On January 17, 1975 a Memorandum of Understanding (40 FR 4025 to 4027) was signed between the Service and the FDA. This agreement sets forth the working arrangements that are being followed or adopted to enable each agency to discharge, as effectively as possible, its obligations in regard to the inspection and standardization activities for fishery products.

Some responsibilities of the service are to:

1. Provide a list of fishery plants under its inspection service to the FDA.
2. Assign only a full grade to a satisfactory product and to so state if only certain factors are inspected or graded.
3. Provide the FDA with any information about specific lots of products to be considered for legal action by the FDA.
4. Shall routinely advise a fishery processing plant about FDA requirements and methods of compliance.

Some responsibilities of the FDA are to:

1. Recognize the services provided by the other agency, which should minimize FDA inspections rather than diminishing FDA authority.
2. Notify the National Marine Fisheries Service about any official legal action taken against any fishery product processed in one of the latter's inspection plants.

It is mutually agreed that:

1. If violation in several fishery plants is apparent, the two agencies shall meet to consider action.
2. Each agency shall keep records and make them available when necessary.
3. If either agency foresees any failure to comply with terms of the agreement, mutual notification shall be made.

More details may be obtained from the original document.

Agreements with State Agencies

The National Marine Fisheries Service has signed Memoranda of Understanding with a number of states at the time of present writing. Samples of such agreements may be obtained from its headquarters; the content of a typical agreement is briefly explained in the following.

The purpose of each cooperative agreement is to:

1. Through cooperation of the parties, make the federal voluntary inspection services for fishery products and the information concerned with inspection and processing and handling practices more widely available than would be possible by each party operating independently.
2. Provide producers, processors, distributors, consumers, and others with current information relative to good methods and practices for handling, processing, standardizing, inspecting, and packaging of fishery products.

Some parts that the National Marine Fisheries Service agrees to carry out include the following:

1. Establish uniform, national qualification standards for all state/federal inspection personnel.
2. Develop inspection regulations, label requirements, and standards for grades for fishery products and other criteria to be used in the inspection process.
3. Base inspection on the appropriate standards for grades of processed fishery products, federal or military specifications, buyer/seller contract specification or any officially approved specifications submitted by an applicant, and/or other minimum quality and standards established by state law.

Some parts that the state agency agrees to carry out include the following:

1. Accept and adopt all standards and grades officially approved by the National Marine Fisheries Service as stated in the agreement.
2. Inform producers and others regarding proper interpretation and application of federal requirements and the inspection process.
3. Encourage state and local government procurement officials and consumers to purchase federal/state inspected fishery products.
4. Furnish facilities and equipment for the performance of inspection services when they are needed.

It is mutually agreed that:

1. The National Marine Fisheries Service will train and license federal/state inspectors.
2. All assignments of state inspectors must be approved by both parties.
3. Procedures and methods employed in the conduct of the inspection process shall be established by the federal agency.
4. With minor exceptions, inspection certificates issued shall be federal certificates.

Consumer and Trade Education

To increase public awareness of the various inspection and grading services offered by the Fishery Products Inspection and Safety Division of the National Marine Fisheries Service, the National Oceanic and Atmospheric Administration issued a statement of interest and intent on April 28, 1975 (40 FR 18480). This statement, entitled "Consumer and trade education and promotion of inspected fishery products," conveys the following messages:

1. Most consumers erroneously assume that fishery products are mandatorily inspected, just as meat, poultry, and eggs are. This is not the case.
2. Unsuccessful approaches have been made to the U.S. Congress concerning mandatory seafood inspection legislation.
3. Many fishery processors are not familiar with the voluntary inspection programs and their benefits.
4. The agency should make a big effort to educate the consumer, the seafood industries, and the public-at-large about the existence of the inspection and grading programs and the many advantages of the inspection and grade marks on the product labels.

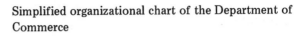

APPENDIX 2-1.   Simplified organizational chart of the Department of
Commerce

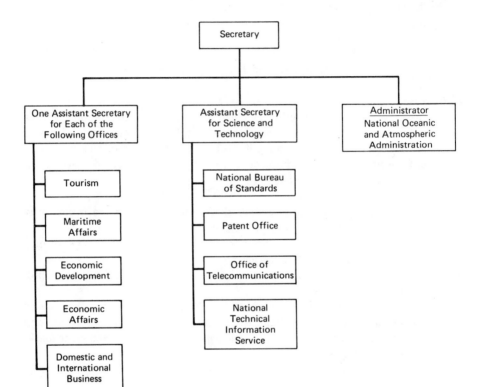

APPENDIX 2-2. Simplified organizational chart for the National Bureau of Standards

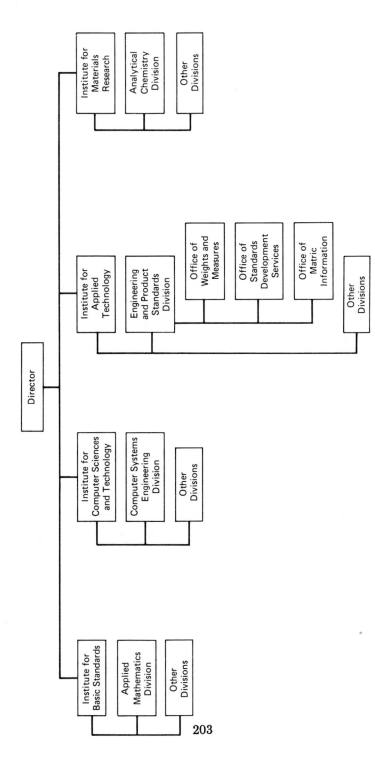

203

APPENDIX 2-3.   Part of NBS Voluntary Product Standard PS 14-69, "Salt
Packages." Reproduced from the original.

PRODUCT STANDARDS

Product Standards are published voluntary standards that establish (1) dimen-
sional requirements for standard sizes and types of various products, (2)
technical requirements for the product, and (3) methods of testing, grading, and
marking these products. The objective of a *Product Standard* is to establish
product requirements which are in accordance with the principal demands of
the industry and, at the same time, are in the interest of the consumer.

Development of a PRODUCT STANDARD

The Bureau's Office of Engineering Standards Services works closely with business firms, trade organizations, testing laboratories, and other appropriate groups
to develop *Product Standards*. The Bureau has the following role in the development process: It (1) acts as an unbiased coordinator in the development of the
standard; (2) provides editorial assistance in the preparation of the standard;
(3) supplies such assistance and review as is required to assure the technical
soundness of the standard; (4) sees that the standard is representative of the
views of producers, distributors, users, and consumers; (5) seeks satisfactory
adjustment of valid points of disagreement; and (6) publishes the standard.
Industry, on the other hand, (1) initiates and participates in the development of
a standard; (2) provides technical counsel on a standard; and (3) promotes the
use of, and support for, the standard. (A group interested in developing a *Product
Standard* may submit a written request to the Office of Engineering Standards
Services, National Bureau of Standards, Washington, D.C. 20234.)

When the Bureau receives a request for a standard, it must first determine that
the standard would be technically feasible and in the public interest. After this
is established, a draft of the proposed standard is developed in consultation with
interested trade groups and is circulated for industry consideration and comment.
Subsequently, a Standard Review Committee is established to review the proposed standard for conformance with the Department of Commerce procedures.
The committee includes qualified representatives of producers, distributors,
and users or consumers of the product being standardized. When the committee
approves a proposal, copies of the recommended standard are distributed for
industry consideration and acceptance. When the acceptances show general agreement by all segments of the industry, and when there is no substantive objection
deemed valid by the National Bureau of Standards, the Bureau announces approval of the *Product Standard* and proceeds with its publication.

Use of a PRODUCT STANDARD

The adoption and use of a *Product Standard* is voluntary. *Product Standards* are
used most effectively in conjunction with legal instrumentalities such as sales
contracts, purchase orders, and building codes. When a standard is made part of
such a document, compliance with the standard is enforceable by the buyer or the
seller along with other provisions of the document. There is no governmental
regulation or control involved.

Product Standards are useful and helpful to both purchasers and manufacturers.
Purchasers may order products that comply with *Product Standards* and determine for themselves that their requirements are met. Manufacturers may refer
to the standards in sales catalogs, advertising, invoices, and labels on their product. Commercial inspection and testing programs may also be employed, together
with grade labels and certificates assuring compliance, to promote even greater
public confidence. Such assurance of compliance promotes better understanding
between buyers and sellers.

Effective Date

Having been passed through the regular procedures of the Office
of Engineering Standards Services, National Bureau of Standards,
and approved by the acceptors hereinafter listed in part, this
Product Standard is issued by the National Bureau of Standards,
effective:

August 1, 1969

Nat. Bur. Stand. (U.S.), Prod. Stand. 14–69, 9 pages (May 1970) CODEN:
XNPSA

APPENDIX 2-3. (continued).

Product Standard PS 14–69

Supersedes Simplified Practice Recommendation 70–54

Salt Packages

Effective August 1, 1969

1. PURPOSE

1.1. The purpose of this Product Standard is to establish, as a standard of practice in production, distribution, and use, the types of packages for the various kinds of salt and the quantities in which such salt is to be packaged. This revision of Simplified Practice Recommendation R 70–54 incorporates changes that are deemed necessary to reflect the current needs and demands of the salt industry, as well as the desires of consumers. The adoption and use of this Standard is voluntary, although widespread conformance to the Standard will allow producers, distributors, retailers, and consumers of salt to benefit from salt package standardization.

2. SCOPE AND CLASSIFICATION

2.1. **Scope**—This Product Standard specifies the recommended salt packages for each kind of salt, the labeled net weight of the packages, and the type and capacity of shipping containers. Definitions and uses for salt are also included. While no attempt is made to list all of the packages, sizes, and containers which might be packed by one or more producer, table 1 includes those items common to the entire industry.

2.2. **Classification**—The chemical term for salt is sodium chloride. Within the industry, salt is classified by methods of production and by the characteristics of the products that are required for particular end uses.

Salt is classified by methods of production as follows: Rock salt, evaporated salt, and solar salt. Rock salt is produced by drilling and blasting natural salt deposits. Evaporated salt is produced by evaporating brine in large covered, steam-heated kettles or pans under vacuum conditions, or in open pans at temperatures less than boiling. Solar salt is produced by pumping brine into shallow ponds for evaporation by the sun and wind.

Salt products are also classified into two major use categories: high grade and common grade. High grade salt products are generally certified or guaranteed to have specific chemical or physical properties or added ingredients that make them especially suitable for certain critical end uses. Included in this category are salts with high sodium chloride content with minimal amounts of impurities. Most high grade salt is produced by the two evaporation methods, although some is produced from solar and rock salt. Common grade salt, while of generally high quality when produced by evaporation or solar methods, is not generally certified or guaranteed to have a specific chemical analysis. Such salt is utilized primarily as a basic chemical (sodium chloride) for a great variety of noncritical end uses.

3. REQUIREMENTS

3.1. **Packaging of salt**—The net weights of the packages of the various kinds of salt are contained in table 1 along with a description

APPENDIX 2-3.   (continued).

TABLE 1. *Salt packages*

Kind of salt	Primary container		Shipping container [1]	
	Net weight of contents—Pounds	Kind	Capacity [2]	Kind
Table	1½ (26 oz)[3]	Round carton	24/1½	Case.
Table	5	Pocket [4]	12/5	Case or bale.
Table	100	Bag		
Rock (coarse sizes)	10	Pocket	6/10	Case or bale.
Rock (coarse sizes)	25, 50, 100	Bag		
Rock (fine and granulated)	25, 50, 100	Bag		
Evaporated granulated	25, 50, 100	Bag		
Undried solar	50, 100, 125	Bag		
Dry solar, kiln dried	10	Pocket	6/10	Bale.
Dry solar, kiln dried	50, 100	Bag		
Blocks	50			[5]
Bricks	4		15/4 [6]	Case.
Medium (flake)	25, 50, 100	Bag		
High grade	5	Pocket	12/5	Case or bale.
High grade	100	Bag		
Mineralized	50, 100	Bag		
Compressed water softener	25, 50, 100	Bag		
Popcorn	1½ (26 oz)	Round carton	24/1½	Case.
Kosher	3	Square carton	12/3	Case.
Hawaiian	1	Bag	12/1	Bale.

[1] Where no shipping container is shown, the primary container also serves as the shipping container.

[2] Capacity indicates the number of primary containers in each shipping container. Thus, 15/4 means 15 four-pound primary containers or packages.

[3] While 1½ pound (26 oz) rounds are standard with all producers, table salt is also available in smaller, convenient consumer sizes, including single serving packets.

[4] The term "Pocket" refers to a bag of 10 pounds or less net weight.

[5] Shipping containers are available for 50-lb trace mineralized blocks at customer's option.

[6] 10/5's instead of 15/4's are packaged in the California and Utah salt producing areas.

APPENDIX 2-3. (continued).

of the primary container and the capacity and description of the shipping container, where appropriate. Only salt packaged according to the limitations set forth in table 1 shall be deemed to be packaged in conformance with this Product Standard.

4. DEFINITIONS AND USES

4.1. **Table salt**—Salt produced for human consumption, normally is an evaporated granulated salt with a grain size between 0.01 and 0.03 inch. Table salt may contain free-flowing and/or anticaking additives and is available as plain or iodized salt.

4.2. **Rock salt (coarse sizes)**—Mined salt that usually is crushed and screened to sizes from 0.08 to 0.75 inch. Rock salt is the mineral Halite, a natural sodium chloride found in the earth in beds a few feet to several thousand feet in thickness. Rock salt is used in refrigeration systems, in water-softening processes, in chemical manufacture, in the salting of hides, and in highway snow and ice removal operations. It contains approximately 95 percent to 99 percent sodium chloride.

4.3. **Rock salt (fine and granulated)**—Mined rock salt that is crushed to a grain size usually less than 0.08 inch. It is used where a fine grade of rock salt is required, such as in free-choice cattle feeding.

4.4. **Evaporated granulated salt**—Salt produced by vacuum pan evaporation of brine under conditions designed to control crystal size and purity. The crystal structure is cubic. Grain size is less than 0.05 inch, generally ranging between 0.01 and 0.03 inch. The sodium chloride content usually exceeds 98 percent, and the color is opaque white.

Evaporated granulated salt is used by meatpackers for dry salting of meat and for pickling and curing (as a brine); by food processors for the processing of sauerkraut, cucumber pickles, and the like; and by chemical and dye industries. It is used as an ingredient in many prepared foods, in feeds for livestock, and in the zeolite process of water softening.

4.5. **Undried solar salt**—A salt produced by evaporation of sea, salt lake, or underground saline waters by sun and wind in shallow ponds. This salt does not normally contain more than 5 percent moisture. The coarse screenings from this process are suitable for most of the purposes for which the coarse sizes of rock salt are used.

4.6. **Dry solar, kiln-dried salt**—A salt that has been dried to a moisture content of less than 0.5 percent in a rotary kiln. It is used for the same purposes as rock salt, except where moisture is a problem.

4.7. **Salt blocks**—Blocks of salt that are produced from evaporated granulated, crushed solar, or rock salt compressed into a standard block of 50 pounds. These blocks are manufactured in plain, sulfur, iodized, trace mineralized, and mineral supplement forms. Although the 50-pound block of plain salt was originally developed for cattle, it is now widely used in certain types of water softening and refrigeration systems.

4.8. **Salt bricks**—Small blocks similar to "salt blocks," pressed into 4-pound bricks, for animal use.

4.9. **Medium (flake) salt**—Salt ranging in size between 0.01 and 0.05 inch. Medium salt is produced by slow evaporation of brine in open pans at temperatures less than boiling. The crystals are cubic but aggregate into hopper-like shapes which break up into fragments known as flakes. Closely screened medium salt is classified as flake salt. The sodium chloride content usually exceeds 96 percent. Medium is

APPENDIX 2-3. (continued).

sold to meatpackers and the agricultural trade. Flake salt is sold primarily for food uses.

4.10. **High grade salt**—An evaporated granulated flake or solar salt which has been selected or processed to provide special features, such as high purity or fewer impurities than are usually found in these types of salt. This salt is used in certain critical applications where a guaranteed analysis is required. The particle sizes are the same as those for evaporated granulated salt.

4.11. **Mineralized salt**—Salt containing trace amounts of minerals. The term "trace mineralized" refers to evaporated granulated solar or rock salts, screened to sizes less than 0.05 inch, to which has been added trace amounts of iron, copper, iodine, cobalt, zinc, manganese, or other compounds to prevent trace mineral deficiencies that may be responsibile for the poor health of farm animals or fowl. The term "mineral supplement" refers to salt products containing calcium and phosphorus and trace minerals which are formulated to supply a balanced ratio of phosphorus and calcium that is necessary for the proper nutrition of livestock.

4.12. **Compressed water softener salt**—A product compressed from evaporated granular or solar salts into "thumbnail" or smaller sizes for regenerating water softening systems. It has the advantage of high quality without the insoluble sediments found in the mined rock salt.

4.13. **Popcorn salt**—Evaporated salt which is finely screened (finer than 0.01 inch), often containing free-flowing agents for ease of application; used in seasoning popcorn.

4.14. **Kosher salt**—A coarse flake salt produced by open pan evaporation under conditions approved by the Orthodox Jewish faith for use in Kosher food.

4.15. **Hawaiian salt**—A solar salt produced by the evaporation of sea water in clay beds. This unwashed salt, used for cooking in Hawaii, contains a small amount of red clay (alae).

5. IDENTIFICATION

5.1. **Labels and literature**—In order that purchasers may identify products complying with the requirements of this voluntary Product Standard, packagers choosing to package such products in compliance with this voluntary Standard may include a statement in conjunction with their name and address on labels, invoices, sales literature, and the like. The following statement is suggested when sufficient space is available:

This salt is packaged and labeled in accordance with the requirements of Product Standard PS 14–69, developed cooperatively with the industry and published by the National Bureau of Standards under the voluntary Product Standards procedures of the U.S. Department of Commerce. Full responsibility for the conformance of this product with the standard is assumed by (name and address of packager or distributor).

The following abbreviated statement is suggested when available space on labels is insufficient for the full statement:

Conforms to PS 14–69, a packaging quantity standard (name and address of packager or distributor).

APPENDIX 2-3. (continued).

6. HISTORY

6.1. Previous editions—A voluntary Standard for salt packages developed under Department of Commerce procedures has existed since 1927, when Simplified Practice Recommendation R 70 was issued. The simplification of the quantities of salt packages was originally initiated at the request of the Salt Producers Association. In 1941, 1942, 1946, and most recently in 1954, the Standard was revised to keep it current with regard to industry's packaging practices. (Additional details regarding the development of previous revisions of this Standard are given in earlier editions of R 70.)

6.2. Current revision—The current revision of SPR 70–54 was requested by the Salt Institute, an organization of natural salt producers, and the successor organization of the Salt Producers Association. This revision further updates the Standard by including certain new quantities of salt packages and by deleting other quantities which are no longer recognized as "standard." It also contains minor changes in nomenclature, and sets forth in one table information formerly found in two separate tables.

Copies of the recommended Standard, designated TS 114b, were distributed to the industry for acceptance July 25, 1968. An analysis of the responses indicated a consensus among producers and packagers, distributors, and users of the product as defined in the published procedures. The new edition of the Standard was designated Product Standard PS 14–69, *Salt Packages*, and became effective on August 1, 1969.

Technical Standards Coordinator:

Charles B. Phucas, Product Standards Section, Office of Engineering Standards Services, National Bureau of Standards, Washington, D.C. 20234

7. STANDING COMMITTEE

7.1. The following individuals comprise the membership of the Standing Committee, which is to review, prior to circulation for acceptance, revisions proposed to keep the Standard up to date. Comment concerning the Standard and suggestions for revision may be addressed to any member of the committee or to the Office of Engineering Standards Services, National Bureau of Standards, U.S. Department of Commerce, which acts as secretary for the committee.

Representing Packagers

Mr. John M. Rankin, Morton Salt Company, 110 North Wacker Drive, Chicago, Illinois 60606 (Chairman)
Mr. H. J. Carey, Jr., President, The Carey Salt Co., 180 Carey Boulevard, Post Office Box 1728, Hutchinson, Kansas 67501
Mr. Edson K. Green, Vice President, International Salt Co., Clarks Summit, Pennsylvania 18411
Mr. Edward M. Dodd, Executive Vice President, Diamond Crystal Salt Co., 916 South Riverside Avenue, St. Clair, Michigan 48079

Representing Distributors

Mr. Walter A. Churchill, Churchill Super Markets, Inc., 2845 West Central Avenue, Toledo, Ohio 43606

APPENDIX 2-4. Simplified organizational chart for the National Marine Fisheries Service

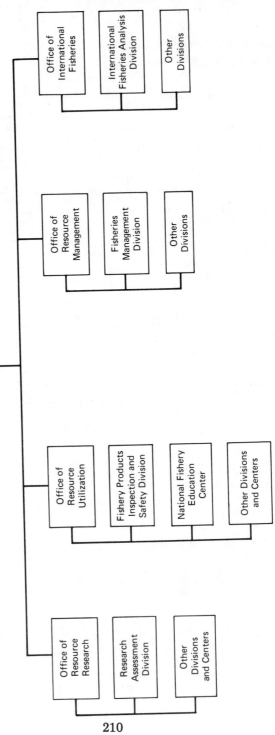

APPENDIX 2-5. Approved identifications for the grading, inspection, and so on of fish and fishery products, reproduced from 50 CFR 260.86 (1977).

§ 260.86 Approved identification.

(a) Grade marks: The approved grade mark or identification may be used on containers, labels, or otherwise indicated for any processed product that (1) has been packed under inspection as provided in this part to assure compliance with the requirements for wholesomeness established for the raw product and of sanitation established for the preparation and processing operations, and (2) has been certified by an inspector as meeting the requirements of such grade, quality or classification. The grade marks approved for use shall be similar in form and design to the examples of Figures 1 to 5 of this section.

APPENDIX 2-5. (continued).

Shield using red, white, and blue background or other colors appropriate for label.

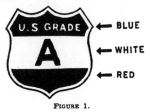

FIGURE 1.

Shield with plain background.

FIGURE 2.

U.S. GRADE A

FIGURE 3.

U.S.
GRADE

B

FIGURE 4.

U.S.
GRADE

C

FIGURE 5.

(b) Inspection marks: The approved inspection marks may be used on containers, labels, or otherwise indicated for any processed product that (1) has been

packed under inspection as provided in this part to assure compliance with the requirements for wholesomeness established for the raw product and of sanitation established for the preparation and processing operations, and (2) has been certified by an inspector as meeting the requirements of such quality or grade classification as may be approved by the Secretary. The inspection marks approved for use shall be similar in form and design to the examples in Figures 6, 7, and 8 of this section.

Statement enclosed within a circle.

FIGURE 6.

Statement without the use of the circle.

PACKED UNDER
FEDERAL
INSPECTION

U.S. DEPARTMENT
OF COMMERCE
FIGURE 7.

Statement without the use of the circle.

PACKED BY

UNDER FEDERAL INSPECTION
U.S. DEPT. OF COMMERCE
FIGURE 8.

(c) Combined grade and inspection marks: The grade marks set forth in paragraph (a) of this section, and the inspection marks, Figures 7 and 8, set forth in paragraph (b) of this section, may be combined into a consolidated grade and inspection mark for use on processed products that have been

§ 260.88   **Title 50—Wildlife and Fisheries**

packed under inspection as provided in this part.

(d) Products not eligible for approved identification: Processed products which have not been packed under inspection as provided in this part shall not be identified by approved grade or inspection marks, but such products may be inspected on a lot inspection basis as provided in this part and identified by an authorized representative of the Department by stamping the shipping cases and inspection certificate(s) covering such lot(s) as appropriate, with marks similar in form and design to the examples in Figures 9 and 10 of this section.

FIGURE 9.

U. S. D. C.

OCT. 3, 1970

ACCEPTED
Per
SPECIFICATIONS

FIGURE 10.

(e) Removal of labels bearing inspection marks: At the time a lot of fishery products is found to be mislabeled and the labels on the packages are not removed within ten (10) consecutive calendar days, the following procedure shall be applicable:

(1) The processor, under the supervision of the inspector, shall clearly and conspicuously mark all master cases in the lot by means of a "rejected by USDC Inspector" stamp provided by the Department.

(2) The processor shall be held accountable to the Department for all mislabeled products until the products are properly labeled.

(3) Clearance for the release of the relabeled products shall be obtained by the processor from the inspector.

(f) Users of inspection services having an inventory of labels which bear official approved identification marks stating "U.S. Department of the Interior" or otherwise referencing the Interior Department, will be permitted to use such marks until December 31, 1971, except that upon written request the Director, National Marine Fisheries Service, may extend such period for the use of specific labels.

[36 F.R. 4609, Mar. 10, 1971]

§ 260.88   **Political activity.**

All inspectors and licensed samplers are forbidden, during the period of their respective appointments or licenses, to take an active part in political management or in political campaigns. Political activities in city, county, State, or national elections, whether primary or regular, or in behalf of any party or candidate, or any measure to be voted upon, are prohibited. This applies to all appointees or licensees, including, but not limited to, temporary and cooperative employees and employees on leave of absence with or without pay. Wilful violation of this section will constitute grounds for dismissal in the case of appointees and revocation of licenses in the case of licensees.

§ 260.90   **Compliance with other laws.**

None of the requirements in the regulations in this part shall excuse failure to comply with any Federal, State, county, or municipal laws applicable to the operation of food processing establishments and to processed food products.

§ 260.91   **Identification.**

Each inspector and licensed sampler shall have in his possession at all times

APPENDIX 2-6. United States standards for grades of frozen salmon steaks, reproduced from 50 CFR 262.201 to 262.231 (1977).

Subpart C—United States Standards for Grades of Frozen Salmon Steaks

§ 262.201 **Product description.**

Frozen salmon steaks are clean, wholesome units of frozen raw fish flesh with normally associated skin and bone and are 2.5 ounces or more in weight. Each steak has two parallel surfaces and is derived from whole or subdivided salmon slices of uniform thickness which result from sawing or cutting dressed salmon perpendicularly to the axial length, or backbone. The steaks are prepared from either frozen or unfrozen salmon (Oncorhynchus spp.) and are processed and frozen in accordance with good com-mercial practice and are maintained at temperatures necessary for the preservation of the product. The steaks in an individual package are prepared from only one species of salmon.

(a) *Species.* Frozen salmon steaks covered by this standard are prepared from salmon of any of the following species:

Silver or coho (O. kisutch).
Chum or keta (O. keta).
King, chinook, or spring (O. tshawytscha).
Red, sockeye (O. nerka).
Pink (O. gorbuscha).

§ 262.202 **Styles.**

(a) *Style I—Random weight pack.* The individual steaks are of random weight and neither the individual steak weight not the range of weights is specified. The steaks in the lot represent the random distribution cut from the head to tail of a whole dressed salmon.

(b) *Style II—Random weight combination pack.* The individual steaks are of random weight and neither the individual steak weight not range of weights is specified. The steaks in the lot represent a combination of cuts from selected parts of the whole dressed salmon.

(c) *Style III—Uniform weight or portion pack.* All steaks in the package or in the lot are of a specified weight or range of weights.

§ 262.203 **Grades.**

(a) "U.S. Grade A". is the quality of frozen salmon steaks that possess good flavor and odor, and that for those factors which are rated in accordance with the scoring system outlined in the following sections the total score is not less than 85 points.

(b) "U.S. Grade B" is the quality of frozen salmon steaks that possess at least reasonably good flavor and odor, and that for those factors which are rated in accordance with the scoring system outlines in the following sections the total score is not less than 70 points.

(c) "Substandard" is the quality of frozen salmon steaks that fail to meet the requirements of the "U.S. Grade B."

§ 262.206 Recommended dimensions.

(a) The recommended dimensions of frozen salmon steaks are not incorporated in the grades of the finished product since dimensions, as such, are not factors of quality for the purpose of these grades. However, the degree of uniformity of thickness among units of the finished product is rated since it is a factor affecting the quality and utility of the product.

(b) It is recommended that the thickness (smallest dimension) of individually frozen salmon steaks be not less than ½ inch and not greater than 1½ inches.

§ 262.211 Ascertaining the grade.

The grade is ascertained by observing the product in the frozen, thawed, and cooked states and is determined by consideration of the following:

(a) *Factors rated by score points.* The quality of the product with respect to all factors is scored numerically. Cumulative point deductions are assessed for variations of quality for the factors in accordance with the schedule in Table I, in the frozen, thawed, and cooked states. The total deduction is subtracted from the maximum possible score of 100 to obtain the "product score."

(b) *Factors governed by "limiting rule".* The factors of flavor and odor, in addition to being rated by score points, are further considered for compliance with the "limiting rule" grade requirements of flavor and odor in Table I, as defined under Definitions § 262.221(g)(9).

(c) *Determination of the final product grade.* The final product grade is derived on the basis of both the "product score" and the "limiting rule" grade requirements of flavor and odor, per Table I.

§ 262.221 Definitions.

(a) "Slight" refers to a defect that is scarcely noticeable and may not affect the appearance, the desirability, and/or eating quality of the steaks.

(b) "Moderate" refers to a defect that is conspicuously noticeable (not seriously objectionable) and does not seriously affect the appearance, desirability and/or eating quality of the steaks.

(c) "Excessive" refers to a defect that is conspicuously noticeable (seriously objectionable) and seriously affects the appearance, desirability, and/or eating quality of the steaks.

(d) "Occurrence" is defined as each incidence of the same or different types of defects.

(e) "Cooked state" means that the thawed, unseasoned product has been heated within a boilable film-type pouch by immersing the pouch with product in boiling water for 10 minutes. Steaks cooked from the frozen state may require about two additional minutes of cooking.

(f) "Actual net weight" means the weight of the salmon steaks within the package after removal of all packaging material, ice glaze or other protective coatings.

(g) "Scored factors" (Table I):

(1) "General appearance defects" refer to poor arrangement of steaks, distortion of steaks, wide variation in shape, between steaks greater than normal number of head and/or tail pieces, imbedding of packaging material into fish flesh, inside condition of package, frost deposit, excessive or non-uniform skin glaze, and undesirable level of natural color.

(2) "Dehydration" refers to the appearance of a whitish area on the surface of a steak due to the evaporation of water or drying of the affected area.

(3) "Uniformity of thickness" means that steak thickness is within the allowed ⅛-inch manufacturing tolerance between the thickest and thinnest parts of the steaks within a package or sample unit.

APPENDIX 2-6. (continued)

TABLE I—SCHEDULE OF POINT DEDUCTIONS FOR FACTORS RATED BY SCORE POINTS [1]

Scored factors	Description of quality variation	Deduct
FROZEN		
1. General appearance defects	Per occurrence:	
	Slight	1-2
	Moderate	3-4
	Excessive	5-10
2. Dehydration	(Per occurrence) for each 1 sq. inch of surface area	1
3. Uniformity of thickness	For each 1/16 inch above 1/8" variation tolerance in steak thickness (max. deduction: 6 points).	2
4. Uniformity of weight and minimum weight	Style I & II—Random weight. For each steak between 2.5 and 3.0 ounces in weight per package, or per pound of product for packages over 1 pound net wt.	4
	Style III—Uniform weight or portion. For each 0.1 ounce beyond the 0.1 ounce tolerance of the specified portion weight range per 5 lbs. of product.	1
THAWED		
5. Workmanship defects: Blood spots, bruises, cleaning, cutting, fins, foreign material, collarbone, girdle, loose skin, pugh marks, sawdust, scales.	Per occurrence:	
	Slight	1
	Moderate	2-5
	Excessive	5-6
6. Color defects:		
(a) Discoloration of fatty portion	Slight	1-5
	Moderate	3-5
	Excessive	6-10
(b) Discoloration of lean portion	Slight	1-2
	Moderate	3-5
	Excessive	6-10
(c) Non-uniformity of color	Slight	1-2
	Moderate	3-4
	Excessive	5-6
7. Honeycombing	Percent sample area affected:	
	26 to 50	1
	51 to 75	2
	75 to 100	3
COOKED		
8. Texture defect (tough, dry, fibrous, or watery)	Slight	1-2
	Moderate	3-5
	Excessive	6-10
9. Odor [2]	Good (A)	0-2
	Reasonably good (B)	3-5
	Substandard (S)	6-15
10. Flavor:		
(a) Lean portion	Good (A)	0-2
	Reasonably good (B)	3-5
	Substandard (S)	6-15
(b) Fatty portion	Good (A)	0-2
	Reasonably good (B)	3-5
	Substandard (S)	6-15

[1] This schedule of point deductions is based on the examination of sample units composed of: (a) An entire sample package and its contents (for retail sized packages) or (b) a representative subsample consisting of about one pound of samon steaks taken from each sample package (for institutional sized packages), except that the entire sample package or its equivalent shall be examined for factor 4.

[2] "Limiting rule" grade requirements of flavor and odor: Salmon steaks which received over 5 deduction points for odor, or flavor of the lean, or flavor of the fatty portion, shall not be graded above substandard, and those which receive between 3 to 5 points shall not be graded above "U.S. Grade B," regardless of the total product score. (This is a "limiting rule" based on flavor and odor as defined under definitions § 262.221(g) (9)).

(4) "Uniformity of weight and minimum weight" is defined in Table I. (Portions are designated by "weight range" or "specified weight." The "weight range" of portions bearing "specified weight" designation on containers shall be taken as the "specified weight" plus or minus 0.5 ounces unless otherwise specified.)

(5) "Workmanship defects" refers to appearance defects that were not eliminated during processing and are considered objectionable or poor commercial practice. They include the following: Blood spots, bruises, cleaning (refers to inadequate cleaning of the visceral cavity from blood, viscera and loose or attached appendages), cutting (refers to irregular, inadequate, unnecessary, or improper cuts and/or trimmings), fins, foreign material (refers to any loose parts, of fish or other than fish origin), collar bone, girdle (refers to bony structure adjacent to fin), loose skin, pugh marks, sawdust and scales.

(6) "Color defects":

(i) "Discoloration of fat portion" means that the normal color of the fat shows increasing degrees of yellowing due to oxidation.

(ii) "Discoloration of lean portion" means that the normal surface flesh color has faded or changed due to deteriorative influences.

(iii) "Nonuniformity of color" refers to noticeable differences in surface flesh color on a single steak or between adjacent steaks in the same package or sample unit. It would also include color variation of the visceral cavity and skin watermarking.

(7) "Honeycombing" refers to the visible appearance on the steak surface of numerous discrete holes or openings of varying size.

(8) "Texture defect" refers to an undesirable increase in toughness and/or dryness, fibrousness, and watery nature of salmon examined in the cooked state.

(9) "Odor" and "flavor:"

(i) "Good flavor and odor" (essential requirement for Grade A) means that the fish flesh has the good flavor and odor characteristic of the indicated species of salmon, and is free from rancidity and from off-flavors and off-odors.

(ii) "Reasonably good flavor and odor" (minimum requirement for Grade B) means that the fish flesh may be somewhat lacking in the good flavor and odor characteristics of the indicated species of salmon, is reasonably free of rancidity, and is free from objectionable off-flavors and off-odors.

(iii) "Substandard flavor and odor" (substandard grade) means that the flavor and odor fail to meet the requirements of "reasonably good flavor and odor."

§ 262.225 Tolerances for certification of officially drawn samples.

The sample rate and grades of specific lots shall be certified on the basis of Part 260 Subpart A of this chapter. (Regulations Governing Processed Fishery Products.)

§ 262.231 Score sheet for frozen salmon steaks.

Label: _____
Size and kind of container: _____
Container mark or identification: _____
Size of lot: _____
Number of packages per master carton: _____
Size of sample: _____
Number of steaks per container: _____
Product style: _____
Actual net weight: _____(ounces)_____(lb.)

Scored factors	Deductions
FROZEN	
1. General appearance defects_____	_____
2. Dehydration_____	_____
3. Uniformity of thickness_____	_____
4. Uniformity of weight_____	_____
THAWED	
5. Workmanship defects_____	_____
6. Color defects_____	_____
7. Honeycombing_____	_____
COOKED	
8. Texture_____	_____
9. Odor (Limiting rule—Table I)_____	_____
10. Flavor (Limiting rule—Table I)_____	_____
Total deductions_____	_____

Product score (100—Total deductions)_____
Flavor and odor rating_____
Final grade_____

CHAPTER 3
CONSUMER PRODUCT SAFETY COMMISSION

Organization, General Activities, and Statutes Administered
Agreement with the Food and Drug Administration
Product Standards

ORGANIZATION, GENERAL ACTIVITIES, AND STATUTES ADMINISTERED

The Consumer Product Safety Act of October 27, 1972 (PL 92-573, 86 Stat. 1207) established the Consumer Product Safety Commission, which was activated on May 14, 1973. The main purpose of the commission is to reduce the unreasonable risk of injury to the public from consumer products. An organization chart of the agency is presented in Appendix 3-1. The main federal statutes administered by the commission are described in Table 3-1. The commissioners are nominated by the U.S. President and confirmed by the U.S. Senate.

TABLE 3-1. Some Federal Statutes Administered by the
Consumer Products Safety Commission

1. The Consumer Product Safety Act of 1972
   (15 U.S.C. 2051 et seq.)

2. The Flammable Fabrics Act as amended of 1967
   (15 U.S.C. 1191 et seq.)

3. The Federal Hazardous Substances Act as amended of 1972
   (15 U.S.C. 1261 et seq.)

4. The Poison Prevention Packaging Act of 1970
   (15 U.S.C. 1471 et seq.)

5. The Refrigerator Safety Act of 1956
   (15 U.S.C. 1211 et seq.)

To accomplish its chief mission, the commission is authorized, among other things:

1. To assist consumers to evaluate the comparative safety of consumer products.
2. To develop and issue consumer product safety standards, establish requirements for warnings and instructions; and minimize conflicting state and local regulations.
3. To declare consumer products banned hazardous products when the public cannot be protected adequately by feasible consumer product safety standards.
4. To promote research and investigation in causes and prevention of product-related deaths, illnesses, and injuries.
5. To require manufacturers, distributors, and retailers to report potential sub-

stantial product hazards associated with consumer products to the commission.

After the commission has established mandatory safety standards for consumer products sold in the United States, it has legislative authority to enforce such standards in the courts with civil penalties of up to $500,000 in fines and criminal penalties of up to $50,000 in fines and one year in jail. The commission also may require--after opportunity for hearing and giving notice--the recall, repair, replacement, or refund of products judged unreasonably hazardous. As stated previously, it has the power to ban such products.

Any interested consumer or consumer organization may petition the commission to begin proceedings to issue, amend, or revoke a consumer product safety rule. The Consumer Product Safety Act also requires that the commission grant or deny the written request within 120 days. If the petition is denied, the commission must publish its reasons in the Federal Register. The petitioners may also appeal the decision in the court.

The commission has two other important functions: a strong congressional mandate to educate and inform the general public about product safety and the maintenance of an injury information clearing house in conjunction with injuries associated with consumer products.

AGREEMENT WITH THE FOOD AND DRUG ADMINISTRATION

On August 13, 1976 the Consumer Product Safety Commission signed a Memorandum of Understanding (41 FR 34342 and 34343) with the FDA. The purpose of this agreement was to delineate the areas of jurisdiction of the respective agencies for administration of the Consumer Product Safety Act and the Federal Food, Drug, and Cosmetic Act with respect to food, food containers, and related articles and equipment.

This agreement provides a very useful and analytical legal background of the two agencies' responsibilities. It is explained in the following outline.

Legal Responsibilities of the Consumer Product Safety Commission

The Commission is authorized by the Consumer Product Safety Act to carry out numerous activities, some of which have been described previously.

According to Section 3(a)(1) of the Consumer Product Safety Act [U.S.C. 2052(a)(1)], a consumer product is defined as follows:

The term "consumer product" means any article, or component part thereof, produced or distributed

(i)   for sale to a consumer for use in or around a permanent or temporary household or residence, a school, in recreation, or otherwise, or

(ii) for the personal use, consumption or enjoyment of a consumer in or around a permanent or temporary household or residence, a school, in recreation, or otherwise; but such term does not include--...

(I)   food. The term "food" as used in this subparagraph means all "food" as defined in section 201(f) of the Federal Food, Drug, and Cosmetic Act....

Thus food is not a consumer product and cannot be regulated under the Consumer Product Safety Act. According to the Federal Food, Drug, and Cosmetic Act, substances that are "food" are also excluded from the definition of "hazardous substance" under Section 2(f)2 of the Federal Hazardous Substances Act [15 U.S.C. 1261(f)2]. Therefore, they cannot be regulated by the commission under that act. However, under Section 2(2)(0) of the Poison Prevention Packaging Act of 1970 [15 U.S.C. 1471(2)(C)], "food" may be made subject by the commission to a child-resistant (special) packaging requirement.

The definition of the term "food" in Section 201(f) of the Federal Food, Drug, and Cosmetic Act [21 U.S.C. 321(f)] is, therefore, critical in delineating the scope of the commission's jurisdiction over "consumer products." The term "food" means: (1) articles used as food or drink for man or animals, (2) chewing gum, and (3) substances used as components for any such article.

Legal Responsibilities of the Food and Drug Administration

The FDA has the responsibility of enforcing the Federal Food, Drug, and Cosmetic Act, which, among other things, prohibits the introduction into interstate commerce of articles of food that are adulterated or misbranded. An "adulterated food" (21 U.S.C. 342) is considered as injurious to health or otherwise unfit for food. A "misbranded food" (21 U.S.C. 343) is considered as false or misleading in any particular of its labeling. The FDA is also responsible for ensuring that "food additives" [21 U.S.C. 321(s)] are safe under the conditions of their intended use.

The need for this agreement arose because of uncertainty concerning the scope of the statutory exclusion under the Consumer Product Safety Act for all articles defined as "food" by the Federal Foods, Drug, and Cosmetic Act. The need for clarification is acute because determination of whether a potentially hazardous consumer article is a "food" determines as well whether consumers are to be protected from risk of injury or illness by the commission pursuant to the Consumer Product Safety Act or by the FDA pursuant to the Federal Food, Drug, and Cosmetic Act.

According to the agreement, the two agencies have agreed on the following principles:

Aerosol Propellants

Aerosol propellants included in a food product may be substantially dissipated before the food is ingested. However, they are "components" of food and are thus considered as food according to the Federal Food, Drug, and Cosmetic Act; they are subject to regulation by the FDA.

Food Contact Surfaces (Migration)

Articles having food contact surfaces, such as food containers and food cooking, eating, and preparation articles, from which there is migration of a substance from the contact surface to the food are food "components" and thus "food" within the meaning of the Federal Food, Drug, and Cosmetics Act and subject to regulation by the FDA. However, in any case where there is migration, the FDA will have regulatory authority over the article as a "food," and the commission will have regulatory authority over the article for hazards unrelated to migration (see text that follows).

Food Contact Surfaces (No Migration)

Articles employed in the preparation or holding of food may cause contamination or spoilage without migrating or otherwise becoming a component of the food, such as home canning equipment that fails to provide a seal adequate to keep air from passing into stored food; pressure cookers, slow cookers, refrigerators, or freezers that fail to perform at proper temperatures, thereby rendering food unfit to eat; and can openers that fail to perform properly, causing metal particles from the can (not from the can opener) to be deposited in food. Because such articles do not present a hazard by becoming components of food, they are subject to regulation as "consumer products" by the Commission under the Consumer Product Safety Act. The FDA may, of course, take action under the Federal Food, Drug, and Cosmetic Act against food contaminated or spoiled by such articles if interstate commerce is involved. The FDA may also regulate the equipment and procedures employed by commercial processors of food that has been or is to be shipped in interstate commerce when necessary to assure the wholesomeness or safety of such food.

Food Containers (Mechanical Hazards)

Food containers may present mechanical risks of injury unrelated to food contamination or spoilage, such as a defect in the container that leads to an explosion or
breakage of the container, sharp edges presented by the container, and defects in
the nozzle. Because such articles do not present hazards by becoming components
of food, they are subject to regulation by the commission under the Consumer
Product Safety Act. However, such articles may also be subject to overlapping
jurisdiction of FDA under the Federal Food, Drug, and Cosmetic Act, because the
FDA has jurisdiction over a food container (even where the container is not a food)
which "is composed, in whole or in part, of any poisonous or deleterious substance
which may render the contents (food) injurious to health," and because the FDA
has jurisdiction as well over a food which "bears...any...deleterious substance"
[Section 402(a)(1), (6) of the Federal Food, Drug, and Cosmetic Act, 21 U.S.C.
342(a)(1), (6)].

Technical Assistance

The FDA will provide, on the request of the commission, technical assistance, such
as evaluation of sealing efficiency of home canning lids, where the FDA determines
that it has the technical and laboratory capability to provide such assistance.
Results of an evaluation are later reported to the commission.

PRODUCT STANDARDS

All regulations promulgated by the Consumer Product Safety Commission are
located in Title 16 of the Code of Federal Regulations. Table 3-2 presents the general content of Chapter II (Consumer Product Safety Commission).
       Has the commission established any product standard that is related to food
or food-preparation equipment? Table 3-2 indicates that 16 CFR 1750 is related to
the Refrigerator Safety Act. Since the regulations are concerned with standards for
devices to permit the opening of household refrigerator doors from the inside, they
are not discussed here. Interested persons may consult the original document.
       Actually, the commission has established very few product standards that are
of interest in this book. However, in the last few years, a number of petitions have
been submitted pursuant to Section 10 of the Consumer Product Safety Act (15
U.S.C. 2059) , which provides that any interested person may petition the commission to commence a proceeding for the issuance of a consumer-product safety rule.
Table 3-3 indicates some of the petitions that were submitted and denied in accordance with established procedure. All these petitions were related to food contain-

TABLE 3-2. Subchapter Titles and Part Numbers of Chapter II (Consumer Product Safety Commission), Title 16, Code of Federal Regulations

Subchapter	Title	Parts
A	General	1009 to 1031
B	Consumer Product Safety Act Regulations	1105 to 1207
C	Federal Hazardous Substances Act Regulations	1500 to 1512
D	Flammable Fabrics Act Regulations	1602 to 1632
E	Poison Prevention Packaging Act of 1970 Regulations	1700
F	Refrigerator Safety Act Regulations	1750

TABLE 3-3. Notices of Denial by the Consumer Product Safety Commission to Establish Safety Standards for Products Indicated

Reference	Product Standard Petitioned and Denied
40 FR 32157 (07/31/75)	Glass containers for malt beverages
41 FR 40216 (09/17/76)	Pull-tab and pull-off lid containers
41 FR 52100 to 52101 (11/26/76)	External surface temperature of ovens
42 FR 831 to 832 (01/04/77)	Five gallon glass bottles
42 FR 832 to 833 (01/04/77)	Glass containers for beverages; bottle caps

ers or food-preparation equipment. In the following, an example of such denial is described.

On January 9, 1976 the commission was petitioned to develop a consumer product safety standard to regulate pull-tab and pull-off lid containers. The petitioner alleged that the products are likely to cause the following injuries:

1. Lacerations to the hand and fingers while opening.
2. Lacerations due to handling or stepping on a lid that has been disposed of improperly.
3. Injuries to small children playing with the inner rim of an opened container.
4. Injuries due to excessive internal pressure.
5. Injuries due to mistaken identification such as automotive products packaged as "six packs."
6. Injuries due to metal fragmenting.
7. Injuries caused when the container does not open by normal means and pliers or other tools must be used.

   The petition requested the following remedies:

1. Coat the removal lids with synthetic materials.
2. Recess the inner rim so that it would not be so accessible as to pose risk of cutting.
3. Provide obvious warning notices on containers stating the chance of injury and how it might occur.

   According to the commission's denial notice, injury data and other available information indicate that containers with self-opening lids do not present a greater hazard than those associated with the problem of sharp edges of conventional metal cans, and in addition, injuries associated with the use of both types of cans appear to be relatively minor. It also appears that there are relatively few injuries associated with pull-tab and pull-off lid containers, most of which are for beer and soft drinks, in comparison with the number of these items in the marketplace. Consequently, the commission denied the petition, and the denial notice was announced in the Federal Register on September 17, 1976.

   Since the commission only started its work on May of 1973, it will be some time before more food-related product standards are issued. However, there are two recent standards of this type that have some bearing on the objective of this book.

   The Poison Prevention Packaging Act of 1970 (15 U.S.C. 1471 to 1475) authorizes the commission to issue standards for the special packaging of any household substances if it makes the following finding. The degree or nature of the hazard to children in the availability of such substance by reason of its packaging is such that special packaging is required to protect them from serious injury or illness resulting from the handling, using, or ingesting of such substance.

Acute accidental poisoning from iron began to occur with greater frequency when it became widely used as a therapeutic agent for the treatment of anemia. Data from the National Clearing House for Poison Control Centers on accidental ingestion of iron preparations by children under 5 years of age for the latest available period, 1969 to 1974, show 2470 such ingestions, of which 632 required hospitalization. In view of this and other data, the commission proposed (40 FR 20148 to 20150, April 18, 1977) to amend 16 CFR 1700, which contains regulations for the Poison Prevention Packaging Act of 1970 (see Table 3-2). This proposal has become a permanent regulation which is described under Section 16 CFR 1700.14 (substances requiring special packaging). Paragraph 16 CFR 1700.14(a)(12) is entitled "Iron containing drugs," and paragraph 16 CFR 1700.14(a)(13) entitled "Dietary supplements containing iron." The latter contains the following information.

With the exception of those preparations in which iron is present solely as a colorant, dietary supplements that contain an equivalent of 250 mg or more of elemental iron, from any source, in a single package in concentrations of 0.025% or more on a weight:volume basis for liquids, and 0.05% or more on a weight:weight basis for nonliquids (e.g., powders, granules, tablets, capsules, wafers, gels, and viscous products such as pastes and ointments) are required to be packaged in special or child-resistant packages in accordance with established standards.

Another relevant standard that has just been established is the following. On June 30, 1977 (42 FR 33276 to 33282), the commission issued mandatory safety requirements for pacifiers in the form of a final regulation banning from interstate commerce pacifiers not meeting the safety requirements. The regulation is designed to address choking and strangulation hazards associated with pacifiers.

Thus a new 16 CFR 1511, entitled "Requirements for Pacifiers," is added to the regulations for the Federal Hazardous Substances Act (see Table 3-2). The statutory authority under which this part was issued was provided by Sections 2(f)(1)(D), (q)(1)(A), (s), 3(e)(1), 74 Stat. 372, 374, 375, as amended; 80 Stat. 1304 to 1305, 83 Stat. 187 to 189; and 15 U.S.C. 1261, 1262.

The need for this regulation was demonstrated by injury data and death reports. About ten deaths and seven nonfatal choking incidents that were associated with pacifiers were reported between 1966 and 1975. Four of the deaths were due to choking and six to strangulation.

The regulation has five parts. The first part requires a guard or shield on the pacifier of sufficient size so that the pacifier cannot be drawn through a test fixture with dimensions similar to a baby's mouth. In addition, the guard or shield is required to have at least two ventilation holes. These holes are intended to provide an emergency oxygen supply as well as a rapid means of removing the pacifier from the child's throat.

The second part prescribes a protrusion limitation requirement designed to address the hazard pattern of a child falling forward or rolling over with the pacifier in his/her mouth. The regulation also has a test for the structural integrity of the pacifier and its component parts. Any components or fragments of the pacifier released when subjected to the structural integrity tests are then subject to a small parts test.

The last two sections of the regulation address the strangulation hazard that results from tying a pacifier around a child's neck with ribbons, string, or similar attachments. A required warning label would alert parents and others to this hazard.

The test procedures in the regulation describe the tests that the commission will perform on pacifiers for compliance and enforcement purposes. Manufacturers, of course, are free to test their own products by more stringent procedures than those described in the standard.

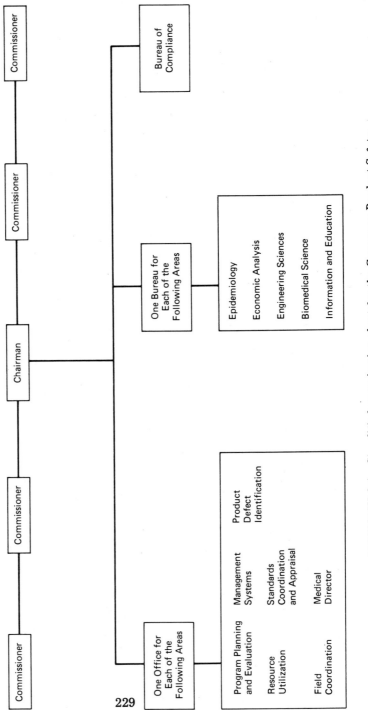

APPENDIX 3-1. Simplified organization chart for the Consumer Product Safety Commission.

CHAPTER 4

ENVIRONMENTAL PROTECTION AGENCY

INTRODUCTION

General Activities, Organization, and Statutes Administered

The Environmental Protection Agency (EPA) is an independent agency created through an executive reorganization plan designed to consolidate certain federal government environmental activities into a single agency. Organizationally, the EPA is headed by an administrator who is supported by a deputy administrator and six assistant administrators. The administrator of the EPA may undertake certain enforcement actions in his own right to ensure compliance, although judicial enforcement actions are undertaken by the Justice Department on request from the administrator or his delegates. An organizational chart of this agency is provided in Appendix 4-1. Each of the six assistant administrators is in charge of one category of activities. One such category is of concern to this book, namely water and hazardous materials.

The activities under the assistant administrator for water and hazardous materials are primarily policy development, standards and criteria development, and support and evaluation of regional activities. Among all the activities of the agency, those that concern this book the most are drinking water safety and protection of food from pesticides. They are presented in detail later.

The EPA administers a number of federal statutes. The most relevant ones are described as follows:

1. The Federal Water Pollution Control Act Amendments of October 18, 1972 (PL 92-500, 86 Stat. 816 et seq., 33 U.S.C. 1251 et seq.).
2. The Clean Water Act of December 27, 1977 (PL 95-217, 91 Stat. 1566).
3. The Safe Drinking Water Act of December 16, 1974 (PL 93-523, 42 U.S.C. 300f et seq., Sections 1401 et seq. of the Public Health Service Act, 88 Stat. 1660 et seq.).
4. The Federal Insecticide, Fungicide, and Rodenticide Act of 1947 as amended in 1972 and 1975 (PL 92-516, October 21, 1972, 86 Stat. 973 et seq., 61 Stat. 163 et seq., 7 U.S.C. 135 et seq.; PL 94-140, November 28, 1975). Sometimes the 1972 amended act is also known as the Federal Environmental Pesticide Control Act of 1972.
5. A provision of the Fish and Wildlife Act of August 1, 1958 (PL 85-582, Section 1, 72 Stat. 479, 16 U.S.C. 742d-1).
6. Sections 406, 408, and 409 of the Federal Food, Drug, and Cosmetic Act (21 U.S.C. 346, 346a, 348).

Office of Water and Hazardous Materials

The assistant administrator for this office serves as a principal adviser to the administrator of the EPA in matters pertaining to water and hazardous materials programs, specifically, the management of water and pesticide programs.

To manage the water and pesticides programs, four different offices (see Appendix 4-1) have been assigned the responsibility. They include the Offices of Water Planning and Standards, Water Program Operations, Water Supply, and Pesticide Programs. Although the last two offices are of major importance to this book, it is unrealistic to discuss the safety of our drinking water supply without some idea of the EPA's work on the pollution of water in general. A brief description for the functions of the first two offices serves this purpose.

The deputy assistant administrator for the Office of Water Planning and Standards is assigned to:

1. Develop, in cooperation with other fellow program offices, a general program strategy for the abatement of water pollution.
2. Coordinate all national water-related activities generated from the overall water program strategy.
3. Monitor national progress regarding the attainment of water quality goals.
4. Develop, within the assigned program responsibilities, water quality standards and effluent guidelines.
5. Develop effective regional and state water quality planning and control agencies.
6. Maintain and develop a centralized data system for water programs, including compatible water quality, discharger, and program data files.

The deputy assistant administrator of Water Program Operations is assigned to:

1. Develop technical policies, national program, guidelines, and regulations for water supply and water pollution control.
2. Provide technical support and direction to various organizations and the respective regional offices.
3. Evaluate regional programs with respect to hazardous materials and oil spills response and prevention, municipal point source control and abatement, manpower development for water-related activities, and water supply improvement and protection.

These delineations of functions have been obtained from the Organization and Functions Manual of the EPA. The work is directly related to the provisions of the Federal Water Pollution Control Act Amendments of October 18, 1972. Details about the Offices of Water Supply and Pesticide Programs are presented later.

Regulations Promulgated

The regulations promulgated by the EPA to implement the statutes administered are contained in Title 40 of the Code of Federal Regulations. Although six parts (40 CFR 141, 142, 143, 146, 149, and 180) have direct relationship with the content of this book, the regulations contained in numerous other parts have a very important direct effect on the quality of our environment, which ultimately affects our water and food supply.

The task of the EPA is to protect the health and welfare of the American people by controlling pollution hazards. To do so, the EPA sets and enforces air and water pollution standards, monitors pollution, controls pesticides, sets standards for noise and general ambient standards for radiation, works on solid waste management, conducts research and demonstration projects, and helps state and local environmental efforts. Most of the regulations relating to these programs are not discussed; details on the relevant aspects are presented later. An idea of what all the regulations involve is provided in the appendix as detailed in the next paragraph.

Thus under Title 40 of the Code of Federal Regulations, Subchapters D, E, and N are entitled Water program, Pesticide programs, and Effluent guidelines and standards, respectively. Appendix 4-2 provides the titles of the parts contained under each subchapter and the statutory authority under which each part was issued.

OFFICE OF WATER SUPPLY

General Activities and Organization

As discussed earlier, under the Assistant Administrator for Water and Hazard Materials, two offices are of importance to this book. One is the Office of Water Supply. The Deputy Assistant Administrator for Water Supply is responsible for:

1.   Implementing the programs established by PL 93-523, the Safe Drinking Water Act of 1974.
2.   Cooperation with state and regional authorities.

3. Developing a national program of public information to encourage citizen participation aimed at the goal, "Safe Drinking Water for all Americans."
4. Coordination with other federal agencies in water supply activities and liaison with the National Drinking Water Advisory Council.
5. Preparation of budget and program status reports for the water supply program.

Under this office there are three main divisions: the Criteria and Standards Division, the State Program Division, and the Technical Support Division (Cincinnati). The Organization and Functions Manual of the EPA provides the following functional statements for each division.

Criteria and Standards Division

This division is under the supervision of a director who is assigned to:

1. Develop and revise guidelines and regulations that will protect the public health and welfare with reference to primary and secondary drinking water criteria.
2. Develop site selection, surveillance, and operations and maintenance regulations and guidelines.
3. Establish, in place of assignable maximum contaminant levels, treatment regulations.
4. Award and monitor contracts needed to assist in the development of regulations.
5. Coordinate other technical program areas.
6. Identify research needs and assure that research results are coordinated and applied.
7. Evaluate and implement suitable demonstration projects.
8. Provide technical guidance and advice to other federal agencies in the establishment of regulations and standards, for example, bottled water standards (FDA).
9. Provide scientific advice to assist in emergency situations.
10. Provide direction and guidance on ground water developments and technology and alternate underground injection techniques and methods.
11. Monitor the National Academy of Sciences with reference to more "acceptable" contaminant levels and treatment of drinking water.

State Program Division

This division is supervised by a director who is assigned to:

1. Establish and revise guidelines and regulations for state water supply programs, state program grants, underground injection control (UIC) programs, and UIC permit programs.
2. Provide policy direction and guidance to the states and regions in the establishment and implementation of UIC programs and their public water system supervision programs.
3. Assure that state program aspects of the Safe Drinking Water Act are implemented by regional authorities in compliance with guidelines and requirements of the national program. The assurance is achieved by constant monitoring.
4. Provide technical, management, and policy guidance and direction to states and regions on how to maintain, process, and collect those data required by the regulations.
5. Provide guidance and advice on exemptions and variances and review of those granted.
6. Monitor, via regional offices, the operations of state programs.
7. Assist in the evaluation programs of each state.
8. Certify loan guarantee applications.
9. Develop policy guidance in regard to the surveillance and monitoring programs for Indian reservations and federal facilities and the interstate carrier water supply certification program.
10. Provide policy guidance for response to local, regional, and national emergencies.
11. Identify research needs.
12. Serve as the program liaison with the National Pollutant Discharge Elimination System program.
13. Provide technical guidance for the protection of rural and nonpublic water supplies.
14. Coordinate the review of all projects that are federally assisted and occur in locations in which a sole-source designation has been made.
15. Provide guidance, in cooperation with the Office of Water Enforcement, to the regional authorities on how to implement enforcement and surveillance programs in those states that do not have primary enforcement responsibility.

Technical Support Division (Cincinnati)

The division is supervised by a director who is assigned to:

1. Provide technical assistance to the states and regions in the discipline of maintenance and operation, surveillance and monitoring, manpower development, and treatment technology programs.

2. Provide technical support for the use of available treatment techniques.
3. Assist in the review and development of substantive and procedural guidelines and regulations as required.
4. Maintain experienced personnel to provide technical support in situations of emergency.
5. Prepare and plan, when requested, investigations of the extent and nature of contaminants in ground water sources and public water supplies; identify the contamination sources and develop recommendations for corrective actions.
6. Develop and improve field techniques to investigate and evaluate the quality of drinking water.
7. Assist in the establishment and implementation of manpower development programs for local and state water supply personnel.

The Safe Drinking Water Act

In 1974, the Safe Drinking Water Act (33 U.S.C. 1251 et seq.) was passed by the U.S. Congress. The act is to provide for the safety of drinking water supplies throughout the United States and enforce national drinking water standards. The EPA has the primary responsibility of establishing the standards and the states, enforcing them and otherwise supervising public water supply systems and sources of drinking water. In the following some major provisions of the act are discussed. The material has been adapted from the original act and the publications in Table 4-1.

The major provisions of the Safe Drinking Water Act are listed as follows;

1. To establish primary regulations for the protection of public health.
2. To establish secondary regulations relating to the taste, odor, and appearance of drinking water.
3. To protect underground drinking water sources.
4. To research and study health, economic, and technological problems of drinking water supplies. Specifically required are studies of viruses in drinking water and contamination by cancer-causing chemicals.
5. To investigate the availability and quality of rural water supplies.
6. To assist the states to upgrade their drinking water program through technical support, personnel, and manpower training and to grant assistance.
7. To file citizen suits against individuals or parties that violate the act.
8. To issue regulations, authorize inspections, and require detailed record keeping and judicial review.
9. To establish a National Drinking Water Advisory Council of 15 members to advise the agency on the scientific and other responsibilities under the act.

10. To require the FDA (see Chapter 6) to develop and issue bottled drinking
water standards that conform to the primary regulations established under
the act--or publish reasons for not complying with the requirement. This requirement is mandatory.

TABLE 4-1. Publications Related to the Safe Drinking Water Act

1. The Environmental Protection Agency: Legislation, programs and organization. U.S. Environmental Protection Agency. Reprinted by the Library System Branch and revised periodically.
2. An environmental law: Highlights of the Safe Drinking Water Act of 1974.
U.S. Environmental Protection Agency. Revised November 1976.
3. Five articles on drinking water in the February 1977 issue of EPA Journal.
4. Is your drinking water safe? U.S. Environmental Protection Agency. March
1977.
5. A drop to drink. U.S. Environmental Protection Agency. Reprinted March
1977.
6. Your drinking water. U.S. Environmental Protection Agency. April 1977.
7. Drinking water standards take effect. EPA Journal 3:12-13 (July/August
1977).
8. What everyone should know about the quality of drinking water. U.S. Environmental Protection Agency. December 1977.
9. Drinking water reform. EPA Journal 4:28-29 (March 1978).
10. Curbing chemicals in drinking water. EPA Journal 4:26-27 (September
1978).
11. Things you should know about the Safe Drinking Water Act. American
Water Works Association.

Other aspects of the act are as follows. The law provides that variances and
exemptions from certain requirements may be granted under certain conditions. A
variance is an official permission from a state or the EPA to disregard certain provisions of the law, provided that this doesn't result in an "unreasonable" risk to
health. The provisions may relate to a required contaminant level or a treatment
technique.

A variance could be granted because of the inability of the water system to
comply, because of the nature of the water source, or because the raw water is of
such good quality that a required treatment is not necessary. The period that variances may be in effect will depend on the condition of the raw water source and
available technology. A variance can last indefinitely, but it has to be reviewed at

least once every 3 years to see that the situation hasn't changed. In addition, a state cannot grant a variance in the first place without first announcing its intention and holding a public hearing on the matter. Publicity is a key part of this law.

An exemption can be granted to systems unable to meet contaminant level or treatment technique requirements "because of compelling reasons, including economic factors." However, once again, no exemption can be granted if it may result in unreasonable risk to health.

Exemptions from contaminant levels or required treatment techniques--extending up to 7 years or up to 9 years for a regional system--may be granted by a state for compelling reasons. Thus exemptions *must* carry a specific time limit. The states must prescribe a formal schedule to be followed by the system to amend the situation that brought about the exemption. Again, public hearings are part of the requirement.

Basically, the Safe Drinking Water Act is to establish uniform national safety and quality water standards. This means the identification of contaminants and the establishment of their maximum acceptable levels in drinking water. The difference between an established primary drinking water regulation and a secondary one is that the enforcement of the former is mandatory, whereas the latter is optional.

To qualify for the primary enforcement (of the primary drinking water standards and regulation) responsibility, a state must submit a program to the EPA and be approved. Whenever a public water system in a state with primary enforcement responsibility does not comply with a primary regulation or a schedule imposed with a variance or exemption, the EPA is directed by a provision of the act to notify the state and to provide advice or technical assistance in an effort to bring about compliance. If noncompliance continues beyond a 60-day grace period, federal action may be taken. Also, the EPA may begin enforcement at the request of a governor or a responsible state agency. In a state without primary enforcement authority, the EPA may take direct civil action or lawsuits against offending utilities, with all the attendant publicity that assures. Whoever the designated authority (state or EPA), a maximum penalty of $5,000 a day may be imposed for willful violation until corrective action is taken. The EPA may hold public hearing on petition of the state, the public water system, or a person served by the system, to assist the state in carrying out the primary enforcement role.

On a community level, a public water supply, whether privately or state owned, must give notice to its consumers if it:

1. Fails to meet the primary drinking water regulations.
2. Fails to perform required monitoring.
3. Has a variance or exemption.
4. Fails to comply with a schedule imposed with a variance or exemption.

The notice must be given at least every 3 months in newspapers of general circulation and must be included in customers' water bills. Other communication media must also be notified.

The law requires issuance of the notices for a violation "as soon as practicable after it discovers that it's in violation." In any case, *notice must go out to news media no later than 36 hours after a violation is confirmed.* A state or the EPA will file lawsuits only if the utility fails to act on its own.

The act has a number of other miscellaneous provisions:

1. If a system runs up against shortages of necessary chemicals, such as chlorine, the agency is specifically authorized to *issue* certifications of need and to *direct* suppliers to deliver needed chemicals to water systems.
2. If a citizen does not like the odor or appearance of the drinking water, he must approach the state authority. Most states either enforce the federal secondary drinking water regulations or have their own.
3. If a citizen is not satisfied with the drinking water, he can bring lawsuits against the responsible water system. However, there are a number of restrictions to discourage frivolous suits. For instance, class action suits are prohibited so that an individual can file only on his own behalf. In addition, the person is required to give notice to the water system, the state and the EPA 60 days in advance, and be subject to their limitations. If the person happens to be an employee of a private water system he is suing, the act protects him from dismissal by his employer.
4. To protect the public at all times, the act has an "emergency powers" provision that allows the EPA to take immediate action if it is advised by a qualified source that a contaminant that is present or likely to enter into a public water system may present "an imminent and substantial endangerment to health... and that state and local authorities have not acted to protect health." After due investigation, the agency may take any necessary action to protect health. Failure to comply with such an order can bring up to $5,000/day fines.
5. The EPA is authorized to provide financial assistance in various ways if the U.S. Congress appropriates the requested money. Some examples are:
   a. If a small public water system is unable to obtain enough financial resources for required improvements, the EPA can guarantee loans made by private banks or others. The EPA is not permitted to loan money directly.
   b. No grants or loans are authorized for construction of facilities.
   c. The EPA is authorized to allot money to states to help them develop and carry out supervisory programs for their water systems.
   d. The EPA is authorized to allot money for grants to develop and demonstrate new or better ways to provide dependably safe drinking water and for reclamation, recycling, and reuse of waste waters for drinking.

e. The EPA is authorized to allow money to states to carry out underground water source protection programs.

f. The EPA plans to finance a great deal of research directly, including studies of viruses and of a variety of suspected carcinogens (cancer causing chemicals) in water supplies.

The Safe Drinking Water Act also provides for the protection of underground sources of drinking water by means of a regulatory program similar to that governing public water systems. To safeguard such sources, the EPA must establish requirements.

The primary responsibility for carrying out these requirements falls to the states where underground source protection programs have been established. If a state fails to assume this responsibility, the EPA will prescribe a control program for that state. The act specifies that regulations will not be established that will interfere with oil or natural gas production, unless such regulations are deemed essential to prevent contamination of underground drinking water sources.

National Drinking Water Standards and Related Regulations

Regulations related to the Safe Drinking Water Act are promulgated in 40 CFR 141, 142, 143, and 149. Appendix 4-2 describes their titles and the issuing statutory authorities. Part 141 establishes the national interim primary drinking water regulations pursuant to Section 1412 of the Public Health Service Act, as amended by the Safe Drinking Water Act (PL 93-523) and related regulations applicable to public water systems.

A brief summary about primary drinking water regulation is as follows:

1. It applies to public water systems.
2. It specifies contaminants that may have any adverse effect on the health of the persons.
3. It specifies the maximum contaminant level for each such contaminant if possible.
4. It specifies treatment technique that may reduce the level of those contaminants for which maximum contaminant levels are impossible to set.
5. It contains criteria and procedures to assure a supply of drinking water which dependably complies with such maximum contaminant levels.
6. It includes quality control and testing procedures to insure:
   a. compliance with maximum contaminant levels
   b. proper operation and maintenance of the system
   c. requirements as to the minimum quality of water that may be taken into

the system and siting for new facilities for public water systems.

It is specifically stated that the regulations shall apply to each public water system, unless the system meets all of the following conditions:

1. Consists only of distribution and storage facilities (and does not have any collection and treatment facilities);
2. Obtains all of its water from, but is not owned or operated by, a public water system to which such regulations apply;
3. Does not sell water to any person; and
4. Is not a carrier that conveys passengers in interstate commerce.

Table 4-2 provides the subpart and section titles of 40 CFR 141. It should be noted that, according to certain provision in the statute, this interim primary drinking water regulation will eventually be replaced by a final and permanent version. According to Subpart A of 40 CFR 141, some definitions are presented as follows. A "contaminant" is any physical, chemical, biological, or radiological substance or matter in water. The "maximum contaminant level" means the maximum permissible level of a contaminant in water that is delivered to the free flowing outlet of the ultimate user of a public water system, except in the case of turbidity where the maximum permissible level is measured at the point of entry to the distribution system. Contaminants added to the water under circumstances controlled by the user, except those resulting from corrosion of piping and plumbing caused by water quality, are excluded from this definition.

TABLE 4-2. Subpart Titles and Section Numbers of 40 CFR 141 (National Interim Primary Drinking Water Regulations)

Subpart	Title	Section Numbers
A	General	141.1 to 141.6
B	Maximum contaminant levels	141.11 to 141.16
C	Monitoring and analytical requirements	141.21 to 141.29
D	Reporting, public notification and record-keeping	141.31 to 141.33

A public water system means a system for the provision to the public of piped water for human consumption, if such system has at least 15 service connections or regularly serves an average of at least 25 individuals daily at least 60 days out of the year. Such term includes:

1. Any collection, treatment, storage, and distribution facilities under control of the operator and used primarily in connection with such system, and
2. Any collection or pretreatment storage facilities not under such control that are used primarily in connection with such system. A public water system is either a "community water system" or a "noncommunity water system."

A community water system means a public water system that serves at least 15 service connections used by year-round residents or regularly services at least 25 year-round residents.

A sanitary survey means an on-site review of the water source, facilities, equipment, operation, and maintenance of a public water system for the purpose of evaluating their adequacy in producing and distributing safe drinking water.

Some siting requirements are as follows. Before a person may enter into a financial commitment for or initiate construction of a new public water system or increase the capacity of an existing public water system, he shall notify the state and, to the extent practicable, avoid locating part or all of the new or expanded facility at a site that:

1. Is subject to a significant risk from earthquakes, floods, fires, or other disasters that could cause a breakdown of the public water system; or
2. Except for intake structures, is within the floodplain of a 100-year flood or is lower than any recorded high tide where appropriate records exist.

The EPA will not seek to override land-use decisions affecting public water systems siting that are made at the state or local government levels.

Some maximum contaminant levels established in Subpart B of 40 CFR 141 are presented in the list that follows. The regulations have established such levels for inorganic chemicals; organic chemicals; turbidity; bacteria; radium-226, radium-228, and gross alpha particle radioactivity in community water systems; and beta particle and photoradioactivity from man-made radionuclides in community water systems. For example, the maximum microbiological contaminant levels for coliform bacteria, applicable to community water systems and noncommunity water systems, are as follows:

1. When the membrane filter technique is used, the number of coliform bacteria shall not exceed any of the following:
   a. 1/100 ml as the arithmetic mean of all samples examined per month.
   b. 4/100 ml in more than one sample when less than 20 are examined per month.

      c. 4/100 ml in more than 5% of the samples when 20 or more are examined per month.

2. a. When the fermentation tube method and 10 ml standard portions are used, coliform bacteria shall not be present in any of the following:

      i. more than 10% of the portions in any month.

      ii. three or more portions in more than one sample when less than 20 samples are examined per month, or

      iii. three or more portions in more than 5% of the samples when 20 or more samples are examined per month.

    b. When the fermentation tube method and 100 ml standard portions are used, coliform bacteria shall not be present in any of the following:

      i. more than 60% of the portions in any month

      ii. five portions in more than one sample when less than five samples are examined per month

      iii. five portions in more than 20% of the samples when five or more samples are examined per month.

3. For community or noncommunity systems required to sample at a rate of less than four per month, compliance with the above will be based on sampling during a 3-month period, except that, at the discretion of the state, compliance may be based on sampling during a 1-month period.

In Subpart C the requirements for monitoring and analyses are described. They include those for various contaminants mentioned in Subpart B. In the following, the microbiological contaminant sampling and analytical requirements are presented. Only selected aspects are discussed.

Suppliers of water for community water systems and noncommunity water systems shall analyze for coliform bacteria for the purpose of determining compliance. Analyses shall be conducted in accordance with the analytical recommendations set forth in "Standard Methods for the Examination of Water and Wastewater," American Public Health Association, 13th Edition, pp. 662 to 688, except that a standard sample size shall be employed. The standard sample used in the membrane filter procedures shall be 100 ml. The standard sample used in the five tube most probable number (MPN) procedure (fermentation tube method) shall be five times the standard portion. The standard portion is either 10 ml or 100 ml The samples shall be taken at points representative of the conditions within the distribution system.

The supplier of water for a community water system shall take coliform density samples at regular time intervals and in number proportionate to the population served by the system. In no event shall the frequency be less than as set forth in the table that follows.

Population Served	Minimum Number of Samples per Month	Population Served	Minimum Number of Samples per Month
25 to 1,000	1	96,001 to 111,000	100
1,001 to 2,500	2	111,001 to 130,000	110
2,501 to 3,300	3	130,001 to 160,000	120
3,301 to 4,100	4	160,001 to 190,000	130
4,101 to 4,900	5	190,001 to 220,000	140
4,901 to 5,800	6	220,001 to 250,000	150
5,801 to 6,700	7	250,001 to 290,000	160
6,701 to 7,600	8	290,001 to 320,000	170
7,601 to 8,500	9	320,001 to 360,000	180
8,501 to 9,400	10	360,001 to 410,000	190
9,401 to 10,300	11	410,001 to 450,000	200
10,301 to 11,100	12	450,001 to 500,000	210
11,101 to 12,000	13	500,001 to 550,000	220
12,001 to 12,900	14	550,001 to 600,000	230
12,901 to 13,700	15	600,001 to 660,000	240
13,701 to 14,600	16	660,001 to 720,000	250
14,601 to 15,500	17	720,001 to 780,000	260
15,501 to 16,300	18	780,001 to 840,000	270
16,301 to 17,200	19	840,001 to 910,000	280
17,201 to 18,100	20	910,001 to 970,000	290
18,101 to 18,900	21	970,001 to 1,050,000	300
18,901 to 19,800	22	1,050,001 to 1,140,000	310
19,801 to 20,700	23	1,140,001 to 1,230,000	320
20,701 to 21,500	24	1,230,001 to 1,320,000	330
21,501 to 22,300	25	1,320,001 to 1,420,000	340
22,301 to 23,200	26	1,420,001 to 1,520,000	350
23,201 to 24,000	27	1,520,001 to 1,630,000	360
24,001 to 24,900	28	1,630,001 to 1,730,000	370
24,901 to 25,000	29	1,730,001 to 1,850,000	380
25,001 to 28,000	30	1,850,001 to 1,970,000	390
28,001 to 33,000	35	1,970,001 to 2,060,000	400
33,001 to 37,000	40	2,060,001 to 2,270,000	410
37,001 to 41,000	45	2,270,001 to 2,510,000	420
41,001 to 46,000	50	2,510,001 to 2,750,000	430
46,001 to 50,000	55	2,750,001 to 3,020,000	440
50,001 to 54,000	60	3,020,001 to 3,320,000	450
54,001 to 59,000	65	3,320,001 to 3,620,000	460
59,001 to 64,000	70	3,620,001 to 3,960,000	470
64,001 to 70,000	75	3,960,001 to 4,310,000	480
70,001 to 76,000	80	4,310,001 to 4,690,000	490
76,001 to 83,000	85	4,690,001 or more	
83,001 to 90,000	90		
90,001 to 96,000	95		

Based on a history of no coliform bacteria contamination and on a sanitary survey by the state showing the water system to be supplied solely by a protected ground water source and free of sanitary defects, a community water system serving 25 to 1000 persons may, with written permission from the state, reduce the sampling frequency given in the preceding table, except that in no case shall it be reduced to less than one per quarter. For further details on 40 CFR 141, consult the original document.

Federal regulations issued to implement the primary drinking water standards are promulgated in 40 CFR 142, with special emphasis on the role of the states. Table 4-3 provides the subpart titles and section numbers of part 142; a brief description of these subparts is as follows.

TABLE 4-3. Subpart Titles and Section Numbers of 40 CFR 142
(Drinking Water Standards Implementation)

	Subpart Titles	Section Numbers
Subpart A	General provisions	142.1 to 142.4
Subpart B	Primary enforcement responsibility	142.1 to 142.15
Subpart C	Review of state-issued variances and exemptions	142.2 to 142.24
Subpart D	Federal enforcement	142.3 to 142.34
Subpart E	Variances issued by administrator	142.4 to 142.46
Subpart F	Exemptions issued by administrator	142.5 to 142.55

Subpart A contains general provisions applicable to the entire part. Subpart B sets forth requirements the states must meet to have primary enforcement responsibility and includes regulations concerning determinations of the EPA administrator relating to primary enforcement responsibility.

Subpart C provides for the statutorily mandated periodic review by the EPA of variances and exemptions granted by states with primary enforcement responsibility. Subpart D covers federal enforcement actions in situations where a state with primary enforcement responsibility does not take appropriate action to deal with violations of the primary drinking water standards. It also provides for EPA hearings on systems in violation of applicable standards and for EPA inspections of public water systems.

Subparts E and F deal with variances and exemptions from national primary drinking water standards granted by the EPA for public water systems in states that do not have primary enforcement responsibility. States that have primary enforcement responsibility and wish to grant variances and exemptions do not have to follow the procedures set forth in Subparts E and F provided that the state procedures comply with sections 1415 and 1416 of the Safe Drinking Water Act (PL 93-523). Selected aspects are discussed in the paragraphs that follow.

According the Subpart B of 40 CFR 142, the requirements for a determination of primary enforcement responsibility are defined as follows. A state has primary enforcement responsibility for public water systems during any period for which the administrator of the EPA determines, based on submitted information, that the state:

1. Has adopted its own primary drinking water standards that are not less stringent than those promulgated by the EPA.
2. Has adopted and is implementing adequate procedures to enforce those standards.
3. Has established and will maintain record keeping and reporting of its activities in accordance with established regulations.
4. Complies with the requirements of the original act in its granting of variances or exemptions.
5. Has adopted and can implement an adequate plan for the provision of safe drinking water under emergency circumstances.

The procedures used by a state to enforce its own standards should include the following:

1. Maintenance of an inventory of all public water systems.
2. A program for conducting sanitary surveys of known water systems, especially those not in compliance with state standards.
3. A program for approval and certification of laboratories to analyze water contaminants in accordance with state standards.
4. Assurance of the availability of such laboratories to handle the specified contaminants.
5. A program to assure that the design and construction of new or substantially modified public water system facilities will comply with state standards.
6. Adequate statutory and regulatory enforcement authority to effect compliance.

According to Subpart D, one aspect of federal enforcement relates to the entry and inspection of public water systems. Some conditions are described as follows:

1. Any supplier of water subject to the national primary drinking water standard

is required to permit authorized EPA personnel with a written notice of inspection to enter the premise to determine whether the requirements or regulations are complied with. Such inspection may include inspection, at reasonable times, of records, files,papers, processes, controls, and facilities or testing of any feature of a public water system, including its raw water source.

2. Prior to entry into a facility for inspection, the EPA will notify the state authority of such intention and the reasons. If the state does not think that such action is in its interest, the EPA will consider the matter before making an entry. However, the EPA shall in any event offer the state agency the opportunity of having a representative accompany the authorized EPA inspector.

3. A state agency is not permitted to notify the person whose premise is involved. If such privilaged information is disseminated, then EPA will not send the state authority any future notice until there is evidence that such violation will not take place.

According to Subpart E of 40 CFR 142, the requirements for a variance are as follows. The EPA may grant one or more variances to any public water system within a state that does not have primary enforcement responsibility from any requirement regarding a maximum contaminant level of an applicable national primary drinking water standard, if it finds that:

1. Because of characteristics of the raw water sources that are reasonably available to the system, the system cannot meet the requirements despite best technology, treatment techniques, or other means that are generally available, taking costs into consideration.

2. The granting of a variance will not result in an unreasonable risk to the health of persons served by the system.

The EPA will also grant one or more variances from any requirement of a specified treatment technique if it finds that the public water system applying for the variance has demonstrated that the technique is not necessary to protect the health of the persons because of the nature of the raw water source of the system.

Since Section 1412(c) of the Safe Drinking Water Act [42 U.S.C. 300 g-l] requires the EPA to establish national secondary drinking water regulations, the EPA released the proposal on March 31, 1977 (42 FR 17143 to 17147). The proposal established a new 40 CFR 143 for the regulations.

Some basic requirements of the secondary drinking water regulations are as follows:

1. Applies to public water systems.

2. Specifies the maximum contaminant levels requisite to protect the public

welfare.
3. Contaminant includes any that may:
    a. Adversely affect the odor, taste, or appearance of such water and thus a substantial number of the persons served by the public water system providing such water to discontinue its use.
    b. Otherwise adversely affect the public welfare.
4. Such regulations may vary according to geographic and other circumstances.

It is important to emphasize that compliance with these regulations is not mandatory. A state does not need to have or it may have its own secondary drinking water regulations.

Thus the proposed 40 CFR 143 establishes the following secondary maximum contaminant levels for public water systems:

Contaminant	Level
Chlorine	250 mg/liter
Color	15 color units
Copper	1 mg/liter
Corrosivity	noncorrosive
Foaming agents	0.5 mg/liter
Hydrogen sulfide	0.05 mg/liter
Iron	0.3 mg/liter
Manganese	0.05 mg/liter
Odor	3 threshold odor number
pH	6.5 - 8.5
Sulfate	250 mg/liter
TDS	500 mg/liter
Zinc	5 mg/liter

The regulations also describe specific technical procedures for monitoring each of the contaminants. For example, hydrogen sulfide is measured by the "titrimetric iodine method" and odor, by the "consistent series method." Both methods are available in the "Methods for Chemical Analysis of Water and Wastes" published by the EPA. For further details, check the original document.

According to Section 1424(e) of the Public Health Service Act, as amended by the Safe Drinking Water Act, PL 93-523, if the EPA determines, on petition or on its own initiative, that an area has an aquifer that is the sole or principal drinking water source for the area and that, if contaminated, would create a significant hazard to public health, it will announce such determination in the Federal Register. After the announcement, no commitment for federal financial assistance such as grant or loan may be entered into for any project that may contaminate such aquifer through a recharge zone so as to create a significant hazard to public health. However, a commitment for federal assistance may, if authorized under another provision of the law, be entered into to plan or design the project to assure that it will not so contaminate the aquifer. Also, the EPA, pursuant to Section 1450 of the same act, may promulgate regulations to govern the review process of such projects.

Thus 40 CFR 149 sets forth, pursuant to Sections 1424(e) and 1450 of the act, interim guidelines relating to the review of major federal financially assisted programs or action that potentially affect the quality of the Edwards Underground Reservoir through the recharge zone, San Antonio, Texas, Part 149 is titled "Review of projects affecting sole source aquifers."

According to the regulations in this part, any person may submit a petition requesting the regional administrator of the EPA to review a project to determine if it will contaminate the Edwards Underground Reservoir to the extent of endangering public health.

As soon as practicable after a study of the petition, public comments, information from the originating federal agency, and on the basis of any other information available to him the regional administrator shall review the project, taking the following factors into account:

1. The extent of possible health hazard by the project.
2. Planning, design, construction, operation, maintenance, and monitoring measures included in the project that could prevent or mitigate the possible health hazard.
3. The extent and effectiveness of state or local controls over possible contaminant releases to the Edwards Underground Reservoir.
4. The expected benefits of the project.
5. The cumulative impact of the proposed project.

The decision of the regional administrator will depend on the specific petition and project. If the regional administrator or administrator of the EPA decides that it has been determined that such project may contaminate the reservoir through the recharge zone so as to create a significant hazard to public health, he will publish the determination in the Federal Register, or he will decline to make such a determination if the facts warrant. Further details on the entire procedure of reviewing such projects may be obtained from the original document.

Part C of the Safe Drinking Water Act adds to the Public Health Service Act (88 Stat. 1660 et seq.) provisions for the protection of present and potential underground drinking water sources from contamination by underground injection of contaminants. The sections of the Public Health Service Act affected include 1421 to 1424 (42 U.S.C. 300-h through 300-h-3). Section 1422 of the Public Health Service Act provides that the administrator of the EPA will list in the Federal Register each state for which in his judgment a state underground injection control program may be necessary to assure that underground injection will not endanger drinking water sources. Within 270 days after a state is listed, it must submit to the administrator a state program adequate to protect underground sources of drinking water. If the state program is not submitted or approved by the administrator, an underground injection control program for the state must be prescribed by the administrator. Thus the EPA proposed on August 31, 1976 (41 FR 36725 to 36745) to add a new part 40 CFR 146 related to state underground injection control. This new part sets forth procedural and substantive requirements which must by met by state programs to obtain the administrator's approval. Any state program approved by the administrator will be subject to the requirements of this part. A state with an approved program in effect shall have primary enforcement responsibility for all (with some exceptions) underground injection activities in the state. The overall contents of the proposed regulations include: general information, requirements applicable to waste disposal wells and engineering wells, requirements applicable to injection wells related to oil and gas production, and requirements applicable to all drainage wells. It is expected that the regulations will eventually be finalized. Further details may be obtained from the original document.

The Safe Drinking Water Act requires a three-stage mechanism for the establishment of comprehensive regulations for drinking water quality:

1. Promulgation of National Interim Primary Drinking Water Regulation (as discussed earlier).
2. A study to be conducted by the National Academy of Sciences (NAS), within 2 years of enactment, on the human health effects of exposure to contaminants in drinking water, and
3. Promulgation of revised National Primary Drinking Water Regulations based upon the NAS report.

On July 11, 1977, the recommendations of the NAS were published (42 FR 35764 to 35779). Based on the completed NAS report and the findings of the administrator, the EPA is expected to publish:

1. Recommended maximum contaminant levels (health goals) for substances in drinking water which may have adverse effects on humans. These recommended levels will be selected so that no known or anticipated adverse effects would occur, allowing an adequate margin of safety. A list of contaminants which may have adverse effects,but which cannot be accurately measured in water, will also be published.
2. Revised National Primary Drinking Water Regulations. These will specify maximum contaminant levels or require the use of treatment techniques. The levels will be as close to the recommended ones for each contaminant as is feasible. Required treatment techniques for those substances which cannot be measured will reduce their concentrations to a level as close to the recommended one as is feasible. Feasibility is defined in the Safe Water Drinking Act as use of the best technology, treatment techniques, and other means which the administrator of EPA finds are generally available (taking costs into consideration).

PESTICIDE PROGRAM

General Responsibilities, Activities, and Organization

A deputy assistant administrator supervises the Office of Pesticide Programs; the overall responsibility of this office is to:

1. Develop strategic plans for the control of the national environmental pesticide situation for application by the Office of Pesticide Programs, other segments within the EPA, and all other concerned parties, including private sections, state, local, and other federal agencies.
2. Register pesticides.

This office is composed of four divisions: criteria and evaluation, registration, technical services, and operations. The activities of each division are described in the following paragraphs; the information is obtained from the Organization and Functions Manual of the EPA.

Criteria and Evaluation Division

This division is supervised by a director who is assigned to:

1. Establish criteria and standards to be applied in the setting of human safety, environmental and efficacy standards, and *food residue tolerances* applicable to product registration.
2. Assess and review the environmental, human safety, and risk/benefit aspects of currently registered pesticide chemicals and their continued use. The findings are reported to the deputy assistant administrator, who will decide on the appropriate regulatory actions.
3. Provide technical support to the Office of General Counsel and Enforcement to assist in the conduct of regulatory actions and statutory appeals.
4. Develop appropriate criteria, guidelines, and standards from the accumulated and comprehensive knowledge of pesticides and their impact on the environment when such information is needed by other governmental agencies and other segments of the EPA.
5. Develop research needs.
6. Develop monitoring requirements for the pesticide area.
7. Provide program policy direction to monitoring activities in the Office of Pesticide Programs.

Registration Division

This division is supervised by a director who is assigned to:

1. *Establish tolerances for pesticide residues in or on feedstuffs and food* and for the registration of pesticides and their use to assure protection of environmental quality and human safety.
2. Specify how samples are to be examined for the purpose of pesticide registration.
3. Provide technical support for and make recommendations to the Office of General Enforcement with respect to enforcement actions.
4. Coordinate registration actions with the Office of General Enforcement.
5. Work closely with the Criteria and Evaluation Division to identify the need for performing reviews of registered pesticide chemicals and the need for new guidelines and standards applicable to the registration process.

Technical Services Division

This division is supervised by a director who is assigned to:

1. Provide technical information and data support to groups outside and other divisions within the Office of Pesticide Programs.
2. Provide routine information on registered tolerances and uses to other agencies and states on a timely basis and to meet the operating information needs of the EPA by directing, planning, and operating within the framework of the overall agency information system, specially designed computer data systems.
3. Provide computer programming, perform statistical analysis, and devise modeling support for the other divisions within the Office of Pesticide Programs.
4. Operate a monitoring program to assess the effects of human exposure to pesticides and to *estimate pesticide residue levels in soil, water, air, crops, livestock, and aquatic and land animals.*
5. Develop scientific publications relevant to the pesticide program and provide reference and library services of a highly technical and specialized field.
6. Provide technical, program, and policy supervision and guidance to the laboratory operations conducted by the Office of Pesticide Programs.
7. Establish and maintain analytical references standards for pesticides to support regulatory and research activities.

Operations Division

This division is supervised by a director who is assigned to:

1. Develop programs to increase the effectiveness of governmental activities in the pesticide field.
2. Provide program policy direction to training programs and technical assistance in the pesticide field.
3. Develop and recommend model legislation and program content for states and, through the regional office, assist states in developing and upgrading their program contents and activities according to recommended models.
4. Participate in federal interagency activities in the pesticide field.
5. Investigate pesticide incidents and accidents.

Federal Insecticide, Fungicide, and Rodenticide Act;
Fish and Wildlife Act;
and Federal Food, Drug, and Cosmetic Act

Pesticides are chemicals used to control harmful insects, diseases, rodents, weeds, bacteria, and other pests that attack man's food and fiber supplies and threaten his health and welfare. Thus pesticides benefit man in the area of agriculture production, sanitation, and disease control.

Most pesticide chemicals are poisons, which, if used improperly or without sufficient knowledge of their side effects, can harm people, animals, and the environment. The widespread use of pesticides, more than half of which is in agriculture, particularly cotton and corn production, has increased the possibility of injury to humans and damage to the environment.

Indirect and direct risks or hazards from the use of pesticides may involve the buildup of persistent pesticide residues in the food chain and consequent damage to fish, birds, and other wildlife; the elimination of beneficial insects; widespread contamination of the environment; and immediate or future hazard to human health.

The EPA pesticide program is based on three specific approaches: (1) pesticides must be registered to ensure their proper use, (2) the use of pesticides is carefully controlled, and (3) research is conducted to determine the health and environmental effects of pesticides. These approaches and their detailed workings are the regulations set up to implement the federal statutes that give the agency authority to control pesticides and their uses.

The EPA is responsible for administering three basic federal laws regulating the marketing and use of pesticides and related chemicals in the United States. These are the Federal Insecticide, Fungicide, and Rodenticide Act, as amended (7 U.S.C. 135 et seq.); certain provisions of the Fish and Wildlife Act (16 U.S.C. 742 d-1; and certain provisions of the Federal Food, Drug, and Cosmetic Act (21 U.S.C. 346, 346a, 348). The first statute, supplemented by the second, authorizes a comprehensive program to regulate the manufacturing, distribution, and use of pesticides as well as major research efforts into the effects of pesticides. The third statute ensures that many foods we eat will be safe with respect to pesticide residues. The first two statutes are discussed in the paragraphs that follow.

The provision in the Fish and Wildlife Act as quoted here is self-explanatory (16 U.S.C. 742 d-1):

> The Administrator of the Environmental Protection Agency is authorized and directed to undertake comprehensive continuing studies on the effects of insecticides, herbicides, fungicides, and pesticides, upon the fish and wildlife resources of the United States, for the purpose of determining the amounts, percentages, and formulations of such chemicals that are lethal to or injurious to fish and wildlife and the amounts, percentages, mixtures, or formulations that can be used safely, and thereby prevent losses of fish and wildlife from such spraying, dusting, or other treatment [PL85-582, Section 1, August 1, 1958, 72 Stat. 479; 1970 Reorganization Plan No. 3, Section 2(a)(2)(i), effective December 2, 1970, 35 FR 15623, 84 Stat. 2086].

Some major provisions of the Federal Insecticide, Fungicide, and Rodenticide Act as amended include the following:

1. Registration with the EPA is required of all pesticide products shipped interstate as well as intrastate.
2. All pesticide chemicals must be classified as "restricted" or "general." Only certified applicators may use or supervise the use of restricted pesticide products; otherwise their use must be specially authorized by the EPA.
3. The EPA sets standards for the certification of applicators of restricted pesticides, and all states must have approved certification programs.
4. The prohibition of misuse of pesticides is achieved in various manners.
   a. The use of a registered pesticide product must be in compliance with the labeling instructions. Violators are subject to criminal and civil penalties as described in items (b) and (c) below.
   b. Private applicators and farmers can be fined up to $1,000 and/or 30 days prison for a knowing violation of the law.
   c. Any distributor, commercial applicator, or pesticide registrant who knowingly violates the law is liable to a $5,000 civil or $25,000 criminal fine or one year in prison or both.
   d. The EPA can issue a "stop sale, use, and removal" order and seize pesticides if they violate the law.
5. Registration with the EPA is required of all plants manufacturing pesticides for sale or distribution.
6. The EPA may conduct research on pesticides and alternatives, monitor pesticide presence and use in the environment, and issue experimental use permits.
7. The law requires the EPA to establish regulations and procedures for the disposal or storage of pesticide containers.
8. States are entitled to federal assistance in the enforcement and administration of various provisions of the law, for example, the applicator certification program.
9. The law authorizes states to register pesticide products or issue experimental permits to meet special local needs.

Some detailed explanation of certain provisions of the statute are described in the following paragraphs. The material is adapted from the original act and the brochure "Pesticides and the law" issued by the EPA in 1974.

Product Registration

Under the Federal Insecticide, Fungicide and Rodenticide Act the EPA issues a registration number only after the manufacturer has supplied sound scientific evidence that such a pesticide product, when used as directed, will: (1) be effective in the control of the particular pest(s) specified on the product label, (2) not harm the environment, injure nontarget animals, plants, or humans, and (3) not result in illegal pesticide residues in or on feed and/or food.

How is the registration enforced? To ensure that registered pesticide products continue to meet EPA registration requirements in the light of new scientific data, trained federal personnel continually check on the marketed products. Samples are collected from pesticide manufacturers and distributors in all parts of the country. These are field tested and analyzed in EPA laboratories for verification of label claims concerning content, effectiveness, and safety. Labels are reviewed to determine that no claims are made other than those accepted at the time of registration. Furthermore, effects of pesticides on the environment are continuously monitored in a national program that includes studies on soil, water, plants, animals, and man. If a product is found to be ineffective or unsafe, the agency may take one of several actions. In the case of a minor violation, an informal notice to the company concerned is usually sufficient to insure that deficiencies are corrected. More serious violations may result in a formal notice of violation, seizure of the company's goods, or initiation of civil or criminal proceedings against the violator.

Regulation of Residues

The amended Federal Insecticide, Fungicide, and Rodenticide Act is supplemented by the special pesticide amendment to the Federal Food, Drug, and Cosmetic Act, namely, Section 408, which is discussed in detail later. This special pesticide amendment authorizes the EPA to establish an allowable limit or tolerance for any detectable pesticide residues that might remain in or on a harvested food or feed crop. This is to protect animal and human health. The tolerance level is, in many cases, many times the actual level expected to produce undesirable health effects in man or animal. Whereas the EPA establishes the tolerances levels, the FDA enforces the regulations. Thus, the latter agency will collect and analyze food samples, mostly agricultural commodities. Residues of pesticides that exceed the established tolerances are considered a violation of the act. The USDA collects and analyzes samples of livestock and poultry. Again, residue levels must be within legal limits to avoid violations.

The EPA and FDA are also responsible for sampling and testing food shipments entering the United States from foreign countries. They also cooperate with state health officials in a testing program for those food commodities intended for intrastate shipment. A shipper or grower is informed if a food shipment contains pesticide residues in excess of promulgated tolerances. Action is taken to avoid shipment of such food items. Feed or food with excessive pesticide residue is subject to destruction and seizure by the USDA or the FDA.

Cancellation and Suspension

Continuous scientific research may yield results or data that raise questions about the safety of some registered pesticide products. If their safety is seriously questioned, the EPA administrator is authorized to suspend or cancel the registration of such a product(s) to protect public interest. Such suspension and/or cancellation may, of course, be petitioned according to established agency procedures by public or private individuals, groups, or organizations that have an interest in the product.

Based on potential or actual hazard to the environment, animals, or people, the registration of a product may be cancelled. If the manufacturer is not satisfied with the cancellation, he must challenge the action within 30 days. If an appeal is filed with the EPA, the manufacturer is authorized to continue marketing the product until all administrative procedures have been completed and a final order issued on the appeal.

Based on an imminent hazard to public health, the registration of a product may be suspended. If the EPA administrator decides to suspend the registration of a product, he must simultaneously publicize his intention to change the classification of the product or to cancel its registration. The manufacturer will receive a notification of such action and if it wants an expedited hearing on the validity of the existence of an imminent hazard, it must act within 5 days after receipt of the notification. Until the hearing has been held and a decision made, the product may still be marketed.

However, if the administrator decides that an emergency exists, he can disregard the expedited hearing procedure and issue a suspension notice before notifying the manufacturer. When the product is suspended under an emergency situation or as a result of an expedited hearing, the manufacturer may appeal the government's action, but he must immediately cease all domestic sale and distribution of the particular product as long as his appeal is being processed under established procedures.

In the case of suspension, the EPA may issue a "stop sale, use and removal" order and/or request the manufacturer to voluntarily recall the product from the wholesalers, retailers, and even users to avoid further danger to the public. Some of the pesticide products that have been subjected to cancellation or suspension include DDT, aldrin, dieldrin, and Mirex. Details on their cases can be obtained from public record or the EPA.

Pesticide Tolerances in Agricultural Commodities

The EPA has published many regulations to implement the provisions in the Federal Insecticide, Fungicide, and Rodenticide Act as amended and the Fish and Wildlife

Act. Their legal references are described in Appendix 4-2; they are contained in Title 40 of the Code of Federal Regulations. Space limitation prohibits further discussion of these regulations except for 40 CFR 180.

Sections 406, 408, and 409 of the Federal Food, Drug and Cosmetic Act (21 U.S.C. 346, 346a, and 348) are administered by the EPA, and 40 CFR 180 contains the regulations that implement those statutory provisions. Part 180 is entitled "Tolerances and exemptions from tolerances for pesticide chemicals in or on raw agricultural commodities," and the subpart titles are described in Table 4-4.

TABLE 4-4. Subpart Titles and Section Numbers of 40 CFR 180 (Tolerances and Exemptions from Tolerances for Pesticide Chemicals in or on Raw Agricultural Commodities)

Subpart	Title	Section Numbers
A	Definitions and interpretative regulations	180.1 to 180.6
B	Procedural regulations	180.7 to 180.35
C	Specific tolerances	180.101 to 180.350
D	Exemptions from tolerances	180.1001 to 180.1029

According to Subpart A of 40 CFR 180, the definitions and interpretative regulations provide legal answers to the following questions:

What do raw agricultural commodities include? They include, among other things, fresh fruits, regardless of whether they have been washed and colored or otherwise treated in their unpeeled natural form; vegetables in their raw or natural state, whether stripped or not stripped of their outer leaves, waxed, prepared into fresh green salads, and so on; and grains, nuts, eggs, raw milk, meats, and similar agricultural products. Such commodities do not include foods that have been processed, fabricated, or manufactured by cooking, freezing, dehydrating, or milling.

When will processed foods be considered safe in regard to pesticide chemicals? For raw agricultural commodities bearing residues that have been exempted from the requirement of a tolerance or are within a tolerance permitted by law, the processed foods will be considered safe if:

1.   The poisonous or deleterious pesticide residues have been removed to the ex-

tent possible in good manufacturing practice.

2. The concentration of the pesticide in the preserved or processed food when ready to eat is not greater than the tolerance permitted on a raw agricultural commodity.

When a tolerance or exemption has been established for certain pesticide chemicals in or on a general category of commodities, what are the applicable specific commodities under each category? Table 4-5 provides answers to this question.

TABLE 4-5. Specific Commodities within Those General Categories of Products with Specific Tolerance or Exemption.[a] Adapted from 40 CFR 180.1(h) (1976).

Column A	Column B
Bananas	Bananas, plantains
Beans	Green beans, lima beans, navy beans, red kidney beans, snap beans, wax beans, cowpeas, blackeyed peas
Celery	Anise (fresh leaves and stalks only), celery
Cherries	Sour cherries, sweet cherries
Citrus fruits	Grapefruit, lemons, limes, oranges, tangelos, tangerines, citron, kumquats, and hybrids of these
Melons	Cantaloupe, casabas, crenshaws, honeydew melons, honey balls, muskmelons, Persian melons, and hybrids of these, watermelons and their hybrids
Onions	Dry bulb onions, green onions, garlic, leeks, shallots, spring onions
Onions (dry bulbs only)	Garlic, onions (dry bulb only)
Peppers	All varieties of peppers including pimentos and bell, hot, and sweet peppers
Tangerines	Tangelos, tangerines
Turnip tops or turnip greens	Broccoli raab (raab, raab salad), hanover salad, turnip tops (turnip greens)

[a] Column A = general categories; column B = specific commodities. A tolerance or exemption for an item in B does not apply to one in A.

Which part of the agricultural product is to be examined? Unless otherwise specified, tolerances and exemptions established under the regulations in 40 CFR 180 apply to residues from only preharvest application of the chemicals, and the raw agricultural commodity to be examined for pesticide residues shall consist of the whole (normally edible part) raw agricultural commodity. Some examples follow:

1. Bananas, when examined for pesticide residues, shall not include any crown tissue or stalk.
2. Nuts without shell shall be examined for pesticide residues.
3. Strawberries without caps (hulls) shall be examined for pesticide residues.
4. Stems shall be removed and discarded from melons before examination for pesticide residues.
5. Roots, stems, and outer sheaths (or husks) shall be removed and discarded from garlic bulbs; only garlic cloves shall be examined for pesticide residues.
6. When a root vegetable is marketed as roots and tops and a tolerance has been established for the vegetable including or with tops, they shall be analyzed separately. The residue on the roots or the tops shall not exceed the tolerance level, although, in the case of carrots, the tops shall be discarded before the analysis.
7. Pineapples shall be analyzed for pesticide residues without the crowns (leaves at the top of the fruit).
8. "Lima beans" include the beans and the pod.

What is the meaning of "negligible residue"? On the basis of adequate scientific data, negligible residue refers to that amount of pesticide chemical remaining in or on a raw agricultural commodity that will be considered as toxicologically insignificant if consumed daily. This will ordinarily add to the diet less than 1/2000th of the amount shown to produce no effect from oral feeding of the most sensitive animals. Regulations require that such tests include at least 90-day feeding studies in two species of animals.

What is the meaning of a "nonperishable raw agricultural commodity"? Such a commodity does not decay or deteriorate rapidly to become unfit for human consumption. They include cocoa beans, coffee beans, field-dried beans, field-dried peas, grains, and nuts. They exclude meat, poultry, eggs, milk, and most fresh fruits and vegetables.

What are the pesticide chemicals not generally recognized as safe? Only the following pesticide chemicals are generally recognized as safe for use: benzaldehyde (when used as a bee repellant in the harvesting of honey), ferrous sulfate, lime, lime-sulfur, potassium polysulfide, sodium carbonate, sodium chloride, sodium polysulfide, sodium carbonate, sodium chloride, sodium polysulfide, and sulfur and, when used postharvest as fungicides, citric acid, fumaric acid, oil of lemon, oil of orange, sodium benzoate, and sodium propionate. All others are not.

What are some special criteria applicable to the tolerances for related pesticide chemicals? Two such criteria are as follows:

1. Pesticide chemicals that produce related pharmacological effects are considered to have an additive deleterious action unless contradicted by scientific evidence. For example, within each of the following groups many pesticide chemicals have related pharmacological effects: chlorinated organic pesticides, arsenic-containing chemicals, metallic dithiocarbamates, and cholinesterase-inhibiting pesticides.
2. Tolerances established for such related pesticide chemicals may limit the amount of a common component (e.g., As_2O_3), or the amount of biological activity (e.g., cholinesterase inhibition), or the total amount of related pesticide chemicals (e.g., chlorinated organic pesticides) that may be present.

What is the meaning of a "zero tolerance"? It means that no amount of a pesticide chemical may remain on the raw agricultural commodity offered for shipment. This requirement is necessary for various reasons, some of which are as follows:

1. A safe level of the pesticide chemical in the diet of two different species of warm-blooded animals has not been reliably determined.
2. The chemical is carcinogenic or has other alarming physiological effects when ingested by one or more species of test animals.
3. The pesticide chemical is toxic but is normally used in such manner and/or at such times that its residue will not remain in the commodity afterward.
4. Any residue of the pesticide chemical is normally removed through good agricultural practices such as brushing or washing, changes in the chemical itself, and/or weathering prior to introduction of the commodity into interstate commerce.

What is the EPA's statement of policy regarding pesticide tolerances in milk, eggs, meat, and/or poultry? This complicated statement of policy is summarized in Table 4-6. Some additional conditions related to the statement in Table 4-6 are as follows:

1. When pesticides are used directly on the animal or administered purposely in the feed or drinking water, the tolerances for residues actually incurred or reasonably expected in eggs, milk, meat, and/or poultry will be handled in accordance with principles in Table 4-6.
2. Apart from toxicological considerations, the establishment of tolerances also

TABLE 4-6. Pesticide Tolerances Regarding Milk, Eggs, Meat, and/or Poultry; Illustration of Statement of Policy by the EPA. Adapted from 40 CFR 180.6 (1976)

Possible scientific conclusion in the evaluation of the occurrence of pesticide residues in products such as milk, eggs, meat, and/or poultry	POLICY STATEMENT	
	The establishment of tolerances in or on raw agricultural commodities that serve as feeds for animals producing the milk, eggs, meat, and/or poultry	The establishment of tolerances for pesticide residues in milk, eggs, meat, and/or poultry produced by animals fed agricultural commodities bearing such pesticide residues
Finite residues will actually be incurred in these foods	Yes	Yes, if a tolerance can be established for the human food shown
It is not possible to establish with certainty whether finite residues will be incurred, but there is a reasonable expectation of finite residues in light of data reflecting exaggerated pesticides levels in feeding studies	Yes	Yes, if a tolerance can be established for the human food shown
It is not possible to establish with certainty whether finite residues will be incurred, but there is no reasonable expectation of finite residues in light of data such as those reflecting exaggerated pesticide levels in feeding studies and those elucidating the biochemistry of the pesticide chemical in the animal	Yes	Not necessary

263

depends on the availability of an analytical method. The method must be sensitive and reliable at the tolerance level or, in special cases, at a higher level. The latter is acceptable if it is safe and unlikely for residue to exceed the tolerance. The official Pesticide Analytical Manual is the standard to be used for enforcement purpose.

Subpart B of 40 CFR 180 explains a number of procedural regulations. Some aspects are as follows: One important procedure is the granting of temporary tolerances. A person holding an experimental permit for a pesticide chemical under the Federal Insecticide, Fungicide, and Rodenticide Act as amended may request for a temporary tolerance or a temporary exemption from a tolerance. The EPA may grant such a status if the applicant submitted scientific justification before obtaining the experimental permit.

A temporary tolerance or exemption from a tolerance may be issued for a period designed to allow the orderly marketing of the raw agricultural commodities produced while testing the chemical under the experimental permit. The EPA must be assured that public health is not jeopardized by the practice. Any evidence to the contrary will immediately revoke the temporary status of the tolerance and/ or permit.

Some requirements usually accompany the temporary tolerance status. They include the following:

1. Restrict the amount of chemical used on designated crops.
2. Limit it to experimental use by qualified personnel.
3. Require the applicant to inform the EPA of any findings that relate to safety.
4. Require the applicant to keep records of production, distribution, and performance for 2 years and make them available to authorized EPA personnel when requested.

There are a number of ways to test the amount of residue remaining in a product. One method is the following. If the pesticide chemical is not absorbed into the living plant or animal when applied (i.e., is not systemic), it may be possible to make a reliable estimate of the residues to be expected on each commodity in a group of related commodities on the basis of less data than would be required for each commodity in the group, considered separately. Table 4-7 provides the grouping of such commodities.

Another method of estimating residue in a product is the following. It may be possible to make a reliable estimate of negligible residues of pesticide chemicals to be expected on each commodity in a designated grouping on the basis of data on a representative number of commodities, such as those listed in Table 4-8.

Subpart C of 40 CFR 180 provides the list of pesticide chemicals for which

TABLE 4-7. Related Raw Agricultural Commodities.[a] Adapted from 40 CFR
180.34(e) (1976).

1	Apples, crabapples, pears, quinces	16	Lettuce, endive (escarole), Chinese cabbage, salsify tops
2	Avocados, papayas		
3	Blackberries, boysenberries, dewberries, loganberries, raspberries	17	Onions, garlic, leeks, shallots (green, or in dry bulb form)
		18	Potatoes, Jerusalem-artichokes, sweet potatoes, yams
4	Blueberries, currants, gooseberries, huckleberries	19	Spinach, beet tops, collards, dandelion, kale, mustard greens, parsley, Swiss chard, turnip tops, watercress
5	Cherries, plums, prunes		
6	Oranges, citrus citron, grapefruit, kumquats, lemons, limes, tangelos, tangerines	20	Tomatoes, eggplants, peppers, pimentos
7	Mangoes, persimmons	21	Pecans, almonds, brazil nuts, bush nuts, butternuts, chestnuts, filberts, hazelnuts, hickory nuts, walnuts
8	Peaches, apricots, nectarines		
9	Beans, peas, soybeans (each in dry form)		
10	Beans, peas, soybeans (each in succulent form)	22	Field corn, popcorn, sweet corn (each in grain form)
11	Broccoli, brussels sprouts	23	Milo, sorghum (each in grain form)
12	Cantaloupes, honeydew melons, muskmelons, pumpkins, watermelons, winter squash	24	Wheat, barley, oats, rice, rye (each in grain form)
13	Carrots, garden beets, sugar beets, horseradish, parsnips, radishes, rutabagas, salsify roots, turnips	25	Clovers, alfalfa, cowpea hay, lespedeza, lupines, peanut hay, pea-vine hay, soybean hay, vetch
14	Celery, fennel	26	Corn forage, sorghum forage
15	Cucumbers, summer squash	27	Sugarcane, cane sorghum

[a] Each of the following groups of crops lists raw agricultural commodities that are considered to be related for the purpose of obtaining a reliable estimate of the residues of those pesticide chemicals that are not absorbed into the living plant or animal when applied (that is, not systemic).

the EPA has established specific tolerance levels in designated commodities. Some general provisions about these data are as follows:

1. The specific tolerances established for the pesticide chemicals apply to residues resulting from their application prior to harvest or slaughter, unless otherwise noted.
2. Tolerances are expressed in terms of parts by weight of the pesticide chemical per one million parts by weight of the raw agricultural commodity.

TABLE 4-8. Grouping of Agricultural Products for Estimating Pesticide Residues.[a]
Adapted from 40 CFR 180.34(f) (1976).

1   Citrus fruits

    Citrus citron, grapefruit, kumquats, lemons, limes, oranges, tangelos, tanger-
    ines, and hybrids of these

2   Curcurbits

    Cantaloupes, casabas, crenshaws, cucumbers, honey balls, honeydew melons,
    melons, melon hybrids, muskmelons, Persian melons, pumpkins, summer
    squash, watermelons and their hybrids, winter squash

3   Forage grasses

    Any grasses (either green or cured) that will be fed to or grazed by livestock,
    all pasture and range grasses, all grasses grown for hay or silage, corn grown for
    fodder or silage, sorghum grown for hay or silage, small grains grown for hay,
    grazing, or silage

4   Forage legumes

    Any crop belonging to the family Leguminosae that is grown for forage (hay,
    grazing, silage, etc.), alfalfa, beans (for forage), clovers, cowpeas (for forage),
    cowpea hay, lespedezas, peanuts (for forage), peanut hay, peas (for forage),
    pea vine hay, trefoil, velvet beans (for forage), vetch, soybeans (for forage),
    soybean hay

5   Fruiting vegetables

    Eggplants, peppers, pimentos, tomatoes

6   Grain crops

    Any crop belonging to the family Graminae that produces mature seed that
    are used for food or feed, barley, buckwheat, corn (field corn, sweet corn, and
    popcorn), milo, oats, rice, rye, sorghum (grain), wheat

7   Leafy vegetables

    Anise (fresh leaf and stock only), beet greens (tops), broccoli, broccoli raab,
    brussels sprouts, cabbage, cauliflower, celery, Chinese cabbage, collards, dande-

TABLE 4-8 (continued)

lion, endive, escarole, fennel, kale, kohlrabi, lettuce, mustard greens, parsley, rhubarb, salsify tops, spinach, sugar beet tops, Swiss chard, turnip greens (tops) watercress

8   Nuts

Almonds, Brazil nuts, bush nuts, butter-nuts, cashews, chestnuts, filberts, hazelnuts, hickory nuts, macadamia nuts, pecans, walnuts

9   Pome fruits

Apples, crabapples, pears, quinces

10   Poultry

Chickens, ducks, geese, guineas, pheasant, pigeons, quail, turkeys

11   Root crop vegetables

Beets, carrots, chicory, garlic, green onions, horseradish, Jerusalem artichokes, leeks, onions, parsnips, potatoes, radishes, rutabagas, salsify, shallots, spring onions, sugarbeets, sweet potatoes, turnips, yams

12   Seed and pod vegetables

Black-eyed peas, cowpeas, dill, edible soybeans, field beans, field peas, garden peas, green beans, kidney beans, lima beans, navy beans, okra, peas, pole beans, snap beans, string beans, wax beans, other beans and peas (except dried beans and peas)

13   Small fruits

Blackberries, blueberries, boysenberries, cranberries, currants, dewberries, elderberries, gooseberries, grapes, huckleberries, loganberries, raspberries

14   Stone fruit

Apricots, cherries (sour and sweet), damsons, nectarines, pawpaws, peaches, plums, prunes

TABLE 4-8 (continued)

15   Stored commodities other than fruits, grain, and vegetables

Cottonseed, dried beans (all), dried peas (all), hay, peanuts

16   Stored fruits and vegetables

Same crops as specified in this list for curcurbits, fruits, nuts, and vegetables

17   Stored grain

Same crops as specified in this list for grain crops

---

^a This grouping assures that a reliable estimate of the negligible residues of pesticide chemicals can be made for the entire group after the values for some representative members are known.

3. The poisonous and deleterious substances for which tolerances are established are named by their common names wherever practicable, otherwise by their chemical names.
4. The analytical methods to be used for determining whether pesticide residues, including negligible residues either in or on raw agricultural commodities, are in compliance with the tolerances established are identified among the methods contained or referenced in the Pesticide Analytical Manual that is maintained by and available from the FDA.

The chemicals in Subpart C of 40 CFR 180 are listed in two ways. One is according to section numbers such as 180.102 to 180.360; the other arranges the chemicals alphabetically. Table 4-9 reproduces the tolerances for the residues of the pesticide picloram (4-amino-3,5,6-trichloropicolinic acid).

Subpart D of 40 CFR 180 lists all those chemicals that have been granted exemptions from tolerances in certain agricultural products. Interested parties may obtain details from the original document.

The Office of Pesticide Programs in the EPA has special responsibility in regard to monitoring pesticide residues. They are as follows:

1. The EPA is required to formulate and periodically revise, in cooperation with other federal, state, or local agencies, a national plan for monitoring pesticides.
2. The EPA is required to undertake such monitoring activities (including the

TABLE 5-9. The Residue Tolerances of Picloram in Various Raw Agricultural
Commodities.[a] Adapted from 40 CFR 180.292 (1976).

Commodity	ppm[a]	Commodity	ppm[a]
Barley, grain	0.5	Horses, fat	0.2
Barley, green forage	1	Horses, kidney	5
Barley, straw	1	Horses, liver	0.5
Cattle, fat	0.2	Horses, meat-by-	0.2
Cattle, kidney	5	products (except	
Cattle, liver	0.5	kidney & liver)	
Cattle, meat-by-	0.2	Horses, meat	0.2
products (except		Milk	0.05
kidney & liver)		Oats, grain	0.5
Cattle, meat	0.2	Oats, green forage	1
Eggs	0.05	Oats, straw	1
Goats, fat	0.2	Poultry, fat	0.05
Goats, kidney	5	Poultry, meat-by-	0.05
Goats, liver	0.5	products	
Goats, meat-by-	0.2	Poultry, meat	0.05
products (except		Sheep, fat	0.2
kidney & liver)		Sheep, kidney	5
Goats, meat	0.2	Sheep, liver	0.5
Grasses, forage	80	Sheep, meat-by-	0.2
Hogs, fat	0.2	products (except	
Hogs, kidney	5	kidney & liver)	
Hogs, liver	0.5	Sheep, meat	0.2
Hogs, meat-by-	0.2	Wheat, grain	0.5
products (except		Wheat, green forage	1
kidney & liver)		Wheat, straw	1
Hogs, meat	0.2		

[a] The pesticide picloram (4-amino-3,5,6-trichloropicolinic acid) is applied in the
acid form or in the form of its potassium triethylamine, or tri-isopropanolamine
salts. The residue is expressed in the form of picloram in parts per million (ppm).

monitoring of air, soil, water, plants, and animals) as may be necessary for the
implementation of the national pesticide monitoring plan.

These responsibilities are the result of certain provisions of the Federal Insecticide, Fungicide, and Rodenticide Act, as amended. The EPA conducts many
programs to carry out such activities which are not discussed here. However, one
publication that provides much useful scientific data is the Pesticides Monitoring
Journal, published by an interagency committee with the EPA as a major partici-

pant. Many of the articles published in this journal are related to the monitoring of pesticide residues in food and feed for man and animal.

Agreements with the Food and Drug Administration

The FDA and the EPA have a close working relationship. The FDA administers the Federal Food, Drug, and Cosmetic Act, as amended. However, Reorganization Plan No. 3 of 1970 published in the Federal Register of October 6, 1970, stated in Section 2, Paragraph (4) (84 Stat. 2086) that the functions vested in the Secretary of Health, Education, and Welfare (i.e., the FDA), of establishing tolerances for pesticide chemicals under the Federal Food, Drug, and Cosmetic Act (Sections 406, 408, and 409 of the act, i.e., 21 U.S.C. 346, 346a, and 348) were transferred to the administrator of the EPA effective December 2, 1970. Also, the EPA administers the Federal Insecticide, Fungicide, and Rodenticide Act, as amended, 7 U.S.C. 135 et seq.). With reference to some provision in the two acts administered by the EPA, certain confusion and misunderstandings have arisen in the actual enforcement of the statutes. Thus four very important Memoranda of Understanding have been signed between the EPA and FDA. The contents of these agreements are briefly described in the following paragraphs; further details may be obtained from the original documents.

Agreement of 1971

On December 22, 1971 an agreement between the EPA and FDA was announced (36 FR 24234 and 24235). The purpose of the agreement was as follows. After considering all the various pesticide uses that had been subject to petition procedures under the relevant provisions of the two acts, the EPA and FDA had concluded that an agreement was needed to coordinate the activities pertaining to pesticides and related chemicals to specify which agency would process the pesticide petitions for each type of use. Because certain products were subject to the requirements of the provisions of both acts, inconvenience, confusion, and misunderstanding had resulted in the past from procedures followed in the proposed marketing of such products. Thus the agreement would establish a new procedure to be followed, and the manufacturer would know which agency exercised primary jurisdiction over his product and that he would not receive approval for the marketing of the product until each agency had approved the marketing under the respective authority.

The agreement also established other procedures that involved:

1.   Issuance of regulations under Section 406 of the Federal Food, Drug, and Cos-

metic Act.
2. Establishment of reference standards for pesticide and related chemicals.
3. Exchange of information on certain programs.
4. Agreements with states and foreign countries on surveillance and enforcement activities on pesticide residues in food.
5. Publication of the Pesticide Analytical Manual.

Some details of the agreement are as follows:

1. Petitions to be processed by the EPA:
    a. Tolerances or exemption from tolerances for residues of pesticide chemicals on raw agricultural commodities.
    b. Food additive regulations required for residues of pesticide chemicals carrying over and concentrating in processed foods manufactured from treated raw agricultural commodities.
    c. Regulations for residues of pesticide and related chemicals from direct treatment of processed foods with fumigants or insecticides.
    d. Food additive regulations to permit the safe use of pesticides and related chemicals to impregnate food-packaging materials such as wrappers or bags to protect raw agricultural commodities from any pest or to protect processed foods from insects.
2. Petitions to be processed by the FDA:
    a. Food additive regulations to permit use of sanitizers on food-contact surfaces.
    b. Food additive regulations to permit the safe use of pesticides or related chemicals on preservatives in processed foods.
    c. Food additive regulations to permit the safe use of pesticides or related chemicals on food-packaging material when such use is not covered by that delegated to the EPA.
3. Applications for approval of drugs, including antibiotics, under the Federal Food, Drug, and Cosmetic Act and for registration of pesticides and related chemicals under the Federal Insecticide, Fungicide, and Rodenticide Act are required to be processed in accordance with a series of arrangements made between the two agencies. Neither agency will approve the marketing of a product under the law administered by it if the product would not be in full compliance with the requirements of a law administered by the other.
4. If the poisonous or deleterious substances referred to in Section 406 of the Federal Food, Drug, and Cosmetic Act (21 U.S.C. 346) is present in food primarily as a result of its use as a pesticide or related chemical, any regulation establishing a tolerance for such substances in food will be promulaged by the EPA. Any other regulations under Section 406 will be promulgated by the FDA.

5. The EPA will have primary responsibility for maintenance of an analytical reference standards repository of pesticides for which tolerances are established.
6. The FDA will continue the responsibility for agreements with states and foreign countries on surveillance and enforcement activities on pesticide residues in food.
7. Publication of the FDA Pesticide Analytical Manual for residues in foods and other environmental substrates will be continued as a joint FDA/EPA sponsorship under editorial management consisting of representatives of both agencies.

Agreement in 1973

On September 6, 1973 an agreement (38 FR 24233 and 24234) between the EPA and FDA agencies was announced. This agreement was to further detail each agency's responsibilities on the regulation of drugs and pesticides; it amended the one made in 1971. Examples of additional arrangements are as follows:

1. The application of a pesticide for any of the uses listed as follows would be considered as both an animal drug and a pesticide. The agency for primary jurisdiction regarding such articles would be the FDA.
    a. Aquatic treatments intended to control parasites and/or disease of fish in ponds or aquariums.
    b. Animal drinking water treatments with direct or implied claims for control of animal parasites or diseases.
2. The application of a pesticide for any of the uses listed as follows would be regarded as a pesticide usage. In these cases the agency for primary jurisdiction would be the EPA.
    a. Aquatic treatments of ponds or aquariums solely for control of algae or bacteria.
    b. Sanitizers applied to inanimate surfaces and/or in drinking water of animals that do not include any direct or implied claims to control disease.

If a product subject to joint jurisdiction was deemed to be either a new human or animal drug prior to registration by EPA, it must be in full compliance with the requirements for FDA approval of a new drug application, which include publication of its approval where required by the Federal Food, Drug, and Cosmetic Act (i.e., new animal drug), regardless of the agency of primary jurisdiction.

If a manufacturer proposing a new product could not determine the agency of primary jurisdiction, a presubmission inquiry might be submitted to either agency. The FDA and EPA would jointly consider the inquiry and advise the manufacturer of their conclusions in this matter.

Agreement in 1974

Because of the particular circumstances surrounding this "agreement," some background information is presented as follows to clarify why certain arrangements must be agreed on by the two agencies. The EPA administers Sections 406, 408, and 409 of the Federal Food, Drug, and Cosmetic Act (21 U.S.C. 346, 346a, and 348). Section 406 has created some problems. This section permits the establishment of tolerances for added poisonous or deleterious substances, including pesticides, when these substances result in food from "unavoidable" sources of contamination. For example, various species of fish do contain residues of pesticides and industrial chemicals, such as dieldrin, DDT, PCB, Mirex, Kepone, and mercury, irrespective of where they are caught. No one has intended that these chemicals be present in fish or directly added to the fish for certain technical purposes. Normally the EPA or FDA simply ban an undesirable pesticide (or related chemical) from or declines to issue an approval for its addition to or use on food as a means of preventing contamination. Obviously, the above mentioned "unavoidable" contaminants cannot be banned since they have never been approved to be used on fish, for example. On the other hand, potential harm from the consumption of these fish cannot be ignored.

Thus among all the unavoidable poisonous substances, pesticide chemicals are one type since they frequently result in environmental contamination. Under Section 406, the EPA has the authority to establish tolerances for "unavoidable" pesticide residues in food, even though the pesticide itself is not registered by the EPA for use with that particular food. However, at present time of writing, that agency has not issued this type of pesticide tolerance. To solve this problem, the term "action level"has been created or developed.

An action level is a temporary criterion used by the FDA for those situations where there are no established tolerances under Sections 406, 408, or 409 and where a regulatory tool is needed for enforcement purposes. This is especially true with those contaminants occurring in food from indirect and unavoidable sources of contamination, pursuant to Section 406.

Because of their joint pesticide responsibilities under the act, the EPA and FDA agree that both agencies have definite roles in respect to action levels for pesticides. Since an action level is an exercise of enforcement discretion and since the FDA is responsible for enforcement under the executive order establishing the EPA, the FDA is responsible for determining when an action level for a pesticide should be established and for issuing such action levels as regulations. Also, since action levels are similar to a formal tolerance in basis and effect and since the EPA has the expertise to establish pesticide tolerances, the EPA is responsible for determining, on request from the FDA, the appropriate level at which a pesticide action level is to be set. And, as mentioned previously, it is FDA's responsibility to implement and enforce pesticide action levels.

Such tolerances or action levels properly recognize the problem of environmental contamination caused by the drift of a pesticide from one area to another or the persistence of the chemical in the environment over a period of time. In no instance, however, does any such action level or tolerance itself authorize use of any pesticide on a food crop for which it has not been registered by the EPA. Except in certain limited instances, no action level or other administrative action will be taken to permit the sale of food contaminated with pesticide that has been used in any manner other than in strict accordance with the label directions approved by the EPA.

The EPA/FDA agreement was informally adopted by the two agencies in 1973 and was formally announced in the Federal Register of December 6, 1974 (39 FR 42737 to 42751, especially pages 42745 and 42746) when FDA issued proposed procedural regulations for formalizing its implementation of the provisions of Section 406 of the Federal Food, Drug, and Cosmetic Act and for establishing tolerances and action levels for unavoidable food contaminants. The latter regulations were later finalized and announced on September 30, 1977 (42 FR 52813 to 52824).

The agreement applies to EPA registered pesticides, their metabolites, and any normally associated impurities. Consequently, whether the EPA will fulfill the agreed-on responsibility will not be determined by the source of food contamination. This also means that the FDA will approach the EPA, even if the unavoidable pesticide contamination is not the result of a pesticide usage. For example, the EPA assisted in developing action levels for Mirex and Kepone in fish that were taken from Lake Ontario and the James River, respectively. Obviously, the contamination problems were unrelated to pesticide usage; rather, they were the result of industrial pollution.

Because of enforcement practicalities, tolerances and action levels for imported food must be the same as for domestically produced food, although levels of unavoidable contamination may differ from country to country. For example, some pesticides are approved for use abroad because of conditions that justify their use but are not registered for use in this country because those conditions do not exist here. In such a case, a regulation issued by the EPA under Section 408 or 409 of the Federal Food, Drug, and Cosmetic Act would apply to any food on which the pesticide was intentionally used. A tolerance may be issued by the EPA or an action level by the FDA (after consultation with the EPA) to be applied to food unavoidably contaminated by the pesticide. That tolerance or action level will be set at a uniform level for all food, including domestic food. However, the establishment of the tolerance or action level will not authorize any use of the pesticide in this country.

Agreement in 1975

On June 12, 1975 an agreement (40 FR 25078 and 25079) signed between the two agencies was announced. The Reorganization Plan of 1970 had authorized the following:

1. The EPA establishes tolerances levels of pesticide residues in food.
2. The FDA enforces those levels.
3. The EPA monitors the compliance with such tolerances and the effectiveness of surveillance and enforcement.

Foods may become contaminated with illegal residues of pesticides through the use of a registered pesticide in a manner inconsistent with the label directions, through the unauthorized use of a nonregistered pesticide, or as a result of environmental or other indirect sources of contamination. Regardless of the source of contamination, the immediate and primary concerns of the FDA under the Federal Food, Drug, and Cosmetic Act are to remove the adulterated food from consumer channels and to prevent further marketing of the food. The immediate and primary concerns of the EPA under the Federal Insecticide, Fungicide, and Rodenticide Act regard the conditions under which pesticide usage has caused the contamination of the food and the issues of whether a violation of that act has occurred or whether use, if approved, is consistent with protecting man and his environment.

Of concern to both the EPA and FDA is the protection of human health from exposure to harmful pesticides and pesticide residues, the prevention of further pesticide abuse and contamination, and the need for cooperation between both agencies to assure the optimum expenditure of public funds. The agreement was signed by both agencies to discharge as effectively as possible their responsibilities related to pesticide enforcement.

It was agreed that the EPA will:

1. Supply concerned FDA offices and personnel with a list of approved pesticides.
2. Supply the FDA with all necessary information if a detected pesticide misuse is suspected to result in illegal residues in food or feed products.
3. Investigate any suspicious report from the FDA for possible violation of the Federal Insecticide, Fungicide, and Rodenticide Act and initiate appropriate regulatory action if necessary and inform the FDA of any results.
4. Provide FDA with document and/or testimony needed to support a pesticide related regulatory action under the Federal Food, Drug, and Cosmetic Act.
5. Inform the FDA of any possible violation of the Federal Food, Drug, and Cosmetic Act during any routine EPA investigation.

It was agreed that the FDA will:

1. Notify the EPA of any possible pesticide misuse or presence of illegal pesticide residues in food or feed.
2. Investigate any suspicious report from EPA for possible violation of the Federal Food, Drug, and Cosmetic Act and initiate appropriate regulatory action if necessary; inform the FDA of any results.
3. Provide the EPA with document and/or testimony needed to support a pesticide related regulatory action under the Federal Insecticide, Fungicide, and Rodenticide Act.
4. Inform the EPA of any possible violation of the Federal Insecticide, Fungicide, and Rodenticide Act during any routine FDA investigation.

It was mutually agreed that each agency will:

1. Maintain a close working relationship.
2. Coordinate investigations, sample analysis, and enforcement actions to avoid duplication.
3. Presume that when information reveals a violation of both acts that involves misuse of pesticides, any punitive action initiated by the EPA under the Federal Insecticide, Fungicide, and Rodenticide Act will represent the interests of both agencies and the public. Such action by the EPA will not preclude the FDA from initiating other legal sanctions of seizure and/or injunction in regard to that violation, but ordinarily the FDA will not initiate separate criminal proceedings under the Federal Food, Drug, and Cosmetic Act.
4. Designate contact points and other communication arrangements.

Agreement with the Department of Agriculture

As indicated earlier, meat and poultry may become contaminated with illegal residues of pesticides because of one or more of the following:

1. Using an unauthorized pesticide.
2. Using an authorized pesticide in a manner inconsistent with its container label.
3. Environmental or other indirect sources of contamination.

In either case the immediate and primary concerns of the United States Department of Agriculture (USDA) under the Federal Meat Inspection Act (21 U.S.C. 601 et seq.) and the Poultry Products Inspection Act (21 U.S.C. 451 et seq.) are to:

1. Remove the adulterated meat and poultry from consumer channels.
2. Prevent further marketing of the contaminated food.

The immediate and primary concerns of EPA under the Federal Insecticide, Fungicide, and Rodenticide Act are:

1. What were the conditions under which the pesticide usage caused the contamination of the meat and poultry?
2. Did a violation of the act occur?
3. Was the use of the pesticide, if approved, consistent with a statutory duty to protect man and his environment?

Thus EPA and USDA have certain related objectives in carrying out their respective statutory authorities. On October 27, 1977, it was announced (42 FR 56629 and 56630) that a Memorandum of Understanding had been signed by the two agencies. The agreement was intended to serve two purposes.

1. It describes the working arrangements being adopted by EPA and USDA in order to discharge as effectively as possible their responsibilities relative to pesticide enforcement.
2. It furthers the will of Congress that EPA and USDA cooperate with other federal agencies in carrying out the provisions of their respective acts [7 U.S.C. 136t, 21 U.S.C. 454(a), and 21 U.S.C. 661(a)].

According to the agreement, the USDA (i.e., the Meat Poultry Inspection Program) will:

1. Supply EPA headquarters with a complete list of all meat and poultry processing and packing establishments operating under USDA's continuous inspection. The EPA will be notified of any changes or additions to this list.
2. Immediately notify the appropriate EPA regional offices and headquarters of findings of illegal pesticide residues in edible tissue samples of meat and poultry, and promptly transmit other relevant information subsequent to the notification.
3. Report to the appropriate EPA regional or headquarters office the results of any USDA investigation initiated because of information made available by that EPA regional or headquarters office.
4. Make available to EPA, to the extent authorized by law, any reports or documents necessary to support regulatory action under the Federal Insecticide, Fungicide, and Rodenticide Act involving pesticide residues. Upon request, make USDA personnel available for testifying at hearings, conferences, and

meetings.

5. Routinely supply EPA headquarters with all reports compiled on the results of USDA meat and poultry residue sampling and testing programs.

6. Submit USDA annual regulatory program to EPA in advance for comments. The transmission will include designation of pesticides to be sought, methods used, and proposed sampling program.

7. Notify EPA headquarters of any findings of illegal residues or industrial chemical residues in tissue samples of meat or poultry, together with notice of actions.

According to the agreement, the EPA will:

1. Immediately notify the appropriate USDA office if and when EPA comes into possession of findings of illegal pesticide residues in feeds intended for food producing animals or results of any other investigation which indicate the likelihood that actionable residues will be present in meat or poultry.

2. Report to the appropriate USDA office the results of any investigation initiated because of information made available by USDA office.

3. Routinely furnish USDA headquarters with all periodic reports compiled on the results of EPA regulatory program involving pesticides in animal feeds, milk, and eggs.

4. Recommend, upon request from the USDA, action levels for pesticide residues in meat or poultry.

5. Continue to periodically notify USDA of experimental use permits issued under Section 5(a to e) of the amended Federal Insecticide, Fungicide, and Rodenticide Act.

6. Submit to USDA in advance of publication a notice of any proposed tolerance of pesticides in meat or poultry. This advance notice will include the proposed method of analysis.

It is mutually agreed that:

1. Both agencies will maintain a close working relationship, both in headquarters and in the field.

2. Each agency will coordinate its investigations with the other agency and with appropriate state officials to the extent necessary to avoid duplication of effort.

3. Regulations proposed by either agency pertaining to the problem of residues in animal feed, meat, and poultry will be referred to the other agency for review and comment prior to issuance.

4. Both agencies will exchange information relative to their analytical methodol-

ogy, methods of development activities and related analytical methodology, and procedures in determining the presence of pesticide residues in feeds, feed ingredients and food derived from animals. Both agencies will agree to the specific analytical methods to be used for the determination of residues of pesticides for regulatory purposes.

5. Each agency will advise the other agency and exchange relevant data whenever it is considering release of information materials that may have an impact on the other agency.

6. The two agencies will exchange information about surveillance programs developed by either agency relating to collection of samples or other information covered in this agreement.

7. An appropriate communication and representation system will be established.

For further details, refer to the original document.

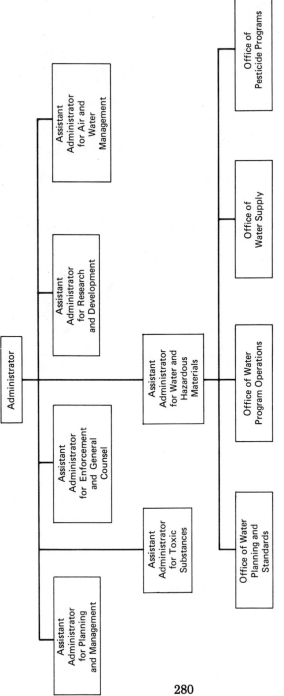

APPENDIX 4-1. Simplified organization chart for the Environmental Protection Agency.

APPENDIX 4-2. Titles and issuing statutory authorities for Parts 104 to 180, 401 to 432, Title 40, Code of Federal Regulations (1976), Chapter I, Environmental Protection Agency

Subchapter D Water Programs

Part | Part title and statutory authority under which part was issued

104 — Public hearings on effluent standards for toxic pollutants. Authority: Sections 501 and 307(a) of the Federal Water Pollution Control Act, as amended, PL 92-500, 86 Stat. 816.

105 — Public participation in water pollution control. Authority: Section 101(e), Federal Water Pollution Control Act (Section 2, Federal Water Pollution Control Act Amendments of 1972, PL 92-500; 86 Stat. 816; 33 U.S.C.

108 — Employee protection hearings. Authority: Section 507(e), PL 92-500, 86 Stat. 816 (33 U.S.C. 1251 et seq.)

109 — Criteria for state, local, and regional oil removal contingency plans. Authority: Section 11(j)(1)(B), 84 Stat. 96, 33 U.S.C. 1161(j)(1)(B).

110 — Discharge of oil. Authority: Section 11(b)(3), as amended, 84 Stat. 92; 33 U.S.C. 1161.

112 — Oil pollution prevention. Authority: Sections 311(j)(1)(C), 311(j)(2), 501(a), Federal Water Pollution Control Act [Section 2, PL 92-500, 86 Stat. 816 et seq. (33 U.S.C. 1251 et seq.)]; Section 4(b), PL 92-500, 86 Stat. 897; 5 U.S.C. Reorg. Plan of 1970 No. 3 (1970), 35 FR 15623, 3 CFR 1966 to 1970 Comp.; E.O. 11735, 38 FR 21243, 3 CFR, unless otherwise noted.

113 — Liability limits for small onshore storage facilities. Authority: Section 311(f)(2), 86 Stat. 867, 33 U.S.C. 1251 (1972).

114 — Civil penalties for violation of oil pollution prevention regulations. Authority: Sections 311(j), 501(a), PL 92-500. 86 Stat. 868, 885 [33 U.S.C. 1321(j), 1361(a)].

120 — Water quality standards. Authority: Section 1, 70 Stat. 506, as amended; 38 U.S.C. 1160(c), unless otherwise noted.

122 — Thermal discharges. Authority: Sections 316(a) and 501(a) of the Federal Water Pollution Control Act, as amended; 86 Stat. 816 et seq.; PL 92-500 [33 U.S.C. 1326(a) and 1361(a)].

Part	Part title and statutory authority under which part was issued
123	State certification of activities requiring a federal license or permit. Authority: Sections 21(b) and (c), 84 Stat. 91; 33 U.S.C. 1171(b) (1970), Reorganization Plan No. 3 of 1970.
124	State program elements necessary for participation in the national pollutant dischange elimination system. Authority: Section 304, 84 Stat. 816, 33 U.S.C. 1251 (1972).
125	National pollutant discharge elimination system. Authority: Sections 402 and 405 of PL 92-500 (86 Stat. 816 et seq., 33 U.S.C. 1251nt).
126	Areawide waste treatment management planning areas and responsible planning agencies. Authority: Sections 208, 501, 86 Stat. 816 [33 U.S.C. 1251, 1288(a)(1)].
128	Pretreatment standards. Authority: Section 307(b) PL 92-500; 86 Stat. 857 (33 U.S.C. 1317).
130	Toxic pollutant effluent standards. Authority: Sections 106, 208(b)(2), 303(d), 303(e), 305(b), 314, 501, 516(b) of the Federal Water Pollution Control Act, as amended; PL 92-500, 86 Stat. 816 (1972); (33 U.S.C. 1251 et seq.).
131	Preparation of water quality management basin plans. Authority: Section 303(e), 86 Stat. 816 (1972); (33 U.S.C. 1251 et seq.).
133	Secondary treatment information. Authority: Sections 304(d)(1), 301(b)(1)(B) Federal Water Pollution Control Act Amendments, 1972 PL 92-500.
135	Prior notice of citizen suits. Authority: Section 505, PL 92-500; 86 Stat. 888 (33 U.S.C. 1365).
136	Guidelines establishing test procedures for the analysis of pollutants. Authority: Section 304(g), 86 Stat. 816 et seq., PL 92-500.
140	Marine sanitation device standard. Authority: Section 13, 70 Stat. 506, as amended, 33 U.S.C. 1163. Interpret or apply Section 13(b)(1), 84 Stat. 100, 33 U.S.C. 1163(b)(1).
141	National interim primary drinking water standards. Authority: Sections 1412, 1414, 1450 of PL 93-523 (42 U.S.C. 300g-1, 300g-3, 300g-4, 300j-9).
142	Drinking water standards implementation. Authority: Sections 1413 to 1416, 1445 and 1450 of PL 93-523 (42 U.S.C. 300g-2, 300g-3, 300g-4, 300g-5, 300j-4, and 300j-9).

Part	Part title and statutory authority under which part was issued

143   National secondary drinking water regulations.
        Authority: Section 1412(c) of PL 93-523 (42 U.S.C. 300g-1), see 42 FR
        17143 to 17146.

146   State underground injection control programs.
        Authority: Sections 1421, 1422, 1423, and 1450 of the Public Health
        Service Act, as amended by the Safe Drinking Water Act (PL 93-523), see
        41 FR 36730 to 36745.

149   Review of projects affecting sole source aquifers.
        Authority: Section 1424(e) of PL 93-523 (42 U.S.C. 300h-3).

Subchapter E Pesticide Programs

Part	Part title and statutory authority under which part was issued

162   Regulations for the enforcement of the Federal Insecticide, Fungicide, and
        Rodenticide Act.
        Authority: Section 6, 61 Stat. 168; 7 U.S.C. 135d.

163   Certification of usefulness of pesticide chemicals.
        Authority: Section 3, 68 Stat. 511; 21 U.S.C. 346a.

164   Rules of practice governing hearings, under the Federal Insecticide, Fungi-
        cide, and Rodenticide Act, arising from refusals to register, cancellations
        of registrations, changes of classifications, suspensions of registrations, and
        other hearings called pursuant to Section 6 of the act.
        Authority: Section 6 of the Federal Insecticide, Fungicide, and Rodenti-
        cide Act, as amended; 38 FR 8670, unless otherwise noted.

165   Regulations for the acceptance of certain pesticides and recommended pro-
        cedures for the disposal and storage of pesticides and pesticides containers.
        Authority: Sections 19(a) and 25(a) of the Federal Insecticide, Fungicide,
        and Rodenticide Act as amended by the Federal Environmental Pesticide
        Control Act of 1972 (86 Stat. 955 and 977), and Section 204 of the Solid
        Waste Disposal Act (PL 89-272 as amended by PL 91-512).

166   Exemption of Federal and State agencies for use of pesticides under
        emergency conditions.
        Authority: Section 25 of the Federal Insecticide, Fungicide, and Rodenti-
        cide Act, as amended by the Federal Environmental Pesticide Control Act
        of 1972 (86 Stat. 997).

167   Registration of pesticide-producing establishments, submission of pesticides
        reports, and labeling.

Part	Part title and statutory authority under which part was issued

Authority: Sections 7, 25, Federal Insecticide, Fungicide, and Rodenticide Act, as amended; 86 Stat. 987, 997.

168   Rules of practice governing proceedings conducted in the assessment of civil penalties under the Federal Insecticide, Fungicide, and Rodenticide Act, as amended.
Authority: Sections 14(a) and 25(a), Federal Insecticide, Fungicide, and Rodenticide Act, as amended; PL 92-516; 86 Stat. 973 (7 U.S.C. 1361(a), 136t(a).

169   Books and records of pesticide production and distribution.
Authority: Sections 8, 25, Federal Insecticide, Fungicide, and Rodenticide Act, as amended by the Federal Environmental Pesticide Control Act of 1972 (86 Stat. 987 and 997).

170   Worker protection standards for agricultural pesticides.
Authority: Section 25, 86 Stat. 997; 7 U.S.C. 136w.

171   Certification of pesticide applicators.
Authority: Sections 4, 25(a), Federal Insecticide, Fungicide, and Rodenticide Act, as amended; 86 Stat. 973, 987, 997.

172   Experimental use permits.
Authority: Sections 5, 24, and 25(a) of the Federal Insecticide, Fungicide, and Rodenticide Act, as amended by the Federal Environmental Pesticide Control Act of 1972 (86 Stat. 983 and 997).

180   Tolerances and exemptions from tolerances for pesticide chemicals in or on raw agricultural commodities.
Authority: Section 408, 68 Stat. 511; 21 U.S.C. 346a, unless otherwise noted.

Subchapter N Effluence guidelines and standards

Part	Part title and statutory authority under which part was issued

401   General provisions.
Authority: Sections 301, 304(b) and (c), 306(b) and (c), 307(b) and (c), and 316(b) of the Federal Water Pollution Control Act, as amended (the "Act"); 33 U.S.C. 1251, 1311, 1314(b) and (c), 1316(b) and (c), 1317(b) and (c), and 1326(c); 86 Stat. 816 et seq.; PL 92-500.

405   Effluent limitations guidelines for standards of performance and pretreatment standards for new sources for the dairy products processing industry point source category.
Authority: Sections 301, 304(b) and (c), 306(b) and (c), and 307(c) of the

Part	Part title and statutory authority under which part was issued

Federal Water Pollution Control Act, as amended (the Act); 33 U.S.C. 1251, 1311, 1314(b) and (c), 1316(b) and (c), and 1317(c); 86 Stat. 816 et seq.; PL 92-500.

406   Grain mills point source category.
Authority: Sections 301, 304(b) and (c), 306(b) and (c), and 307(c) of the Federal Water Pollution Control Act, as amended; 33 U.S.C. 1251, 1311, 1314(b) and (c), 1316(b) and (c), and 1317(c); 86 Stat. 816 et seq.; PL 92-500.

407   Canned and preserved fruits and vegetables processing point source category.
Authority: Sections 301, 304(b) and (c), 306(b) and (c), and 307(c) of the Federal Water Pollution Control Act, as amended; 33 U.S.C. 1251, 1311, 1314(b) and (c), 1316(b) and (c), and 1317(c); 86 Stat. 816 et seq.; PL 92-500.

408   Canned and preserved seafood processing point source category.
Authority: Sections 301, 304(b) and (c), 306(b) and (c), and 307(c) of the Federal Water Pollution Control Act, as amended; 33 U.S.C. 1251, 1311, 1314(b) and (c), 1316(b) and (c), and 1317(c); 86 Stat. 816 et seq.; PL 92-500.

409   Sugar processing point source category.
Authority: Sections 301, 304(b) and (c), 306(b) and (c), 307(c), and 316(b) of the Federal Water Pollution Control Act, as amended [33 U.S.C. 1251, 1311, 1314(b) and (c), 1316(b) and (c), 1317(c), and 1326(c)], 86 Stat. 816 et seq., PL 92-500.

412   Feedlots point source category.
Authority: Sections 301, 304(b) and (c), 306(b) and (c), and 307(c) of the Federal Water Pollution Control Act, as amended; 33 U.S.C. 1251, 1311, 1314(b) and (c), 1316(b) and (c), and 1317(c); 86 Stat. 816 et seq.; PL 92-500.

418   Fertilizer manufacturing point source category.
Authority: Sections 301, 304(b) and (c), and 307(c) of the Federal Water Pollution Control Act, as amended [33 U.S.C. 1251, 1311, 1314(b) and (c), 1316(b), 1317(c)]; 86 Stat. 816 et seq., PL 92-500.

432   Meat products point source category.
Authority: Sections 301, 304(b) and (c), 306(b) and (c), and 307(c) of the Federal Water Pollution Control Act, as amended; 33 U.S.C. 1251, 1311, 1415(b) and (c), 1316(b) and (c), 1317(c); 86 Stat. 816 et seq.; PL 92-500.

CHAPTER 5

FEDERAL TRADE COMMISSION

INTRODUCTION

Organization, Activities, and Statutes Administered

The Federal Trade Commission Act of 1914 permitted the establishment of an independent administrative agency in 1915--the Federal Trade Commission (FTC). The act authorizes the FTC to act as a law enforcement arm of the federal government to protect the public consumer and businessman alike against anticompetitive behavior and unfair and deceptive business or trade practices. The basic objective of the FTC is the maintenance of a strongly competitive enterprise as the keystone of the American economic system. The FTC is given many duties by the U.S. Congress but the foundation of public policy underlying all these duties is essentially the same--to keep business or trade competition both free and fair. In addition to the Federal Trade Commission Act, the FTC also finds its primary expression in the Clayton Act. Both were passed in 1914 and successively amended in the years that have followed.

At present the FTC has authority and power over more than ten different federal statutes; this book is concerned only with the Federal Trade Commission Act (38 Stat. 717; 15 U.S.C. 41 to 51). Although the FTC also administers the Packaging and Labeling Act of 1966, it does not have specific authority over the packaging and labeling of foods and drugs.

To tell businessmen what they can and cannot do, the FTC issues "industry guides" (formerly called "trade practice rules") and "trade regulation rules" periodically. The agency supplements these issuances with "advisory opinions" that are given to corporations and individuals requesting them. To ensure that every interested party has an opportunity to participate, the proposal of any new rules, guides, or regulations is preceded by ample and widespread notice or announcement in the Federal Register. An interested party may comment on its provisions either in writing or at a public hearing. The publication of the final forms of these rules, and so on, is again accompanied by a wide publicity so that all parties concerned--consumers,businesses, and industries--are fully aware of their releases. These preventive measures have proved to be effective deterrents to unfair and deceptive practices occurring throughout an entire industry.

Recently, the guidance and prevention functions of the FTC are strengthened by legislation authorizing it to sue an entire industry for civil penalties and to obtain redress, including damages, for violation of a trade regulation rule.

In the case of violation by an individual or one specific corporation, the FTC issues complaints and entering orders to halt fraudulent selling or false advertising or to prevent a businessman or corporation from using unfair tactics against competitors. Depending on the specific cases, civil penalties and consumer redress can be brought against individuals who violate these orders.

The FTC has the widest authority over business or trade practices in the United States. It accomplishes three unique purposes: (1) guides and advises corporations and businessmen that are anxious to trade legally, (2) eliminates trade practices that violate the law, and (3) provides the consumers with a focal point at which complaints about trade may be registered.

An organization chart of the Commission is attached to Appendix 5-1. Each of the FTC's five commissioners is appointed for a term of 7 years by the president of the United States, with the advice and consent of the U.S. Senate. The chairman of the FTC is assisted by five offices of functions and served by an executive director who supervises various bureaus, one of which is the Bureau of Consumer Protection. This book is concerned mainly with this bureau.

The organization and general activities of the FTC are described in two simple brochures issued by the agency: (1) FTC, Orientation Manual, Office of the Secretary and (2) FTC, Your FTC: What It Is and What It Does. Although both are undated and unnumbered, they are revised periodically. Both publications may be obtained from the agency. Further, the FTC Annual Report and the latest issue of the Government Manual also serve as good reference sources. Much of the information discussed previously and immediately following has been derived from these published materials. However, comprehensive details contained in the Code of Federal Regulations is referred to later in this chapter. To obtain the name of an officer-in-charge of a specific office or division within the agency, one should request a copy of the latest FTC telephone directory, which usually contains both organizational and alphabetical listings.

With reference to the Bureau of Consumer Protection, its functions are to: (1) make rules and regulations for various trade practices, (2) investigate and litigate alleged deceptive or unfair trade practices, (3) advise and coordinate consumers, businessmen, and officials of the local, state, and federal governments, to foster understanding among them and to encourage compliance with trade rules and regulations voluntarily, and (4) educate the consumer to detect deceptive trade practices and to assist the FTC to correct them.

The Bureau of Consumer Protection is partitioned into five specialized divisions, each of which has specific responsibilities and all of which concern this book. The five divisions are: Compliance, Marketing Practices, National Advertising, Special Projects, and Special Statutes. These divisions carry out the bureau's many functions mainly through case-by-case enforcement and development of trade regulation rules. Although each division carries out specific responsibilities, their works are interrelated. No attempt is made here to discuss each division separately. Instead, relevant and specific details of the bureau's work, in conjunction with the overall duty of the FTC, are presented.

To maintain a fair and competitive business enterprise in this country, the

FTC, among other statutory provisions, depends heavily on four important sections of the Federal Trade Commission Act as amended. These four sections are cited as follows:

> Unfair methods of competition in commerce, and unfair or deceptive acts or practices in commerce, are hereby declared unlawful. [*Section 5(a)(1)*, Federal Trade Commission Act (38 Stat. 719; 15 U.S.C. 45)]

> To gather and compile information concerning, and to investigate from time to time the organization, business, conduct, practices, and management of any person, partnership, or corporation engaged in or whose business affects commerce. [*Section 6(a)*, Federal Trade Commission Act (38 Stat. 721; 15 U.S.C. 46)]

> From time to time to classify corporations and...to make rules and regulations for the purpose of carrying out the provisions of this Act. [*Section 6(g)*, Federal Trade Commission Act (38 Stat. 721; 15 U.S.C. 46)]:

> (a) It shall be unlawful for any person, partnership, or corporation to disseminate, or cause to be disseminated, any false advertisement:
>
>   (1) By United States mails, or in or having an effect upon commerce by any means, for the purpose of inducing, or which is likely to induce, directly or indirectly, the purchase of food, drugs, devices, or cosmetics; or
>   (2) By any means, for the purpose of inducing, or which is likely to induce, directly or indirectly, the purchase in or having an effect upon commerce of food, drugs, devices, or cosmetics.
>
> (b) The dissemination or the causing to be disseminated of any false advertisement within the provisions of subsection (a) of this section shall be an unfair or deceptive act or practice in or affecting commerce within the meaning of Section 5.
>
> [*Section 12*, Federal Trade Commission Act (52 Stat. 114; 15 U.S.C. 52)]

In regard to the Fair Packaging and Labeling Act (see Section 10 of the act or 80 Stat. 1301), the FTC is specifically excluded from having authority over the regulation of products such as drugs, devices, cosmetics, and food products, including alcoholic beverages, meat or meat product, poultry or poultry product, and all other food items.

Agreement with the Food and Drug Administration

As can be observed in the preceding discussion, the FTC protects the public from a variety of unfair business practices. This book is concerned mainly with its authority over the advertisement of food and food-related products. To do so, the FTC uses Sections 5, 6, and 12 of the Federal Trade Commission Act as amended frequently. However, it should be noted that this act, its amendments, and certain other federal statutes provide the FTC with no authority over the advertisement of alcoholic beverages and prescription drugs.

It seems clear that the Fair Packaging and Labeling Act and the Federal Trade Commission Act delineate the responsibilities of the FTC and the FDA separately. Thus the FDA monitors the labeling but not the advertisement of food and food products. However, even in advertising there is the possibility of concurrent jurisdiction because the FDA-administered Federal Food, Drug, and Cosmetic Act (discussed in Chapter 6 of this book) defines labeling as "all labels or other written, printed or graphic matter (1) upon any article or any of its containers or wrappers, or (2) accompanying such article" [21 U.S.C. 601(p)]. Such a definition can be interpreted to include advertisement. Because of possible overlaps, the two agencies have signed a Memorandum of Understanding (36 FR 18539, September 16, 1971). Some relevant sections of this agreement are described in the following. It is thus specifically agreed that:

1. The FTC has primary authority over the advertising (excluding labeling) of foods, drugs (excluding prescription drugs), devices, and cosmetics.
2. The FDA has primary jurisdiction over the advertising of prescription drugs and the labeling of foods, drugs, devices, and cosmetics.
3. Coordinated activities and actions by the two agencies will be conducted in cases where both agencies have a concern and the actions of one agency may affect the proceedings by the other. Such special cases include: (1) when both labeling and advertising contains similar claims and (2) when written, printed, or graphic material may be construed as either advertising or as accompanying labeling or both, depending on the circumstances of distribution.
4. If a consumer commodity does fall under the jurisdiction of both agencies, they will ensure that uniform regulations are promulgated.

Further details about the agreement may be obtained from the original document. However, it must be emphasized that this agreement of 1971 can be amended, revised, revoked, or terminated in accordance with established procedures. Therefore, it is advisable that an interested party ascertain the existence of the *latest* Memorandum of Understanding between the FDA and FTC.

Law Enforcement Functions

How do the FTC and its Bureau of Consumer Protection really enforce the intentions of the statutes administered by the agency? A simplified answer to this question is found in the Government Manual or other brochures mentioned previously. The following description is adapted from these resource materials.

The FTC's law enforcement work falls into two general categories: (1) actions to foster law observance voluntarily and (2) formal litigation leading to mandatory orders against offenders. These two processes are discussed in detail in the following paragraphs.

Voluntary Compliance

Voluntary and cooperative procedures are used extensively by the FTC to "prevent" the use of unfair and deceptive practices in commerce, as required by statutory directive. The FTC achieves this by relying on staff level advice and the issuance of advisory opinion, trade regulation rules, and industry guides. These procedures provide industry and business with certain measure of certainty and much authoritative guidance as to what they are legally permitted to practice in reference to the federal statutes administered by the FTC.

Staff level advice is of assistance in making decisions, but it is not binding on FTC. If circumstances permit, the FTC will provide an *advisory opinion* in regard to the likely action of the FTC in response to certain proposed course of activity by an industry or individual. Such opinions are binding on the FTC but, if it serves the public interest, it may reconsider and rescind the opinion. However, the FTC will not use any information submitted by a firm or an individual to institute a proceeding against the latter. It will most likely give the requesting party an opportunity to modify or discontinue the proposed activity that it has pursued because of the advice of the FTC.

Although the FTC has been given many federal statutes to administer, most of them contain broad terms and generalizations. Consequently, the U.S. Congress has also assigned the FTC specific but limited legislative authority to make rules and regulations [Section 6(g) of the Federal Trade Commission Act] to effectively "regulate" the complex and changing trade practices. Rulemaking is essentially the establishment of regulations that specify which particular practices are unlawful. With very few exceptions, trade regulation rules are used exclusively in the consumer protection field, and, hence, the Bureau of Consumer Protection assumes most of the responsibility in formulation of the rules. *Trade regulation rules* express the experience and judgment of the FTC as an entity, "based on facts of which its knowledge is derived from studies, reports, investigations, hearings, and other proceedings, or within official notice, concerning the substantive requirements of the statutes which it administers." These rules may be nationwide in effect and cover all applications of a particular statutory provision or may be limited to particular areas, industries, products, or geographic markets. Once effective, a rule has the force of law; a violation of a rule is considered to be a violation of the Federal Trade Commission Act. The FTC needs only to show that a firm is engaged in a practice forbidden by the rule to make a case. The following lists the basic steps in the normal rulemaking procedure as established by the Bureau of Consumer Protection within the FTC:

1. Complaints or inquiries from consumers, businessmen, members of Congress, or others direct FTC attention to a particular situation that has broad impact on an industry, group of industries, particular business, practice, or product.
2. Through the proper chain of authority, the appropriate staff within the Bureau of Consumer Protection is assigned to research the area and draft a rule for review.
3. If the staff recommendations warrant a rule, the FTC will, after review and approval by the regular chain of authority, issue the draft rule as a proposed rule.
4. The FTC issues the draft rule in the Federal Register and announces the date, usually 60 days later, for public hearings when all interested parties may comment and make recommendations.
5. The staff then collects all the comments and suggestions, rewrites a final rule, and submits a staff report to the proper FTC officer. The period between draft and final rule may vary from a few months to a few years. This is because the public hearings may be repeated many times.
6. The final rule is reviewed by the Bureau of Consumer Protection and the FTC as a whole before it is approved and published in the Federal Register, the entire project may be aborted even at the final stage, if it is the general consensus.
7. Once the rule is issued and finalized, affected firms are given a period of time to modify or eliminate their practices to conform with the new rule. The usual length of time is 90 days after the effective date.

Industry guides are intended to clarify legal approaches to such single industry concerns as cigarette advertising and the dog and cat food industry. Other guides may discuss illegalities such as deceptive pricing, bait advertising, and other violations of the law. Not only do the guides alert the industries involved, they also educate consumers and protect them from being victimized by improper sales practices.

To guide the public to conform to the legal requirements of the laws that it administers the FTC establishes industry guides that are actually administrative interpretations of the laws. Based on these guides, members of an industry may voluntarily abandon any unlawful practices. Of course, the FTC can and will pursue corrective actions under applicable statutory provisions in cases of noncompliance with the guides. Industry guides may be applicable to certain specific practices of a particular industry or to a practice common to many industries. In the past, a number of these industry guides have been promulgated and referred to as "trade practice rules," although these designations are no longer in use.

Industry guides may be initiated and promulgated by the FTC under two general circumstances:

1. Petition, or informal application filed with the FTC secretary by an interested party, whether an individual or a group.
2. The FTC's own initiative in view of possible benefit to the public interest when guidance as to the legal requirements applicable to particular business practices may serve to bring about more widespread and equitable observance of laws administered by the FTC.

To promulgate an industry guide, the FTC may conduct investigations, studies, conferences, or hearings as it deems appropriate. They are carried out in accordance with established procedures.

Industry guides do not relieve anyone of the necessity of complying with the legal requirements of other provisions of other existing federal statutes, especially the pure food laws, which are of major concern to this book. Industry guides are established by the FTC to eliminate unfair competitive and deceptive practices in the interest of the public and to assist in general law enforcement to this end.

Formal Litigation

To begin with, the FTC is usually initiated into investigating a case. The initiation may originate through complaint by a consumer or a competitor, the U.S. Congress, or from Federal, state, or municipal agencies. The complaint is usually in the form of a letter generally known as "applications for complaints" to distinguish them from formal complaints brought by the FTC that may initiate any investigation itself to determine possible violation of the laws administered by the FTC.

When a party submits an application for complaint, no formal procedure is required. The application should be in the form of a letter that should describe the facts of the case in detail, accompanied by whatever evidence the party may have in support of the charges made. Unless required by law, the FTC does not make known the identity of the party that applies for a complant. On receipt of a complaint, various criteria are applied in determining whether the particular matter should be docketed for investigation. The questioned trade practice must, of course, involve one or more of the following: public interest, violation of a law administered by the FTC, and anything affecting interstate or intrastate commerce. Within the limits of FTC resources, investigations are initiated which are considered to best support FTC goals of maintaining competition and protecting consumers. An investigation may start with correspondence from the FTC requiring the business concerned to file a special report, or with a request of a subpoena for information by the staff of a bureau or regional office of the FTC.

After a careful study of the materials gathered from an investigation, the FTC proceeds to make a decision. The decision may follow one of the following possibilities:

1. Dismissal of the case for lack of evidence or public interest.
2. Informal settlement of the case. This is the usual procedure when compliance does not seem to be a problem and the case is of minor importance to the public interest.
3. Notification of the company regarding a possible issuance of a formal complaint, suggesting the company or individual to sign a consent order under the FTC's consent order procedure.
4. Issuance of a formal complaint, accompanied by a cease and desist order.

If the FTC decides to issue a complaint, the company or individual is served with a notice of the FTC's intention and is furnished a copy of the intended complaint and proposed order. Prior to the hearings, the company and the FTC counsels may negotiate a cease and desist order to which the company agrees to consent. Many of the complaints issued by the FTC are settled by a consent order, in which the company or businessman signs a document stating that the challenged practices will be discontinued or corrected. Before the FTC finalizes the order, it studies the comments received from the public sector, which is given an opportunity to comment on the proposed order. Sometimes, a statement is included in the order to emphasize that the signed consent order is for settlement purposes only and does not constitute an admission of guilt or violation of the law by the company or individual. For noncompliance with the substance of the consent order, the FTC can bring a suit against the company or businessman for civil penalties that can run up to $10,000 a day for each violation of the order.

If an agreement containing a consent order is not entered into, the FTC thereafter issues its complaint and litigation usually ensues. An administrative law judge of the FTC tries the case using informal rules of court procedure. An FTC attorney acts as prosecutor, and the company or individual may be represented by an attorney. After taking testimony at public hearings, the judge issues an initial decision. Within a set period of time, the decision becomes a decision of the FTC unless the FTC places the case on its own review, the FTC stays the effective date of the decision, or the company or the FTC attorney appeals the decision to the five FTC commissioners.

When the FTC reviews the case or studies the appeal, it may sustain, modify, or dismiss the initial or original decision. If the case is modified or sustained, a cease and desist order is issued. Of course, any modification may involve the dismissal of some of the charges.

Under the Federal Trade Commission Act, the order to cease and desist or to take other corrective action such as affirmative disclosure, divestiture, or restitution usually becomes final 60 days after the date of service of the order on the respondent, unless within that period the latter appeals the decision to an appropriate U.S. Court of Appeals to review the order. Either side may ultimately appeal to the U.S. Supreme Court. In case of review, the order of the FTC becomes final after affirmance by the Court of Appeals or by the Supreme Court if taken to that court on *writ of certiorari*. If the case is finally decided against the company, it usually has 60 days to comply with the order.

If the losing company makes no appeal or its appeal fails and it still continues the practices in question, it is in violation of an order to cease and desist. This subjects the offender to a suit by the FTC, via the U.S. Justice Department, in a U.S. District Court to enforce its subpoenas and obtain preliminary injunctions to sue for civil penalties for recovery of up to $10,000/day per violation. If found guilty, the violator has to pay penalties for each day it continues the practice after the order has become final (i.e., 60 days after all appeals are settled and the case closed).

As cited previously, the FTC has specific authority to prohibit the advertisements of drugs, devices, cosmetics, and food intended for use in the prevention, treatment, and diagnosis of disease whenever it believes that the prohibition is in the public interest (also see Sections 14 and 15 of the Federal Trade Commission Act, 15 U.S.C. 54 and 55). Actually, the FTC can issue a preliminary injunction against the offending company or businessman in such cases. The injunction will remain in effect until a cease and desist order is issued and becomes final. Such an order will also be channeled through the detailed procedure described previously. Thus, the order may be dismissed by the FTC or set aside by the court on review or appeal, respectively.

In reference to drugs, devices, cosmetics, and food, the violation may be a misdemeanor if the false advertisement results in the use of an advertised commodity that is injurious to health or if there is intention to defraud or mislead. If convicted, this misdemeanor violation carries a penalty of 6 months of maximum imprisonment and/or $5,000 maximum fine. Succeeding convictions may result in 1 year maximum imprisonment and/or $10,000 maximum fine. The FTC has specific statutory authority to refer this type of case to the U.S. attorney general for the institution of appropriate court proceedings.

In making judgments, the FTC listens to and evaluates the validity of the legal arguments and other facts presented by its own staff and the company involved.

The FTC must establish priorities with reference to action against unfair and deceptive trade practices. Action simply cannot be brought against all offenders. Members of the public must report any known violations, reputable businessmen must voluntarily be aware of and obey trade rules and laws, and advertising media and agencies must maintain high ethical standards if all of us want to keep deception and anticompetitive practices under control.

Through systematic and continuous review, the FTC obtains and maintains compliance with its cease and desist orders. Once an order has been issued against a firm or an individual, the latter is required to submit reports to the FTC to substantiate their compliance. In the case of noncompliance and subsequent violation, the FTC may institute proceedings. Violation of an FTC order that has been affirmed by a decree of a U.S. Court of Appeal makes the respondent further subject to contempt proceedings.

FEDERAL REGULATIONS PROMULGATED

General Procedures, Nonadjudicative and Adjudicative Proceedings

The official source of much of the materials discussed so far is the Code of Federal Regulations. Chapter I of Title 16 of the Code is devoted almost entirely to the FTC. Table 5-1 shows the content of Chapter I, which is divided into six subchapters, each covering a number of parts. Some of these parts concern this book and the most relevant ones are grouped under Subchapter A (see Tables 5-1 and 5-2), that is, Parts 0 to 15. A brief discussion of some parts is presented in the following paragraphs.

Part 1 describes the general procedures whereby the promulgation of advisory opinions, industry guides, and trade regulation rules is achieved. It states the policy, procedure, advice, and public disclosures for advisory opinions, purpose, and method of promulgation for industry guides, and the initiation and procedure of trade regulation rules. Also, 16 CFR 17 provides more information on the application of industry guides (formerly called "trade practice rules") and various definitions and meanings of terms used.

Voluntary compliance by an industry or a corporation, as discussed earlier,

TABLE 5-1. Subchapter Titles and Part Numbers of Chapter I (FTC) of Title 16
of the Code of Federal Regulations

Subchapter	Title	Parts
A	Procedures and rules of practice	0 to 15
B	Guides and trade practice rules	17 to 254
C	Regulations under specific acts of U.S. Congress	300 to 303
D	Trade regulation rules	400 to 432
E	Rules, regulations, statement of general policy or interpretation and exemptions under the Fair Packaging and Labeling Act	500 to 503
F	Statements of general policy or interpretations under the Fair Credit Reporting Act	600

TABLE 5-2. Part Titles of Subchapter A (Procedures and Rules of Practice) of
Chapter I (FTC) of Title 16 of the Code of Federal Regulations

Part	Part title
0	Standards of conduct
1	General procedures
2	Nonadjudicative procedures
3	Rules of practice for adjudicative proceedings
4	Miscellaneous rules
13	Prohibited trade practices
14	Administrative interpretations, general policy statements, and enforcement policy statements
15	Administrative opinions and rulings

may involve signing a consent order. Part 2 (see Table 5-2), entitled "nonadjudicative procedures," provides details whereby such an agreement may be reached.
Thus if the FTC believes the public interest will be fully safeguarded, it may dis-
pose of a matter under investigation by accepting a promise that the questioned
practice will be discontinued. A number of factors are considered by the FTC in
the cases in which it accepts such a promise, including: (1) the nature and gravity
of the practice in question, (2) the prior record and good faith of the party, and (3)
other factors that may play a part in the assurance of voluntary compliance.

The nonadjudicative procedures described in 16 CFR 2 are divided into three
subparts. Subpart A is related to the investigation of a complaint and it provides

information such as how initiated, investigational policy, by whom conducted, subpoenas, hearings, rights of witnesses, deposition, orders requiring access, noncompliance, disposition, testimonial immunity, and other relevant information. The definition of voluntary compliance is explained in Subpart B. Of course, the details for entry or negotiation for a consent order procedure are explained fully in Subpart C, and a brief summary of this procedure has been presented earlier.

If a consent order is not entered, the FTC may proceed with the adjudicative procedures, the details of which are described in 17 CFR 3. Adjudicative proceedings are those formal proceedings conducted under one or more of the statutes administered by the FTC that are required by statute to be determined on the record after opportunity for an agency hearing. Thus after a company has failed to sign a consent order voluntarily , the FTC may issue and serve a formal complaint; after this, all parties involved shall follow the rules of practice for an adjudicative proceeding in accordance with established regulations. .

The adjudicative proceedings as described in 16 CFR 3 are divided into eight subparts, including the scope of rules and nature of adjudicative proceedings; pleadings; rehearing procedures, motions, interlocutory appeals, summary decisions; discovery and compulsory process; hearings; decisions; reports of compliance; and reopening of proceedings. A brief summary of an adjudicative proceeding has been described earlier and further legal details are not discussed. Interested parties should consult the original document.

The provisions contained in 16 CFR 1 to 3 were issued under the authority of Section 6, 38 Stat. 721; 15 U.S.C. 46, unless otherwise noted.

To illustrate the activities of the FTC, we must use concrete examples. The discussion provided thus far will be very difficult to understand without describing some case histories of "deceptive" advertisements with reference to the quality, safety, nutrition, and other related aspects of food and food products. Some selected examples are given in the remaining sections of this chapter.

In sum, the FTC can charge a company with violation of any of three kinds of legal provisions that it establishes, namely: (1) prohibited trade practices, (2) industry guides, and (3) trade regulation rules.

Prohibited Trade Practices and Affirmative Corrective Actions

In this highly complex, changing, and competitive world of business, unfair and deceptive trade practices, and especially false claims, can be many and varied. Not only will it be difficult to police their occurrences, but the task of making valid or "provable" charges can also be monumental. It is obvious that a single charge of unfair or deceptive business practice and/or false advertisement is too vague and general. To delineate specific charges against certain unfair trade practices, the FTC makes use of the authority inherent in Section 6(g) of the Federal Trade Commission Act to make rules and regulations by establishing a list of prohibited trade practices and certain acceptable remedies. They are contained in 16 CFR 13, and this part is entitled "Prohibited trade practices and affirmative corrective actions." The authority for the provisions of this part was issued under Sections 6(g), 5, 38 Stat. 722 and 719; Sections 2(a), (c), (d), and (e), 49 Stat. 1526 and 1527; and 15 U.S.C. 46, 45, and 13(a), (c), (d), and (e), unless otherwise noted. The 1977 edition of the Code describes more than 1000 such officially listed practices and actions. The FTC adds new ones as time progresses. The list may continue to increase, although occasionally some old ones may be deleted, especially when special industry guides or trade regulation rules are developed to take their places. Thus Part 13 contains 20 subparts, each of which includes a number of sections. Also, each section represents a prohibited trade practice or corrective action. Table 5-3 lists the subparts in the order they appear in the Code, and each subpart is given a chronological number. These numbers do not appear in the original documents; they are added by this author for convenience. The section(s) included under each subpart are also shown in Table 5-3.

Not all the prohibited practices and corrective actions listed in 16 CFR 13 are applicable to "deceptive" trade practices that are related to the safety, quality, nutritional values, and other factors of foods. Certain sections most relevant to this book are found in subparts 1, 2, 4, 8, 9 to 12, 18, and 19 of 16 CFR 13 and are presented on pp. 302 and 303. Note that each section has its own title and number.

Let us set up a hypothetical situation. Assume that a company trying to sell some vitamin tablets distributes some promotional pamphlets and advertises in television commercials about the products. The company "falsely" claims that the National Athletic Association endorses the products because they help a person to develop athletic ability and good physical fitness. The FTC charges that the company and its advertising firm have violated Section 13.330-60 (see Subpart 2). The FTC requests the firms to cease and desist from such a practice and make corrective action such as described in Section 13.533-20 (see Subpart 4). Of course, whether the companies will agree or not is another matter, and either voluntary compliance or formal litigation proceedings must be conducted in accordance with established regulations.

Because of various social, political, and legal changes, the number of complaints filed by the FTC against advertisements related to food qualities and so on have increased recently. But that does not mean that the number of signed consent orders will increase simultaneously. However, it is only fair to state that a food corporation prefers voluntary compliance to litigation whenever the accusation is justified.

Where can one locate information about a specific complaint, consent order, decision, or case history? If a case is recent, one may find practically all

Table 5-3. Subpart Titles and Section Numbers of 16 CFR 13 (Prohibited Trade Practices and Affirmative Corrective Actions)

a	Title of Subpart	Section(s) in Subpart
1	Advertising falsely or misleadingly	13.10 to 13.285
2	Claiming or using indorsements or testimonials falsely or misleadingly	13.330
3	Collecting, assembling, furnishing, or utilizing consumer reports	13.382
4	Corrective actions and/or requirements	13.533
5	Delaying or withholding corrections, adjustments, or action owed	13.675 to 13.677
6	Delivering short measure	13.680
7	Disparaging competitors and their products	13.895 to 13.1040
8	Furnishing means and instrumentalities of misrepresentation or deception	13.1055 to 13.1057
9	Misbranding or misleading	13.1170 to 13.1355
10	Misrepresenting oneself and goods	13.1365 to 13.1843
11	Neglecting, unfairly or deceptively, to make material disclosures	13.1845 to 13.1900
12	Offering unfair, improper and deceptive inducements to purchase or deal	13.1925 to 13.2090
13	Packaging or labeling of consumer commodities unfairly and/or deceptively	13.2100
14	Securing agents or representatives by misrepresentation	13.2117 to 13.2165
15	Securing orders by deception	13.2170
16	Simulating another or product thereof	13.2205 to 13.2245
17	Substituting product inferior to offer	13.2263
18	Using deceptive techniques in advertising	13.2275
19	Using misleading name	13.2280 to 13.2465
20	Using patents, rights, or privileges unlawfully	13.2485 to 13.2515

a These numbers do not appear in the original document; they are used here to indicate the order in which the subparts are presented.

1. Subpart: Advertising Falsely or Misleadingly

13.10	Advertising falsely or misleadingly	13.170-52	Medicinal, therapeutic, healthful, etc.
13.45	Content	13.170-64	Nutritive
13.73	Formal regulatory and statutory requirements	13.170-74	Reducing non-fattening, low-calories, etc.
13.85	Government approval, action, connection, or standards	13.175	Quality of product or service
		13.180	Quantity
13.85-30	Federal Trade Commission orders or indorsement	13.180-30	In stock
		13.190	Results
		13.195	Safety
13.85-60	Standards, specifications, or source	13.195-60	Product
		13.205	Scientific or other relevant facts
13.110	Indorsements, approval, and testimonials		
		13.210	Scientific tests
13.135	Nature of product or service	13.230	Size or weight
		13.255	Survey
13.170	Qualities or properties of product or service	13.280	Unique nature or Advantage
13.170-12	Auxiliary, improving, or supplementary		

2. Subpart: Claiming or Using Indorsements or Testimonials Falsely or Misleadingly

13.330	Claiming or using indorsements or testimonials falsely or misleadingly	13.330-45	Health authorities, hospitals, nursing profession, etc.
		13.330-60	National organizations
13.330-33	Doctors and medical profession	13.330-90	United States Government
		13.330-90(h)	Federal Trade Commission
13.330-36	Druggists of America	13.330-94	Users in general

4. Subpart: Corrective Actions and/or Requirements

13.533	Corrective actions and/ or requirements	13.533-45	Maintain records
		13.533-45(a)	Advertising substantiation
13.533-20	Disclosures	13.533-45(k)	Records, in general

8. Subpart: Furnishing Means and Instrumentalities of Misrepresentation or Deception

13.1055	Furnishing means and instrumentalities of misrepresentation or deception	13.1057	Packaging deceptively
		13.1057-40	Oversized containers

9. Subpart: Misbranding or Misleading

13.1170	Advertising and	13.1315	Safety
	promotion	13.1323	Size or weight
13.1200	Content		

10. Subpart: Misrepresenting Oneself and Goods

13.1575	Comparative data or	13.1710	Qualities or properties
	merits	13.1715	Quality
13.1590	Composition	13.1720	Quantity
13.1605	Content	13.1730	Results
13.1623	Formal regulatory and	13.1740	Scientific or other
	statutory requirements		relevant facts
13.1632	Government indorsement	13.1743	Size or weight
	or recommendation	13.1757	Surveys
13.1645	Government standards	13.1770	Unique nature or
	or specifications		advantages
13.1665	Indorsements	13.1775	Value
13.1685	Nature		

11. Subpart: Neglecting, Unfairly or Deceptively, to Make Material Disclosure

13.1845	Composition	13.1885	Qualities or properties
13.1850	Content	13.1886	Quality, grade, or type
13.1852	Formal regulatory and	13.1890	Safety
	statutory requirements	13.1895	Scientific or other
13.1870	Nature		relevant facts

12. Subpart: Offering Unfair, Improper, and Deceptive Inducements to Purchase or Deal

| 13.2063 | Scientific or other | 13.2075 | Television "mock ups," |
| | relevant facts | | etc. |

18. Subpart: Using Deceptive Techniques in Advertising

| 13.2275 | Using deceptive tech- | 13.2275-65 | Labeling depiction |
| | niques in advertising | 13.2275-70 | Television depictions |

19. Subpart: Using Misleading Name

| 13.2325 | Qualities or properties | 13.2335 | Results |

related materials in public record for inspection or copying at any FTC center or its headquarters by writing to the headquarters and requesting such records. However, if a specific case is old, one will probably have to request its record from the headquarters since all related materials may have been placed on an "inactive" file. If there is any formal litigation related to a case that is more than 2 or 3 years old, one may find the information in the Federal Trade Commission Decisions, a publication available in a law or document library. Of course, if a case does involve formal litigation, one can also obtain the legal proceedings from various legal publications obtainable in a law library. These methods of search assume one knows which company is involved, the approximate time of occurrence, and a general idea of what is involved.

The biggest problem arises when one does not have any specific case in mind but is interested in learning about the types of food company, product, advertisement, compliance, FTC decision and legal proceeding, and so forth that may have taken place or are involved. Quite often, the public record available at an FTC center does not arrange the materials by a specific subject index. Rather, the filing system usually uses the alphabetic listing of companies. This also applies to legal publications such as the Federal Reporter, Federal Supplement, Supreme Court Reporter, and others, most of which index the companies' names. Also, practically all finalized consent orders are published in the Federal Register. Again we have the same problem here; index to the Federal Register also lists names of companies only. This is not to mention the trouble and inconvenience one encounters in using the microfilms because past issues of the Federal Register are very cumbersome to keep. Thus the main obstacle is the number of companies involved in various types of unfair trade practices. It is difficult to discern the practice in question by a simple inspection of the campany's name.

In view of these facts, a careful search of the Federal Register has been conducted for the period 1971 to 1976. Most relevant cease and desist orders are summarized in Tables 5-4 to 5-9. Hopefully, such listing will provide a useful source of reference for any interested party, especially educators in nutrition, food science, and law. The materials may also be of assistance to attorneys and companies that deal with the Federal Trade Commission in food-related matters.

It should be stressed that most of the final orders described have been complied with voluntarily by the affected firms or individuals. However, if one is interested in any specific case history, one should use the information provided in the tables to obtain further details from an FTC center. This is especially important in situations where noncompliance or further litigation may have later taken place and no notice has been issued in the Federal Register.

TABLE 5-4. Cease and Desist Orders Announced in the Federal Register in 1971 by the FTC

Reference Source	FTC Date of Issue (Docket No.)	Corporation (Individual)	Examples of Violated Sections in 16 CFR 13	Substance of Order to Cease and Desist
36 FR 1047 (01/22/71)	12/08/70 (C-1833)	Carnation Co.	45, 170, 170-64, 1200, 2275, 2275-70	To cease making unwarranted nutritional claims in advertising its "Carnation Instant Breakfast"
36 FR 11282 (06/11/71)	04/21/71 (C-1904)	Borden, Inc.	175, 2275, 2275-70	To cease misrepresenting that depictions or demonstrations of its products such as "Kava Instant Coffee" are actual proof of quality of product
36 FR 17994 (09/08/71)	08/02/71 (C-1992)	Swift & Co. [a]	45, 170, 170-52, 1605, 1710	To cease misrepresenting that its baby food product is a "health food" because of its special nutritional or therapeutic value
36 FR 18521 and 18522 (09/16/71)	08/17/71 (C-2015)	ITT Continental Baking Co., Inc.; Ted Bates & Co.	170, 170-74, 255, 1757	To cease misrepresenting the nutritional value of its "Profile Bread" (e.g., weight-reduction result) and to make affirmative and corrective action
36 FR 19690 and 19691 (10/09/71)	08/27/71 (C-2020)	Mr. Beef Inc., (Donald Bevelheimer)	73, 230, 1623	To cease failing to disclose the weight loss from buying untrimmed meat

305

TABLE 5-4 (continued)

Reference Source	FTC Date of Issue (Docket No.)	Corporation (Individual)	Examples of Violated Sections in 16 CFR 13	Substance of Order to Cease and Desist
36 FR 19679 and 19680 (10/09/71)	09/02/71 (C-2023)	T-Ville Freezer Meats, Taftville Beef Co., Beef-land Beef Co. (Angelo Cofone)	73, 175, 230 1852	To cease misrepresenting meat grade, and meat loss from cutting, trimming, dressing, and shrinkage
36 FR 19683 and 19684 (10/09/71)	09/03/71 (C-2025)	General Sales Corp.; Farmers Quality Meats, Inc., (Raymond Barlow, Willard L. Gettle)	73, 175, 180, 180-30, 230	To cease failing to disclose ungraded meats as such and fat trim, bone, and shrink loss of its meat
36 FR 20588 (10/27/71)	09/09/71 [b] (C-2037)	J.B. Williams Co., Inc.; Parkson Advertising	170, 170-64, 170-74, 210, 2275, 2275-70, 2325	To cease misrepresenting that its products such as "Proslim" or "Proslim 7-Day Reducing" wafers and diet drink mix are effective in weight reduction
36 FR 20586 (10/27/71)	09/13/71 C-2038	General Foods Corp.; Benton & Bowles, Inc.	170, 170-64, 2275 2275-70	To cease misrepresenting that its product such as "Toast 'em Pop Ups" is a nutritionally sound substitute for a regular meal

| 36 FR 20591 and 20593 (10/27/71) | 09/21/71 (C-2045) | Natpac Inc.; Natpac of New Jersey, Inc.; Natpack of New York, Inc.; Natpac of Connecticut, Inc.; (and 10 other firms) | 175, 230, 1623, 1625, 1647, 1715, 1743, 1852 | To cease misrepresenting the grade of meat sold, and representing that a home economist will supervise customers' menus and that nonmeat foods are packaged by national firms |

[a] A New York advertising agency (McCann-Erickson, Inc.) was simultaneously charged with the same violations (see 36 FR 17991, September 8, 1971).

[b] A modification to this order was later issued (36 FR 23869, December 16, 1971).

TABLE 5-5. Cease and Desist Orders Announced in the Federal Register in 1972 by the FTC

Reference Source	FTC Date of Issue (Docket No.)	Corporation (Individual)	Examples of Violated Sections in 16 CFR 13	Substance of Order to Cease and Desist
37 FR 5366 and 5367 (03/15/72)	02/11/72 (8828)	G.R.I Corp.	170, 170-52	To cease misrepresenting the quality of its products, such as potency of vitamin pills
37 FR 6394 and 6395 (03/29/72)	02/14/72 (C-2148)	Procter & Gamble Co.	170, 170-64, 170-74, 2275, 2275-70	To cease misrepresenting that its product such as Crisco Oil is unique, has less calories, and results in less grease in fried foods
37 FR 10923 and 10924 (06/01/72)	05/04/72 (C-2211)	Cattlemens Quality Meat, Inc. (William David Evans); Glen Park Meats, Inc.	70, 73, 85, 175, 230, 1623, 1852, 1886	To cease misrepresenting the quality and quantity of meat and meat products
37 FR 16483 and 16484 (08/15/72)	06/23/72 (8840)	Ocean Spray Cranberries, Inc.; Ted Bates & Co., Inc.	135, 170, 170-64	To cease misrepresenting the composition and nutritive value of the beverage product Ocean Spray Cranberry Juice Cocktail and to take affirmative and corrective action
37 FR 21932 (10/17/72)	09/13/72 (C-2284)	Cumberland Packing Corp.	10, 170, 170-64, 280, 1710, 1770	To cease misrepresenting nutritional value of the product suggar, claiming that it is organically grown and has not been processed

37 FR 25495 (12/01/72)	11/01/72 (C-2309)	Sugar Information, Inc.; Sugar Associates, Inc. [a]	170, 170-74, 205, 280, 1710, 1740, 1770	To cease making false weight-reduction claims for its product refined sugar, and misrepresenting its nutritional value in weight-reduction dieting; and to make corrective advertisements
37 FR 28502 (12/27/72)	11/28/72 (C-2323)	Beatrice Foods Co.; I/Mac, Inc.	110, 175, 330, 1665, 1710	To cease misrepresenting the endorsements, qualities, and properties of its bakery and confectionery products

[a] A cease and desist order was simultaneously issued against the advertising company, Leo Burnett Company (see 37 FR 25494, December 1, 1972).

TABLE 5-6. Cease and Desist Orders Announced in the Federal Register in 1973 by the FTC

Reference Source	FTC Date of Issue (Docket No.)	Corporation (Individual)	Examples of Violated Sections in 16 CFR 13	Substance of Order to Cease and Desist
38 FR 971 and 972 (01/08/73)	12/07/72 (C-2329)	William Freihofer Baking Co., Inc.	135, 170, 170-74, 1575, 1590, 1605, 1710, 1740, 2275	To cease misrepresenting nutritional value of its bread
38 FR 10257 and 10258 (04/26/73)	03/15/73 (8880)	Seekonk Freezer Meats, Inc. (Lawrence Fontes)	10, 73, 85, 85-60, 175, 180, 230, 1623, 1645, 1715, 1720, 1886	To cease misrepresenting quantity and quality of any meat or other food products
38 FR 12333 and 12334 (05/11/73)	04/11/73 (C-2379)	MCP Foods, Inc.; The Mayne Agency, Inc. (Lawrence W. Pendleton)	10, 170, 170-64, 1710, 1845, 1885	To cease misrepresenting composition or nutrient value of its products such as imitation orange juice
38 FR 18366 (07/10/73)	05/29/73 (C-2406)	Thomas J. Lipton, Inc.; Knox Gelatine, Inc.	170, 170-52, 170-64, 205, 1710, 1740	To cease misrepresenting that its products such as Knox Gelatine Drink make a substantial contribution to general health or to nutritional needs
38 FR 21627 and 21628 (08/10/73)	07/13/73 (C-2424)	RJR Foods, Inc.; William Esty Company, Inc.	45, 135, 175, 1605, 1685, 1710, 1850, 1870, 1885, 2275, 2275-65	To cease misrepresenting natural fruit juice content of its fruit-flavored beverage products such as Hawaiian Punch

38 FR 29315 and 29316 (10/24/73)	09/25/73 (C-2459)	American Dairy Association; Leo Burnett Company, Inc.	10, 45, 170, 170-64, 170-74, 1605, 1710	To cease misrepresenting fat content and nutritional value of its milk and milk products
38 FR 30869 to 30871 (11/08/73)	10/02/73 (8887)	Amstar Corporation; Lewis & Gilman, Inc.; Dailey and Associates	10, 110, 135, 170, 170-52, 170-64, 205, 280, 330, 330-60, 1575, 1665, 1685, 1710, 1730, 1740, 1770	To cease misrepresenting endorsements and nutritional value of its products such as Domino sugar

TABLE 5-7. Cease and Desist Orders Announced in the Federal Register in 1974 by the FTC

Reference Source	FTC Date of Issue (Docket No.)	Corporation (Individual)	Examples of Violated Sections in 16 CFR 13	Substance of Order to Cease and Desist
39 FR 2081 to 2083 (01/17/74)	12/11/73 (C-2481)	Biochemic Research Foundation; Biochemical Research Foundation (Robert W. Reid and Allan A. Reid)	135, 170, 170-52, 205, 1575, 1685, 1690, 1710, 1740	To cease misrepresenting medicinal and therapeutic value of its products such as natural flake salt
39 FR 17759 (05/20/74)	03/20/74 (C-2496)	New Orleans Meats, Inc., doing business as Hutcheson Meats (Robert E. Brannan)	10, 73, 85, 85-60, 175, 180, 1623, 1715, 1720, 1743, 1852, 1886	To cease misrepresenting the quality and quantity of its meat and meat products
39 FR 14940 (04/29/74)	03/20/74 (C-2501)	Bi-Rite, Inc., trading and doing business as Bargain Barn	10	To cease advertising cheese, fowl, or fish as meat or meat products
39 FR 33506 and 33507 (09/18/74)	07/15/74 (C-2522)	Carnation Company; Erwin Wasey, Inc.	10, 135, 170, 170-64, 1575, 1685, 1710	To cease misrepresenting nutritional value of its products such as instant chocolate flavored nonfat dry milk

39 FR 35139 and 35140[a] (09/30/74)	07/23/74 (C-2524)	Wasem's, Inc., (Clifford W. Wasem and Weldon B. Wasem)	10, 85, 85-30, 135, 170, 170-12, 170-52, 205, 210, 330, 330-90(h), 1632, 1685, 1685-15, 1710, 1762, 2315	To cease misrepresenting medicinal and therapeutic value of its products such as vitamins and minerals
39 FR 41838 and 41839 (12/03/74)	09/20/74 (C-2547)	Nevada Meats, Inc. (Edgar S. Stacy)	10, 135, 180, 205, 1685, 1720, 1740	To cease misrepresenting quality and quantity of its meat and meat products

[a] A correction for printing error appeared in 39 FR 38097 (October 29, 1974).

313

TABLE 5-8. Cease and Desist Orders Announced in the Federal Register in 1975 by the FTC

Reference Source	FTC Date of Issue (Docket No.)	Corporation (Individual)	Examples of Violated Sections in 16 CFR 13	Substance of Order to Cease and Desist
40 FR 12775 and 12776 (03/21/75)	12/03/74 (C-2606)	General Foods Corp.	10, 45, 170, 170-52, 170-64, 195, 195-60, 205, 285, 533, 533-20, 1055, 1605, 1710, 1730, 1740, 1775, 1850, 1885, 1890, 1895, 2063	To cease misrepresenting nutritional needs of pets and contents of company's products such as dog food
40 FR 14303 and 14304 (03/31/75)	12/05/74 (C-2613)	Shaklee Corp.	10, 45, 170, 170-53, 170-64, 205, 533, 533-45, 533-45(a), 1605, 1710, 1740, 2063	To cease misrepresenting nutritional value of its products such as concentrated protein supplement
40 FR 40149 (09/02/75)	07/21/75 (C-2707)	Morton-Norwich Products, Inc.; Needham, Harper & Steers Advertising, Inc.	10, 205, 1740	To cease misrepresenting safety, medicinal, and therapeutic value of its products such as Morton Lite Salt
40 FR 40154 and 40155 (09/02/75)	07/21/75 (C-2708)	Lumberjack Meats, Inc. (Harold Abrams)	10, 45, 135, 170, 170-64, 205, 1575, 1605, 1710, 1740	To cease misrepresenting nutritional composition and general quality of its products such as meat and meat soy protein concentrate

314

40 FR 41756 and 41757[a] (09/09/75)	07/29/75 (C-2713)	Commerce Drug Company, Inc.; Del Laboratories, Inc.	10, 135, 170, 170-52, 205, 533-45, 533-45(k), 1710, 1730, 1740	To cease misrepresenting medicinal, therapeutic, and healthful value of its products such as vitamin and/or mineral products
40 FR 51419 and 51420[b] (11/05/75)	10/01/75 (C-2733)	General Foods Corporation	10, 170, 195, 205, 1740, 2063, 2275, 2275-70	To cease using depictions and descriptions in certain food-related advertisement capable of influencing children to engage in harmful activities

[a] A cease and desist order was simultaneously issued against the advertising company, Levine, Huntley & Schmidt, Inc. (see 40 FR 42202, September 11, 1975).

[b] A cease and desist order was later issued against the advertising company, Benton & Bowles, Inc. (see 41 FR 32120, August 3, 1976).

TABLE 5-9. Cease and Desist Orders Announced in the Federal Register in 1976 by the FTC

Reference Source	FTC Date of Issue (Docket No.)	Corporation (Individual)	Examples of Violated Sections in 16 CFR 13	Substance of Order to Cease and Desist
41 FR 14729 and 14730 (04/07/76)	03/01/76 (8979)	Vitamin Education Institute, Certified Research Foundation, Natural Vitamin Research Council, Marketing Group One (Herbert B. Pastor)	10, 110, 175, 190, 205, 330, 330-94, 533, 533-45, 533-45(a), 1665, 1685, 1715, 1730, 1740, 1870, 1886, 1895, 2063	To cease using deceptive weight loss claims regarding its products such as vitamin supplements and dietary regime to be used with supplements; using words implying professional or institutional connections as part of corporate or trade name; representing *Research Report* as bona fide medical or scientific research report
41 FR 31527 and 31528 (07/29/76)	07/06/76 (C-2827)	Richard Foods Corp. (Louis P. Richard)	10, 45, 110, 135, 170, 170-52, 170-64, 195, 195-60, 205, 330, 330-33, 533, 533-20, 1055, 1605, 1665, 1685, 1710, 1740, 1850, 1870, 1885, 1890, 1895, 2063	To cease misrepresenting nutritional and medicinal values and safety of its protein food supplements; to recall all advertised materials and add a warning label on its product
41 FR 34939 (08/18/76)	07/20/76 (8987-o)	National Commission on Egg Nutrition; Richard Weiner, Inc.	10, 170, 170-52, 205, 1710, 1740, 1885, 1895	To cease misrepresenting physiological effects of consuming dietary cholesterol or eggs and using a misleading trade name

316

| 41 FR 40458 and 40459 (09/20/76) | 08/18/76 (C-2834) | Nagle, Spillman & Bergman, Inc. | 10, 110, 135, 170, 170-52, 170-70, 190, 195, 195-60, 205, 330, 330-33, 330-45, 533, 533-20, 533-45, 1665, 1685, 1710, 1730, 1740, 1870, 1885, 1890, 1895, 2063 | To cease misrepresenting nutritional, medicinal, and therapeutic value of its products such as Adolph's Salt Substitute and safety of the product |

318 Federal Trade Commission

The following presents details of eight cease and desist orders published in the Federal Register that should be consulted if additional information is needed.

Swift & Co. (see Table 5-4). On August 2, 1971 the FTC issued a consent order involving Swift & Co., a major meat packing company with headquarters in Chicago, Illinois, which also marketed baby foods.

With reference to its baby food products such as Swift's Strained Meats, Junior Meats, Strained High Meat Dinners, and Junior High as Swift's Meats for Babies, the company was ordered to cease and desist from disseminating any advertisement claiming that any such product:

1. Was a "health food," with special and exclusive dietary qualities necessary to promote health. (However, the company would not be prohibited from claiming that any such product was a healthy food.)
2. Had a direct, substantial, and essential relationship with strong bones and teeth because of its B vitamin content.
3. Should contain adequate iron, when consumed in normal or average quantities, to meet a baby's minimum daily iron requirements, or to prevent anemia.
4. Should prevent germs and infections from entering the body, prevent colds, or possess qualities or ingredients that would be uniquely effective in promoting a baby's appetite or sleep.
5. Was as important as milk in the diets of babies.
6. Contained 100% meat even if water had been added.
7. After the addition of water, contained as much vitamins, minerals, and proteins as an equivalent quantity of product that was all meat.

Cattlemens Quality Meat, Inc., et al. (see Table 5-5). On May 4, 1972 the FTC issued a consent order involving two affiliated meat retailers of Oak Park, Illinois and Gary, Indiana. With reference to their meat and meat products, the companies were ordered to cease and desist from disseminating any advertisement that:

1. Would fail to disclose clearly and conspicuously:
    a. That beef sides, hindquarters, and other untrimmed pieces of meat offered for sale were sold subject to the average weight loss due to dressing, trimming, and cutting.
    b. That the price charged for such untrimmed meat was based on the hanging weight before dressing, trimming, and cutting.
    c. The average range of weight loss of such meat due to dressing, trimming, and cutting.
2. Would fail to include:
    a. The statement that "This meat has not been graded by the USDA" when

meat not graded by the USDA was advertised.

    b. The statement that "This meat is of a grade below U.S. Prime, U.S. Choice, and U.S. Good" when the advertised USDA graded meat was below the grade of "USDA Good."

    c. A statement indicating the portion that was ungraded and the percentage of such ungraded portions, by weight, of the total meat, if such ungraded meat was a portion of the total meat offered and advertised for sale.

3. Must not misrepresent in any manner:

    a. The amount of ground beef that would be contained in beef orders when the same were packaged and ready for home freezer storage.

    b. The amount, grade, quality, identity, or classification of meat that would be received by a purchaser.

Further, the company was prohibited from discouraging the purchase of, or disparaging in any manner, any meat or other food products it had advertised for sale so that the customers would purchase some other high-priced meat items.

RJR Foods, Inc. et al. (see Table 5-6). On July 19, 1973 the FTC issued a consent order involving RJR Foods, a New York City manufacturer, seller, and distributor of beverages designated Hawaiian Punch, and its New York City advertising agency, William Esty Company, Inc. The FTC defined the beverage in question as any fruit-flavored, noncarbonated beverage sold under the Hawaiian Punch trade mark as a frozen concentrate, liquid, liquid concentrate, powder, or other physical form, with or without natural fruit juice.

With reference to Hawaiian Punch, the company was ordered to cease and desist from disseminating certain prohibited advertisement for a period of one year and thereafter until it submitted to the Commission the results of a survey conforming in protocol, procedure, and results to Appendix A of this order. The survey was to gauge the need for continuing certain disclosures in the advertisements.

The prohibited advertisement included the use of words, depictions, photographs, or other representation of fruit or juice:

1. To indicate that the natural fruit content of the product was greater than its actual fruit juice content;

2. Unless (a) the total percentage of single strength fruit juice contained in a concentration at which the product was intended to be served was clearly disclosed, or (b) the product contained 100% single strength fruit juice in a concentration at which the product was intended to be served.

However, the use of the word"fruit" or name of a fruit(s) to describe the taste or flavor of the product was expressedly permitted by this order.

With reference to the disclosure of percentage of fruit juice, it would be, for compliance purposes, deemed clear and conspicuous in television advertising if:

1. It appeared at least once in each television commercial.
2. It was presented simultaneously in both the video and audio portions of the commercial.
3. The video portion
   a. Was of a sufficient size so that it could be easily read on all commercially available tube sizes, and
   b. Appeared on the screen for a sufficient period to permit it to be read by the viewer, but not for less than the audio portion.
4. Any other video or audio material accompanying the disclosure would be consistent with normal artistic and technical standards.

For the purpose of compliance, the advertising agency, William Esty Company, Inc., might rely in good faith upon information concerning the composition of any such product supplied by the manufacturer or processor provided that the agency was not aware that any claim for the product was false or negative.

Other requirements of the order pertained to specific disclosures on the labels of the products. The company would be in compliance with these disclosures if the latter should appear on labels placed into production within 60 days after service of this order. Such requirements are described below:

1. The company was prohibited from depicting fruit or juice on the label unless the percentage of fruit juice was disclosed in the same manner as in the advertisement.
2. However, the company could comply with this requirement by following the regulations or standards of labeling issued by the FDA (see Chapter 6).
3. To comply with the labeling requirements, the disclosures would be deemed clear and conspicuous if they
   a. Appeared on any appropriate information panel as that term was used by the FDA;
   b. Appeared in numbers of color or shade that readily contrasted with the background;
   c. Appeared in a type face of not less than 6 point on a 46-fluid ounce container, 4 point on a 12-fluid ounce container, and in proportional type sizes for other container sizes; and
   d. Appeared as part of any tabular, charted, or graphic presentation and the label showed a compositional comparison between "Hawaiian Punch" and any other product.

Due to space limitation, the Appendix A to the order is not included here. Consult the original document for details.

Wasem's, Inc., et al. (see Table 5-7). On July 23, 1974 the FTC issued a consent order involving Wasem's, Inc., a Clarkston, Washington, retail drug and general merchandise store. The company was ordered to cease and desist from representing in any manner that vitamin and/or mineral products, and its Super B Vitamins in particular:

1. Would make people feel better, make people better to live with, improve job performance, or build up blood and nerves.
2. Should be used for the treatment or relief of symptoms such as tiredness, nervousness, and run-down conditions without prior medical consultation.
3. Would aid in the betterment of human physical or mental condition.

unless the company could provide reasonably scientific basis for such claims, made available for public inspection at the point of sale.

With reference to Super B Vitamins, the company was ordered to cease and desist from representing in any manner that:

1. The products were scientifically tested and approved by acceptable standards to be the best or superlative in any respect unless such was the fact.
2. The FDA or any other federal, state, local, or private agency or source whatever had tested the particular products and found them to be worthy of recommendation on any basis.
3. The FTC or similar agency had accepted the company's claims that its particular products are satisfactory and agreed to publicizing the results of its investigation.
4. Most people did not receive enough vitamins or minerals through their normal diet and needed to supplement their diet with its particular products.
5. A highly concentrated dosage of vitamins or minerals was in some way beneficial or better than the "Recommended Daily Allowances" as established by the Food and Nutrition Board of the National Research Council, National Academy of Sciences.

The company was ordered to cease and desist from disseminating any advertisement, promotional or other materials, for a period of one year from the final effective date of this order, about its vitamin and/or mineral products unless the company should devote 25% or more of the expenditures (excluding production cost) for each medium in each market used to advertising, in a manner authorized by representatives of the Seattle Regional Office of the FTC that, contrary to prior advertising, Wasem's Super B Vitamins:

1. Did not have the previously claimed health benefits.
2. Had not been recommended or approved by any outside source.
3. Were not in any way necessary or helpful in larger than "recommended daily allowance" dosages.

The advertisements should also contain the statement that they are being run pursuant to an order of the FTC.

The company was also specifically ordered to place seven 60 second retractive advertisements on consecutive days with the same television stations at the same approximate time of day used for previous Wasem's Super B Vitamins advertisements. They should follow the same general format as previous television advertisements with Clifford Wasem making the following audio presentation:

> This advertisement is run pursuant to an order of the Federal Trade Commission. I have previously been advertising Wasem's Super B Vitamins and have made various claims which are erroneous and misleading. Contrary to what I have told you previously, Super B will not make you feel better nor make you better to live with nor work better on the job. There is no need for most people to supplement their diet with vitamins or minerals. Excess dosages over the recommended daily adult requirements of most vitamins will be flushed through the body and be of no benefit whatsoever. Contrary to my previous ads neither the FDA nor the FTC nor anyone else has recommended Super B or approved our prior claims. Super B Vitamins are sold on a money-back guarantee, so if you are not fully satisfied, then return them to me at Wasem's Rexall Drug Store in Clarkston for a refund.

Such advertisement should be run no later than 60 days after service of this order.

The company was also prohibited from representing in advertisement, labels, or packages that their vitamin and/or mineral products have "super potency" and from using the word "super" or any word of similar meaning as a part of the trade name of their products.

General Foods Corp. (see Table 5-8). On October 1, 1975 the Commission issued a consent order involving General Foods Corp., a White Plains, New York producer, distributor, and seller of food products.

The consent order as published in the Federal Register does not provide a background history of the original government complaint. The information is as follows. The company employed a prominent person to advertise for one of its food products, Grape Nuts. While promoting the product in a television commercial, the person pointed to a certain wild plant and indicated that it was edible, though the plant was not the advertised or promoted product. The Commission complained that unsuspecting individuals such as children might be influenced by such depiction and start eating wild plants without adult supervision. The company signed the consent order and the content of this order is described below.

In connection with the advertising and promotional sale of its food products, the company was ordered to cease and desist from presenting, through depictions or otherwise, that:

1. A plant was suitable for human consumption in its raw state by showing in the advertisement or promotional material a visual depiction of
   a. The plant in its growing state or natural surroundings when such a depiction was not a clear portrayal of conditions of domestic cultivation for human consumption.
   b. The consumption of a raw plant which was simultaneously described as wild in the advertisement.
   The plant depicted or described was not the advertised product or an ingredient of the advertised product.
2. Any given thing, other than items that were commonly recognized as foods or lawful food additives, was suitable for human consumption as a food where it was reasonably foreseeable through inquiry that such a representation had the tendency to influence certain members of the audience who were in reasonably good health to engage in behavior that might create an imminent risk of physical harm to them or to others.

The above description of the order defined specific prohibitions in an advertisement. It was worded in such a manner as to be applicable to all situations. However, a simplified summary of the consent order is described below.

The company was prohibited from using certain depictions and descriptions in an advertisement for its food products because such presentation might influence children viewers to engage in harmful activities. Specifically, the prohibited presentation included the visual impression that a certain plant not grown for human consumption was edible in the raw state or that a raw plant was shown being consumed and described at the same time as wild. The plant was not the advertised food product.

Richard Foods Corp. (see Table 5-9). On July 6, 1976 the Commission issued a consent order involving Richard Foods Corp., a Melrose Park, Illinois, manufacturer and seller of protein food supplements. The order contained four parts: definitions; prohibited representations; affirmative and corrective actions; and special requirement.

Definitions

1. Fearn Natural Soya Powder referred to the product marketed by the company and any other protein supplement for infant use.
2. A "protein supplement for infant use" was any protein food product marketed for infant use as a protein dietary supplement.

Prohibited representations

With reference to Fearn Natural Soya Powder, the company was ordered to cease and desist from representing in any manner that:

1. Its baby formula for soya milk or any other substantially similar formula for the preparation of soya milk was an adequate nutritional replacement for human or cow's milk for the feeding of infants under one year of age.
2. Soya milk was nutritionally adequate in protein content and availability to support normal cell and body growth in infants under one year of age.
3. Soya milk was nutritionally adequate in calorie, vitamin, and mineral (such as calcium and iodine) contents to support normal growth and development in infants under one year of age.
4. The calcium content of soya milk was well assimilated in infants under one year of age for normal growth of bones, teeth, and muscular tissue.
5. Running noses, stomach ache, gas and diarrhea in infants under one year of age were symptoms confined to food allergies.
6. Food allergies in infants under one year of age might be safely determined by self-diagnosis without the need for any medical consultation.
7. Attacks of food allergies in infants under one year of age might be adequately treated without medical authorization by adding soya powder to their diets.
8. Infants under one year of age were normally allergic to vitamins contained in natural foods.
9. Infants under one year of age could normally ingest enough soya milk to satisfy daily energy requirements and maintain sufficient nutrition for adequate growth and development.
10. Infants under one year of age might subsist on soy milk without other nutritional supplements for a significant period of time without suffering any nutritional risk to health, growth, or development.
11. Soya milk was approved by medical authorities as being nutritionally adequate for consumption by infants under one year of age.

12. Fearn Soya Powder should be added to the diets of infants under one year of age in the absence of medical authorization.

Affirmative and corrective actions

1. The company was ordered to disclose the following warning clearly and conspicuously on the label of Fearn Natural Soya Powder and any other protein supplement for infant use to be marketed by the company.

    NOTICE: Not for use in diets of infants under one year of age unless recommended by a physician

    The smallest letter of the notice should be no smaller than one-sixteenth of an inch and the NOTICE should not be obscured by background contrast, designs or vignettes, or crowding with other written, printed, or graphic matter.
2. The company was ordered to disclose a specific warning in its advertisement or promotional material (excluding labels) for its product for a period of two years after the effective date of the order. The products include Fearn Natural Soya Powder or any other protein supplement for infant use to be marketed by the company.

    NOTICE: Not for use in diets of infants under one year of age unless recommended by a physician

    The notice must be clear and conspicuous, in print of a size and type no less prominent than the majority of the text of the document in which it was required to be stated. Certain advertisements or promotional materials (excluding labels) were exempted from carrying the above warning notice. They included those that:
    a. limited their contents to the name and price of the product and a general description of the product of no more than one sentence or phrase.
    b. limited their contents to no more than four sentences of description relating to the product and not directing to infants or young children as users of the product. Instead, the notice of warning should be: Use as directed by label.
3. The company was ordered to take all necessary actions to retrieve all known copies of promotional leaflets advertising their soya milk infant formula from distributors and retail store customers.

Special Requirement

1. The company would not be held responsible if their distributors or franchisees violated any requirement of the order unless it had actual knowledge of the violation and failed to take corrective action within a reasonable period of time, such as terminating the act.
2. However, the company would be held responsible for the violation if it had actual knowledge that a violation had occurred more than once and had failed to take any corrective action within a reasonable period of time. Also, any repeated violation must have occurred after the company had taken appropriate action to correct a previous violation.

National Commission on Egg Nutrition et al. (see Table 5-9). On July 20, 1976, the Commission issued a final cease and desist order against the National Commission on Egg Nutrition, a Park Ridge, Illinois, egg industry trade association, and a New York City public relations firm, Richard Weiner, Inc. With reference to its claim about egg nutrition, the trade association was ordered to cease and desist from disseminating any advertisement which represented that:

1. There was no scientific evidence that eating eggs could increase the risk of heart attacks, heart disease, atherosclerosis, arteriosclerosis, or any attendant condition.
2. There was scientific evidence that dietary cholesterol including that in eggs could decrease the risk of heart attacks, heart disease, atherosclerosis, arteriosclerosis, or any attendant condition.
3. There was scientific evidence that avoiding dietary cholesterol, including that in eggs, could increase the risk of heart attacks, heart disease, atherosclerosis, arteriosclerosis, or any attendant condition.
4. Eating eggs could not increase the blood cholesterol level in a normal person.
5. Dietary cholesterol intake could not raise or lower blood cholesterol level.
6. The human body could increase its manufacture of cholesterol in an amount equal to a decrease in dietary cholesterol intake.
7. The average human body could eliminate the same amount of cholesterol as that eaten.
8. The body required dietary cholesterol including that in eggs to build sex hormones, for transmitting nerve impulses and for maintaining life in cells.

With reference to its claim on egg nutrition, the trade association was specifically prohibited from:

1. Utilizing the name "National Commission on Egg Nutrition" unless it disclosed

clearly in close proximity that such a name was composed of egg producers and other individuals and organizations of the egg industry.

2. Misrepresenting in any manner the physiological effects of consuming dietary cholesterol or eggs.

At the time of current writing, the trade association is appealing its case in a United States Court of Appeal. Therefore, an interested party should consult regular legal literature for any future development.

Hudson Pharmaceutical Corp. On January 13, 1977 the FTC issued (Docket No. C-2860) a consent order (42 FR 12041 and 12042, March 2, 1977) involving Hudson Pharmaceutical Corp., a Borough of West Caldwell, N.Y., manufacturer and distributor of children's vitamin supplements. The company was required, among other things, to cease disseminating any advertisements related to vitamin supplements or preparations designed primarily for use by children where such advertisements are directed to children. Some aspects of the cease and desist order are discussed in the following.

The term "children" includes persons under 12 years of age. The term "advertisement directed to children" is defined as follows:

1. Any advertisement with a dominant appeal to a child audience and disseminated by broadcast over any television network or station and appearing in any print media.
2. Any television advertisement with more than 50% of the audience composed of children and appearing on the program itself or in a spot announcement during the program break.
3. Any advertisement broadcasted over any television network or station from 6 a.m. to 9:05 p.m. local time.
4. Any television advertisement that uses a hero figure, including but not limited to "Spider-Man," which has a special appeal for children, and which endorses or appears in conjunction with the product. This provision will not apply if a depiction of the product's container or package on which a hero figure appears is limited to less than one-third of the size of the screen.
5. Any advertisement that appears in a comic book where the printed matter is directed primarily to children.
6. Any advertisement that appears in print media where 50% or more of the trim area or a page of the advertisement consists of the depiction of a hero figure which has a special appeal for children, including but not limited to "Spider-Man."
7. Any advertisement:
   a. that states that it is addressed to children, or

b. that is sent through the mail and addressed to children, or whose addresses
include the names of children, or whose content is not sealed within an
envelope.

INDUSTRY GUIDES FOR THE DOG AND CAT FOOD INDUSTRY

The prohibited trade practices discussed in the preceding section are effective in
handling many of the unfair practices perpetuated by certain individuals and corporations. However, the FTC also employs industry guides as voluntary/mandatory
enforcement tools. These guides may be focused on a practice common to many
industries or specific practices of a particular industry. (Refer to the earlier discussion on this topic.) Once a guide has been established, it guides the public in conducting its affairs in conformity with legal requirements. In Title 16 of the Code of
Federal Regulations, Parts 1 and 17 (see Tables 5-1 and 5-2) provide certain legal
definition and explanation for an industry guide. Suffice it to say that an industry
guide provides the basis for voluntary and simultaneous abandonment of unlawful
practices by members of an industry. Failure to comply with the guides may result
in corrective action by the FTC under applicable statutory provisions. For a
number of years since the 1940s, trade practice rules (an old term for industry
guides) have been established for the frozen food industry, kosher food products
and kosher products industry, preserve manufacturing industry, macaroni and
noodle products industry, tomato paste manufacturing industry, oleomargarine
manufacturing industry, wine industry, sardine industry, tuna industry, ripe olive
industry, yeast industry, candy manufacturing industry, and cocoa and chocolate
industry. These guides or trade practice rules have been concerned with the quality,
quantity, grades, standards, safety, nutrition, or other related aspects of the food
products of these industries. However, since 1975 the FTC has been issuing
proposals regarding the rescissions of these rules or guides because of legal and
technological changes. Such proposals are referred to in 40 FR 20147 and 20148
(May 15, 1975), 41 FR 2382 and 2383 (January 16, 1976), 41 FR 2398 and 2399
(January 16, 1976), and 42 FR 12171 (March 3, 1977). Most likely, these out-of-
date guides are expected to be eliminated. The references in the Federal Register
will show that some of them have been withdrawn and encountered no public or
industry opposition. As a result, this book does not discuss them. However, there is
one relevant industry guide that has been established quite recently and is actively
enforced by the FTC, the Guides for the Dog and Cat Food Industry, described in
16 CFR 241. There are 17 sections in this part, and each section is considered as
one guide. The provisions of Part 241 were issued under the authority of 38 Stat.
717, as amended; 15 U.S.C. 41 to 58, unless otherwise noted. The guides were officially finalized and issued on February 28, 1969 (34 FR 3619).

Federal statute defines food as articles for both human and animal consumption (see Chapter 6). In this country, dog and cat foods are categorized as a multimillion dollar business. To protect the consumer, there must be effective guides that will govern those unfair or deceptive business practices and competition in the pet food industries. At the same time, these guides must be of assistance to the consumers who are exposed to various kinds of advertising and promotional materials even when pet food is considered.

Space limitation does not permit detail analysis or description of each section or guide in 16 CFR 241. In the following, the title of each section is given, and one or two examples of the type of information contained in the section or guide is described. Further details may be obtained from the original document.

Guide 1: Definitions. A food for dogs or cats includes all types of canned, frozen, semimoist, dry, and other commercial items marketed specifically for the pets. Animal medicine or remedy is not considered a dog or cat food.

Guide 2: Misuse of Terms. The names of ingredients should not be used in advertising, labeling, and so on so as to misrepresent the identity of an ingredient or the composition of an industry product.

Guide 3: Misrepresentation in General. There should be no dissemination of any advertisement or promotional materials that may deceive the prospective customers with reference to the substance, composition, identity, content, quantity, appearance, consistency, shape, form, flavor, color, cost, origin, grade, value, quality, suitability, nutritional properties, manner of processing, methods of manufacture, or novelty of a product or ingredient.

Guide 4: Misrepresenting Composition, Form, Suitability, or Quality in Labeling. The label for pet food should contain sufficient information to enable the customer to determine the nature and composition of the product and the purpose for which it is suitable; thus the product may be a supplemental food or a special food for puppies or other animals.

The name of a particular ingredient should not be so conspicuous as to mislead the customer into believing that there is greater portion of such ingredient in the product than there is in fact.

Guide 5: Misrepresenting Composition, Form, Suitability, or Quality in Advertising. A product should not be described in advertising as "all meat" or "100 percent meat," or "all tuna," or "all chicken," if it contains other ingredients such as the byproducts of meat, poultry, or fish.

A product should not be described as fortified with fresh eggs if the product in fact contains no fresh eggs or an inappreciable amount or only dried or powdered eggs or egg yolks or whites.

Guide 6: Misrepresentation of Color in Advertising. Do not misrepresent in advertising the actual color of a product; thus do not represent that the color of a product is natural when such color has been formed by artificial means. Do not represent that a product does not contain an artificial coloring ingredient unless this is true.

Guide 7: Misrepresentation of Flavor in Advertising. Do not represent in advertising that a product has a particular flavor unless the product has that flavor.

Guide 8: Diet and Nutrient Misrepresentation. Do not represent in any manner that a product meets the requisites of a complete or balanced ration for dogs or cats unless this is true.

Do not represent in any manner that any listing of nutrients is equal to or exceeds the amounts recommended by a recognized authority on animal nutrition, such as the Committee on Animal Nutrition of the National Academy of Sciences, unless such listing utilizes the same units of measure and lists in equal or excess amounts all of the essential nutrients contained in the most recent nutrient list of that authority.

Guide 9: Misrepresentation of Medicinal and Therapeutic Benefits. Do not represent in any manner that a product or its ingredients will provide any therapeutic benefit, prevent and cure any disease, or in any way improve the health or condition of the animal when such is not the case.

Guide 10: Human Food Representation. Do not represent in any manner that a product is fit for human consumption or made under the same sanitary conditions as food for humans.

Guide 11: Misrepresentation of Processing Methods. Do not misrepresent in any manner the methods used in the manufacturing or processing of a product. For example, do not represent that a product has been broiled, braised, baked, or otherwise cooked, preserved, or processed in a specific manner unless such is the case.

Guide 12: Defamation of Competitors or False Disparagement of Their Products. Do not falsely disparage the quality, grade, composition, or other characteristic about the competitor's product(s).

Guide 13: Misrepresentation of the Character and Size of Business, Extent of

Testing, and so on. Do not misrepresent in any manner that one owns or operates a laboratory, breeding or experimental kennel, or that one's products have been tested in any particular manner, for any period of time, or with any particular results.

Guide 14: Deceptive Endorsements, Testimonials, and Awards. Do not represent by endorsement, testimonial, or other means that a product or an ingredient has been inspected by the U.S. Government or any governmental agency and that it has passed that inspection unless such is the case.

Guide 15: Bait Advertising. Do not offer for sale any product when the offer is not a bona fide effort to sell the product so offered as advertised and at the advertised price.

Guide 16: Guarantees and Warranties. Do not represent in any manner that a product is guaranteed without clear and conspicuous disclosure of the nature and extent of the guarantee.

Guide 17: Deceptive Pricing. Do not represent in any manner that a product may be purchased for a specified price or at a saving when such is not the fact.

TRADE REGULATION RULES

The trade regulation rules promulgated by the FTC are described in Subchapter D of chapter I of Title 16 of the Code of Federal Regulations. They are included in Parts 400 to 435, some of which are reserved and do not carry any rules. The 1977 edition of the code indicates that there are 24 such rules promulgated by the FTC. None of them is specifically concerned with the quality, grades, standards, nutrition, safety, and related aspects of any food products. However, the FTC has been working diligently since 1974 to add new parts that will promulgate trade regulation rules relevant to food quality, nutrition, and so on. Three such proposed new parts include "food advertising," "labeling and advertising of protein supplements," and "children's advertising." Although they have not yet been finalized at the present time of writing, they are briefly presented in the following sections.

Food Advertising

In 1974 the FTC proposed the issuance of a new trade regulation rule to establish a new 16 CFR 437. The new part will be titled "Food advertising." According to established regulations and procedures, such a proposal must be open to public hearing and analysis. At this time, the proposal is still in the "hearing" and "comment" stage. However, to learn about the content of this proposed rule, public comments, FTC position, and so forth, one should consult the following: 39 FR 39842 to 39862 (November 11, 1974), 40 FR 23086 to 23091 (May 28, 1975), 41 FR 8980 to 8984 (March 2, 1976), and 43 FR 11834 (March 22, 1978). The proposal has generated much controversy, and it is generally expected that it will be a long time before a final decision on its acceptance can be reached. Favorable and adverse comments have been expressed by both food industries and consumer groups. Irrespective of the final legal status of 16 CFR 437, the following provides a brief description of this proposed rule.

The proposed Part 437 is divided into two aspects: general and voluntary claims. Under "general" there are two sections: definitions and form, content, and method of making disclosures. Under "voluntary claims," there are seven sections: emphatic nutrition claims; nutrient comparison claims; nourishment claims; natural and organic food claims; claims for foods intended for combination with other foods; energy and calorie claims; fat, fatty acid, and cholesterol content claims, and health-related claims. Because of legal uncertainty and space limitation, only sample information contained in some sections are discussed. For further details, refer to the references cited.

Definitions.   The proposed rule provides definitions for: advertisement, food, nutrients, United States Recommended Daily Allowances (USRDA), serving, portion, "clearly and conspicuously disclose," representation, and Protein Efficiency Ratio (PER).

Form, Content, and Method of Making Disclosures.   The proposed rule states that any reference to nutrient(s) in advertisement will trigger certain required information to be disclosed and prescribes the form and style of presentation of this information. To explain how this is to be accomplished, the proposed rule discusses: nutrients, protein, analytical methods, calories, serving or portion, identification and designation of foods, television advertisements--method and form of disclosures. Some of the information prescribed is presented in the paragraphs that follow.

When a claim mentions a nutrient of an advertised product, it is assumed to imply that the nutrient is present at a level of 10% or more of the USRDA. If this is not the case, the claim is misleading.

Representations in advertising of the presence of protein may be made only if a serving of the advertised food contains protein at a level of 10% or more of the USRDA and the total protein in the advertised food alone has a protein efficiency ratio of 20% or more of that for casein.

The energy content of a food shall be stated in calorie per serving, expressed to the nearest 2 calorie increment up to and including 20 calories, to the nearest 5 calorie increment above 20 calories and up to and including 50 calories, and to the nearest 10 calorie increment above 50 calories.

To ensure that the required disclosures are comprehensive and visible, the proposal prescribes specific methods of disclosure for specific types of advertising medium, namely, television and print media.

With reference to television advertising, any required disclosure should be made in the same portion (audio or video) of the advertisement in which the voluntary claim is made. The disclosure is also required to be in immediate conjunction with the claim. Video disclosure shall be easily and completely read and/or seen in all commercially available television sets.

With reference to print advertisements, the proposal prescribes details on type-size requirements. If the printing does not meet such requirements, it is a violation of the rule. The use of condensed type is prohibited. Also, the type shall be set on a slug at least one point larger than the point size of the type (not solid), using only normal word and letter spacing.

Emphatic Nutrition Claims. To use a descriptive adjective such as "good" or "excellent" in reference to an advertised food as a source of a particular nutrient, the food must contain at least 35% of the USRDA for that nutrient.

Nutrient Comparison Claims. Representations in advertising that make a comparative claim for the amount of any nutrient contained in an advertised food are not permitted unless a number of conditions are satisfied. For example, one condition is that the comparison is made with an equalized serving of a commercially available food.

Nourishment Claims. An advertisement shall not represent a food to be "nourishing," "wholesome," or "nutritious" or use any other terms of similar import that suggest that such food is a valuable or significant source of nutrition, unless a serving of the food contains at least four nutrients, including protein, each of which is present in an amount of at least 10% of the USRDA per 100 calories and unless at least one of such nutrients is present in a serving of such food in an amount of at least 10% of the USRDA.

Claims for Foods Intended for Combination with Other Foods. If an advertised food is frequently, but not necessarily, combined with any other food(s) or ingredient(s) for consumption, any representation regarding nutrition shall be based on the nutritional value of the advertised food alone (e.g., breakfast cereal and milk).

Energy and Calorie Claims.   An advertisement shall not represent that a food or nutrient is a source of "energy" or "food energy" unless it discloses clearly in immediate conjunction with the claim that "energy" or "food energy" is supplied by calories. The advertisement must also state the number of calories contained in a specified serving of the advertised food.

An advertisement shall not claim that consumption of a food or nutrient by itself will produce or provide health, general vigor, sustained energy, or alertness or that the energy from calories by itself will produce or provide strength, endurance, intellectual performance, or the prevention or relief of fatigue.

Advertising and Labeling of Protein Supplements

A publication titled "Health hazards and marketing deceptions: A staff report to the federal trade commission" was issued by the FTC on August 8, 1975. Partly based on this report, the FTC in late 1975 proposed a new 16 CFR 454, to be titled "Advertising and labeling of protein supplements." Since this proposal must be discussed by the public under established procedures, it will be some time before a final decision can be reached. However, information about this proposed rule and its related public comments may be found in 40 FR 41144 to 41148 (September 5, 1975), 41 FR 10232 and 10233 (March 10, 1976), and 41 FR 22593 to 22595 (June 4, 1976); 43 FR 33258 (July 31, 1978). At this time the proposal is in the "comment" stage, and a brief description of its contents is as follows.

The proposal is composed of three subparts containing 18 sections. Subpart I, titled "General," contains the following sections: definitions; methods of calculation; form, content, and method of making disclosures; inconsistent or derogating representations; and interpretation and conformity with related regulations. Subpart II, titled "Affirmative Disclosures," contains the following sections: protein content disclosure; health hazard disclosures; and protein need disclosure. Subpart III, titled "Voluntary Claims," contains the following sections: use of protein supplements by infants or young children; quick energy presentations; energy and calorie representations; athletic or activity representations; aging, senility, or therapeutic representations; weight reduction representations; emphatic nutrition representation; protein comparison representations; and protein need representations.

In view of the uncertainty about the legal status of this proposal, this book does not discuss this rule in detail. However, some interesting points are mentioned.

What will the proposed rule do? In connection with the "protein need" disclosure, the United States Public Health Service has determined that the daily diet of most Americans contains adequate protein and that protein supplements are hence unnecessary for most Americans. Further, the disclosure must also indicate that protein in excess of the body's daily needs may contribute calories that can cause weight gain and that weight reduction can occur only if the body uses more calories than it ingests from all sources, including protein.

The "health hazards" disclosure refers to those associated with improper use of concentrated protein supplements by infants, young children, and persons with liver or kidney disorders.

With reference to the "content" disclosure, the amount or percentage of protein in the supplement, the product's protein source, and the quality of the protein must be stated.

What are some deceptive and unfair nutritional and other health claims? The proposed rule prohibits such misrepresentations as the following:

1. That protein supplements are sources of "quick energy."
2. That protein will reduce weight or that by itself protein will produce general good health, vigor, sustained energy, or alertness.
3. That protein supplements can improve athletic performance, act as an antidote to the effects of aging or prevent or cure diseases or minor ailments.
4. That protein supplements are more economical sources of protein than are some ordinary protein-rich foods such as steak or eggs, without the concurrent disclosure of inferiority of these supplements in terms of overall nutritional value.
5. Deceptive comparisions of protein supplements and ordinary protein-rich foods with regard to the concentration of protein in the compared foods.
6. That protein deficiency can be effectively and economically met by the consumption of protein supplements.

Children's Advertising

After releasing the study, "Staff Report on Televised Advertising to Children," the FTC announced on April 27, 1978 (43 FR 17967 to 17972) that it was proposing a new 16 CFR 461, titled "Children's advertising." The FTC invited comment on the advisability and manner of implementation of a trade regulation rule which would include the following three elements:

1. Ban all televised advertising for any product which is directed to, or seen by, audiences composed of a significant proportion of children who are too young to understand the selling purpose of or otherwise comprehend or evaluate the advertising.
2. Ban televised advertising for sugared food products directed to, or seen by, audiences composed of a significant proportion of older children, the con-

sumption of which products poses the most serious dental health risks.

3. Require televised advertising for sugared food products not included in "2" above, which is directed to, or seen by, audiences composed of a significant proportion of older children, to be balanced by nutritional and/or health disclosures funded by advertisers.

In addition, the FTC solicits comments on the appropriateness and workability of the following alternative remedial approaches and welcomes other possible alternatives:

1. Affirmative disclosures located in the body of advertisements for highly cariogenic products directed to children.
2. Affirmative disclosures and nutritional information contained in separate advertisements, funded by advertisers of highly cariogenic products advertised to children.
3. Limitations upon particular advertising messages and/or techniques used to advertise to very young children, or to advertise highly cariogenic products to all children.
4. Limitations upon the number and frequency of advertisements directed at very young children; limitations upon the number and frequency of all advertisements of highly cariogenic products directed at all children.

Consult the original documents for further details.

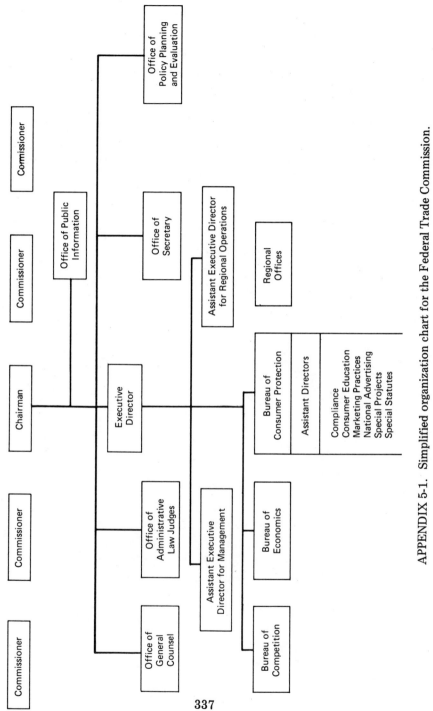

APPENDIX 5-1. Simplified organization chart for the Federal Trade Commission.

337

CHAPTER 6

DEPARTMENT OF HEALTH, EDUCATION AND WELFARE
Food and Drug Administration

INTRODUCTION

The FDA is one of the many agencies within the Department of Health, Education, and Welfare. Appendix 6-1 shows a simplified organization chart of this department.

The FDA is the federal government's primary consumer protection agency in regard to food and drugs. It acts under laws passed by the U.S. Congress, most of the provisions of which also apply to imported products. The U.S. Bureau of Customs works closely with the FDA to ensure that all requirements are met by foreign products. This chapter focuses on the food aspect.

The FDA performs numerous activities; some examples are as follows:

1. It makes periodic inspections of food establishments and examines samples of their products for adulteration or misbranding.
2. It establishes standards of identity, quality, and fill of containers for food products.
3. It develops and enforces regulations for proper food labeling.
4. It assists the food industry in voluntary compliance with the law and issues regulations designed to prevent violations.
5. It makes decisions on the safety of food additives and regulates the conditions of their usage.
6. It determines the safety of food colors and tests batches of those subject to certification.
7. It enforces safe limits on the amount of pesticide residues that may remain on food crops, if any.
8. It regulates drugs and feeds that are for human food-producing animals.
9. It enforces sanitation and safety regulations for food and water served to passengers traveling in regular interstate vehicles.
10. It monitors food supply to detect possible contamination with industrial chemicals or other deleterious substances and takes proper regulatory actions.
11. It maintains adequate communication with and extends maximal cooperation to state authorities and other federal agencies in urgent situations such as massive food contamination by floods, explosions, fires, and food poisoning.
12. It inspects the import of food products to assure compliance with domestic federal laws.
13. It warns the general public when a hazardous food product is identified.
14. It initiates court proceedings against firms and individuals that have violated the law(s).

Since many misconceptions exist regarding the FDA's legal authority, the following provide some examples that define what the agency can and cannot do:

1. In general, the FDA can only regulate food manufacturers or firms that engage their products in interstate commerce. State officials have direct control over those products processed and sold solely within the state.

2. Although the FDA has authority over the safety of a food product before or after it enters interstate commerce, it cannot *prevent* a person from selling a worthless or harmful product. However, *after* such a product has been marketed, the FDA can challenge its value and safety and the agency bears the burden of proof.

3. The FDA's authority in dealing with a food product it regulates is as follows:
   a. It cannot recall a food product that is discovered to be defective, but it can request a manufacturer to do so under threat of legal action.
   b. It can obtain a court order to seize a lot of defective food products.
   c. It can request a recall or legally seize certain food products if *new* scientific evidence shows that they may be hazardous or unacceptable although their interstate shipment and marketing were legal previously.

4. The FDA can take action against false and misleading labeling on the food products it regulates.

5. The FDA cannot regulate local and state food service sanitation, such as restaurants, delicatessens, drive-ins, fast-food counters, vending machines, and others.

6. The FDA cannot regulate food prices and food advertising.

7. The FDA cannot regulate cigarettes.

8. The FDA cannot regulate any food items containing more than 2% poultry and/or 3% meat product. Such products are regulated by the USDA.

9. The FDA cannot regulate the quality as well as the sanitation of Grade A pasteurized fluid milk. It cooperates with and assists state authorities that have primary responsibility over the product.

10. The FDA cannot regulate unsolicited food products or related literature in the *mail* even if they are deceptive. The U.S. Postal Office has direct regulatory authority.

Statutes Administered

The FDA administers a number of federal statutes (see Table 6-1). In the following a brief description is provided for each; further details are presented later.

The Federal Food, Drug, and Cosmetic Act of 1938, as Amended

This book is only interested in those provisions that are related to food. This act is intended to assure the consumer that foods are pure and wholesome, safe to eat,

TABLE 6-1. Major Federal Statutes Administered by the FDA

The Federal Food, Drug, and Cosmetic Act of 1938, as amended
(52 Stat. 1046 et seq.; 21 U.S.C. 301 et seq.)

The Fair Packaging and Labeling Act of 1966
(80 Stat. 1296 et seq.; 15 U.S.C. 1453 et seq.)

The Radiation Control for Health and Safety Act of 1968
(Section 358, 82 Stat. 1177; 42 U.S.C. 263f)

The Public Health Service Act of 1944
(Section 361 and 362 of the act; 42 U.S.C. 264, 265)

The Tea Importation Act of 1897 as amended
(Sections 1, 10, 29 Stat. 604, 607; 21 U.S.C. 41, 50)

Import Milk Act of 1927
(44 Stat. 1101 et seq., as amended; 21 U.S.C. 142 et seq.)

Federal Meat Inspection Act of 1967
[Sections 402, 409(b) of the act; 21 U.S.C. 672 and 679(b)]

Poultry Products Inspection Act of 1957, as amended
[Sections 19 and 24(b) of the act; 21 U.S.C. 462 and 467(b)]

Egg Products Inspection Act of 1970
(21 U.S.C. 1031 et seq.)

and produced under sanitary conditions and that the packaging and labeling of these products is truthful and informative. The Food Additives Amendment of 1958 prohibits the introduction of new food additives until the manufacturer can prove their safety; the Color Additive Amendments of 1960 give the FDA authority to control the conditions for safe use of a color additive, including the amount used in a product.

The Fair Packaging and Labeling Act of 1966

This act requires that the net weight of a food product as well as other information be accurately stated in a uniform location on the label.

The Radiation Control for Health and Safety Act of 1968

This act protects the public from unnecessary exposure to radiation from electronic products such as microwave ovens and color television sets. The FDA sets performance standards for these and similar products.

The Public Health Service Act of 1944

The FDA enforces a number of provisions of this act. The most relevant sections concern the following: the safety of pasteurized milk and shellfish and the sanitation of food services; and the food, water, and sanitary facilities for train, airplane, and bus passengers.

The Tea Importation Act of 1897, as Amended

The act assures that all teas imported into the United States meet the quality standards set by the U.S. Board of Tea Experts. Samples of imported teas are examined before being allowed on the market.

The Import Milk Act of 1927

This act regulates the importation of milk and cream into the United States for the purpose of promoting the dairy industry of the United States and of protecting the public health.

Miscellaneous Statutory Provisions

One Provision of the Federal Meat Inspection Act of 1967, as Amended. The FDA is authorized to detain any carcass or its part, meat, or meat product of cattle, sheep, swine, goats, or equines for adulteration or other violation.

One Provision of the Poultry Products Inspection Act of 1957, as Amended. The FDA is authorized to detain any poultry carcass, its part or poultry products for adulteration or other violation.

The Egg Products Inspection Act of 1970, as Amended. The FDA shares responsibility with the USDA in administering this act. The FDA has exclusive jurisdiction over the quality of eggs served or used in certain establishments such as restaurants and others.

Program Management

One of the best ways to understand the overall activities of the FDA is through its program management system. This is an agency-wide system consisting of the vital processes necessary to manage the FDA, including such information as planning, budgeting, reporting, and evaluation. It provides an insight into the total responsibility and the huge amount of work that has to be accomplished by this agency. The system was introduced in 1970, designed to be of minimum complexity and systematically organized into meaningful and readily identified program elements. Each year, the FDA publishes a "PMS (Program Management System) Blue Book" that outlines the program management data for the next fiscal year. This practice is expected to be continued. The information presented here is obtained from the Blue Book published in 1976.

Integral to the system is a framework of a number of programs (nine for fiscal year 1977; described in Table 6-2) that are further subdivided into projects. These projects are the basic building blocks for all management activities. For example, in Table 6-2, one program is food safety, under which one project is shellfish safety. The amount of allotted funds spent on each program or project varies from year to year. The Blue Book makes an estimate annually.

Project priorities and consequently the amount of money spent are planned according to four criteria: risk, sensitivity, potential effectiveness, and negative impact. Risk is the real loss or injury experienced by the public and also involves the remaining hazard or problem to be eliminated. Sensitivity is the intensity of interest as expressed by consumers, the U.S. Congress, the Executive Branch, and industry. High sensitivity is typically engendered by high consumer vulnerability and lack of product substitutes. Potential effectiveness is the expected impact of additional resources on risk reduction. Negative impact is the expected impact of a reduction in resources.

Most of those projects that are related to food and described in Table 6-2 are covered to a certain degree in this chapter.

Sources of Information

To assist state and other federal agencies, industries, lawyers, scientists, and the general public to understand the work and actions of the FDA, it has made available numerous publications, most of which may be obtained from the FDA through established procedures. Although some of the literature is intended for lay persons, most of it has been prepared for use by FDA personnel. Some are free of charge, others priced items. The following list presents these different sources of information.

TABLE 6-2. Program Management System Project Structure for Use in Fiscal Year 1977. Adapted from "FY 77 PMS Blue Book," FDA, July 1976

1. Food safety
(1) Chemical contaminants
(2) Food additives
(3) Food sanitation control
(4) Food service
(5) Interstate travel
(6) Mycotoxins and other natural poisons
(7) Nutrition
(8) Quality control
(9) Shellfish safety

2. Food economics
(1) Economic deception
(2) Food standards

3. Cosmetics
(1) Cosmetics

4. Human drugs
(1) Antibiotic and insulin certification
(2) Biopharmaceutics
(3) Clinical investigation evaluation
(4) Drug abuse treatment monitoring
(5) Drug efficacy study implementation (DESI)
(6) Drug experience and trends analysis
(7) Drug listing
(8) Drug quality assurance
(9) New drug evaluation
(10) Over-the-counter drug evaluation
(11) Poison control
(12) Prescription drug advertising
(13) Prescription drug labeling and compendium

5. Animal drugs and feeds
(1) Animal drugs: bio-research monitoring
(2) Animal drug safety
(3) Animal feed safety
(4) Antibiotics in animal feeds
(5) Drug residues

6. Medical devices and diagnostic products
(1) Classification
(2) Devices requiring general controls
(3) Devices requiring premarket approval
(4) Devices requiring standards
(5) Diagnostic products requiring standards

7. Biologics
(1) Bacterial and allergenic products
(2) Biologics: bio-research monitoring
(3) Biologics safety, efficacy, and labeling study
(4) Blood and blood products
(5) Viral and rickettsial products

8. Radiological health
   - (1) Ionizing radiation: products and devices
   - (2) Ionizing radiation: use control
   - (3) Light and sonic radiation
   - (4) RF microwave

9. National center for toxicological research
   - (1) Carcinogenesis
   - (2) Mutagenesis
   - (3) Teratogenesis

A. *General*

1. "Public information," 21 CFR 20.
2. Annual report.
3. The FDA Informational Materials for The Food and Cosmetic Industries.
4. The FDA Consumer.
5. Extracts from annual subject indexes published by the Federal Register relating to food and drugs from 1967 to date.
6. Chronological document listing 1936-1976. FDA Federal Register Documents.
7. Statements of policy and interpretations adopted by the FDA and not published in the Federal Register.
8. Index of administrative staff manuals and instructions to staff.
9. Federal Register.
10. Memoranda of Agreements with state or other federal agencies and with foreign governments.
11. Fact sheets and numerous general materials to educate the consumers.

B. *Administrative affairs*

1. Administrative guidelines manual.
2. Staff manual guides--organization and delegations, three volumes.
3. Field management directives.
4. Telephone directory of FDA.

C. *Regulatory activities*

1. Compliance policy guide.
2. Compliance program-guidance manual.
3. Hazard analysis and critical control point--a system for inspection of food processors.
4. Inspector operations manual.
5. Inspector training manual.
6. Inspector's manual for state food and drug officials.
7. Inspector's technical guide.
8. Regulatory procedures manual.
9. Supervisory inspectors guide.
10. Import procedure manual.
11. FDA enforcement report.

D. Technical and scientific publications

1. Food additives analytical manual.
2. Laboratory operations manual.
3. Pesticide analytical manual.
4. FDA by-lines.
5. Bacteriological and analytical manual.
6. Training manual for analytical entomology in the food industry.

E. Legal interpretation

1. Requirements of the United States Food, Drug, and Cosmetic Act.
2. Food Packaging and Labeling Act Requirements.

A number of private publications are devoted to food laws and their developments. Information on the activities and legal decisions of the FDA is a frequent topic. They are mainly for professionals such as academicians, attorneys, corporate officials, and governmental regulatory personnel. They are listed as follows:

1. Food Drug Cosmetic Law Journal.
2. Association of Food and Drug Officials Quarterly Bulletin.
3. Food Technology.
4. Food Production Management.
5. Food Product Development.
6. Food Engineering
7. Food Chemical News

There are other useful FDA publications mentioned later in connection with the relevant discussion sections.

ORGANIZATION AND SPECIFIC ACTIVITIES

Introduction

The FDA issues a huge Staff Manual Guide, Food and Drug Administration, Organization and Delegations Manual, which is constantly updated by replacement sheets and inserts. It describes in detail the organizational structure of the agency and the specific function and activities of each office, bureau, division, and so on. Such information is also described in general terms in other educational materials issued by the agency. All materials presented below have been adapted from the master Staff Manual Guide.

Appendix 6-2 provides an overall organizational chart for the FDA, the major components of which are offices, bureaus, regional directors, and others. Space limitation permits a discussion of only certain selected subdivisions.

The FDA is headed by a commissioner who supervises a number of bureaus, one of which is the Bureau of Foods. Each bureau is headed by a director who supervises a number of offices or branches. Appendixes 6-3 to 6-7 described the organizational structures of the Bureau of Foods and its various offices and branches.

Office of Technology, Bureau of Foods

According to Appendix 6-6, the Associate Director for Technology in the Bureau of Foods supervises four different divisions, one of which is the Division of Food Technology. One branch supervised by this division is the Dairy and Lipid Products Branch, which manages and coordinates FDA activities in relation to the quality and sanitation of milk, milk products, and frozen desserts. Some activities of this branch are as follows:

1. It certifies milk rating officers. This is one aspect of the nationwide, voluntary, cooperative federal/state Interstate Milk Shipper's Certification Program, administered by the FDA in cooperation with the National Conference on Interstate Milk Shipments.
2. It develops milk production model ordinances and codes, criteria, standards, and related program guides, for example, the Pasteurized Milk Ordinance and sanitary standards for milk equipment.
3. It assists state and local community officials in administrative and technical matters relating to such models and codes, which they are encouraged to adopt and apply in their jurisdictions.
4. It evaluates milk equipment to monitor compliance with recommended requirements and standards.
5. It determines the type and quantity of deleterious substances and other undesirable changes, including those of decomposition, in dairy and lipid products.
6. It evaluates the possible contamination of food with biotoxins, disseminates preventive measures to avoid mold growth, and observes and analyzes factories and processing plants.
7. It cooperates with FDA's Cincinnati Training Facility to develop and carry out training programs for FDA and other authorized personnel in milk sanitation.

8. It participates in other activities such as pasteurized milk radiation surveillance
    networks, evaluation of food additives petitions in connection with milk and
    milk products, and developing standards for dairy food.

It is important to realize that the FDA *does not have actual regulatory power*
over the quality and sanitation of milk and milk products within a given state.
According to Section 361 of the Public Health Service Act (PL 78-410, 42 U.S.C.
264), which is administered by the FDA, the traditional programs in these areas
are *advisory* and *stimulatory* in nature and operate under the broad authority of
the act. The FDA can recommend but cannot require certain practices to guarantee
the quality and safety of pasteurized milk. Although milk moving interstate is subject to the Federal Food, Drug, and Cosmetic Act, the state and local regulatory
programs have been very successful in achieving a high sanitary quality of market
Grade A milk and milk products. The FDA has not found it necessary to routinely
inspect market milk plants or farms.

Also, the FDA has promoted the establishment and maintenance of effective
milk sanitation programs that will provide protection for all dairy foods involved,
regardless of whether they move in inter- or intrastate commerce. Table 6-3 provides a list of those relevant publications issued and maintained by the FDA to
achieve its goal.

For example, the publication "Procedures governing the cooperative State-
Public Health Service Program for certification of interstate milk shippers" provides some background material on the "national conference" and the "certification program." At the present time of writing, the National Conference on Interstate Milk Shipments is a conference comprised of the milk sanitation agencies
within 49 states with the participation of FDA personnel. The main objective of
the conference is to "promote the best possible milk supply for all the people,"
and it utilizes the FDA for training program and for disseminating information
about milk sanitation. The publication provides details on: types of standards used,
supervision requirements, rating and certification, uniform bill of lading and seals,
responsibilities of participating state agencies, responsibilities of the Public Health
Service and the FDA, procedure for handling complaints and challenges of validity
of ratings, and application of conference agreements. Other publications listed in
Table 6-3 are invaluable references for the dairy industries, teaching profession, and
regulatory personnel and for enforcement purposes such as court evidence. They
are mostly standards and guidelines developed and recommended by the FDA.
Most of them have been reviewed and approved by all parties concerned, including
state regulatory agencies and the industries.

As an example, the "Grade A pasteurized milk ordinance" is a very comprehensive handbook containing recommendations by the FDA. The ordinance is
composed of the following:

352   Department of Health, Education, & Welfare (FDA)

TABLE 8-3. FDA publications on the sanitation of milk and milk products;

Procedures governing the cooperative State-Public Health Service Program for certification of Interstate Milk Shippers (1975 revision)

Grade "A" pasteurized milk ordinance (1965 recommendations)[a]

Grade A condensed and dry milk products and condensed and dry whey--Recommended sanitation ordinance for condensed and dry milk products and condensed and dry whey used in grade A pasteurized milk products--Supplement I to the grade A pasteurized milk ordinance (1965 recommendations)[a]

Methods of making sanitation ratings of milksheds (1966 edition)[a]

Fabrication of single-service containers and closures for milk and milk products. Guide for sanitation standards. (1965 recommendations)[a]

Milk laboratories approved by federal and state agencies (1975 edition)

Sanitation compliance and enforcement ratings of interstate milk shippers (Quarterly)

---

[a] At time of current writing, these publications are either being revised or to be replaced with new editions or recommendations. For more information either consult 42 FR 6001-6002 (February 1, 1977) or write to the appropriate office in the FDA.

1. Defining milk, certain milk products, milk producer, pasteurization, and other terms.
2. Prohibiting the sale of adulterated and misbranded products.
3. Requiring permits for the sale of the products.
4. Regulating the inspection of dairy farms and milk plants and the examination, labeling, pasteurization, distribution, and sale of milk and milk products.
5. Providing for the construction of future dairy farms and milk plants.
6. Prescribing standards for milk and milk products.

Some standards for the products are as follows:

1. Chemical, bacteriological, and temperature standards for Grade A milk and milk products.
2. Sanitation requirements for Grade A raw milk for pasteurization.
3. Sanitation requirements for Grade A pasteurized milk and milk products.

Further details may be obtained from the publications listed in Table 6-3.

The Journal of Food Protection, formerly the Journal of Milk and Food Technology, is another reference source for information on the latest technical and legal developments in dairy industries and food services.

The Division of Food Technology also supervises the Shellfish Sanitation Branch, which manages and supervises a cooperative Federal-State-Industry National Shellfish Sanitation Program. Activities relating to this program are as follows:

1. It develops and recommends programs for the production, processing, and interstate shipment of fresh or frozen mollusks and crustaceans.
2. It develops and maintains standards and criteria in the Sanitation Program Manual of Operations in close cooperation with state authorities and the shellfish industry.
3. It compiles and disseminates a bimonthly list of certified interstate shellfish shippers.
4. It monitors the compliance of industries with requirements of the program.
5. It serves as the FDA's focal point for technical and administrative matter for shellfish by providing technical advice to industries, state agencies, and foreign countries, preparing shellfish sanitation agreements with foreign governments when officially requested, and supervising training programs for authorized personnel.

Shellfish include fresh or frozen oysters, clams, or mussels. A good sanitary control program is necessary because shellfish grow in easily contaminated coastal waters and some species are eaten raw. Since 1925 a close and interlocking cooperation has existed among shellfish-producing states, the industry, and the U.S. Public Health Service.

All operation controls have been exercised by the states in accordance with established standards. State health personnel continually inspect and survey bacteriological conditions in all shellfish-growing areas, and any contaminated location is supervised or patrolled and declared restricted. Shellfish obtained from polluted waters are indistinguishable from safe ones. Prohibited harvesting is the only way to keep them off the market.

State inspectors check harvesting boats and shucking plants before issuing approval "certificates," which are equivalent to operating licenses. Such approved plants place a certification number on each shellfish package shipped. It indicates that the shipper is under state inspection and meets the requirements of the cooperative program. Also, in the rare event of accidental contamination, any offending shipment can be traced and seized.

Recently, the ability of shellfish to concentrate radioactive material, insecticides, or other chemicals from their environment has raised additional concern. Thus one broad phase of the shellfish-control program is to solve the sanitation problem by ensuring that shellfish-growing areas are free from sewage pollution and/or toxic industrial waste. Any contaminated area is isolated.

The other safety problem of shellfish is the control of natural toxicity. This is different from sanitation. The poison that causes paralytic shellfish poisoning is found in planktonic organisms known as "dinoflagellates." The survival and multiplication of these organisms do not depend on sewage or other pollutants as food sources. With the exception of Alaska and to a lesser degree the West Coast and New England states, the control of this toxicity is not a major problem in the United States. Again, it is achieved by a careful survey followed by the prohibition of harvesting from locations inhabited by toxic shellfish.

The Shellfish Sanitation Branch and the field inspectors of the FDA conduct continuing review of state programs, including an annual inspection of selected processing plants. Twice a month, the FDA publishes a list of valid interstate shipper permits with the certificate number issued by those state authorities that have been endorsed by the agency. Wholesale buyers should check this list to make sure that the products for sale are obtained from FDA-approved establishments. Adulterated or mislabeled shellfish (contaminated, decomposed, etc.), if shipped in interstate commerce, are subject to seizure and shippers may be prosecuted or enjoined under the Federal Food, Drug, and Cosmetic Act. Shellfish industry contributes to the program by complying voluntarily with all instructions and sanitary precautions prescribed for the entire process from harvesting to shipping.

Again, the FDA does not have regulatory power over shellfish sanitation if the product is not shipped interstate. Basic statutory responsibility derives from Section 361 of the Public Health Service Act (42 U.S.C. 264), which authorizes the FDA to make recommendations and to cooperate with local and state authorities in assuring the safety and wholesomeness of these products.

Table 6-4 describes the publications issued by the FDA for use in the National Shellfish Sanitation Program. Parts I and II of the Manual of Operations for the program have been very useful for inspection personnel and the industries. Some of their contents are briefly described as follows.

The publication "Sanitation of shellfish growing areas" provides information on the following: general adminstrative procedures, laboratory procedures, growing area survey, and classification; preparation of shellfish for marketing; control of harvesting from closed areas; and bacteriological criteria for shucked oysters at the wholesale market level. The publication "Sanitation of the harvesting and processing of shellfish" provides details on the following: harvesting and handling shell-stock, shucking and packing shellfish, packing and shipping shell-stock, repacking of shellfish, reshippers, inspection of certified shellfish shippers, code-dating system for shucker-packers and repackers, cooling rates of fresh oysters,

TABLE 6-4. Food and Drug Administration Publications on Shellfish Sanitation

National Shellfish Sanitation Program, Manual of Operations, Part I, Sanitation of
   Shellfish Growing Areas, 1965 Revision, edited by L. S. Houser, Sanitarian
   Director. PHS, Shellfish Sanitation Branch.

National Shellfish Sanitation Program, Manual of Operations, Part II, Sanitation of
   the Harvesting and Processing of Shellfish, 1965 Revision, compiled and edited
   by E. T. Jensen, Sanitary Engineer director.

Interstate certified shellfish shippers list. Monthly publication.

The National Shellfish Sanitation Program (FDA) 72-2016. Undated.

and heat shock method. For further details, consult the original documents.

Office of Nutrition and Consumer Sciences, Bureau of Foods

According to Appendixes 6-3 and 6-7, the Office of Nutrition and Consumer
Sciences supervises three divisions, one of which is the Division of Food Service.
The activities of this Division are listed as follows:

1. It manages and supervises activities to reduce consumer hazards such as food
   poisoning from commercial and institutional food servicing, including restaurants, cafeterias, drive-ins, delicatessens, commissaries, fast-food counters,
   vending machines, and retail food marketing.
2. It prepares and interprets model ordinances and codes for food service sanitation and retail food marketing, promotes their adoption and uniform application by state and municipal authorities, and cooperates with regional operations of the FDA in all related activities.
3. It develops and supervises training programs for authorized personnel relating
   to food service sanitation in the FDA's Cincinnati Training Facility.
4. It assists in the development of food and water sanitation programs for interstate travel. Further details on this aspect are presented later.
5. It assists regional operations in the inspection of food service establishments in
   federal buildings under reimbursable agreements with the General Services
   Administration.
6. It provides technical advice to other government agencies, educational institutions, health-related organizations, and industries in all matters relating to
   food service sanitation and vending equipment.

7. It develops programs for laboratory and field investigations to solve current and emerging problems of food safety in food service operations and evaluates potential hazards of industry innovations.

Again, the FDA does not have direct regulatory power over the sanitation of food served in restaurants, delicatessens, and other public locations, except interstate travel vehicles. The statutory responsibility under Section 361 of the Public Health Service Act (42 U.S.C. 264) authorizes the FDA to make recommendations and cooperate with local and state officials in achieving the main objective, protection of public health in the food service arena. One of the most important activities of the FDA is to issue a number of model ordinances and recommendations in the form of publications described in Table 6-5. They have been used as references by many state agencies and the food service industries. They are especially valuable in college food service courses. Their titles are self-explanatory. In the following, a brief summary of the contents is presented. For example, the contents of the Food Service Sanitation Manual include the following:

1. Need, purpose, and scope of a food service sanitation program.
2. Conducting an effective food sanitation program.
3. Adoption by reference form--FDA food service sanitation ordinance.

TABLE 6-5. Food and Drug Administration Publications on Food Service Sanitation

Food service sanitation manual including a model food service sanitation ordinance, 1976.

Procedure for evaluating food service sanitation programs, 1976.[a]

Procedure for the standardization and certification of food service sanitation survey officers, 1967.

Sanitary food service. Instructor's guide, 1969.
(United States Department of Agriculture, Public Health Service, Department of the Army, Department of the Navy, and Department of the Air Force.)

The vending of food and beverages including a model sanitation ordinance, 1977.[a]

Model retail food store sanitation ordinance, 1977.[a]

[a] At time of current writing, these publications are in the revision process. Final printed forms are not yet available. For more information consult either 42 FR 54626-54627 (October 7, 1977) and 42 FR 56367 (October 25, 1977) or write to the appropriate office in the FDA.

In the same publication, the 1976 recommendations of the FDA food service sanitation ordinance provides information on the following: food care; personnel; equipment and utensils; cleaning, sanitization, and storage of equipment and utensils; sanitary facilities and controls; construction and maintenance of physical facilities; mobile food units or pushcarts; temporary food service; and compliance procedures.

The publication "Procedure for evaluating food service sanitation programs" includes data collection and tabulation, interpreting the food service establishment average rating score and administrative numerical scores, and the total food service sanitation program rating score. The contents of the publication "Sanitary food service. Instructor's guide" include the following: importance and magnitude of the food service industry and the need for food service worker's training; microbiology and foodborne disease; methods for the prevention of foodborne disease; personal hygiene, self-protection, and salesmanship; proper methods of washing and sanitizing utensils and equipment; insect and rodent control; housekeeping and waste disposal practices; and follow-up training and application of information learned. For further details, consult the original documents in Table 6-5.

At the present time of writing, there is much controversy over government regulations, both state and federal, and the food service industry. Two major problems are: (1) regulations and recommendations governing food service sanitation are not uniform and specific, and (2) food service operators are usually not sufficiently trained in handling the sanitation problems.

The increasing public and media attention devoted to food served in restaurants, drive-ins, and other establishments has focused both government and consumer attention to food service sanitation. This concern is also closely related to the social trend of increasing number of Americans "eating out." At present, the FDA, in cooperation with the National Institute for the Food Service Industry, has initiated a voluntary program of training and certifying food-service managers. This is a timely and obvious attempt to improve the sanitation and safety of food served to the public. For further information on the FDA, government regulations, the food service industry, and the training-certification program, consult the following reference sources:

1. The impact of food regulations on the food service industry. A symposium presented during the Food Service Division program at the 37th Annual Meeting of the Institute of Food Technologists, Philadelphia, Pennsylvania, June 1977.
2. H. R. Roberts. The food service industry--a view from Washington. Speech presented to the International Food Service Executive Association Annual Conference at Orlando, Florida, August 1975.
3. W. F. Bower and A. S. Davis. The Federal food service program. Journal of

Milk Food Technology, February, 1976.
4. C. D. Clingman. Food service manager certification--The NIFI Program. Journal of Food Protection, March 1977.
5. Food service manager training and certification program. Recommendations for a training course to improve food protection practices in food service establishments. Pamphlet distributed by the FDA in 1976.
6. R. P. Morrison and R. R. Carter. Certification of food service manager--why and how? Journal of Milk Food Technology, March 1975.
7. A. L. Banks. Standardization and certification in food service sanitation. Speech presented at the N.Y. Conference of health officers and food and drug officials, New York, N.Y., December 1974.

REGIONAL OPERATIONS

To coordinate the network of field activities and personnel, the FDA has established the office of the Executive Director of Regional Operations, which is headquartered in Washington, D.C. and supervises three divisions as well as the regional food and drug directors field organizations which are referred to later (see Appendix 6-8). The three divisions are: Federal-State Relations, Field Operations, and Planning and Analysis. The first two divisions are briefly discussed in the following paragraphs.

Division of Federal-State Relations

This division supervises three branches: the State Services Branch, the Program Development Branch, and the State Training Branch (Cincinnati Training Facility). The overall major activities of the division are as follows:

1. It maintains the latest information on those state laws that pertain to products regulated by the FDA.
2. It commissions state and local officials to perform federal regulatory activities.
3. It maintains a State Inspector's Manual relating to investigational and inspectional procedures in cooperation with the Association of Food and Drug Officials, a private body.
4. It manages the National Regional State Telecommunications Network, which connects the state food and drug agencies with the FDA field offices and headquarters to provide a focal point for emergency health and enforcement communications and information exchange.
5. It administers federal/state contracts.

6. It coordinates FDA field personnel, state and local authorities involved in the sanitation of food service, milk and milk products, shellfish, animal feed, and radiological health.
7. It administers training and education programs for state, local, and federal personnel.

Training programs are conducted at the Cincinnati Training Facility. This facility has developed manuals, course materials, publications and audiovisual aids needed for the effective conduct of classroom, correspondence, and on-the-job training programs.

In April 1971 the FDA submitted a report titled "A Report on FDA's Current and Future Reliance Upon the States" to the Secretary of Health, Education, and Welfare. This report still contains current information on such topics as description of the states' current FDA-related functions, major gaps and federal versus state role in the current performance of these functions, and a proposed program for states assistance. It should be consulted for more information on federal/state relationship.

Division of Field Operations

This division supervises the Mexican Liaison Staff, the Field Compliance Branch, and the Field Investigations Branch. Some overall major activities of this division are as follows:

1. It coordinates the communication, liaison, and activities between the FDA and Mexican authorities with reference to: imported food products, compliance with official agreements, cooperative quality assurance programs, training of Mexican officials, and maintenance of bilingual capabilities.
2. It exercises direct control over all field program guidance materials and compliance operating manuals and procedures. These include: Compliance Programs, Administrative Guidelines, Compliance Policy Guides, Regulatory Procedures Manual and the Import Procedures Manual, and other new materials.
3. It supervises field emergency preparedness plans to manage, with other government units, natural disasters or national emergencies that are related to food supply.
4. It supervises all investigational and inspectional problems and practices such as communication, program adequacy, equipment and supplies, personnel training and exchanges, foreign inspection programs, FDA/industries quality assurance programs, disease outbreaks and injuries, and investigational and inspectional manuals.

Memoranda of Understanding

The FDA signs official agreements, usually known as Memoranda of Understanding, with state authorities, other Federal agencies, and foreign governments. Many of them relate to the quality and safety of food.

Those federal agencies that sign agreements with the FDA include the Department of Agriculture, Department of Commerce, Department of Defense, General Services Administration, Veterans Administration, and others. Many of these agreements involve inspection of food products and establishments, confirming food grades and specifications, monitoring of harmful chemical contaminants, sharing legal authority, and other related duties. Some of these agreements have been discussed elsewhere.

The FDA is currently conducting an import source country certification program. It was established to improve FDA control over certain imported food products through the operation of agreements with the foreign exporting countries. It involves the negotiation of Memoranda of Understanding that establish production controls and end-products specifications for specific commodities. Such agreements result in intensive control of shipments at the point of production and are supplemented by FDA audit over selected lots entering the United States. At the present time of writing, a number of such Memoranda of Understanding have been signed (see Table 6-6). Such agreements are announced in the Federal Register, and copies may be obtained from or consulted at the FDA headquarters or a District Office. As an example, some arrangements written in the agreement between the United States (FDA) and Japan on shellfish sanitation (see Table 6-6) are as follows:

1. Shellfish products are defined to include fresh or frozen oysters, clams, and mussels intended for shipment from Japan to the United States.
2. The principles of FDA recommendations on the practice for sanitary control of the shellfish industry will apply to shellfish production and certification of exporters in Japan.
3. The Japanese Ministry of Health and Welfare will notify the FDA of the state of compliance including lists of shippers holding operating permits and complying with prescribed principles.
4. If acceptable, the FDA will also place their names and permit numbers on its bi-monthly list of certified shellfish shippers. They may be removed from the list if the product has not been produced and handled in accordance with prescribed requirements or in a public health emergency.
5. The shellfish products shipped from Japan to the United States will, in addition, be subject to the provisions of the Federal Food, Drug, and Cosmetic Act.

6. Shellfish exported from the United States to Japan will be subject to a corresponding arrangement.

Since the FDA has such extensive field operations and partnership with state authorities, a number of Memoranda of Understanding have been signed between the two parties. Table 6-7 lists those in effect at the present time of writing. Their titles are indicative of the general contents. Some sample information contained in some of those documents concerning work-sharing arrangement include the following:

1. Purpose of the agreement.
2. Work-sharing programs such as goals, responsibilities, and commitments.
3. General provisions: information exchange on inspection reports, samples, and complaints; work planning such as inspection scheduling; compliance follow-up; recall and emergency; program review; training; and performance evaluation.

With reference to all FDA Memoranda of Understanding, a few points should be noted. They are usually negotiated by the FDA headquarters and the Division of Field Operations of the Executive Director of Regional Operations. The FDA maintains an updated list of such agreements for public reference. It is obvious that periodic renewal of the arrangements by the parties concerned is needed. Therefore, the latest agreements should always be requested.

State Food Laws and Regulatory Agencies

As mentioned previously, to have effective regional operations, the FDA maintains the most updated knowledge about the laws and regulatory agencies of each state with reference to food and feed products. The information helps to avoid duplicating efforts and facilitates enforcement actions of the FDA field offices. The office of the Executive Director of Regional Operations has prepared three important charts for this purpose (see Tables 6-8 to 6-10). Each chart matches the relevant information with each of the 50 states, the District of Columbia, and Puerto Rico. For example, Table 6-8 presents the following: type of food law enforced, enforcing agency, food additives amendment, color additives amendment, pesticide residues amendment, adoption of federal regulations, and enrichment requirements. Table 6-9 presents the following: type of feed law enforced, enforcing agency, adoption of the Federal Insecticide, Fungicide, and Rodenticide Act, and the Pesticide Applicator Act. Table 6-10 shows the specific agency within the state responsible for controlling foods in general, fluid milk, restaurants, shellfish, and

TABLE 6-6. Examples of Memoranda of Understanding Signed between the FDA and Foreign Countries

Number in Guide[a]	Agency in Foreign Country	Agreement Topic	TN[b]	Date
7155a.02	The National Commission of Quality for Export Products (CONACALPE) of Mexico	Covers numerous aspects relating to the commerce of products between the two countries such as inspection, analysis, etc.	74-28	09/10/74
7155a.03	The Ministry of Agriculture of Belgium	Sanitary quality of dry milk products exported to the United States	75-6	02/14/75
7155a.04	The Ministry of Agriculture and Fisheries of the Netherlands	Sanitary quality of dry milk products exported to the United States	75-6	02/14/75
7155a.07	The Ministry of Agriculture of France	Exporting dry milk products to the United States (sanitary quality)	75-13	06/03/75
7155a.07	Department of National Health and Welfare of Canada	Monitoring of food, beverage, and sanitary services provided on common carriers operating between the two countries	75-18	10/28/75
7155a.08	Ministry of Agriculture and Fisheries, New Zealand	Exporting dry milk products to the United States (sanitary quality)	76-1	01/15/76
7155a.09	Ministry of Foreign Trade, India	Sanitary quality of frozen frog legs	76-33	05/12/76
7155a.10	Ministry of Agriculture, Denmark	Sanitary quality of dry milk products exported to the United States	76-35	05/13/76
7155a.11	Swedish National Board of Health and Welfare	Exchange of inspectional information	76-68	07/12/76

7155a.13	Japan	Shellfish sanitation	77-26	04/07/'77
7155a.15	Canada	Sanitary control of shellfish industry	77-28	04/07/'77

[a] Guide = Compliance Policy Guide, FDA.

[b] TN = Transmittal number which appears in the Compliance Policy Guide.

TABLE 6-7. Examples of Memoranda of Agreements Signed between the FDA and a State Agency and Related to Food and Feed[a]

State Agency	Agreement Number	Period Covered	Description of Agreement
Delaware Department of Agriculture	225-76-4009	04/22/76 to 04/30/77	Work-sharing agreement concerning inspections of Delaware medicated feed mills and livestock
Delaware Department of Health and Social Services	225-76-4010	06/01/76 to 05/31/77	Work-sharing agreement concerning inspections of Delaware food processing and storage facilities
Iowa State Department of Agriculture	225-77-4001	03/23/77 to 03/24/78	Work-sharing agreement concerning inspections and related activities to ensure the safety of foods for humans and animals
Maryland Environmental Health Administration	225-75-4073	08/01/75 to 07/31/76	Work-sharing agreement concerning inspections of Maryland food processing and storage facilities
Minnesota Department of Agriculture	225-76-4001	07/01/75 to ?	Work-sharing agreement concerning inspections of Minnesota food and medicated feed facilities
Oregon State Department of Agriculture	225-77-1000	10/01/76 to 11/01/77	Work-sharing agreement concerning regulatory investigations involving drug, pesticides, and industrial chemical residues in animal feeds and in meat and poultry
Pennsylvania Department of Agriculture	225-77-4000	09/08/76 to 10/30/77	Work-sharing agreement concerning inspection of Pennsylvania food processing and storage facilities
Virginia Department of Health	225-76-4005	01/01/76 to 12/31/76	Work-sharing agreement concerning inspections of Virginia crabmeat plants
Virginia Department of Agriculture and Commerce	225-76-4004	10/01/75 to 09/30/77	Work-sharing agreement concerning inspections of Virginia food processing and storage facilities

West Virginia Department of Agriculture	225-76-4008	04/12/76 to 04/30/78	Work-sharing agreement concerning inspections of West Virginia food warehouses and medicated feed mills
West Virginia Department of Health	223-76-4011	07/01/75 to 06/30/77	Work-sharing agreement concerning inspections of West Virginia food processing industry
Wisconsin Department of Agriculture	225-76-4000	07/01/75 to ?	Work-sharing agreement concerning inspections of Wisconsin dairy products and canning and freezing plants and monitoring of pesticides on raw and processed foods

[a] Since each agreement includes the effective time period, always request the latest information if one is interested.

[b] Question mark indicates "indefinite" date.

TABLE 6-8. State Food Laws Chart Showing Enforcement Agencies and Principal Provisions[a]

	Alabama	Alaska	Arizona	Arkansas	California	Colorado	Connecticut	Delaware
Type of law enforced	Food & Drug Act 1907	Uniform FDCA	Uniform FDCA	Uniform FDCA	Uniform FDCA	Uniform FDCA	Uniform FDCA	Food & Drug Act 1907
Enforcing agency	Agric	Health	Health	Health	Health	Health	Consumer protection	Health
Food additives amendment	No	No	Yes 1971	No	Yes 1959	Yes 1970	Yes 1963	No
Color additives amendment	No	No	Yes 1971	No	Yes 1961	Yes 1970	Yes 1963	No
Pesticide residues amendment	No	No	Yes 1971	No	Yes 1959	Yes 1970	Yes 1963	No
Adoption of federal regulations	No reg	By reg	By reg	By reg	Automatic	Automatic	By reg	By reg
Enrichment requirements	Yes 1943	Yes 1947	Yes 1972	Yes 1945	Yes 1945	Yes 1949	No	No

366

	Florida	Georgia	Hawaii	Idaho	Illinois	Indiana	Iowa	Kansas
Type of law enforced	Uniform FDCA	Uniform FDCA	Uniform FDCA	Uniform FDCA	Uniform FDCA	Uniform FDCA	Food Act 1906	Uniform FDCA
Enforcing agency	Agric	Agric	Health	Health	Health	Health	Agric	Health
Food additives amendment	Yes 1963	No	Yes 1941	No	Yes 1967	Yes 1971	No	Yes 1953
Color additives amendment	Yes 1963	No	Yes 1967	No	Yes 1967	Yes 1971	No	Yes 1953
Pesticide residues amendment	Yes 1963	No	Yes 1957	No	Yes 1967	Yes 1971	No	Yes 1953
Adoption of federal regulations	By reg	By reg	By reg	By reg	Automatic	By reg	By reg	By reg
Enrichment requirements	No	Yes 1945	Yes 1947	Yes 1949	No	Yes 1945	No	Yes 1947

	Mississippi	Missouri	Montana	Nebraska	Nevada	New Hampshire	New Jersey
Type of law enforced	Food & Drug Act 1907	Uniform FDCA	Uniform FDCA	Uniform FDCA	Uniform FDCA	Uniform FDCA	Uniform FDCA
Enforcing agency	State chemist	Health	Health	Agric	Health	Health	Health
Food additives amendment	No	No	Yes 1967	Yes 1965	No	Yes 1965	No
Color additives amendment	No	No	Yes 1967	Yes 1965	No	Yes 1965	No
Pesticide residues amendment	No	No	Yes 1967	Yes 1965	No	Yes 1965	No
Adoption of federal regulations	By reg	By reg	By reg	Automatic	By reg	By reg	By reg
Enrichment requirements	Yes 1944 Health	No	No	Yes 1940	No	Yes 1945	Yes 1946

	New Mexico	New York	N. Carolina	N. Dakota	Ohio	Oklahoma	Oregon
Type of law enforced	Uniform FDCA	Uniform FDCA	Uniform FDCA	Uniform FDCA	Uniform FDCA	Uniform FDCA	Uniform Food Act
Enforcing agency	Health	Agric	Agric	State lab	Agric	Health	Agric
Food additives amendment	No	Yes 1966	No	Yes 1967	No	No	Yes 1961
Color additives amendment	No	Yes 1966	No	Yes 1967	No	No	No
Pesticide residues amendment	No	Yes 1966	No	Yes 1967	No	No	Yes 1961
Adoption of federal regulations	By reg	By reg	By reg	By reg	By reg	By reg	By reg
Enrichment requirements	Yes 1955	Yes 1945	Yes 1945	Yes 1945 State lab	Yes 1949	Yes 1949	Yes 1971

	Pennsylvania	Rhode Island	S. Carolina	S. Dakota	Tennessee	Texas	Utah
Type of law enforced	Uniform Food Act	Uniform FDCA	Uniform FDCA	Food & Drug Act 1907	Uniform FDCA	Uniform FDCA	Uniform FDCA
Enforcing agency	Agric	Health	Agric/Health	Agric	Agric	Health	Agric
Food additives amendment	Yes (Regs)	No	Yes	No	Yes 1961	Yes 1961	Yes 1957
Color additives amendment	Yes (Regs)	No	Yes	No	Yes 1961	No	No
Pesticide residues amendment	Yes (Regs)	No	Yes	No	Yes 1961	Yes 1961	Yes 1957
Adoption of federal regulations	No provision	By reg	Automatic	No provision	By reg	No provision	Automatic
Enrichment requirements	No	Yes 1948	Yes 1942	Yes 1945	No	Yes 1943	No

	Vermont	Virginia	Washington	West Virginia	Wisconsin	Wyoming	District of Columbia	Puerto Rico
Type of law enforced	Uniform FDCA	Uniform Food Act	Uniform FDCA	Food & Drug Act 1907	Food & Drug Act 1907	Food & Drug Act 1907	Act Supplementing Federal Act	Uniform FDCA
Enforcing agency	Health	Agric	Agric	Agric	Agric	Agric	Health	Health
Food additives amendment	No	No	Yes 1963	No	Yes 1959	No		No
Color additives amendment	No	No	Yes 1963	No	No	No		No
Pesticide residues amendment	No	No	Yes 1963	No	Yes 1959	No		No
Adoption of federal regulations	By reg	By reg	By reg	No provision	No provision	By reg		By reg
Enrichment requirements	No	No	Yes	Yes 1945	No	No	Federal standards	Yes, rice only 1949

a Reproduced from an original chart prepared by the Program Development Branch, Division of Federal-State Relations, Office of the Executive Director of Regional Operations, Food and Drug Administration, July 1972, revised March 1974.

Abbreviations: FDCA = Food, Drug, & Cosmetic Act; Agric = Agriculture; Reg = Regulation; Regs = Regulations

TABLE 6-9. State Feed and Pesticide Laws Chart and the Corresponding Enforcing Agencies[a]

State	Type of law enforced	Enforcing agency	IFRA	PAA
Alabama	CFL 1927	Agric	Yes/Agric	Yes/Agric
Alaska	none		Yes/Agric	Yes/Agric
Arizona	CFL 1956[b]	State chemist	Yes/State chemist	Yes/Agric
Arkansas	CFL 1951[b]	State plant board	Yes/State plant board	Yes/State plant board
California	CFL 1967[b]	Agric	Yes/Agric	Yes/Agric
Colorado	CFL 1961[b]	Agric	Yes/Agric	Yes/Agric
Connecticut	CFL 1965[b]	Agric Exp Sta	Yes/Agric	Yes/Agric
Delaware	CFL 1967[b]	Agric	Yes/Agric	Yes/Agric
District of Columbia	None		Federal Act	No
Florida	CFL 1955[b]	Agric	Yes/Agric	Yes/Agric
Georgia	CFL 1972[c]	Agric	Yes/Agric	No
Hawaii	CFL 1959[b]	Agric	Yes/Agric	Yes/Agric
Idaho	CFL 1953	Agric	Yes/Agric	Yes/Agric
Illinois	CFL 1961[b]	Agric	Yes/Agric	Yes/Agric
Indiana	CFL 1971[c]	Agric Exp Sta	Yes/Agric Exp Sta	No
Iowa	CFL 1964[b]	Agric	Yes/Agric	Yes/Agric
Kansas	CFL 1971[c]	Agric	Yes/Agric	Yes/Agric
Kentucky	CFL 1954[b]	Agric Exp Sta	Yes/Agric Exp Sta	No
Louisiana	CFL 1948[b]	Agric & Agric Exp Sta	Yes/Agric	Yes/Agric
Maine	CFL 1971[c]	Agric	Yes/Agric	Yes/Board of Pest Control
Maryland	CFL 1958[b]	Agric	Yes/Agric	Yes/Agric
Massachusetts	CFL 1972[c]	Agric Exp Sta	Yes/Health	Yes/Health
Michigan	CFL 1965[b]	Agric	Yes/Agric	Yes/Agric
Minnesota	CFL 1971[c]	Agric	Yes/Agric	Yes/Agric
Mississippi	CFL 1972[c]	Agric & State chemist	Yes/State plant board	Yes/State plant board

TABLE 6-9 (continued)

State	Type of law enforced	Enforcing agency	IFRA	PAA
Missouri	CFL 1972[b]	Agric	Yes/Agric	No
Montana	CFL 1963[b]	Agric	Yes/Health	No
Nebraska	CFL 1971[c]	Agric	Yes/Agric	No
Nevada	none		Yes/Agric	Yes/Agric
New Hampshire	CFL 1971[c]	Agric	Yes/Agric	Yes/Agric
New Jersey	CFL 1971[c]	Agric	Yes/State chemist	No
New Mexico	CFL 1961[b]	Agric	Yes/Agric	Yes/Agric
New York	CFL 1958[b]	Agric	Yes/Agric	Yes/Agric
N. Carolina	CFL 1909	Agric	Yes/Agric	Yes/Agric
N. Dakota	CFL 1967[b]	State lab	Yes/State chemist	Yes/Aero-nautics
Ohio	CFL 1963[b]	Agric	Yes/Agric	Yes/Agric
Oklahoma	CFL 1955[b]	Agric	Yes/Agric	Yes/Agric
Oregon	CFL 1971[c]	Agric	Yes/Agric	Yes/Agric
Pennsylvania	CFL 1971[c]	Agric	Yes/Agric	No
Rhode Island	CFL 1936	Natural Resources	Yes/Nat. Resources	Yes/Nat Resources
S. Carolina	CFL 1910	Agric	Yes/Agric	No
S. Dakota	CFL 1970[c]	Agric	Yes/Agric	Yes/Agric
Tennessee	CFL 1972[c]	Agric	Yes/Agric	Yes/Agric
Texas	CFL 1957[b]	Agric Exp Sta	Yes/Agric	Yes/Agric
Utah	CFL 1957[b]	Agric	Yes/Agric	Yes/Agric
Vermont	CFL 1971[c]	Agric Exp Sta	Yes/Agric	Yes/Agric
Virginia	CFL 1919[b]	Agric	Yes/Agric	No
Washington	CFL 1965[b]	Agric	Yes/Agric	Yes/Agric
W. Virginia	CFL 1965[b]	Agric	Yes/Agric	No
Wisconsin	CFL 1951	Agric	Yes/Agric	No
Wyoming	CFL 1917	Agric	Yes/Agric	No
Puerto Rico	CFL 1923	Agric	Yes/Health	Yes/Health

TABLE 6-9 (continued)

a
Abbreviations: IFRA = Insecticide, Fungicide, and Rodenticide Act; PAA = Pesticide Applicator Act; CFL = Commercial Feed Law consistent with; Agric = Agriculture; Exp Sta = Experimental Station.

Source: This chart has been reproduced from an original prepared by Program Development Branch, Division of Federal-State Relations, Office of the Executive Director of Regional Operations, July 1972, revised March 1974.

b
Association of American Feed Control Officials Uniform State Feed Bill, 1958.

c
Association of American Feed Control Officials Uniform State Feed Bill, 1970.

TABLE 6-10. Primary State Agencies Responsible for Food Control.[a]

State	Foods General	Fluid Milk	Restaurants	Shellfish	Weights and Measures
Alabama	Agriculture	Health	Health	Health	Agriculture
Alaska	Health	Natural Resources	Health	--	Commerce
Arizona	Health	Health, Dairy Commerce	Health	--	Agriculture
Arkansas	Health	Health	Health	--	Plant Board
California	Health	Agriculture	Health	Health	Agriculture
Colorado	Health	Health	Health	--	Agriculture
Connecticut	Consumer Protection	Agriculture	Health	Health	Consumer Protection
Delaware	Health	Health	Health	Health	Agriculture
District of Columbia					
Florida	Agriculture	Health, Agriculture	Health	Health	Agriculture
Georgia	Agriculture	Agriculture	Health	Health	Agriculture
Hawaii	Health	Health	Health	--	Agriculture
Idaho	Health	Health	Health	--	Agriculture

375

TABLE 6-10. (continued)

State	Foods General	Fluid Milk	Restaurants	Shellfish	Weights and Measures
Illinois	Health	Health	Health	--	Agriculture
Indiana	Health	Health	Health	--	Health
Iowa	Agriculture	Health	Agriculture	--	Agriculture
Kansas	Health	Health, Agriculture	Health	--	Agriculture
Kentucky	Health	Health	Health	--	Agriculture
Louisiana	Health	Health	Health	Health	Agriculture
Maine	Agriculture	Agriculture	Health	Health	Agriculture
Maryland	Health	Health	Health	Fisheries	Agriculture
Massachusetts	Health	Health, Agriculture	Health	Health	Agriculture
Michigan	Agriculture	Agriculture	Health	Health	Agriculture
Minnesota	Agriculture	Agriculture	Health	--	Public Service
Mississippi	State chemist	Health	Health	Health	Agriculture
Missouri	Health	Health	Health	--	Agriculture
Montana	Health	Health, Livestock Board	Health	--	Agriculture
Nebraska	Agriculture	Health	Agriculture	--	Agriculture

State					
Nevada	Health	Health	Health	--	Agriculture
New Hampshire	Health	Health	Health	Health	Agriculture
New Jersey	Health	Health	Health	Environmental Protection	Agriculture
New Mexico	Health	Health	Health	--	Law & Public Safety
New York	Agriculture	Health, Agriculture	Health, Agriculture	Environmental Conservation	Agriculture
N. Carolina	Agriculture	Agriculture	Health	Health	Agriculture
N. Dakota	State Chemist	Agriculture	State Chemist	--	Public Service
Ohio	Agriculture	Health	Health	--	Agriculture
Oklahoma	Health	Health	Health	--	Agriculture
Oregon	Agriculture	Agriculture	Health	Health	Agriculture
Pennsylvania	Agriculture	Agriculture	Health	Health	Justice
Rhode Island	Health	Health	Health	Health	Labor
S. Carolina	Health	Health, Dairy Commission	Health	Health	Agriculture
S. Dakota	Agriculture	Agriculture	Health	--	Agriculture
Tennessee	Agriculture	Health	Environmental Health	--	Agriculture
Texas	Health	Health	Health	Health	Agriculture

TABLE 6-10. (continued)

State	Foods General	Fluid Milk	Restaurants	Shellfish	Weights and Measures
Utah	Agriculture	Health	Health, Social Service	--	Agriculture
Vermont	Health	Agriculture	Health	--	Agriculture
Virginia	Agriculture	Health, Agriculture	Health	Health	Agriculture
Washington	Agriculture	Agriculture	Health	Health	Agriculture
W. Virginia	Agriculture, Health	Health	Health	--	Labor
Wisconsin	Agriculture	Agriculture	Health	--	Agriculture
Wyoming	Agriculture	Agriculture	Health	--	Agriculture
Guam					
Puerto Rico					
Virgin Islands					

[a] Source: Reproduced from "A Report on FDA's Current and Future Reliance upon the States," Office of the FDA's Assistant Commissioner for Field Coordination, April 1971.

"Non-state" status: There is no information in the original source for the following--District of Columbia, Guam, Puerto Rico, and Virgin Islands.

weights and measures.

These charts are reproduced here because they are not available elsewhere, at least not in such systematic form. They are also very useful for teaching and enforcement purposes. However, the most updated version should always be requested if one is interested in the information.

REGULATIONS PROMULGATED

Introduction

Section 201 of the Federal Food, Drug, and Cosmetic Act (21 U.S.C. 321) defines "food" as the following. "The term 'food' means: (1) articles used for food or drink for man or other animals, (2) chewing gums, and (3) articles used for components of any such article." The act is intended to assure the consumer that foods are pure and wholesome, safe to eat, and produced under sanitary conditions. It prohibits distribution in the United States or importation of articles that are adulterated or misbranded. "Adulteration" is related to the content of the product, whereas "misbranding" includes any statements in labels or labeling that are false or misleading in any particular context.

Most of the regulations promulgated by the agency are aimed at implementing the various provisions of the act. The FDA has issued a small booklet titled "Requirements of the United States Food, Drug, and Cosmetic Act," which explains the act in easy-to-read terms and which is updated periodically. At the present time of writing the edition is February 1972. Part of the material in the following list has been adapted from this publication. Also, Table 6-11 presents the titles of the various sections of the act, showing the legal citations. Below is a synopsis of the principal requirement of the act as related to foods.

Health Safeguards

1. A food is illegal if it contains a natural or added deleterious substance that may render it injurious to health or unsafe [21 U.S.C. 342(a)(1) and (2)].
2. Food additives must be cleared for safety before they may be used in a food or become a part of a food as a result of processing, packaging, transporting, or holding the food (21 U.S.C. 348).
3. Raw agricultural products containing residues of pesticides not authorized by, or in excess of, tolerances established by regulations of the EPA are illegal (21 U.S.C. 346a).
4. A food is illegal if it is prepared, packed, or held under insanitary conditions

TABLE 6-11. Contents of the Federal Food, Drug, and Cosmetic Act, as Amended through 1972[a].

Chapter Number	Chapter Title	Section of		Section Title
		Act	21 U.S.C.	
I	Short title	1	301	Short title
II	Definitions	201	321	Definitions
III	Prohibited acts and penalties	301	331	Prohibited acts
		302	332	Injunction proceedings
		303	333	Penalties
		304	334	Seizure
		305	335	Hearing before report of criminal violations
		306	336	Report of minor violations
		307	337	Proceedings in name of United States; provision as to subpoenas
IV	Food	401	341	Definitions and standards for food
		402	342	Adulterated food
		403	343	Misbranded food
		404	344	Emergency permit control
		405	345	Regulations making exemptions
		406	346	Tolerances for poisonous ingredients in food
		407	347	Oleomargarine or margarine
		408	346a	Tolerances for pesticide chemicals in or on raw agricultural commodities
		409	348	Food additives
		410	349	Bottled drinking water
V	Drugs and devices	501	351	Adulterated drugs and devices
		502	352	Misbranded drugs and devices

	503	Exemptions in case of drugs and devices
	505	New drugs
	506	Certification of drugs containing insulin
	507	Certification of antibiotics
	508	Authority to designate official names
	509	Nonapplicability to cosmetics
	510	Registration of producers of drugs
	512	New animal drugs
VI	Cosmetics	
	601	Adulterated cosmetics
	602	Misbranded cosmetics
	603	Regulations making exemptions
VII	General administrative provisions	
	701	Regulations and hearings
	702	Examinations and investigations
	702a	Seafood inspection
	703	Records of interstate shipment
	704	Factory inspection
	705	Publicity
	706	Listing and certification of color additives for foods, drugs, and cosmetics
	707	Revision of U.S. Pharmacopeia; development of analysis and mechanical and physical tests
VIII	Imports and exports	
	801	Imports and exports
IX	Miscellaneous	
	901	Separability clause
	902	Effective date and repeals

a Reproduced from Federal Food, Drug, and Cosmetic Act as amended, August 1972, FDA.

whereby it may have been rendered injurious to health [21 U.S.C. 342(a)(4)].

5. Food containers must be free from any poisonous or deleterious substance that may cause the contents to be injurious to health [21 u.s.c. 342(a)(6)]. Some packaging materials, such as tamarind seed kernel powder and alkyl ketene dimers, may be "food additives" subject to regulations (21 U.S.C. 348).

6. Colors added to food must be only those established by the FDA as being safe [21 U.S.C. 342(c) and 376]. Unless exempt, colors for use in food must be from batches tested and certified by the FDA [21 U.S.C. 376(c)].

7. Confectionery, including candy, must not contain any alcohol, except alcohol less than 0.5% derived solely from the use of flavoring extract. Unless authorized, it is not permitted to contain any nonnutritive object. Nonnutritive ingredients such as food additives may be used only if they are safe; serve some practical and functional purpose in the manufacture, packaging, or storage of the confectionery; and do not deceive the consumer or violate other provisions of the act.

Sanitary Safeguards

1. A food is illegal if it is filthy, putrid, or decomposed [21 U.S.C. 342(a)(3)].
2. A food is illegal if it is prepared, packed, or held under insanitary conditions whereby it may have become contaminated with filth [21 U.S.C. 342(a)(4)].
3. A food is illegal if it is the product of a diseased animal or one that has died otherwise than by slaughter [21 U.S.C. 342(a)(5)].

Economic Safeguards

1. Food labels or labeling (circulars, etc.) must not be false or misleading in any particular [21 U.S.C. 343(a)]. Labeling is misleading not only if it contains false statements, but also if it fails to reveal material facts [21 U.S.C. 321(n)].
2. Damage or inferiority in a food must not be concealed in any manner [21 U.S.C. 342(b)(3)]. For example, adding artificial coloring and/or flavoring to a food to make it appear a better grade than it is, such as adding yellow coloring to make a food appear to contain more eggs than it actually contains.
3. A food must not be sold under the name of another food [21 U.S.C. 343(b)].
4. A substance recognized as being a valuable constituent of a food must not be omitted or abstracted in whole or in part, nor may any substance be substituted for the food in whole or in part [21 U.S.C. 342(b)(1) and (2)] (e.g., an article labeled "milk"or "whole milk" from which part of the butter fat has been skimmed).
5. Food containers must not be so made, formed, or filled as to be misleading [21 U.S.C. 343(d)] (e.g., a closed package filled to less than its capacity).

6. Required label information must not only be conspicuously displayed, but must also be in terms that the ordinary consumer is likely to read and understand under ordinary conditions of purchase and use [21 U.S.C. 343(f)].

The regulations promulgated by the FDA to implement the various provisions of the Federal Food, Drug, and Cosmetic Act and other acts under its jurisdiction may be grouped into categories. For example, one category of regulations are all related to food standards. All FDA official regulations are published in the Code of Federal Regulations and described in Appendixes 6-9 to 6-11. These appendixes present the title of each part and the statutory authority under which each part was issued. In the following paragraphs the different categories of regulations are discussed.

Administrative Policies

The regulations governing the conduct and policies of the FDA are described in the following legal documents:

21 CFR 5	Delegations of authority and organization
21 CFR 10	Administrative practices and procedures
21 CFR 12	Formal evidentiary public hearing
21 CFR 13	Public hearing before a public board of inquiry
21 CFR 14	Public hearing before a public advisory committee
21 CFR 15	Public hearing before the commissioner
21 CFR 16	Regulatory hearing before the FDA
21 CFR 19	Standards of conduct and conflicts of interest
21 CFR 21	Protection of privacy
21 CFR 25	Environmental impact consideration

Their titles are self-explanatory and space limitation prohibits a detailed discussion of each part. In the following, two selected aspects are presented: (1) certain common definitions used by the FDA and (2) the procedure whereby it issues regulations, standards, and other criteria and guidelines that form the core of the FDA's role in protecting public health in regard to food.

Some of the most common terms used by the FDA in its administrative practices are as follows, most of which have been adapted from 21 CFR 10.

Administrative Action. This refers to every form and kind of act, including the refusal or failure to act, involved in the implementations of the laws administered by the agency, except that it excludes the referral of apparent violations to U.S. attor-

neys for the institution of civil and criminal proceedings and all associated prepara-
tory and incidental acts.

Administrative File. This refers to the file maintained by the FDA, in which all
documents pertaining to an administrative proceeding, including internal working
memoranda and recommendations, are retained.

Administrative Proceeding (or Sometimes Termed "proceeding"). It means any
undertaking to issue, amend, or revoke a regulation or order or to take or refrain
from taking any other form of administrative action.

Agreements. These are all formal agreements, Memoranda of Understanding, or
other similar written documents executed by the FDA and another person or
organization, all of which are in public file. Any such document not included in the
public file is deemed to be rescinded and will have no force or effect whatever.

Advisory Committee or Public Advisory Committee. This is any committee, board,
commission, council, conference, panel, task force, or other similar groups or any
subgroups, not composed wholly of full-time officers or employees of the federal
government and established or utilized by the FDA to obtain advice or recommendations.

Advisory Opinion. An advisory opinion represents the formal position of the FDA
on the matter involved, and with certain exceptions, obligates the FDA to follow
it until it is amended or revoked. The FDA will not recommend legal action against
any person or product with respect to any action taken in conformity with an advisory opinion that has not been amended or revoked. A statement made or advice
provided by an FDA employee shall constitute an advisory opinion only if it is
issued in writing pursuant to established procedures. If it is given orally or given in
writing but not pursuant to prescribed rules, it is an *informal* communication that
represents the best judgment of that employee at that time but does not constitute an advisory opinion, does not necessarily represent the formal position of the
agency, and, consequently, does not bind or otherwise obligate or commit the
agency to the views expressed.

Communication, Ex Parte. This refers to an oral or written communication not on
the public record with respect to which reasonable prior notice to all parties is not
given. It does not include requests for status reports on any matter or proceeding.

Guidelines. Guidelines establish principles or practices of general applicability and
do not include decisions or advice limited to particular situations. They relate to

technical or policy criteria such as manufacture practices, product standards, compliance criteria, ingredient specifications, and labeling. They state procedures or standards of general applicability that are not legal requirements but are acceptable to the agency for a subject matter that falls within the laws administered by the FDA. A guideline represents the formal position of the FDA on the matter involved and, with few exceptions, obligates the agency to follow it until it is amended or revoked. The FDA will not recommend legal action against any person or product with respect to any action taken in conformity with a guideline issued and that has not been amended or revoked.

Meeting. This refers to any oral discussion, whether by telephone or in person, between an FDA employee and an individual from outside.

Order. This refers to any final FDA disposition, other than the issuance of a regulation, in a proceeding concerning any matter. It includes action on any new drug application, new animal drug application, or biological license; or, simply, it is the final agency disposition of an administrative proceeding.

Petition. This refers to any petition, application, or other document requesting the FDA to establish, amend, or revoke a regulation or order or to take or refrain from taking any other form of administrative action, under the laws administered by the FDA.

Regulation. This refers to any FDA rule of general or particular applicability and future effect implementing or applying any law administered by the FDA or relating to administrative practices and procedures. All FDA regulations having general applicability and legal effect shall be promulgated in the Federal Register and codified in the Code of Federal Regulations. Regulations may contain provisions that will be enforced as legal requirements or are intended only as guidelines and recommendations.

The promulgation of a rule or regulation by the FDA is a very important procedure and detailed information is provided in 21 CFR 10. Some aspects of the process are described in the following paragraphs.

The FDA may propose and promulgate regulations for the efficient enforcement of the laws administered by the agency whenever it is necessary or appropriate to do so. The issuance, amendment, or revocation of any such regulation may be initiated in any of the specified ways. The FDA may publish the regulation proposed by a petitioner if the reasons and interest are sound. It may publish two or more alternative proposed regulations on the same subject to obtain comment on the different alternatives. Any such regulation shall be the subject of a notice of proposed rule making published in the Federal Register. Such notice will contain the following:

1. A general statement at the beginning describing the substance of the document in easily understandable terms.
2. A preamble that summarizes the proposal and the facts and policy underlying it.
3. References to all data and information on which the FDA relies for the proposal, copies or a full list of which will be a part of the administrative file on the matter, kept in the office of the hearing clerk.
4. The statutory authority under which the regulation is proposed.
5. Either the terms or substance of the proposed regulation or a description of the subjects and issues involved.
6. A proposed effective date.
7. A reference to the existence or lack of need for an environmental impact statement.
8. The time, place, and method for interested persons to submit written comments on the proposal and a statement that comments should be submitted in accordance with the requirements specifically stated.
9. The docket number of the matter, which will be used to identify the administrative file established by the hearing clerk for all submissions relating to the matter, as provided in the regulation.

Such proposal shall ordinarily provide 60 days for comment, although the FDA may reduce or extend this time period for good cause. In no event will the time for comment be less than 10 days. After publication of the notice of proposed rule making, any interested person may request the FDA to extend the comment period for an additional specified length of time by submitting a written request to the hearing clerk stating the reasons. Such requests must follow established procedures and shall bear the heading, "REQUEST FOR EXTENSION OF COMMENT PERIOD." Any such request is required to show either why comments could not reasonably be submitted within the time permitted, that important new information will shortly be available, or that sound public policy otherwise supports an extension of the time for comment. The FDA may grant or deny such request or may grant an extension for a time period different from that requested. Extensions will not ordinarily be granted. It is limited to specific persons who have made and justified such a request but will ordinarily apply to all interested persons.

Any extension of 30 days or longer will be the subject of a notice published in the Federal Register and applicable to all interested persons. Any extension less than 30 days will be the subject either of a letter or memorandum filed with the hearing clerk or of a notice published in the Federal Register.

Four copies of all comments will be submitted to the hearing clerk, except that individuals may submit single copies of comments. Comments will be stamped with the date of receipt and will be numbered chronologically. Persons submitting comments critical of a proposed regulation are encouraged to include alternative wording that they believe would be preferable.

After the time for comment on a proposed regulation has expired, the FDA will review the entire administrative record on the matter, including all comments, and will determine the proceeding, issue a new proposal, or promulgate a final regulation, by notice published in the Federal Register.

The quality and persuasiveness of the comments will determine the FDA's decision with respect to such comments. The number or length of comments will not ordinarily be a significant factor in such decision. However, the number may be material where the degree of public interest is a legitimate factor for consideration. The decision of the agency with reference to the matter will be based solely on the administrative record.

The preamble to a final regulation published in the Federal Register will contain, in the first and second paragraphs, reference to prior notices relating to the same matter plus a general statement describing the substance of the document in easily understandable terms and will summarize each type of comment submitted on the proposal and the FDA's conclusions with regard to each such type of comment. The preamble will contain a thorough and comprehensive articulation of the reasons for FDA decisions on each issue.

The notice promulgating a final regulation published in the Federal Register will specify the effective date, which will not be less than 30 days after the date of publication in the Federal Register, except for any regulation: (1) that grants an exemption or relieves a restriction or (2) where the FDA finds and states in the notice good cause for an earlier effective date. Such rule making procedure will not apply to situations such as food additive and color additive petitions and new animal drug regulations, all of which are subject to special procedures.

In addition to the notice and public procedure required pursuant to these procedures, the FDA may, in its discretion, also subject any proposed or final regulation, before or after publication in the Federal Register, to any of the following procedures where they are reasonably applicable to the matter involved:

1. Conferences, meetings, discussions, and correspondence in accordance with established procedures.
2. A formal evidentiary public hearing according to 21 CFR 12.
3. A public hearing before a public board of inquiry according to 21 CFR 13.
4. A public hearing before a public advisory committee according to 21 CFR 14.
5. A public hearing before the commissioner according to 21 CFR 15.
6. A notice published in the Federal Register requesting data, information, and views before the FDA determines whether to propose a regulation.

7. A draft of a proposed regulation placed on public display in the office of the hearing clerk. If this procedure is used, the FDA will publish an appropriate notice in the Federal Register stating that the document is available and specifying the time within which comments may be submitted orally or in writing on the draft of the proposed regulation.

8. A revised proposal published in the Federal Register, which will be subject to all the provisions relating to proposed regulations.

9. A tentative or revised final regulation placed on public display at the office of the hearing clerk and, if deemed desirable by the FDA, published in the Federal Register. If the tentative regulation is placed on display only, the FDA will publish an appropriate notice in the Federal Register stating that the document is available and specifying the time within which comments may be submitted orally or in writing and will mail a copy of the document and the notice to each person who submitted comments on the proposed regulation if one has been published.

10. A final regulation published in the Federal Register that provides an opportunity for the submission of further comments, in accordance with established procedures, to determine whether the regulation should subsequently be modified or revoked.

11. Any other specific public procedure established by the FDA and explicitly made applicable to the matter by the terms of certain provisions.

Any party interested in obtaining further details or information on other administrative aspects of the FDA such as delegations of authority and organization should consult the original legal documents.

Food Standards

Section 401 of the Federal Food, Drug, and Cosmetic Act (21 U.S.C. 341) states:

Whenever in the judgment of the Secretary such action will promote honesty and fair dealing in the interest of consumers, he shall promulgate regulations fixing and establishing for any food, under its common or usual name so far as practicable, a reasonable definition and standard of identity, a reasonable standard of quality, and/or reasonable standards of fill of containers. However, no definition and standard of identity or standard of quality shall be established for fresh or dried fruits, fresh or dried vegetables, or butter, except that definitions and standards of identity may be established for avocados, cantaloupes, citrus fruits, and melons.

The "Secretary" refers to the Secretary of Health, Education, and Welfare who has delegated his authority to the FDA. Thus to "promote honesty and fair dealing in the interest of consumers," the FDA has issued the three kinds of standards. prescribed in the preceding quotation (viz., identity, quality, and fill of containers) for a number of food products. The premises and criteria for each of the standards are explained briefly in the following list in simple terms.

Standards of Identity

1. It establishes or defines what a given food product is; for example, it specifically establishes which ingredients the food must contain.
2. It specifies the correct name of the food and other required label information.
3. It limits the amount of water permitted.
4. It sets the required amounts of expensive ingredients and limits the inexpensive ones.
5. It defines the kind and amount of certain vitamins and minerals that must be present in foods labeled "enriched."
6. In prescribing a standard of identity for a food in which optional ingredients are permitted, the FDA must designate those to be named on the label.
7. If a proposed amendment or alteration of an existing food standard involves a food additive, all federal regulations relating to the use of a food additive in food must be complied with.
8. Temporary permits may be issued for interstate shipment of experimental packs of food varying from the requirements of definitions and standards of identity, assuming all established procedures have been followed.
9. A food standard is based on the assumption that the food is properly prepared from clean and sound materials. It usually does not relate to such factors as harmful impurities, filth, decomposition, and bacteria. However, there are exceptions, such as standards for products containing whole egg, egg white or yolk, and milk and milk products shipped interstate, requiring that they be pasteurized or otherwise treated to destroy all viable microorganisms, such as *Salmonella*.
10. A food represented as or purporting to be a food for which a standard of identity has been promulgated must comply with the specifications of the standard or definition in every respect. It is in noncompliance if it:
    a. Contains an ingredient not prescribed in the standard (however, under certain circumstances,if such an ingredient is an incidental additive, it may be permitted).
    b. Does not contain one or more of the prescribed ingredients in the standard.

    c. Contains an ingredient or component that deviates from the prescribed
       quantity.
11. Any standard of identity prescribed for avocados, cantaloupes, citrus fruits,
     or melons is related only to maturity and the effects of freezing.

The standards of identity are the basic food standards issued by the FDA.
They protect consumers from being cheated by inferior products or confused by
misleading labels. At the time of current writing, they number in the hundreds,
some of which are supplemented by standards of quality and fill of containers.

Standards of Quality

1. They are minimum standards for canned fruits and vegetables and establish
    specifications for quality requirements or factors such as ripeness, tenderness,
    color, and freedom from defects.
2. They protect the buyer from unknowingly receiving such products as stringy
    string beans, hard peas, or tomatoes with excess core and peeling.
3. If a food for which a standard of quality has been promulgated falls below
    such standard, it must bear special labeling: "BELOW STANDARD IN QUAL-
    ITY," followed by either "GOOD FOOD--NOT HIGH GRADE" or a state-
    ment showing the kind of defect, such as "Excessive Peel" or "Excessively
    Broken." The statements must be in prescribed size and style of type.
4. Standards of quality must not be confused with the "standards for grades"
    issued by the USDA for agricultural products and the Department of Com-
    merce for fishery products. Standards of quality are minimum standards only,
    whereas standards for grades may classify the products from average to excel-
    lent in quality. Standards for grades are not required to be stated on the label.
    However, if they are stated, the product must comply with the specifications
    of the declared grade.

Standards of Fill of Containers

1. They specify how full the container must be to avoid deception of the con-
    sumer and charges of "slack-filling."
2. They are especially needed for products composed of a number of units or
    pieces packed in a liquid or products that shake down after filling.
3. Formal standards of fill of containers have been issued for some fruits and
    vegetables, canned tuna, oysters, shrimp, and packed nuts.
4. Informal guidelines have been set for the fill of spices, olives, and pickles.
5. If a food for which a standard of fill of container has been promulgated falls
    below such standard, it must bear a general statement of substandard: "BE-

LOW STANDARD IN FILL." Such a statement must follow certain prescribed size and style of type.

6. In prescribing any standard of fill of container, due consideration must be given to the natural shrinkage in storage and in transit of fresh natural food and to the need for the necessary packing and protective material.

The technical details and requirements that explain how the three types of standards for food products are established can be located in 21 CFR 130, "Food standards: general." The legal administrative procedure whereby such standards are promulgated is the same as the one for promulgating rule or regulation by the FDA, which has been discussed in detail previously.

At the time of current writing, the FDA has established food standards for 21 categories of food. They are described alphabetically as follows, with the legal references:

Bakery products	21 CFR 136	Frozen vegetables	21 CFR 158
Cacao products	21 CFR 163	Fruit butters, jellies, preserves, and related products	21 CFR 150
Cereal flours and related products	21 CFR 137		
Canned fruit juices	21 CFR 146	Fruit pies	21 CFR 152
Canned fruits	21 CFR 145	Macaroni and noodle products	21 CFR 139
Canned vegetables	21 CFR 155		
Cheese and cheese products	21 CFR 133	Margarine	21 CFR 166
		Milk and cream	21 CFR 131
Eggs and egg products	21 CFR 160	Nonalcoholic beverages	21 CFR 165
Fish and shellfish	21 CFR 161		
Food dressings and flavorings	21 CFR 169	Sweeteners and table sirups	21 CFR 168
Frozen desserts	21 CFR 135	Tree nut and peanut products	21 CFR 164
		Vegetable juices	21 CFR 156

The various items included under each category of food products indicated in the preceding list are described as follows:

Bakery products (six items); 21 CFR 136

Bread, rolls, and buns

Enriched bread, rolls, and buns

Milk bread, rolls, and buns

Raisin bread, rolls, and buns

Enriched raisin bread, rolls, and buns

Whole wheat bread, rolls, and buns

Cacao products (14 items); 21 CFR 163

Cacao nibs

Chocolate liquor

Breakfast cocoa

Cocoa

Low-fat cocoa

Cocoa with diocytl sodium sulfo-
succinate for manufacturing

Sweet chocolate

Milk chocolate

Buttermilk chocolate

Skim milk chocolate

Mixed dairy product chocolates

Sweet cocoa and vegetable fat
(other than cacao fat) coating

Sweet chocolate and vegetable fat
(other than cacao fat) coating

Milk chocolate and vegetable fat
(other than cacao fat) coating

Cereal flours and related products (33 items); 21 CFR 137

Flour

Bromated flour

Enriched bromated flour

Enriched flour

Instantized flours

Phosphated flour

Self-rising flour

Enriched self-rising flour

Cracked wheat

Crushed wheat

Whole wheat flour

Bromated whole wheat flour

White corn flour

Yellow corn flour

Durum flour

Whole durum flour

Corn grits

Enriched corn grits

Quick grits

Yellow grits

White corn meal

Bolted white corn meal

Enriched corn meals

Degerminated white corn meals

Self-rising white corn meal

Yellow corn meal

Bolted yellow corn meal

Degerminated yellow corn meal

Self-rising yellow corn meal

Farina

Enriched farina

Semolina

Enriched rice

Canned fruit juices (42 items); 21 CFR 146

Cranberry juice cocktail

Artificially sweetened
  cranberry juice cocktail

Canned fruit nectars

Lemonade

Frozen concentrate for lemonade

Frozen concentrate for artificially
  sweetened lemonade

Colored lemonade

Frozen concentrate for colored
  lemonade

Limeade

Canned pineapple/grapefruit drink

Orange juice

Frozen orange juice

Pasteurized orange juice

Canned orange juice

Orange juice from concentrate

Frozen concentrated orange juice

Canned concentrated orange juice

Orange juice for manufacturing

Orange juice with preservatives

Concentrated orange juice for
  manufacturing

Concentrated orange juice with preservatives

Orange juice drink

Concentrate for orange juice drink

Powdered orange juice drink

Orange juice drink blend

Powdered orange juice drink blend

Orange drink

Concentrate for orange drink

Powdered orange drink

Orange flavored drink

Concentrate for orange flavored drink

Powdered orange flavored drink

Water-extracted soluble orange solids

Dehydrated water-extracted soluble
  orange solids

Comminuted oranges

Dehydrated comminuted oranges

Extract of comminuted oranges

Dehydrated extract of comminuted
  oranges

Juicy orange pulp for manufacturing

Dehydrated juicy orange pulp for
  manufacturing

Canned pineapple juice   Canned prune juice

Canned fruits (25 items); 21 CFR 145

Canned applesauce

Canned apricots

Artificially sweetened canned apricots

Canned apricots with rum

Canned berries

Canned cherries

Artificially sweetened canned cherries

Canned cherries with rum

Canned figs

Artificially sweetened canned figs

Canned preserved figs

Canned fruit cocktail

Artifically sweetened canned fruit
  cocktail

Canned seedless grapes

Canned grapefruit

Canned peaches

Artificially sweetened canned peaches

Canned peaches with rum

Canned pears

Artificially sweetened canned pears

Canned pears with rum

Canned pineapple

Artificially sweetened canned pineapple

Canned plums

Canned prunes

Canned vegetables (11 items); 21 CFR 155

Canned green beans and canned
  wax beans

Canned corn

Canned field corn

Canned peas

Canned dry peas

Canned tomatoes

Tomato paste

Tomato puree

Catsup

Certain other canned vegetables

Canned mushrooms

Cheese and related cheese products (73 items); 21 CFR 133

Asiago fresh and asiago soft cheese

Asiago medium cheese

Asiago old cheese

Blue cheese

Brick cheese

Brick cheese for manufacturing

Caciocavallo siciliano cheese

Cheddar cheese

Cheddar cheese for manufacturing

Low sodium cheddar cheese

Colby cheese

Colby cheese for manufacturing

Low sodium Colby cheese

Cold-pack and club cheese

Cold-pack cheese food

Cold-pack cheese food with fruits, vegetables, or meats

Cook cheese, koch kaese

Cottage cheese

Dry curd cottage cheese

Low fat cottage cheese

Cream cheese

Cream cheese with other foods

Washed curd and soaked curd cheese

Washed curd cheese for manufacturing

Edam cheese

Gammelost cheese

Gorgonzola cheese

Gouda cheese

Granular and stirred cured cheese

Granular cheese for manufacturing

Grated cheeses

Grated American cheese food

Hard grating cheeses

Gruyere cheese

Hard cheese

Limburger cheese

Monterey cheese and Monterey jack cheese

High-moisture jack cheese

Mozzarella cheese and scamorza cheese

Low-moisture mozzarella and scamorza cheese

Part-skim mozzarella and scamorza cheese

Low-moisture part-skim mozzarella and scamorza cheese

Muenster and munster cheese

Muenster and munster cheese for manufacturing

Neufchatel cheese

Nuworld cheese

Parmesan and reggiano cheese

Pasteurized blended cheese

Pasteurized blended cheese with fruits, vegetables, or meats

Pasteurized process cheese

Pasteurized process cheese with fruits, vegetables, or meats

Pasteurized process pimento cheese

Pasteurized process cheese food

Pasteurized process cheese food with fruits, vegetables, or meats

Pasteurized cheese spread

Pasteurized cheese spread with fruits, vegetables, or meats

Pasteurized neufchatel cheese spread with other foods

Pasteurized process cheese spread

Pasteurized process cheese spread with fruits, vegetables, or meats

Provolone and pasta filata cheese

Soft ripened cheeses

Romano cheese

Roquefort, sheep's milk blue-mold, and blue-mold cheese from sheep's milk

Samsoe cheese

Sap sago cheese

Semisoft cheeses

Semisoft part-skim cheeses

Skim milk cheese for manufacturing

Spiced cheeses

Part-skim spiced cheeses

Spices, flavored standardized cheeses

Swiss and emmentaler cheese

Swiss cheese for manufacturing

Eggs and egg products (10 items); 21 CFR 160

Eggs

Dried eggs

Frozen eggs

Liquid eggs

Egg whites

Dried egg whites

Frozen egg whites

Egg yolks

Dried egg yolks

Frozen egg yolks

Fish and shellfish (17 items); 21 CFR 161

Oysters

Extra large oysters

Large oysters

Medium oysters

Small oysters

Very small oysters

Olympia oysters

Large Pacific oysters

Medium Pacific oysters

Small Pacific oysters

Extra small Pacific oysters

Canned oysters

Canned Pacific salmon

Canned wet pack shrimp and canned dry pack shrimp in non-transparent containers

Frozen raw breaded shrimp

Frozen raw lightly breaded shrimp

Canned tuna

Food dressings and flavorings (11 items); 21 CFR 169

French dressing	Concentrated vanilla flavoring
Mayonnaise	Vanilla powder
Salad dressing	Vanilla/vanillin extract
Vanilla extract	Vanilla/vanillin flavoring
Concentrated vanilla extract	Vanilla/vanillin powder
Vanilla flavoring	

Frozen desserts (eight items); 21 CFR 135

Frozen custard	Mellorine
Fruit sherbets	Nonfruit sherbets
Ice cream	Nonfruit water ices
Ice milk	Water ices

Frozen vegetables (one item); 21 CFR 158

Frozen peas

Fruit butters, jellies, preserves, and related products (five items); 21 CFR 150

Fruit butter	Fruit preserves and jams
Fruit jelly	Artificially sweetened fruit preserves and jams
Artificially sweetened fruit jelly	

Fruit pies (one item); 21 CFR 152

Frozen cherry pie

Macaroni and noodle products (15 items); 21 CFR 139

Macaroni products	Enriched macaroni products with fortified protein
Enriched macaroni products	Milk macaroni products

Nonfat-milk macaroni products

Enriched nonfat-milk macaroni
  products

Vegetable macaroni products

Enriched vegetable macaroni products

Whole wheat macaroni products

Wheat and soy macaroni products

Noodle products

Enriched noodle products

Vegetable noodle products

Enriched vegetable noodle products

Wheat and soy noodle products

Margarine (one item); 21 CFR 166

Margarine

Milk and cream (18 items); 21 CFR 131

Milk

Concentrated milk

Sweetened/condensed milk

Nonfat dry milk

Nonfat dry milk fortified with
  vitamins A and D

Evaporated milk

Lowfat milk

Skim milk

Heavy cream

Light cream

Light whipping cream

Sour cream

Acidified sour cream

Sour cream dressing

Half-and-half

Sour half-and-half

Acidified sour half-and-half

Sour half-and-half dressing

Nonalcoholic beverages (one item); 21 CFR 165

Soda water

Sweeteners and table sirups (nine items); 21 CFR 168

Dextrose anhydrous

Dextrose monohydrate

Glucose sirup

Dried glucose sirup

Lactose

Cane sirup

Maple sirup	Table sirup
Sorghum sirup	

Tree nut and peanut products (three items); 21 CFR 164

Mixed nuts	Peanut butter
Shelled nuts in rigid or semirigid containers	

Vegetable juices (two items); 21 CFR 156

Tomato juice	Yellow tomato juice

To illustrate the food standards established by the FDA, Appendixes 6-12 and 6-13 reproduce some examples from the Code of Federal Regulations. Appendix 6-12 describes the standard of identity for mayonnaise, 21 CFR 169, and Appendix 6-13, the standards of identity, quality, and fill of container for canned peas, 21 CFR 155.

The Codex Alimentarius Commission is an international body with various activities concerning food. Details on this organization are discussed in Chapter 1 of this book. One of its major functions is to establish food standards to facilitate international commerce in food products. The regulation contained in 21 CFR 130.6 explains how the United States, that is, the FDA, will handle such standards. All food standards adopted by the commission will be reviewed by the FDA and either accepted without change, accepted with change, or not accepted. The review will be accomplished, by official publication in the Federal Register for comments, in one of the following ways:

1. An interested party may petition the FDA to adopt a standard, with or without change, by proposing a new standard or an appropriate amendment of an existing standard.
2. The FDA may initiate the proposal.
3. A standard not handled by one of the above two methods will be published for public comments.

After reviewing all comments from any of these three channels, the FDA will make a decision on the standard. Any partial or total adoption of such a food standard will, of course, make that standard legally enforceable in this country.

The FDA encourages all interested parties to confer with different interest groups such as consumers, industries, academic communities, and professional organizations in formulating petitions or comments.

According to the Staff Manual Guide of the FDA, the Office of Sciences within the Bureau of Foods supervises a number of divisions, one of which is the Division of Microbiology (see Appendix 6-5). This division oversees, among others, the Food Microbiology Branch, which performs a number of activities and functions. For example, this branch develops "the technical and microbiological basis for recommended limits, guidelines, and practices applied to food in Current Good Manufacturing Practices and used by Federal, State, and municipal health control agencies." This particular functional statement should not be taken to mean that the FDA has promulgated "microbiological quality standards" for many foods. At the present time of writing the FDA has just started promulgating bacteriological standards for food. As a matter of fact, it is a very controversial issue.

When establishing microbial limits for food, the FDA distinguishes between pathogens and those bacteria that are at least nonpathogenic when present in small numbers. Thus the latter are usually implied when the microbiological quality of a food is referred to by the FDA. Those foods that have some kind of bacteriological guidelines established by the FDA are discussed as follows:

1. The FDA has promulgated "standards of quality" for bottled water. In the standards the FDA specifies the limits or counts of a number of bacteria permitted to be present.
2. According to the standards of identity established by the FDA for eggs, egg whites, and egg yolks, including dried, frozen and liquid forms, each product is not permitted to contain viable *Salmonella*. The FDA considers this as a factor of safety and not quality since *Salmonella* is a pathogen.
3. The official FDA standards of identity for milk and milk products do not specify the bacterial counts, although they require the process of pasteurization or similar treatment. However, the FDA has *recommended* microbiological standards for such products to be used by state and local authorities in their regulatory control. If these products are shipped interstate or served in interstate travel vehicles, the recommendations may become requirements and such standards will be fully enforceable.
4. The FDA has *recommended* bacteriological standards for certain shellfish such as oysters, clams, or mussels, either shucked or in the shell, fresh, or frozen. Again, local and state officials use them for sanitary control, although the FDA will enforce them if the products are shipped interstate.
5. The FDA issues unofficial or informal microbiological guidelines or criteria to its field personnel. These guidelines define bacteriological limits for a number of food products, and the data are based on what is attainable in the products

under the conditions of processing, assuming good manufacturing practices have been exercised. They are used primarily in conjunction with inspectional findings to support observations of insanitary practices.

The parameters used by the FDA to indicate bacteriological quality of a food are usually total aerobic plate counts and counts of *Escherichia coli*, coagulase-positive *Staphylococcus aureus*, and coliforms. The FDA's inclination to promulgate more microbiological quality standards for food has generated much controversy. Some basic problems that have been debated frequentely are indicated below:

1. If a state or local authority also sets up microbial limits for food, the manufacturer who ships his products interstate will encounter a great problem.
2. Informal and internal microbiological guidelines used by the FDA field personnel in food processing plants for inspection and products monitoring have created some problems because food processors do not have access to them. At the present time of writing, because of new agency policies, the food manufacturer may be able to obtain the data and incorporate them into their own quality control procedures.
3. Various organoleptic tests of food products have shown that food quality cannot be equated to its microbial counts.
4. The selection of indicator bacteria and the method of measuring them are not uniform and reliable.
5. It is difficult to ascertain whether the manufacturer can attain the limits required.
6. The cost that will pass on to the consumers is high.
7. One basic problem is how to account for abuses and contamination due to the handling of the products at the distribution and retail levels.

Food Packaging and Labeling

The two federal statutes that regulate food packaging and labeling are the Federal Food, Drug, and Cosmetic Act and the Fair Packaging and Labeling Act (15 U.S.C. 1453 et seq.). The relevant provisions of the latter are explained in detail in the FDA publication, "Food Packaging and Labeling Act Requirements." The relevant regulations promulgated by the FDA are listed as follows:

21 CFR 1   General regulations for the enforcement of the Federal Food, Drug, and Cosmetic Act and the Fair Packaging and Labeling Act (Subpart A, General Provisions, and B, General Labeling Requirements)

21 CFR 101 Food labeling

21 CFR 102   Common or usual name for nonstandardized foods

The following discussion has been adapted from the original regulations, various FDA fact sheets, and articles published in the FDA Consumer (e.g., June 1977 issue).

A "label" is the display of written, printed, or graphic matter on the immediate container or package of a consumer commodity; it may be affixed to the package. "Labeling" generally refers to all associated printed or graphic material such as would appear on a display case, sign, placard, or similar, near or adjacent to the immediate container at any time while such article is in interstate commerce or held for sale after shipment or delivery in interstate commerce.

The "principal display panel" of a food package is the surface of the package that, either by design or through general use, is customarily displayed to the consumer. The "information panel" means that part of the label immediately contiguous and to the right of the principal display panel as observed by an individual facing the principal display panel. There are many exceptions to this definition.

The labeling of meats and poultry products, with some exceptions, is regulated by the USDA (see Chapter 1). The labeling of all alcoholic beverages is regulated by the Bureau of Alcohol, Tobacco, and Firearms (see Chapter 7). The advertisement and literature relevant to food products and their labels is regulated by the FTC (see Chapter 5). Also, the FDA has exempted a number of food products from complying with its labeling requirements.

The FDA does not have legal authority to restrict the number of different package sizes in which a food may be sold. It does, however, have the authority to define the range of package sizes--for example, "small," "medium," "large," and "extra large." Thus, the "large" size of one manufacturer's product will not be the "medium" size of a competitor. Certain provisions of the Fair Packaging and Labeling Act authorize the Department of Commerce, through the National Bureau of Standards (see Chapter 2), to seek voluntary agreement from manufacturers so that a single commodity will not be offered in a confusing array of packaging sizes.

The information on the label or other location of a food package is categorized into the following:

    I.   Mandatory information
        1. Statement of identity
        2. Language requirement
        3. Net quantity of food contents
        4. Name and address of business or manufacturer
        5. Ingredients
        6. Manufacturing code
        7. Prominence of required statements

II. Mandatory wordings of certain information if it is included on the food label
1. Nutrition labeling
2. Grades
3. Labeling for special dietary use
4. Saving representations
5. Warning statement
III. Optional information
1. Universal Product Code
2. Dates
3. Symbols
4. Others

In the following some of the relevant legal information relating to food labels are discussed, and the discussion follows the format or different categories presented in the preceding outline.

I. Mandatory Information

1. Statement of Identity

a. In the case of a standardized food, the complete name as designated in the standard of identity.
b. For nonstandardized foods, the common or usual name, an appropriately descriptive term, or a fanciful name commonly used by the public.
c. The form of the product must also be included, such as "sliced," "whole," or "chopped" (or other type), unless it is depicted by vignette or the product is visible through the container.
d. All words should be in bold type, in a size reasonably related to the most prominent printed matter and should be in lines generally parallel to the base on which the package rests as it is designed to be displayed.
e. Imitation food must bear the word "imitation." For example, the word "imitation" must be used when the product is not as nutritious as the product that it resembles and for which it is a substitute. If a product is similar to an existing one and is equally nutritious, a new name can be given to it rather than calling it "imitation." For example, eggless products that are nutritionally equivalent to eggs have been given names such as "eggbeaters" and "scramblers."
f. A label may be required to bear the percentage(s) of a characterizing ingredient(s) or information concerning the presence or absence of an ingredient(s) or the need to add an ingredient(s) as part of the common or usual name of a nonstandardized food item (see examples that follow).

The labels of some foods may be deceptive or misleading. To prevent possible deception, such foods are required to have a "common or usual" name that gives accurate information about the content. For example, a beverage that resembles orange juice but actually contains very little orange juice must carry a name such as "diluted orange-juice drink." Some such products are required to declare on the label the percentage of characterizing ingredient they contain. In the example given, the common or usual name might be "diluted orange-juice beverage, contains 10% orange juice."

A noncarbonated beverage that appears to contain a fruit or vegetable juice but actually does not must state on the label that it contains no fruit or vegetable juice. Another special label requirement concerns packaged foods in which the main ingredient or component of a recipe is not included, as in the case of some "main dishes" or "dinners." On such foods, the common or usual name consists of the following:

i. The common name of each ingredient in descending order by weight, for example, "noodles and tomato sauce."
ii. Identification of the food to be prepared from the package, for example, "for preparation of chicken casserole."
iii. A statement of ingredients that must be added to complete the recipe, for example, "you must add chicken to complete the recipe."

2. Language Requirement. If the food is packaged for interstate shipment in the United States, the mandatory and optional information must appear on the label in the English language. If the label of a food bears representations in a foreign language, the label must bear all of the required statements in the foreign language, as well as in English. (Note: The Tariff Act of 1930 requires that all imported articles be marked with the English name of the country of origin.)

3. Net Quantity of Food Contents. The net quantity of food in the package must be declared. This shall be expressed in terms of weight, measure, numerical count, or a combination; it must be in terms of liquid, solid, semisolid, or viscous products accordingly. The declaration must facilitate value comparisons by consumers and should accurately reveal the quantity of food in the package, exclusive of wrappers and other material packed therewith. There are numerous requirements relating to the declaration of food contents. In the following some examples are given; complete details should be obtained from the original document (21 CFR 101.105):

a. The basic units of measure are in terms of the avoirdupois pound and ounce and the U.S. gallon of 231 cubic inches and quart, pint, and fluid ounce subdivisions thereof.

b. The quantity declaration must appear on the principal display panel of the label in lines generally parallel to the base of the package when displayed for sale. If the principal display panel area is larger than 5 square inches, the declaration should appear within the lower 30% of the label. It must be in a type size based on the area of the principal display panel of the package as described in the regulation and must be separated from other information.

c. The new weight on packages containing one pound (avoirdupois) or more and less than 4 pounds must be declared first in total avoirdupois ounces followed by a second statement in parentheses in terms of pounds and ounces, or pounds and common or decimal fractions of the pound. Examples are: "Net Wt. 24 oz (1 lb 8 oz)," "Net Wt. 24 oz (1½ lb)," or "Net Wt. 24 oz (1.5 lb)." The contents of packages containing less than one pound must be expressed as total ounces (e.g., "Net Wt. 12 oz").

d. Net volume of liquid products in packages containing 1 pint or more and less than 1 U.S. gallon must be declared first in total fluid ounces followed by a second statement in parentheses in terms of quarts, pints, and fluid ounces or fractions of the pint or quart. Examples are: "Net contents 56 fluid ounces (1 quart 1½ pints)" or "Net 56 fluid oz (1 qt 1 pt 8 oz). The declaration "Net 56 fluid oz (1 quart 24 ounces)" is incorrect. Volume of packages containing less than 1 pint must be declared in fluid ounces (e.g., 5 fluid oz).

e. The metric system of weight or measure may also be used to declare the quantity, in addition to the English system.

f. If the label of any food package also represents the contents in terms of the number of servings, the size of each serving must be indicated and stated in the same printing size in immediate conjunction with the serving statements.

g. "The declaration of net quantity of contents shall express an accurate statement of the quantity of contents of the package. Reasonable variations caused by loss or gain of moisture during course of good distribution practice or by unavoidable deviations in good manufacturing practice will be recognized. Variations from stated quantity of contents shall not be reasonably large." [21 CFR 101.105(q); see also National Bureau of Standards, Chapter 2 of this book].

4. Name and Address of Business or Manufacturer. The name, street address, city, state, and zip code of either the manufacturer, packer, or distributor must be given. The street address may be omitted by a firm listed in a current city or telephone directory. A firm whose address is outside the United States may omit the zip code. If the food is not manufactured by the person or company whose name appears on the label, the name must be qualified by "Manufactured for," "Distributed by," or similar expression.

5. Ingredients. The ingredients in a food must be listed by their common names in the order of predominance by weight unless the food is standardized, in which case the label must include those ingredients that the regulation requires to be declared. The word "ingredients" does not refer to the chemical composition, but to the individual food components of a mixed food.

The *presence* of any artificial flavoring, coloring, and/or chemical preservatives must be stated. Each food additive must be listed by name; spices, flavors, and colors may be listed as such without naming the specific materials. Butter, cheese, and ice cream, however, are not required to state the presence of artificial color.

When the presence of a single, expensive ingredient is promoted as significant to the value of the food, a declaration of the percent of the expensive ingredient present may be required. For example, a label designation of "cottonseed oil and olive oil" for a mixture containing 80% or more cottonseed oil may require a declaration of the percent of each type of oil present.

With reference to the designation of ingredients for standardized foods, the following should be noted:

a.   The FDA has set "standards of identity" for some foods. These standards require that all foods called by a particular name (e.g., mayonnaise or catsup) contain certain mandatory ingredients. Manufacturers are also permitted to add certain optional ingredients.

b.   At the present time of writing, federal law does not require the declaration of mandatory ingredients on the label of standardized foods.

c.   Consumers want the labels of standardized foods to bear complete information on the ingredients contained in the food. In the absence of statutory authority to require that the label bear such information, the FDA encourages all manufacturers, packers, and distributors to voluntarily make such disclosure.

d.   The FDA intends to amend the definitions and standards of identity of food by enforcing Section 401 of the Federal Food, Drug, and Cosmetic Act (21 U.S.C. 341) to require label declaration of all optional ingredients with the exception of optional spices, flavorings, and colorings that may continue to be designated as such without specific ingredient declaration.

e.   For *some* definitions and standards of identity for food, there is a requirement that designated optional ingredients such as sweeteners, flavor enhancers, stabilizers, preservatives, spices, colorings, flavorings, and emulsifiers be declared in a specified manner on the label wherever the name of the standardized food appears. The declaration must be conspicuous so as to be easily seen under customary conditions of purchase.

f.   Some manufacturers of standardized foods do declare both mandatory and optional ingredients on the labels.

6. Manufacturing Code. Many companies use code dating on products that have a long "shelf life." The code gives the manufacturer and the store precise information about where and when the product was manufactured and/or packaged. This facilitates the recall or segregation of specific food lots that may have become contaminated and unfit for human consumption. Such a code may appear anywhere on the product package. Some codes are visible to the human eye and some not, requiring a special machine for reading or decoding.

7. Prominence of Required Statements. Some situations when the required statements will not be legally considered as prominent and conspicuous are the following:

a. The terms used are confusing to the ordinary customer under conditions of purchase and use.
b. They fail to appear on the part of the label displayed under customary conditions of purchase.
c. Nonrequired information such as words or designs have occupied the label area and there is insufficient space for the required statements.
d. The printing suffers from any or all of the following: (i) small type, (ii) unclear style of type, (iii) insufficient background contrast, (iv) obscuring designs or vignettes, (v) crowding with other material such as printing, writing, or graphics.

II. Mandatory Wordings of Certain Information if It Is Included on the Food Label

1. Nutrition Labeling. Nutritional labeling has been termed a "voluntary" program. However, it becomes mandatory if one or both of the following conditions are applicable:

a. A nutrient such as protein, mineral, or vitamin has been added to the food (e.g., vitamin C added to fruit drinks, or vitamins A and D added to skim milk).
b. A nutritional claim is made about the food on the package, in product literature, through public media, and other forms of communication. Some examples are:
   i. The statement, "This food is nutritious."
   ii. The statement, "Vitamins have been added." Mention of any of the following will require full nutrition labeling on the package: protein, carbohydrate, fat, vitamin, mineral, fatty acids, cholesterol, or calories.
   iii. The phrases, "low calorie," "high protein," "low fat," and "low cholesterol."

However, many food manufacturers state nutrition information on products when not required to do so.

Nutrition labels list the number of calories and quantities of protein, carbohydrate, and fat in a serving of the product. They also declare the percentage of the U.S. Recommended Daily Allowances (USRDAs) of protein and seven important vitamins and minerals that each serving of the product contains. The information is intended to assist the consumers to shop for more nutritious food and plan more nutritionally balanced meals for the American family. Some details of nutrition labeling are described in the following paragraphs.

The label states the size of a serving (e.g., one cup, two ounces, 1 tablespoon), the number of servings in the container, the number of calories per serving, and number of grams of protein, carbohydrate, and fat per serving. Protein is listed twice on the label: in grams and as a percentage of the USRDA. The vitamins and minerals must be shown in the order shown: vitamin A, vitamin C (ascorbic acid), thiamin (vitamin B1), riboflavin (vitamin B2), niacin, calcium, and iron. The listing of 12 other vitamins and minerals, and of cholesterol, fatty acid, and sodium content is optional.

The USRDAs are the approximate amounts of protein, vitamins, and minerals that an adult should eat every day to maintain health. If interested in the technical and complicated details whereby the values of the USRDAs are obtained, one should consult 21 CFR 101 and/or the latest edition of the Recommended Dietary Allowances, published by the Food and Nutrition Board, National Academy of Sciences/National Research Council. Nutrition labels list the USRDA by percentage. For example, the label may state that one serving of the food contains 35% of the USRDA of vitamin A and 25% of the USRDA of iron. The total amount of food an individual eats in a day should supply the USRDA of all essential nutrients.

Nutrition labels show amounts in grams rather than ounces because grams are a smaller unit of measurement and many food components are present in very small amounts. An example of conversion of units is "1 pound (lb) = 454 grams (g)."

Many foods today are manufactured into products that are different from traditional foods. Some examples include: frozen dinners; breakfast cereals; meal replacements; noncarbonated breakfast beverages fortified with vitamin C; and main dishes such as macaroni and cheese, pizzas, stews, and casseroles. To assist the consumer to obtain adequate nutrient intakes from such foods, the FDA is estabishing voluntary nutritional guidelines for them. The regulations are described in 21 CFR 104 and are discussed in further detail later. A product that complies with such official guideline may include on its label the statement that it meets the U.S. nutritional quality guideline for that particular class of food.

2. Grades. Some food products carry a grade on the label, such as "U.S. Grade A."

Grades are set by various federal and state agencies:

a. The USDA sets grades for a number of agricultural products, based on the quality levels inherent in the product such as taste, texture, and appearance. No nutritional factors are involved.
b. The National Marine Fisheries Service of the Department of Commerce sets grades for fishery products. Nutrients are not considered.
c. Milk and milk products in most states carry a "Grade A" label. This grade is based on FDA recommended sanitary standards for the production and processing of milk and milk products, which are regulated by the states. The grade is not related to nutritional factor. However, the FDA has established certain standards for milk that require certain levels of vitamins A and D when they are added to milk.

Federal food grading is a voluntary program. However, the quality of product that bears a federal grade mark on its label must be what it claims to be.

3. Labeling for Special Dietary Use. Examples of foods for special dietary use include protein, vitamin, and/or mineral supplements, infant formulas, foods for certain allergic patients, and others. The label must describe the dietary properties in a prescribed manner to inform the purchasers fully as to their value for such uses. The label is specifically prohibited from:

a. Any claim, with certain exceptions, that products intended to supplement diets are sufficient in themselves to prevent, treat, or cure disease(s).
b. Any implication that a diet of ordinary foods cannot supply adequate nutrients.
c. All claims that inadequate or insufficient diet is due to the soil in which a food is grown.
d. All claims that transportation, storage, or cooking of foods may result in inadequate or deficient diet.
e. Nutritional claims for nonnutritive ingredients such as rutin, other bioflavonoids, para-aminobenzoic acid, inositol, and similar ingredients. Their combinations with essential nutrients are also prohibited.

The regulations do not preclude a manufacturer or distributor who has adequate scientific data from claiming a higher nutrient retention in his product than in a competitive product, nor do they prohibit a claim that a particular food has a higher nutrient content because of the soil in which it is grown if that claim is substantiated by scientific data. The regulations permit a manufacturer to identify which vitamins are naturally present and which are added to his product. For further information on foods for special dietary use, consult 21 CFR 105.

4. Savings Representations. If the sponsor of a food product includes a representation on the label about savings to the consumer in various forms, the labeling must comply with special regulations, some of which are described as follows:

a. The container may bear a representation of economy by virtue of its size (e.g., "economy size," "thrifty pack," and "bargain size"). However, one requirement is that the sponsor must offer, at the same time, the same brand of that commodity in at least one other packaged size or label form. The promoted package must be sold 5% less than the lowest price per unit weight, volume, or measure of the regular packages of the same product sold at the same time.
b. The container may bear a "cents-off" promotion. However, one requirement is that the sponsor must include on the label the single price to be paid by the consumer and the statement "Price Marked is...Cents Off the Regular Price," or the regular price must be posted on a placard or listed on a shelf marker.

5. Warning Statement. The label of a food packaged in a self-pressurized container and intended to be expelled from the package under pressure is required to bear certain prescribed warning statement. For example, "WARNING--Avoid spraying in eyes. Contents under pressure. Do not puncture or incinerate. Do not store at temperature above 120°F. Keep out of reach of children." In the case of products intended for use by children, the phrase "except under adult supervision" may be added at the end of the last sentence in the warning statement just described.

III. Optional Information

The materials described as follows are not regulated by the FDA or other federal agencies at the present time of writing. However, because they appear so frequently on food packages, a brief description will provide some background information.

1. Universal Product Code. Many food labels now include a small block of parallel lines of various widths, with accompanying numbers, usually on the bottom and sides. This is the Universal Product Code; each code on a label is unique to that product. The numbers identify the category of products, the company manufacturing the product, and the size and contents of the package. With the use of a computerized checkout apparatus that can read the code, a variety of information can be obtained. The basic items include tax computation, recording sale, dispensing a receipt, and inventory control. If proper programs are incorporated into the machine, other duties can be performed, such as sales, check authorization, trading stamps, food stamps, credit references, and the degree of acceptability of a product

to the consumer. Because the code may eventually prove to be a money-saving device to grocery merchants, its popularity is increasing. (The firm that handles this new system is Distribution Codes, Inc., 401 Wyeth Street, Alexandria, Virginia 22314).

2. Dates. To help consumers obtain food that is fresh and wholesome, many manufacturers date their products. Open dating, as this practice often is called, is at present at the center of dispute. This dispute results from the indecision as to the kind of open dating that should be used. Four kinds are available and they are briefly described as follows:

a. Expiration date: the last date the food should be consumed.
b. Freshness date: similar to the expiration date but may allow for normal home storage.
c. Pack date: the date on which the food was packed or manufactured.
d. Pull or sell date: the last date the product should be sold, assuming it has been stored and handled properly. The pull date allows for some storage time in the home refrigerator.

3. Symbols on Food Labels. The symbol that consists of the letter "U" inside the letter "O" is one whose use is authorized by the Union of Orthodox Jewish Congregations of America, more familiarly known as the Orthodox Union, for use of foods that comply with Jewish dietary laws. (Further information may be obtained from its headquarters, 116 East 27th St., New York, New York 10016).

The symbol that consists of the letter "K" inside the letter "O" is used to indicate that the food is "kosher" (complying with the Jewish dietary laws and processed under the direction of a rabbi).

The symbol "R" or letter "R" inside a letter "O" on a label signifies that the trademark used on the label is registered with the U.S. Patent Office. The symbol "C" indicates that the literary and artistic content of the label is protected against infringement under the copyright laws of the United States. Copies of such labels have been filed with the Copyright Office of the Library of Congress.

4. Others. Other information may appear on the labels, such as brand name, suggested recipes, storage and cooking instructions or recommendations, games, comics, or competitions. None of these is authorized or regulated by the FDA or other federal agencies, at least not at the present time of writing.

Quality and Definition for Certain Foods

Regulations have been promulgated for governing the properties of certain foods, as follows:

21 CFR 103   Quality standards for foods with no identity standards
21 CFR 104   Nutritional quality guidelines for foods
21 CFR 105   Foods for special dietary use

Each of these three sets of regulations is briefly discussed as follows:

Quality Standards for Foods with No Identity Standards. The quality of a food depends on numerous characteristics including physical factors such as odor, flavor, color and turbidity, and biological factors such as microorganism count. They inform us of the general quality of the raw ingredients, the degree of quality control practiced in the processing, and the conditions of packaging, storage, handling, and distribution. To ensure that the consumer buys a good product, individual standards of quality are required to be established for different types of food. The label of a product that fails to meet the established requirements must show a statement of substandard quality as prescribed by regulation or the label may bear the statement "Below Standard in Quality--_____," with the blank to be filled in with whichever of the following are applicable: "Contains Excessive Bacteria," "Excessively Turbid," "Abnormal Color," and any other quality deviation as specified.

The statement of substandard quality should appear on the principal display panel, and the name of the food should either immediately precede or follow the statement. Such quality standards apply to certain class of food and are not standards of identity for the products involved. Compliance with a standard of quality promulgated does not exempt the product from compliance with all other requirements of the Federal Food, Drug, and Cosmetic Act. For example, evidence obtained through factory inspection indicating a violation of sanitation renders the food unlawful, even though the food contains levels of microorganisms lower than those prescribed by an applicable quality standard. Thus standards of quality for the following foods have been established: frozen ready-to-eat banana, coconut, chocolate, or lemon cream-type pies; food grade gelatin; and bottled water. For example, a frozen ready-to-eat banana cream type pie is required to have the physical and compositional characteristics of a cream-type pie, including semisolid filling and/or topping, to contain flavoring and/or fruit ingredients corresponding to the banana flavor, and to be prepared with or without a crust. The geometric mean of the aerobic plate count should be less than or equal to 50,000 per gram. The average coliform count should be less than or equal to 50 per gram. For further details on these three products, consult the original document (21 CFR 130). At present time of writing, some of these quality standards are being revised so that future microbiological standards can be prepared in a form consistent with international microbiological specifications.

Nutritional Quality Guidelines for Food. A nutritional quality guideline prescribes the minimum level or range of nutrient composition (nutritional quality) appropriate for a given class of food. The label of such a product may state that "This product provides nutrients in amounts appropriate for the class of food as determined by the U.S. Government," except that the words "this product" are optional. The size and location of this statement must follow regulations. Noncompliance products cannot use this statement. The label of the product in compliance must follow the following instructions:

1. Provide the common name of the product.
2. Include nutritional labeling.
3. No claim may be made implying any nutritional or other differences between a product to which a nutrient has or has not been added to meet the guidelines.
4. The addition of an "unnecessary" nutrient must bear the statement, "The addition of _____ to (or "The addition of _____ at the level contained in) this product has been determined by the U.S. Government to be unnecessary and inappropriate and does not increase the dietary value of the food."

Some specific nutritional guidelines have been established for frozen "heat and serve" dinners. Each such product should contain at least the following three components:

1. One or more sources of protein derived from meat, poultry, fish, cheese, or eggs.
2. One or more vegetables or vegetable mixtures other than potatoes, rice, or cereal-based product.
3. Potatoes, rice, or cereal-based product (other than bread or rolls) or another vegetable or vegetable mixture.

The components, including their sauces, gravies, and breading, must also satisfy the following conditions:

1. Contribute a minimum amount of certain prescribed nutrients, for example, 4 g of protein per 100 kilocalories of the components.
2. The protein source(s) of the flesh or dairy component should provide not less than 70% of the total protein supplied by the three components.
3. Any addition of nutrient should result in a total of under 150% of the mini-

mum prescribed level for each nutrient.

For further information, consult the original document (21 CFR 105).

Foods for Special Dietary Use. The term "special dietary use" as applied to food for human consumption refers to the following:

1. Supplying a special dietary need because of a physical, physiological, pathological, or other condition such as disease, convalescence, pregnancy, lactation, infancy, allergic hypersensitivity to food, underweight, overweight, or the need to control sodium intake.
2. Supplying a vitamin, mineral, or other ingredient to supplement a human diet. There are regulations prescribing the composition and labeling of such dietary supplements.
3. Supplying a special dietary need because it is the sole item of the diet.

The use of artificial sweetener, unless otherwise exempted, is considered a use for regulation of the intake of calories and available carbohydrate or for diabetics and thus constitutes a special dietary use.

The regulations define the daily amounts of vitamins and minerals as included in the USRDA. They provide the chemical structures for the vitamins and define those vitamins and minerals for which no USRDA have been established. With reference to the labels of food for special dietary use, the regulations indicate mandatory information, prohibitions, labeling statements for hypoallergic, low sodium and low caloric foods, and vitamin and mineral supplements.

The regulations also provide complete details on the standards of identity for dietary supplements of vitamins and minerals, including type and amount, acceptable ingredient sources, format of listing, and certain labeling prohibitions.

Food and Color Additives, Pesticides and Related Substances, and Unavoidable Chemical Contaminants

Food Additives

Since 1970 the safety of the use of food additives probably has been one of the most publicly debated topics in relation to the FDA and the products it regulates. This situation is expected to remain unchanged for a long period. The information presented in the following paragraphs concentrates on the legal issues and does not pertain to the controversy of the use of such substances.

In 1958 a Food Additives Amendment was added to the original Federal

Food, Drug, and Cosmetic Act passed by Congress in 1938. This amendment contains four important aspects:

1. It defines what a food additive is.
2. It authorizes the FDA to "license" the use of food additives.
3. It permits the proposed use of a food additive if it can be proven safe when present at a certain level in the food.
4. If a food additive is a proven carcinogen in animals or men, its addition to food is not permitted. This provision is popularly known as the Delaney Amendment.

Section 201(s) of the Federal Food, Drug, and Cosmetic Act, as amended [21 U.S.C. 321(s)], defines a food additive as

> any substance the intended use of which results or may reasonably be expected to result, directly or indirectly, in its becoming a component or otherwise affecting the characteristics of any food (including any substance intended for use in producing, manufacturing, packing, processing, preparing, treating, packaging, transporting, or holding food; and including any source of radiation intended for any such use), if such substance is not generally recognized, among experts qualified by scientific training and experience to evaluate its safety, as having been adequate shown through scientific procedures...to be safe under the conditions of its intended use.

According to the Federal Food, Drug, and Cosmetic Act, if a chemical substance is legally a food additive then its use will be restricted. The party interested in proposing a use for the substance is required to submit a petition to the FDA, requesting the issuance of a regulation that prescribes various requirements such as the exact chemical structure of the substance, the food to which it can be added, the amount permitted, and other criteria. However, the complete provision of Section 201(s) of the act [21 U.S.C. 321(s)] has made two types of exemptions:

1. Certain substances are specifically excluded from the legal definition of a food additive, for example, pesticide and related substances, color additives, and new animal drugs. They are regulated by other provisions of the act.
2. Certain chemical substances, although technically food additives, are exempt from following the restrictive regulations in their usage. These are listed as follows:
   a. A chemical substance will not be legally a food additive if it is "generally recognized as safe" (GRAS) under the conditions of intended use, by

scientists qualified by experience and training to evaluate food safety. The regulations define the necessary expertise as "sufficient training and experience in biology, medicine, pharmacology, physiology, toxicology, veterinary medicine, or other appropriate science to recognize and evaluate the behavior and effects of chemical substances in the diet of man and animals." Substances generally recognized as safe are commonly called GRAS, as shown by the acronym. The law also specifically indicates that the general recognition of safety of such a substance may rely on experience based on common use in food prior to January 1, 1958.

b. A chemical substance will not be legally a food additive if it is used in accordance with sanctions granted prior to the passage of the Food Additives Amendment [PL 85-929, 72 Stat. 1784, 21 U.S.C. 321(s)(4)]. In actual practice, these "prior-sanctioned" chemicals may be divided into three categories.

  i. Those used in food products that have been standardized by the FDA.
  ii. Those approved by the USDA for use under the Meat Inspection Act and the Poultry Products Inspection Act.
  iii. Those approved specifically by the FDA before the passage of the Food Additives Amendment. The approval was usually granted by a written statement, such as letters, memoranda, and other evidence through direct communications.

A legal food additive can be an intentional additive, in which case it is added purposely to food to achieve certain specific technical functions. It can also be an incidental additive, in which case it is not intended to be in food but has become a part of the food through some aspects of food production, processing, storage, or packaging. The latter occurrence has no function in the finished product. Thus the first type is sometimes called "direct" and the second, "indirect," food additives. Also, the irradiation of food with radioactive rays is considered to add a food additive since it is usually used to destroy bacteria and thus achieve a technical function.

The regulations issued by the FDA on food additives and their legal citations are described as follows:

21 CFR 170   Food additives
21 CFR 171   Food additive petitions
21 CFR 172   Food additives permitted for direct addition to food for human consumption
21 CFR 173   Secondary direct food additives permitted in food for human consumption
21 CFR 174   Indirect food additives, general
21 CFR 175   Indirect food additives--adhesive coatings and components

21 CFR 176	Indirect food additives--paper and paperboard components
21 CFR 177	Indirect food additives--adjuvants, production aids, and sanitizers
21 CFR 179	Irradiation in the production, processing, and handling of food
21 CFR 180	Food additives permitted in food on an interim basis or in contact with food pending additional study
21 CFR 181	Prior-sanctioned food ingredients
21 CFR 182	Substances generally recognized as safe
21 CFR 184	Direct food substances affirmed as generally recognized as safe
21 CFR 186	Indirect food substances affirmed as generally recognized as safe
21 CFR 189	Substances prohibited from use in human food

The regulations described in 21 CFR 170 and 171 provide some general information about food additives and their petitions such as opinion letters on food additives status, food additives in standardized foods, exemption for investigational use, tolerances for related food additives, pesticide chemicals in processed foods, general principles for evaluating the safety of food additives, safety factors to be considered, eligibility for classification as GRAS, determination of food additive status, and the procedural details for food additive petitions. Selected aspects are discussed in the following paragraphs.

The FDA has established more than 40 categories of food products to group specific, related foods together for the purpose of establishing tolerances or limitations for the use of direct human food ingredients. For example, three such categories are as follows:

1. Beverages and beverage bases, nonalcoholic, including only special or spiced teas, soft drinks, coffee substitutes, and fruit and vegetable flavored gelatin drinks.
2. Fish products, including all prepared main dishes, salads, appetizers, frozen multicourse meals, and spreads containing fish, shellfish, and other aquatic animals, but not fresh fish.
3. Processed fruits and fruit juices, including all commercially processed fruits, citrus, berries, and mixtures; salads, juices, and juice punches, concentrates, dilutions, "-ades," and drink substitutes therefrom.

By adopting from the National Academy of Sciences/National Research Council national survey of food industries, the FDA will use the following terms to describe the physical or technical functional effects for which direct human food ingredients may be added to foods:

| 1. | Anticaking and free-flow agents | 3. | Antioxidants |
| 2. | Antimicrobial agents | 4. | Colors and coloring adjuncts |

5. Curing and pickling agents	20. Nutrient supplements
6. Dough strengtheners	21. Nutritive sweeteners
7. Drying agents	22. Oxidizing and reducing agents
8. Emulsifiers and emulsifier salts	23. pH control agents
9. Enzymes	24. Processing aids
10. Firming agents	25. Propellants, aerating agents, and
11. Flavor enhancers	gases
12. Flavoring agents and adjuvants	26. Sequestrants
13. Flour treating agents	27. Solvents and vehicles
14. Formulation aids	28. Stabilizers and thickeners
15. Fumigants	29. Surface-active agents
16. Humectants	30. Surface-finishing agents
17. Leavening agents	31. Synergists
18. Lubricants and release agents	32. Texturizers
19. Non-nutritive sweeteners	

Assume a food manufacturer wants to introduce a new chemical as a direct food additive or a new use for an old one and the law requires him to file a petition with the FDA and request the issuance of a regulation sanctioning the proposed use of the substance. Some of the information needed in the petition includes the following:

1. Chemical identity and composition of the substance and its physical, chemical, and biological properties.
2. Amount specified for use and purposes for which it is proposed, together with all directions, recommendations, and suggestions regarding the proposed use.
3. Data establishing that the food additive will have the intended physical or other technical effect or that it may reasonably be expected to become a component of the food.
4. Practicable methods to determine the amount of the food additive in the raw, processed, and/or finished food.
5. Full reports of investigations made with respect to the safety of the food additive. The reports ordinarily should include detailed data derived from appropriate animal and other biological experiments in which the methods used and the results obtained are clearly set forth. The petition should not omit without explanation any reports of investigations that would bias an evaluation of the safety of the food additive.
6. Proposed tolerances for the food additive, if tolerances are required, so as to ensure its safety.
7. The environmental impact analysis report assessing the environmental impact of the manufacturing process and the ultimate use or consumption of the food additive.

How will the FDA decide about the safety of a food additive in the petition? Some basic considerations are as follows [21 U.S.C. 348(c)(5)]:

1. "The probable consumption of the additive and of any substance formed in or on food because of the use of the additive."
2. "The cumulative effect of such additive in the diet of man or animals, taking into account any chemically or pharmacologically related substance or substances in such diet."
3. "Safety factors which in the opinion of experts qualified by scientific training and experience to evaluate the safety of food additives are generally recognized as appropriate for the use of animal experimentation data."

The FDA recommends two important guidelines on safety to any petitioner for a food additive:

1. The petitioner should follow the principles and procedures for establishing the safety of food additives stated in current publications of the National Academy of Science/National Research Council, although this is not binding.
2. A food additive for use by man will not be granted a tolerance that will exceed 1/100th of the maximum amount demonstrated to be without harm to experimental animals. The FDA regards this as the safety factor.

It is expected that, after an adequate and unbiased review of the petition, the FDA will not issue a regulation for the proposed use of the food additive if the data confirm one or more of the following:

1. The safety of the proposed use is not established.
2. Deception of the consumer may result from the intended use.
3. The intended technical or physical effect will not be accomplished by the proposed use.
4. It may possibly not be safe for a person to accumulate potentially the substance taken in from more than one food source.
5. The substance can cause cancer in animals.

How will the FDA determine the eligibility for the classification of a substance as GRAS? The FDA has issued the following guidelines:

1. If a chemical substance satisfies the following two conditions, it "will ordinarily be regarded as GRAS without specific inclusion" in any official list:
   a. A food ingredient of natural biological origin that has been widely con-

sumed for its nutrient properties in the United States prior to January 1, 1958 without known detrimental effects and for which no known safety hazard exists.

   b. Same as (a), except that the substance is one that is "subject only to conventional process as practiced prior to January 1, 1958."

2. The status of the following food ingredients has to be reviewed and "affirmed as GRAS." In case such a substance is not affirmed, the FDA will either determine it to be a legal food additive or subject it to the prior-sanction clause.

   a. Any substance of natural biological origin that has been widely consumed for its nutrient properties in the United States prior to January 1, 1958 without known detrimental effect. No health hazard is known about this substance and it has been modified by processes first introduced into commercial use after January 1, 1958, which may reasonably be expected to significantly alter the composition of the substance.

   b. Any substance of natural biological origin that has been widely consumed for its nutrient properties in the United States prior to January 1, 1958 without known detrimental effect. No health hazard is known about this substance and it has had significant alteration of composition by breeding or selection after January 1, 1958, where the change may be reasonably expected to alter the nutritive value or the concentration of toxic constituents.

   c. Distillates, isolates, extracts, concentrates, of extracts and reaction products of GRAS substances.

   d. Substances not of a natural biological origin, including those showing evidence of being identical to a GRAS counterpart of natural biological origin.

   e. Substances of natural biological origin intended for consumption for other than their nutrient properties.

3. The GRAS classification will not be assigned if a substance has no history of food use or if its safe use requires setting a limitation.

What is the process of affirmation of a GRAS substance status? Such a process may be initiated by the FDA or any other interested party. The latter is required to file a petition with the FDA. In either case all available information will be published in the Federal Register and a specific period of time allotted for receiving public comments. The FDA will study the whole file including the comments and make a decision. Some of the information required in the petition is as follows:

1. A description of the substance, such as name or chemical structure.
2. Use of the substance, such as date when use began and foods in which used.
3. Methods for detecting the substance in food, with details such as their sensi-

tivity and reproducibility.
4. Information to establish the safety and functionality of the substance in food, such as published scientific literature and other supporting data.

The affirmation process is less complex than a food additive petition since it does not require the animal feeding studies that are mandatory for a food additive petition.

Any group of scientists, whether government employed or not, may render their opinion or judgment about the general recognition of safety on a chemical substance. Of course, any private and independent determination of such a status may be jeopardized if the FDA and/or their scientists disagree, in which case the substance will not *generally* be regarded as safe. However, a private group--the Flavor and Extract Manufacturer's Association--has published long lists of substances used in food flavors that have been determined as GRAS by a panel of independent scientists. Their opinions are published in the journal Food Technology. The FDA has expressed both explicit and tacit approval of the decisions of this expert panel.

Before 1969 the granting of a GRAS status by the FDA was somewhat less demanding. However, because of increasing consumer dissatisfaction with the criteria granting a chemical substance GRAS status and distrust of the safety of food additives in general, President Nixon, in a Consumer Protection Message of 1969, directed the FDA to reevaluate the safety of all items included on the GRAS list. As a result, the FDA has been placing many former GRAS substances on review and periodically releasing a reapproved list. The process is still continuing and, consequently, some substances are on the "interim" list. Further details on the listing of food additives are described as follows.

Those food additives permitted for direct addition to food for human consumption are described in 21 CFR 172. Regulations prescribing conditions under which food additive substances may be safely used always specify that normal good manufacturing practices be exercised. The latter are defined to include the following:

1. The quantity of the substance used does not exceed the amount reasonably required to accomplish its intended physical, nutritive, or other technical effect in food.
2. The substance is of appropriate food grade and is prepared and handled as a food ingredient.
3. The existence of any regulation prescribing the safe conditions of use for a nutrient substance does not constitute a finding that it is useful or required as a supplement to the diet of humans.
4. The substance must also comply with all other provisions of the Federal Food, Drug, and Cosmetic Act.

This list classifies the additives into eight types, which include:

1. Food preservatives, such as butyrated hydroxy toluene (BHT), sodium nitrite, and heptyparaben.
2. Coatings, films, and related substances, such as polyacrylamide.
3. Special dietary and nutritional additives, such as amino acids, vitamins, and minerals.
4. Anticaking agents, such as calcium silicate, and silicon dioxide.
5. Flavoring agents and related substances, such as disodium inosinate.
6. Gums, chewing gum bases, and related substances, such as furcelleran.
7. Other specific usage additives, such as calcium lignosulfonate.
8. Multipurpose additives, such as aspartame, glycine, and polysorbate 60.

Those secondary direct food additives permitted in food for human consumption are listed in 21 CFR 173. They are divided into four different types, which include:

1. Polymer substances for food treatment, such as acrylate/acrylamide resins and polyvinylpolypyrrolidone.
2. Enzyme preparations and microorganisms, such as amylglucosidase (derived from *Ryizopus niveus*) and milk-clotting enzyme.
3. Solvents, lubricants, release agents, and related substances, such as acetone, hexane, hydrogenated sperm oil and tricholorethylene.
4. Specific usage additives such as boiler water additives, defoaming agents, dichlorodifluoromethane, and sodium methyl sulfate.

A number of *indirect* food additives are described in 21 CFR 174 to 178. Again, the usage of such substances must follow, in addition to other requirements, good manufacturing practices which include the following:

1. The quantity of any such substance that may be added to food as a result of use in articles that contact food:
   a. Is not permitted to exceed any prescribed limitations.
   b. Is not permitted to exceed, where no limits are specified, the amount that results from use of the substance in a portion not more than reasonably required to accomplish the intended physical or technical effect in the food-contact article.
   c. Is not intended to accomplish any physical or technical effect in the food itself, except as permitted by regulation.
2. Any substance used as a component of articles that contact food should be of a purity suitable for its intended use.

3. The substance must not violate other provisions of the Federal Food, Drug, and Cosmetic Act.

Various types of indirect food additives with examples are given as follows:

1. As components of adhesives, such as calcium ethyl acetoacetate and 1,4-butanediol modified with adipic acid.
2. As components of coatings, such as acrylate ester copolymer coatings and poly(vinyl fluoride) resins.
3. As components of paper and paperboard, such as slimicides, sodium nitrate/urea complex, and alkyl ketene dimers.
4. As basic components of single and repeated use food contact surfaces, such as cellophane, ethyleneacrylic acid copolymers, isobutylene polymers, nylon resins, and polyvinyl alcohol film.
5. As components of articles intended for repeated use, such as ultrafiltration membranes and textiles and textile fibers.
6. Controlling growth of microorganisms, such as sanitizing solutions.
7. Antioxidants and stabilizers, such as octyltin stabilizers in vinyl chloride plastics.
8. Certain adjuvants and production aids, such as animal glue, hydrogenated castor oil, synthetic fatty alcohols, and petrolatum.

As mentioned previously, radiation is legally considered as a food additive. Regulations prescribing irradiation in the production, processing, and handling of food are described in 21 CFR 179. Some aspects are presented in the following paragraphs.

Some sources of radiation for the inspection of foods before and after packaging and for controlling food processing may be safely used under certain conditions, some of which are:

1. The radiation source is from X-ray tubes producing X-radiation from operation of the tube source at energy levels of 300 kV peak or lower.
2. The label of the sources should specifically identify the source of information and the maximum energy of radiation emitted by X-ray tube sources.

The gamma radiation for the treatment of certain foods may be safely used under certain conditions:

1. The radiation source consists of sealed units containing the isotope cobalt-60 or cesium-137.
2. The technique is permitted for use on wheat, wheat flour from unirradiated

wheat, and white potatoes.
3.   To ensure safe use, the label should bear a statement of "Treated with ionizing radiation" or "Treated with gamma radiation" on retail packages.

When gamma radiation is used in the treatment of prepackaged foods, the packaging materials that may be subject to a dose of radiation, not to exceed 1 Mrad (megarad), include nitrocellulose-coated or vinylidene chloride copolymer-coated cellophane, glassine paper, and acrylonitrile copolymers. All these must also comply with indirect food additive regulations. There are other examples.

Those food additives permitted in food on an interim basis or in contact with food pending additional study are listed in 21 CFR 180. Substances having a history of use in food for human consumption or in food contact surfaces may at any time have their safety or functionality brought into question by new information that in itself is not conclusive. An interim food additive regulation for the use of any such substance is promulgated if the following criteria are satisfied:

1.   New information raises a substantial question about the safety or functionality of the substance.
2.   There is a reasonable certainty that the substance is not harmful.
3.   No harm to the public health will result from the continued use of the substance for a limited period of time while the question raised is being resolved by further study.

No interim additive regulation will be promulgated if the following conditions prevail:

1.   The new information is conclusive with respect to the question raised.
2.   There is a reasonable likelihood that the substance is harmful.
3.   Continued use of the substance will result in harm to the public health.

An interim food additive petition may be initiated by the FDA or by an outsider. The FDA uses the following major criteria to determine the interim status:

1.   Is the interim food additive regulation justified?
2.   What are the types of study necessary and appropriate to resolve questions raised about a substance?
3.   Do the interim results indicate the reasonable likelihood that a health hazard exists?
4.   Do the data available at the conclusion of those studies justify a food additive regulation?

Some examples of interim food additives are mannitol, brominated vegetable oil, and "saccharin and its salts."

The list of prior-sanctioned food ingredients are described in 21 CFR 181. It should be noted that even for this list there are regulations and requirements that control their usage. The list divides the substances into the following classes:

1. Certain substances employed in the manufacture of food packaging materials.
2. Antioxidants, such as gum guaiac, propyl gallate, and thiodipropionic acid.
3. Antimycotics, such as sorbic acid, sodium benzoate, and methylparaben.
4. Driers, such as cobalt linoleate, iron caprylate, and manganese tallate.
5. Drying oils as components of finished resins, such as linseed oil, chinawood oil (tung oil), and tall oil.
6. Plasticizers, such as triethyl citrate, and diphenyl-2-ethylhexyl phosphate.
7. Release agents, such as oleamide, stearamide, and linoleamide.
8. Stabilizers, such as ammonium citrate, calcium phosphate, potassium oleate, and sodium stearate.
9. Substances used in the manufacture of paper and paperboard products used in food packaging, such as borax, titanium dioxide, polymerized methyl acrylate, nitrocellulose, and polyvinyl acetate.
10. Acrylonitrile copolymers and resins.

Substances generally recognized as safe are described in 21 CFR 182, although only some are listed for the practical reason of limited space. The list classifies the substances into the following:

1. Spices and other natural seasonings and flavorings such as paprika, mace, capers, and grains of paradise.
2. Essential oils, oleoresins (solvent free), and natural extractives (including distillates), such as clove leaf, hops, and immortelle.
3. Natural substances used in conjunction with spices and other natural seasonings and flavorings, such as brown algae.
4. Natural extractives (solvent free) used in conjunction with spices, seasonings, and flavorings, such as peach kernel and quince seed.
5. Certain other spices, seasonings, essential oils, oleoresins, and natural extracts, such as white and green cognac oil and musk.
6. Synthetic flavoring substances and adjuvants, such as acetoin, diacetyl(2,3-butandeione), and 1-malic acid.
7. Substances migrating from cotton and cotton fabrics used in dry food packing, such as corn dextrin, sorbose, urea, and zinc chloride.
8. Substances migrating to food from paper and paperboard products, such as aluminum oleate, reduced iron, and sulfamic acid.

9. Adjuvants for pesticide chemicals.
10. Multipurpose GRAS food substances, such as tartaric acid, caffeine, papain, rennet, triacetin, and beeswax.
11. Anticaking agents, such as calcium silicate and sodium aluminosilicate.
12. Chemical preservatives, such as ascorbic acid and sodium bisulfite.
13. Emulsifying agents, such as cholic acid and ox bile extract.
14. Nutrients and/or dietary supplements, such as carotene, inositol, and lysine.
15. Sequestrants, such as calcium phytate, tetrasodium pyrophosphate, and stearyl citrate.
16. Stabilizers such as agar/agar and sodium alginate.

Those direct food substances affirmed as GRAS are listed in 21 CFR 184. Some examples are benzoic acid, methylparaben, and oil of rue. Those indirect food substances affirmed as GRAS are listed in 21 CFR 186. Some examples are acacia (gum arabic) and pulp.

Substances that are prohibited from use in human food are listed in 21 CFR 189. The FDA has determined that they present a potential risk to the public health or have not been shown by adequate scientific data to be safe for use in human food. Use of any of these substances in violation of regulations causes the food involved to be adulterated and thus a violative product. The list includes only some of those substances prohibited from use in human food, for easy reference purposes, and is not a complete list. The substances prohibited from *direct* addition or use as human food include calamus and its derivatives, cobaltous salt and its derivatives, coumarin, cyclamate and its derivatives, diethylpyrocarbonate, dulcin, monochloroacetic acid, nordihydroguairetic acid, P-4000, safrole, and thiourea. For information on the chemical structure, reference to reasons for the banning, and official method of detection, consult the original document. The substances prohibited from *indirect* addition to human food through food-contact surfaces include flectol H, mercaptoimidazoline, and 2-mercaptoimidazoline 4,4'-metyl-enebis (2-chloroanaline).

Color Additives

In 1960 the Color Additive Amendments were added to the Federal Food, Drug, and Cosmetic Act (21 U.S.C. 376). According to regulations promulgated by the FDA, a color additive is defined to include the following:

1. Any material, unless otherwise exempted, that is a dye, pigment, or other substance synthesized or extracted from a vegetable, animal, mineral, or other source.
2. When the substance is added or applied to a food, it is capable of imparting a

color.

3. Substances capable of imparting a color to a container for foods are not color additives unless the customary handling of the container may reasonably be expected to result in the transmittal of the color to the contents of the package.

4. Food ingredients such as cherries, green or red peppers, chocolate, and orange juice that contribute their own natural color when mixed with other foods are not regarded as color additives.

5. When a food substance such as beet juice is deliberately used as a color, as in pink lemonade, it is a color additive.

6. Chemicals permitted in standardized foods are color additives.

7. An ingredient of an animal feed whose intended function is to impart, through the biological processes of the animal, a color to the meat, milk, or eggs of the animal is a color additive and is not exempt from statutory requirement.

8. The definition will apply irrespective of whether such ingredient has nutritive or other functions in addition to the property of imparting color.

9. The term "color" includes black, white, and intermediate grays.

10. Substances including migrants from packaging materials that do not contribute any color apparent to the naked eye are not color additives.

11. Assume a substance fits the definition of a color additive. If it is to be exempt from all accompanying prescribed requirements because it will be used solely for a purpose other than coloring, it must be used in such a way that any color imparted is clearly unimportant insofar as the appearance, value, marketability, or consumer acceptability is concerned.

At present, statutory requirements for the usage of color additives in food are the following:

1. All color additives for use in food must receive safety clearance from the FDA before the color can be marketed or used in food.

2. Approval may be obtained by filing a color additive petition.

3. Any officially approved color additive is required to be listed as either certified or uncertified.

4. Certification means that the manufacturer is required to submit a sample of the color to the FDA for chemical analysis. This analysis is compared with the specifications officially listed, and, if it complies in all aspects, a lot number is assigned, and a certificate is issued to that particular batch of color. Since the specifications are based primarily on the analysis of the color used in toxicological testing, this procedure ensures that the batch is chemically similar to the color subjected to the animal feeding safety studies. To be ex-

empted from certification, the petition must show cause why it is not necessary for the protection of public health.

5. In the listing of color additives, the FDA is authorized to indicate their specific usage and tolerances (limitations or safe levels) permitted in food.

6. Whenever the data submitted to the FDA fail to show that it would be safe to list the color additive for all the uses or levels proposed, the FDA will allocate the safe tolerance for the straight color in the color additive among the competing needs. The submission of data by all interested parties is required before allocations are made. Also, the FDA's intention must be announced in the Federal Register.

7. If the question of safety has arisen regarding any of the color additives previously listed as safe, the FDA is authorized to require a new study of such substances, using modern scientific methods and procedures to reestablish their safety.

8. If a color additive is shown to be carcinogenic to animals or men, it is not permitted to be used in food. However, if the sponsor of the petition so requests, the entire matter will be placed under the review of an Advisory Committee.

9. The FDA is authorized to make possible, on an interim basis and for a reasonable period, through provisional listings, the use of commercially established color additives to the extent consistent with the public health, pending the completion of the scientific investigations needed as a basis for making determinations as to the listing of such additives. In general, the FDA has been making decisions as to the closing date of each provisional listing.

10. Many of the factors used to evaluate the safety of food colors are the same as those for food additives.

The information discussed above has been adapted from 21 CFR 70 and 71. The FDA has promulgated the following regulations concerning color additives:

21 CFR 70   Color additives
21 CFR 71   Color additive petitions
21 CFR 73   Listing of color additives exempt from certification
21 CFR 74   Listing of color additives subject to certification
21 CFR 80   Color additive certification
21 CFR 81   General specifications and general restrictions for provisional color additives for use in foods, drugs, and cosmetics
21 CFR 82   Listing of certified provisionally listed colors and specifications

In the following, food color additives exempted from certification are described (21 CFR 73) alphabetically:

Annatto extract

Beta-apo-8'-carotenal

Canthazanthin

Caramel

Beta-carotene

Carrot oil

Cochineal extract; carmine

Corn endosperm oil

Dehydrated beets (beet powder)

Dried algae meal

Ferrous gluconate

Fruit juice

Grape skin extract
    (enocianina)

Paprika

Paprika oleoresin

Riboflavin

Saffron

Synthetic iron oxide

Tagetes (Aztec marigold)
    meal and extract

Titanium dioxide

Toasted partially defatted
    cooked cottonseed flour

Turmeric

Turmeric oleoresin

Ultramarine blue

Vegetable juice

Those food color additives subject to certification (21 CFR 74) are FD&C Blue No. 1, Orange B, Citrus Red No. 2, FD&C Red No. 3, FD&C Red No. 40, and FD&C Yellow No. 5. The abbreviation FD&C stands for Food, Drug and Cosmetics. At present, the FDA is intensely reviewing the safety of all food colors, whether certified or not. A number of color additives are placed on the provisional listing. Because of the unstable legal status of such substances, they are not discussed here.

Pesticides and Related Substances

A pesticide chemical is legally not a food additive. However, since they may occur in food for human consumption as a result of any aspect of food harvesting, processing, storage, and other handling, Section 409 of the Federal Food, Drug, and Cosmetic Act (21 U.S.C. 348) requires that tolerances be established for them. The EPA establishes such tolerances, and the FDA enforces them. Thus 21 CFR 193 presents those pesticide chemicals for which tolerances have been established in food for human consumption. Some examples are: captan, copper, 2,2-dichlorovinyl dimethyl phosphate, diquat, hydrogen cyanide, and simazine. Some examples of tolerance levels are as follows:

1. Ethion: 10 ppm in dried tea and 4 ppm in raisins.
2. Phosalone: 40 ppm in or on dried prunes, 20 ppm in or on raisins, and 8 ppm in or on dried tea.

Unavoidable Chemical Contaminants

Recently, one of the most troublesome food protection problems is the presence of "unintentional" or "unavoidable" chemical contaminants. This problem is expected to persist. Some typical examples are: mercury in seafood, DDT in a number of food products, aflatoxin in peanuts, PCB in food packages, lead in evaporated milk, and Kepone and Mirex in fish.

Some basic problems with this kind of contaminants are as follows:

1. Legally, such substances have never been approved for use in or on the food that they have contaminated. They do not serve any technical, physical, or other useful purposes in those foods.
2. Most likely the contamination is a result of environmental pollution, biological concentration of food chains, and the drifting of water, wind, and soils. Some sources of these pollutants include the past ill-controlled disposal of industrial chemicals, widespread use and misuse of pesticde chemicals, recycling of raw materials, and feeding of food producing animals indiscriminately with various wastes. Rigid legal control to curtail such practices is a preventive measure, but it is only for the future. It will not help to remove what already exists in the water, soil, air, and food chain.
3. Either voluntarily or through the court, the FDA can effect massive removal of contaminated food from the market. This approach has some basic inherent disadvantages. The FDA must prove that the contaminated products are injurious to health, which is only possible if they occur in dangerous or potentially dangerous amounts. Money and time pose another problem. Also, it is unrealistic to ban all contaminated peanuts, milk, meat, fish, and other foods even though the chemicals are present in reasonably harmless levels. This calls for the setting of safety limits or tolerances.
4. The potential hazard from consuming these contaminated products cannot be ignored.

This important aspect of unavoidable chemical contaminants is discussed in the paragraphs that follow. The information has been adapted from: "Poisonous or deleterious substances in peanuts, evaporated milk, fish and shellfish," 39 FR 42737 to 42752, December 6, 1974; "Unavoidable contaminants in food and food-packaging material," 21 CFR 109; and "Regulation of food contaminants," by J. R. Wessel, Association of Food and Drug Officials Quarterly Bulletin, January 1977. "Poisonous or deleterious substances in food," 42 FR 52813 to 52824, September 30, 1977.

The FDA has to surmount several legal and technical barriers to protect public health from such contaminants.

Basically, Section 402 of the Federal Food, Drug, and Cosmetic Act (21 U.S.C. 342) states that it is illegal to add any poisonous or deleterious substances to a food unless they are pesticides and food additives, the uses of which are required to comply with other provisions of the act. Section 408 of the act (21 U.S.C. 346a) states that if a pesticide is to be used in or on an agricultural product, its usage must be consistent with good agronomical practices, and the safe amount of residue left in the product must be established by the EPA. Section 409 of the act (21 U.S.C. 348) states that if a food additive is to be used in food, it must have been approved by the FDA with reference to numerous requirements such as general condition of use, chemical composition, and safety limits.

EPA definitely has never approved the use of DDT on seafood. The FDA has never approved the use of PCB in packaging materials or lead in evaporated milk. Sections 408 and 409 prove to be ineffective in controlling unavoidable contaminants. Section 406 of the act (21 U.S.C. 346) provides the FDA with the necessary authority to establish tolerances or safety limits for unavoidable contaminants in food. In accordance with official regulations, to establish a formal tolerance under Section 406 requires a public hearing, supporting data and evidence, and a stable situation. The last condition pertains to how transient the evidence is and how long the formal tolerance will be useful. For example, the "unavoidable" occurrence may be decreasing as industrial practices are improving under rigid legal control. Also, as additional toxicological data are available, the setting of a safety limit will vary. Thus to establish a formal tolerance with insufficient data and unstable or unsure environmental conditions will cost an unnecessary and large amount of time and money. To have regulatory control over these contaminants, the FDA resorts to "action level" under authority of Section 306 of the act (21 U.S.C. 336). This provision permits the FDA to use a written notice or warning for minor violations instead of using prosecution and other legal proceedings.

Thus the FDA has issued action levels for certain contaminants in food under the combined authority of Sections 306, 402(a), and 406 of the Federal Food, Drug, and Cosmetic Act. Some basic criteria for establishing the action levels are as follows:

1. The substance is present despite good manufacturing practice.
2. The action levels must be those necessary for the protection of the public health, taking into account the extent to which the substance cannot be

avoided and the other ways in which the consumer may be affected by the same or other poisonous or deleterious substances.

3. An action level is similar to a formal tolerance in basis and effect. Although it is based on the same criteria as a formal tolerance, it is temporary until the appearance of more stable circumstances permits the setting of a formal safety limit. The FDA refers to the action level as an exercise of enforcement discretion.

Therefore, to control the different unavoidable contaminants, the FDA has been using informal action levels. For example, if a certain food product contains a contaminant at or under its action level, the FDA will not take any legal action. However, any excess over the level will precipitate the removal of the food from the market by the FDA. Since 1973 the FDA has issued formal tolerances for such unavoidable substances. At the time of current writing, only one such tolerance, PCB, has been established and is located in 21 CFR 109. In the meantime, the FDA continues to use action levels to exercise regulatory controls over such contaminants.

On September 30, 1977 (42 FR 52813 to 52824), the FDA announced the final rule that established procedures for regulating food contaminants and naturally occurring poisonous or deleterious substances in food. This action was taken to implement those provisions of the Federal Food, Drug, and Cosmetic Act that permit the FDA to set tolerances and action levels to control the levels of unavoidable contaminants in food. These procedures, which also permit the identification and listing of naturally occurring poisonous or deleterious substances in food, apply to all poisonous or deleterious substances in food, including food contact surfaces, pet food, and animal feed.

Food Manufacturing: Sanitation and Wholesomeness

One major purpose of the Federal Food, Drug, and Cosmetic Act is to ensure that human food is free from repulsive or offensive matter classed as filth regardless of whether they: (1) may be injurious to health, (2) can be detected by laboratory procedures, or (3) are very likely to be present because of the conditions under which the food is prepared and handled.

"Filth" includes contaminating elements such as rat and mouse hairs and excreta, whole insects, insect parts and excreta, maggots, larvae, parasitic worms, pollution from the excrement of man and animal, as well as other extraneous materials that because of their repulsiveness would not knowingly be eaten or used. The presence of such filth renders foods adulterated, regardless of whether harm to health can be shown.

The maintenance of sanitary conditions requires extermination and exclusion of rodents, inspection and sorting of raw materials to eliminate the insect-infested and decomposed portions, fumigation, quick handling and proper storage to prevent insect development or contamination, use of clean equipment, control of possible sources of sewage pollution, and supervision of personnel who prepare foods so that acts of misconduct may not defile the products they handle.

Fumigation of commodities already infested with insects will not result in a legally permissible product since dead insects or evidence of past insect activity are objectionable. Fumigation should be employed where necessary, to prevent infestation but avoid accumulation of nonpermitted chemical residues from fumigation.

The FDA exercises rigorous regulatory control over the conditions under which human food is manufactured. Such food must be free from filth, disease causing bacteria, illegal pesticide residues, food and color additives, and other deleterious substances. The regulations promulgated to implement such control are as follows:

21 CFR 1	General regulations for the enforcement of the Federal Food, Drug, and Cosmetic Act and the Fair Packaging and Labeling Act (Subpart E, Imports and Exports)
21 CFR 2	General administrative rulings and decisions
21 CFR 108	Emergency permit control
21 CFR 110	Current good manufacturing practice in manufacturing, processing, packing, or holding human food
21 CFR 113	Thermally processed low-acid foods packaged in hermetically sealed containers
21 CFR 118	Cacao products and confectionery
21 CFR 122	Smoked and smoke-flavored fish
21 CFR 123	Processing and bottling of bottled drinking water
21 CFR 197	Seafood inspection program

These regulations are discussed according to the following three aspects: (1) some mandatory regulations and food manufacturing, (2) food safety programs, and (3) special seafood-inspection program.

Some Mandatory Regulations and Food Manufacturing

Emergency Permit Control System and Low-Acid Canned Food. In the United States, botulism poisonings are mostly associated with home-canned food products. The few cases that resulted from commercially canned foods were followed by extensive product recalls. As a result, the National Canners Association in 1971 was prompted to petition the FDA to exercise the authority in Section 404 of the Federal Food, Drug, and Cosmetic Act (21 U.S.C. 344). This emergency permit control provision authorizes the FDA to issue regulations governing the processing, manufacturing, and/or packing of commercial food products that may be hazardous to human health because of bacteria contamination. The latter cannot be adequately detected or eliminated once the products are in interstate commerce. The regulation for such an emergency system is described in 21 CFR 108. Briefly, it is as follows.

The first part of the regulation explains the conditions that govern exemption from and compliance with established requirements and actions taken by government for noncompliance. It includes information on the need, denial, suspension, reinstatement, and violation of a permit. If a manufacturer fails to meet certain requirements, a permit will be necessary before he can introduce food into interstate commerce. Emergency permits are granted after the violative conditions are corrected. The second part contains those requirements and conditions established for a specific food manufacturing. At the present time of writing, the conditions have been established for the thermal processing of low-acid foods packaged in hermetically sealed containers. Thus the processor must register his plant, file his processes with the FDA, process each low-acid food in conformity with the scheduled process, report to the FDA any instance involving a danger to public health from a food that has entered distribution, and have a formalized and written recall procedure. In addition, the processor must employ supervisors at critical heat processing operations and container closure inspectors who have satisfactorily completed a prescribed course in a school approved by the FDA. Imports are regulated in the same way as domestic products, although the FDA requests the Bureau of Customs to refuse their entry rather than issuing or denying a permit during an emergency.

The emergency permit control system is intended to protect the consumer from unsafe food while averting economic waste of raw food materials. Such control may be removed by the FDA when the canner or food processor shows that he has met all the requirements for exemption. Until that time, the plant is subject to surveillance by the agency.

Good Manufacturing Practice Regulations. A Good Manufacturing Practice (GMP) is one that sets forth both recommended and required practices in the operation of an establishment. It provides reasonable assurance to the FDA that the food product will, when distributed in interstate commerce, be safe and wholesome. The regulation is used to determine whether the facilities, methods, practices, and controls used in the manufacture, processing, packing, or holding of food are in conformance with good manufacturing practices for safety and sanitation. It deals specifically with the quality of raw materials, processing and quality-control methods, equipment, environmental conditions in the plant, sanitary practices of employees, recordkeeping, and qualifications of certain key employees.

The GMP program began in 1969 when the FDA published its first such regulation (21 CFR 110) for food plants in general. The latter has often been referred to as the "umbrella GMP." Its initial enforcement presented some difficulty because vague terms such as "sufficient," "proper," and "adequate" were used. However, the most important objective of that regulation was to provide guidance to the food industry on good manufacturing practices so that they could be incorporated into their long range program of plant facilities and practices improvement. Selected information contained in 21 CFR 110 is described as follows.

First, the cleanliness of plant personnel should be ensured. For example, all persons, while working in direct contact with food ingredients and preparation, should wear clean outer garments, maintain a high degree of personal cleanliness, and conform to hygienic practices while on duty, to the extent necessary to prevent the contamination of food products. They should remove all insecure jewelry and, during periods where food is manipulated by hand, remove from hands any jewelry that cannot be adequately sanitized. They should wear hairnets, headbands, caps, or other effective hair restraints.

All food utensils and product-contact surfaces of equipment should be cleaned as frequently as necessary. Nonproduct-contact surfaces of equipment should be kept free from dust, dirt, food particles, and other debris. Single-service articles (e.g., paper cups and paper towels) should be stored in appropriate containers and handled, dispensed, used, and disposed of in a manner that does not contaminate food or food-contact surfaces. All food utensils and product-contact surfaces of equipment should be cleaned and sanitized prior to use and following any interruption during which they may have become contaminated.

All reasonable precautions should be taken to ensure that production procedures do not contribute contamination such as filth, harmful chemicals, undesirable microorganisms, or any other objectionable material to the processed product. For example, raw materials and ingredients should be inspected and segregated as necessary to ensure that they are clean, wholesome, and fit for processing into human food and stored under conditions that prevent contamination and minimize deterioration. Raw materials should be washed or cleaned as required to remove soil or other impurities. Water used for washing, rinsing, or conveying of food products should be of adequate quality, and such water should not be reused.

In the FDA files are official photographs taken during inspections of food processing or storage establishments of some examples of poor employee practices, including the following (adapted from FDA Papers, now FDA Consumer, March, 1968):

1. Stacked bags of beans in a warehouse were sprinkled with sodium fluosilicate, a rodenticide, and later analysis showed the product to be contaminated with

this deadly poison.

2. Residue was shown built up on shredding machinery in a potato processing plant and remained for several hours, inviting bacterial growth.
3. A plant's laxity in keeping its lavatory in sanitary condition is apparent.
4. Access of rodents to stored bags of pretzels in a distributor warehouse is confirmed by the presence of excreta pellets.
5. Frequently used electric power switch shows food residue from hands of employee.
6. Employee moving a piece of dough carelessly, bringing it into contact with his clothes.

Some foods, even when produced under current good manufacturing and/or processing practices, contain natural or unavoidable defects at lower levels that are not hazardous to health. Whenever necessary and feasible, the FDA establishes maximum levels for such defects in food products and uses them for recommending regulatory actions. Defect action levels are varied according to new technology and information. Compliance with these levels does not permit violation of other provisions of the Federal Food, Drug, and Cosmetic Act. For example, evidence obtained through factory inspection indicating a violation of other requirements of the act renders the food unlawful, even though the amounts of natural or unavoidable defects are lower than the currently established action levels.

A food manufacturer must at all times utilize quality control procedures to reduce such defects to the lowest level currently feasible. The mixing of a food in violation of current defect action levels with another lot of food is not permitted and renders the final food unlawful regardless of its defect level. Current action levels that have been adopted on a temporary basis for natural and unavoidable defects in food for human consumption that present no health hazard may be obtained from the FDA. Some examples of defects include rot, insect fragments, excreta, mold, larvae, drosophila eggs, and foreign particles.

The FDA also issues, in cooperation and sponsorship with seven types of food and related industries, a booklet titled "Voluntary industry sanitation guidelines for food distribution centers and warehouses" (1974), to assist individual food manufacturers.

Ever since the beginning of the GMP program in 1969, the FDA has been systematically issuing specific GMP regulations, each of which applies to a particular food industry. At present, such regulations are in effect for the low-acid canned food industries (21 CFR 113), cacao products and confectionery (21 CFR 118), smoked and smoke-flavored fish (21 CFR 122), frozen raw breaded shrimp (21 CFR 123), and processing and bottling of bottled drinking water (21 CFR 129). Each such regulation contains different sections, which are briefly described as follows (not all sections are usually included):

1. Definitions. They are usually relevant to a particular industry.
2. Emphasis on the applicability of the umbrella GMP regulations (21 CFR 110).
3. Plants and grounds. Conditions intended to prevent contamination from without and crosscontamination between different operations from within factory.
4. Equipment and utensils. Stress general overall designated criteria for equipment that are unique for that industry or where special controls for safety and sanitation are required.
5. Personnel sanitation facilities.
6. Cleaning and sanitizing of equipment.
7. Operations and process, probably the most important.
8. Records and recordkeeping. Data should be kept for at least the average life of the product in distribution.

With the exception of the low-acid canned food (21 CFR 113), the GMPs do not spell out specific equipment details. In the following, selected aspects of the specific regulation for cacao products and confectionery (21 CFR 118) are described.

Regulations for the general good manufacturing practices (21 CFR 110) also apply to this industry. Cacao products include any form of chocolate, cocoa, and their products. Such foods include cacao nibs, sweet chocolate, milk chocolate, other standardized foods, and chocolate sirup. They exclude raw cacao bean, extracts, flavoring derived from such extracts, and chocolate- or cocoa-flavored foods. "Confectionery" means candy and food products made with sweeteners, and frequently prepared with colorings, flavorings, milk products, cacao products, nuts, fruits, starches, and other materials, Such foods include frostings, toppings, and cake decorations. They exclude chewing gums, sauces, sirups, jellies, jams, preserves, cakes, or cookies.

To prevent contamination, the following operations should be separated by partition, location, air flow, enclosed systems or other effective means: receiving; raw material storage; cacao bean cleaning, roasting, cooling, cracking, and fanning; cacao product milling, pressing, mixing, refining, conching, tempering, and molding; pulverizing or separating of cocoa and other dusty operations; cacao product and confectionery processing; portable equipment and utensil cleaning and sanitizing; packaging and packing; and finished product storage and shipping.

Some aspects of the regulations for processes and controls are as follows. Raw materials such as milk and milk products; egg products; gelatin, dried coconut, nuts; and other susceptible items should be free of pathogenic microorganisms before being incorporated into the finished products. Pasteurization before use or otherwise treated during the processing operations is recommended.

Peanuts, Brazil nuts, pistachio nuts, filberts, walnuts, almonds, pecans, cornmeal, and other raw materials susceptible to aflatoxin contamination must comply with current action levels or tolerances for poisonous or deleterious substances before incorporation into the finished products. Nuts, raisins, cacao beans, spices, rework, return, and other raw materials susceptible to infestation or contamination by animals, birds, vermin, microorganisms, or extraneous material must comply with current FDA action levels for natural or unavoidable defects before incorporated into the finished products. Compliance of these above raw materials with all requirements may be accomplished by purchasing them under a supplier's guarantee or certification or verified by analyzing these materials for the presence of contaminant.

Some aspects of the processing operations are as follows. Frozen egg products should be defrosted in a sanitary manner and without adversely affecting their wholesomeness. For example, defrost at $40^{\circ}F$ or lower or defrost at $40+^{\circ}F$ for less than 24 hours. Every part of the defrosted liquid should be under $50^{\circ}F$. The pasteurization process or treatment to destroy harmful bacteria should be standardized for a given product to ensure destruction of unwanted microorganisms. Rework and return should be considered as raw materials. They should be held in properly identified containers to prevent product contamination. Hold waste in properly identified containers and remove it daily from the processing area. Use effective measures to prevent cross contamination between raw materials and finished products/refuse. When any of these items is unprotected, do not handle simultaneously in a receiving, loading, or shipping area. Raw materials and products transported by conveyor should be protected from extraneous material. Use effective means to exclude metal or other extraneous materials from finished products. Achieve this by using suitable equipment such as sieves, magnets, electronic metal detectors, or other means.

Use effective means to remove extraneous material from molding starch before it is reused in molding operations. Achieve this by passing the starch through a sieve and a metal trap or by other means. The cooling and winnowing of roasted cacao beans and the processing and storage of cocoa nibs should be carried out in such a manner as to prevent product contamination. Cacao bean shell, dust, and other residue particles resulting from cracking operations should be handled and held in such a manner as to prevent product contamination. Adulterated materials should be disposed of in such a manner as to avoid cross contamination. If feasible, they may be reconditioned, reexamined, and reused if found to be wholesome.

Permanently legible code marks should be placed at a readily visible location on each product container, such as the package delivered to the retail purchasers, and be visible on the unopened package. They should identify at least the plant where packed and the product or packaged lot.

Finished products should be handled in storage, during shipment, and while being held for sale in such a manner as to prevent product contamination. Transportation equipment, warehouses, and other facilities used for storing, holding, or transporting finished products should have such design and construction as to prevent contamination or adulteration of the products. Such facilities and equipment should be free of vermin or other objectionable conditions.

Imports and Exports. According to Section 801 of the Federal Food, Drug, and Cosmetic Act (21 U.S.C. 381), the provisions regarding imports and exports contain the following requirements:

1. The Bureau of Customs is authorized to deliver samples of imported foods to the FDA, simultaneously informing the owner who, if necessary, may appear before the FDA officials to present an explanation and introduce testimony.
2. If the analysis shows that such article has been manufactured, processed, or packed under insanitary conditions or is forbidden or restricted for sale in the country of origin, it will be refused entry.
3. The FDA may destroy any such refused article unless it is exported within 90 days of the date of official notice of refusal or within such authorized additional time.
4. If an imported shipment is being held pending decision, the FDA may release it to the owner or consignee. However, the latter is required to pose an acceptable bond for the payment of such liquidated damages in the event of default as required by regulations.
5. At the discretion of the FDA, an importer may be permitted to try to bring an illegal shipment into compliance with the law before a final decision is made as to whether it may be admitted. The owner or consignee must make an application and post a bond. On approval, all corrective actions such as relabeling must be done under the supervision of FDA personnel.
6. All expenses in connection with destruction, supervision of corrective actions, and storage, cartage, or label incidental to a refused shipment must be paid by the owner or consignee. Failure to do so will constitute grounds for lien against any future importations made by the same party.
7. A food intended for export will not be deemed adulterated or misbranded if it:
   a. Complies with the specifications of the foreign purchaser.
   b. Is not in conflict with the laws of the country to which it is intended for export.
   c. Is labeled on the outside of the shipping package to show that it is intended for export.

To implement these provisions, the FDA has issued regulations in Subpart E of 21 CFR 1. They are related to the detailed procedure of: notice of sampling, payment for samples, hearing on refusal of admission, application for and grant of authorization to relabel and recondition and associated chargeable costs, and bonds. To provide detailed instruction for field personnel, the FDA has also issued an Import Procedures Manual or similar publication. It should be consulted for further information on the topic. Some useful additional reference sources are:

1. Customs and FDA. FDA Papers, April 1968.
2. New directions in import coverage. FDA Papers, November 1971.
3. J. R. Brooker. How to export fishery products to the United States. Food Drug Cosmetic Law Journal, May 1976.
4. Keeping an eye on imports. FDA Consumers (formerly FDA Papers), March 1977.
5. Detentions compound coffee problem. FDA Consumers, September 1977.

Some methods used in the coverage of imported products by the FDA follow:

Customs Review of Invoices. This is the traditional method and is still being practiced. On reviewing entry documents received at a large customs port, an official identifies those that list food products and notifies the local FDA inspector who determines whether to perform on-site products examination or sample analyses. The Bureau of Customs admits or detains the shipment according to FDA's report. At times, information on an invoice does not denote that the shipment is under FDA's jurisdiction. Its own examination of some samples may, if reasons exist, result in the samples being referred to the FDA promptly.

Analyses of Samples. Both the FDA and the Bureau of Customs do sample testings. The FDA is interested in the cleanliness or adulteration, the quality, and the possible dangers of the shipment. Customs is interested in learning the percentage of certain ingredients to determine the rate of duty under U.S. tariffs.

Mobile Laboratories. Regular FDA laboratories are quite often overloaded with sample analyses generated by the inspection staffs. The use of small, maneuverable, mobile laboratories operated by inspectors and inspector technicians has solved part of the problems. This approach permits the sanitation and economic samples collected to be examined at the pier with no additional inspector manpower. This also frees the regular analyst for other tasks.

Ship-to-Ship Coverage. This technique requires that an FDA inspector be placed at the point of discharge, a pier, airport, or container terminal to inspect, examine, and/or sample cargo as it is discharged from the carrier. His decisions as to which products require checking for adulteration or misbranding are made from actual visual observations instead of a review of documents that merely identify the importation and ownership. Thus more suspect imports come under scrutiny for possible violations. This method is especially applicable to commodities suitable for field testing and obviates the need for sampling of many products for laboratory examination. Visual observation can also detect cargo with physical damage or adulteration from polluted harbor water or spillage of toxic chemicals. This method also provides quick delivery for many shipments when compliance can be rapidly determined and reduces the probability of demurrage charges to the impporter who will especially be pleased if his products are perishable in nature.

Circuit Rider Program. This program involves regular but not prescheduled visits by FDA inspectors to certain remote ports, for example, those situated along the Texas/Mexico border. The FDA makes an official agreement with the customs office at each port, in which is described the method by which the nearest FDA district office will be notified of entries, types of entries from which customs will take samples, and other elements. Quite often, because of the unique location, the port is "specialized," that is, handling only one or two types of food products. Apart from increasing surveillance of import shipments, this program permits the FDA inspector to improve local FDA/Bureau of Customs relations, check products entering these ports, and advise customs officials of current priorities and problems as he is "riding the circuit."

Inspection of Foreign Plants and Products

a. Increase consultative type inspections of foreign plants and products by FDA personnel. However, this involves willing requests from foreign manufacturers who must also cover the costs. This is a topic of discussion and negotiation among all parties concerned, including FDA officials, import associations, trade groups, foreign processors, commercial attaches, and foreign consuls and representatives. The problem becomes more urgent when a non-compliance product involving detention is at issue, especially multiple detentions of shipments.

b. The FDA has recently signed official agreements with a number of foreign governments. In each agreement, it is agreed that the foreign government will inspect the food manufacturing plant and its products and certify the extent of wholesomeness and/or safety from certain hazards. Examples of such agreements are shown in Table 6-6. This is generally known as the "import source country certification program."

Food Safety Programs

At present, the FDA has two important food safety programs, one traditional and the other recent. They are: (1) factory inspection, and (2) hazard analysis and critical control point (HACCP) inspection program.

Factory Inspection. The following information has been adapted from inspection manuals, fact sheets, FDA Consumer, and other FDA publications.

The FDA periodically dispatches an inspector to inspect food production, storage, and distribution firms; investigate complaints of injury and poisoning; and report evidence of violation of the various acts enforced by the FDA.

The agency has published and maintained three current important publications: Inspector Operations Manual, Inspector Training Manual, and Inspector's Technical Guide. They provide guidelines and instructions for an FDA inspector or, as is presently known, a Consumer Safety Officer.

After the officer has been given an assignment, he studies the standard agency publications and reviews the guidelines and enforcement programs for the specific inspection assignment. He then examines the previous record(s) of the firm such as the reports of previous inspection, possible violations and corrections, legal status, plant personnel attitude, and consumer complaints. From the record he should understand the nature of its product, its method of operation, and its past performance.

In addition to plant sanitation, the officer is instructed to:

1. Review the firm's analytical data.
2. Perform tests, whenever feasible, to determine product adulterations and contaminations and ingredient stability.
3. Be alert to and check use and misuse of food ingredients, food and color additives, accuracy of product label (including net contents), and adequate package of the product.
4. Be prepared to document all evidence of violations.
5. Encourage corrective actions at the source.

He must check the inspectional equipment assigned to him and assemble any special equipment he will need. A list of the accessories is as follows:

1. A flashlight is used for poorly lit areas and for examination of equipment such as vats.
2. A set of portable scales to weight products to check label declaration.
3. A black ultraviolet light is used to examine material that can suffer from rodent contamination. The light makes rodent urine stains glow brightly.
4. A camera is used to document certain violations.
5. Sample collection equipment such as sterile sieves, triers, and spoons.
6. Sample containers such as sterile vials, jars, and plastic bags.

7. Chlorine test kit for special tests.
8. The vehicle also contains a dictating mechanism and typewriters, used for preparing reports while in travel status.
9. Clean protective clothing and gear, such as some sort of head cover for protection and sanitation, smocks, and coveralls when the operation conditions require.

The officer arrives at the plant unannounced, except in rare instances where the FDA wants to see special files or other materials to which it would not normally have access. In accordance with Section 704(a) of the Federal Food, Drug, and Cosmetic Act (21 U.S.C. 374), the officer is authorized to enter the food establishment at a reasonable time, within a reasonable limit, and in a reasonable manner and is required to present the management with a written Notice of Inspection, after identifying himself with the proper credential. If, as sometimes happens, a plant authority refuses to consent to inspection, the officer may return with an "inspection warrant" obtained through a federal court.

The officer invites the management to assign a representative to accompany him in the inspection. If other government inspectors such as those of the USDA and National Marine Fisheries Service are present, the inspectors or officers will team up.

The officer then usually has a preliminary interview or discussion with the management or its representative. The officer will request the following information about the firm:

1. Name of the officers, their responsibility, recent personnel changes, and the same information for any related firms.
2. Current legal status.
3. Products: kind, volume with percentage engaged in interstate commerce, trade names, method of distribution, and other data.
4. Providing or receiving food guarantees.
5. Ability to produce wholesome and safe products.
6. Hiring consultants in laboratory work, sanitation, and labeling.
7. Floor plans and operation flow charts.

Some of the information may be obtained from the management at the end of the inspection. Then the officer begins an inspection of the interior of the plant and pays very careful attention to the following aspects:

1. Raw materials
   a. Receiving, handling, and storage.
   b. Decomposition, parasites, filth such as rat hair, ants, metals, and stones.

     c.   Sampling for pesticide, bacteria, food and color additives, and other analyses.

2. Plant construction and design
   a. General condition in relation to type of food processing.
   b. Floors, ceilings, walls, doors, windows, ease of cleaning, and maintenance.
   c. Different operations partitioned to avoid cross contamination.
   d. Location of lighting.
   e. Location for washing equipment utensils.
   f. Ventilation to prevent airborne contamination.
   g. Mechanical exclusion of dogs, cats, birds, insects, rodents, vermin, by means such as windows, doors, pipings, and other outside connections.

3. Equipment and utensils
   a. Appropriate for the work.
   b. Easy to repair and clean.
   c. Ease and frequency of contact with clothes and person.
   d. Ease of contamination with metal pieces, lubricants, fuel, and unclean water.

4. Personnel
   a. Rules about diseases such as colds, wounds, and boils.
   b. Appearance and cleanliness.
   c. Special clothing gear, such as hairnet and gloves.
   d. Rules about hand washing and sanitizing.
   e. Training for food handling, contamination, and protection, such as removal of jewelry.

5. Sanitary controls
   a. Facilities for the sanitation.
   b. Clean water sources.
   c. Toilet and hand- washing facilities.
   d. Sanitizing solutions and facilities.
   e. Sewage-disposal systems, floor drains.
   f. Garbage and other waste disposal.

6. Sanitary operations
   a. Condition of physical facilities.
   b. Cleaning practices.
   c. Insects, rodents, vermin, and animal control.
   d. Pesticides usage and control.
   e. Cleaning and sanitizing of equipment.
   f. Effective and safe sanitizing agents.
   g. Clean equipment and utensil storage and handling.

7. The controls and processing of food
   a. Raw materials: type, condition, handling, storage, containers.

b. Processing equipment and their ease of cleaning.
c. Legal use of food and color additives.
d. Packaging and analysis procedures.
e. Product coding and record keeping.
f. Methods to avoid contamination of food by biological, chemical, and foreign particles and the deterioration of the food.
g. Controls and operations, such as temperature, pressure, humidity, flow rate, time, freezing, sterilization, dehydration, and refrigeration.

Bacterial contamination may occur in the processing of specialty products such as frozen, precooked, ready-to-eat seafoods and prepared salads. A bacteriological inspection is also known as a "comprehensive sanitary inspection." Although an inspector or officer can conduct a bacteriological inspection alone, the officer/microbiologist team approach is often used. It is quite similar to a regular inspection although much more intense. The following is essential to ensure the personal cleanliness of the inspection team:

1. The inspectors follow the firm's sanitation program for employees and often beyond the normal requirements.
2. They wear clean coveralls and sometimes change clothes several times during a single inspection.
3. They use clean paper or plastic bags both to store clothing before and after use to avoid contamination.
4. They wear disposable coverings for the head and wash their hands frequently.
5. In area where cross contamination may be important, disposable coverings for hands and feet are used.
6. They use aseptic techniques in collecting raw material and in-line and finished-product samples for bacteriological examination.

The inspectors pay attention to the following;

1. Bacteriological contamination of raw materials.
2. Source and nature of water supply and method of in-plant treatment, if any.
3. Source and condition of the air throughout the plant.
4. Sanitizing practices.
5. Cleanliness of and supplies for toilet facilities.
6. Usage for certain items such as brushes, scrapers, brooms, containers, and wiping cloths.
7. Appearance and practices of all employees such as clothing, head coverings, colds, sores, bandages, and contact with products.

Some other aspects of a factory inspection process should be noted, such as the following:

1. The law requires that if a sample is taken for analysis, a receipt must be provided the management, which is also encouraged to take a sample of its own. A copy of the result of the sample analysis is required to be sent to the management promptly.
2. Photographs of evidence of violations should be taken.
3. If an unfit lot of raw ingredient or finished product is detected and the management decides to destroy it, the officer should witness the destruction and make a note in his report.
4. An inspection of the outside of the food plant is usually made and attention paid to possible uncut and tall grass and weed, scattered trash, collection of mud, garbage, water pool, and other situations where rodents and other animals or bacteria may thrive, and to broken glass, woodpiles, and other undesirable aspects.
5. Special attention is paid to any delays that may occur in the food manufacturing process. Examples are:
   a. Accumulated raw materials or residues in equipment and utensils should be removed as soon as possible since they may contaminate clean food.
   b. Determine time/temperature relationships for products subject to tempering, aging, drying, and other holding operations. Adequacy of cooking operations, cooling and storage of cooked raw materials, and freezing and packaging practices.
6. Each inspection process may take from half a day to one or more weeks, depending on the plant and conditions. However, the average inspection takes a day.

The postinspectional procedures follow:

Discussion with the Management. The law, fairness, and common courtesy require a detailed discussion between the officer and the management. The latter should be informed of all violative conditions that will be confirmed in writing. The officer stresses that they should be corrected as soon as possible. However, he does not specify exactly what action should be taken or how it should be done. The methods of correction are not his concern provided that they are effective and will not result in new problems. The management is encouraged to broach disagreement with the officer's findings.

Certain findings that are not required to be confirmed in writing include net weight deficiencies, questionable use of food and color additives, and other apparent labeling errors. The officer advises the management to obtain assistance from the FDA District Office or Headquarters in Washington, D.C.

Written Report. Section 704(b) of the Federal Food, Drug, and Cosmetic Act (21 U.S.C. 374) states that:

> Upon completion of any such inspection of a factory, warehouse...and prior to leaving the premises, the officer...making the inspection shall give to the owner...a report in writing setting forth any conditions or practices observed by him which, in his judgment, indicate that any food...in such establishment (1) consists in whole or in part of any filthy, putrid, or decomposed substance, or (2) has been prepared, packed, or held under insanitary conditions whereby it may have become contaminated with filth, or...have been rendered injurious to health.

Thus the officer will prepare this written report, "Report of Observations," including all details of findings and observations, field test results, samples collected, and any photographic evidence of violative conditions. The report lists all samples collected for analysis, which are coded and dispatched to the appropriate laboratories. The analysis is for bacteriological and chemical contamination, filth, decomposition, additives, and pesticide residues. The results of the analysis should confirm and/or supplement the information in the report. A copy of the report is given to the management.

After the FDA District Office or Headquarters has studied the report, they will take action against any violations. A letter will be sent to the management and request a reply within 10 days on what corrective actions will be taken. In most cases the firm agrees to correct the deficiencies, and the FDA follows up to ensure that the corrections are made. If violations continue and/or dangerous products are involved, the agency will take other appropriate enforcement actions.

The question of how a food plant is selected for inspection has frequently been raised. The FDA is fully aware that its number of consumer safety officers is limited, not every food establishment can be inspected, and questions may be raised regarding the safety and sanitation of a considerable number of food products being sold commercially. The FDA has developed a procedure to remedy this.

Decision as to which plants to inspect is made by supervisory investigators in each FDA District Office with the assistance of a computer which takes into consideration a number of factors. For example:

1. Some plants are regularly inspected by other local, state, and federal health authorities. They are thus inspected less frequently by the FDA.
2. Certain industries, such as flour mills, warehouses, beverage bottlers, bakeries, and grain elevators, are inspected by state agencies having signed agreements

with the FDA concerning work-sharing responsibility.

3. Some firms engage in a very small amount of interstate commerce.
4. Some plants have a history of high quality products from a good quality control. They are self-regulatory and usually report to the FDA of any recalls or severe problems.
5. Some plants are known to pay little attention to quality control. They are the ones most frequently inspected by the FDA.
6. Recommendation is made by each officer and his supervisor in regard to certain plant and is stated in each inspection report.

The total information is fed into a computer, which will alert the FDA to conduct an inspection of a certain firm at the appropriate time.

Some aspects of food establishment inspections by the FDA were discussed in the 21st annual educational conference of the Food and Drug Law Institute, Inc., and the FDA, held in Washington, D.C. on December 13 and 14, 1977.

Hazard Analysis and Critical Control Point (HACCP) Inspectional Program. Detailed information about the HACCP system may be obtained from the publications listed in Table 6-12.

The National Aeronautics and Space Administration, the U. S. Army Natick Laboratories, and the Pillsbury Company jointly developed the basic concept of the HACCP system. The Natick Laboratories first developed the Models of Failure, a system consisting of examining the product, the components, and the manufacturing process and deciding which aspect can make a mistake. Such a concept became the basis of the HACCP system which actually applies a zero-defects program to the production of food. Eventually, the FDA adopted this concept in its inspection programs.

The system consists of the analysis of the processing of food products and identifies all those points that may pose potential hazards to public health. Such an analysis begins with the incoming raw materials and ends with the final distribution of the product. Each such point is labeled as a critical control point where the hazard must be removed by proper control. The analysis concentrates on three types of hazards:

1. Extraneous substances, such as pebbles, metal, and glass.
2. Chemical contaminants, such as industrial chemicals, pesticide residues, and related substances. Examples include polychlorinated biphenyls, DDT, mercury, and others.
3. Biological contaminations such as pathogenic bacteria and harmful molds, including *C. perfringens, C. botulinum,* coagulase positive *staphylococci, E. coli, salmonella, shigella,* and *A. flatus,* and aflatoxin and botulism toxin.

TABLE 6-12. Publications on the Hazard Analysis and Critical Control Point (HACCP)

1. Hazard Analysis and Critical Control Point. A system for inspection of food processors. Published by the FDA and completely updated at all times since it is one of the many inspection manuals.

2. Scientific symposium on HACCP. Food Microbiology Division Symposium on Microbiological Considerations of HACCP Systems, at the 34th Annual Meeting of the Institute of Food Technologists, New Orleans, Louisiana, May 12 to 15, 1974. Completely reproduced in the September 1974 issue of Food Technology.

3. HACCP--A new approach to FDA inspections. Presented by J. P. Hile before the Food & Drug Institute in cooperation with FDA, Washington, D.C., December 11, 1973.

4. HACCP Status and future. Presented by R. M. Schaffner at the Cornell University Management Seminar for food processors, Batavia, New York, March 14, 1974.

5. J. E. Curtis and G. E. Huskey. HACCP analysis in quality assurance. Food Product Development, April, 1974.

6. Control of critical points in food processing. The Food Processors Institute, 1977.

Any of these three types of hazard can endanger life if they exist in sufficient quantity, although some contaminations require only a small amount to be hazardous. Thus the basic analysis must search the entire system and identify those points where potential hazards can enter. Critical control points should be established at various positions in food processing, packaging, and distribution.

Some basic premises to remember about the HACCP system are as follows:

1. Most food industries already have some kind of safety program to test their products for sanitation and wholesomeness. However, the HACCP provides a systems approach for estimating risk, evaluating possible hazards, devising methods for their elimination, and prescribing acceptable limits for "unavoidable hazards." The elimination of hazard at the earliest critical control point will prevent its progressing to the next point.

2. Hazards and control points vary with the types of ingredient and their packag-

ing, the overall processing procedures, products acceptance criteria, and conditions of product handling and storage.
3. The type of product determines the place, method, and quantity of sample to be analyzed.

Some examples of critical control points in the production of frozen vegetables are described as follows:

1. The washing of raw vegetables is a critical control point. Water quality at washing and equipment sanitation can be critical since it determines whether harmful bacteria has contaminated the product. This is especially important since the later blanching of the raw vegetables will not eliminate the microorganisms although their number may be decreased. Since heat treatment is not needed in the preparation of frozen vegetables, controls at subsequent location will be of no benefit.
2. Another critical control point is when the vegetable is cut, sliced, and diced. Bacterial contamination at this stage is highly possible since the fluid coming out of the cut surface is a good medium for bacterial growth and the equipment can directly contribute undesirable microorganisms. Any contamination at this stage will nullify the controls instituted previously.

As can be observed, to control the bacterial contamination at these two points is critical and requires careful planning and testing.

At present the FDA has instituted the new HACCP inspection approach, whereas in the past the traditional FDA inspection involved on-the-site observation of operating conditions by an inspector on any particular day or days. This type of inspection is still in full force, especially for such establishments as warehouses. However, it is obvious that such an inspection does not inform the FDA what the manufacturing or operating practices are when the inspector is not present. The inspector also will not know how the management monitors and controls the continuous operations of the plant. The HACCP inspectional program is aimed at correcting these deficiencies. The procedure is divided into three parts:

1. Conduct a traditional inspection of the establishment for one or more days. It should follow the processing procedures with a flow chart and identify the critical control points in the process.
2. Review the quality control system of the company, with emphasis on the critical control points.
3. Document the degree that the management has adhered to its own quality control program.

By studying the past conduct of the firm's product processing through its quality control records and by a site observation of its operation, the inspector will have a good idea about the plant's operation through the entire year. The approach identifies problems and defines corrective actions. It assures the firm of a safe product and serves as an investigative tool by the plant management to verify its own quality control system.

The general outline of an HACCP inspection by the FDA is as follows. When an FDA inspector arrives at the plant, he conducts a conference with the management, wherein decision is reached regarding the inspection/program objectives and an introduction to all pertinent personnel data and plant operation records. The inpsector then conducts an inspection of the plant at a predetermined time. Afterwards, an Establishment Inspection Report is filed with the FDA District Office and eventually its headquarters at the Bureau of Foods. Each report categorizes the food establishment into any of the following three classes:

1. Only routine follow-up is needed.
2. Prompt attention is needed because of some major deviations from the requirements of good manufacturing practices.
3. Immediate remedy is necessary because of one or more critical deviation(s) from proper manufacturing practices.

Each food plant will be informed of the finding, although one with deviation(s) will receive a formal notification from the inspector or authorized personnel, which may be: (1) a written statement immediately following the inspection, (2) a postinspection letter, or (3) an invitation requesting a meeting between FDA personnel and authorized plant officers. Such notifications have resulted in corrective actions taken in food establishments, such as replacement of inadequate and improper equipment, improvement or initiation of controls at critical points, and record keeping.

There are some aspects of this inspectional approach that should be noted:

1. It takes longer and requires more records and personnel participation of the firm.
2. Although unannounced inspections will still be the primary investigative tool, the element of surprise does not play such an important role in the HACCP approach.
3. The number of inspectors needed will depend on the complexity and size of the plant.
4. The approach is preventive in nature, ensuring corrective actions before any real health hazard has occurred.
5. The approach is applicable to any of the FDA's program areas. The technique

was started in the fall of 1972 when the low-acid canned food industries were first tested by this program. It is expected that the FDA will continue the use of this technique.

During the HACCP inspections of food establishments in 1973, some significant deviations from good manufacturing practices were recorded in a food establishment (see Table 6-13).

To guarantee the safety of the food supply, the FDA uses good manufacturing practices, unannounced factory inspections, and hazard analysis and critical control point inspection system as investigative and preventive measures. It should be stressed that it is not possible to discuss these three programs separately since they are interrelated. However, each has its own distinct characteristics.

Special Seafood Inspection Program

According to the Federal Food, Drug, and Cosmetic Act, any interstate shipment of seafood is prohibited from adulteration and misbranding. Seafood manufacturing and processing is subjected to all applicable regulations promulgated by the FDA. When the U.S. Congress was preparing this act, it gave additional attention to the inspection of seafood products. It authorized the FDA to provide certain voluntary fee-for-service inspection program.

Thus according to Section 702a of the act (21 U.S.C. 372a), the program is as follows:

1. On application by a seafood packer engaged in interstate commerce, the FDA may designate inspectors to examine and inspect such food and the production, packing, and labeling of the products.
2. Product compliance will be marked.
3. Such inspection services must be financed by the applicant in terms of prescheduled fees.
4. The FDA is authorized to promulgate regulations governing the sanitary and other conditions under which the service is needed or granted.
5. Misrepresentation of government or official marks or stamps will be guilty of a misdemeanor and shall on conviction be subject to imprisonment for not more than one year or a fine of not less than $1,000 nor more than $5,000, or a combination of such imprisonment and fine.

Accordingly, at the present time of writing, the FDA has issued specific regulations for canned oysters and processed shrimp. They are located in 21 CFR 197.

The regulation issued for canned oyster inspection consists of: application for inspection service, granting or refusing inspection service and cancellation of ap-

TABLE 6-13. Commonly encountered deviations from good manufacturing practice in an establishment.[a]

---

1. Inadequate control of filling conditions and inadequate records of fill weights, drained weights, and initial temperature, which are critical processing factors.

2. Inaccurate mercury thermometers. Disagreement between recording thermometers and mercury thermometers. Use of recording thermometer as the criterion for process temperature instead of the mercury thermometer.

3. Inadequate or unconventional venting techniques. Venting under water, and using vent lines of excessive length. Use of globe valves for venting.

4. Faulty retort construction. Inadequate bleeders, valves, and piping. No steam regulators. Improper location of bleeders and vents.

5. Lack of scheduled processes, and lack of procedures of handling process deviations. Firms that have shortened process times, and firms unable to verify processes used.

6. Inadequate records. Processing records lacking information regarding minimum initial temperature, mercury and recording thermometer readings, actual process temperature, time steam on, and venting parameters.

7. Improper use of filling equipment creating conditions that could prevent proper heat penetration.

8. Inadequate steam supplies. Steam pressures observed varying or never reaching the recommended minimum pressure. Steam regulated by manual valves only. No heat distribution studies to determine adequacy of the pressures actually utilized.

9. Lack of knowledge of critical control points of the process and lack of clear understanding of process flow on a system basis.

10. Lack of appropriate training of plant personnel in critical areas, such as retort operators, and use of personnel with language difficulties without adequate means to overcome these difficulties.

---

[a] Adapted from the presentation by J. P. Hile (an FDA official) before the Food and Drug Law Institute in Washington, D.C., December 1973 (see Table 6-12).

plication, suspension and withdrawal of inspection service, inspection periods, assignment of inspectors, uninspected products excluded from inspected establishments, general requirements for plant and equipment, general operating conditions,

code marking, processing, examination after canning, labeling, certificates of inspection, warehousing and export permits, and inspection fees. Selected aspects
are discussed as follows:

Separate all shucking sheds and packing rooms, and construct and arrange all
fixtures and equipment to permit thorough cleaning. They should be adequately
lighted and ventilated, and the floors should be tight and arranged for thorough
cleaning and proper drainage. Open drains from shucking shed should not enter
packing room. If the shucking shed and packing room are in separate buildings,
they should be less than 100 yards apart, unless adequate provisions are made to
enable efficient inspection.

One or more suitable washing device and inspection belt should be installed
for the washing and subsequent inspection of the oysters before delivery for steam-
ing or other means of opening. If steam boxes are used for opening the oysters,
they should be provided with adequate steam inlets, exhausts, drains, a safety
valve, and a pressure gauge. Shells and debris should be removed from the shucking
shed by suitable means. One or more suitable devices should be provided for removing shell and grit from shucked oysters, for washing such oysters, and for their
subsequent drainage. Suitable belts should be installed for the inspection of
shucked oysters. An automatic container-counting device should be installed in
each cannery line, and each sterilizing retort should be fitted with the minimum
required equipment. The inspector should be provided with suitable space and
facilities to prepare records and examine samples and for the safekeeping of records
and equipment.

With reference to the general operating conditions, some details are as follows.
Before being steamed or opened by other means, the oysters are washed with clean,
unpolluted water and then passed over the inspection belt and culled to remove
dirty, muddy, dead, or decomposed oysters and extraneous material. Return
muddy oysters to the washer for rewashing. Wash unloading platforms and equipment with clean, unpolluted water and remove all debris. Remove the shells from
the shucking shed continuously. Do not permit any offal, debris, or refuse from any
source to accumulate in the cannery or, except for shells, about the premises. Do
not permit shells to accumulate about the premises to such an extent as to create
a nuisance. Do not permit the delivery of steamed oysters to shuckers by manually
rolling, trundling, or wheelbarrowing such oysters on or above shucking tables.
Before use each day, thoroughly wash shucking knives and cups with soap and
water and chlorinate them. The concentration of the chlorine solution should be
200 ppm.

If an inspector condemns some oysters as filthy, decomposed, putrid, or unfit
for food, the packer should destroy them for food purposes under the immediate
supervision of the inspector. Do not take into the cannery any oysters condemned
on the boat or the unloading platform. Destroy them or return to the abedding
ground.

Further details on this special seafood inspection program may be obtained from the original document, 21 CFR 197.

Interstate Travel Sanitation

The U.S. Public Health Service has enforced regulations to prevent the spread of communicable diseases between states since 1893. In June 1969 the responsibility was transferred to the FDA. Such authority is based on Section 361 of the Public Health Service Act (PL 78-410, 42 U.S.C. 264), which encompasses the Interstate Quarantine Regulations. Within the FDA, the Interstate Travel Sanitation Branch (see Appendix 6-4) has the primary responsibility of coordinating programs to assure the safety of food and water service and waste disposal on interstate public carriers and/or support facilities.

Regulations promulgated to enforce interstate travel sanitation are described in 21 CFR 1240 and 1250. The authority under which they were issued was derived from Sections 215, 361, 58 Stat. 690, 703, as amended (42 U.S.C. 216 and 264).

The title of 21 CFR 1240 is "Control of communicable disease," which contains regulations on the restrictions on travel of persons, specific administrative decisions regarding interstate shipments, and source and use of potable water. A brief discussion of potable water is as follows.

Unless otherwise exempted, only potable water is permitted for drinking and culinary purposes in a conveyance engaged in interstate traffic. Such water should either have been obtained from officially approved water points or, if treated aboard a conveyance, should have been subjected to approved treatment.

The FDA will approve any water point if the water supply meets the standards prescribed by federal statute and the methods of delivery of such water to the conveyance prevent the introduction, transmission, or spread of communicable diseases. The approval may be based on the recommendation of the health authorities of a state or a contiguous foreign nation.

The title of 21 CFR 1250 is "Interstate conveyance sanitation," and it describes regulations of food service sanitation on land and air conveyances, and vessels, such as equipment, operation, and servicing areas for land and air conveyances and sanitation facilities and conditions on vessels. In the following, some aspects of food service sanitation on interstate vehicles are discussed.

All food and drink served must be clean, wholesome, and free from spoilage and must be prepared, stored, handled, and served in accordance with prescribed requirements. Operators of conveyances are required to identify, when requested by FDA officials, the vendors from whom they have acquired their food supply. The FDA may inspect any source of such food supply to determine whether sanitation and safety regulations have been met. The approval or recommendation of other government health authority is also accepted.

Some regulations regarding requirements for serving certain special foods are as follows. Milk and fluid-milk products, including cream, buttermilk, skim milk, milk beverages, and reconstituted milk, should be pasteurized and obtained from an approved source. Containers of these products should be labeled to show the contents, with the word "pasteurized" and the identity of the manufacturing plant by name and address or acceptable code. Ice cream and other frozen desserts, cheese, and butter should be manufactured from milk or milk products that have been pasteurized or subjected to equivalent heat treatment. Milk, buttermilk, and milk beverages should be served in or from the original individual containers in which received from the distributor, or from a bulk container equipped with a dispensing device so designed, constructed, installed, and maintained as to prevent the transmission of communicable disease.

Shellfish purchased for consumption on any conveyance should originate from a dealer currently listed by the FDA as holding an unexpired and unrevoked certificate issued by a state authority. Shucked shellfish should be furnished in the containers in which they are placed at the shucking plant and should be kept in them until used. The state abbreviation and certificate number of the packers should be permanently recorded on the container.

Some other requirements are as follows. All perishable food or drink should be kept at or below $50^\circ F$, except when being prepared or kept hot for serving. Ice coming in contact with food or drink and not manufactured on the conveyance should be obtained from approved sources. All food and drink should be stored and handled in such a manner as to avoid contamination.

All kitchens, galleys, pantries, and other places where food is prepared, served, or stored should be adequately lighted and ventilated except where cold storage is employed. They should also be free from flies, rodents, and other vermin. For more details, consult the original document.

The Interstate Travel Sanitation Branch of the FDA develops and maintains sanitation standards and handbooks for the design, construction, and operation of interstate public carriers and support facilities. They are especially interested in the facilities and equipment used for food and water service and waste disposal. They issue Letters of Acceptance to the operators if their conveyances have been approved. They also issue the annual List of Accepted Equipment for Interstate Carrier Use and Official Classification Lists. All handbooks, standards, and other relevant materials issued by the FDA in connection with interstate travel sanitation are described in Table 6-14. They are of tremendous value to the transportation industries and the field inspection personnel, both state and federal. Interested parties should consult them for further information.

As a result of the Railroad Car Sanitation Conference held on September 10

TABLE 6-14. List of Publications Issued by the FDA and related to Activities of the Interstate Travel Sanitation Branch

Publication Number	Publication Title	Publication Date
308	Handbook on Sanitation of Airlines	Revised 1964, Reprinted 1974
1454	Handbook on Sanitation of Buses	1966
95	Handbook on Sanitation of Railroad Passenger Cars	Revised 1964
66	Handbook on Sanitation of Railroad Servicing Areas	Reprinted 1963
393	Handbook on Sanitation of Vessel Construction	Revised 1965
274	Handbook on Sanitation of Vessel Watering Points	Reprinted 1967
None	Guidelines for evaluating aircraft lavatory servicing vehicle construction	Reprinted 1976
None	Guidelines for evaluating aircraft potable water servicing vehicle construction	None
None	Guidelines for the treatment of railroad conveyance wastes for enroute disposal	December 1972
None	Official interstate carrier classification list, acceptable vessel watering points as of *date*.	Constantly updated

and 11, 1974, in Washington, D.C. (see Food Drug Cosmetic Law Journal, October 1974 issue) and subsequent Task Force meetings, a second compliance program is currently being implemented by the FDA to direct the inspection of food transport vehicles in conjunction with routine, regularly scheduled food sanitation inspections to reduce the incidence of contamination and/or insanitary condition aboard such vehicles, which consist of railroad cars and trucks.

Meat, Poultry, and Eggs

Federal regulatory control over these three products is mainly assigned to the USDA. However, either by specific statutory provisions or by official interagency agreements, the FDA has some degree of authority over these products or food containing them as ingredients. In the following paragraphs, a legal analysis of this jurisdictional conflict is presented. Any interested party should consult the original legal or government documents to make one's own analyses and interpretations if necessary.

Jurisdiction of the FDA over Meat Food Products

According to the FDA's Compliance Policy Guides, Section 7 of the Food Additives Amendment of 1958 states that none of the provisions in this amendment intends to exempt a meat product from any requirement prescribed under the Federal Meat Inspection Act and the Poultry Products Inspection Act, both of which are administered by the USDA. Both the FDA and USDA have regulatory control over a food additive if it is used in a poultry or meat product. Either agency may publish its own food additive regulation or accede to the other's. In the absence of such a regulation, a meat product is not permitted to contain a food additive that does not have approval from both agencies.

Section 902(b) of the Federal Food, Drug, and Cosmetic Act [21 U.S.C. 392(b)] indicates that the adulteration and misbranding of meat and meat products will be exempt from FDA control to the extent that they are covered by the Federal Meat Inspection Act, which is administered by the USDA. The Wholesome Meat Act of 1967 gave USDA authority over the complete process of production of meat and meat products. Thus the USDA has jurisdiction over these products beyond the official inspection establishment, to include their subsequent adulteration and misbranding. This is equivalent to FDA jurisdiction over all other foods. The 1967 Wholesome Meat Act [21 U.S.C. 679(a)] provides that, Section 902(b) of the Federal Food, Drug, and Cosmetic Act notwithstanding, the provisions of the Wholesome Meat Act shall not derogate from any authority conferred by the Federal Food, Drug, and Cosmetic Act prior to the enactment of the Wholesome Meat

Act. This particular provision ascertains that the FDA will not be displaced from its jurisdiction over meat and meat products. On August 17, 1972, in an opinion of the U.S. Attorney General (Volume 42, Op. No. 44), the USDA was informed that legislative history had shown that the U.S. Congress intended to give the USDA and FDA concurrent jurisdiction over misbranding and adulteration of meat products after USDA inspection. At present, the policy of the FDA with respect to these products is as follows.

Assume a meat or poultry product, after it has left an establishment under USDA supervision, is involved in a violation that comes to the FDA's attention. The FDA will inform the USDA; this is to prevent duplication of effort if the USDA prefers to take regulatory action or is already in the process of doing so. Normally, the FDA will not initiate any action unless it has been informed that the USDA does not wish to handle the matter. Under appropriate circumstances, the FDA may exercise its jurisdiction under the Federal Food, Drug, and Cosmetic Act over meat and poultry products in interstate commerce.

According the Section 1(j) of the Federal Meat Inspection Act (21 U.S.C. 601), "meat food product" is defined as:

> any product capable of use as human food which is made whole or in part from any meat or other portion of the carcass of any cattle, sheep, swine, or goats, excepting products which contain meat or other portions of such carcasses only in a relatively small proportion or historically have not been considered by consumers as products of the meat food industry, and which are exempted from definition as a meat food product by the Secretary under such conditions as he may prescribe to assure that the meat or other portions of such carcasses contained in such product are not adulterated and that such products are not represented as meat food products.

This exemption also applies to food products of equines.

Since the "Secretary" in the preceding quote refers to the U.S. Secretary of Agriculture, the USDA states its position in 9 CFR 301.2(vv) (see Chapter 1) by asserting that the Administrator of the Meat Poultry Inspection Program of the USDA will determine what is or is not a meat food product. At present, a formal regulation has not yet been issued by the USDA, and *red* meat food product exemptions from USDA control are handled on a case-by-case basis, using the general and informal criterion that products with less than 3% meat will be regulated by the FDA. A copy of the Meat Poultry Inspection memorandum or letter exempting an interstate product is sent to the FDA, which then assumes active jurisdiction.

According to Section 4(f) of the Poultry Products Inspection Act (21 U.S.C.

441), "poultry product" is defined as:

> any poultry carcass, or part thereof, or any product which is made wholly or in part from any poultry carcass or part thereof, excepting products which contain poultry ingredients only in a relatively small proportion or historically have not been considered by consumers as products of the poultry food industry, and which are exempted by the Secretary from definition as a poultry product under such conditions as the Secretary may prescribe to assure that the product ingredients in such products are not adulterated and that such products are not represented as poultry products.

The U.S. Secretary of Agriculture, through its Meat Poultry Inspection Program, has issued relevant formal regulation to handle this statutory clause. According to 9 CFR 381.15 (see Chapter 1) the following food articles contain poultry ingredients only in a relatively small proportion or historically have not been considered by consumers as products of the poultry food industry. Therefore, they are exempted from the definition of "poultry product," the requirements of the act, and the applicable regulations, if they comply with the following specified conditions:

1. Any human food product in a consumer package, unless otherwise exempted, if:
   a. It contains less than 2% cooked poultry meat (deboned white or dark poultry meat, or both).
   b. It contains less than 10% of cooked poultry skins, giblets, or fat, separately, and less than 10% of cooked poultry skins, giblets, fat, and meat (itself less than 2%).
   c. The poultry ingredients used in the product were prepared under authorized domestic or foreign governmental supervision or inspection.
   d. The name of the product appears in authorized form on its label.
   e. The product is not represented as a poultry product.
   These percentages of ingredients should be computed on the basis of the moist, deboned, cooked poultry in the ready-to-serve product when prepared according to the serving directions on the consumer package.
2. Any human food product in a consumer package, unless otherwise exempted, if:
   a. It is prepared for sale only to institutional users, such as hotels, restaurants, and boarding houses, for use as a soup base or flavoring.
   b. It contains less than 15% cooked poultry meat (deboned white or dark poultry meat, or both), computed on the basis of the moist deboned,

cooked poultry meat in such product.

   c. It complies with the criteria cited about ingredients inspection, label name, and nonrepresentation as poultry product.

3. Bouillon cubes, poultry broths, gravies, sauces, seasonings, and flavorings, unless otherwise exempted, if:

   a. They contain poultry meat or poultry fat only in condimental quantities.

   b. They comply with the criteria cited about ingredients inspection, label name, and nonrepresentation as poultry product.

   c. In the case of poultry broth, it will not be used in the processing of any poultry product in any official USDA supervised establishment.

4. Fat capsules and sandwiches containing poultry products if they comply with the criteria cited about ingredients inspection, label name, and nonrepresentation as poultry product.

5. For those items under (1) and (2) above, the products will be deemed to be represented as poultry products if the kind name (chicken, turkey, etc.) is used in the product name without appropriate qualification. For example, a consumer packaged noodle soup product containing less than 2% chicken meat on a ready-to-serve basis may not be labeled "Chicken Flavored Noodle Soup."

The regulation also declares that all products exempted under the provision of 9 CFR 381.15 are subject to the requirements of the Federal Food, Drug, and Cosmetic Act and thus are under FDA authority.

Detention of Carcasses
<u>Detention of Carcasses</u>

Sections 402 and 409(b) of the Federal Meat Inspection Act [U.S.C. 672, 679(b)] and Sections 19 and 24(b) of the Poultry Products Inspection Act [21 U.S.C. 462, 467(b)] provide the FDA with the following authority. Food and Drug Administration officials are authorized to detain any carcass, its part, meat, or meat food product of cattle, sheep, swine, goats, or equines, and any poultry carcass, its part, or product for a period of 20 days if the following conditions are satisfied:

1. They are located in a premise that is outside any official establishment under the supervision of the USDA inspectional personnel.

2. They are located in such a premise for the purposes of, or during or after distribution in, commerce.

3. The FDA officials have reason to believe that any such article is adulterated or misbranded and is capable of use as human food or is in violation of any other federal law or the laws of any state or territory, or the District of Columbia.

Such detained product is subject to seizure and condemnation as authorized by the other provisions of the relevant acts.

Egg Products Inspection

The Egg Products Inspection Act of 1970 as amended (21 U.S.C. 1031 to 1056) is administered jointly by the FDA and the USDA. On February 4, 1972 an official Memorandum of Understanding between the two agencies was announced (37 FR 2686 and 2687), which delineates the specific responsibility and authority of each agency in regard to the act. The specific duties of the USDA have been presented in Chapter 1; those of the FDA are described in the following paragraphs.

The FDA will have exclusive jurisdiction over restaurants, institutions, food manufacturing plants, and other similar establishments that break and serve eggs or use them in their products to determine, among other things, that the eggs used do not contain a precentage of restricted eggs greater than that allowed in U.S. Consumer Grade B (see Chapter 1). The FDA will perform the following specific functions:

1. Exercise the administrative detention authority provided in the act with respect to shell eggs and egg products located on the premises of establishments for which the FDA has jurisdiction.
2. Notify the USDA of violations committed in establishments under FDA jurisdiction. The USDA can then check on the seller of the restricted eggs for a possible violation of the act. If food manufacturers decide to break eggs below U.S. Consumer Grade B, the egg breaking portion of their operation would require USDA inspection.
3. Establish standards of identity for egg products.
4. Assume responsibility for food products containing eggs that are not egg products as defined by the act, except where on an individual basis. The two agencies have agreed that the USDA will have authority over such food products being produced in an egg product plant.
5. Notify the USDA of any unwholesome egg products it encounters, including imported shell eggs that contain restricted eggs not complying with USDA regulations and labeling requirements.
6. Monitor imported and domestic shell eggs for the presence of pesticides and other contaminants.

Recall of Food Products with Meat or Poultry Ingredients

During the Class I or II recall of a product processed in accordance with the Federal Meat Inspection Act and/or the Poultry Products Inspection Act, which name recalled ingredients subject to FDA jurisdiction, both the FDA and USDA have common or related objectives in carrying out their respective regulatory and service activities. A Class I recall concerns products that may be life threatening; Class II recall concerns products thay may directly or indirectly be responsible for immediate/long-range and potentially life-threatening effects. To delineate the duties of each agency in such an effort of recall, an official Memorandum of Understanding between the FDA and USDA was announced on June 12, 1975 (40 FR 25079). The specific duties of the USDA under this agreement have been presented in Chapter 1; those of the FDA are described as follows.

1. It will expeditiously furnish the USDA's compliance staff, the rationale on which the recall is based, and the identity of USDA inspected firms known by the FDA to have received the products being recalled. This information will relate to ingredients under the exclusive jurisdiction of FDA that were subsequently used in meat and poultry products in a USDA inspected plant.
2. It will assist the USDA, when requested, in its investigation and evaluation to determine the need for the secondary recall of a meat and/or poultry product processed in a USDA inspected plant.
3. It will furnish the USDA compliance staff pertinent evidence to support a USDA request to a U.S. attorney for seizure (if necessary) under Section 403(a) of the Federal Meat Inspection Act (21 U.S.C. 673) and Section 20 of the Poultry Products Inspection Act [21 U.S.C. 469(b)].
4. It will keep customary records and make relevant information available to the USDA.
5. It will collaborate in furnishing reports of work progress.

Drug, Pesticide, and Industrial Chemical Residues in Animal Feeds, Meat, and Poultry

The FDA ensures that foods for human and animal consumption are safe and wholesome and that animal feeds are free of illegal drug, pesticide, and industrial chemical residues. It accomplishes this by inspecting the processing and distribution of animal feeds and examining samples to assure compliance with the Federal Food, Drug, and Cosmetic Act. The USDA samples and analyzes edible tissues derived from livestock and poultry at the time of slaughter to ensure, among other things, that meat and poultry products do not contain illegal residues of those substances. Such products may become contaminated with illegal residues from several sources, including the presence of these residues in animal feeds at actionable levels. On April 10, 1975 the FDA and USDA announced (40 FR 16228 and 16229) that they had signed a Memorandum of Understanding to detail the working arrangements so that proper regulatory control is exercised over any illegal residues. The specific duties of the USDA under this agreement have been presented in Chapter 1; those of the FDA are described as follows:

1. It will immediately notify the USDA headquarters of findings of illegal residues in feeds and feed ingredients intended for food-producing animals or results of any other FDA investigation that indicate the likelihood that actionable residues will be present in meat or poultry.
2. It will report to the appropriate USDA regional office the results of any FDA investigation initiated because of information made available by the USDA.
3. It will provide the USDA headquarters with FDA inspectional, sampling, and testing programs for drugs, pesticides, and industrial chemicals in animal feeds, feed ingredients, dairy products, and eggs. It will also periodically furnish the results of such programs, including the number and location of samples tested, the residues for which tests were conducted, the methodology used, and other related information.
4. It will recommend on request from the USDA, action levels for industrial chemical residues in meat or poultry.
5. It will advise USDA headquarters whenever it plans to establish an action level for a pesticide residue in animal feeds, feed ingredients, dairy products, or eggs so that the USDA may also consider the need for an action level for that pesticide residue in meat and poultry.

The USDA can and does condemn meat and poultry when the product contains illegal drug residues, as well as for other reasons. They could not, however, take action against the causative factor, namely, the producer and shipper of those animals. The FDA can and does enforce legal sanction against the producers for their violative products.

Microwave Ovens

According to Appendix 6-2, one bureau within the FDA is the Bureau of Radiological Health. Among its numerous activities, one that concerns this Chapter is its responsibility to ensure that there is no consumer hazard from the use of microwave cooking ovens. The Radiation Control for Health and Safety Act of 1968 (42 U.S.C. 216; see Table 6-1) established an electronic product radiation control program within the FDA. Sections 354 to 360F of the Public Health Service Act (see Table 6-1; 42 U.S.C. 263b to 263n) specifically relate to electronic product radiation control and are administered by the FDA. Accordingly, the FDA has promulgated regulation to govern the construction and other aspects of microwave ovens to limit radiation from U.S. manufactured and imported electronic products for the protection of public health. They are located in 21 CFR 1030 and are titled "Performance standards for microwave and radio frequency emitting products." It was issued under the authority of Section 358, 82 Stat. 1177; 42 U.S.C. 263f. Some aspects are presented as follows:

The regulation describes: definitions, requirements for the performance standards for a microwave oven such as power density limit, door and safety interlocks, measurements and test conditions, and availability of instructions. The provisions of this standard are applicable to microwave ovens manufactured after October 6, 1971.

According to the regulation, a microwave oven refers to a device to heat, cook, or dry food through the application of electromagnetic energy at frequencies assigned by the Federal Communications Commission in the normal ISM (Industrial, Scientific, Medical) heating bands ranging from 890 MH_2 to 6000 MH_2. It is limited to those manufactured for use in homes, restaurants, food vending, or service establishments, interstate carriers, and similar facilities.

The maximum limit for the amount of radiation that can escape or leak from the oven is 1 mW/cm^2 at the time of purchase and no more than 5 mW during the useful life of the oven.

The requirements for door and safety interlocks of a microwave oven are as follows. A "microwave oven cavity" refers to that portion of the equipment in which food may be heated, cooked, or dried. "Door" means the movable barrier that prevents access to the cavity during operation and whose function is to prevent emission of microwave energy from the passage or opening that provides access to the cavity. "Safety interlock" means a device intended to prevent generation of microwave energy when access to the cavity is possible. Each oven is required to have a minimum of two operative safety interlocks, one of which must not be operable by any part of the body or a rod 3 mm or greater in diameter and with a useful length of 10 cm. A magnetically operated interlock is considered to be concealed only if a test magnet, held in place on the oven by gravity or its own attraction, cannot operate it. The test magnet must have a pull at zero air gap of at least 4.5 kg and a pull at 1 cm air gap of at least 450 g when the face of the magnet, which is toward the interlock switch when the magnet is in the test position, is pulling against one of the large faces of a mild steel armature having dimensions of 80 x 50 x 8 mm.

Service adjustments or procedures on the oven should not cause the safety interlocks to become inoperative or the radiation emission to exceed the power density limits. Insertion of an object into the oven cavity through any opening while the door is closed should not cause emission from the oven to exceed the applicable power density limits.

The primary required safety interlock should prevent emission in excess of the requirement; the secondary interlock should prevent emission in excess of 5 mW/cm^2 at any point 5 cm or more from the external surface of the oven. The service instructions for the oven should designate the two required safety interlocks as primary or secondary.

If the required safety interlock(s) should fail to perform the specified functions, there should be a mechanism to render the oven inoperable and remain so until repaired. Interlock failures should not disrupt such monitoring function.

The FDA conducts sample testing of microwave ovens in homes, commercial establishments, dealer and distributor premises, factories, and in its own laboratories to assure that they comply with federal requirements. It also evaluates manufacturers' radiation testing and quality control programs. When a problem is identified, the FDA requires the manufacturer to correct all noncomplying ovens at no cost to the consumer.

The regulations promulgated by the FDA in 21 CFR 1010, "Performance standards for electronic products: general," also apply to microwave ovens. This part was issued under the authority of Section 358, 82 Stat. 1177; 42 U.S.C. 263f. The regulations describe the various procedures whereby the manufacturers of microwave ovens will conform to the specifications described in 21 CFR 1030, which were discussed in the preceding paragraphs. Thus 21 CFR 1010 describes the certification, identification, variances, special test procedures, and exportation of electronic products with performance standards. Further details should be obtained from the original document.

Tea Importation

The following information is adapted from "Compliance program evaluation," FDA By-lines, July 1977.

The FDA administers the Tea Importation Act, passed in 1897 and amended in July 1943 (29 Stat. 604 et seq.; 21 U.S.C. 41 et seq.). It requires that all whole or broken leaf tea offered for importation into the United States be sampled and examined by the Board of Tea Experts, who ascertain its purity, quality, and fitness for consumption. The Bureau of Customs, working closely with the FDA, refuses entry of nonapproved shipments.

The FDA regulates instant tea under the authority of the Federal Food, Drug, and Cosmetic Act and the Fair Packaging and Labeling Act because it was developed after passage of the Tea Importation Act.

The U.S. Board of Tea Experts is made up of seven recognized tea experts from the FDA and industry. They are appointed by the Secretary of Health, Education, and Welfare annually. It meets once a year to establish the criteria for examining tea samples. An importer whose tea has been rejected may formally appeal to the U.S. Board of Tea Appeals, a body comprised of three FDA Tea Examiners designated by the U.S. Secretary of Health, Education, and Welfare. If the rejection is confirmed by this board, the tea cannot be reexamined.

Each year, based on samples submitted by trade members, the Board of Experts establishes standards for tea. One standard specimen is available for each major type of tea imported. The names and number of the standard teas may vary from year to year. Some examples are Formosa Oolong, Scented Black Tea, Black Tea, China, Formosa, and Japan Type. In picking a standard, the board tries to select one at least equal in quality to that of the previous year. Duplicate tins of the standards are supplied to board members and FDA Tea Examiners. Members of the tea trade can obtain these at cost. The law requires that each importer pay a prescheduled fee for the inspection service. For a lot of tea to be accepted to the United States, it must compare favorably with the standard in the analyses performed by an FDA Tea Examiner.

The three general types of tea, namely, green, black, and oolong, come from the same plant species. The major differences among them result from the method of processing, although growing conditions and location do affect the quality and other characteristics of each type. A fourth major type of tea, "mixed tea" can be a mixture of two of the above three types. A "mixed tea" can also be a combination of one type of tea with an observable quantity of another substance, such as orange peel.

A sample from each lot of tea offered for import is collected by the importer and shipped to the nearest FDA Tea Examiner. Food and Drug Administration Tea Examiners are located in New York, Boston, and San Francisco. These cities are thus considered the ports of examination. New York District's Tea Examiner, in the role of Supervisory Tea Examiner, coordinates the entire program. He prepares quarterly and annual reports that include the amount of tea examined, rejected, and passed. This information is tabulated by month, port of examination, type of tea, and country of origin. The FDA conducts spot checks to determine whether importers are submitting representative samples of tea.

The official regulation promulgated by the FDA under the Tea Importation Act is described in 21 CFR 1220. It contains information on: general provisions; shipment and storage; customs requirements; sampling procedures; establishment of standards; individual standards; inspection, testing, and grounds for rejection; and administration procedures based on examination. Selected aspects are described in the following paragraphs.

Tea packages and contents should constitute a unit for either exportation or destruction. No separation of tea from its covering is permitted except under the following two conditions:

1.   If a lot of imported tea contains an excessive quantity of dust and siftings, the

tea may be sifted and admitted to entry if found up to the standard. Under certain circumstances, the dusts and siftings may also be admitted.

2. If, by reason of damage, a tea otherwise equal in quality to the standard has been rejected, the damaged portion may be removed and exported or destroyed under the Bureau of Customs' supervision, and the sound remainder may be resubmitted for examination and admitted to entry if found up to the standard.

With reference to inspection, testing, and grounds for rejection, the following requirements are described.

The examination of tea in comparison with the standards should be made according to the usages and customs of the tea trade, including the testing of an infusion in boiling water and, if necessary, chemical analysis; and examiners are advised, inasmuch as they must not under the law admit any tea inferior to the standards in purity, quality, and fitness for consumption, to employ the present methods of determining the presence of artificial coloring and other impurities.

In comparing with standards, examiners are to test all the teas for quality, for impurity consisting of artificial coloring or facing matter and other impurity, and for quality of infused leaf. Quality should be ascertained by drawing, according to the custom of the tea trade, with the weight of a silver half dime to the cup. The quality must be equal to standard, but the flavor may be that of a different district, as long as it is equally fit for consumption. As an illustration, a Teenkai may be equal to a Moyune, but a distinctly smoky or rank Fychow or Wenchow of sour character is not considered equal to the first two mentioned. Tea dust, fannings, siftings and offgrades, including broken tea, broken mix, and Bohea when so marked and for which there are no specific standards, should be tested for quality, purity, and fitness for consumption in comparison with their respective leaf standards.

If the examiner suspects the presence of paraffin or any similar substance, he should perform a comparison test against the standard by spreading the tea between two sheets of unglazed white paper and placing a hot iron thereon. The greasy substance, if any, will appear on the paper, and if not equal to the standard, the tea would justly be rejected.

For further details on the regulation, consult 21 CFR 1220. Another interesting reference source is "Putting tea to the taste," FDA Consumer, September 1974.

Milk Importation

The chief purpose of the Federal Import Milk Act of 1927 (44 Stat. 1101, 21 U.S.C. 141 to 149) is to regulate the importation of milk and cream into the United States for the purpose of promoting the dairy industry of this country and protecting the public health of its people. The regulations promulgated by the FDA to implement this act are located in 21 CFR 1210, which were issued under the authority of Sections 2, 3, 44 Stat. 1101, 1102, as amended, and 21 U.S.C. 142 and 143. With reference to milk and cream product, all proper cross references, including the standards established by the FDA, and the grading and inspection of the USDA should be taken into consideration.

The content of 21 CFR 1210 is as follows: general provisions, inspection, and testing, permit control, permit suspension and revocation, hearing procedure, evidence, and appeals procedures. Selected aspects are discussed in the following paragraphs.

With reference to inspection and testing, the following requirements should be noted. Dairy farms and plants from which milk or cream is shipped or transported to the United States should be open at all reasonable times to authorized FDA agents for the necessary examinations and inspections. Failure to permit entry may be considered cause for the suspension or revocation of the official permit. The sanitary conditions of such farms and plants is required to score at least 50 out of 100 points according to the officially prescribed method of scoring. The physical examination of any and all cows in herds producing the milk or cream must be made by an authorized veterinarian of the United States or of any state or municipality of the country of origin so as to ascertain the healthy conditions of the animals. Such examination is required to be made whenever the FDA considers it necessary and, in any event, should have been made within one year prior to the time of importation.

All machines for pasteurization should be of a type easily cleaned and of sanitary construction capable of holding every portion of the milk or cream at the required temperature for the required time. The time and temperature recording devices should be accurate and kept in good working order at all times. The temperature at the time of heating and holding should be recorded on thermograph charts, initialed, numbered, and dated by the official having jurisdiction over such farms and plants. All such charts should be held for 2 years unless within that period they have been examined and released by an authorized agent of the FDA.

The permit to ship the products to the United States may be suspended for cause at any time. It may also be revoked for cause, although the permittee will be given a hearing. He may provide a reason why the permit should not be revoked by appearing in person, by letter, or through an attorney. While a hearing is being conducted to decide on a possible revocation, the FDA may temporarily suspend the permit.

If interested, one should consult the original document for further details. According to Table 6-6, the FDA has signed a number of official agreements with foreign countries, in which both countries agree to control the sanitary quality of dry milk products to be imported by the United States.

Drugs and Feeds for Food-Producing Animals

Section 201(f) of the Federal Food, Drug, and Cosmetic Act (21 U.S.C. 321) defines "food" as to include articles used for food or drink for animals. Section 201(g) of the same act [21 U.S.C. 321(g)] defines drugs as "articles intended for use in the diagnosis, cure, mitigation, treatment, or prevention of disease in man or other animals," and/or "articles (other than food) intended to affect the structure or any function of the body of man or other animals." Although this chapter is not concerned with human drugs, it is interested in animal feeds, drugs, and devices, the interstate marketing of which is regulated by the FDA. The regulations promulgated by the FDA to govern such items are many, and Appendix 6-14 presents their legal citations in the Code of Federal Regulations. It includes the title of each part and the statutory authority under which each part was issued.

Appendix 6-2 shows that one bureau within the FDA is the Bureau of Veterinary Medicine. The basic responsibility of this bureau is as follows:

1. It assures that all drugs and devices intended for the treatment of animals are safe and effective. Proper labeling must accompany such articles; it must be informative as to the recommendations for use and also bear precautions against misuse. If the drug is intended for use in food-producing animals, the labeling must bear instructions regarding its use that will preclude its becoming a residue in edible products (milk, meat, or eggs) derived from treated animals.
2. It ensures that ingredients, drugs, and additives used in animal feeds are safe for the animals and with reference to potential residues. All animal foods must not be misbranded.

This bureau works closely with the USDA.

Some drugs and feed additives intended for inclusion in food of animals may serve to improve weight gain and feed efficiency, as sources of nutrients, for nutrient deficiencies, and for prevention of certain metabolic diseases.

Any application for the use of investigational new animal drugs must contain adequate residue data to show that the edible products are safe since the applicant may be permitted to slaughter for food those that have been used for investigational and unapproved new drugs in clinical or field trials.

There are approximately 13,000 feed mills of all sizes in the United States that manufacture about 45 million tons of medicated feed annually. Apart from approving drugs, additives, and ingredients used in the feeds, the FDA also performs routine inspection of the mills. The law requires that there be one inspection every 2 years. Since the FDA does not have sufficient resources to accomplish this, it has contracted with a number of state authorities which enforce compliance by frequent inspection.

Other work of the bureau includes the following:

1. It monitors animal feeds for possible contamination with mycotoxins, bacteria, and heavy metals.
2. It reviews labeling claims for pet foods.
3. It cooperates with the EPA in assuring that pesticides and related products for animal and livestock pests and insect control are registered, safe, and effective, and that their labeling statements are accurate.

The FDA has issued a number of regulations to control the unavoidable contaminants, effectiveness, use of additives, proper composition, labeling, manufacturing, and sanitation for animal feeds. They include 21 CFR 501, 503, 507, 508, 509, 564, 570, 571, 573, and 582. The titles of these regulations in Appendix 6-11 show that the information included are quite similar to those for human food. They are not discussed here. As an example, Table 6-15 presents some food additives permitted in feed and drinking water of animals (21 CFR 573).

The FDA also issued a number of regulations concerning animal drugs and medicated feeds; they are included in 21 CFR 500, 505, 510, 511, 514, 520, 522, 524, 529, 536, 539, 540, 544, 546, 548, 555, 556, and 558. Refer to Appendix 6-11 for further details. In the following, 21 CFR 556 and 558 are briefly discussed.

The tolerances for residues of new animal drugs in human food are described in 21 CFR 556. The tolerances prescribed are based on residues of the drugs in edible products of food-producing animals treated with such drugs. When an appropriate tolerance is considered for a drug, the conclusion can be any of the following:

1. A finite tolerance is required if finite residues will be present in the edible products.
2. A tolerance for negligible residue is required if it is not possible to determine whether finite residues will be incurred but there is reasonable expectation that they may be present.
3. The drug can induce cancer in man or animal; however, it does not adversely affect the animals for which it is intended, and no residue of the drug is found in any edible portion of such animals after slaughter. The analysis of the residue must be done by prescribing methods that are either published or referenced.
4. No tolerance is required if it may or may not be possible to determine whether finite residues will be incurred but there is no reasonable expectation that they

TABLE 6-15. Food Additives Permitted in Feed and Drinking Water of Animals. Adapted from 21 CFR 573.

Acrylamide-acrylic acid resin
Ammoniated cottonseed meal
Ammoniated rice hulls
Anhydrous ammonia
Condensed animal protein
  hydrolysate
Feed-grade biuret
Calcium periodate
Calcium silicate
Feed-grade calcium stearate
Choline xanthate
Diammonium phosphate
Diatomaceous earth
Disodium EDTA
Ethoxyquin in animal feeds
Ethoxyquin in certain dehydrated
  forage crops
Ethyl cellulose
Ethylene dichloride

Formaldehyde
Formic acid
Condensed, extracted glutamic acid
  fermentation product
Hemicellulose extract
Hydrolyzed leather meal
Iron ammonium citrate
Iron-choline citrate complex
Lignin sulfonated
Menadione dimethyl-pyrimidinol
  bisulfite
Methyl esters of higher fatty
  acids
Methyl glucoside-coconut oil
  ester
Mineral oil
Sodium nitrite
Petrolatum

Odorless light petroleum hydrocarbons
Poloxalene
Polyethylene
Polyethylene glycol (400) mono and
  dioleate
Polyoxyethylene glycol (400) mono
  and dioleates
Polysorbate 60
Polysorbate 80
Normal propyl alcohol
Pyrophyllite
Selenium
Silicon dioxide
Sorbitan monostearate
Taurine
Verxite
Yellow prussiate of soda

may be present.
5. No tolerance is required if the drug is metabolized in such a manner that any residue is indistinguishable from normal tissue constituents.
6. A finite tolerance is required if finite residues are present in the edible products. No tolerance established under such condition will be set at any level higher than that reflected by the permitted use of the drug.

The method of analysis for residue must be practicable, sensitive, and reliable. In the following, some examples of those drugs for which tolerances for residues have been established in edible animal products are provided. The original document should be consulted for further details.

Arsenic. In uncooked chicken muscle: 0.5 ppm. In uncooked swine liver and kidney: 2 ppm.

Dihydrostreptomycin. Zero tolerance in uncooked edible tissues of calves, in milk from dairy animals, and in any food in which such milk has been used.

Ethopabate. In uncooked liver and kidney of chicken: 1.5 ppm.

Testosterone propionate. No residues may be found in the uncooked edible tissues of heifers.

Tetracycline. For negligible residues in uncooked edible tissues of calves, swine, sheep, chickens, and turkeys: 0.25 ppm.

Virginiamycin. For negligible residues in the edible tissues of swine: 0.1 ppm.

Zeranol. No residues in the uncooked edible tissues of cattle and sheep.
The new animal drugs for use in animal feeds are described in 21 CFR 558. Two examples are given here. Only partial information for the example is provided. For further details and examples, consult the original document.

Carbadox. Premix level containing 2.2% (10 g/pound). Finished feed 75% to 125% of labeled amount. Do not use in feeds containing bentonite. In swine, 10 to 25 g/ton of feed, for increase in rate of weight gain and improvement of feed efficiency. Do not feed to swine weighing more than 75 pounds, within 10 weeks of slaughter, and do not use in complete feeds containing less than 15% crude protein.

Coumaphos. Premix levels 1.12%, 2%, 11.2%, and 50%. Finished feed must contain 80% to 120% of the labeled amount. Adequate directions and warnings for use must be given and shall include a statement that it is a cholinesterase inhibitor and that animals being treated with coumaphos should not be exposed during or within a few days before or after treatment to any other cholinesterase inhibiting drugs, insecticides, pesticides, or chemicals. For beef and dairy cattle, 0.00012 pound/100 pounds body weight/day. As an aid in the reduction of fecal breeding flies through control of fly larvae. Feed for the duration of fly seasons in a complete feed containing 0.0033% or in a feed supplement containing under 0.0066%. Do not feed to animals less than 3 months old and do not use in pelleted feeds.

Those pesticides for which tolerances have been established in animal feeds by the EPA are described in 21 CFR 561. Some examples of such pesticides are given in Table 6-16.

Animal drugs can be misused, for example, by not following labeling and use instruction. This abuse has created three kinds of problems.

1. Health Hazards to Animals. Improper, and sometimes even proper, use may produce allergy or hypersensitivity, influence intestinal microflora adversely, and be toxic to the organ systems. Any one of these effects may interfere with the veterinarian's diagnosis and treatment.

2. Health Hazards to Humans. There are two major concerns here. First, residues in the meat, milk, dairy products, poultry, and eggs always carry a potential threat. If the drug residue happens to be antibiotic, consumption of such products may produce sensitization and possibly cause adverse reactions. The uncontrolled and/or abusive use of antibiotics in animals may be responsible for bacterial drug resistance that can be transferred to bacteria in humans. Thus certain strains of bacteria may become resistant to a specific antibiotic. If a human or an animal becomes infected with these bacteria, the use of the same or related antibiotic may be ineffective.

3. Economic Loss. The condemnation and destruction of animal products such as meat, eggs, and poultry contaminated with excessive residues is definitely a loss to the producer. If it occurs in large scale, the consumer may have to bear part of the loss through price increase.

As can be observed from the preceding discussion, residues of drugs, pesticides, and industrial chemicals may occur in animal products. The USDA, FDA, and EPA share the information gathered through the residue monitoring and surveillance program with appropriate state agencies. The EPA establishes pesticide tolerances and FDA drug and additive tolerances in food and feed. The USDA assures the absence of illegal residues in meat, poultry, and eggs. The FDA monitors milk, other dairy products, and all other foods derived from living animals

TABLE 6-16. Pesticides for which Tolerances Have Been Established for Animal Feeds by the Environmental Protection Agency. Adapted from 21 CFR 561.

Acephate	Dioxathion
Aldicarb	Diuron
Aluminum phosphide	Ethion
Benomyl	Fluometuron
sec-Butylamine	Formetanate hydrochloride
Carbophenothion	Inorganic bromides
Chlordimeform	Malathion
(2-Chloroethyl-)trimethyl-ammonium chloride	Methanearsonic acid
2,4-D	Phorate
Dalapon	Phosalone
DDT	Piperonyl butoxide
Demeton	Procyazine
Dialifor	Propargite
3'4'-Dichloropropionanilide	Pyrethrins
0,0-Diethyl S-2-(ethylthio) ethyl phosphorodithioate	Simazine
Dimethoate including its oxygen analog	Succinic acid, 2,2-dimethyl-hydrazide
0,0-Dimethyl S-[4-oxo-1,2,3-ben-zotriazin-3(4H)-ylmethyl] phosphorodithioate	Synthetic isoparaffinic petroleum hydrocarbons
0,0-Dimethyl 2,2,2-trichloro-1-hydroxyethyl phosphonate	TDE(DDD)
2,4-Dinitro-6-octylphenyl crotonate and 2,6-dinitro-4-octylphenyl crotonate	Thiabendazole
	S,S,S -Tributyl phosphoro-trithioate
	Tricyclohexyltin hydroxide
	Zinc ion and maneb coordination product

except meat, poultry, and eggs to ensure the absence of illegal residues.

Some additional information on the FDA and animal drug safety are described as follows:

1. Drug firms are required to report unexpected adverse reactions to their new animals drug products within 15 days of receipt, and veterinarians are encouraged to volunteer this information. The original approval of these drugs was based on studies performed with a relatively small sample of the "target" population. This mandatory reporting informs the FDA about the drug perfor-

mances in actual field conditions within the total target population.

2. For mass education of the use of drugs in animals, the FDA issues a Drug Use Guide for sheep and dairy goats; swine; beef cattle and calves; dairy cattle and calves; and chickens, turkeys, and other poultry. Each guide emphasizes reading labels and instruction. Specifically it provides information on the active ingredients in each drug, the withdrawal days, milk discard times, and brand name examples.

In the following, the FDA offers some tips to animal drug users on how to avoid leaving drug residues:

1. Follow directions and use drugs as directed.
2. Do NOT overdose; an overdose is more expensive and may be toxic.
3. Use intravenous injection site when permitted on the labeling when administering irritating drugs.
4. Do NOT inject into the peritoneal cavity.
5. Do NOT combine products in the same syringe.
6. Do NOT combine products at the same injection site unless in an approved combination.
7. Do NOT use the same site for repeated treatment.
8. If given intramuscularly, do not give too large an amount in one injection.
9. Observe withdrawal period.
10. Properly identify treated animals.
11. Do NOT allow delivery of animals for slaughter if NOT sufficiently withdrawn from medicated feeds or therapeutic drugs.

At present, because of some of the problems discussed earlier, the FDA is conducting an intensive review of using antibiotics in animal feeds. As a result, the legal status of such usage is not certain at time of current writing. For a review of this subject, consult the following references:

1. Report to the Commissioner of the Food and Drug Administration by the FDA Task Force on the Use of Antibiotics in Animal Feeds (FDA) 72-6008. January 1972.
2. Relationships of antibiotics in animal feeds and salmonellosis in animals and man. Presented as part of a Symposium, The Use of Antimicrobials and Hormones for Livestock Production, at the 66th Annual Meeting of the American Society of Animal Science at the University of Maryland, College Park, July 1974.
3. G. B. Guest. Status of FDA's program on the use of antibiotics in animal feeds. Invitational paper presented as part of the symposium on Feed Use of Anti-

biotics held during the 67th Annual Meeting of the American Society of Animal Science at Fort Collins, Colorado, July 1975.

4. G. B. Guest. Antibiotics in animal feeds: current status. Report delivered at the Twentieth Annual Educational Conference of the Food Drug Law Institute and the FDA, held at Washington, D.C., December 7 to 8, 1976.
5. T. Larkin. Using drugs in food animals. FDA Consumers, April 1977.
6. C. D. Van Houweling. Draft environmental impact statement subtherapeutic antibacterial agents in animal feeds. FDA, July 1978.
7. A. Hecht. Medicated feed: the view from the farm. FDA Consumers, September 1978.
8. New animal drugs for use in animal feeds, 21 CFR 558, latest edition and/or changes.

Further information on the work of the Bureau of Veterinary Medicine may be obtained from "The responsibility of FDA to the livestock industry and the consumer," presented as a symposium at the 64th Annual Meeting of the American Society of Animals Science, Blacksburg, Virginia, August 1972.

ENFORCEMENT

Introduction

As mentioned previously (see Appendix 6-8), the executive director of Regional Operations supervises the regional directors, each of whom is in charge of a district office of the FDA. Each regional director supervises, among numerous other duties, one group of men and women sometimes considered the "front line" of the FDA. They are the consumer safety officers, formerly known as "inspectors." They perform a variety of duties. One any given day, an officer may be at a dockside checking on an import, conducting an inspection of a food processing plant, testifying in court about a violation of the law, investigating a consumer complaint of manufacturing violations or of illnesses and injuries from a product, or in a supermarket buying a product for testing. When a violation is detected, the compliance officer within the district office is informed. Depending on the violation and the circumstances, the FDA regional director and headquarters may use a number of "semilegal" and legal tools to handle the situations.

Tools

The enforcement tools employed by the FDA include publicity, information and regulatory letters, recalls, seizure, injunction, and prosecution. Section 705 of the Federal Food, Drug, and Cosmetic Act (21 U.S.C. 375) provides the FDA with the necessary statutory authority to make *publicity* about its administrative and legal actions. It is one of the few government agencies given such power.

Accordingly, the FDA publishes in the FDA Consumer the following: reports summarizing seizures and postal service cases; notices of judgment on seizure actions and criminal action; and decrees and court orders. All of these have been rendered under the Federal Food, Drug, and Cosmetic Act; they include the nature of the charge and its disposition. The FDA is specifically authorized to disseminate information regarding food in situations involving imminent danger to health or gross deception of the consumer. Thus it issues the weekly FDA Enforcement Report, which describes that week's cases of prosecution, seizures, injunctions, and recalls. Periodic reports are distributed concerning factory inspection findings for selected industry segments. The FDA also publishes in the Federal Register information regarding regular administrative actions such as the approval, denial, or withdrawal of approval of food and color additives and veterinary drugs, and some of these may actually be direct enforcement actions.

Other means of publicity used by the FDA include formal news or press conferences, briefings or releases, articles in private journals and the FDA Consumer, interviews, consumer educational forums, speeches, and, as claimed by some, "leaks." At present, the FDA is trying to issue official regulation that will delineate the conditions and requirements governing FDA use of publicity. For example, why does the FDA wish to make publicity, what special precautions apply to any publicity, and how will the FDA handle publicity about court proceedings? On March 4, 1977, the FDA announced (42 FR 12436 to 12441) its intention to add new administrative practices and procedures governing publicity policy to 21 CFR 2. The proposal is a very complicated one and will not be detailed here. However, two aspects of the background materials are briefly described in the following paragraphs.

The FDA seeks publicity for several purposes, among which are to:

1. warn against the use of marketed products that may be hazardous.
2. warn against gross economic deception.
3. encourage public comment on proposed regulations or actions and other public participation in FDA activities.
4. report to the public on adjudicated court proceedings.
5. present to the public FDA's views on matters of public interest.
6. report on studies or investigations that may form the basis for an FDA regulatory action.

Despite these positive objectives of publicity, there are occasions when publicity can have a negative or adverse effect. Some examples are described in the
following:

1. An excess of negative information could make the public indifferent or insensi-
   tive to important warnings about a potentially dangerous product.
2. Adverse publicity may prejudice a defendant's right to a fair trial in a criminal
   prosecution, or might improperly influence civil litigation.
3. Under certain circumstances, the issuance of publicity could create a greater
   hazard by causing a panic-type reaction.
4. Adverse publicity can cause economic harm to both individuals and firms.
   For example, one type of publicity often considered to be adverse by manufacturers of regulated products is that which accompanies a product recall.
   More information on product recall is discussed in another section.

Further details about publicity policy should be obtained from the original document.

Section 306 of the Federal Food, Drug, and Cosmetic Act (21 U.S.C. 336)
provides the FDA with another type of enforcement tool. According to this provision, the FDA is not required to report for prosecution, or for the institution of
libel or injunction proceedings, minor violations of the act if it believes that the
public interest will be adequately served by a suitable written notice or warning.
This authority is used in three ways: (1) establishment of action levels for unavoidable chemical contaminants and defects in food product (discussed previously),
(2) information letter, and (3) regulatory letter.

The *information letter* is used in the following manner. If a food product's
labeling deviates slightly from the prescribed requirements, the FDA may consider
this a minor violation. It will send an information letter to the firm, mentioning or
affirming no specific citation of violation of the Federal Food, Drug, and Cosmetic
Act. It raises questions about the legality of how the product has been marketed
and usually allows about 30 days for response. The firm is expected to provide an
explanation for its conduct and to indicate whether actions will be taken to prevent occurrence. This shows that the firm is given certain flexibility in its response.
There is a willingness on the part of the FDA to assist the firm with explanation
and problems in net weight, labeling, packaging, and other similar requirements in
product marketing.

A *regulatory letter* is stronger than an information letter. The FDA uses it to
inform the management of a firm that they have violated certain provision(s) of
the Federal Food, Drug, and Cosmetic Act and if corrective actions are taken, there
will be no legal action.The intention of the FDA is as follows: (1) the company will
comply, and the FDA wants to be flexible; (2) the violation poses no health risk to

the consumer; and (3) if a violation is not remedied, there is adequate legal cause for court action.

A regulatory letter has a specific format. It identifies itself as a regulatory letter and cites the specific statutory provision(s) of the act that has been violated and the specific manner of violation. The letter indicates that corrective actions must be taken for compliance. The firm management is required to provide a response within a specified period, usually 10 days. The letter is ended with a warning stating that if the company ignores the content of the letter, the FDA will resort to court action to effect compliance.

The FDA uses the regulatory letter because it feels that the violations committed have not been intentional and flagrant. The company has not shown a pattern of noncompliance. The regulatory letter is expected to save the amount of time and money spent by the government, which may be used for other necessary court actions. This kind of warning will also give the company an opportunity to correct the violations with no immediate and significant economic loss. All regulatory and information letters are on public record. An interested party may examine the public file for such communications. On June 23, 1978, the FDA proposed regulations (43 FR 27497 to 27502) describing the practices and procedures for two forms of compliance correspondence for judicially and administratively enforced sanctions, namely, a "notice of adverse findings" or a "regulatory letter."

Recall, seizure, injunction, and prosecution are regular enforcement tools of the FDA. With the exception of recall, the other enforcement mechanisms are specifically authorized by the U.S. Congress as described in Sections 301 to 307 of the Federal Food, Drug, and Cosmetic Act (21 U.S.C. 331 to 337). Penalties, including fines and imprisonments for these violations are also stated in the act. These legal proceedings require court actions and as such must follow civil and criminal procedures as prescribed in the U.S. judicial system. Details on these procedures may be obtained from some basic legal reference sources. For background information, some simple definitions are provided in the following paragraphs.

Seizure is an action taken to remove a product from commerce because it is in violation of the law. The FDA initiates a seizure by filing a complaint with the U.S. district court where the goods are located. A U.S. marshal is then directed by the court to take possession of the products until the matter is resolved. The date when a seizure is requested must be distinguished from the actual date of seizure since a court order is needed. *Injunction* is a civil action filed by the FDA against an individual or firm seeking, in most cases, to stop a company from continuing to manufacture or distribute products that are in violation of the law. Again, filing an injunction does not necessarily mean that it is automatically concluded and carried out since the court must approve the action. *Prosecution* is a criminal action filed by the FDA against a company and/or individual charging violation of the law. As is well known by the general public, filing a prosecution is only the beginning since court trial and conclusion including appeals must be taken into consideration before the entire matter ends.

The use of *recalls* as an enforcement tool has been practiced by the FDA for a long time. On June 16, 1978, the FDA established final regulations (43 FR 26201 to 26221, also see 41 FR 26924 to 26930, June 30, 1976) intended as guidelines that set forth the agency's policy and procedures for product recalls and that provide guidance to manufacturers and distributors of products regulated by the agency so that they may more effectively discharge their recall responsibilities. The recall guidelines apply to all FDA-regulated products such as food (including animal feed) except electronic products subject to the Radiation Control for Health and Safety Act. Some selected aspects of these guidelines are discussed briefly in the following paragraphs.

"Recall" means a firm's removal or correction of a marketed product that the FDA considers to be in violation of the laws it administers and against which the agency would initiate legal action, e.g., seizure. Recall does not include a market withdrawal or a stock recovery. "Market withdrawal" means a firm's removal or correction of a distributed product which involves a minor violation that would not be subject to legal action by the FDA or which involves no violation, e.g., normal stock rotation practices, routine equipment adjustments and repairs, etc. "Stock recovery" means a firm's removal or correction of a product that has not been marketed or that has not left the direct control of the firm, i.e., the product is located on premises owned by, or under the control of, the firm and no portion of the lot has been released for sale or use.

At present, the FDA has defined three classes of recalls. A Class I recall is a situation in which there is a reasonable probability that the use of, or exposure to, a violative product will cause serious adverse health consequences or both. A Class II recall is a situation in which use of, or exposure to, a violative product may cause temporary or medically reversible adverse health consequences or where the probability of serious adverse health consequences is remote. A Class III recall is a situation in which use of, or exposure to, a violative product is not likely to cause adverse health consequences.

The FDA delineates three important aspects of its recall policy:

1. Recall is an effective method of removing or correcting consumer products that are in violation of laws administered by the FDA. It is any voluntary action that takes place because manufacturers and distributors carry out their responsibility to protect the public health and well-being from products that present a risk of injury or gross deception or are otherwise defective.
2. Recall may be undertaken voluntarily and at any time by manufacturers and distributors, or at the request of the FDA. A request by the FDA is reserved for urgent situations and is to be directed to the firm that has primary respon-

sibiłity for the manufacture and marketing of the product that is to be recalled.

3. Recall is generally more appropriate and affords better protection for con-
    sumers than seizure, when many lots of product have been widely distributed.
    Seizure, multiple seizure, or other court action is indicated when a firm re-
    fuses to undertake a recall requested by the FDA, or where the agency has
    reason to believe that a recall would not be effective, determines that a recall
    is ineffective, or discovers that a violation is continuing.

The FDA will promptly make available to the public in the weekly FDA Enforcement Report a descriptive listing of each new recall according to its classification, whether it was FDA-requested or firm-initiated, and the specific action
being taken by the recalling firm. The report will not include a firm's product
removals or corrections which the FDA determines to be market withdrawals or
stock recoveries. Further details on recall regulations may be obtained from the
original documents..

Many of the FDA's enforcement actions depend on the criterion of "imminent hazard to the public health." To clarify this standard of evaluation, the FDA
provides the following explanation in 21 CFR 2.5:

1. An imminent hazard to the public health exists when there is sufficient evi-
    dence to show that a product or practice, posing a significant threat of danger
    to health, creates a public health situation that should be corrected immediate-
    ly to prevent injury and should not be permitted to continue while a hearing
    or other formal proceeding is being conducted.
2. The "imminent hazard" may be declared at any point in the chain of events
    that may eventually result in harm to the public health.
3. The occurrence of the final anticipated injury is not essential to establish that
    an "imminent hazard" of such occurrence exists.
4. On deciding the existence of an "imminent hazard," the FDA will consider the
    number of injuries anticipated and the nature, severity, and duration of such
    injury.

To illustrate the trend of enforcement actions by the FDA in regard to food,
Table 6-18 shows the number of seizures, prosecutions, and injunctions in the
period 1965 to 1977.

Criminal Prosecution

Usually, any court action to which the FDA resorts is taken after careful and de-

TABLE 6-17. Seizures, Prosecutions and Injunctions under the
Federal Food, Drug and Cosmetic Act[a]

Fiscal year[b]	Seizures	Prosecutions	Injunctions
1965	522	67	11
1966	566	59	4
1967	657	77	10
1968	384	70	3
1969	232	45	5
1970	267	33	23
1971	510	47	11
1972	547	65	10
1973	515	96	8
1974	272	92	7
1975	348	43	15
1976	168	30	12
1977	271	25	22

[a] All legal actions are related to foods only. The information has
been derived from FDA Annual Reports 1965-1974, 1976 and
1977.

[b] Fiscal year 1976 ended on June 30, 1976. Because of reorgani-
zational changes, fiscal year 1977 covered the period October
1, 1976, through September 30, 1977. Activities for the tran-
sitional period July 1, 1976, through September 30, 1976 are:
seizures, 57; prosecutions, 7; and injunctions, 1.

tailed consideration. This applies especially to criminal prosecution. The following reference sources provide some information on the FDA's enforcement pos-
ture and activities, especially in regard to prosecutional sanction:

1. Enforcement policy, 21 CFR 7. Also see 42 FR 6801 (February 4, 1977).
2. R. E. Keating. "Compliance officers: Enforcing the FD&C Act," FDA Con-

sumer, October 1974.

3. J. E. Hoffman. "Enforcement trends under the Federal Food, Drug and Cosmetic Act--A view from outside." Food Drug Cosmetic Law Journal, June 1976.

4. S. D. Fine. "Enforcement philosophy." Speech delivered at the Food and Drug Law Institute Enforcement Week Session, Washington, D.C., March 17, 1976.

5. C. R. McConachie. "The role of the Department of Justice in enforcing the Food, Drug and Cosmetic Act." Speech delivered at the Food and Drug Law Institute Enforcement Week Session, Washington, D.C., March 17, 1976.

Criminal prosecution is a serious action, and the FDA has set up a very careful and exhaustive review system for the purpose of arriving at a final decision to prosecute. Assume that an FDA inspector or consumer safety officer has identified a violation; the simple chart shown in Figure 6-1 illustrates the chain of events or reviews that will take place. Of course, a violation can be brought to the FDA's attention in another manner.

The chart on page 485 shows that, before the district office sends in the recommendation to prosecute to the headquarters, it issues a Notice of Hearing to the affected firm and/or individual(s). This notice provides them with a final opportunity to defend themselves before formal court action. Although not required to appear before the hearing, the affected parties are advised by the FDA not to ignore the notice and its charges. Whether the case will be dismissed after the hearing will depend on the argument presented and any contemplated or progressing corrective actions.

There is only one type of criminal prosecution recommendation that the district office can send to the Regulatory Management Staff directly, bypassing the Bureau of Foods. This is the sanitation violation in a food warehouse, and it has to satisfy a number of stringent requirements before it is qualified for such direct action.

The Summary and Recommendation File contains a lot of information. Some most pertinent ones are as follows:

1. Type and importance of the violation(s).
2. Inspectional and analytical evidence.
3. Name of company and officers charged with the violations.
4. A comprehensive statement that details the reasons why a prosecution recommendation is necessary or appropriate.
5. Hearing record, if any.
6. Numerous other data.

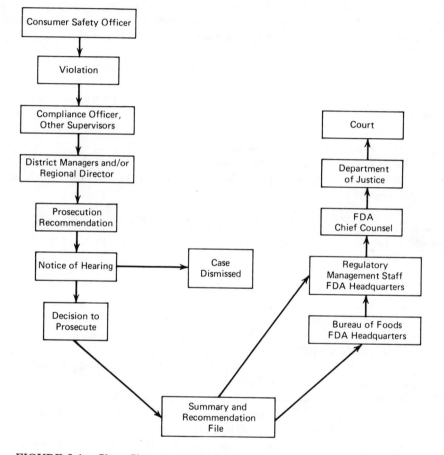

FIGURE 6-1. Chart Showing the Major Review Processes Normally Preceding a Criminal Prosecution by the FDA

The basic guideliness that the agency uses to recommend prosecution are as follows:

1. How serious is the violation?
2. Is the violation intentional?
3. Does the management have knowledge of the violative conditions?
4. Will this particular prosecution coerce the management into better compliance in the future? Will the management remedy other similar existing situations?
5. Does the FDA have sufficient resources to conduct a thorough investigation for a successful prosecution?
6. To what extent will this prosecution benefit the consumers in this particular industry? For example, will other industries align for more compliance when they are aware of this prosecution? This will benefit the consumers if other members of the trade shun similar violations.
7. What is the collective judgment of all parties involved within the FDA, such as compliance officers, regional and headquarters managers, technical staffs, and attorneys?

When a case is reviewed for prosecution, and, in order that it will, one or more of the following violative characteristics must be evident before it can receive approval from each link of the review chain or mechanism:

1. The firm has demonstrated continuous violation. It is aware of a violation, has been warned a number of times, but has failed to take corrective action. This is applicable to the situation when recalls and other civil court proceedings have been sanctioned against the firm; examples of civil actions are multiple seizures and injunctions.
2. The violations are gross or flagrant, such as excessive molds and animal excrements around or in food products.
3. The violations are obvious, for example, fire-damaged food packages, appearance of metals and other foreign objects in the food products, and foul smelling working areas in a food manufacturing plant.
4. The violations threaten life or cause injuries, for example, botulism from canned foods and excessive use of a harmful amount of coloring on candies.
5. Violations are deliberate or intentional and resort to fraud, for example, submitting false records, shortweighing, and using decomposed products in packages.

Thus when the file of a recommended prosecution is being reviewed by the different offices within the FDA, every responsible officer will have a chance to ensure that all prosecution requirements have been satisfied and the criteria have been applied uniformly throughout the country. The review must be fair and impartial and all FDA policy guidelines have been adhered to. The chief counsel of the FDA and the Department of Justice request precise and accurate information, as they want to make sure that there is sufficient legal ground to file a prosecution with the court.

There are two other aspects that should be explained. The FDA will not prosecute a firm or an individual for technical violations since they can be corrected by less stringent means. Another most important consideration of the agency is its position of not prosecuting a corporation only. Some specific individuals will be charged since a firm cannot commit a crime by itself. These persons must be in a responsible position, aware of the violations, and have the authority to make changes but have failed to do so. This particular philosophy of corporate responsibility is one of the most controversial topics in the food industries and regulatory agencies circle at the present time of writing.

Corporate Responsibility

The FDA holds high ranking corporate officers *personally* responsible for any violative conditions in their warehouses, food manufacturing plants, and/or products. The FDA's legal authority to do so has been challenged twice in the U.S. Supreme Court. The government won both times. Information on these two controversial and "classical" court actions may be obtained from the following lawsuit and literature references:

1. *U.S.* v. *Dotterweich* 320 U.S. 277 (1943).
2. *U.S.* v. *Park* 421 U.S. 658 (1975).
3. D. F. O'Keefe, Jr. and M. H. Shapiro. "Personal criminal liability under the Federal Food, Drug, and Cosmetic Act The Dotterweich Doctrine." Food Drug Cosmetic Law Journal, January 1975.
4. J. W. Sloat. "Executive's personal risk is high if FDA cites unsanitary storage or holding." Food Product Development, September 1975.
5. R. A. Merrill. "The Park Case." Food Drug Cosmetic Law Journal, December 1975.
6. W. F. Janssen. "Personal responsibility and the Food and Drug Law." FDA Consumer, November 1975.

The following brief discussion has been adapted from the FDA Consumer (November 1975). On June 30, 1941 J. H. Dotterweich appeared in the Rochester, New York Federal District Court. He was charged with interstate shipment of adulterated and misbranded cascara compound tablets, and subpotency digitalis tablets and posterior pituitary solution. The company lawyer informed the FDA that the firm would plead guilty if the charges against Dotterweich were dropped. The offer was not accepted.

It was and still is the policy of the FDA to charge the corporation as well as an individual defendant. At least one individual is responsible for the activities of a firm. In this case Dotterweich was responsible for the actions of Buffalo Pharmacal. For example, a former employee testified that nothing could be done at the firm without Dotterweich's knowledge, consent, and instructions. No FDA inspector was permitted to inspect the plant unless he was accompanied by Dotterweich personally. The defense attorney explained to the jury that if the firm was found guilty, its 26 employees would be laid off. Job scarcity during a depression must be taken into consideration. The judge's instruction to the jury was: "Are you satisfied from the evidence that shipment(s) were made under his supervision by him as 'General Manager'? It is not necessary for the Government to prove that he personally and physically made the shipment himself. It is sufficient if the evidence establishes to your satisfaction that it was made under authority conferred by him as general manager upon his subordinates."

The jury acquitted the corporation and found Dotterweich guilty. The defense attorney argued that Dotterweich's verdict was inconsistent with the jury's failure to convict the corporation. The verdict against his client should be disregarded. The judge ruled otherwise and fined him $500 on each of the three charges, and payment was suspended on two charges. In addition, a 60 day probation on each count (to run concurrently) was imposed.

On appeal the conviction was reversed on the technical grounds that he was not a "person" within the meaning of the Federal Food, Drug, and Cosmetic Act. There was no personal relationship between Dotterweich and the violative shipments although he had instructed the employees to process the orders. The court of appeals stated that "for some unexplainable reason, it (the jury) disagreed as to the corporation's guilt." It could not distinguish between agents of high or low rank in a company; the law must be applicable to all, including manager, shipping clerk, or any other employee involved in causing the violative shipments. Therefore, Dotterweich was found not guilty of the violations.

After being denied a rehearing before the court of appeals, the FDA approached the U.S. Supreme Court, which on November 22, 1943 reversed the Court Appeals in a 5-4 decision. Associate Justice Felix Frankfurter delivered the majority opinion.

The U.S. Supreme Court believed that Dotterweich was a "person" within the meaning of the Federal Food, Drug, and Cosmetic Act and that the corporation was not the only "person" subject to prosecution. Buffalo Pharmacal was primarily a repacker of drugs that it obtained from other sources and sold by mail to physicians under its own label. The original manufacturers of these drugs guaranteed that they were in compliance with the act. If valid, such guaranties, authorized by section 303(e) of the act [21 U.S.C. 333(e)], would grant immunity from prosecution to distributors, such as wholesale or retail grocers or druggists. The court of appeals held that Dotterweich and Buffalo Pharmacal were protected by these guaranties. The U.S. Supreme Court considered this as a restrictive and weakening interpretation, stating that federal food and drug laws were written and passed to "touch phases of the lives and health of people which, in the circumstances of modern industrialism, are largely beyond self-protection," and that "regard for these purposes should infuse construction of the legislation if it is to be treated as a working instrument of government and not merely a collection of English words." Penalties under the act "serve as an effective means of regulation" and "such legislation dispenses with the conventional requirement for criminal conduct--awareness of some wrongdoing. In the interest of the larger good, it puts the burden of acting at hazard upon a person otherwise innocent but standing in responsible relation to a public danger."

The Dotterweich decision forcefully confirmed that company officials could be held personally responsible for violations, even without any "awareness" of "wrongdoing." Many food and drug cases since have been settled on the basis of the Dotterweich doctrine. Top officials, ranging from president to department head to group leader of a company, have been criminally prosecuted. For 34 years this doctrine was not challenged, at least not to the highest court. On June 9, 1975 the U.S. Supreme Court ruled again on a similar subject.

The case of *United States* v. *Park* was very different from *United States* v. *Dotterweich*. It involved food products and a large corporation. J. R. Park was the president of Acme Markets, a large food chain distributor, with headquarters in Philadelphia. A prosecution filed by the FDA in the U.S. District Court of Maryland charged Acme and Park with five instances of violating the Federal Food, Drug, and Cosmetic Act by causing food to be held in a Baltimore warehouse where it was exposed to contamination by rodents. Under the act, food is adulterated if it is "held under insanitary conditions," and actual contamination of the food is not a prerequisite. Acme pleaded guilty to the charges; Park pleaded innocent.

The following information was made available at the trial. In April 1970 the FDA informed Park in a letter about the insanitary conditions in Acme's Philadelphia warehouse. In January 1972 Park received a second warning letter about similar conditions in Acme's Baltimore warehouse. When the latter was inspected again in March 1972, there was some improvement, although rodent infestation was still apparent.

According to the testimony, the president of the firm delegated "normal operating duties," including sanitation matters, but retained "certain things, which are the big, broad principles of the operation of the company," and had "the responsibility of seeing that they all work together." The defense attorney claimed that "the evidence...has shown that Mr. Park is not personally concerned in his violation" and that Park should be acquitted.

Park was the only defense witness. He testified that company responsibilities were "assigned to individuals who, in turn, have staff and departments under them." He identified the individuals responsible for sanitation and said that he discussed the FDA letter of January 1972 with the company's legal counsel. Park was informed that the division vice president at Baltimore "was investigating the situation immediately and would be taking corrective action and would be preparing a summary of the correction to reply to the letter." Park doubted that there was anything he could have done more constructively than what was being done. During his testimony, Park admitted the following:

1. In the entire operation of the company he was responsible for providing sanitary conditions for the manufacturing of food products for public consumption.
2. The sanitation problem was one of the many phases of the operation of the company that he assigned to "dependable subordinates."
3. He received the FDA 1970 letter concerning insanitary conditions at the Philadelphia warehouse, indicating that the same individuals were responsible for the warehouses at both Baltimore and Philadelphia.
4. With reference to the Baltimore warehouse, the system for handling sanitation "wasn't working perfectly," and he stated that he was responsible for "any result which occurs in our company."

The judge denied the motion for acquittal and issued instructions to the jury. The defense counsel objected and argued that they failed to define a "responsible relationship" between the defendant and the violation. This would not fairly reflect the Dotterweich doctrine, in which case the U.S. Supreme Court ruled that the burden of acting was placed on persons otherwise innocent but "standing in responsible relation to a public danger." The objection was overruled; and Park was found guilty. He was fined $250, $50 per count.

The court of appeals overturned the conviction because the FDA had failed to show any "wrongful...acts of commission or omission" on the defendant's part that "would 'cause' the contamination of food." It held that the Dotterweich decision had dispensed with the element of "an awareness of wrongdoing" but not that of "wrongful action." The FDA presented its case to the U.S. Supreme Court, which by a vote of 6:3 upheld the Dotterweich doctrine. Chief Justice Burger issued the following salient points:

1. In a corporation, a ranking officer with authority and responsibility to enforce

compliance with company and government regulations has a "responsible share" or "responsible relationship" in any incidents of violation.

2. Management officials have "not only a positive duty to seek out and remedy violations...but also, and primarily, a duty to...insure that violations will not occur."

3. "The requirements of foresight and vigilance imposed on responsible corporate agents are beyond question demanding, and perhaps onerous...but they are no more stringent than the public has a right to expect of those who voluntarily assume positions of authority in business enterprises whose services and products affect the health and well-being of the public that supports them."

4. Although company officials may delegate compliance responsibilities, they continue to have the responsibility to ascertain that the assignments have been completed satisfactorily.

5. "The Government establishes a prima facie case when it introduces evidence sufficient to warrant a finding...that the defendant had...responsibility and authority either to prevent in the first instance, or promptly to correct, the violation complained of, and that he failed to do so."

The U.S. Supreme Court emphasized its position by quoting the statement made by the prosecutor's summation to the jury: "Mr. Park was responsible for seeing that sanitation was taken care of, and he had a system set up that was supposed to do that. This system didn't work. It didn't work three times. At some point in time Mr. Park has to be held responsible for the fact that his system isn't working."

According to the chief counsel of the FDA, this Park case reaffirmed certain basic ground rules maintained by the FDA:

1. The FDA will almost always "include one or more individuals as defendants; corporations alone do not commit crimes."

2. The FDA "will not include individuals who lack authority to prevent or correct violations or who could not be expected to have been aware of violations in the reasonable exercise of their corporate duties."

3. "Even if investigation discloses the elements of liability," the FDA ordinarily does not "recommend prosecution unless the defendant, after learning of the violations, fails to correct them or to make changes to prevent their occurrence."

The FDA refers cases to the Department of Justice according to the following standards: (1) "continuing violations," (2) "violations of an obvious and flagrant nature," and (3) "intentionally false or fraudulent violations."

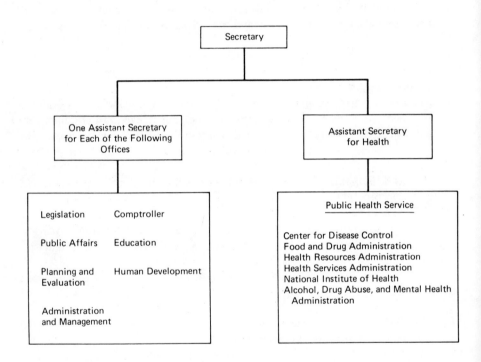

APPENDIX 6-1. Simplified organizational structure of the Department of Health, Education, and Welfare

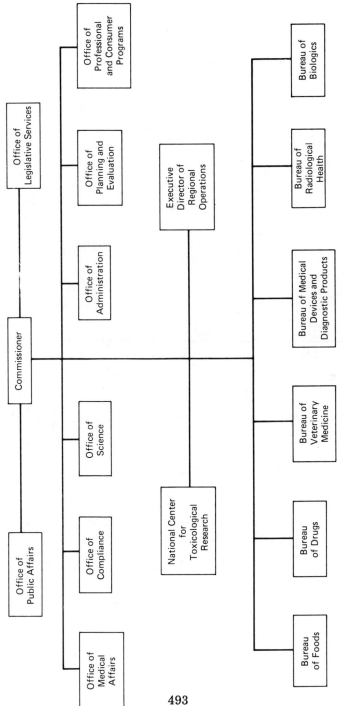

APPENDIX 6-2. Simplified organizational structure of the Food and Drug Administration.

493

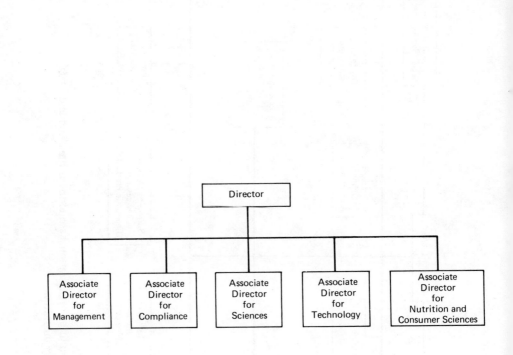

APPENDIX 6-3. Simplified organizational chart for the Bureau of Foods, Food and Drug Administration.

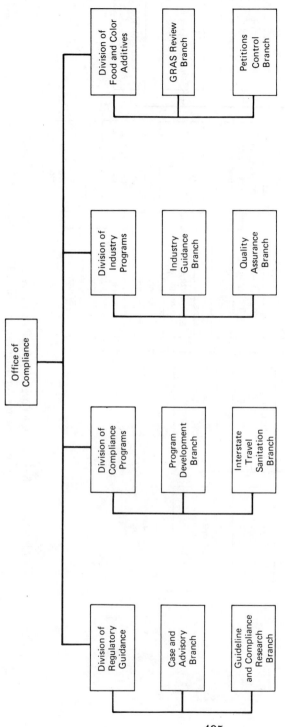

495

APPENDIX 6-4. Simplified organizational structure of the office of the Associate Director for Compliance, Bureau of Foods, Food and Drug Administration.

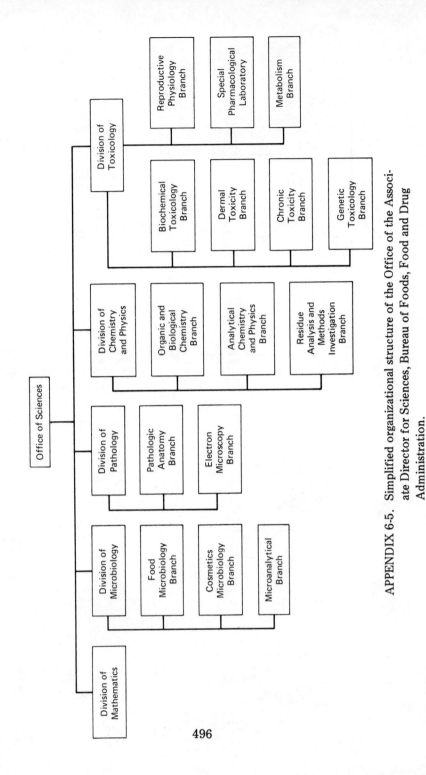

APPENDIX 6-5. Simplified organizational structure of the Office of the Associate Director for Sciences, Bureau of Foods, Food and Drug Administration.

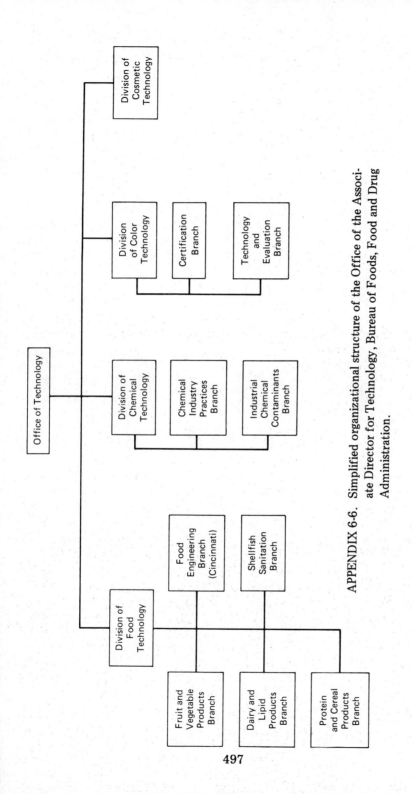

APPENDIX 6-6. Simplified organizational structure of the Office of the Associate Director for Technology, Bureau of Foods, Food and Drug Administration.

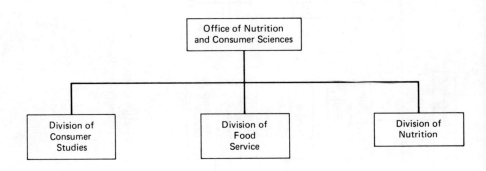

APPENDIX 6-7. Simplified organizational structure of the Office of the Associate Director for Nutrition and Consumer Sciences.

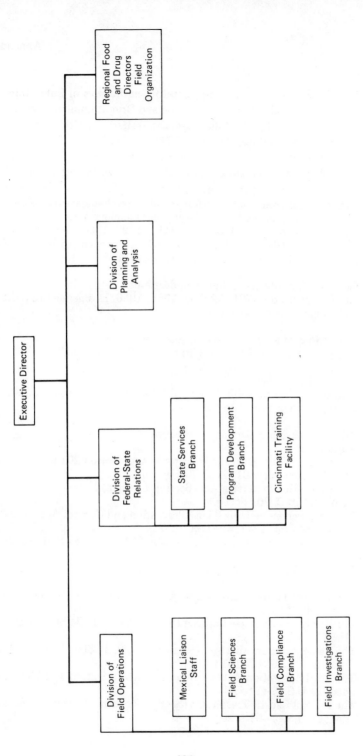

APPENDIX 6-8. Simplified organizational structure of the Executive Director of Regional Operations.

499

APPENDIX 6-9.   Part titles and issuing statutory authorities of Subchapter A
                (General) of Chapter 1 (Food and Drug Administration, Depart-
                ment of Health, Education, and Welfare) of Title 21 of the Code
                of Federal Regulations (1977)

Part	Part title and statutory authority under which part was issued
1	General regulations for the enforcement of the Federal Food, Drug, and Cosmetic Act and the Fair Packaging and Labeling Act. Authority: Sections 4, 6, 80, Stat. 1297, 1299, 1300; Sections 403, 602, 701, 52 Stat. 1047, 1050, 1054 to 1056, as amended; 15 U.S.C. 1453, 1455, 21 U.S.C. 343, 352, 362, 371, unless otherwise noted.
2	General administrative rulings and decisions. Authority: Section 701, 52 Stat. 1055, 1056, as amended (21 U.S.C. 371), unless otherwise noted.
5	Delegations of authority and organization. Authority: Section 701(a), 52 Stat. 1055 (21 U.S.C. 371).
7	Enforcement policy. Authority: Sections 305, 701(a), 52 Stat. 1045, 1055 [21 U.S.C. 335, 371(a)], unless otherwise noted.
10	Administrative practices and procedures. Authority: The Federal Food, Drug, and Cosmetic Act (Section 201 et seq., 52 Stat. 1040, as amended; 21 U.S.C. 321 et seq.). The Public Health Service Act (Section 1 et seq., 58 Stat. 682, as amended; 42 U.S.C. 201 et seq.). The Comprehensive Drug Abuse Prevention and Control Act of 1970 (Section 4, 84 Stat. 1241; 42 U.S.C. 257a). The Controlled Substances Act (Section 301 et seq., 84 Stat. 1253; 21 U.S.C. 821 et seq.). The Federal Meat Inspection Act [Section 409(b), 81 Stat. 600; 21 U.S.C. 679(b)]. The Poultry Products Inspection Act [Section 24(b), 82 Stat. 807; 21 U.S.C. 467f(b)]. The Egg Products Inspection Act (Section 2 et seq., 84 Stat. 1620; 21 U.S.C. 1031 et seq.). The Federal Import Milk Act (Sections 1 to 9, 44 Stat. 1101-1103, as amended; 21 U.S.C. 141 to 149). The Tea Importation Act (Sections 1 to 10, 29 Stat. 604 to 609, as amended; 21 U.S.C. 41 to 50). The Federal Caustic Poison Act (Section 2 et seq., 44 Stat. 1406, as amended; 15 U.S.C. 401 et seq.).

Part	Part title and statutory authority under which part was issued

The Fair Packaging and Labeling Act (Section 1 et seq., 80 Stat. 1296, as amended; 15 U.S.C. 1451 et seq.).

12   Formal evidentiary public hearing.
      Authority: Same as that for Part 10.

13   Public hearing before a public board of inquiry.
      Authority: Same as that for Part 10 and other statutory authority delegated to the Commissioner (21 CFR 5.1).

14   Public hearing before a public advisory committee.
      Authority: Same as that for Part 10.

15   Public hearing before the Commissioner.
      Authority: Same as that for Part 10 with the following modifications:
      The Federal Import Milk Act (44 Stat. 1101; 21 U.S.C. 141 et seq.).
      The Tea Importation Act (21 U.S.C. 41 et seq.).
      The Federal Caustic Poison Act (44 Stat. 1406; 15 U.S.C. 401 to 411 notes).
      The Fair Packaging and Labeling Act (80 Stat. 1296; 15 U.S.C. 1451 et seq.)
      All other statutory authority delegated to the Commissioner (21 CFR 5.1).

16   Regulatory hearing before the Food and Drug Administration.
      Authority: Same as that for Part 15.

19   Standards of conduct and conflicts of interest.
      Authority: Same as that for Part 15.

20   Public information.
      Authority: Section 201 et seq., PL 717, 52 Stat. 1040 et seq., as amended (21 U.S.C. 321 et seq.); Section 1 et seq., PL 410, 58 Stat. 682 et seq., as amended (42 U.S.C. 201 et seq.); PL 90-23, 81 Stat. 54 to 56, as amended by 88 Stat. 1561 to 1565 (5 U.S.C. 552).

21   Protection of privacy.
      Authority: Section 201 et seq., PL 717, 52 Stat. 1040 et seq., as amended (21 U.S.C. 321 et seq.); Section 1 et seq., PL 410, 58 Stat. 682 et seq., as amended (42 U.S.C. 201 et seq.); PL 90-23, 81 Stat. 54 to 56, as amended (5 U.S.C. 552); PL 93-579, 88 Stat. 1896 (5 U.S.C. 552a).

25   Environmental impact considerations.
      Authority: Section 701, 52 Stat. 1055, 1056, as amended by 70 Stat. 919 and 72 Stat. 948, 21 U.S.C. 371; Section 102(2)(C), 83 Stat. 853, 42 U.S.C. 4332; the Guidelines issued by the Council on Environmental

Part	Part title and statutory authority under which part was issued

Quality (36 FR 7724); Executive Order 11514 of March 4, 1970 (35 FR 4247).

70 Color additives.
Authority: Sections 701, 706, 52 Stat. 1055, 1056, as amended; 74 Stat. 399 to 407, as amended (21 U.S.C. 371, 376), unless otherwise noted.

71 Color additives petitions.
Authority: Sections 701, 706, 52 Stat. 1055, 1056, as amended; 74 Stat. 399 to 407, as amended (21 U.S.C. 371, 376), unless otherwise noted.

73 Listing of color additives exempt from certification.
Authority: Sections 701, 706, 52 Stat. 1055, 1056, as amended; 74 Stat. 399 to 407, as amended (21 U.S.C. 371, 376), unless otherwise noted.

74 Listing of color additives subject to certification.
Authority: Sections 701, 706, 52 Stat. 1055, 1056, as amended; 74 Stat. 399 to 407, as amended (21 U.S.C. 371, 376), unless otherwise noted.

80 Color additive certification.
Authority: Sections 701, 706, 52 Stat. 1055, 1056, as amended; 74 Stat. 399 to 407, as amended (21 U.S.C. 371, 376), unless otherwise noted.

81 General specifications and general restrictions for provisional color additives for use in foods, drugs, and cosmetics.
Authority: Title II of PL 86-618, Section 203(c), (d), 74 Stat. 405 (21 U.S.C. 376, note), unless otherwise noted.

82 Listing of certified provisionally listed colors and specifications.
Authority: Sections 406, 504, 604, 701, 702, 706, 52 Stat. 1049, as amended, 1055, 1056 as amended, 1058, as amended (21 U.S.C. 346, 354, 364, 371, 372, 376), unless otherwise noted.

APPENDIX 6-10. Part titles and issuing statutory authorities of Subchapter B
(Food for human consumption) of Chapter 1 (Food and Drug
Administration, Department of Health, Education, and Welfare)
of Title 21 of the Code of Federal Regulations (1977)

Part	Part title and statutory authority under which part was issued

100   General.
Authority: Section 701, 52 Stat. 1055, 1056, as amended (21 U.S.C.
371), unless otherwise noted.

101   Food labeling.
Authority: Sections 4, 6, PL 89-755, 80 Stat. 1297, 1299, 1300 (15
U.S.C. 1453, 1455); Sections 403, 602, 701, PL 717, 52 Stat. 1047, 1054,
1055, as amended (21 U.S.C. 343, 362, 371), unless otherwise noted.

102   Common or usual name for nonstandardized foods.
Authority: Sections 201(n), 403, 701(a), 52 Stat. 1041, as amended,
1047, 1048, as amended, 1055 [21 U.S.C. 321(n), 343, 371(a)].

103   Quality standards for foods with no identity standards.
Authority: Sections 401, 403, 701, 52 Stat. 1046 to 1048, as amended;
1055, 1056, as amended by 70 Stat. 919 and 72 Stat. 948 (21 U.S.C. 341,
343, 371), unless otherwise noted.

104   Nutritional quality guidelines for foods.
Authority: Sections 201, 403, 701(a), 52 Stat. 1040 to 1042, as amended;
1047, 1048, as amended, 1055 [21 U.S.C. 321, 343, 371(a)], unless
otherwise noted.

105   Foods for special dietary use.
Authority: Sections 403, 701, 52 Stat. 1047, 1048, as amended; 1055,
1056, as amended (21 U.S.C. 343, 371), unless otherwise noted.

108   Emergency permit control.
Authority: Sections 402, 404, 701, 52 Stat. 1046, 1047 as amended,
1048, 1055, 1056, as amended by 70 Stat. 919 and 72 Stat. 948 (21
U.S.C. 342, 344, 371).

109   Unavoidable contaminants in food and food-packaging material.
Authority: Sections 402(a), 406, 409, 701, 52 Stat. 1046, as amended;
1049, as amended, 1055, 1056 as amended by 70 Stat. 919 and 72 Stat.
948, 72 Stat. 1785 to 1788, as amended [21 U.S.C. 342(a), 346, 348,
371].

110   Current good manufacturing practice in manufacturing, processing, pack-

Part	Part title and statutory authority under which part was issued

ing, or holding human food.
Authority: Sections 402(a)(4), 701(a), 52 Stat. 1046, 1055 [21 U.S.C. 342(a)(4), 371(a)], unless otherwise noted.

113   Thermally processed low-acid foods packaged in hermetically sealed containers.
Authority: Sections 402(a)(4), 701(a), 52 Stat. 1046, 1055 [21 U.S.C. 342(a)(4), 371(a)].

118   Cacao products and confectionery.
Authority: Sections 402(a)(4), 409, 701(a), 52 Stat. 1046, 1055; 72 Stat. 1785 to 1788 [21 U.S.C. 342(a)(4), 348, 371(a)].

122   Smoked and smoke-flavored fish.
Authority: Sections 402(a)(4), 701(a), 52 Stat. 1046, 1055 [21 U.S.C. 342(a)(4), 371(a)].

123   Frozen raw breaded shrimp.
Authority: Sections 402(a)(4), 701(a), 52 Stat. 1046, 1055 [21 U.S.C. 342(a)(4), 371(a)].

129   Processing and bottling of bottled drinking water.
Authority: Sections 402(a)(4), 409, 701(a), 52 Stat. 1046, 1055; 72 Stat. 1785 to 1788 [21 U.S.C. 342(a)(4), 348, 371(a)].

130   Food standards: general.
Authority: Sections 401, 701, 52 Stat. 1046, as amended; 1055, 1056, as amended (21 U.S.C. 341, 371).

131   Milk and cream.
Authority: Sections 401, 701, 52 Stat. 1046, as amended; 1055, 1056, as amended by 70 Stat. 919 and 72 Stat. 948 (21 U.S.C. 341, 371).

133   Cheeses and related cheese products.
Authority: Sections 401, 701, 52 Stat. 1046, as amended; 1055, 1056, as amended (21 U.S.C. 341, 371), unless otherwise noted.

135   Frozen desserts.
Authority: Sections 401, 701, 52 Stat. 1046, as amended; 1055, 1056, as amended (21 U.S.C. 341, 371).

136   Bakery products.
Authority: Sections 401, 701(e), 52 Stat. 1046, as amended; 70 Stat. 919, as amended [21 U.S.C. 341, 371(e)].

Part	Part title and statutory authority under which part was issued

145   Canned fruits.
        Authority: Sections 401, 701, 52 Stat. 1046, as amended; 1055, 1056, as
        amended (21 U.S.C. 341, 371), unless otherwise noted.

146   Canned fruit juices.
        Authority: Sections 401, 701, 52 Stat. 1046, as amended; 1055, 1056, as
        amended (21 U.S.C. 341, 371).

150   Fruit butters, jellies, preserves, and related products.
        Authority: Sections 401, 701, 52 Stat. 1046, as amended; 1055, 1056, as
        amended (21 U.S.C. 341, 371).

152   Fruit pies.
        Authority: Sections 401, 701, 52 Stat. 1046, as amended; 1055, 1056, as
        amended (21 U.S.C. 341, 371).

155   Canned vegetables.
        Authority: Sections 401, 701, 52 Stat. 1046, as amended; 1055, 1056, as
        amended (21 U.S.C. 341, 371), unless otherwise noted.

156   Vegetable juices.
        Authority: Sections 401, 701, 52 Stat. 1046, as amended; 1055, 1056, as
        amended (21 U.S.C. 341, 371).

158   Frozen vegetables.
        Authority: Sections 401, 701, 52 Stat. 1046, as amended; 1055, 1056, as
        amended (21 U.S.C. 341, 371).

160   Eggs and egg products.
        Authority: Sections 401, 701, 52 Stat. 1046, as amended; 1055, 1056, as
        amended (21 U.S.C. 341, 371), unless otherwise noted.

161   Fish and shellfish.
        Authority: Sections 401, 701, 52 Stat. 1046, as amended; 1055, 1056, as
        amended (21 U.S.C. 341, 371), unless otherwise noted.

163   Cacao products.
        Authority: Sections 401, 701, 52 Stat. 1046, as amended; 1055, 1056, as
        amended (21 U.S.C. 341, 371), unless otherwise noted.

164   Tree nut and peanut products.
        Authority: Sections 401, 701, 52 Stat. 1046, as amended; 1055, 1056, as
        amended (21 U.S.C. 341, 371).

Part	Part title and statutory authority under which part was issued

165   Nonalcoholic beverages.
Authority: Sections 401, 701, 52 Stat. 1046, as amended; 1055, 1056, as amended by 70 Stat. 919 and 72 Stat. 948 (21 U.S.C. 341, 371), unless otherwise noted.

166   Margarine.
Authority: Sections 401, 701, 52 Stat. 1046, as amended; 1055, 1056, as amended by 70 Stat.919 and 72 Stat. 948 (21 U.S.C. 341, 371), unless otherwise noted.

168   Sweeteners and table sirups.
Authority: Sections 401, 701, 52 Stat. 1046, as amended; 1055, 1056, as amended by 70 Stat. 919 and 72 Stat. 948 (21 U.S.C. 341, 371).

169   Food dressings and flavorings.
Authority: Sections 401, 701, 52 Stat. 1046, as amended; 1055, 1056, as amended by 70 Stat. 919 (21 U.S.C. 341, 371), unless otherwise noted.

170   Food additives.
Authority: Sections 409, 701, 52 Stat. 1055, 1056, as amended; 72 Stat. 1785 to 1788, as amended (21 U.S.C. 348, 371), unless otherwise noted.

171   Food additive petitions.
Authority: Sections 409, 701, 52 Stat. 1055, 1056, as amended; 72 Stat. 1785 to 1788, as amended (21 U.S.C. 348, 371), unless otherwise noted.

172   Food additives permitted for direct addition to food for human consumption.
Authority: Sections 409, 701, 52 Stat. 1055, 1056, as amended; 72 Stat. 1785 to 1788, as amended (21 U.S.C. 348, 371), unless otherwise noted.

173   Secondary direct food additives permitted in food for human consumption.
Authority: Sections 409, 701, 52 Stat. 1055, 1056, 72 Stat. 1785, 1786, as amended (21 U.S.C. 348, 371), unless otherwise noted.

174   Indirect food additives: general.
Authority: Sections 409, 72 Stat. 1785 to 1788 as amended (21 U.S.C. 348, 371).

175   Indirect food additives: adhesive coatings and components.
Authority: Sections 409, 701, 52 Stat. 1055, 1056, as amended; 72 Stat. 1785 to 1788, as amended (21 U.S.C. 348, 371), unless otherwise noted.

176   Indirect food additives: paper and paperboard components.

Part	Part title and statutory authority under which part was issued
	Authority: Sections 409, 701, 52 Stat. 1055, 1056, as amended; 72 Stat. 1785 to 1788, as amended (21 U.S.C. 348, 371), unless otherwise noted.
177	Indirect food additives: polymers. Authority: Sections 409, 701, 52 Stat. 1055, 1056, as amended, 72 Stat. 1785 to 1788, as amended (21 U.S.C. 348, 371), unless otherwise noted.
178	Indirect food additives: adjuvants, production aids, and sanitizers. Authority: Sections 409, 701, 52 Stat. 1055, 1056, as amended, 72 Stat. 1785 to 1788, as amended (21 U.S.C. 348, 371), unless otherwise noted.
179	Irradiation in the production, processing, and handling of food. Authority: Sections 409, 701, 52 Stat. 1055, 1056, as amended, 72 Stat. 1785 to 1788, as amended (21 U.S.C. 348, 371), unless otherwise noted.
180	Food additives permitted in food on an interim basis or in contact with food pending additional study. Authority: Sections 409, 701, 52 Stat. 1055, 1056, as amended; 72 Stat. 1785 to 1788, as amended (21 U.S.C. 348, 371), unless otherwise noted.
181	Prior-sanctioned food ingredients. Authority: Sections 409, 701, 52 Stat. 1055, 1056, as amended; 72 Stat. 1785 to 1788, as amended (21 U.S.C. 348, 371), unless otherwise noted.
182	Substances generally recognized as safe. Authority: Sections 409, 701, 52 Stat. 1055, 1056, as amended; 72 Stat. 1785 to 1788, as amended (21 U.S.C. 348, 371), unless otherwise noted.
184	Direct food substances affirmed as generally recognized as safe. Authority: Sections 409, 701, 52 Stat. 1055, 1056, as amended, 72 Stat. 1785 to 1788, as amended (21 U.S.C. 348, 371), unless otherwise noted.
186	Indirect food substances affirmed as generally recognized as safe. Authority: Sections 201(s), 409, 701(a), 52 Stat. 1055, 72 Stat. 1784 to 1788, as amended [21 U.S.C. 321(s), 348, 371(a)].
189	Substances prohibited from use in human food. Authority: Sections 409, 701, 52 Stat. 1055, 1056, as amended; 72 Stat. 1785 to 1788, as amended (21 U.S.C. 348, 371), unless otherwise noted.
193	Tolerances for pesticides in food administered by the Environmental Protection Agency. Authority: Section 409, 72 Stat. 1785 (21 U.S.C. 348).
197	Seafood inspection program. Authority: Section 701, 52 Stat. 1055, 1056, as amended (21 U.S.C. 371).

APPENDIX 6-11. Part titles and issuing statutory authorities of Subchapter E
(Animal drugs, feeds, and related products) of Chapter 1 (Food
and Drug Administration, Department of Health, Education,
and Welfare) of Title 21 of the Code of Federal Regulations
(1977)

Part	Part title and statutory authority under which part was issued

500   General.
Authority: Sections 512, 701(a), 52 Stat. 1055; 82 Stat. 343 to 351 [21
U.S.C. 360b, 371(a)].

501   Animal food labeling.
Authority: Sections 4, 6, 80 Stat. 1297, 1299, 1300 (15 U.S.C. 1453,
1455) and Sections 403, 602, 701, 52 Stat. 1047, 1048 as amended;
1054 to 1056, as amended (21 U.S.C. 343, 362, 371), unless otherwise
noted.

503   Common or usual names for nonstandardized animal foods.
Authority: Sections 201(n), 403, 701(a), 52 Stat. 1041, as amended;
1047, 1048, as amended, 1055 [21 U.S.C. 321(n), 343, 371(a)].

505   Interpretive statements Re: Warnings on animals drugs for over-the-
counter sale.
Authority: Sections 502, 503, 506, 507, 701, 52 Stat. 1050, as amended;
1052, as amended; 1055, 1056, as amended; 52 Stat. 854; 55 Stat. 851;
59 Stat. 463, as amended (21 U.S.C. 352, 353, 356, 357, 371).

507   Thermally processed low-acid animal foods packaged in hermetically
sealed containers.
Authority: Sections 402(a)(4), 701(a), 52 Stat. 1046, 1055 [21 U.S.C.
342(a)(4), 371(a)].

508   Emergency-permit control.
Authority: Sections 402, 404, 701, 52 Stat. 1046, 1047, as amended;
1048, 1055, 1056, as amended by 70 Stat. 919 and 72 Stat. 948; 21
U.S.C. 342, 344, 371.

509   Unavoidable contaminants in animal food and food-packaging material.
Authority: Sections 402(a), 406, 409, 701, 52 Stat. 1046, as amended;
1049, 1055, 1056, as amended by 70 Stat. 919 and 72 Stat. 948; 72 Stat.
1785 to 1788, as amended; 21 U.S.C. 342(a), 346, 348, 371.

510   New animal drugs.
Authority: Sections 512, 701(a), 52 Stat. 1055, 82 Stat. 343 to 351 (21
U.S.C. 360b, 371), unless otherwise noted.

Part	Part title and statutory authority under which part was issued

511   New animal drugs for investigative use.
        Authority: Sections 512, 701(a), 52 Stat. 1055, 82 Stat. 343 to 351; [21 U.S.C. 360b, 371(a)], unless otherwise noted.

514   New animal drug applications.
        Authority: Sections 512(i), (n), 701(a), 52 Stat. 1055; 82 Stat. 343 to 351 [21 U.S.C. 360b(i), (n)], unless otherwise noted.

520   Oral dosage form new animal drugs not subject to certification.
        Authority: Section 512(i), 82 Stat. 347 [21 U.S.C. 360b(i)].

522   Implantation or injectable dosage form new animal drugs not subject to certification.
        Authority: Section 512(i), 82 Stat. 347 [21 U.S.C. 360b(i)].

524   Ophthalmic and topical dosage form new animal drugs not subject to certification.
        Authority: Section 512(i), (n), 82 Stat. 347, 350, 351 [21 U.S.C. 360b(i), (n)].

529   Certain other dosage form new animal drugs not subject to certification.
        Authority: Section 512(i), 82 Stat. 347 [21 U.S.C. 360b(i)].

536   Tests for specific antibiotic dosage forms.
        Authority: Section 507, 59 Stat. 463, as amended (21 U.S.C. 357).

539   Bulk antibiotic drugs subject to certification.
        Authority: Section 507, 59 Stat. 463, as amended (21 U.S.C. 357).

540   Penicillin antibiotic drugs for animal use.
        Authority: Sections 507, 512, 59 Stat. 463, as amended; 82 Stat. 343 to 351 (21 U.S.C. 357, 360b), unless otherwise noted.

544   Oligosaccharide certifiable antibiotic drugs for animal use.
        Authority: Sections 507, 512, 59 Stat. 463, as amended; 82 Stat. 343 to 351 (21 U.S.C. 357, 360b).

546   Tetracycline antibiotic drugs for animal use.
        Authority: Sections 507, 512, 59 Stat. 463, as amended; 82 Stat. 343 to 351 (21 U.S.C. 357, 360b).

548   Certifiable peptide antibiotic drugs for animal use.
        Authority: Sections 507, 512, 59 Stat. 463, as amended; 82 Stat. 343 to 351 (21 U.S.C. 357, 360b).

Part	Part title and statutory authority under which part was issued

555   Chloramphenicol drugs for animal use.
Authority: Sections 507, 512, 59 Stat. 463, as amended; 82 Stat. 343 to 351 (21 U.S.C. 357, 360b).

556   Tolerances for residues of new animal drugs in food.
Authority: Section 512, 701(a), 52 Stat. 1055, 82 Stat. 343 to 351 [21 U.S.C. 360b, 371(a)].

558   New animal drugs for use in animal feeds.
Authority: Section 512, 701(a), 52 Stat. 1055, 82 Stat. 343 to 351 [21 U.S.C. 360b, 371(a)], unless otherwise noted.

561   Tolerances for pesticides in animal feeds administered by the Environmental Protection Agency.
Authority: Section 409, 72 Stat. 1785 (21 U.S.C. 348).

564   Definitions and standards for animal food.
Authority: Sections 401, 701, 52 Stat. 1046, 1055, as amended; 21 U.S.C. 341, 371.

570   Food additives.
Authority: Sections 409, 701, 52 Stat. 1055, 1056, as amended; 72 Stat. 1785 to 1788, as amended (21 U.S.C. 348, 371), unless otherwise noted.

571   Food-additive petitions.
Authority: Sections 409, 701, 52 Stat. 1055, 1056, as amended; 72 Stat. 1785 to 1788, as amended (21 U.S.C. 348, 371), unless otherwise noted.

573   Food additives permitted in feed and drinking water of animals.
Authority: Section 409, 72 Stat. 1785 to 1788, as amended (21 U.S.C. 348), unless otherwise noted.

582   Substances generally recognized as safe.
Authority: Sections 201(s), 409, 701, 52 Stat. 1055, 1056, as amended; 72 Stat. 1784 to 1788, as amended [21 U.S.C. 321(s), 348, 371], unless otherwise noted.

§ 169.140 Mayonnaise.

(a) *Description.* Mayonnaise, mayonnaise dressing, is the emulsified semisolid food prepared from vegetable oil(s), one or both of the acidifying ingredients specified in paragraph (b) of this section, and one or more of the egg yolk-containing ingredients specified in paragraph (c) of this section. One or more of the ingredients specified in paragraph (d) of this section may also be used. The vegetable oil(s) used may contain an optional crystallization inhibitor as specified in paragraph (d)(7) of this section. All the ingredients from which the food is fabricated shall be safe and suitable. Mayonnaise contains not less than 65 percent by weight of vegetable oil. Mayonnaise may be mixed and packed in an atmosphere in which air is replaced in whole or in part by carbon dioxide or nitrogen.

(b) *Acidifying ingredients.* (1) Any vinegar or any vinegar diluted with water to an acidity, calculated as acetic acid, of not less than 2½ percent by weight, or any such vinegar or diluted vinegar mixed with an optional acidifying ingredient as specified in paragraph (d)(6) of this section. For the purpose of this paragraph, any blend of two or more vinegars is considered to be a vinegar.

(2) Lemon juice and/or lime juice in any appropriate form, which may be diluted with water to an acidity, calculated as citric acid, of not less than 2½ percent by weight.

(c) *Egg yolk-containing ingredients.* Liquid egg yolks, frozen egg yolks, dried egg yolks, liquid whole eggs, frozen whole eggs, dried whole eggs, or any one or more of the foregoing ingredients listed in this paragraph with liquid egg white or frozen egg white.

(d) *Other optional ingredients.* The following optional ingredients may also be used:

(1) Salt.

(2) Nutritive carbohydrate sweeteners.

(3) Any spice (except saffron or turmeric) or natural flavoring, provided it does not impart to the mayonnaise a color simulating the color imparted by egg yolk.

(4) Monosodium glutamate.

(5) Sequestrant(s), including but not limited to calcium disodium EDTA (calcium disodium ethylenediaminetetraacetate) and/or disodium EDTA (disodium ethylenediaminetetraacetate), may be used to preserve color and/or flavor.

(6) Citric and/or malic acid in an amount not greater than 25 percent of the weight of the acids of the vinegar or diluted vinegar, calculated as acetic acid.

(7) Crystallization inhibitors, including but not limited to oxystearin, lecithin, or polyglycerol esters of fatty acids.

(e) *Nomenclature.* The name of the food is "Mayonnaise" or "Mayonnaise dressing".

(f) *Label declaration of ingredients.* Each of the ingredients used in the food shall be declared on the label as required by the applicable sections of Part 101 of this chapter.

(xii) Sodium carbonate, sodium bicarbonate, sodium hydroxide, calcium hydroxide, magnesium hydroxide, magnesium oxide, magnesium carbonate, or any mixture or combination of these in such quantity that the pH of the finished canned peas is not more than 8, as determined by the glass electrode method for the hydrogen ion concentration.

(3) The food may be seasoned with one or more of the following optional seasonings:

(i) Green peppers or red peppers. which may be dried.

(ii) Mint leaves.

(iii) Onions, which may be dried.

(iv) Garlic, which may be dried.

(v) Horseradish.

(vi) Lemon juice or concentrated lemon juice.

(vii) Butter or margarine in a quantity not less than 3 percent by weight of the finished food. When butter or margarine is added, safe and suitable emulsifiers or stabilizers, or both, may be added. When butter or margarine is added, no spice, flavoring, or coloring simulating the flavor or color imparted by butter or margarine is used.

(4) The name of the optional pea ingredient is "early" or "June" or "early June", "sweet" or "sweet wrinkled" or "sugar".

(5) If artificial coloring is present, the label shall state that fact in such manner and form as provided in paragraph (b) (3) of this section.

(6) The name of the food is "peas". The name of the food shall include a declaration of any flavoring that characterizes the product as specified in § 101.22 of this chapter, and a declaration of any spice or seasoning that characterizes the product; for example, "with added spice", "seasoned with red peppers", "seasoned with butter". Whenever the name "peas" appears on the label so conspicuously as to be easily seen under customary conditions of purchase, the name of the optional pea ingredient present as specified in paragraph (a) (4) of this section, shall immediately and conspicuously precede or follow such name, without intervening written, printed, or graphic matter, except that the specified varietal name of the peas may so intervene.

(7) Each of the optional ingredients used shall be declared on the label as required by the applicable sections of Part 101 of this chapter.

(b) *Quality*—(1) The standard of quality for canned peas is as follows:

(i) Not more than 4 percent by count of the peas in the container are spotted or otherwise discolored;

(ii) Standard canned peas are normally colored, not artificially colored;

(iii) The combined weight of pea pods and other harmless extraneous vegetable

§ 155.170   Canned peas.

(a) *Identity*—(1) Canned peas is the food prepared from one of the optional pea ingredients, specified in paragraph (a)(1), of this section, and water. The food may contain one or more of the optional ingredients specified in paragraph (a)(2) of this section and one or more of the optional seasonings specified in paragraph (a)(3) of this section. The food is sealed in a container and so processed by heat as to prevent spoilage. The optional pea ingredients are:

(i) Shelled, succulent peas (*Pisum sativum*) of Alaska or other smooth skin varieties.

(ii) Shelled, succulent peas (*Pisum sativum*) of sweet, wrinkled varieties.

(2) The following optional ingredients may be used:

(i) Salt.

(ii) Monosodium glutamate.

(iii) Disodium inosinate complying with the provisions of § 172.535 of this chapter.

(iv) Disodium guanylate complying with the provisions of § 172.530 of this chapter.

(v) Hydrolyzed vegetable protein.

(vi) Autolyzed yeast extract.

(vii) Sugar.

(viii) Dextrose.

(ix) Spice.

(x) Flavoring (except artificial)

(xi) Artificial coloring.

material is not more than one-half of 1 percent of the drained weight of peas in the container;

(iv) The weight of pieces of peas is not more than 10 percent of the drained weight of peas in the container;

(v) The skins of not more than 25 percent by count of the peas in the container are ruptured to a width of $\frac{1}{16}$ inch or more;

(vi) Not less than 90 percent by count of the peas in the container are crushed by a weight of not more than 907.2 grams (2 pounds); and

(vii) The alcohol-insoluble solids of Alaska or other smooth skin varieties of peas in the container are not more than 23.5 percent, and of sweet, wrinkled varieties, not more than 21 percent.

(2) Canned peas shall be tested by the following methods to determine whether or not they meet the requirements of paragraph (b)(1) of this section:

(i) After determining the fill of the container as prescribed in paragraph (c)(1) of this section, distribute the contents of the container over the meshes of a circular sieve made with No. 8 woven-wire cloth which complies with the specifications for such cloth set forth on page 3 of "Standard Specifications for Sieves," published October 25, 1938, by United States Department of Commerce, National Bureau of Standards. The diameter of the sieve used is 8 inches if the quantity of the contents of the container is less than 3 pounds, or 12 inches if such quantity is 3 pounds or more. Without shifting the peas, so incline the sieve as to facilitate drainage. Two minutes from the time drainage begins, remove the peas from the sieve and weigh them. Such weight shall be considered to be the drained weight of the peas.

(ii) From the drained peas obtained in paragraph (b)(2)(i) of this section, promptly segregate and weigh the pea pods and other harmless extraneous vegetable material, and the pieces of peas.

(iii) From the drained peas obtained in paragraph (b)(2)(i) of this section, take at random a subdivision of 100 to 150 peas, and count them. Immediately cover these peas with a portion of the liquid obtained in paragraph (b)(2)(i) of this section, and add the remaining liquid to the drained peas from which the subdivision was taken. Count those peas in the subdivision which are spotted or otherwise discolored, and also those peas the skins of which are ruptured to a width of $\frac{1}{16}$ inch or more.

(iv) Immediately after each pea is examined by the method prescribed in paragraph (b)(2)(iii) of this section, test it by removing its skin, placing one of its cotyledons, with flat surface down, on the approximate center of the level, smooth surface of a rigid plate, lowering a horizontal disc to the highest point of the cotyledon, and measuring the height of the cotyledon. The disc is of rigid material and is affixed to a rod held vertically by a support through which the rod can freely move upward or downward. The lower face of the disc is a smooth, plane surface horizontal to the vertical axis of the rod. A device to

which weight may be added is affixed to the upper end of the rod. Before lowering the disc to the cotyledon, adjust the combined weight of disc, rod, and device to 100 grams. After measuring the height of the cotyledon, and shifting the plate, if necessary, so that the cotyledon is under the approximate center of the disc, add weight to the device at a uniform, continuous rate of 12 grams per second until the cotyledon is pressed to one-fourth its previously measured height, or until the combined weight of disc, rod, and device is 907.2 grams (2 pounds). A pea so tested shall be considered to be crushed when its cotyledon is pressed to one-fourth its original height.

(v) Drain the liquid from the peas which remained after taking the subdivision as prescribed in paragraph (b)(2)(iii) of this section. Transfer the peas to a pan, and rinse them with a volume of water equal to twice the capacity of the container from which such peas were drained in paragraph (b)(2)(i) of this section. Immediately drain the peas again by the method prescribed in paragraph (b)(2)(i) of this section. After the 2 minutes' draining, wipe the moisture from the bottom of the sieve. Comminute the peas thus drained, stir them to a uniform mixture, and weigh 20 grams of such mixture into a 600 cc beaker. Add 300 cc. of 80 percent alcohol (by volume), stir, cover beaker, and bring to a boil. Simmer slowly for 30 minutes. Fit a Buchner funnel with a previously prepared filter paper of such size that its edges extend $\frac{1}{2}$ inch or more up the vertical sides of the funnel. The previous preparation of the filter paper consists of drying it in a flat-bottomed dish for 2 hours at 100° C, covering the dish with a tight-fitting cover, cooling it in a desiccator, and promptly weighing. After the

APPENDIX 6-13. (continued)

filter paper is fitted to the funnel, apply suction and transfer the contents of the beaker to the funnel. Do not allow any of the material to run over the edge of the paper. Wash the material on the filter with 80 percent alcohol (by volume) until the washings are clear and colorless. Transfer the filter paper with the material retained thereon to the dish used in preparing the filter paper. Dry the material in a ventilated oven, without covering the dish, for 2 hours at 100° C. Place the cover on the dish, cool it in a desiccator, and promptly weigh. From this weight, subtract the weight of the dish, cover, and paper, as previously found. The weight in grams thus obtained, multiplied by 5, shall be considered to be the percent of alcohol-insoluble solids.

(3) If the quality of canned peas falls below the standard prescribed in paragraph (b)(1) of this section, the label shall bear the general statement of substandard quality specified in § 130.14(a) of this chapter, in the manner and form therein specified; but in lieu of such general statement of substandard quality when the quality of canned peas falls below the standard in only one respect, the label may bear the alternative statement "Below standard in quality _____

_____", the blank to be filled in with the words specified after the corresponding subparagraph number of paragraphs (b)(1) of this section which such canned peas fail to meet, as follows: (i) "Excessive discolored peas"; (ii) "Artificially colored"; (iii) "Excessive foreign material"; (iv) "Excessive broken peas"; (v) "Excessive cracked peas"; (vi) "Not tender"; (vii) "Excessively mealy". Such alternative statement shall immediately and conspicuously precede or follow without intervening written, printed, or graphic matter, the name "Peas" and any words and statements required or authorized to appear with such name by paragraph (a)(4) of this section.

(c) *Fill of container*—(1) The standard of fill of container for canned peas is a fill such that, when the peas and liquid are removed from the container and returned thereto, the leveled peas (irrespective of the quantity of the liquid), 15 seconds after they are so returned completely fill the container. A container with lid attached by double seam shall be considered to be completely filled when it is filled to the level 3/16 inch vertical distance below the top of the double seam; and a glass container shall be considered to be completely filled when it is filled to the level 1/2 inch vertical distance below the top of the container.

(2) If canned peas fall below the standard of fill of container prescribed in paragraph (c)(1) of this section, the label shall bear the general statement of substandard fill specified in § 130.14(b) of this chapter, in the manner and form therein specified.

514

APPENDIX 6-14. Part titles and issuing statutory authorities of Subchapter L
(Regulations under certain other acts administered by the Food
and Drug Administration) of Chapter 1 of Title 21 of the Code
of Federal Regulations (1977)

Part	Part title and statutory authority under which part was issued
1210	Regulations under the Federal Import Milk Act. Authority: Sections 2, 3, 44 Stat. 1101, 1102, as amended; 21 U.S.C. 142, 143.
1210	Regulations under the Tea Importation Act. Authority: Sections 1, 10, 29 Stat. 604, 607; 21 U.S.C. 41, 50, unless otherwise noted.
1230	Regulations under the Federal Caustic Poison Act. Authority: Section 9, 44 Stat. 1049, as amended; 15 U.S.C. 409.
1240	Control of communicable diseases. Authority: Sections 215, 361, 58 Stat. 690, 703, as amended (42 U.S.C. 216, 264).
1250	Interstate conveyance sanitation. Authority: Sections 215, 361, 58 Stat. 690, 703, as amended (42 U.S.C. 216, 264).

CHAPTER 7

DEPARTMENT OF THE TREASURY
Bureau of Alcohol, Tobacco, and Firearms

INTRODUCTION

Organization and Activities

According to Section 201(f) of the Federal Food, Drug, and Cosmetic Act of 1938, as amended (21 U.S.C. 321), the term "food" includes alcoholic beverages (see Chapter 6); and the regulatory control over their quality, standards, manufacture, and other related aspects is of concern to this book.

Prior to July 1, 1972 the Alcohol, Tobacco, and Firearms Division was part of the Internal Revenue Service. The director of such a division was responsible for the administration and enforcement of all internal revenue laws and regulations relating to distilled spirits and other beverages and products having an alcoholic content, and to cigars, cigarettes, and cigarette paper and tube. On February 29, 1972 the secretary of the Treasury announced that the division would be transferred on July 1, 1972 as a new bureau in the Treasury Department. This specific authority of the secretary originated from Reorganization Plan No. 26 of 1950, and the transfer was established in Treasury Department Order No. 22.

The order transferred the functions, powers, and duties arising under laws relating to alcohol, tobacco, firearms, and explosives from the Internal Revenue Service (IRS) to the bureau completely. Information about the mission, organization, and functions of the new Bureau of Alcohol, Tobacco, and Firearms and the federal statutes it administers is described in a small publication issued by the bureau (see ATF 0 1100.1 in Table 7-1). The source of this and other publications issued by this bureau is explained in detail later. The following discussion is partly derived from this publication.

The headquarters of the bureau is located in Washington, D.C. but since it is decentralized, most of its personnel are stationed throughout the country where many of its operational functions are performed.

The bureau is supervised by a director who is appointed by the secretary of the Treasury Department. However, the director is under the direct supervision of the assistant secretary of Enforcement, Tariff and Trade Affairs, and Operations within the Treasury Department. See Appendix 7-1 for a simplified version of the organizational structure of the Treasury Department.

The main objective of the bureau's programs is to maximize voluntary compliance with the laws under its jurisdiction and to minimize willful or involuntary violations of the laws. To achieve these goals, the bureau has two basic functions: criminal enforcement and regulatory enforcement. The objectives of the criminal enforcement activity are to suppress the traffic in illicit distilled spirits; to eliminate illegal possession and use of explosives, destructive devices, and firearms; and to cooperate with state and local law enforcement agencies to reduce crime and

TABLE 7-1. Some Publications Related to and published by the Bureau of Alcohol, Tobacco, and Firearms

Publication Number	Date	Title
ATF P 1200.3	March, 1976	Index of Materials required by the Freedom of Information Act
ATF 0 110.1	March 12, 1974	Mission, organization, and functions
ATF P 5600.1	May, 1975	Rulings and procedures relating to alcohol, tobacco and wagering matters. Compiled from Revenue Rulings and Revenue Procedures Published During the Period January 1, 1953 through June 30, 1972
None	Monthly	Alcohol, Tobacco and Firearms Bulletin
None	See footnote "a"	Alcohol, Tobacco and Firearms Cumulative Bulletin

a Annual publication, first issue in 1974.

violence. The regulatory enforcement activity determines and assures full collection of revenue due from legal alcohol and tobacco industries; fulfills the bureau's responsibility in the prevention of commercial bribery, consumer deception, and other improper trade practices in the distilled spirits industry; and assists other federal, state, and local government agencies in the resolution of problems relating to industrial development, ecology, revenue protection, public health, and other areas of jurisdictional concern.

The bureau administers a number of federal statutes. Those that are of main concern to this book include certain sections of the Internal Revenue Codes of 1918 and 1954 and the Federal Alcohol Administration Act of 1935. These statutes are discussed in detail later. The following proceeds to a discussion of the organization and specific activities of the bureau.

A detailed organizational chart of the bureau is shown in Appendix 7-2. The director of the bureau supervises five main offices of functions, each of which is headed by an assistant director. The office of the assistant director of Regulatory Enforcement is of major concern to this book. This office is in charge of various divisions and the headquarters of the regional offices throughout the country. The three major divisions of interest are: Regulations and Procedures, Industry Control, and Trade and Consumer Affairs. An organizational chart of the Office of Regulatory Enforcement is provided in Appendix 7-3. To obtain the names of the officers in charge of each office and division within the bureau, one should obtain the latest issue of the telephone directory of the Treasury Department. The following presents a discussion of certain responsibilities and activities within each division of the Office of Regulatory Enforcement.

The Regulations and Procedures Division is specifically responsible for the preparation of the bureau's regulations, methods, and procedures for the control and supervision of the legal liquor and tobacco industries. This division is in charge of two branches: the Research and Regulations Branch and the Procedures Branch.

The Research and Regulations Branch has the following responsibilities:

1. It researches and makes analytical studies of regulations aimed at more effective and economical administration of laws. It achieves this goal by recognizing technological changes and trends and by evaluating related methods and procedures to determine effectiveness, assure uniform application, and identify problem areas.
2. It tests proposals to evaluate feasibility prior to amendment of regulations.
3. It implements legislation and administration decisions.
4. It conducts studies of existing and proposed laws and develops recommendations for, and provides technical assistance in connection with, new or amendatory legislation.
5. It provides technical advice, as requested, to other divisions in the preparation and processing of regulations.

The Procedures Branch is responsible for a number of activities. Those of relevance to this book include: amending the statement of procedural rules and regulations relating to procedure and administration in regulatory enforcement functions, furnishing general information to the industry and the public, and reviewing field office forms and issuances.

The Industry Control Division formulates decisions and takes definitive action over the operations of the legal liquor and tobacco industries. Thus it provides advice and information on such matters to industry and other concerned parties. This division supervises two branches of activities, one of which is the Rulings Branch. This branch is of great importance and it is responsible for the following:

1. It develops and publishes procedural statements relating to the procedures whereby the applicable laws and regulations may be complied with by industry members.

2. It acts on special applications involving proposals for conducting operations or installing, using, or constructing equipment or premises in a manner other than as prescribed by law or regulations. The operations are usually related to alcoholic beverages.
3. It develops and publishes formalized rulings on any bureau actions related to alcohol, tobacco, firearms, and allied industries. These actions are of precedent-setting nature and are related to matters that may have general area-wide or industry-wide application.
4. It acts on *offers* submitted by industry members *in compromise* of tax liabilities or violations of internal revenue law or the Federal Alcohol Administration Act.

The Trade and Consumer Affairs Division is probably the division having the most impact on the consuming public and the money they spend on alcoholic beverages. It directs control over trade and consumer affairs by classifying, for tax and regulatory purposes, alcoholic beverage products and tobacco under the Internal Revenue laws. It has authority over the advertising and labeling of alcoholic beverages under the Federal Alcohol Administration Act. It makes decisions and takes action on a wide variety of matters related to industry trade practices. It provides advice on the laws and regulations to foreign and domestic industries, the bureau's field offices, public and private organizations, and the staff of foreign embassies. This division supervises two branches of activities: the Commodity Classification Branch and the Trade Affairs Branch.

The Commodity Classification Branch is responsible for the following:

1. It examines, for proper classification, statements of processes filed by proprietors of distilled spirits plants and breweries.
2. It acts on formulas for rectified distilled spirits and wines to determine applicable tax rates and to assure that products are manufactured in accordance with regulations and laws.
3. It acts on applications for certificates of label approval for alcoholic beverages and applications for exemptions from label approval.
4. It provides general information to the general public and industry members.
5. It acts on requests for tax classification of various tobacco products.

The Trade Affairs Branch is responsible for the following:

1. It makes decisions on the advertising of alcoholic beverages in all media by acting on the acceptability of existing as well as newly proposed advertising themes.
2. It makes decisions on the legality of various industry trade practices in accor-

dance with established regulations under the Federal Alcohol Administration Act and advises the bureau's field offices in regard to such practices.

3.   It acts on applications for approval of containers as distinctive liquor bottles.

4.   It holds public hearings in regard to proposals for amendment of the Federal Alcohol Administration Act regulations in the areas of consumer protection and trade practices. It makes recommendations and offers technical advice in regard to such proposals.

5.   It acts on applications for interlocking directorates with the view of deterring and preventing monopolistic growth within the distilled-spirits industry.

6.   It provides for interchange of technical advice with representatives of foreign governments relative to the laws and regulations for alcoholic beverages.

Statutes Administered

What are the federal statutes administered by the bureau? Because of the limited interest of this book, only certain pertinent statutes are discussed. The bureau administers certain sections of the Internal Revenue Code of 1954. Specifically, this includes Subtitles E and F of Title 26 of the United States Code. Subtitle E covers "alcohol, tobacco, and certain other excise taxes," including Sections 5001 to 5862. Subtitle F covers "procedure and administration," including Sections 6001 to 7852. This book is concerned mainly with Chapter 51 of Subtitle E of Title 26 of the United States Code. Chapter 51, titled "Distilled spirits, wines, and beer," is divided into 10 subchapters, which are listed in Table 7-2. It should be pointed out that Chapter 51 actually incorporates some of the relevant provisions of the Internal Revenue Code of 1918. For further details concerning the contents of Chapter 51 of Title 26 of the United States Code, consult the original document.

Perhaps, the major responsibility of the bureau with respect to Chapter 51 may be summarized in one sentence. The bureau makes sure that the proper amount of tax is being paid to the federal government by individuals or corporations engaged in all phases of production, storage, transport, sale, import, export, and/or all other aspects relating to doing business in alcoholic beverages. To achieve this, the information in Chapter 51 of Title 26 describes in some details the definitions of alcoholic beverages, the equipments used in their productions, the types of ingredients used, the chemical formulas involved, and various other criteria of importance to this book. Of course, the bureau has further promulgated more regulations in the Code of Federal Regulations to implement, supplement, or complement the materials described in the Internal Revenue Code. Consequently, much of the material prescribed in Chapter 51 of Title 26 is reiterated in the Code of Federal Regulations, but in a different form. All these are discussed in further detail later.

TABLE 7-2. Subchapter Titles of Chapter 51 (Distilled Spirits, Wines, and Beer),
Subtitle E (Alcohol, Tobacco, and Certain Other Excise Taxes),
Title 26 (Internal Revenue Code), United States Code

Subchapter	Title	Sections
A	Gallonage and occupational taxes	5001 to 5148
B	Qualification requirements for distilled spirits plants	5171 to 5181
C	Operation of distilled spirits plants	5201 to 5252
D	Industrial use of distilled spirits	5271 to 5275
E	General provisions relating to distilled spirits	5291 to 5315
F	Bonded and taxpaid wine premises	5351 to 5392
G	Breweries	5401 to 5417
H	Miscellaneous plants and warehouses	5501 to 5523
I	Miscellaneous general provisions	5551 to 5562
J	Penalties, seizures, and forfeitures relating to liquors	5601 to 5691

There is one other section of the Internal Revenue Code of 1954 that is of interest to this book. This is the concept of "offers-in-compromise." Information on this topic is found in 26 U.S.C. 7122 and 26 CFR 601.203. Thus according to 26 U.S.C. 7122, the secretary of the Treasury, the director of the bureau, or other authorized personnel, may compromise any civil or criminal case arising under the Internal Revenue laws prior to reference to the Department of Justice for prosecution or defense; and the Attorney General of the United States may compromise any such case after reference to the Department of Justice for prosecution or defense. Thus 26 CFR 601.203 describes in detail the procedure and conditions of "offers-in-compromise." An example of a required condition mandates that if the violations involving certain regulatory provisions are deliberate and with intent to defraud, the criminal liabilities will not be compromised. Another stated condition requires that an offer in compromise be evaluated according to the magnitude of the violation.

An offer in compromise is first considered by the director having jurisdiction. Except in certain penalty cases, an investigation of the basis of the offer is required. The examining officer makes a written recommendation for acceptance or rejection of the offer. If the director has jurisdiction over the processing of the offer, he will: (1) reject the offer, (2) accept the offer if it involves a civil liability under $500, (3) accept the offer if it involves a civil liability of $500 or more, but less than $100,000, or involves a specific penalty and the regional counsel concurs

in the acceptance of the offer, or (4) recommend to the national office the acceptance of the offer if it involves a civil liability of $100,000 or over.

Let us illustrate the concept of offers in compromise with a simple example.
A certain proprietor of a plant is charged with manufacturing distilled spirits that
have been labeled with a slightly (but illegal) higher alcoholic content than they actually contain. The bureau may agree to accept an offer in compromise in return
for nonprosecution as well as corrective actions to be taken by the proprietor.

The other federal statutes administered by the bureau and of interest to this
book is the Federal Alcohol Administration Act of August 19, 1935 (49 Stat. 977,
27 U.S.C. 201 to 211). The general content of this act is given in Table 7-3. This
act is very consumer oriented. It gives the bureau broad authority to make sure
that industry members of the alcoholic beverage industry do not deceive the consuming public. As an example, Section 5 of the act makes it unlawful for any person engaged in the business to sell alcoholic beverages that are not properly labeled
or to disseminate any false advertisement about their products. This applies to all
transactions in interstate or foreign commerce. The industry must not deceive the
consumer with respect to the quantity and quality of the product, such as the percentage of alcohol, types of ingredients, taste, flavor, and other aspects. Section
17(a) of the act provides the definitions for distilled spirits, wine, malt beverage
and bottle, all of which are related to the composition and standards of the products. Further details are presented later.

SOURCES OF INFORMATION

One of the main objectives of this book is to present the sources of information
discussed. The bureau's system of dissemination of information for the general
public is very well organized. Table 7-1 lists those materials that are available to the
general public and will provide most of the information needed to understand the
bureau, the statutes it administers, and its overall regulatory activities. They are the
basis of the discussion presented in the first half of this chapter; the rest is drawn
from the Code of Federal Regulations.

Index of Materials Required by the Freedom of Information Act

At present the bureau has established the Office of the Assistant to the Director
for Disclosure (see Appendix 7-2). This office was established pursuant to the passage by the U.S. Congress of the Freedom of Information Act. It is the focal point
of communication with inquiries from the general public for information about the
bureau and its work. To provide more efficient service, the Office of Disclosure has
compiled a booklet titled "Index of Materials Required by the Freedom of Infor-

TABLE 7-3. General Contents of the Federal Alcohol Administration Act
(Act of August 19, 1935, 49 Stat. 977, 27 U.S.C. 201 to 211)

	Section of	
General Title as given in the Original Act	Act	27 U.S.C.
General	None	201
	2(e)	202(a)
	2(f)	202(b)
	2(g)	202(c)
	2(h)	202(d)
Unlawful business without permit	3	203
Permits	4	204
Unfair competition and unlawful practices	5(a) to 5(f)	205
Bulk sales and bottling	6	206
Penalties	7	207
Interlocking directorates	8	208
Miscellaneous	17(a) to 17(c)	211

mation Act" (see Table 7-1), a new issue of which is published periodically. This index, listing most of the materials issued by the bureau, is divided into three main parts. The contents of the first part relevant to this book are described in Table 7-4. In general, this part contains many of the bureau's past rulings and decisions related to alcohol, tobacco, and firearms, most of which are precedent-setting in nature and have an area- or industry-wide general application. Some examples are presented later. The second part of the index contains current ATF (Alcohol, Tobacco, and Firearms) orders and handbooks, while the third part contains current ATF notices. Those subject titles under which the materials in the second and third parts are categorized are listed in Table 7-5. Publication ATF 0 1100.1 mentioned in Table 7-1 is categorized under "organization, authorities, and functions" in Table 7-5.

According to Table 7-5, there is one category called "regulatory enforcement." The publications issued under this heading are useful in understanding the

TABLE 7-4.   Alphabetical Listing of Subject Titles under Which are Categorized
Bureau's Rulings on Matters Relating to Alcohol (Compiled from
Index of Materials Required by the Freedom of Information Act
ATF P 1200.3 3/76)

Administration	Exportation	Qualifying documents
Advertising	Exporters	Records
Aircraft	Fiduciaries	Rectification
Alcohol	Foreign embassies and	Redistillation
Applications	legations	Refunds and credits
Articles	Foreign-trade zones	Reports
Beer	Forms	Retail liquor dealers
Blending	Formulas	Returns
Bonded wine cellars	Gauge	Samples
Bonds	Hospitals, clinics, and	Seizures
Books and records	blood banks	Special tax
Bottlers	Importation	Specially denatured
Breweries	Importers	spirits
Cereal beverages	Inducements	Stamps
Claims	Inspections and	States
Coloring, flavoring,	investigations	Stills
and blending	Labels	Tanks
Construction	Laboratories	Tax
Containers	Liens	Taxpaid wine bottling
Cordials	Limitation period	houses
Corporations	Liqueurs and cordials	Trade names
Credits	Losses	Transfers
Customs	Marks and brands	Users
Dealers	Materials	Vessels and aircraft
Deficiencies	Nonbeverage	Vinegar
Delinquency	manufacturers	Violations
Denaturants	Nonbeverage products	Virgin Islands
Distillates	Offers in compromise	Volatile fruit-flavor
Distilled spirits	Overpayments	concentrates
Distilled spirits plants	Packages	Waivers
Drawback	Partnerships	Warehouses
Ecology considerations	Penalties	Wholesale liquor dealers
Equipment and supplies	Proprietary solvents	Wine
Exemptions	Puerto Rico	Wineries

inspection routines and techniques of the bureau. Selected examples of these publications are given in Appendix 7-4. Let us take a couple of examples from this list
and study them.

Refer to Order ATF 0 5110.8A (Revenue Protection Inspections; Distilled

TABLE 7-5.   Subject Titles under Which are Categorized Bureau's Publications
Such as "Current ATF Orders and Handbooks" or "Current ATF
Notices," in Order as Listed in "Index of Materials Required by the
Freedom of Information Act (ATF P 1200.3, March 1976)

1	Classification codes, checklists, and indexes
2	Civil rights
3	Organization, authorities, and function
4	External relationships
5	Management systems and standards
6	Travel and transportation
7	Administrative support
8	Distribution
9	Protective programs
10	Logistics management
11	Fiscal management
12	Personnel management
13	Criminal enforcement
14	Regulatory enforcement
15	Technical and scientific services
16	Inspection

Spirits Bottling Phase) of Appendix 7-4. This order establishes the techniques and
procedures to be used in making a revenue protection inspection of distilled spirits
plant bottling premises. The provisions of this order apply to headquarters and
field regulatory enforcement offices. Each officer is instructed to use these techniques and procedures to the extent necessary to satisfy himself that the proprietor
operates in accordance with law and regulations and properly accounts for all
spirits and wines received, rectified, bottled, packaged, or otherwise disposed of.
He may, when circumstances justify, either omit certain techniques and procedures
or extend the inspection into areas not specifically covered in this order. Some examples of inspection techniques are as follows.

Inquire into the methods used by the proprietor in determining quantities of
eligible and ineligible spirits dumped for rectification, bottling, and so on. Ascertain that products are being manufactured in accordance with approved formulas,
where required, being especially careful to determine whether products on which
standard export drawback rates have been established conform to formulas and
meet the requirements of regulations. Also ascertain the proprietor's use of nonbev-
erage drawback alcoholic flavorings to determine whether they are used within prescribed limits. Spot check the identity, proof, and fill of bottled distilled spirits to

determine whether the proprietor is properly filling bottles as required by the bureau's regulation. For further details, consult the original document.

Refer to Order ATF 0 5110.12 (Product Integrity Phase Inspections--Distilled Spirits Plants) of Appendix 7-4. This order establishes the techniques and procedures to be used in making product integrity inspections at distilled spirits plants. The provisions of this order apply to headquarters and field regulatory offices. The Product Integrity Phase Inspection is made at a distilled spirits plant as a part of the Consumer Protection Program. The goal is to offer protection to the consumer by ensuring that the product he purchases is exactly what it is claimed to be and not misrepresented by the proprietor. The basic procedures for this type of inspection are observation of operations and examination and analysis of records. The officer should check enough records and operations to satisfy himself that the proprietor is operating within the law and correctly representing his products. When circumstances justify, one may omit certain procedures or extend the inspection into areas not listed in this order. Some examples of inspection procedures are as follows.

In evaluating the integrity of the proprietor's products, the officer should determine whether the proprietor is producing spirits in accordance with approved statements of process, whether packages are marked and branded as required by regulations, whether proper procedures are followed when spirits are mingled or consolidated, and whether denaturations are made according to approved formulas.

Other Bureau Publications

Apart from the "index" described in the preceding section, the bureau also issues a very informative publication, the "Alcohol, Tobacco, and Firearms Bulletin." This bulletin is published monthly and is obtainable through the Government Printing Office. The cover of this bulletin contains the subtitle "Treasury Decisions, Rulings, and Procedural and Administrative Matters Concerning Alcohol, Tobacco, Firearms, Explosives, and Wagering, Department of the Treasury, Bureau of Alcohol, Tobacco, and Firearms" (refer to Table 7-1).

The background and content of this bulletin is discussed here, and the material is obtained from the introduction of one such issue. The bulletin is the authoritative instrument of the director of the bureau for announcing official procedures and rulings of the bureau and for publishing Treasury Decisions, legislation, administrative matters, a list of court decisions, announcements, and other items of interest. The announcements may include notices of hearing and notices of proposed rule making published in the Federal Register and administrative actions taken by the bureau. An example of administrative action is the description of a specific violation by a specific individual or corporation and the acceptance of an offer-in-compromise by the bureau. For further details relating to administrative actions, consult: ATF Bulletin No. 1976-1, January 12, 1976, pages 14 to 15, announcement 76-5, "Administrative Action Guidelines." The bulletin incorporates into one publication all matters of the bureau that are of public record.

It is the policy of the bureau to publish in the bulletin all substantive rulings necessary to promote a uniform application of all laws administered by the bureau as well as all rulings that supersede, revoke, modify, or amend any of those previously published in the bulletin (including those published prior to July 1, 1972 in the Internal Revenue Bulletin). All rulings apply retroactively unless otherwise indicated. Procedures relating solely to matters of internal mangement are not published. However, industry regulations appearing in internal management documents and statements of internal practices and procedures that affect the rights and duties of the public are published.

Bureau rulings represent the conclusions of the bureau on the application of the law to the entire state of facts involved. In those that are based on positions taken in rulings to industry members or technical advice to bureau field offices, identifying details and confidential information are deleted, to prevent unwarranted invasions of privacy and to comply with statutory requirements concerning disclosure of information obtained from the public.

Rulings and procedures reported in the bulletin do not have the force and effect of Treasury regulations, but they may be used as precedents. In applying published rulings and procedures, the effect of subsequent legislation, regulations, court decisions, rulings, and procedures must be considered. Concerned parties are cautioned against reaching the same conclusions in other cases unless the facts and circumstances are substantially the same.

Bulletin contents of a permanent nature are consolidated each calendar year into cumulative issues (see Table 7-1 for Cumulative Bulletin). Nonpermanent nature materials include most of the announcements, such as administrative actions and hearing notices. Examples of some rulings and administrative actions are presented later in this chapter. As for the meaning of bureau procedure, the following discussion provides an example.

Refer to Bulletin No. 1976-19 (September 10, 1976), ATF Procedure 76-3, "Manufacture and use of plastic containers." In this notice the bureau set forth its position regarding the manufacture and use of plastic containers in the bottling of distilled spirits and provides procedural guidelines for affected industries.

Some time before 1973 the bureau authorized an experimental program to use polyvinyl chloride plastic bottles for distilled spirits. The program was terminated on May 11, 1973 because of suspected migration of the material into the alcohol. In 1976 the bureau concluded that it might be possible to use plastic resins instead of polyvinyl chloride for alcoholic beverage packaging. Thus the bureau issued the new guidelines.

Some primary considerations of such guidelines required data on well-established bottle specifications, laboratory tests regarding the suitability of such packaging, and preparation of environmental impact statements pertaining to such liquor bottles. Specifically, the bureau permitted a preliminary testing program that would not involve consumers and requested industry application for approval for permanent use. Further, all application must be supported by scientific evidence and samples of plastic containers must be made available to the bureau. The bureau indicated that to reach a final action for approval would require a long time.

Apart from Bulletin No. 1976-19 mentioned above, in May, 1975, the bureau issued a publication entitled "Rulings and Procedures Relating to Alcohol, Tobacco and Wagering Matters, compiled from Revenue Rulings and Revenue Procedures Published During the Period January 1, 1953 through June 30, 1972" (see Table 7-1). Prior to the establishment of the bureau, revenue rulings and procedures relating to alcohol, tobacco, and other matters, were published by the IRS in the Internal Revenue Bulletin. In January, 1973 the bureau began publishing the bulletin instead. This particular publication contains the full text of all revenue rulings and procedures relating to alcohol, tobacco, and so on, published in the period shown, and which remaining in effect on and after May 1, 1975. This publication, together with sebsequent and new issues of the bulletin, provides a useful research guide to all current and past rulings and procedures.

It should be pointed out that much of the information contained in the first part (see Table 7-4) of the Index of Materials Required by the Freedom of Information Act is actually derived from this publication and other bulletins issued.

Finally, practically most of the information described in these resource materials are required to be first published in the Federal Register in conformity with federal regulations. Thus the Federal Register remains the most updated reference source for information relating to the Bureau of Alcohol, Tobacco, and Firearms.

The most recent regulations governing public access to bureau information are located in 27 CFR 71, T.D. ATF-47 (Bulletin No. 1978-4, pages 5 to 28), and 43 FR 10687 (March 15, 1978).

BUREAU'S REGULATIONS, RULINGS, AND ADMINISTRATIVE ACTIONS

Many details on regulatory controls and the various phases of the production of alcoholic beverages are found in Title 27 of the Code of Federal Regulations. Table 7-6 lists those parts of special concern to this chapter and the statutory authority under which each part was issued. The remainder of this chapter is devoted mostly to a discussion of the materials described in Table 7-6.

TABLE 7-6. Selected Federal Regulations Related to Alcoholic Beverages, Published in Code of Federal Regulations and Issued by Bureau of Alcohol, Tobacco, and Firearms

Subject Matter	Title of Specific Part in CFR	Reference	Authority under which Specific Part Was Issued (Unless Otherwise Noted)
Wine	Labeling and advertising of wine	27 CFR 4	49 Stat. 981, as amended; 27 U.S.C. 205
	Wine	27 CFR 240	Section 7805, 68A Stat. 917; 26 U.S.C. 7805
Distilled spirits	Labeling and advertising of distilled spirits	27 CFR 5	49 Stat. 981, as amended; 27 U.S.C. 205
	Distilled spirits plants	27 CFR 201	Section 7805, 68A Stat. 917, 26 U.S.C. 7805
	Liquors and articles from Puerto Rico and the Virgin Islands	27 CFR 250	Sections 7651, 7652, 7805, 68A Stat. 906, 907, 917; 26 U.S.C. 7651, 7652, 7805
Other alcoholic beverages	Labeling and advertising of malt beverages	27 CFR 7	49 Stat. 981, as amended; 27 U.S.C. 205
	Beer	27 CFR 245	Section 7805, 68A Stat. 917; 26 U.S.C. 7805
Import and export of alcoholic beverages	Importation of distilled spirits, wines, and beer	27 CFR 251	Section 7805, 68A Stat. 917; 26 U.S.C. 7805
	Export of liquor	27 CFR 252	Section 7805, 68A Stat. 917; 26 U.S.C. 7805

531

TABLE 7-6 (continued)

Subject Matter	Title of Specific Part in CFR	Reference	Authority under which Specific Part Was Issued (Unless Otherwise Noted)
Other relevant regulations	Production of volatile fruit-flavor concentrate	27 CFR 18	Section 7805, 68A Stat. 917; 26 U.S.C. 7805
	Production of vinegar by the vaporizing process	27 CFR 195	Section 7805, 68A Stat. 917; 26 U.S.C. 7805
	Gauging manual	27 CFR 186	Section 7805, 68A Stat. 917; 26 U.S.C. 7805
	Basic permit requirements under the Federal Alcohol Administration Act	27 CFR 1	49 Stat. 977, as amended; 27 U.S.C. 202 note
	Bulk sales and bottling of distilled spirits	27 CFR 3	49 Stat. 985, as amended; 27 U.S.C. 206
	Procedure and administration	27 CFR 70	(26 U.S.C. 7805, 18 U.S.C. 926, 847); 68A Stat. 917, 82 Stat. 234, 84 Stat. 959. Statutory provisions interpreted or applied are cited in parentheses in text. 5 U.S.C. 301, 552
	Statement of procedural rules	27 CFR 71	68A Stat. 895, 917; 72 Stat. 1314, 1373, 1374, 1402; 26 U.S.C. 5001, 5291, 5301, 5605, 5606, 7502, 7805
	Return of substances, articles, or containers	27 CFR 173	
	Stills	27 CFR 196	Section 7805, 68A Stat. 917; 26 U.S.C. 7805
	Rules of practice in permit proceeding	27 CFR 200	Section 7805, 68A Stat. 917; 26 U.S.C. 7805
	Taxpaid wine bottling houses	27 CFR 231	Section 7805, 68A Stat. 917; 26 U.S.C. 7805

Wine

According to Table 7-6, the title of 27 CFR 4 is "Labeling and advertising of wine." Appendix 7-5 describes the section title for this Part 4. The following paragraphs discuss those sections related to definition, standards of identity, and certain labeling requirements for wine.

Wine is defined in accordance with Section 17(a)(7) of the Federal Alcohol Administration Act (27 U.S.C. 211). Thus wine:

1. Is as defined in Sections 610 and 617 of the Revenue Act of 1918 (40 Stat. 1109 to 1112; 26 U.S.C. 5373, 5381 to 5387, 5392). This lengthy and complicated definition for wine is presented later in connection with the standards of identity for wine.
2. Includes other alcoholic beverages not so defined, but made in the manner of wine, such as: carbonated and sparkling wine; wine made from condensed grape must; wine made from other agricultural products that are not the juice of sound and ripe grapes, imitation wine, and compounds sold as wine, vermouth, cider, perry and sake, provided that they contain 7% to 24% of alcohol by volume and are not meant for industrial use.

What are the standards of identity for wine? Table 7-7 lists the classes and types of wine as described in 27 CFR 4. Let us examine Class 1 wine--grape wine. The definition given in the following paragraph is similar to the one detailed in the Internal Revenue Code of 1918.

Grape wine is the wine produced by the normal alcoholic fermentation of the juice of sound and ripe grapes, including restored or unrestored pure condensed grape must. However, grape brandy or alcohol may be added, and pure condensed grape must may also be added after fermentation. No other addition or abstraction of substances is permitted with the exception of those approved and used in cellar treatment of wine. However, before, during, and after fermentation, the product may be ameliorated by any of the following procedures:

1. The wine may be ameliorated by adding a certain amount of sugar that will increase the volume by 35% or less. Sugar and water may be added separately or in combination. After such amelioration, the product is not permitted to have:
   a. More than 13% of alcohol by volume because of fermentation.
   b. Less than 5 parts per thousand (ppt) of natural acid   content after the addition of water.
   c. A total solid content of more than $22g/100cm^3$.
2. The wine may be ameliorated by adding separately or in combination 20% or

TABLE 7-7. Classification and Types of Wine. Adapted from 27 CFR 4,
            "Standards of Identity for Wine"

Class of Wine	Name of the Class of Wine	Types of Wine within the class
1	Grape wine	Grape wine, table wine, and dessert wine
2	Sparkling grape wine	Sparkling grape wine, champagne, champagne style, and crackling wine
3	Carbonated grape wine	Carbonated grape wine, including carbonated wine, carbonated red wine, and carbonated white wine
4	Citrus wine	Citrus wine, citrus table wine, citrus dessert wine, and other varieties of wine related to citrus wine (consult 27 CFR 4 for details)
5	Fruit wine	Fruit wine, berry wine, fruit table wine, fruit dessert wine, and other varieties of wine related to fruit wine (consult 27 CFR 4 for details)
6	Wine from other agricultural products	Table wine, dessert wine, raisin wine, sake, and other varieties of related wine (consult 27 CFR 4 for details)
7	Aperitif wine	Aperitif wine and vermouth
8	Imitation and substandard wine	Imitation wine and substandard wine can be of various varieties (consult 27 CFR 4 for details)
9	Retsina wine	Retsina wine

less by weight of sugar and 10% or less by weight of water.

In the case of domestic wine, the maximum volatile acidity must not be more than $0.14g/100cm^3$ ($20^{\circ}C$) for natural red wine and 0.12 g for other grape wine. Volatile acidity is calculated as acetic acid exclusive of sulfur dioxide.

Grape wine may be designated as "red wine," "pink (or rose) wine," "amber wine," or "white wine," depending on the presence or absence of the red coloring matter of the skins, juice, or pulp of grapes. Any grape wine containing no added grape brandy or alcohol may be further designated as "natural."

Dessert wine is grape wine having an alcoholic content of 14% to 24% by volume. Further designation of various dessert wine is given in Table 7-8. For further details on the standards of identity for other classes and types of wine, refer to the original document.

TABLE 7-8. Various Designations of Dessert Wine. Adapted from 27 CFR 4, "Standards of Identity of Wine"

Taste, Aroma, and Characteristics Generally Attributed to	Percent of alcoholic content by volume (derived in part from added grape brandy or alcohol)	Designation
Sherry	17+	"sherry"
Angelica, madeira, muscatel, port	18+	"angelica," "madeira," "muscatel," or "port," respectively
Sherry	14 to 17	"light sherry"
Angelica, madeira, muscatel, port	14 to 18	"light angelica," "light madeira," "light muscatel," or "light port," respectively

What are certain labeling requirements for wine? According to 27 CFR 4, no person in the alcoholic beverage business is permitted to handle the products in any manner unless such wine is packaged and the packages are labeled in conformity with specific requirements. Examples of these requirements are given in the following paragraphs.

Each label on a package of beverage must carry certain mandatory label information. It is required to include: a legal brand name; class, type, or other specific designations; name and address of domestic (or foreign) manufacturer; percentage of foreign wine present in the product if any foreign origin is claimed; alcoholic content; net contents; and certain required information for imported wine.

The statement of alcoholic content must conform to the following criteria. The statement is needed if the wine contains more than 14% of alcohol by volume. For wines with less than 14% alcohol by volume, either the alcoholic content or the type designation such as "table" wine (or "light" wine) must be stated. The description of alcoholic content must be in terms of percentages of alcohol by volume, such as:

1. "Alcohol....% by volume"--In general, when the wine contains 14+% or 0% to
    14% of alcohol by volume, the permitted tolerance is respectively ± 1% or
    ± 1.5%.
2. "Alcohol....% to....% by volume"--In general, when the wine contains 14+% or
    0% to 14% of alcohol by volume, a range of 0% to 2% or 0% to 3% will be per-
    mitted between the minimum and maximum percentages stated, and no toler-
    ance will be permitted either below such minimum or above such maximum.

Also, the statement of alcoholic content must be consistent with that of the class
and type of wine indicated.

When a standard of fill is prescribed for a wine, its net content must be stated
according to established criteria as described in 27 CFR 4. If no standard of fill is
prescribed for a wine, its net content must use the following metric criteria:

1. If the content is more than 1 liter, use decimal portions of a liter accurate to
    the nearest one-hundredth of a liter.
2. If the content is less than 1 liter, use milliliters (ml). However, if the wine was
    bottled before December 31, 1978, the net content may be stated in U.S. fluid
    measure.

When the volume of wine within the container is indicated by the net content,
the following tolerances are permitted:

1. Discrepancies due exclusively to errors in measuring. These may occur in fill-
    ing even if good commercial practice is complied with.
2. Discrepancies due exclusively to differences in the capacity of containers.
    These may result from the unavoidable difficulties in manufacturing containers
    of uniform capacity.
3. Discrepancies in measure due to differences in atmospheric conditions in vari-
    ous places. These are usually unavoidable and may result from the ordinary
    and customary exposure of alcoholic beverages in containers to evaporation.
    However, the degree in discrepancies in this situation is subjected to the con-
    sideration of the Bureau of Alcohol, Tobacco, and Firearms.

In addition to mandatory information, all labels are required to be so designed
that all statements are readily legible under ordinary conditions and set on a con-
trasting background. The size of the script, type, or printing must follow specified
requirements. Further, all mandatory label information must be stated in the English language. However, the brand name, the place of production, and the name of

the manufacturer, producer, blender, bottler, packer, or shipper appearing on the label need not be in the English language if the words "product of" immediately precede the name of the country of origin stated in accordance with regulations of the Bureau of Customs. Additional statements in foreign language may be made on the labels, if they are not contrary to the regulations of the Bureau of Alcohol, Tobacco, and Firearms. It is emphasized that only selected information from the Code of Federal Regulations is discussed here; interested parties should consult 27 CFR 4 and 43 FR 37672 to 37678 (August 23, 1978).

According to Table 7-6, 27 CFR 240 is another important part devoted entirely to the wine business; it is titled simply "Wine." Appendix 7-6 describes the subpart titles of Part 240. The titles show that the regulations in this part relate to the production and removal of wine, including special natural wine and effervescent wine, from bonded wine cellars. They describe the establishment and operation of bonded wine cellars for (either or all):

1. The production, amelioration, sweetening, addition of wine spirits, blending, and other cellar treatment; storage; taxpayment, transfer to customs manufacturing warehouse and removal for exportation.
2. Experimental or research purposes by scientific institutions.
3. Analysis or testing by or for the proprietor of a bonded wine cellar.
4. Use of the Government of the United States.
5. Analysis, testing, research, or experimentation by the governments of the several States.
6. Use as distilling material.
7. Use in the manufacture of vinegar.

It should be pointed out that federal regulations are not really "how-to" handbooks. They do not describe a process of production or manufacture from "a" to "z." Rather, they emphasize the do's and don't's in the process. To illustrate the contents of 27 CFR 240, some aspects of selected sections are discussed in the following paragraphs.

According to Appendix 7-6, Subpart B explains some terms used in the wine industry. "Amelioration" means the addition to juice or wine of water, sugar, or both at any stage before, during, or after fermentation. The sugar may be dry sugar, liquid sugar, or invert sugar syrup. Amelioration adjusts the acid content or develops alcohol by fermentation.

Bonded wine cellars are defined as the officially registered premises for wine production operations. Premises must be provided by any person wishing to establish operation for the production, blending, cellar treatment, storage, bottling, packaging, or repackaging of untaxpaid wine (other than cider, family wine, or experimental wine produced free of tax). The person must apply and file bond with the bureau's regional office and must be granted official permission to operate a bonded wine cellar. The procedure for application and approval varies with the production and storage capacity desired.

"Lees" means the settlings of wine.

Proof denotes the ethyl alcohol content of a liquid at $60^\circ F$ and is stated as twice the percent of ethyl alcohol by volume. A proof gallon contains 50% of ethyl alcohol by volume and is the alcoholic equivalent of a U.S. gallon at $60^\circ F$.

Pure sugar is pure refined sugar produced from cane, beets, or fruit, or from grain or other sources of starch. It is suitable for human consumption and contains a dextrose equivalent of not less than 95% on a dry basis.

Liquid sugar is a near colorless sugar and water solution with at least 60% of pure sugar by weight (60° Brix). An invert sugar syrup is a solution of invert sugar prepared by a standard method of inversion from pure sugar. It is near colorless with at least 60% of sugar by weight (60° Brix).

Subpart O (see Appendix 7-6) describes the production of wine. Some aspects of this subpart are summarized as follows. The kinds of wine authorized to be produced on bonded wine cellar premises and in accordance with established regulations include: (1) natural wine, including sparkling wine and artificially carbonated wine, (2) specially sweetened natural wine, (3) special natural wine, (4) agricultural wine, and (5) wine other than standard wine.

What is the juice used for the production of standard wine? It may be: (1) a concentrated fruit juice reduced with water to any degree of Brix between its original density and 22° Brix or (2) an unconcentrated fruit juice reduced with water to not less than 22° Brix. When a proprietor receives a concentrated fruit juice on bonded wine cellar premises, he must obtain from the producer a certificate stating the kind of fruit juice from which it was produced and total solids content of such juice before and after concentration. Also, if the shipment is received from a concentrate plant, the producer must also state whether the volatile fruit flavor has been removed and if so, whether the identical flavor has been restored. If the proprietor receives an unconcentrated fruit juice processed at a concentrate plant, he is required to obtain a certificate from the producer stating similar information regarding the volatile fruit flavor.

Concentrated or unconcentrated fruit juice may be used in juice or wine made from the same kind of fruit for purposes of developing alcohol by fermentation or for sweetening. Concentrated fruit juice or juice that has been concentrated and reconstituted is not permitted for use in standard wine production if it has been concentrated to more than 80° Brix.

What is the regulation regarding the use of essences, flavors, or coloring? Essences, flavors, or coloring are permitted for use in accordance with established regulations and include the use of: (1) natural essences, natural flavors, or caramel coloring in the production of special natural wine, (2) hops in the production of honey wine, and (3) volatile fruit-flavor concentrate in the production of natural grape and fruit wines.

The use in wine of essences, flavoring, or coloring, other than as authorized by established regulations, results in the production of an imitation or compound wine, with liability to rectification tax, and is permitted only on the bottling premises of a distilled spirits plant.

What is the regulation regarding the use of volatile fruit-flavor concentrated in cellar treatment of natural wine? In the cellar treatment of natural wine, volatile fruit-flavor concentrate produced from: (1) the same variety of grape or the same kind and variety of berry may be added to natural grape or berry wine of the winemaker's own production, or (2) the same kind of fruit may be added to natural fruit wine other than grape or berry of the winemaker's own production.

What is the regulation regarding the use of juice or must from which volatile fruit flavor has been removed? Even though volatile fruit flavor has been removed, the juice, concentrated juice, or must processed at a concentrate plant is considered as pure as long as equivalent quantity of volatile fruit-flavor concentrate is added back at the concentrate plant or added to wine of the winemaker's own production made from such juice or must. Of course, the fruit-flavor concentrate must have derived from the corresponding grape, berry, or fruit.

Subpart P (see Appendix 7-6) describes the production and treatment of natural wine. Only the regulations relating to the production of wine without the use of sugar are presented in the following paragraph.

In the production of natural grape wine without the use of sugar, only the following materials may be added to the juice or crushed grapes at the time of starting fermentation:

1. Water. This serves to reduce the juice to not less than 22° Brix of total solids.
2. Yeast, or yeast cultures grown in grape juice. No limit on the amount added.
3. Yeast foods, sterilizing agents, or other fermentation adjuncts. They must all belong to an approved list issued by the Bureau of Alcohol, Tobacco, and Firearms.

With reference to the use of water at the time of crushing, including that necessary to flush equipment, it is noted in (1) (above) that the density of the juice must not be reduced below 22° Brix in the production of natural wine. However, if the wine is not produced from high acid grapes and the total solids content of the juice is less than 23° Brix, water used to flush equipment is permitted to reduce the total solids content of the juice by less than 1° Brix. On removal of wine from fermenters, the quantity of liquid should be determined and recorded accurately. Also, the quantity of liquid in the fermenters at the close of each month must be reported on a special form provided.

Natural grape wine produced without the use of sugar may be sweetened before or after the addition of wine spirits with concentrated or unconcentrated grape juice. However, the total solids content of the finished wine should not exceed 21% by weight. Any natural grape wine produced without the use of sugar may be sweetened with pure dry or liquid sugar after removal from the fermenters if the following criteria are met:

1. The initial and final total solids content by weight of the wine does not exceed 12%.
2. The alcoholic content of the finished wine is not more than 14% by volume.
3. The use of liquid or dry sugar will not result in a final volume exceeding the maximum permitted.
4. A record of sweetening must be kept in accordance with established procedures if liquid sugar is used.
5. The gallons of wine determined before and after sweetening must be recorded in accordance with established procedures if concentrated or unconcentrated grape juice or pure dry sugar is used.

To correct the natural deficiencies in the fruit, juice, or wine made from certain grapes, only acids of the kinds occurring in such grapes may be used. However, the finished wine must not contain more than 8 ppt of fixed acid (calculated as tartaric acid). If authorized ameliorating material is used in the production of grape wine, no acid may be used to correct the deficiencies. However, the bureau permits the use of citric acid to stabilize any grape wine. Only tartaric, citric, or malic acid may be added to the juice or wine of grapes to correct the natural deficiencies, and the use of any acid must be recorded in accordance with regulations. However, if acids other than those authorized are to be used, special requirements must be followed.

Subpart ZZ (see Appendix 7-6) describes the materials authorized by the bureau for the treatment of wine. These substances have been approved as being consistent with good commercial practice, for use by proprietors of bonded wine cellars in the production, cellar treatment, or finishing of wine (including distilled material). These substances should not alter the character of the wine to the extent inconsistent with good commercial practice. Also, there are specific limitations in the use of some of the chemicals. Further, if the FDA removes any substance on this approved list from the status of generally recognized as safe (see Chapter 6), the bureau may also cancel its approved use. In the following, some examples of such substances are described and their uses indicated, although the specific references or limitations are not included. Complete details are available in the original document.

Acetic acid	To correct natural deficiencies in grape wine
Acidex	To reduce excess natural acidity in wine
Activated carbon	To assist precipitation during fermentation, clarify and purify wine, and remove excess color in white wine
Atmos 300	As antifoaming agent
Bentonite	To clarify wine
Bentonite slurry	To clarify wine
Bone charcoal	To clarify wine
Calcium sulfate	For production of Spanish type or Flor sherry wine
Carbon	To clarify and purify wine
Carbon dioxide	To stablize and preserve wine and maintain counterpressure during transfer of finished sparkling wines
Citric acid	To increase the acidity of wine
Compressed air	For aeration of sherry wine
Copper sulfate	To clarify and stabilize grape wine and for treatment of distilled material
Cufex	To remove trace metal from wine
Diatomaceous earth and agar/agar	For filtering and clarifying wine
Eggs (albumen or yolks)	To clarify wine
Fermcozyme Vin	To clarify and stabilize wine
Ferrix	To remove trace metal from wine
Gelatin	To clarify wine
Gum arabic	To clarify and stablize wine
Ion-exchange resins	For treatment of wine
Klerzyme H. T.	To clarify and stabilize wine and facilitate separation of fruit from juice
Oak chips (charred)	To treat Spanish type blending sherry
Oxygen	In baking or maturing wine
Phosphates	As yeast food in distilling material and wine production and to start secondary fermentation in manufacturing champagne and sparkling wines
Potassium carbonate	To reduce excess natural acidity in wine
Promine-D	To clarify and stabilize wine
Sodium caseinate	To clarify wine
Sorbic acid	As a sterilizing and preservative agent and to inhibit mold growth and secondary fermentation
Tannin	To clarify grape wine
Tartaric acid	To increase acidity of grape wine
Urea	To facilitate fermentation of wine
Veltol (maltol)	As a stabilizing and smoothing agent
Veltol plus	For smoothing and stabilizing wine
Yeastex	To facilitate fermentation

To illustrate the specific limitations imposed on some of these substances, we examine some examples. Thus when cufex is used to remove trace metal from wine, no insoluble or soluble residue in excess of 1 ppm is permitted to remain in the finished wine and the basic character of the wine should not be changed by such treatment. When oxygen is used in baking or maturing wine, it should not produce changes in the wine other than those occurring during the usual storage in wooden cooperage over a period of time. The user must file an application. When urea is used to facilitate fermentation of wine, the amount used should not exceed 2 pounds per 1000 gallons of wine.

If the proprietor desires to use materials or methods not specifically authorized, he must file a notice or application of his intention. The notice should show the name and description of the material or method, the purpose, the manner and the extent to which it is to be used, and any other information pertinent to the material or method. If requested, a sample of the material should be forwarded to the bureau. The notice may be accompanied by any data or written statements purporting to indicate that the proposed use of the material or method is a cellar treatment consistent with good commercial practice. The proprietor is not permitted to use such method or material until an official decision or approval has been issued by authorized bureau personnel.

We have completed a brief discussion of the regulations contained in 27 CFR 4 and 240.

When the "sources of information" were presented earlier, the term "rulings" was used frequently. In the following an example of the bureau's ruling on regulations related to wine is provided. Alcohol, Tobacco, and Firearms (ATF) Ruling 74-10 is referenced in the 1974 Cumulative Bulletin of the bureau, and the following is adapted from the original ruling.

The bureau was asked whether small amounts of coumarin would be permitted in "May wine" if its presence were a natural result of using the leaves or essences of woodruff herbs as a flavoring material.

When the bureau takes an action or makes a ruling relating to the use of material in wine production, it follows the published regulations of the FDA, since the latter determines the use of an additive in a food product and wine is defined as a food product by federal statute.

Because of the toxicity of coumarin, the FDA had declared that foods and beverages to which coumarin had been added would be regarded as adulterated. That declaration resulted in the issuance of Internal Revenue Ruling 56-627 (C.B. 1956-2, 1043, IRS) to inform winemakers and rectifiers that formulas containing that substance as an ingredient would not be approved. In response to the bureau's request for amplification of the regulations governing the use of coumarin in food and beverage products, the FDA advised that the presence of a small amount of coumarin in a product would be acceptable if it was there as a result of the use of woodruff herbs, leaves, or essences (i.e., naturally) and not otherwise added to the product. However, if coumarin was added as a separate ingredient, the resultant product would be regarded as adulterated.

In view of these facts, the bureau held that "May wine," a product made from light natural white grape wine flavored with woodruff herbs, leaves, or essences, was permitted to contain coumarin in such quantity as not to exceed 5 ppm and would not be regarded as adulterated if the presence of that substance were the natural result of the use of woodruff herbs, and so on. Thus Revenue Ruling 56-627, C.B. 1956-2, 1043 (Internal Revenue) was thereby modified.

Another topic presented earlier was "offers in compromise" of criminal and/or civil liabilities incurred. The bureau began to publish some of such "administrative actions" in its monthly bulletin, beginning with the January 1976 issue, although such data would not be included in the annual Cumulative Bulletin. In the following some administrative actions relating to offers in compromise that have been accepted by the bureau are listed. They have been obtained from the monthly issues of the ATF Bulletin for 1976 and whenever available show the specific violation of federal laws and regulations governing wine production, sale, and other aspects.

Announcement 76-12
Reference in bulletin: January 12, 1976, page 19
Sections violated: Not specified
Amount offered in compromise: $2,000 per winery, with a total of $4,000
Case description: The proprietor of two bonded wineries removed from each winery wine bearing unapproved labels, engaged in operations under a tradename without approval for the use of the tradename and bottled and removed wine bearing labels and case markings that did not identify the winery where the wine was bottled.

Announcement 76-16
Reference in bulletin: January 12, 1976, page 19
Sections violated: 26 U.S.C. 5364; 26 U.S.C. 5388(b), 27 U.S.C. 205(e), and 27 CFR 240.488
Amount offered in compromise: $5,000
Case description: The proprietor of a bonded winery produced and stored substandard wine on winery premises not qualified to produce substandard wine. In addition, the proponent removed substandard wine with improper labels from such premises.

Announcement 76-29
Reference in bulletin: February 13, 1976, page 15

Sections violated: 26 U.S.C. 5364, 27 CFR 240.488; 26 U.S.C. 5388, 27 U.S.C.
                     205(e)
Amount offered in compromise: $20,000
Case Description: The proprietor of a bonded winery produced and stored substandard wine on standard winery premises. The proprietor also removed such wine
with improper labels.

Announcement 76-35
Reference in bulletin: March 13, 1976, pages 10, 11
Sections violated: 26 U.S.C. 5041, 5368, 5382, 5387; 27 CFR 240.465, 240.566,
                     240.1052
Amount offered in compromise: $1,000
Case description: The proprietor of a bonded winery bottled and sold honey wine
produced without an approved formula. The proponent also produced, bottled,
and sold two kinds of grape wine containing alcohol in excess of 14% by volume
that were labeled and taxpaid as not more than 14% by volume.

Announcement 76-89
Reference in bulletin: September 10, 1976, page 23
Sections violated: 27 U.S.C. 205(e), 27 CFR 4.40(b)
Amount offered in compromise: $7,500
Case description: Banfi Products Corporation, Farmingdale, New York, a whole-
saler and importer of alcoholic beverages, altered Forms 1649, Application for and
Certification of Label Approval. Banfi submitted such altered certificates of label
approval to the U.S. Customs Service to obtain the release of wine from customs
custody.

Announcement 76-113
Reference in bulletin: December 14, 1976, page 19
Sections violated: 27 U.S.C. 205(f), 27 CFR 4.64(a)(1), 26 U.S.C. 5662
Amount offered in compromise: $10,000
Case description: Heublein, Inc., Hartford, Connecticut, caused to be published
during July and August 1975, at various locations throughout the country, adver-
tisements representing a still wine to be an effervescent wine. Although artificial-
ly carbonated, the wine is within the permissible carbon dioxide limits of still wine
for tax purposes, in accordance with 26 U.S.C. 5041, and is taxed as a still wine.
The wine had originally been imported into the United States as a "crackling rose."
However, at a later date it was found that the product was artificially carbonated
and thus not entitled to the "crackling" designation.

Announcement 76-114
Reference in bulletin: December 14, 1976, page 19
Sections violated: 27 U.S.C. 205(e), 27 CFR 4.36(b)(1), 4.30(a)
Amount offered in compromise: $7,500
Case description: Robin Fils & Cie., Ltd., Batavia, New York, a wholesaler and proprietor of a bonded winery, bottled, labeled, and shipped in interstate commerce wine that was mislabeled as to alcoholic content. An inspection of the proprietor's operations and premises, conducted in 1975, disclosed that in 1974 the proponent bottled and removed 7764 wine gallons of wine bearing labels that improperly stated the alcohol content.

Distilled Spirits

According to Table 7-6, the title of 27 CFR 5 is "Labeling and advertising of distilled spirits." Appendix 7-7 describes the complete section titles for this Part 5. In the following, selected information contained in some sections are presented, including definitions, standards of identity, labeling requirements, and advertising of distilled spirits.

Subpart B of 27 CFR 5 (see Appendix 7-7) provides some useful definitions. Thus age is the period during which, after distillation and before bottling, distilled spirits have been stored in oak containers. For example, age for bourbon whisky, rye whisky, wheat whisky, malt whisky, or rye malt whisky, and straight whiskies other than straight corn whisky, refer to the period when the whisky has been stored in charred new oak containers.

The term "distilled spirits" refers to ethyl alcohol, hydrated oxide of ethyl, spirits of wine, whisky, rum, brandy, gin, and other distilled spirits, including all dilutions and mixtures for nonindustrial use. However, the term excludes any mixture containing wine that has been bottled at 48° proof or less, and the mixture contains more than 50% wine on a proof:gallon basis. A "gallon" is a U.S. gallon of 231 cubic inches of alcoholic beverage at 60°F.

Subpart C of 27 CFR 5 describes the standards of identity for distilled spirits, the classes and types of which are presented in Table 7-9. Class 2, whisky, is discussed in the following paragraph.

Whisky is an alcoholic distillate from a fermented mash of grain produced at less than 190° proof in such a manner that the distillate possesses the taste, aroma, and characteristics generally attributed to whisky, usually stored in oak containers, and bottled at 80° or more proof. It also includes mixtures of such distillates for which no specific standards of identity have been prescribed.

One type of Class 2 distilled spirit is blended whisky or whisky--a blend. This mixture contains at least 20% of straight whisky on a proof:gallon basis and, sep-

TABLE 7-9. Classification and Type of Distilled Spirits. Adapted from 27 CFR 5,
"Standards of Identity for Distilled Spirits"

Class of Distilled Spirits	Name of the Class of Distilled Spirits	Types of Distilled Spirits within Class
1	Neutral spirits or alcohol	Vodka; grain spirits.
2	Whisky	Bourbon (rye, wheat, malt, rye malt, or corn) whisky; straight bourbon (rye, wheat, malt, rye malt or corn) whisky; whisky distilled from bourbon (rye, wheat, malt, or rye malt) mash; light whisky, blended whisky; blended rye (wheat, malt, rye malt, or corn) whisky; a blend of straight whiskies; a blend of straight rye (wheat, malt, rye malt, or corn) whiskies; spirit whisky; Scotch whisky; Irish whisky; blended Irish whisky; Canadian whisky; blended Canadian whisky.
3	Gin	Gin; distilled gin; dry gin; Geneva gin; old Tom gin.
4	Brandy	Brandy, fruit brandy; grape brandy; immature grape brandy; peach (apple or other fruit) brandy; cognac; dried fruit brandy; raisin brandy; lees brandy; pomace brandy; grappa brandy; residue brandy; neutral brandy; neutral citrus residue brandy; substandard brand (variety of such brandy, consult 27 CFR 5 for details).
5	Blended applejack	Blended applejack
6	Rum	Rum
7	Tequilla	Tequilla
8	Cordials and liqueurs	Cordials and liqueurs; sloe gin; rye liqueur; bourbon liqueur; rock and rye; rock and bourbon; rock and brandy; rock and rum; dry cordial or liqueur.
9	Flavored	Flavored brandy; flavored gin; flavored rum; flavored vodka; flavored whisky.
10	Imitations	A variety of imitation distilled spirits (consult 27 CFR 5 for more details).

Class of Distilled Spirits	Name of the Class of Distilled Spirits	Types of Distilled Spirits within Class
11	Geographical designations	Eau de Vie de Dantzig; Ojen; Swedish punch; Cognac; Armagnac; Greek brandy; Pisco brandy; Jamaica rum; Puerto Rico rum; Demerara rum; Scotch; (consult 27 CFR 5 for details).
12	Products without geographical designations but distinctive of a particular place	Consult 27 CFR 5 for details.

arately or in combination, whisky or neutral spirits. A blended whisky containing 50% or more on a proof:gallon basis one of the many types of straight whisky is designated by that specific type of straight whisky, for example, blended rye whisky (or rye whisky--a blend).

Gin is a Class 3 distilled spirit. It is a product obtained by mixing neutral spirits with or over juniper berries and other aromatics, by redistillation of distilled spirits, or by original distillation from mash, and includes mixtures of gin and neutral spirits. It derives its main characteristic flavor from juniper berries and is bottled at 80° or more proof. Gin produced exclusively by original distillation or by redistillation may be further designated as "distilled." "Dry gin" (London dry gin), "Geneva gin" (Hollands gin), and "old Tom gin" (Tom gin) are types of gin known under such designations.

There are many specific requirements for the labels of distilled spirits. The following discusses two aspects mentioned in Subpart D of 27 CFR 5 (see Appendix 7-7).

Thus the alcohol content must be stated by proof for distilled spirits, except it may be stated in percentage by volume for cordials and liqueurs, cocktails, highballs, bitters, and such other specialties as specified by the Bureau of Alcohol, Tobacco, and Firearms. Some details about the statements of age and percentage of alcohol on the labels are given in the following paragraph.

In the case of most straight whiskies 4 or more years old, statements of age and percentage are optional. All other whiskies are required to carry a specific statement. Thus in the case of whisky, whether or not mixed or blended, but containing no neutral spirits, the age of the youngest whisky must be stated, for example, "...years old." Age may, but need not, be stated on labels of rums, brandies, and tequila, except that an appropriate statement with respect to age must appear on the brand label in case of certain brandy not stored in oak containers for a period of at least 2 years. The statement should be "...years old," with the blank to be filled in with the age of the youngest distilled spirits in the product.

In case of grain spirits, the period of storage in oak containers may be stated in immediate conjunction with the required percentage statement, for example, "...% grain spirits stored...years in oak containers."

Subpart H of 27 CFR 5 (see Appendix 7-7) prescribes detailed information on the advertising of distilled spirits. Thus strict federal regulations prohibit any person engaged in business as a distiller, rectifier, importer, wholesaler, or warehouseman and bottler of distilled spirits from disseminating any false advertisement for the purpose of inducing sales of his products. The mandatory statements in an advertising medium must include the name and address of the permittee responsible for its publication or broadcast, the class and type of the product, the alcoholic content, and the percentage of neutral spirits and the name of commodity. Further, the lettering of any printed advertisement is required to be conspicuous and readily legible. Some prohibited statements in an advertisement for distilled spirits are described as follows:

1. Any statement that is false or untrue in any particular.
2. Any statement that is disparaging of a competitor's product.
3. Any obscene or indecent statement.
4. The words "double distilled," "triple distilled," or similar representations.
5. Any statement inconsistent with representations on product label.
6. Any statement concerning age or maturity of any brand of product unless such a statement also appears on the product label.
7. Any statement claiming that the use of the product has curative or therapeutic effects if such is not the case.
8. Any statement claiming that the distilled spirits have been manufactured in or imported from a place or country other than that of their actual origin.
9. Two or more different brands of product are not permitted to appear in one advertisement if the latter tends to create the impression that the representations made as to one brand apply to the other.
10. Any statement or design that may be construed as related to the Armed Forces of the United States or the American flag.
11. Any statement that is untrue in any particular or tends to create a misleading impression.

For further details about 27 CFR 5, consult the original document.

In the past the bureau has issued numerous rulings concerning the regulations in 27 CFR 5. The following cites an example of such rulings (ATF Ruling 76-3, as referenced in the 1976 Cumulative Bulletin).

The bureau was asked to clarify its position on the use of the words "charcoal filtered" appearing on labels to be used on bottles of vodka treated with activated carbon. In the past, the bureau considered that such labeling might be deceptive and in violation of 27 CFR 5.42 because of the method of treatment and filtration employed in some instances.

The regulations in 27 CFR 5.22 prescribe that vodka is a neutral spirit so distilled, or so treated after distillation with charcoal or other materials, as to be without distinctive character, aroma, taste, or color. The regulations in 27 CFR 5.42 prohibit the use of any labels that contain any statement that is false or untrue in any particular or that tends to create a misleading impression.

At the time of the inquiry there was an increase in the use of "activated carbon" in the treatment and filtration of distilled spirits and in the use of bottle labels bearing the designation "charcoal filtered." According to standard government publication, "activated carbon" is the same as "activated charcoal." After considering various methods for treating vodka with activated carbon for the purpose of determining what would constitute charcoal filtering for labeling purposes, the bureau concluded and held that the treatment (and subsequent filtration) of vodka with not less than one ounce of activated carbon or activated charcoal per 100 wine gallons of spirits would entitle it to be labeled as "charcoal." See Revenue Ruling 69-496, CB 1969-2, 272 (Internal Revenue) for other labeling requirements for vodka.

"Distilled spirits plants" is the title of 27 CFR 201 (see Table 7-6). The regulations in this part relate to the location, construction, equipment, arrangement, qualification, and operation (including activities incidental to such operation) of distilled spirits plants. Appendix 7-8 describes all the subparts contained in Part 201 and the corresponding sections each covers. In the following, some aspects of Subparts B, F, and I are presented.

Subpart B provides a number of definitions. Thus premises are defined as those of a distilled spirits plant that are specifically identified in the application for federal registration and on which operations relating to the production, storage, denaturation, or bottling of spirits prior to payment or determination of tax are authorized to be conducted.

When the term "in bond" is used with respect to spirits, it refers to such spirits processed under bond to secure the payment of the internal revenue tax. The plant number is the number assigned to a distilled spirits plant by an authorized bureau personnel, preceded by the abbreviation of the state in which the plant is located and the letters "DSP" (e.g., "DSP-Md-17").

Proof of distillation is the composite proof of the spirits at the time the production gauge is made. Or, if the spirits had been reduced in proof prior to the production gauge, the proof of the spirits prior to such reduction becomes the proof of distillation unless the spirits are subsequently redistilled at a higher proof than the proof prior to the reduction.

A rectifier describes two types of individuals. First, a rectifier is any person who rectifies, purifies, or refines distilled spirits or wines by any process other than by original and continuous distillation, or original and continuous processing from mash, wort, wash, or any other substance, through continuous closed vessels and pipes, until the product is complete. Second, a rectifier is any person who, without rectifying, purifying, or refining distilled spirits, mixes distilled spirits, wine, or other liquor with any material to manufacture any spurious, imitation, or compound liquors for sale, under the name of whisky, brandy, rum, gin, wine, spirits, cordials, wine bitters, or any other name. A rectifier is considered as being engaged in the business of rectifying.

A tax gallon is the unit of measure of spirits for the imposition of tax. When spirits are 100° proof or more at the time of tax determination, the tax is determined on a proof:gallon basis. When spirits are less than 100° proof at the time of tax determination, the tax is determined on a wine gallon basis.

"Wine spirits" mean brandy or wine spirits produced in a distilled spirits plant (with or without the use of water to facilitate extraction and distillation) exclusively from fresh or dried fruit or their residues, the wine or wine residues therefrom, or special natural wine. However, there are many limitations to the definition of wine spirits, and the original document should be consulted for further details.

In Subpart F of 27 CFR 201 (see Appendix 7-8), the qualification of a distilled spirits plant is described in detail. Some aspects are discussed as follows. A person is required to make application for the bureau's legal approval of engaging in the business of a distiller, bonded warehouseman, rectifier, or bottler of distilled spirits. Such application for registration, as is officially known, should be made on a specific form and submitted to the nearest assistant regional commissioner of the bureau. Each application, including all written statements, affidavits, and other supporting documents, must be executed under penalties of perjury. Among numerous other data and information to be included in the application form, the following are of special interest to this chapter. They include the statement of the business to be conducted; details of the plant such as location, plat, and plants; description and list of major equipment; and other required information in accordance with the business desired. Thus if the application is for the business of a distiller, the application must include a statement of the following:

1.   Daily production capacity in proof gallons.
2.   Maximum proof gallons that will be produced during a period of 15 days and in transit to the bonded premises. This is not necessary if the maximum sum has been rendered for the qualification bond.
3.   Process.

4. The inclusion of denaturing operations if such is the case.
5. Title to the bonded premises and interest in the equipment used for the production of distilled spirits. If required, the applicant must submit a statement of consent on a special form.

If the applicant desires to be in the business of a bonded warehouseman, he must provide a statement of:

1. The maximum proof gallons that will be stored on, and in transit to, the bonded premises. This is, again, not required if the qualification bond is in the maximum sum.
2. Storage capacity (bulk, packages, and cases), including a description of the system of storage.
3. The type of operations, whether denaturing or "bottling in bond."

Other information will be required of the applicant who desires to be in the business of rectifier, bottling after tax determination, and other operations to be conducted on the plant premises. For further details, consult the original document. One requirement mentioned in the preceding paragraph that is of special interest is the statement of process. Such a statement in the application for registration is required to provide a step-by-step description of the process employed to produce spirits, commencing with the treating, mashing, or fermenting of the raw materials or substances and continuing through each step of the distilling, redistilling, purifying, and refining processes to the production gauge. The statement should detail the kind and approximate quantity of each material or substance used in the process. If the proprietor desires to produce a new product or make a change in a production process that may affect the designation or character of the original product, he must file an application and receive approval. The new or changed process may not be used prior to official approval.

Subpart I of 27 CFR 201 (see Appendix 7-8) describes the use of materials in the production of spirits. The proprietor may produce spirits in the production facilities from any suitable material in accordance with the statements of process in his notice of registration. The distillation or processing of nonpotable chemical mixtures is considered as an original or continuous distillation of the spirits in such mixtures and constitutes a production of spirits. Materials from which alcohol will not be produced may be used in the production processes only if the use of such materials is described in the approved statements of process.

Regulations govern the removal or destruction of distilling material. The latter is not permitted to be removed from the production facilities before being distilled, except where such removal is authorized by the proper bureau official. The residue of distilling material not introduced into the production system may be removed from the premises after notifying the officer on duty after expressing liquid from the material before removal and assuring that such liquid will not be received at any distilled spirits plant or bonded wine cellar. Residues of beer used as distilled material may be returned to the producing brewery. Distilling material produced and wine and beer received for use as distilling material may be destroyed after giving proper notice to the officer on duty.

Some details about the distilling process are as follows. It is specifically required that the process of distillation in the production facilities be such that the spirits pass through continuous, closed stills, pipes, and vessels from the first still until the production process is completed. The distiller may, in the course of manufacture, carry his product through as many distilling operations as he may desire, provided that the process is closed and continuous. Distilling processes are deemed to be continuous where the spirits are carried through the various steps of production as expeditiously as plant operation will permit. The collection of unfinished spirits for the purpose of redistillation is not considered a break in the continuity of the process. However, the quantity and proof of any unfinished spirits produced from distilling materials must be determined and recorded before any mingling with other materials or before any further processing of the unfinished spirits. Where spirits are percolated through oak chips or otherwise treated, the temporary retention of the spirits in tanks pending such treatment is permissible. Spirits may be held prior to the production gauge only for so long as is reasonably necessary to complete the production process.

Some aspects of the treatment during production of spirits are as follows. In the course of original and continuous distillation in the production facilities, the spirits may be purified or refined through any material that will not remain incorporated in the finished product. Juniper berries and other natural aromatics may be used in the distillation of gin. Spirits may be percolated through oak chips that have not been treated with any chemical. The introduction of any substances into the tanks during hours not directly supervised by bureau personnel must be accomplished by mechanical devices that effectively prevent the removal of spirits. Materials used in the treatment of spirits must be destroyed after having served the purpose, to prevent unauthorized extraction of potable spirits from such materials.

According to Table 7-6, 27 CFR 250 describes the regulations for "liquors and articles from Puerto Rico and the Virgin Islands." These regulations are related to the production, bonded warehousing, and withdrawal of distilled spirits; the manufacture of articles in Puerto Rico and the Virgin Islands to be brought into the United States free of tax; and the collection of internal revenue taxes on taxable alcoholic products coming into the United States from Puerto Rico and the Virgin Islands. Appendix 7-9 provides the subpart titles of 27 CFR 250 and the sections each subpart covers. In the following, some aspects of Subparts C and D are discussed.

According to Subpart C titled "Products coming into the United States from Puerto Rico," most liquors coming into the United States from Puerto Rico are subject to a tax equal to that levied on domestic products. Products exempt from tax include industrial and denatured spirits. Containers of distilled spirits brought into the United States from Puerto Rico having a capacity of not more than 1 gallon (3.768 liters) should conform to established requirements. All labels affixed to bottles of liquors should follow provisions of the Federal Alcohol Administration Act and related regulations in 27 CFR 4, 5, and 7. To be shipped to the United States, each case, barrel, cask, or similar container filled with distilled spirits is required to be serially numbered by the distiller, rectifier, or bottler. Also, on a designated location of each container, there must be plainly printed, stamped, or stenciled with durable coloring material, in letters and figures ½ inch or more in height, the name of the distiller, rectifier, or bottler, the brand name and kind of liquor, the wine and proof gallon contents, the serial number of the approved formula under which made, and, in the case of barrels or casks, the serial number of the withdrawal permit. All these printings must not be obliterated or obscured until after the contents have been removed. After the contents have been emptied, the printing on the containers may be removed in accordance with established regulations. To determine the rate of taxation, the bureau may require samples of liquors to be submitted whenever necessary for laboratory analysis.

Subpart D of 27 CFR 250 (see Appendix 7-9) describes the regulations covering the formulas and processes for products from Puerto Rico. In advance of shipping to the United States, a person must submit to the bureau formulas and processes covering the manufacture of such liquors. Each formula should be given a serial number, beginning with number 1 for the first and continuing in series thereafter. However, any person who has filed formulas before should continue to use the series he has adopted. Formulas for liquors (except beer) must show on the application form the kind, brand name, proof of the product, and all ingredients composing the product. If wine only or wine and distilled spirits are used in any product, the quantity or percentage by volume of each and the percent of alcohol by volume of the wine must be shown. If used, the percentage of coloring, flavoring, sweetening, or blending materials must also be shown. If any of the liquors named in the formula are made outside of Puerto Rico, the country of origin must be stated.

The statement of process must set out in sequence each step used in the manufacture of the finished product. If it is for distilled spirits, the statement must indicate what kind, if any, of liquors 190° or less proof are blended together to manufacture the finished product. Therefore, are the liquors of different ages? Do they differ in kind according to known standards of identity? Most important of all, are the liquors distilled from different materials, by different distillers, at different distilleries, or from different combinations of the same materials? Also, the statement of process must show whether spirits that have been subjected to a certain treatment that alters their characters are to be mixed with spirits not so treated or treated with other procedures. For example, will quick-aged or wood chips treated spirits be mixed with untreated spirits? Or will spirits stored in plain, reused, or metal cooperage be mixed with spirits stored in charred new oak containers?

If the statement includes still wine and the addition of carbon dioxide to such wine, the method or process and the type of equipment used must be stated. The amount of carbon dioxide allowed in the wine should be as follows:

	Maximum limit	Maximum limit permitted due to unavoidable mechanical variations
Gram of carbon dioxide per 100 ml of still wine	0.392 or less	0.401

The tolerance shown is not permitted if the data continuously or intentionally exceed 0.392 or if the variation results from the use of equipment or methods not considered as good commercial practices.

The proprietor must submit a new form and application if there is any change in the ingredients composing a product covered by an approved formula or in the manufacture process. Approval and changed rate of taxation will be issued by the bureau. For further details on 27 CFR 250, consult the original document.

The following describes some of the administrative actions ("offers in compromise") taken by the bureau and published in the bulletin of 1976. They are all related to violations of laws and regulations governing the production, sale, and other aspects related to distilled spirits.

Announcement 76-43
Reference in bulletin: April 9, 1976, page 23
Sections violated: Several sections not specified
Amount offered in compromise: $7,500
Case description: The proprietor of a distilled spirits plant failed on numerous occasions to accurately gauge and properly record quantities of distilled spirits and flavoring materials used in rectifying and bottling operations.

Announcement 74-46
Reference in bulletin: April 9, 1976, page 23
Sections violated: 26 U.S.C. 5301(c); 27 CFR 173.41, 173.42, 173.43, 194.261, 194.262

Amount offered in compromise: $50
Case description: Larry D. Shipman, a retail liquor dealer of Morones, Inc., Marion, Indiana, refilled a liquor bottle that was in his possession with spirits other than those contained in such a bottle at the time of stamping.

Announcement 76-59
Reference in bulletin: May 14, 1976, page 22
Sections violated: 26 U.S.C. 5301(c); 27 CFR 173.41, 173.42, 194.261, 194.262
Amount offered in compromise: $150
Case description: John M. Burnie, a retail liquor dealer for Band Box Cocktail Lounge, Middletown, Ohio, refilled liquor bottles that were in his possession with spirits other than those contained in such bottles at the time of stamping.

Announcement 76-82
Reference in bulletin: August 13, 1976, page 18
Sections violated: 27 U.S.C. 205(e); 27 CFR 5.55
Amount offered in compromise: $1,250
Case description: A distilled spirits plant proprietor failed to obtain certificates of label approval, Forms 1649, or label exemption, Forms 1650, for labels used on spirits bottled and shipped in interstate commerce. Also, the proponent bottled, labeled, and shipped in interstate commerce, spirits that were mislabeled as to proof.

Announcement 76-83
Reference in bulletin: August 13, 1976, page 18
Sections violated: 27 U.S.C. 205(e); 27 CFR 5.55(a)
Amount offered in compromise: $2,000
Case description: A wholesale liquor dealer and importer, Murand Brothers Beverage Company, Chicago, Illinois, affixed labels to various distilled spirits products sold and shipped to retailers prior to official approval of such labels.

Announcement 76-88
Reference in bulletin: September 10, 1976, page 23
Sections violated: Numerous sections of law and regulations, not specified
Amount offered in compromise: $10,000
Case description: The proprietor of Frank-Lin Distillers Products, Ltd., DSP-CA-33, San Jose, California, failed to segregate control stock from other stock on control premises, to affix labels to filled bottles of distilled spirits that were in sealed cases, and to place mandatory marks on cases of distilled spirits. The proprietor also failed to destroy the marks on cases of distilled spirits emptied at the plant premises; failed to mark less than full cases as remnant cases; stored uncased,

labeled, and stamped bottles of distilled spirits off bottling premises; failed to determine the proof gallon content of wine dumped for use in rectification; and failed to furnish the assigned officer with a written schedule of operations or copies of completed Forms 122. In addition, the proprietor failed to mark bonded storage tanks containing distilled spirits as to kind of spirits, to submit a written application to relabel spirits, and to prepare an accurate record of removals from control stock for each day and for each return period.

Announcement 76-98
Reference in bulletin: October 15, 1976, page 5
Sections violated: 26 U.S.C. 5201(a); 27 CFR 201.422, 201.424
Amount offered in compromise: $75,000
Case description: The proprietor of a distilled spirits plant used alcoholic flavorings in which drawback had been claimed, in an intermediate product, pursuant to an approved formula that stipulated the use of alcoholic flavorings on which drawback had not been claimed. The distiller also used alcoholic flavorings on which drawback had been claimed in excess of the regulatory limitation of 2.5 of the total proof gallons in the finished product.

Announcement 76-99
Reference in bulletin: October 15, 1976, page 5
Sections violated: 26 U.S.C. 5201(a); 27 CFR 201.424, 201.425; 26 U.S.C. 5025(b), 27 U.S.C. 204(d), 205(e)
Amount offered in compromise: $10,000
Case description: The proprietor of Schenley Distillers, Inc., Schenley, Pennsylvania, used an excessive quantity of alcoholic flavoring materials in manufacturing rectified products and in manufacturing rum without an approved formula. The proprietor also failed to produce vodka in accordance with an approved formula, resulting in improper labeling of the finished product.

Announcement 76-108
Reference in bulletin: November 12, 1976, page 23
Sections violated: 26 U.S.C. 5301(c)
Amount offered in compromise: $500
Case description: John Furla and Gus Pathenos, proprietors of a retail liquor store, Press Cafeteria and Annex, St. Louis, Missouri, refilled liquor bottles that were in their possession, with spirits other than those contained in such bottles at the time of stamping.

The bureau also publishes another type of administrative action in the monthly issues of the bulletin that is not included in the cumulative bulletin. These are the recalls of alcoholic beverages; reasons for the recall vary. Some examples are described as follows.

Announcement 76-37 (ATF Bulletin, March 12, 1976, page 11). Consolidated Distilled Products, Inc., DSP-ILL-26, Chicago, Illinois, produced and distributed alcoholic beverages that were underproof. Consolidated bottled fifths and ½ pints of Aberdeen Walnut Cow having labels that indicated the product to be 30 proof, but which was actually only 29 proof. Consolidated also bottled fifths and ½ pints of Aberdeen Chocolate Mint having labels that indicated the product to be 30 proof but was actually 29.5 proof. To allow for normal losses in proof during bottling operations, the regulations in 27 CFR 201.459 permit a tolerance of as much as 0.3 proof below label proof. Therefore, since the drop in proof exceeded such tolerance in this case, a recall of the underproof products was initiated. Consolidated released to the market 297 cases of fifths and 59 cases of ½ pints of such underproof Aberdeen Walnut Cow; 31 cases of fifths and four cases of ½ pints were returned. Consolidated released to the market 311 cases of fifths and 80 cases of ½ pints of such underproof Aberdeen Chocolate Mint; four cases of ½ pints were returned. All such underproof merchandise that was not shipped or was returned, was to be reprocessed and rebottled within the limits prescribed by regulations before being released again to the market.

Announcement 76-77 (ATF Bulletin, July 9, 1976, page 26). "Vodka City" brand vodka, bottled by Montebello Brands, Inc., DSP-MD-18, Baltimore, Maryland, was withdrawn from the market after it was found to be underproof by the bureau. Montebello had sold to a distributor in Rochester, New York 15 cases of pints and 46 cases of quarts of Vodka City labeled as 110 proof before analyses of samples of the product taken by the bureau disclosed the proof to be below the tolerance of 0.3 degrees proof prescribed by 27 CFR 201.459. No other underproof Vodka City vodka had been removed from the Montebello premises. The Rochester distributor is returning 16 cases of quarts that were on hand at his premises. The returned vodka, along with other underproof vodka not removed from the Montebello premises, will be reprocessed and rebottled within the limitations prescribed by regulations before being released to the market.

Announcement 76-91 (ATF Bulletin, September 10, 1976, page 24). Jacquin-Florida Distilling Company, DSP-FL-8, Auburndale, Florida, bottled and distributed Jacquin's Grande Reserve Napoleon Brand French Brandy, which was subsequently found to be underproof by the bureau. Laboratory analysis disclosed the actual proof to be 79.45 degrees, whereas the bottle labels showed the proof to be 80 degrees. A recall of the brandy was initiated by the company. A total of 265 cases of 4/5 quarts and 250 cases of quarts of the deficient product had been shipped to wholesalers in Central and Southern Florida. Jacquin had been able to recover from the market 152 cases and seven bottles of quarts and 11 cases and 11 bottles of 4/5 quarts of the product. All such recovered merchandise will be reprocessed and rebottled within the limits prescribed by regulations before being released again to the market.

Announcement 76-112 (ATF Bulletin, December 14, 1976, page 19). Further investigations (refer to Announcement 76-91, above) indicated that gin, rum, and other liquors bottled by Jacquin-Florida Distilling Company, DSP-FL-8, Auburndale, Florida, were also low in proof. As many as 14,946 cases of such products were bottled below proof. The proprietor had dumped and reprocessed 6890 cases of the deficient products that had not been released to the market. In addition, all wholesalers were alerted to the problem, and, as a result, another 430 cases of such products had been returned for dumping and reconditioning. Jacquin was continuing its efforts to recover additional amounts of such underproof products. Before being released again to the market, all deficient merchandise found in the proprietor's inventory or recovered from the market would be reprocessed and rebottled within the proof limits prescribed by the regulations.

Beer

According to Table 7-6, 27 CFR 7 is related to labeling and advertising of malt beverages. The complete section titles of Part 7 are described in Appendix 7-10. Some aspects of definitions and labeling requirements are described as follows.

Subpart B of 27 CFR 7 provides the following definitions. A malt beverage is one prepared by the alcoholic fermentation of an infusion, decoction, or combination of both in potable brewing water of malted barley with hops, including their parts or products. The fermenting material may contain other malted cereals, unmalted or prepared cereals, other carbohydrates or their products, added carbon dioxide, and other wholesome products suitable for human consumption. A "container" means any can, bottle, barrel, keg, or other closed receptacle, irrespective of size or of the material from which made, for use for the sale of malt beverages in containers of a capacity of 1 gallon or less. A packer means any person who places malt beverages in containers of a capacity in excess of 1 gallon.

With reference to labeling requirements, subpart C of 27 CFR 7 (see Appendix 7-10) prescribes detail regulations, some of which are explained as follows. The class of the malt beverage must be stated on the label and, if desired, the type may also be stated. Statements of class and type must conform to the designation of the product as known to the trade. For further information on the class and type of malt beverages, refer to 27 CFR 245.5 and later discussion. If the product is not *known to the trade* under a particular designation, a distinctive or fanciful name should be stated and accompanied by a truthful and adequate statement of the composition of the product. Malt beverages concentrated by partial dehydration and reconstituted by the addition of water and carbon dioxide must be labeled in the same way as those not concentrated and reconstituted. However, the former must be accompanied by the statement "produced from...concentrate" (the blank to be filled in with the appropriate class designation). The class designation must be of the same size and kind of letterings.

The designation "half and half" is permitted only if the product is of equal parts of two classes of malt beverages the names of which are conspicuously stated with the designation "half and half."

No product containing less than 0.5% of alcohol by volume is permitted to use the class designations "beer," "lager beer," "lager," "ale," "porter," or "stout," or any other class or type designation normally used for malt beverages with higher alcoholic content.

To bear the class designation of "ale," "porter," or "stout," the product must be a malt beverage fermented at comparatively high temperature, possessing the unique characteristics generally attributed to such products and produced without the use of coloring or flavoring materials other than those recognized in standard brewing practices.

Geographical names for distinctive types of malt beverages must not be applied to malt beverages produced in any place other than the particular region indicated by the name unless special conditions are met. For example, it will be acceptable if, in direct conjunction with the name, there appears the word "type," the word "American," or some other term indicating the true place of production in lettering substantially as conspicuous as such name; or the malt beverages to which the name is applied conform to the type so designated, or the bureau has ruled that certain geographic names have become generic.

The following are examples of distinctive types of beer with geographical names that have not become generic: Dortmund, Dortmunder, Vienna, Wein, Weiner, Bavarian, Munich, Munchner, Salvator, Klumbacher, Wurtzburger, and Pilsen (Pilsener and Pilsber). However, beer produced in the United States may be designated as "Pilsen," "Pilsener," or "Pilsner" without further modification, if it conforms to such type. An example of a geographical name that the bureau has ruled as generic is India Pale Ale.

The alcoholic content and the percentage and quantity of the original extract of a malt beverage is not permitted on the label unless required by state law. The specific requirements of the state law should then be followed. However, when statement as to alcoholic content is required but the manner of statement is not specified in the state law, it must be stated in percentage of alcohol by weight or by volume, and not by proof or by maximums or minimums.

According to the regulations, certain statements are prohibited on the label for a malt beverage. Some examples are described as follows:

1. Any statement or representation relating to analyses, standards, or tests that the bureau considers as misleading to the consumer is prohibited. This applies irrespective of the falsity or validity of the statement.
2. With certain minor exceptions, the label cannot bear a tradename or brand name that is the name of any living individual of public prominence or existing private or public organization if the use of such name is likely to mislead the consumer to believe that the product has been endorsed by or produced in accordance with the specifications of such individual or organization.
3. The label is not permitted to use words such as "bonded," "bottled in bond," "aged in bond," "bonded age," "bottled under customs supervision," or similar phrases that imply governmental supervision over production, bottling, or packing.
4. The label is prohibited from using words such as "strong," "full strength," "extra strength," "high test," "high proof," "pre-war strength," "full old time alcoholic strength," or similar statements, since they may be considered as statements of alcoholic content. These words are acceptable if they are part of the requirements of a state law.
5. The label shall not contain any statements or designs, whether in the form of numerals, letters, characters, figures, or otherwise since they may be considered as statements of alcoholic content, unless, of course, such statements are required by a state law.

Refer to 27 CFR 7 for further details on the labeling and advertising of malt beverages.

An example of the bureau's rulings on some aspects of the regulations contained in Part 7 is described as follows (ATF Ruling 76-1, 1976 Cumulative Bulletin). The bureau was asked to comment on its position on caloric and carbohydrate references in malt beverages labeling and advertising.

In general, Sections 5(e) and 5(f) of the Federal Alcohol Administration Act (see Table 7-3) and regulations 27 CFR 7.29 and 7.54 prohibit the use of certain statements in advertisements for and on labels of malt beverages introduced into interstate commerce, if the laws of the state into which the malt beverages are to be shipped impose similar requirements. Prohibited statements include those that are untrue in any particular, tend to create a misleading impression, disparage a competitor's product, or imply that the use of any malt beverage has curative or therapeutic effects.

In 1955 the Alcohol Tobacco Tax Division of the Internal Revenue Service (the predecessor of the present bureau) completed a consumer survey to determine whether misleading implications were made through malt beverage advertising. It found that a substantial percentage of the consumers contacted received the impression that so-called "low caloric" beers were either entirely nonfattening or at least negligible in caloric content, that they were less fattening than other competitive beers, that the consumer could lose weight by drinking them, that those products were approximately equal in food value to the food items with which their calorie content was compared, or that the advertised product could be substituted for such food items with the same nutritional results. In view of this, the malt beverage industry was advised in Industry Circular 55-7 and in Revenue Ruling 55-404, C.B. 1955-1, 615 (Internal Revenue), of the misleading aspects of low caloric themes and was requested to promptly desist from the use of any further references to the calorie content of their products and to more specific implications, however made, that their products were not fattening or virtually so.

During the 1960s the Alcohol and Tobacco Tax Division held extensive conferences with the FDA concerning the labeling of various so-called "low calorie/low carbohydrate" beers being introduced into the commercial market. By mutual agreement, statements of average analysis on labels for these beers were permitted, provided no further carbohydrate claim was made. However, a truthful caloric comparison between a low calorie product and that of an equal volume of the brewer's regular beer was permitted to be shown, such as "96 calories--1/3 fewer calories than our regular beer."

Subsequently, although the bureau's position was generally being adhered to, a number of advertisements had been asked to make corrective actions because they exceeded allowable claim. Because of this and numerous industry inquiries, the bureau issued the following formal ruling. Caloric and carbohydrate representations made in labeling and advertising of malt beverages without qualification would be considered as misleading and contrary to the provisions of 27 CFR 7.29(e) and 7.54(e) since they would create the impression that the product had value as a dietary aid.

The bureau would not sanction any labeling or advertising references that indicated or implied the presence of calories or carbohydrates in malt beverage products, unless such references were a part of or made in conjunction with a truthful statement of average analysis. For example:

12-oz size-average analyses	
Calories	96
Carbohydrate	2.8 grams
Protein	0.9 grams[a]
Fat	0.0 grams[a]

[a] "Same as our regular beer."

However, the bureau would permit a truthful statement of caloric comparison between the low-calorie product and an equal volume of the brewer's regular beer, such as "96 calories--approximately 1/3 fewer calories than our regular beer." If such a statement of caloric comparison should appear in advertising material other than in the statement of average analysis, the bottle contents [e.g., "per 12 oz bottle (serving)"] must be included as part of such statement, in equally conspicuous lettering or audio presentation. Revenue Ruling 55-404, C.B. 1955-1, 615 (Internal Revenue) was superseded.

According to Table 7-6, 27 CFR 245 is titled "Beer." The regulations in this part are related to beer and cereal beverages and describe the location, construction , equipment, and operations of breweries and pilot brewing plants and the qualification of such establishments, including ownership, control, and management. Appendix 7-11 describes the subpart titles of 27 CFR 245 and the sections they cover. In the following, some aspects of subparts B, C, F, and 0 are presented.

Subpart B provides the following definitions. "Beer" is defined as beer, ale, porter, stout, and other similar fermented beverages (including sake or similar products) of any description containing 0.5% or more of alcohol by volume and brewed or produced wholly or in part from malt or other substitute (68A Stat. 612; 26 U.S.C. 5052). A "cereal beverage" is defined as a fermented or unfermented malt beverage containing less than 0.5% of alcohol by volume when ready for consumption.

Subpart C explains the location and use of the brewery. Unless permitted otherwise, the brewery is to be used exclusively for:

1. Producing, packaging, and storing beer, cereal beverages, ice, malt, vitamins, malt sirup, and other by-products and for soft drinks and other nonalcoholic beverages.
2. Processing spent grain, carbon dioxide, and yeast.
3. Storing packages and supplies necessary for such operations.

However, if the brewer wishes to use the brewery for other purposes, he must obtain permission from the bureau. Generally, permission is granted if the planned purposes are not related to the production of alcoholic beverages, will not jeopardize the revenue, will not impede the effective administration of regulations in 27 CFR 245, and are not contrary to the specific provision of any law. These other uses of the brewery usually conform to one or more of the following additional criteria:

1. They require the use of by-products or wastage from the production of beer or utilize buildings, rooms, areas, or equipment not fully employed in the production or packaging of beer.
2. They are reasonably necessary to realize the maximum benefit from the prem-

ises and equipment and to reduce the overhead of the plant.

3. They are in the public interest because of emergency conditions.

4. They involve experiments or research projects related to equipment, materials, processes, products, by-products, or wastage of the brewery.

Subpart F of 27 CFR 245 describes regulations governing the use of beer meters. Brewers are required to provide, at their own expense, approved meters for measuring beer to be packaged. When the brewer receives a meter from the manufacturer or from another source he must notify an authorized bureau personnel. The notice should state the make, model, serial number of the meter, and the source and date of acquisition. The meter is prohibited from use for measuring beer until it has been tested for accuracy and proper function. Beer meters should be located and installed so that all beer to be packaged passes through the meters, and they must be readily accessible for examination by IRS officers. The meter installations, including piping, valves, and electrical circuitry, are so arranged that official testing equipment and procedures may be readily accommodated.

Brewers are required to maintain meters to accurately and reliably measure and record beer metered for packaging. The frequency of meter tests, the equipment used, procedures employed in testing meters, and other facets of repair and maintenance must be approved by the bureau. The allowable variation of beer meters, as established by approved tests, must not exceed plus or minus 0.5%. Any variation exceeding such limits must be corrected immediately by suitable adjustments that should reduce the error to as near zero as practicable. If the meter does not record accurately after adjustment or repair, a suitable replacement must be installed.

Subpart O of 27 CFR 245 pertains to the marks, brands, and labels of beer containers. Some aspects of the regulations are as follows. The brewer's name or tradename and the place of production (city and, where necessary for identification, state) must be embossed on, indented in, or branded on each barrel and keg of beer. However, it will be sufficient if the place of production is clearly shown on the bung or on the tap cover or on a label securely affixed to each barrel or keg. Statement as to payment of taxes is not permitted. Where two or more breweries are owned and operated by the same person or corporation, the location(s) of one or more of such breweries may be so stated. If the marking includes a location or locations other than that at which the beer currently in the container was produced, the location of the brewery at which the beer was produced must be shown on the bung, on the tap cover, or on a label securely affixed to each barrel or keg. If more than one commonly owned brewery is located in the same city, the location by street number should also be shown on the label.

Unless authorized under certain circumstances, it is prohibitive to use as container for beer any barrel or keg that bears the name of more than one brewer or a brewer other than the producing brewer. If a brewer has purchased some barrels or kegs from another brewer or obtained them by legitimate means, he should remove the original marks and brands permanently or durably cover them after he has informed the bureau personnel of such intention. However, if a brewer adopts a tradename substantially identical to the name appearing on the barrels or kegs he has acquired, he may use the container in their original brands. The successor to a brewer who has discontinued business may place additional marks and brands on the barrels and kegs in accordance with established regulations to indicate successorship without removing the original marks and brands. For further details about 27 CFR 245, consult the original document.

Import and Export of Alcoholic Beverages

According to Table 7-6, 27 CFR 251 is titled "Importation of distilled spirits, wines, and beer." Appendix 7-12 provides the subpart titles of this part and the corresponding sections covered by each subpart. The regulations in this part present the procedural and substantive requirements related to the importation of distilled spirits, wines, and beer into the United States from foreign countries, including special (occupational) and commodity taxes; permits; marking, branding, labeling, and stamping of containers and packages; and records and reports. Some aspects of Subparts B, E, and N are discussed in the following paragraphs.

Subpart B provides some definitions. The definition for beer is the same as given previously. Distilled spirits or spirits are defined as "substance known as ethyl alcohol, ethanol, or spirits of wine, and all mixtures or dilutions thereof, from whatever source or by whatever process produced, including alcohol, whisky, brandy, gin, rum, and vodka, but not including wine as defined in this subpart." The definition of wine is slightly different from that presented earlier. Thus wine in Subpart B is defined to include:

1. Still wine, including vermouth or other aperitif wine, artificial or imitation wines or compounds sold as still wines, champagne or sparkling wine, and artificially carbonated wine.
2. Flavored or sweetened and fortified or unfortified wines containing not over 24% alcohol by volume. It is immaterial as to the name under which the wine is sold.

Subpart E of 27 CFR 251 explains the general requirements for the importation of alcoholic beverages. Some aspects are as follows. Under the Federal Alcohol Administration Act and related regulations, any person or agency intending to import wines, beer, or distilled spirits for human consumption is required to obtain a permit. Distilled spirits imported for sale must be packaged in liquor bottles conforming to regulations and stamped in accordance with the law. Empty bottles imported for the packaging of distilled spirits must also conform to the requirements. Table 7-10 delineates some of these requirements.

Further, samples of distilled spirits, wines, and beer in containers of 1.75 liters or less, imported solely for quality control purposes (laboratory testing and analysis) and not for sale or use in the production of any article for sale, are exempt from any requirements relating to stamps, marks, bottles, labels, and standards of fill. However they are not exempt from the payment of any importation tax.

Subpart N of 27 CFR 251 describes the requirements for liquor bottles in the import business. They are applicable, with some exceptions, to liquor bottles having a capacity of 200 ml or more.

Distilled spirits are required to be imported into the United States in liquor bottles if each package is for sale and contains 1 gallon (3.785 liters) or less. The liquor bottles include those less than 200 ml capacity, and all must conform to the applicable standards of fill provided for the standards of identity for various distilled spirits.

Liquor bottles must bear the indicia prescribed by regulations, and only those conforming to requirements may be used for importing distilled spirits into the United States. However, additional information, if approved, may be permanently marked on such bottles. On application, an assistant regional commissioner of the bureau may authorize distilled spirits to be imported into the United States in liquor bottles not bearing the indicia required by regulations. However, because of their unique or distinctive shape or design, such bottles must be judged to pose no jeopardy to revenue collection and are suitable for the intended purpose of packaging distilled spirits. Before such request of importation is granted, there must be an initial approval of the distinctive liquor bottle in question. An application for such an approval must be accompanied by a specimen bottle or an authentic model acceptable to the bureau. Photographs of specific size and number must be submitted. The application should specify whether the bottles are to be used for packaging liqueurs, cordials, bitters, cocktails, and other specialties, or for packaging other distilled spirits.

The director of the bureau is authorized to disapprove any bottle, including a bottle of less than 200 ml capacity, for use as a liquor bottle if he determines that it is deceptive. The customs officer at the port of entry, when advised by the bureau, will deny entry into the United States of such bottle containing distilled spirits, irrespective of whether it bears the required indicia.

Empty liquor bottles may be imported into the United States and furnished to liquor dealers for display purposes. Each bottle must be marked to show that it is to be used for such purpose. Any paper strip used to seal the bottle must be of

TABLE 7-10. Labeling and Marking of Imported Alcoholic Beverages. Adapted from 27 CFR 251

Alcoholic Beverage	Container Circumstance	Legal Requirement for Labeling and Marking of Containers
Distilled spirits	In imported containers in excess of 1 gallon or 3.785 liters	Marked and stamped according to customs regulations (19 CFR 11 and 12)
	In imported containers or containers of spirits bottled in customs custody: 1. 1 gallon (3.785 liters) or less 2. for sale at resale	Covered by an official certificate of approval
	Containers of spirits bottled after taxpayment and withdrawal from customs custody	Covered by a certificate of label approval or exemption from label approval
Wines (7%-24% alcohol by volume)	In imported containers	Marked, branded and labeled according to customs regulations (19 CFR 11 and 12)
	All imported wines, prior to removal from customs custody	Packaged, marked, branded, and labeled in conformity with the Federal Alcohol Administration Act and related regulations
	Imported wines bottled or packaged after taxpayment and withdrawal from customs custody	Covered by a certificate of label approval or exemption from label approval
Beer	Imported containers	Marked and labeled in accordance with customs regulations (19 CFR 11 and 12)
	All imported beer to be released from customs custody	Must conform to the Federal Alcohol Administration Act and related regulations

solid color with no other design or printing except the legend "not genuine--for display purposes only." Importers should keep a record of the receipt and disposition of such bottles, including the names and addresses of consignees, dates of shipment, and size, quantity, and description of bottles.

Sometimes, after receiving application through the proper procedure, the nearest assistant regional commissioner may authorize the release from customs custody of distilled spirits in bottles denied entry because of noncompliance with certain provisions of the bureau's regulations. Usually such special authorization ascertains that the liquor bottles are not deceptive, that their releases do not jeopardize proper revenue collection, that the incidents are nonrecurring cases, and that noncompliance constitutes unintentional errors.

The director may, after receiving proper application, authorize an importer to receive used liquor bottles assembled for him in accordance with regulations. Used liquor bottles so received may be stored at any suitable location pending exportation or reuse. Records of the receipt and disposition of such bottles must be maintained. Consult 27 CFR 251 for further details on the regulations governing the importation of alcoholic beverages.

In the following, an example is described concerning the Bureau's rulings on some aspects of such regulations (ATF Ruling 74-34, referenced in the 1974 Cumulative Bulletin). The bureau was asked to review the internal revenue tax applicable to certain imported beverage products bottled at less than 48 degrees of proof and produced by adding distilled spirits, other than wine spirits or brandy, to wine. Because of the complexity of this ruling, the bureau's complete analysis is reproduced in the following:

Under 26 U.S.C. 5002(a)(6), the term "distilled spirits" is defined as that substance known as ethyl alcohol, ethanol, or spirits of wine, including all dilutions and mixtures thereof, from whatever source or by whatever process produced, and shall include whisky, brandy, rum, gin, and vodka. The regulations promulgated under that section as found in 26 CFR 201.11, repeats that definition and eliminates denatured spirits, unless specifically stated. With the intent, however, of relieving certain products from the requirements of 26 CFR 201 dealing with liquor bottles, labels, and strip stamps, a sub-classification is established within such definition which states: "Effective July 1, 1972, for the purpose of the requirements of this part relating to liquor bottles, labels, and strip stamps, the term "spirits" or "distilled spirits" shall not include mixtures containing wine bottled at 48 degrees proof or less, if the mixture contains more than 50 percent wine on a proof gallon basis." Similarly, under 27 CFR 5.11, mixtures containing wine, bottled at 48 degrees of proof or less, which contain more than 50 percent wine on a proof gallon basis are excluded from the labeling and advertising requirements for distilled spirits found under 27 CFR 5. However, neither of the above regulations affects the tax rate applicable to products that fall into the broader definition found under 26 U.S.C. 5001(a)(8) of the statute, which provides that imported liqueurs and cordials, or similar compounds, containing distilled spirits, shall be taxed as distilled spirits.

The regulations promulgated under 26 U.S.C. 5001 (at 26 CFR 251.43 and 251.44) provide equity in tax treatment in regard to foreign and domestic wines that have been produced in the same manner as domestic wines by recognizing the addition of wine spirits or brandy, made from the same kind of fruit from which the wine was produced, as an accepted method of increasing the alcohol content of the wine. Those regulations provide that foreign wine, as in the case of domestic wine, does not lose its tax status as wine when only eligible wine spirits or brandy has been added by stating under 26 CFR 251.43 that, when imported into the United States, fortified or unfortified wines containing not over 24 percent alcohol by volume, to which sweetening or flavoring materials, but no distilled spirits (except those eligible wine spirits or brandies added in the production of fortified wine) have been added are not classified as liqueurs, cordials or similar compounds, but are considered to be flavored wines only and are subject to the internal revenue tax at the rates applicable to wines. Conversely, under 26 CFR 251.44, compounds and preparations containing distilled spirits, which are fit for beverage purposes, when imported into the United States, are subject to the internal revenue tax applicable to distilled spirits.

It is held, therefore, that compounds and preparations fit for beverage use which are made by adding to wine any distilled spirits (other than wine spirits or brandy that has become an integral part of the fortified wine as part of the wine production process), whether or not such compounds and preparations are 48 degrees of proof or less, or whether or not they contain more than 50 percent wine on a proof gallon basis, are subject to the internal revenue tax at the rate applicable to distilled spirits upon importation into the United States.

(NOTE: All references to Title 26 of the Code of Federal Regulations in the above quotation are now located in Title 27 instead, with the section numbers unchanged.)

Table 7-6 indicates that 27 CFR 252 is titled "The exportation of liquors." The regulations in this part are concerned with the following:

1. Exportation, lading for use on vessels and aircraft, and transfer to a foreign-

trade zone or a manufacturing bonded warehouse (Class 6 as defined by U.S. Customs Regulations) of beer, wine, and distilled spirits, including specially denatured spirits.

2. Transfer, in the case of distilled spirits only, to a customs bonded warehouse as required by a specific provision of the Internal Revenue Code.
3. Requirements in regard to removal, shipment, lading, deposit, evidence of exportation, losses, claims, and bonds.
4. The application of regulations related to items (1) to (3) (above) to all alcoholic beverages, whether they be without payment of tax, free of tax, or with benefit of drawback.

Appendix 7-13 provides the subpart titles contained in 27 CFR 252 and the corresponding sections each subpart covers. Subpart E is titled "Withdrawal of distilled spirits without payment of tax for exportation, use on vessels and aircraft, transfer to a foreign-trade zone, or transportation to a manufacturing bonded warehouse." According to the regulations, distilled spirits on which the internal revenue tax has not been paid or determined may be withdrawn from the bonded premises of a distilled spirits plant without payment of tax for either:

1. Exportation.
2. Use on the vessels or aircraft.
3. Transfer to and deposit in a foreign-trade zone for exportation or for storage pending exportation.
4. Transportation to and deposit in a manufacturing bonded warehouse.
5. Transfer to and deposit in a customs bonded warehouse.

All such withdrawals must be made under the applicable bond prescribed by regulations. The application for such withdrawal must be made by the exporter on a special form that provides the name of the carrier to be used in transporting the spirits from the bonded premises of the distilling plant to the port of export, to the customs bonded warehouse, to the manufacturing bonded warehouse, or to the foreign-trade zone, as the case may be. If the spirits are shipped on a through bill of lading and not all carriers handling the spirits while in transit are known, the application must state the name of the carrier to whom the distilled spirits are to be delivered at the shipping premises.

Both the withdrawal of and the containers used for distilled spirits must be authorized. The gauging, packaging, bottling, casing, marking, stamping, and reporting of distilled spirits prior to withdrawal should be carried out in accorance with regulations.

Whenever the exporter desires to transfer distilled spirits from packages filled in internal revenue bond to other packages specially designed for export, the transfer must be done according to the bureau's regulations relating to consolidation of packages, and prior to the preparation of the form covering the removal of the distilled spirits.

Internal Revenue Service officers do not permit the withdrawal for exportation of distilled spirits that have remained in bonded storage after the expiration of the 20-year bonded period prescribed by law. In such cases, the officer notes his disapproval across the face of all copies of application and returns them to the proprietor. At the same time, he will inform the proprietor of the distilled spirits plant in which the spirits are stored that the bonded period has expired, determine the tax on the spirits, and forward a report to authorized bureau personnel so that proper tax may be assessed.

The regulations contained in Subpart E of 27 CFR 252 also describe the procedure for inspection and regauge of withdrawn spirits. The proprietor will inspect all containers to be withdrawn according to specific instruction and will regauge all packages. However, if the spirits are contained in bottle, tin, glass, or similar containers, in sealed metal drums, or where they are to be withdrawn on the filling or original gauge as authorized, a regauge of such spirits is not necessary. Any container bearing evidence of tampering or unusual loss that cannot be satisfactorily explained will be detained pending further investigation in accordance with regulations. In case regauge is required for any withdrawal, it should be done by the proprietor under the direct supervision of the IRS officer and reported on a special form.

The regulations in Subpart E also explain the reduction in proof in distilled spirits with reference to export. Spirits contained in packages filled in internal revenue bond may be reduced in proof for exportation or for transfer to a foreign-trade zone by the addition of pure water only after the packages have been regauged as required. The amount of water added to the spirits in any package is strictly controlled by the permissible space in the package, and it is prohibitive to transfer spirits from one package to another for the purpose of reduction. The proprietor is required to perform the reduction or dilution under the direct supervision of an IRS officer. After an authorized reduction is done, the proprietor must again gauge the packages under supervision and report the details. If the reduction process results in any unusual loss, the proprietor is required to report the details according to specific regulations. Each such report of gauge must bear the statement "Gauge After Reduction."

The regulations also describe how packages are to be stamped. Every package and authorized bulk conveyance of spirits (including tank cars and tank trucks but not pipelines) withdrawn without taxpayment as detailed in regulations must bear a distilled spirits stamp, overprinted with the word "Export" and affixed at the time of its removal from the bonded premises. Such stamps should be issued by the IRS officer on receipt of the withdrawal form and after completion of any required gauge or regauge of the packages or bulk conveyances. The stamps should be over-printed, affixed, and cancelled in accordance with bureau regulations. Similar procedures exist for the stamping of bottles containing distilled spirits.

With reference to the marks and brands required on the packages of spirits, the regulations provide the following details. In addition to the regular marks and brands required to be placed on packages and cases of distilled spirits at the time they are filled, the proprietor must include additional specific marks on each such container before removal from the bonded premises. They are as follows:

1. "Export--Without Payment of Tax."
   This applies to spirits to be withdrawn for export from the United States or for shipment to the Armed Services for export.
2. "Use on Vessels (or Aircraft)--Without Payment of Tax."
   This applies to spirits to be withdrawn for use on vessels or aircraft.
3. "Deposit in C.M.B.W.--Cl. 6" [to be followed by the name and address (city or town and state) of the consignee proprietor].
   This applies to spirits to be withdrawn for transportation to and deposit in a manufacturing bonded warehouse. However, these markings are not required on containers removed for transfer to a contiguous manufacturing bonded warehouse, where authorized bureau personnel find that their omission will not constitute a jeopardy to the revenue.
4. "Export--Without Payment of Tax" "via F.T.Z. No.____."
   This applies to spirits to be withdrawn for deposit in a foreign-trade zone, and the blank should be filled in by the number of the zone.
5. "Deposit in C.B.W." [to be followed by the address (city or town and state)] of the customs bonded warehouse.
   This applies to spirits to be withdrawn for deposit in a customs bonded warehouse.

With reference to the "certificates of origin," the regulations prescribe the following. Since the entry of distilled spirits at ports in certain foreign countries is permitted only on the filing by the importer of an official certificate showing the origin and age of such spirits, an IRS officer may, on request by the applicant, furnish him with a certificate showing the origin and age of the spirits described in the entry for withdrawal. Such information is determined from the marks and brands on the packages or cases containing the spirits. Such certificates are to be furnished on special forms and may also be issued for distilled spirits removed to a foreign-trade zone, in which case the number and location of the foreign-trade zone will replace the name of the foreign country on the form. Consult 27 CFR 252 for further details on the export of alcoholic beverages.

General Regulations

According to Table 7-6, the "Production of volatile fruit-flavor concentrates" is described in 27 CFR 18. The regulations in this part are related to the:

1. Location, construction, arrangement, equipment, and qualification of plants for the manufacture of volatile fruit-flavor concentrates (essence).
2. Production, removal, sale, transportation, and use of such concentrates and of the fruit mash or fruit from which they are produced.

Appendix 7-14 describes the subpart titles and the sections covered by each subpart in 27 CFR 18. Some aspects of subparts B, E, and H are presented. Subpart B provides some definitions. The term "concentrate" refers to any volatile fruit-flavor concentrate (essence) produced by any process which includes evaporation from any fruit mash or juice. "Flash mash" or "juice" refers to the spent fruit mash or juice from which the volatile fruit flavors have been removed. "Fold" is the volume ratio of fruit mash or juice to the concentrate it produces. For example, 1 gallon of concentrate 100-fold will be the product from 100 gallons of fruit mash or juice. The fruit used includes all products commonly known and classified as fruit, berries, or grapes. "High-proof concentrate" refers to a concentrate (essence) having at least 24% by volume of alcohol and deemed unfit for beverage use because of its natural constituents.

"Restrictions as to location" is defined to mean the following. It is prohibitive to establish a concentrate plant in any dwelling house, on board any vessel or boat, or on any premises where other business is conducted. This restriction is to prevent jeopardizing of the revenue or the effective administration of bureau regulations. Thus the premises and equipment of a concentration plant are permitted to be used only for the business stated in the approved application for registration. Any other uses must be approved by the bureau director.

Subpart E of 27 CFR 18 explains the qualification of volatile fruit-flavor concentrate plants. A person is not permitted to engage in the business of manufacturing concentrates unless he has made an application for registration to the bureau and received approval. Each application form must include the following:

1. Serial number, name, and principal business address of the applicant and the location of the plant if different from the business address.
2. Statement of purpose for which filed.
3. Statement of information regarding proprietorship, supported by required organizational documents.
4. Plat and plants.
5. Description of major apparatus and equipment, listing separately each tank,

evaporator, and separator by serial number and showing the capacity of each in wine gallons, and listing separately each still and condenser by serial number, kind, capacity and intended use.

6. Statement of plant capacity.
7. Statement of process to be employed.
8. Statement of other business, if any, to be conducted on concentrate plant premises and identifying approved application for such business.

The application should contain a complete description of the buildings containing the concentrate plant, including the location, dimensions, material of construction, and means of protection and security. All rooms or areas comprising the concentrate plant must be described. The description must include the dimensions of each room or area and its use-specific name.

Statement as to the capacity of the plant should describe the following:

1. Kind of processing materials to be used, including the name of fruit.
2. Maximum quantity of each kind of processing material that will be processed in 24 hours.
3. Maximum quantity of concentrate (in wine gallons) that will be produced in 24 hours.
4. Minimum and maximum folds to which the volatile fruit flavors will be concentrated and the maximum percent of alcohol that will be contained in the concentrates. This applies to the concentrate obtained from each kind of processing material.

The statement of process in the application should include a step-by-step description of the process employed to produce fruit concentrates, beginning with the juicing from the fruit and continuing through each step of the concentration to the removal of the concentrate from the system. In the case of high-proof concentrates (essences), the statement must also indicate any step in the process at which any spirits may be potable.

Subpart H of 27 CFR 18 provides the details of the operations related to the production of volatile fruit-flavor concentrates. Thus with reference to the processing material, the following regulations are in force:

1. It may be produced by the proprietor or obtained elsewhere.
2. If it is fermented, it is prohibited from use in the manufacture of concentrates.
3. It may be used if it contains no more alcohol than is reasonably unavoidable; it should be used when produced or as soon as practicable.
4. If it is removed from the concentrate plant for any purpose, the proprietor is required to record the kind and quantity removed, the name and address of

the consignee, and the reasons for the removal.

5. When it is fed to the evaporator, the number of gallons used should be determined and recorded, and the quantity and alcohol content of the concentrate produced must also be determined and recorded according to prescribed regulations.

Concentrates may be used on the concentrate plant premises in the manufacture of any product authorized by the bureau inasmuch as such product contains less than 0.5% of alcohol by volume.

With reference to the production of high proof concentrate, the following should be noted. Except for authorized samplings, concentrates having at least 24% alcohol by volume may not be produced in a volatile fruit-flavor concentrate plant, unless such product is considered by the bureau as unfit for use as a beverage because of its natural constitutents. Thus the production of high proof concentrate and the kind of concentrate used must be approved by the bureau. Each application for approval must be accompanied by an 8-ounce sample for laboratory analysis. If it is found to be naturally (i.e., without addition of other substances) unfit for use as a beverage, the application may be approved. However, the sample should be representative of the concentrate to be produced and should be labeled to include: (1) name, plant number, and address of producer, (2) in bold type, HIGH-PROOF CONCENTRATE--NOT FOR BEVERAGE USE, (3) kind of concentrate, (4) percentage of alcohol by volume, and (5) fold.

The proprietor may reduce the alcohol content of any concentrate to the required legal level by the addition of water provided the final concentrate will not be less than 100-fold. Each container of concentrate must carry a label identifying the product and describing: (1) name of proprietor, (2) plant registry number, (3) plant address as shown on application form, (4) number of wine gallons, and (5) percentage of alcohol by volume. Consult 27 CFR 18 for further details on the production of volatile fruit-flavor concentrates.

According to Table 7-6, 27 CFR 195 is titled "Production of vinegar by the vaporizing process." The regulations in this part are related to the requirements governing the equipment; construction; location; qualification; changes in equipment, premises, and proprietorship; action by the assistant regional commissioner; plant operations; and records and reports of operations at vinegar plants. Appendix 7-15 describes the subpart titles contained in this part and the corresponding sections each subpart covers.

How are distilled spirits related to vinegar? Subpart B of 27 CFR 195 provides the answer. Distilled spirits, as defined earlier, refer to the substance known as ethyl alcohol, ethanol, spirits, or spirits of wine produced from any source or by any process. They include all dilutions and mixtures of such liquids and, legally, include low wines produced by the vaporization process in the manufacture of vinegar.

To illustrate some of the information contained in 27 CFR 195, the following discusses some aspects of Subpart K, the plant operation of vinegar production by the vaporization process. To conduct any operation in connection with the production of low wines to be used in the manufacture of vinegar, a person must: (1) comply with all the requirements of law and regulations, (2) receive approval for all required and supporting documents, and (3) obtain permission to operate.

All persons manufacturing vinegar by the vaporization process must permit an internal revenue officer to inspect at any reasonable hour the premises, equipment, stocks, and records as required by law and regulations.

Apart from using the vapor to produce low wines for the manufacture of vinegar, it is not permitted to be converted into distilled spirits. To make sure that this will not occur, the regulations specifically prohibit the connection of any vaporizing apparatus used for the manufacture of vinegar with contrivance of any description including conductor, reflux line, pipe, gooseneck that may convey away the vapor and convert it to distilled spirits. The alcoholic vapor is not permitted to be conducted in any manner into a receptacle where self-condensation or condensation with a minute quantity of water may occur and produce spirits of more than 30 degrees proof. The proof of water or liquid used to receive the vapor must be checked constantly to guarantee that it will be below 30°.

All low wines are required to be conveyed promptly into receiving tanks so arranged that the proprietor can ascertain the daily production for record keeping. The operation must be organized so that in case more than a day's vapor runs into the same tank, it is possible to measure the production of one full day or more. The quantity noted as the production of a particular date must be the quantity actually produced on that day.

The low wines may be transferred by pipeline from the receiving tanks to low wine storage tanks or directly to the vinegar factory proper for use in the manufacture of vinegar. The quantity thus removed or used must be determined and recorded by the proprietor.

The proprietor is also required to determine, record, and report each month the quantity of low wines lost in receiving or storage tanks. No application for allowance of loss is necessary if the loss of low wines during any calendar month does not exceed 1% of the aggregate quantity on hand the first of the month and produced during that month. This assumes, of course, that none of the lost low wines was removed and used unlawfully. It is also stipulated that the allowance of 1% loss during any one month is not cumulative.

If the loss is more than 1%, the proprietor may apply for remission of tax on the total losses during the month. Application for such allowances must be made within a specific period after the losses have occurred and must provide all the related material facts, including the nature and cause of the loss such as leakage, evaporation, casualty, theft, or other unavoidable cause, as well as the extent of the loss. Such application must follow stringent procedures and all requirements for approval must be satisfied.

The proprietor must pay internal revenue taxes on any distilled spirits produced in or removed from the premises of a vinegar plant in violation of law or regulations. It is prohibitive to remove from a vinegar plant any vinegar or fluid containing more than 2% proof spirits. The vinegar removed from the factories is analyzed periodically to make sure that the proof does not exceed the legal limit. Consult 27 CFR 195 for further details on the production of vinegar by the vaporization process.

According to Table 7-6, 27 CFR 186 is titled "Gauging manual." The complete subpart and section titles of Part 186 are described in Appendix 7-16. This manual relates to the gauging of distilled spirits. By "gauging" is meant the determination of the proof and the quantity of distilled spirits. To make this possible, the bureau has issued seven technical tables in Subpart E of 27 CFR 186. These tables and their respective instructions are intended to be used, wherever applicable, in making the necessary computations from gauge data. Refer to Appendix 7-16 for the title of each of these tables.

With reference to gauging instruments (Subpart C), some important instructions are as follows. All IRS officers must use only hydrometers and thermometers furnished by the U.S. Government. However, some exceptions are:

1. If precision grade specific gravity hydrometers are needed, the officers may use those furnished by the proprietor in accordance with regulations.
2. The bureau director may authorize the use of any other approved gauging instruments of unusual or costly design provided by the proprietor.

Internal Revenue Service officers are required to verify the accuracy of hydrometers and thermometers used by the proprietors. The proof of distilled spirits and rectified products must be determined by the use of gauging instruments according to established regulations. Some details on hydrometers and thermometers are described as follows.

The hydrometers furnished to IRS officers are graduated to read the proof of aqueous alcoholic solutions at 60°F, that is, 0 for water, 100 for proof spirits, and 200 for absolute alcohol. If read at above or below 60°F, the reading will be respectively greater or lesser than the true percentage of alcohol proof. Hence corrections are necessary for hydrometer readings at temperatures other than 60°F. Table 1 as described in Subpart E of 27 CFR 186 serves this purpose. Precision hydrometers are to be used for gauging large quantities of spirits, such as bulk gauging for taxpayment. In general, hydrometers and thermometers are to be used to determine the true percentage of proof in a manner prescribed by regulations. The construction of these two instruments is quite simple. A brief description is provided in the following paragraphs; further details should be obtained from the original document.

Hydrometers are designated by letters according to range of proof and are provided in ranges and subdivision of stems. For example, a U.S. standard hydrometer "B" covers 80 to 120 proof of alcohol, and the subdivision is 0.5°. A precision hydrometer "M" covers 105 to 125 proof of alcohol, and the subdivision is 0.2°.

Thermometers are designated by type according to range of degrees Fahrenheit and are provided in ranges and subdivision of degrees. For example, a "pencil type" thermometer covers 10° to 100°F and has a subdivision of 1°.

There are numerous details relating to the use of precision hydrometers and thermometers. One such detail is precaution. To obtain accurate hydrometer and thermometer readings, some precautions and steps are as follows:

1. Bulk spirits should be thoroughly agitated so that the test sample will be representative of the lot.
2. The hydrometer should be kept clean and free of any oily substance.
3. Immediately before readings are taken, the glass cylinder containing the thermometer should be rinsed several times with the spirits that are to be gauged. This allows the thermometer and its cylinder to reach the temperature of the spirits. If possible, it is desirable to bring both the instruments and the spirits to room temperature.
4. If the outer surface of the cylinder becomes wet, it should be cleaned dry to avoid the cooling effect of rapid evaporation.
5. During the readings, any temperature variation of the thermometer/cylinder should be prevented by proper protection from drafts or other conditions. For example, the hands should not be placed on the cylinder in such a manner as to warm the fluid contained within.
6. The hydrometer should be inserted in the liquid and the hydrometer bulb raised and lowered from top to bottom five or six times to obtain an even temperature distribution over its surface, and, while the hydrometer bulb remains in the liquid, the stem should be dried and the hydrometer allowed to come to rest without wetting more than a few tenths degrees of the exposed stem.
7. Special care should be taken to ascertain the exact point at which the level of the surface of the liquid intersects the scale of proof in the stem of the hydrometer.
8. The hydrometer and thermometer should be immediately read, as nearly simultaneously as possible.
9. In reading the hydrometer, a sighting should be made slightly below the plane

of the surface of the liquid, and the line of sight should then be raised slowly, being kept perpendicular to the hydrometer stem, until the appearance of the surface changes from an ellipse to a straight line. The point where this line intersects the hydrometer scale is the correct reading of the hydrometer.

10. When the correct readings of the hydrometer and the thermometer have been determined, the true percentage of proof will be ascertained from Table 1 as described in Subpart E of 27 CFR 186.

11. Another sample of the spirits should then be taken and tested in the same manner so as to verify the proof originally obtained.

12. Hydrometer readings should be made to the nearest 0.05°, thermometer readings should be made to the nearest 0.1°, and instrument correction factors, if any, should be applied.

13. It is necessary to interpolate in Table 1 (see Subpart E) for fractional hydrometer readings.

Further details about the Gauging Manual should be obtained from 27 CFR 186.

Table 7-6 indicates that there are at least 13 more parts in Title 27 of the Code of Federal Regulations that have not been discussed. In the following, space limitation permits only a presentation of the brief summaries of the contents of some selected parts. An interested party should refer to Title 27 for complete information.

<u>27 CFR 1</u> Basic Permit Requirements under the Federal Alcohol Administration Act

The regulations in this part relate to the requirements governing the issuance, amendment, denial, revocation, suspension, automatic termination, and annulment of basic permits and the duration of permits, except that the provisions of 27 CFR 200, Rules of Practice in Permit Proceedings, are also made applicable to administrative proceedings with respect to the application for, and to the suspension, revocation, or annulment of, basic permits under the Federal Alcohol Administration Act.

<u>27 CFR 3</u> Bulk Sales and Bottling of Distilled Spirits

This part contains the substantive requirements relative to bulk sales and bottling of distilled spirits under the Federal Alcohol Administration Act, including the terms of warehouse receipt for distilled spirits in bulk. No procedural requirements are prescribed.

27 CFR 70 Procedure and Administration

This part sets forth the procedural and administrative rules of the bureau for the issuance and enforcement of summonses, examination of books of account and witnesses, administration of oaths, entry of premises for examination of taxable objects, granting of rewards for information, canvass of regions for taxable objects and persons, and authority of officers of the bureau.

27 CFR 71 Statement of Procedural Rules

This part sets forth the procedural rules of the bureau regarding matters of official record in the bureau, including the procedures for disclosure of information to the public and the information and publication of rules, regulations, and forms by the bureau.

27 CFR 173 Returns of Substances, Articles, or Containers

This part relates to the returns and records of the disposition of articles from which distilled spirits may be recovered, of substances of the character used in the manufacture of distilled spirits, and of containers of the character used for the packaging of distilled spirits and to the manufacture and disposition of liquor bottles.

27 CFR 196 Stills

This part relates to the manufacture, taxpayment, removal, use, and registration of stills and condenser and the exportation or transfer to foreign-trade zones of stills and condensers with benefit of drawback of internal revenue tax or without payment of tax.

27 CFR 200 Rules of Practice in Permit Proceedings

The regulations in this part govern the procedure and practice in connection with the disapproval of applications for basic permits, and for the suspension, revocation and annulment of such permits under Sections 3 and 4 of the Federal Alcohol Administration Act (27 U.S.C. 201 et seq.) and disapproval, suspension, and revocation of permits under the Internal Revenue Code (26 U.S.C.). The regulations in this part shall also govern, insofar as applicable, any adversary proceeding involving adjudication required by statute to be determined on the record, after opportunity for hearing, under laws administered by the bureau.

27 CFR 231 Taxpaid Wine Bottling Houses

The regulations in this part relate to the bottling and packaging of taxpaid U.S. and foreign wines, at premises other than the bottling premises of a distilled spirits plant operated under 27 CFR 201.

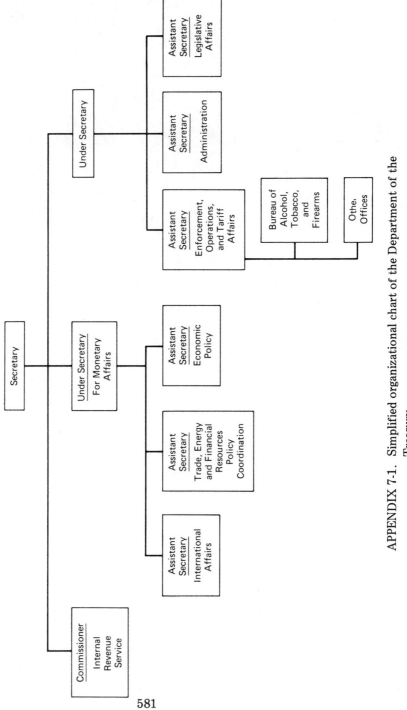

APPENDIX 7-1. Simplified organizational chart of the Department of the
Treasury.

581

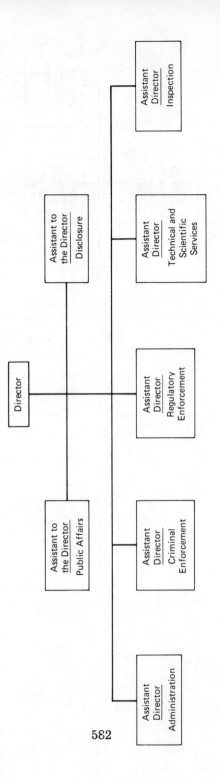

APPENDIX 7-2. Simplified organizational chart of the Bureau of Alcohol, Tobacco, and Firearms.

582

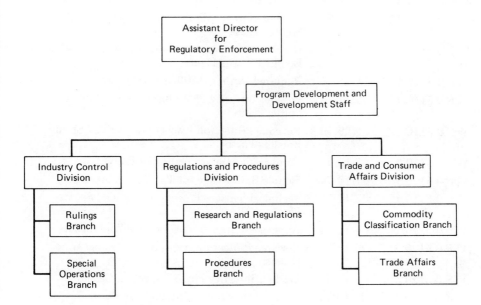

APPENDIX 7-3. Simplified organizational chart of the Office of the Assistant
Director for Regulatory Enforcement within the Bureau of
Alcohol, Tobacco, and Firearms.

583

APPENDIX 7-4. Selected Publications Related to Regulatory Enforcement and Issued either by or of Primary Interest to Regulations and Procedures Division, unless Otherwise Indicated

Publication Number	Date [a]	Publication Title or Subject
ATF 0 5000.1	05/17/64	Regulatory Enforcement Inspection Program
ATF 0 5000.2A	06/18/75	Inspection Frequency
ATF 0 5030.2	10/15/74	Related Inspection Activities
ATF 0 5030.3	05/17/74	Unscheduled Inspections--General
ATF 0 5110.3	05/17/74	Application Inspections--Distilled Spirits Plants
ATF 0 5110.4A	12/24/75	Revenue Protection Inspection--Distilled Spirits Storage Phase
ATF 0 5110.5	05/17/74	Unscheduled Inspections--Inspectors Assigned to Distilled Spirits Plants
ATF 0 5110.6	11/25/75	Required Duties--Distilled Spirits Plants
ATF 0 5110.7	05/17/74	Product Integrity Phase Inspections--Distilled Spirits Plants
ATF 0 5110.8A	01/29/76	Revenue Protection Inspection--Distilled Spirits Bottling Phase
ATF 0 5110.9	07/10/74	Comparative Determination of Proof
ATF 0 5110.10	07/10/74	Sample Bulk Gauge for Tax Determination
ATF 0 5110.12	07/17/75	Technical Services Procedure--Distilled Spirits Plants
ATF 0 5120.1	05/17/74	Application Inspections--Bonded Wine Cellars
ATF 0 5120.2	05/17/74	Revenue Protection Inspections--Bonded Wine Cellars
ATF 0 5120.3	05/17/74	Product Integrity Phase Inspection Cellars
ATF 0 5120.4	07/10/74	Winery Inspections--Optional Use Forms
ATF 0 5120.5	08/29/75	Technical Services Procedure--Wineries
ATF 0 5130.1	05/17/74	Application Inspections--Breweries
ATF 0 5130.2	05/17/74	Product Integrity Phase--Consumer Protection Inspections--Breweries
ATF 0 5130.3	11/03/75	Revenue Protection Inspections--Breweries
ATF 0 5130.4	07/17/75	Technical Services Procedure--Breweries
ATF 0 5140.1	05/17/74	Consumer Protection Inspections of Taxpaid Wine Bottling Houses
ATF 0 5140.2	05/17/74	Application Inspection--Taxpaid Wine Bottling Houses

Publication Number	Date	Publication Title or Subject
ATF 0 5140.3	09/04/75	Technical Services Procedure--Taxpaid Wine Bottling Houses
ATF 0 5160.3	07/10/74	List of Preparations, Formulas, or Processes
ATF 0 5170.1	05/17/74	Application Inspection--Wholesale Liquor Dealers and Importers
ATF 0 5170.2	05/17/74	Consumer Protection Inspection--Wholesale Liquor Dealers and Importers
ATF 0 5170.5	07/25/75	Technical Services Procedures--Wholesalers and Importers
ATF 0 5190.1	09/11/75	Determining Compliance or Non-Compliance of Alcoholic Beverage Advertising[b]
ATF 0 5510.1	05/17/74	Application Inspections--Vinegar Plants (Vaporizing Process)
ATF 0 5510.2	05/17/74	Revenue Protection Inspections--Vinegar Plants
ATF 0 5510.3	08/29/75	Technical Services Procedures--Vinegar Plants Vaporizing Process
ATF 0 5520.1	05/17/74	Application Inspections--Volatile Fruit-Flavor Concentrate Plants
ATF 0 5520.2	05/17/74	Revenue Protection Inspections--Volatile Fruit-Flavor Concentrate Plants
ATF 0 5520.3	09/04/75	Technical Services Procedures--Volatile Fruit-Flavor Concentrate Plants
ATF 0 5540.1	05/17/74	Consumer Protection Inspections--Bottle Manufacturers

[a] If interested, always request the latest issue.

[b] Primary interest is the Trade and Consumer Affairs Division.

APPENDIX 7-5. Subpart and Section Titles of 27 CFR 4[a] (Labeling and Advertising of Wine)

Subpart	Subpart Title	Section	Section Title	Section	Section Title
B	Definitions	4.10	Meaning of terms		
C	Standards of identity for wine	4.20	Application of standards	4.23	Grape type designations
		4.21	The standards of identity	4.24	Generic, semi-generic, and non-generic designations of geographic significance
		4.22	Blends, cellar treatment, alteration of class or type	4.25	Appelations of origin
D	Labeling requirements for wine	4.30	General	4.35	Name and address
		4.31	Misbranding	4.36	Alcoholic content
		4.32	Mandatory label information	4.37	Net contents
		4.33	Brand names	4.38	General requirements
		4.34	Class and type	4.39	Prohibited practice
E	Requirements for withdrawal of wine from customs custody	4.40	Labeling approval and release	4.46	Certificate of nonstandard fill
		4.45	Certificates of origin and identity		
F	Requirements for approval of labels of wine domestically bottled or packed	4.50	Certificates of label approval	4.52	Photoprints
		4.51	Exhibiting certificates to Government officials		
G	Advertising of wine	4.60	Application	4.63	Legibility of requirements
		4.61	Definitions	4.64	Prohibited statements
		4.62	Mandatory statements		
H	Standards of fill for wine	4.70	Application	4.73	Metric standards of fill
		4.71	Standard wine containers	4.74	Bottles per shipping case
		4.72	Standards of fill		
I	General provisions	4.80	Exports		

[a] Also consult 43 FR 37672 to 37678 (August 23, 1978).

586

APPENDIX 7-6. Subpart Titles of 27 CFR 240 (Wine) and Section Numbers They Cover

Subpart	Subpart Title	Sections Included
A	Scope	240.1 to 240.2
B	Definitions	240.10 to 240.56
C	Establishment of premises	240.120 to 240.123
D	Use of bonded wine cellars	240.130 to 240.134
E	Construction	240.140 to 240.145
F	Equipment	240.160 to 240.174
G	Qualifying documents	240.190 to 240.213
H	Bonds and consents of surety	240.220 to 240.237
I	Termination of bonds	240.250 to 240.259
J	Plat	240.270 to 240.274
K	Requirements governing changes in name, proprietorship, and control	240.280 to 240.296
L	Requirements governing changes in location, premises, and equipment	240.310 to 240.313
M	Discontinuance of business	240.320 to 240.322
N	Special (occupational) taxes as wholesale and retail liquor dealers	240.340 to 240.345
O	Production of wine	240.350 to 240.359b
P	Production and treatment of natural grape wine	240.360 to 240.388
Q	Production and treatment of natural fruit wine	240.400 to 240.412
R	Specially sweetened natural wine	240.430 to 240.431
S	Special natural wine	240.440 to 240.448
T	Agricultural wine	240.460 to 240.466
U	Wine other than standard wine	240.480 to 240.491
V	Refermentation of wine and wine lees	240.500 to 240.501
W	Production of effervescent wine	240.510 to 240.513
X	Storage and finishing of wine	240.520 to 240.539
Y	Tax-free production	240.540 to 240.550
Z	Containers for removal of wine	240.560 to 240.583
AA	Taxpayment of wine	240.590 to 240.600
BB	Transfer of wine in bond to other bonded wine cellars	240.610 to 240.620
CC	Removal of wine for use as distilling material	240.630 to 240.634
DD	Removal of still wine for manufacture of vinegar	240.650 to 240.662
EE	Withdrawal of wine without payment of tax for exportation, use on vessels and aircraft, transfer to a foreign-trade zone, or transportation to a manufacturing bonded warehouse class six	240.670 to 240.672

587

Subpart	Subpart Title	Sections Included
HH	Removal of wine for federal or state use	240.720 to 240.726
II	Other tax-free removals	240.730 to 240.732
JJ	Tax-free samples of wine	240.740 to 240.746
KK	Destruction of wine	240.750 to 240.753
LL	Disposition of lees, including filter wash and other residues	240.760 to 240.763
MM	Change of sparkling and artificially carbonated wine into still wine	240.770 to 240.773
NN	Losses of wine in bond	240.780 to 240.790
OO	Return of unmerchantable taxpaid wine to bonded wine cellar	240.800 to 240.809
PP	Withdrawal of wine spirits for wine production	240.820 to 240.839
QQ	Losses of wine spirits in bond	240.850 to 240.859
RR	Disposition of unused wine spirits	240.870 to 240.874
SS	Tax liability for wine spirits withdrawn for wine production	240.880 to 240.881
TT	Production and storage of allied products	240.890 to 240.892
UU	Records and reports	240.900 to 240.925
VV	Miscellaneous provisions	240.940 to 240.943
WW	Examination of premises	240.950
XX	Calculations for wine production	240.960 to 240.1019
YY	Withdrawal of distillates containing aldehydes	240.1041 to 240.1043
ZZ	Materials authorized for treatment of wine	240.1051 to 240.1052

APPENDIX 7-7. Subpart and Section Titles of 27 CFR 5 (Labeling and Advertising of Distilled Spirits)

Sub-part	Subpart Title	Section	Section Title	Section	Section Title
A	Scope	5.1	General	5.2	Related regulations
B	Definitions	5.11	Meaning of terms		
C	Standards of identity for distilled spirits	5.21 5.22	Application of standards The standards of identity	5.23	Alteration of class and type
D	Labeling requirements for distilled spirits	5.31 5.32 5.33 5.34 5.35 5.36 5.37	General Mandatory label information Additional requirements Brand names Class and type Name and address Alcoholic content	5.38 5.39 5.40 5.41 5.42	Net contents Presence of neutral spirits and coloring, flavoring, and blending materials Statements of age and percentage Bottle cartons, booklets, and leaflets Prohibited practices
E	Standards of fill for bottled distilled spirits	5.45 5.46	Application Standard liquor bottles	5.47 5.48	Standards of fill Exceptions
F	Requirements for withdrawal from customs custody of bottled imported distilled spirits	5.51	Label approval and release	5.52	Certificates of age and origin
G	Requirements for approval of labels of domestically bottled distilled spirits	5.55	Certificates of label approval	5.56	Certificates of age and origin
H	Advertising of distilled spirits	5.61 5.62 5.63	Application Definition Mandatory statements	5.64 5.65	Lettering Prohibited statements

589

APPENDIX 7-8. Subpart Titles of 27 CFR 201 (Distilled Spirits Plants) and Sections They Cover

Subpart	Subpart Title	Sections Included
A	Scope	201.1 to 201.4
B	Definitions	201.11
C	Taxes	201.21 to 201.49
D	Administrative and miscellaneous provisions	201.61 to 201.104
E	Location and use	201.111 to 201.120
F	Qualification of distilled spirits plants	201.131 to 201.176
G	Bonds and consents of surety	201.191 to 201.223
H	Construction and equipment	201.231 to 201.249
I	Production	201.261 to 201.281
J	Storage in bond	201.291 to 201.313
K	Bottling on bonded premises	201.321 to 201.352
L	Transfers and withdrawals	201.361 to 201.395
M	Denaturation	201.401 to 201.413
N	Operations on bottling premises other than bottling in bond	201.421 to 201.470
Na	Bottling in bond after tax determination	201.470a to 201.470q
O	Losses after tax determination	201.481 to 201.496
P	Containers and marks and brands	201.501 to 201.533
Pa	Liquor bottle and label requirements	201.540a to 201.540v
Q	Stamps	201.541 to 201.552
R	Voluntary destruction	201.561 to 201.563
S	Return of spirits to bonded premises	201.581 to 201.588
T	Samples	201.601 to 201.607
U	Records and reports	201.611 to 201.634

APPENDIX 7-9. Subpart Titles of 27 CFR 250 (Liquors and Articles from Puerto Rico and the Virgin Islands) and Sections They Cover

Subpart	Subpart Title	Sections Included	
A	Scope of regulations	250.1	to 250.2
B	Definitions	250.11	
C	Products coming into the United States from Puerto Rico	250.35	to 250.45
D	Formulae and processes for products from Puerto Rico	250.50	to 250.55
E	Taxpayment in Puerto Rico of liquors withdrawn before rectification or bottling	250.61	to 250.119
F	Liquors and articles purchased by tourists in Puerto Rico	250.125	to 250.128
G	Procurement and use of red strip stamps for distilled spirits from Puerto Rico	250.135	to 250.146
H	Records and reports of liquors from Puerto Rico	250.163	to 250.165
I	Taxpayment in Puerto Rico upon withdrawal after rectification or bottling	250.180	to 250.186
Ia	Tax-free shipments to the United States from Puerto Rico	250.191	to 250.195
J	Products coming into the United States from the Virgin Islands	250.220	to 250.211
K	Formulae and processes for products from the Virgin Islands	250.200	to 250.226
L	Red strip stamps for distilled spirits from the Virgin Islands	250.230	to 250.258
M	Procedure at port of entry from the Virgin Islands	250.260	to 250.266
N	Records and reports of liquors from the Virgin Islands	250.270	to 250.277
O	Tax-free shipments to the United States from the Virgin Islands	250.291	to 250.293
P	Requirements for liquor bottles	250.311	to 250.319
Q	Miscellaneous provisions	250.331	

APPENDIX 7-10. Subpart and Section Titles of 27 CFR 7 (Labeling and Advertising of Malt Beverages)

Sub-part	Subpart Title	Sec-tion	Section Title	Sec-tion	Section Title
A	Scope	7.10	General	7.2	Territorial extent
B	Definitions	7.10	Meaning of terms		
C	Labeling requirements for malt beverages	7.20	General	7.25	Name and address
		7.21	Misbranding	7.26	Alcoholic content
		7.22	Mandatory label information	7.27	Net contents
		7.23	Brand names	7.28	General requirements
		7.24	Class and type	7.29	Prohibited practices
D	Requirements for withdrawal of imported malt beverages from customs custody	7.30	Application	7.31	Label approval and release
E	Requirements for approval of labels of malt beverages domestically bottled or packed	7.40	Application	7.42	Exhibiting certificates to government officials
		7.41	Certificates of label approval		
F	Advertising of malt beverages	7.50	Application	7.53	Legibility of requirements
		7.51	Definitions	7.54	Prohibited statements
		7.52	Mandatory statements		
G	General provisions	7.60	Exports		

APPENDIX 7-11. Titles of Subparts of 27 CFR 245 (Beer) and Sections They Cover

Subpart	Subpart Title	Sections Included	
A	Scope of regulations	245.1	to 245.2
B	Definitions	245.5	
C	Location and use of brewery	245.10	to 245.13
D	Construction	245.15	to 245.17
E	Equipment	245.25	
F	Beer meters	245.30	to 245.36
G	Notices	245.40	to 245.44
H	Bonds, continuation certificates, and consents of surety	245.45	to 245.61
I	Plats	245.65	to 245.69
J	Approval of documents	245.70	to 245.71
K	Special taxes	245.75	to 245.84
L	Changes in name, proprietorship, control, location, premises, and equipment	245.85	to 245.100
M	Notice of discontinuance of business	245.105	
N	Tax on beer	245.110	to 245.118
O	Marks, brands, and labels	245.125	to 245.129
P	Removal of brewer's yeast and other articles	245.135	to 245.136
Q	Transfers to another brewery of same ownership	245.140	to 245.148
R	Removal of beer unfit for beverage use	245.150	to 245.153
S	Beer returned to brewery or voluntarily destroyed	245.155	to 245.158
T	Refund and credit of tax or relief from liability	245.160	to 245.165
U	Exportation	245.170	
W	Beer procured from another brewer	245.205	to 245.208
X	Cereal beverage	245.210	to 245.211
Y	Removals for analysis, research, development, or testing	245.215	to 245.219
Z	Miscellaneous provisions	245.220	to 245.222
AA	Records, reports, and returns	245.225	to 245.233
BB	Concentration and reconstitution of beer	245.235	to 245.245
CC	Pilot brewing plants	245.251	to 245.258

APPENDIX 7-12. Subpart Titles of 27 CFR 251 (Importation of distilled Spirits, Wines, and Beer) and Sections They Cover

Subpart	Subpart Title	Sections Included	
A	Scope of regulations	251.1	to 251.2
B	Definitions	251.11	
C	Special (occupational) tax	251.30	to 251.31
D	Tax on imported distilled spirits, wines, beer, and imported perfumes containing distilled spirits	251.40	to 251.49
E	General requirements	251.55	to 251.75
F	Red strip stamps to be affixed in a foreign country	251.80	to 251.92
G	Red strip stamps affixed under customs supervision	251.110	to 251.112
H	Importation of distilled spirits in bulk	251.120	to 251.122
I	Importer's records and reports	251.130	to 251.137
K	Disposition of red strip stamps	251.160	
L	Transfer of distilled spirits from customs custody to bonded premises of distilled spirits plant	251.171	to 251.175
M	Withdrawal of imported distilled spirits from customs custody free of tax for use of the United States	251.181	to 251.186
N	Requirements for liquor bottles	251.201	to 251.209
O	Miscellaneous provisions	251.221	

APPENDIX 7-13. Subpart Titles of 27 CFR 252 (Exportation of Liquors) and
Sections They Cover

Subpart	Subpart Title	Sections Included	
A	Scope	252.1	to 252.3
B	Definitions	252.11	
C	Miscellaneous provisions	252.21	to 252.48
D	Bond and consents of surety	252.51	to 252.80
E	Withdrawal of distilled spirits without payment of tax for exportation, use on vessels and aircraft, transfer to a foreign-trade zone, or transportation to a manufacturing bonded warehouse	252.91	to 252.118
F	Withdrawal of wine without payment of tax for exportation, use on vessels and aircraft, transfer to a foreign-trade zone, or transportation to a manufacturing bonded warehouse	252.121	to 252.133
G	Removal of beer without payment of tax for exportation, use as supplies on vessels and aircraft, or transfer to a foreign-trade zone	252.141	to 252.148
Ga	Removal without payment of tax for exportation or transfer to a foreign-trade zone of concentrate produced from beer	252.150a	to 252.150k
H	Withdrawal of specially denatured spirits, free of tax, for exportation or transfer to a foreign-trade zone	252.151	to 252.163
I	Exportation of distilled spirits with benefit of drawback	252.171	to 252.196
J	Exportation, with benefit of drawback, of distilled spirits in casks or packages filled in internal revenue bond	252.201	to 252.204
K	Exportation of wine with benefit of drawback	252.211	to 252.218
L	Exportation of beer with benefit of drawback	252.221	to 252.230
M	Shipment or delivery for export	252.241	to 252.253
N	Proceedings at ports of export	252.261	to 252.290
O	Losses	252.301	to 252.321
P	Action on claims	252.331	to 252.335

APPENDIX 7-14. Subpart Titles of 27 CFR 18 (Production of Volatile Fruit-Flavor Concentrates) and Sections They Cover

Subpart	Subpart Title	Sections Included	
A	Scope	18.1	to 18.3
B	Definitions	18.11	
C	Administrative and miscellaneous provisions	18.21	to 18.28
D	Location and use	18.41	to 18.43
E	Qualification of volatile fruit-flavor concentrate plants	18.51	to 18.82
F	Bonds and consents of surety	18.91	to 18.102
G	Construction and equipment	18.111	to 18.113
H	Operations	18.121	to 18.128
I	Records and reports	18.141	to 18.145

APPENDIX 7-15. Subpart Titles of 27 CFR 195 (Production of Vinegar by the Vaporizing Process) and Sections They Cover

Subpart	Subpart Title	Sections Included	
A	Scope of regulation	195.1	to 195.2
B	Definitions	195.10	to 195.28
C	Location and use	195.35	to 195.36
D	Construction	195.40	to 195.43
E	Sign	195.50	
F	Equipment	195.55	to 195.69
G	Qualifying documents	195.75	to 195.88
H	Plats and plans	195.95	to 195.103
I	Requirements governing changes in name, proprietorship, control, location, premises and equipment	195.110	to 195.132
J	Action by Assistant Regional Commissioner	195.140	to 195.145
K	Plant operation	195.150	to 195.167
L	Proprietor's records and reports	195.175	to 195.177
M	Suspension and resumption of operations	195.185	to 195.187
N	Registry of stills	195.195	
O	Change of persons interested in business	195.200	to 195.203
P	Discontinuance of business	195.210	to 195.212
Q	General provisions relating to vinegar factories	195.222	to 195.226
R	Inspection of vinegar factories	195.235	to 195.237
S	Losses	195.245	to 195.254
T	Rules for computing capacity of stills	195.260	to 195.262

APPENDIX 7-16. Subpart and Section Titles of 27 CFR 186 (Gauging Manual)

Subpart	Subpart title	Section	Section Title
A	Scope of regulations	186.1	Gauging of distilled spirits
B	Definitions	186.11	Meaning of terms
C	Gauging instruments	186.21	General requirements
		186.22	Hydrometers and thermometers
		186.23	Use of precision hydrometers and thermometers
		186.24	Use of U.S. standard hydrometers and thermometers
		186.24a	Specific gravity hydrometers
		186.24b	Use of precision specific gravity hydrometers
		186.25	Gauging instruments of unusual or costly design
D	Gauging procedures	186.31	Determination of proof
		186.32	Determination of proof obscuration
	(Determination of quantity)	186.36	General requirements
	(Determination of quantity by weight)	186.41	Bulk spirits
		186.42	Denatured spirits
		186.43	Packaged spirits
		186.44	Entry or filling gauge for packages
		186.45	Withdrawal gauge for packages
	(Determination of quantity by volume)	186.51	Procedure for measurement
E	Prescribed tables	186.61	Table 1, showing the true percent of proof spirit for any indication of the hydrometer at temperatures between zero and 100 degrees Fahrenheit
		186.62	Table 2, showing wine gallons and proof gallons by weight
		186.63	Table 3, for determining the number of proof gallons from the weight and proof of spirituous liquor

599

APPENDIX 8. Addresses of Federal Agencies Discussed in the Book.

1. Department of Agriculture
   Fourteenth Street and
   Independence Avenue SW.
   Washington, D.C. 20250

2. Department of Commerce
   Fourteenth Street Between
   Constitution Avenue and
   E Street NW.
   Washington, D.C. 20230

3. National Bureau of Standards
   Department of Commerce
   Washington, D.C. 20234

4. National Oceanic and Atmospheric
   Administration
   Department of Commerce
   6010 Executive Boulevard
   Rockville, Maryland 20852

5. National Marine Fisheries Service
   National Oceanic and Atmospheric
   Administration
   Department of Commerce
   Washington, D.C. 20235

6. Consumer Product Safety
   Commission
   1750 K Street NW.
   Washington, D.C. 20207

7. Federal Trade Commission
   Pennsylvania Avenue at Sixth
   Street NW.
   Washington, D.C. 20580

8. Department of Health, Education,
   and Welfare
   330 Independence Avenue SW.
   Washington, D.C. 20201

9. Food and Drug Administration
   200 C Street SW.
   Washington, D.C. 20204

10. Department of the Treasury
    Fifteenth Street and
    Pennsylvania Avenue NW.
    Washington, D.C. 20220

11. Bureau of Alcohol, Tobacco, and
    Firearms
    1200 Pennsylvania Avenue NW.
    Washington, D.C. 20226

INDEX

603

RENNER LEARNING RESOURCES CENTER
ELGIN COMMUNITY COLLEGE
ELGIN, ILLINOIS